Durga's Mosque

The **Institute of Southeast Asian Studies (ISEAS)** was established as an autonomous organization in 1968. It is a regional centre dedicated to the study of socio-political, security and economic trends and developments in Southeast Asia and its wider geostrategic and economic environment.

The Institute's research programmes are the Regional Economic Studies (RES, including ASEAN and APEC), Regional Strategic and Political Studies (RSPS), and Regional Social and Cultural Studies (RSCS).

ISEAS Publications, an established academic press, has issued more than 1,000 books and journals. It is the largest scholarly publisher of research about Southeast Asia from within the region. ISEAS Publications works with many other academic and trade publishers and distributors to disseminate important research and analyses from and about Southeast Asia to the rest of the world.

Durga's Mosque

Cosmology, Conversion and Community in Central Javanese Islam

Stephen C. Headley

INSTITUTE OF SOUTHEAST ASIAN STUDIES
Singapore

First published in Singapore in 2004 by ISEAS Publications
Institute of Southeast Asian Studies
30 Heng Mui Keng Terrace
Pasir Panjang
Singapore 119614

E-mail: publish@iseas.edu.sg
Website: <http://bookshop.iseas.edu.sg>

The responsibility for facts and opinions in this publication rests exclusively with the author and his interpretations do not necessarily reflect the views or the policy of the publisher or its supporters.

ISEAS Library Cataloguing-in-Publication Data

Headley, Stephen Cavanna.
    Durga's mosque: cosmology, conversion and community in Central Javanese Islam.
    1. Islam—Indonesia—Jawa Tengah.
    2. Javanese (Indonesian people)—Indonesia—Jawa Tengah—Religious life and customs.
    3. Kinship—Indonesia—Jawa Tengah.
    4. Durgā (Hindu deity)—Cult—Indonesia—Jawa Tengah.
    5. Jawa Tengah (Indonesia)—Religious life and customs.
    I. Title.
DS646.29 J43H43   2004

ISBN 981-230-242-5 (hard cover)

Cover photograph: Northern flank of the volcano Merapi, Central Java, by author.

Typeset by Superskill Graphics Pte Ltd
Printed in Singapore by Utopia Press Pte Ltd

CONTENTS

PART IV: COSMOLOGY, CONVERSION AND COMMUNITY IN CENTRAL JAVANESE ISLAM TODAY

LIST OF FIGURES

LIST OF TABLES

PREFACE

What's in the *umma*? The *umma* is not a congregation (*jamā'a*, Arabic; *jemaah*, Indonesian)[1] of a given mosque, but the entire community of faithful. For the word *umma* (Ind. Jav. *umat*) there can be no translation into English, only a paraphrase for an attempted definition. Can an *umma* be localized, that is to say, does it have boundaries, whether ethno-linguistic, national, or otherwise? Can we write a book, for instance, about the Javanese *umma* as a vector for the introduction of individualism in Java? There certainly is an *umma* in Java, but clearly it is not only made up of Javanese. Recently, the leader (*penghulu*) of the largest mosque in Surakarta (Central Java) came from the eastern island of Sumbawa, and no one found this unusual. Indeed, the *umma* is cosmopolitan. Does this mean that the *umma* is as ethnically varied as the entire Indonesian archipelago? Should we include in it the Muslims of Malaysia, Sulu (the Philippines), and Petani (southern Thailand)? If one begins to think in terms of a transnational virtual *umma*, it often becomes so vague, that locality disappears as a pertinent marker of identity. In this study, we are committed to describing the development of the *umma* of a given area, Kaliasa. Central Java is the historic heartland of the island and our focus precludes a broader comparative perspective.

Arjun Appadurai (1996, ch. 8) pointed out that ethnographers have long been occupied with studying how local subjects are produced by particular rites of passage. But the "local" *umma* in Central Java has become over time, since 1660, less and less preoccupied with incarnating locality, with taking over the social space and clientele of older "Javanese" deities like Durga. In the course of eighteenth century, this network of mosques spread from city to city and then out into the countryside once royal patronage became a burden as much as an advantage. The urban mosques and rural Koranic schools, began to realize that their teachers who had studied in Medina and Mecca and their faithful who had done the *ḥajj* (Ind. *haj*), were much less motivated in incarnating local identity than in propagating a renewed vision of what it meant to be a Muslim based on contacts with currents of Muslim thinking in the Middle East. The recent flood of Muslim publication from Yogyakarta (LKiS) and Bandung (Mizan) indicates that this interest is on the increase. Paradoxically while these ongoing connections to Middle Eastern Muslim thought in all its diversity is still being strengthened, Javanese Islam remains very Javanese. Though increasingly sophisticated in its understanding of contemporary Muslim reflection throughout the world, the *umma* in Java may not be made up only of Javanese, it nonetheless remains very self-reflective and Javanese.

Let me give an example of the applicability of one kind of Middle Eastern Muslim thinking. Following the Gulf War in May 1991 (Talal Assad 1993, ch. 6), a debate in Saudi Arabia began with an open letter to King Fahd from a hundred of *'ulamā* claiming that the "rights of the individual and society" were not being guaranteed. Since this criticism (*nasīha*) dealt with issues affecting the entire "local" Saudi *umma*, it could be made public. The juridical precedent of Ibn Taymiyya (1263–1328) was cited as a justification of this effort to hold the king accountable as a moral person in the public domain. As al'Za'ayr, a well-known Saudi preacher and lecturer on moral and political criticism (*nasīha;* Assad 1993, pp. 214–23) had been saying, the virtuous Muslim is not judged on what he believes, but on how he lives in that moral space (*umma*) which links all those who are bound to Allah. "The first foundation of independence for the *umma* is to know that it is indissolubly bound to God." This requires not blind obedience but self-evaluation. "If one doesn't secure one's own independent thinking the *umma* is made into an appendage of others. And if that happens, the *umma's* essence (*huwiyya*) and its independence disappear together." This view helps us to understand that the social space of the *umma* is indeed a "singular plural". Based on the monadic character of Allah to whom all submit unconditionally, the *umma* is inconceivable without this focus, but this community is realized by personal piety and a common religious life of individual Muslims. This kind of pious lifestyle has been transposed to Java for centuries now. Recently it has again been applied in *da'wa* campaigns to "purify" rural Islam of its Javaneseness, and in urban contexts to criticize the government of the Indonesian Republic for its corruption and irresponsibility towards its people. If Muslim religion is as much about virtue than about credos, it is because lacking virtue, no practical reasoning can be undertaken by a Muslim. For as Za'ayr shows, the *umma's* piety is deployed not in a secular social space but in a divine and eternal religious *and* civil space where Muslim criticism, punishment, and power have their place.

This book provides one explanation of how Islam in Java stayed Javanese for so long and how now (2004) it has rejuvenated itself, changing in the light of "purer" Muslim models and a renewed Muslim fervour, at the same time as splintering into political factions as post-colonial independence offered it the possibility, not only to deploy its moral authority, but also to gain and exercise power. All this is deliberately seen from the locality of a rural area north of the city of Surakarta, where one can perceive how the holism of Javanese cosmology was lost and then sought after anew as the urban fibre of Surakarta began to tear apart under the Soeharto dictatorship in the 1980s. Reinventions of lost cosmologies are rarely successful, but they do reveal on the part of those who rediscover them a degree of self-understanding. Those Javanese Muslims whose lives have been jeopardized by the unfulfilled promises of democracy are an ethnic majority; they are not the worst off among the ethnic components of what was supposed to become a republic. Society as a project of modernity in Indonesia is now being called into question using such concepts as society without the state (*masyarakat tanpa negara*). Just as the attributes of religion are seen as too visible, too liable to political manipulation (vote Muslim!), so too are the pretensions of popular representation seen to be an illusion in an ongoing crisis where downscaling, using the local resources of the neighbourhood to protect one's family against state terror is envisioned at the local level as more viable than the large scale networks of a governance that are manipulated top to bottom.

Over the last thirty years, so many Javanese have taken of their time to help me understand their language and culture that I could not acknowledge or thank them all here. The earliest contacts I had in 1973 with the village of Krendawahana, the stepping off point in the upper Solo river basin of the volume, was with *radèn*[2] Sastrodiwiryo who was its *lurah* (mayor) until the early 1980s. In October 2003, his family was still surviving, barely, as was that of the elderly *modin* (muezzin), Amah Achiar, who lives directly behind the widow of Sastrodiwiryo. The economic crisis of 1997 had left deep wounds, despite what the macro economic surveys say about current recovery.

Radèn Tanaya, an almanac writer and literati living modestly in the shadow of the Dutch fort Vastenburg, introduced me in 1973 to the Javanese use of corresponding sets of classifications and the mythology that deploys these networks of categorical relations. Many literati at the Reksapustaka, the Mangkunagaran palace library in Surakarta some fifteen kilometres to the south of the village of Krendawahana, helped me locate and read the descriptions of this palace's *Maesa Lawung* offerings at the tertre of the goddess Durga in that village. Friends in Surakarta lodged me with their families and helped me to transcribe recordings and translate texts that proved difficult for me. Cornelios Reismartono, Yeremia Prasetyo Yidi Modorumpoko, Yustina Ramtina Wulandari, and Stephanos Siagalaksana were my assistants in gathering and analysing the materials for Chapters 12, 13, and 14. Without their help the work would have taken much more time and would not have been as interesting. Kyai Haji Dian Nafi' director of the Windan (Makam Haji, Kartasura) branch of the al-Muayyad (Mangukuyudan) Koranic school (*pondok* pesantren), as well as his collaborators, introduced me to many other Muslims in the Surakarta area who helped me to understand how they analysed sociologically the current situation using their Muslim values.

In Europe over the years, I have received much encouragement and criticism from anthropologists, historians, and philologists interested in Java. These friends not only took a professional interest in my writing, but also helped me believe in the conclusion of a project that at times seemed too ambitious an undertaking. I am deeply aware of how much support I received from Ben Arps, Andrew Beatty, Tim Behrend, Valdimir Braginsky, Clara Brakel, Peter Carey, Robert Hefner, Frans Huskens, Charles Macdonald, Jan Mrazek, David Parkin, Merle Ricklefs, and Jessica Rose. Since 1998 I have received a great deal of support from the ERASME (CNRS, Paris). from its members Cécile Barraud and André Itéanu, and especially from Daniel de Coppet (+2002) who supported my overall approach to Java as an instance of a hybrid holistic society.

The support of Triena Ong, Managing Editor and Head of the Publications Unit, and Rahilah Yusuf, Production Editor, of the Institute of Southeast Asian Studies (ISEAS) in Singapore have made the completion of the manuscript a professional and a pleasurable experience.

On a more personal note, the presence of my wife, to whom this book is dedicated, and my children, both in Java (where my daughter was born) and later in France as they waited for me to return from a dozen sojourns in the Solo area, always gave me the assurance that I was not struggling on alone.

NOTES

1. Spelling conventions of foreign words in Indonesian and Javanese are not fixed. The first time a term is used in this book, we have tried to give its Arabic or Indonesian/Javanese spellings in parentheses. When an Indonesian or Javanese author uses a term in his native language or cites a foreign term we have tried to adopt the spelling he or she used if this is recognizable. Abbreviations: Ar. (Arabic); Ind. (Indonesian); Jav. (Javanese); San. (Sanskrit).
2. Javanese titles. Some are capitalized (Ki Dhalang XXXX) as if they were the proper name and others are lower-cased and in italics (*ki dhalang* XXX). We need to flag this ambiguity; the Javanese practice (to leave them capitalized as if they were part of the proper name, which any Javanese know they aren't) is confusing to the non-Javanese.

ACKNOWLEDGEMENTS

This book, long in its gestation, is the result of many years of research. Certain ideas have been treated partially in the author's previously published articles, published in French or in English, listed below. Chapters 6, 10, and 13 are revised versions of these previously published articles.

Ch. 1:   "The Body as a House in Javanese Society". In *De la Hutte au Palais, sociétés "à maison" en Asie du sud-est insulaire*, edited by Charles Macdonald, pp. 133–52. Paris: Editions du CNRS, 1987.

            "The Idiom of Siblingship". In *De la Hutte au Palais sociétés "à maison" en Asie du sud-est insulaire*, edited by Charles Macdonald, pp. 209–17. Paris: Editions du CNRS, 1987.

Ch. 2:   "Le Lit Grenier et la déesse de la fécondité à Java: rites nuptiaux?". *Dialogue 'Le Lit'* no. 82 (4è trimestre 1983): 77–86.

Ch. 4:   "De l'Apanage au Métayage, l'exemple de Java central". In *Sociétés Paysannes du Tiers-Monde*, edited by Catherine Coquery-Vidrovitch, pp. 111–24. Lille: Presses Univ. de Lille, 1980.

Ch. 5:   "Recyclage Rituel au Centre de Java: Le 're-lancement' du Buffle de Durga". *Cheminements, écrits offerts à Georges Condominas. Asie du Sud-Est et Monde Insulindien*, vol. XI, no. 1–4 (1980): 401–13.

Ch. 6:   "The Islamisation of Central Java: The Role of Muslim Lineages in Kalioso". *Studia Islamika* 4, no. 2 (1997): 52–82.

Ch. 7:   "The Javanese Exorcisms of Evil: Betwixt India and Java". In *The Art and Culture of South-East Asia*, edited by Lokesh Chandra, pp. 73–110. Delhi: Aditya Prakashan, 1991.

Ch. 8:   "The Ritual Lancing of Durga's Buffalo in Surakarta and the Offering in the Krendowahono Forest of Its Blood". In *Between People and Statistics. Essays on Modern Indonesian History presented to P. Creutzberg,* edited by Francien van Anrooij et al., pp. 49–58. The Hague: Martinus Nijhoff, 1979.

Ch. 10: "Javanese Cosmogonies and Muslim Cosmographies: An Encompassing Knowledge". *Indonesia and the Malay World* 28, no. 82 (2000): 280–300.

Ch. 11: "Sembah/Salat: The Javanisation of Islamic Prayer; the Islamisation of Javanese Prayer". In *Inside and Outside the Mosque: Islamic Prayer across the Indian Ocean,* edited by David Parkin and Stephen C. Headley, pp. 169–212. Richmond, Surrey: Curzon, 2000.

"Afterword: The Mirror in the Mosque." In *Inside and Outside the Mosque: Islamic Prayer across the Indian Ocean,* edited by David Parkin and Stephen C. Headley, pp. 213–39. Richmond, Surrey: Curzon, 2000.

Ch. 12: "Nier Allah? Réflexions javanaises sur la conversion à l'islam". In *Nier les Dieux. Nier Dieu,* edited by Gilles dorival and Didier Pralon, pp. 393–404. Aix-en-Provence: Publications de l'Université de Provence, 2002.

Ch. 13: "Of Sacred Wells and Shopping Malls: Glimpses of the Reconstruction of Social Confidence in Solo after Soeharto". In *Puppet Theater in Contemporary Indonesia: New Approaches to Performance-Events,* edited by Jan Mrazek, pp. 227–41. Ann Arbor: University of Michigan Press, 2003.

*Introduction*_____

COSMOLOGY, CONVERSION, AND COMMUNITY IN JAVANESE ISLAM

1. JAVANESE ISLAM IN MONSOON SOUTHEAST ASIA

Since unbiased presentations of a culture and religion foreign to one's own are difficult, the reader needs to be aware of the author's assumptions, those of historical anthropology. The present volume on the development of Islam in Java is the sequel to *From Cosmogony to Exorcism in a Javanese Genesis: The Spilt Seed* (Headley 2000). The first volume studied the marginalization of a major Javanese origin myth which had begun as a cosmogony, but ended up an exorcism. What had explained the creation of the world and the social relations of mankind and the gods started to be used in a much more private way, for curing persons of their bad destiny. In this second volume the accent is no longer on the Javanese half-man myths, cosmogonies used to compensate for personal and social lack of fulfilment, but the introduction and eventual encompassment of the Javanese pantheon by a "higher" God, Allah, who eventually plays the principal role in the restoration of social and personal wholeness. In fact, the very nature of social and cosmic wholeness for the Javanese changes with Islamic monotheism. The norms which the socio-cosmic "fit" guarantees are slowly being replaced by another hierarchy of values.

By describing two very different kinds of holism,[1] Javanese and Muslim, and the growth of individualism in both of them, one can see the overall coherence, indeed the simplicity of Javanese social morphology. Our task is therefore an ethnographic one. Here we will try to explore not only religious praxis, but how a village, a social community, with a sacred forest called Krendawahana which had become the site of the royal cult of Durga, north of the Central Javanese palace city of Surakarta, later became just another Javanese "Muslim village with a minor offering site behind its mosque". The Javanese were aware of foreigners coming to Java from the outside world, from "other shores" (*sabrang*), well before they encountered Islam. But during what Anthony Reid (1993, Vol. II, Ch. 3), has called the age of commerce (1450–1680), there occurred a religious revolution during which half the population of Southeast Asia adopted a monotheism.

Christian and Islamic rivalry redefined the political boundaries of many of these kingdoms, but not Java. After the sixteenth century, Islam contributed to greater openness. Then, in the nineteenth century the exploitive character of the Dutch colonial export economy lent a defensive character to the Javanese hierarchy of values. *Vis-à-vis* this outside world, Islam became the higher value for the Javanese, recognizable in the eyes of those who continued to ignore what it meant to be Javanese. On the other hand, when the Javanese were oriented towards the insular traditions of this island, the situation was reversed and the values of their ancestral praxis, "Javanism", again became primordial. Such an inversion shows that there is a higher value, which the simple juxtaposition of two "religions", Javanism and Islam, cannot account for. As will be seen in the closing chapters of this volume, this inversion of the hierarchy of values also goes a long way to explain the emergence of an intolerant communalism[2] in the period after the fall of the Soeharto dictatorship (May 1998).

If communalism is the "hyperenchantment" of religion (Richard Fox 1996), then that communalism which is the widest possible extension of local autonomy, in the case of Islam, has a non-local reference in the Middle Eastern polities who have kept or adopted the *sharī'ah* (Jav. *syari'at, saréngat*; Ar. *shar*) as their civil law. In Indonesia, this "enemy within" for the Muslims are the Christians, in part, because Muslims cannot afford to call into question the unity of the Muslim community without aggravating existing intra-Muslim conflicts. In this introductory chapter we will try to sketch out the complexity of these social parameters of the Javanese Muslim community, simply mentioning some, treating others briefly and focussing more deeply on those that will be taken up in subsequent chapters. Given the dearth of social history for Java this will require switching back and forth between centuries in order to gain a comparative depth of focus and to highlight that data which is available. Many of descriptive claims made in this introduction are not backed up by extensive proofs, but such an overall sketch is necessary to lay out the broader background against which the more detailed anthropology of Islam will later be explored. We have tried to give the reader in each case the bibliographical references allowing him or her to check these claims.

In Java, the appearance of the older indigenous cosmology for use in rituals of exorcism in the seventeenth century marked the beginning of the end of its use as providing explicit origin myths of Javanese society. Their displacement towards a more discreet and "private" use in the ritualized theatre of purification by shadow puppet occurred in Java as Islam was becoming more important, during the sixteenth and seventeenth centuries (Headley 2000). A comparison with Balinese religion suggests that Javanese practice must once have resembled Balinese praxis, but that it has become more discreet and in a sense less explicit over the centuries since the fall of the last "Hindu" Javanese kingdom of Majapahit at the beginning of the sixteenth century. Yet in Bali, where Islam had hardly penetrated, the same cosmogony (*Purwa Bhumi*) was also taken up by *wayang* (shadow puppet theatre) for exorcisms, so this evolution in Java cannot be attributed to the influence of Islam. Other Javanese origin myths survive in agricultural practice, such as the Sri and Sadana, but even here their ritualization has faded from its earlier prominence in planting and harvest rites. What accounts for Java's growing disenchantment with its religious cosmology and origin myths? It may have nothing to do with the presence of Islam and much to do with the evolution of Javanese society *per se*.

The pre-Islamic cosmology, just like pre-Islamic mantra and invocations were gradually interlaced, "enriched" with Islamic elements. The coexistence of Javanese ancestral religious practices and Islam under the self-same cosmology lasted some four centuries up to the twentieth century. Certainly the emergence of the notion of "heterodox" in sixteenth century Java reveals the appearance of a sociology of religion, an orthodoxy explaining the diversity, ruling on the legitimacy of other cults. This signals the marginal position of Islam in Java from its first appearance until about 1650. It is present in the earliest Muslim writings that have come down to us from the sixteenth century (Drewes 1978). While royal sponsorship, as well as local promotion of "foreign", i.e. Hindu Buddhist, cults was common to Java from the sixth or seventh centuries onward, disapproval of local "illicit polytheistic" cults appeared for the first time a thousand years later in these as yet barely indigenized Javanese Muslim circles. The competition between different royal and local religious practices does not indicate a permanent conflictual bifurcation; there seems to have been a *modus vivendi*, which included mutual understanding, if not approval. Although data is scarce prior to the arrival of Islam, a similar divergence existed, this time between royal and village cults (cf. the sixteenth century *Deśawarṇana* 1995 by Mpu Prapañca). During the Hindu-Javanese period rural cults rarely, to our knowledge, challenged royal authority as Islam was later to do. They were part and parcel of the same social morphology. This volume will consider how, during several centuries, Islam's cohabitation with ancestral rural Javanese cults was piloted by Javanese social morphology.

In the second, raja-centric, period of Islamization (1650–1750), these differences were expressed harmoniously on the political level, even if Amangkurat I slaughtered several thousand *ulama* following a 1637 plot against him. From the late seventeenth century, Muslims and non-Muslims alike were starting to focus on a common, non-Javanese enemy, the Dutch foreigners who colonized their land, who made no pretence of any respect for the Javanese "Moors" or animists. The foreigners not only galvanized the Javanese amongst themselves, but given the scale of the colonial enterprise, reinforced what would later become pan-Indonesian Islamic solidarity.

The third period begins in the eighteenth century, after the Java War against the Dutch colonialists (1825–30). The Dutch East Indies government henceforth regularly suspected Muslims of fermenting revolts and kept them under surveillance. This accounted for both the segmentary nature of Javanese Islamic linkages and their autonomy and independence from the native rulers under close Dutch supervision.

In a fourth period after independence from the Dutch (1949), the Muslims did achieve greater linkage between their various branches, but even then they could hardly be described as centrally organized. Their loosely structured community relied heavily on the shared and common faith (*iman*), which provided latent bonds even if these worked slowly and weakly. The permanent difficulty for a more complete development of this Middle Eastern soteriology in Java, however, was, to use Max Weber's expression, the "fetters of kinship" that structured every village.

Javanese society involved a shared hierarchy of values. This meant that their manner of evaluating social facts relied on values largely held in common, and individually evolved values were less frequently found. This similarity of evaluative procedures produced in the Javanese a "social" confidence that these values were not only commonly held, but also cosmic (we would say "Javanese") in origin. Defined negatively, "shared" means that there was little individual indifference in the values as they were ordered by society. The conception of personhood, kinship, and the household benefited from a socio-cosmological fit, a higher level context that would not go away. To speak of Javanese society without some reference to this micro-macrocosmic fit is impossible. One cannot isolate it using labels from traditional religious practice. It is part and parcel of the day-to-day social practice of the Javanese speakers on the island, even if they never describe it in exactly the same terms.

The ascribed status of the person was enmeshed in a socio-cosmic webbing which individual could only step out of with difficulty.

From the sixteenth to the nineteenth century the place of Muhammad, the seal of the prophets in an island without prophets, was still being negotiated into this Javanese hierarchy of values. Only in the twentieth century does one have a fully-fledged Islamic puritan movement, the Muhammadiyah, promoting Muslim "individualism", i.e. personal responsibility for *orthopraxis* of the faith, in urban and later in rural Java, in order to create a "genuine and authentic" Islam. The duration of Islamization, some four hundred years, created a need for renovation and "reinvention" of Muslim tradition. Conversion had been so slow; waves of *Muslimin* had turned towards Allah, crested, and then receded back into the sea of *habitus* with monotonous regularity over centuries. If in the past individuals had converted, when had society at large been converted?

The use of the term "reinvention" does not imply that something new was discovered, for what is new for the neophyte is familiar for the initiated.[3] There is some sense of invention in this notion of rejuvenating tradition, for the fullness of it has escaped certain backwards (*plosok*) Muslims. The risk is that the "genuineness" of the tradition can be lost in these reinventions, if the will and consciousness necessary to revive it leads to artificiality. The example of the effects of the Second Vatican Council's effects on Western European Catholicism comes to mind; in the guise of reviving the fullness of the tradition, the Roman church in Western Europe found itself instead moving towards an individualistic watered down Protestantism. Perhaps this could be cited as an example of what Stéphane Vibert (2001) has signalled out as a tendency in Russia to rely on the notion of community to reinforce the social integration of the individuals whose vertical link with God is weakened by the effects of rationality, individualism, and capitalism. Then the appropriation of modernity via reinforced notions of community in some cases is nothing more than what Louis Dumont (1983) called an "intensification of individualism".

Not surprisingly, the Puritan movement in Java, motivated by the existence of remainders of pagan praxis and neo-Wahabi thought, also adopted from Western modernity a certain strain of individual responsibility as ammunition for their own religiously inspired attacks on pre-scientific and outmoded cosmologies, i.e., Javanese ancestral modes of conceiving the social whole in relation to the cosmos (cf. Abdul Munir Mukhan 2000). How in fact did this Islamic conception of personhood and the hierarchy of social values spread? This book is a case study of that change, starting from one single locality north of the capital of Surakarta in south Central Java.

Many more such studies will be necessary before we have a clear general picture of this development.

First of all we need to decide on the unit of measurement for our description. What was the social scale in which Muslim life unfolds? Should the mosque and its community of faithful at prayer, the *jama'at* (Arabic, *jamā'a*), be taken as the unit of composition, or the community at large, the *umat* (Jav.; Ar. *umma*[4]) a de-territorialized collection of *jama'at* dispersed throughout the island? The mosque is rarely the defining centre of a Javanese village territorial unit as in Bosnian villages, for example (Bringa 1995, p. 200). The *umat* or community at large is a more realistic reference for religious groupings since the Javanese traditionally migrate small and great distances to fulfil their individual preferences for pilgrimage, both mosque-oriented and otherwise. The choice has the disadvantage of being deterritorialized, divorced from connection with a specific community. An intelligent compromise seems to be to take as a reference the local Koranic schools around Kaliasa, which combine both features: local implantation and diversified recruitment.

Is such a community (*umat*) a transposable landscape of belief? If so, what does the transposable landscape of Muslim belief consist of when it arrives on the shores of a distant land? To what norms does the *umat* conform? It is not enough to say that Islam is egalitarian by virtue of its aspiring to be ruled directly by Allah. One needs to specify the religious nature of the communitarian bond in a given Islamic locality. It is often claimed (e.g., Gardet 1981, pp. 195–97) that their common good and the bond of unity is their book, a miracle in itself, since Muhammad recited it word by word under the dictation of the archangel Gabriel. The great hope of the Puritan reformers of Islam has always been the unification of Islam around the Koran and its commentary. The "people of the *qibla* (direction for praying)" formed an ensemble (*jamā'a*) from the very beginning of Islam. Personal error is effaced by a common accord (*ijmā'*); in this sense the community (*umma*) is a state of law, or *hukm*. Muslim confidence in the excellence of this divinely inspired law of society gave them dignity and pride. All men belong to this community, thanks to a pre-eternal covenant (*mīthāq*).

While the pillars of Islam are personal and individual (the creed, or *shahāda*; prayer; alms; fasting; and pilgrimage), there is one collective duty, the "effort (*jihad*)" to spread the rights of Allah (*huqūq Allāh*) to the ends of the earth. Such a conception of the unity of the community does not permit cessation. An apostate is to be put to death. The severity of the traditional conception of this *umat* is not fanaticism says Gardet (1981, p. 202), but simply the spiritual and temporal expression of its cohesion. Fundamentally there existed only the house of Islam (*dār al-Islām*) and the world of war (*dār al-harb*). The approach of the former to the latter is that of the *jihad*, which in periods of religious reform usually takes on a missionary character addressed first of all to lukewarm Muslims. What is the place of the person in this community whose solidarity is a reflection of the unity of the Godhead? Each Muslim derives his dignity from the fact that Allah placed him there. By belonging to the *umat* he acquires a nobility which is existential, expressed by a living sense of fraternity riveted to Allah's monadic unity. So, asks Gardet (1981, p. 205), is the community of the *umat* a communion? While Islam requires outward conformity to its law, it does not judge inward adherence, all the while recognizing that the believer must have correct intentions or *niyat* (Arabic, *niyya*). However, if man exists religiously only through his community (*umma*), he nonetheless presents himself alone before his Maker. Intercession, mediation on another's behalf, as stressed by the Sufis, should not replace private individual action. This provides an entrance point for contemporary Western individualism. While the *umat* is man's sole spiritual community, as "society" the *umat* remains outside of man. It can be asked whether this corresponds to people's experience. One can feel solitude in a Muslim crowd and fraternity in a pagan land.

Where everyone continues to have "religious" beliefs, as in Java, the sociological distinction of F. Tonnïes (1855–1936) between community (i.e., *gemeinschaft*, based on co-operation and custom) and society (or association, *gesellschaft*, based on convention and law) does not seem to allow for the dilemma of disenchantment and secularization (Burger 1967, ch. 5). Praxis and belief remain, but their engagement is more individualistic. Today everywhere Islam is confronted by a modern conception of man's destiny: modern individualism, in which there is no distinction between person and individual, leading towards democratic ideologies; and a materialist individualism where the earthly city is the ultimate finality of all social communities. Because Islam does not distinguish between the temporal and the spiritual, the distinctions made above formally are not deemed pertinent. But the Muslim individual is not always nourished by the *umma*, and modern Western individualism was spread by colonialism throughout the globe. A Muslim is not always capable of respecting difference and alterity (believer: non-believer). The other people of the book, Jews and Christians, can be demonized. Since the *umma* does not transcend earthly cities but unifies them, the danger of ethnic and religious cleansing is ever present. The case of Bosnia, where there is a majority of Muslims and yet a minority culture confronting Catholic and Orthodox "worlds", is a better known instance of this precariousness (Bringa 1995, ch. 6).

Yet in Java where the Muslims are in the immense majority, numbers are not everything. The community of Muslims derives its implantation from the conviction that Islam is both religion and city (*Al-Islām, dīn wa dawla*). Churchless, but nonetheless international, the community of the prophet (*umat al-nabī*) is a world (*dār al-Islām*) unto itself, united by its faith into a believing collectivity (*al-jamā'a al-islāmiyya*). Not only are its values a source of unity and solidarity, but also it is collectively responsible for ordering the good and banning evil. This means to apply the laws of Allah revealed in the Koran to the society in which they are living, eventually to Muslims and non-Muslims alike.

The problem of regionalism, the dispersal of an archipelago, has created the need for continual reform movements. The Muslim community presents itself as universal since Allah's sovereignty is universal and exclusive. Fellow believers are supposed to be brothers. So, cogently, the coat of arms of Islam is the social character of religious duties, although unlike the Jewish law of Leviticus and Deuteronomy, large sectors of life go unqualified in the *sharī'ah*. As Gardet says (1981, p. 232), underneath the rigidity of the forms, there is a whole world of suppleness and imprecision. *Entraide*, interdependence and solidarity are important dimensions of daily life and a Muslim is "encouraged to identify his personal drama with the primordial destiny and defence of the interests of the community": what Gardet called the "mutual understanding and faithfulness guaranteed by the promises of God" (1981, p. 239). While the predominance of social relations and a collective mentality over the individual is a reality in Java, individuality, as anywhere, is expressed in a certain scepticism and suspicion of others. This negative individuality however is rapidly swept aside when confronted by a foreigner; one closes ranks for the offensive moments of *jihad* and missionary endeavour (*dakwah*; Ar., *da'wa*). The desire to live independent of foreign influence, which should be obvious to any one using common sense, is even deeper where the adaptation to modern technology is accepted.

It is obvious that after the First World War, with the collapse of the Ottoman Empire, there occurred a painful readjustment, which neither the sombre Puritanism sponsored by Saudi Arabia nor the orthodox reformers like the Muslim Brothers could wholly resolve in the course of the twentieth century. Muslims are still looking for ways in which to reorganize their common life. Their shared values, which construct this common lifestyle, are their most natural defence against individualism, nationalism or belonging to a given social class. Potentially there lies here a democracy of a non-secularized personhood. Yet the way forward has not been clear. For example, of the two countries that escaped European colonization in the eighteenth and nineteenth centuries and potentially have the greatest resource for effective self-government, Turkey was laicized but suffered from ethnic cleansing, while Iran created an Islamic Republic whose *mollah*-cracy has created as many problems as it pretended to solve. The way forward for Indonesia, a non-Islamic Republic, has not been clear either; internal Islamic separatist movements have created divisions of Islam generally. The latent values of the *umma* are so many covert "dominants" that determine only some of the daily behaviour of people. Local culture and religious traditions have reappeared in Islamic guise. There have always been regional syntheses of Islam, as with the Persian reconciler of Zoroastrian dualism and Muslim monotheism, Sohravardi (1154–91), who wrote: "Read the Koran as if it was revealed only for you!" This was usually treated as non-modern regionalism, until such time, as was the case in the central Celebes and the Malukas recently, when the nation-state having totally lost control of the situation, it has had to appeal to traditional peace pacts with their local customary law to reduce the violence (cf. Davis 2002).

Threatened by the neo-paganism (*jāhilīyah*) of Western authoritarian nationalism and materialism, the leading Muslim thinkers of the twentieth century Egyptian Sayyid Qutb (1906–66) and the Pakistani Abū-l-'Alā Mawdūdī (1903–79), turned to the hope of a reconstituted *umma* on the model of the one created by the Prophet: the command of good (*al-amr bi l-ma'ūf*). The latest groups of Neo-Wahabi came to Java as recently as May 1998, after the fall of Soeharto. The Tarbiyah movement, with its congregations (*jamaah salaf*) among Muslim students in many universities, illustrate these transnational sources being used by a minority of Javanese Muslims to purify Islam of anything that can be identified as Javanese. The universal orthopraxis, which these Neo-Wahabi groups promote throughout the Indonesian archipelago, has become mixed with local political ambitions. Whenever possible in this volume we will try to establish the local sources of such reforming pretensions in order to better understand the forces for fragmentation that are exercised on the shape of the *umat* in Java. I avoid saying the Indonesian *umat*, although this has its legitimacy, in order to factor in the cultural heterogeneity of the archipelago as it effects the articulation of the quite similar Muslim communities: Acehnese (Snouck Hurgronje 1996), Minang (Dobbin 1992), southeastern Sumatra (Peeters 1997; Gadjahnata 1986), Banjar (Alfani Daud 1997), Bugis (Pelras 1996), Lombok (Erni

Budiwanti 2000), etc. Their Islam may be the same but their societies are certainly different, as would have to be said, for instance, of Portuguese and German Catholicism.

2. THE SOCIOLOGY OF A "PLURALISTIC" COSMOS

The transformation of the canopy of the macrocosm during the period of multi-ethnicity on the Javanese north coast's "age of commerce" (1450–1680) has been discussed (Hefner 2001, pp. 1–58) in terms of the creation of plural societies, flexible ethnicity, canopied pluralism, alternative pluralities, and much later during the twentieth century, in terms of repetitive "foundational crises" caused by the temptation to differentiate citizenship on ethnic grounds. All of these issues are linked consciously to the relationship of religion and citizenship.

Indeed until now Javanese Islam was committed to a multi-ethnic Islam (Bugis, Banjar, Minangkabau, Acehnese, Lombok, etc.), as well as to a multi-religious state. In Indonesia the relationship between religion and citizenship was supposedly solved by the national ideology. Pancasila rejected the Western (especially French and American) privatization of religious belief, where the practice of religion is to be personal, even private but not social. Since everyone in Indonesia had beliefs in Allah/God, there would exist no primordial divides in Java between Muslims and non-Muslims, whatever their orthodoxy. In the Javanese case, political scientists' analysis of shared identity and citizenship ignored the extent to which the Javanese shared hierarchy of values suffered under the impact of these modern communities organized around the requirements of production as opposed to social life. Just as the aristocratic tax farmers compromised themselves increasingly with the colonial government during the nineteenth century, so did the Pancasila ideologist fail to realize that they were undercutting the social bonds on which society rested. A Javanese historian said of the nineteenth century,

> the composition and hierarchy of rural values, the specific allocation of authority in peasant communities, and the characteristic symbols, goals, and action — patterns of agrarian politics was radicalised (Sartono Kartodirdjo 1972, p. 73).

Part of the discredit of the urban aristocrats was recuperated as credit by the *santri* teachers established in the rural Koranic schools (*pondok pesantrèn*), a lesser part by the Sufi brotherhoods and a more significant part by the millenarian movements the villages engendered in large numbers. Although many of these latter movements were peaceful, they were produced by economic deprivation, cultural disintegration and political oppression. Nonetheless

Kartodirdjo (1972, p. 75) is at pains to insist that colonial rule and modernization do not explain the existence of millenarian uprisings, only their frequency. The disintegration of Javanese culture associated with the colonial regime increased the numbers of these movements, which prior to the nineteenth century had been more limited to inter-dynastic crises. These peasant counter-élites held religious ideals which, when challenged by alien values, reasserted themselves forcefully. The charismatic authority of religious leaders in a way corresponded to those the bureaucratic élite had betrayed. Whether Muslim or *kejawèn*, the rural peasants movements had large followings. The recent monograph on the beggar king, Embah Wali, and his awaited "just king" (Ratu Adil; here the Sultan of Yogya) shows the continued strength of these cultural paradigms (Rahardjo Suwandi 2000). Shadow-puppet theatre or *wayang* is still being used to interpret their world during the period 1930–80. Respect (*tepa slira*), equality (*pada-pada*) and mutual self-help (*sambatan*) gave and give the villagers the independence, denied them elsewhere, to found communities. These village value systems, I repeat, have their counterparts in the older urban aristocratic ethics (*priyayi*; Kumar 1997, pt. IV), hence their inherent competition with the ruling circles of the principalities prior to the latter's demise in 1945.

Then what of the north coast Javanese merchants' so-called multi-ethnic hierarchy of values? Its Javanese component was gradually weakened in the seventeenth and eighteenth centuries, for as Hefner points out (2001, p. 20):

> The commercial middle class or *orang kaya* (lit. rich or powerful persons) that had occasionally challenged aristocratic power and promoted more individualistic social styles, then, were the first victims of the European order, the reappearance of the Malay or *pribumi* business class would have to wait until the late twentieth century.

Not only did the numbers of the Javanese trading community dwindle, but even amongst their natural audience, the inhabitants of western Austronesia, their Javanese cultural matrix was not transposable onto the multi-ethnicity of the common Malay culture. Java remained a well-used source of prestigious "royal manners" which Sumatrans, Banjar, Bugis, and Malays all adapted to their own local authority. Java remained an outside or overseas (*sabrang*) to their inside, or home base, however coastal and insular. Robson (1981, p. 277) retains Tomes Pires' distinction (written *circa* 1513; Cortesão edition 1944) of merchants and mullahs established on the north coast of Java, saying that,

> The former came in order to trade and get rich, and when they settled the teachers came "from outside"... The Muslim population consisted of the

descendants of various foreigners who had become Javanese by virtue of their long residence in Java and probably by intermarriage. However, there seems to be no hint of "preaching" to the indigenous population with the aim of converting them or of any kind of missionary campaign. Muslim teachers came in order to give instruction to a community that already existed, not in order to set it up.

For almost four centuries before the appearance of a Wahabite reform movement in the late eighteen hundreds, there was a long and gradual accommodation of Islam to Javanese culture itself. The following example of this mode of acculturation is taken from the village of Krendawahana, the initial focus of this volume. In a nineteenth century Javanese poem, the *Suluk Nala Kirdha*,[5] we read of a wandering Muslim scholar, by the same name, who seeks wisdom from five successive teachers in order to understand the meaning of Allah's name. His fifth and final teacher is not a Muslim, but the goddess Durga. She has a traditional sanctuary, an altogether different kind of mosque, an invisible kingdom in a sacred forest. Nonetheless she knows more about the meaning of Allah's name than the four Islamic teachers Nala Kirdha has consulted previously. The figure of the goddess Durga who can penetrate the meaning of the name of Allah shows the extent to which Java took possession of Islam on her own terms. This feature of the inversion of values — Islam being higher *vis-à-vis* the outside world and Javanese tradition being superior *vis-à-vis* the insular world — is what is meant by the deliberately paradoxical title given to this volume, *Durga's Mosque*.

The adjective "syncretic" does not capture the nature of Javanese Islam any more than in other ethno-linguistic areas of the archipelago. There existed a gradual adaptation of the Islamic landscape of belief to an earlier Javanese one which, by the end of the twentieth century, was in the process of being marginalized. The causes and consequences of this marginalization will be examined in following chapters. It is important to notice from the beginning, however, that the development of Islam in such a context had structural effects on the construction of the Javanese *umat* also. Let us return to our example.

Nala Kirdha meets Durga on the "mountain" of Krendawahana. Since there is no such hill, let alone mountain, in the cartographical village of that name, the only possible conclusion is that the forest of Krendawahana, too, is a transposable landscape of belief, like Islam. Krendawahana was initially an Indian toponym in the first book of the Indian epic, the Mahābhārata; the site of an apocalyptic fire started by Agni. Transposed to Java, Krendawahana has followed the changing sites of royal palaces (*kraton*) in Java for centuries. While Nala Kirdha's earlier Islamic teachers resided in "physical" places identified by the text (Mt Merapi, a village in the plane below, Mt Lawu to the east and the Muslim centre of Demak to the north) the *topos* of Krendawahana is an invisible forest accessible, to Muslim Javanese and non-Muslim alike, only through a passage into mystery. The cult of Durga in the present day village of Krendawahana had many earlier precedents in other forest villages in central and eastern Java. The closest Durga temple geographically, but not temporally, is a ninth century temple to Durga and Siwa studied by archaeologists to the north of Solo in the village of Nusukan, some ten kilometres to the south of present day Krendawahana. There is no proof that the Nusukan Durga was associated with a toponym Krendawahana. Having earlier had a distinctly benign aspect, for instance in Singasari, twelfth century, Durga, in the intervening millennium, has lost her protective function as the destroyer of the demon enemies of the gods, the great goddess Mahishamardanî, to become the leader of demon forces in the Javanese shadow puppet theatre (*wayang*). These changing places in the Javanese pantheon occur in the same period when Allah will emerge as the highest divinity In Java.

So we are confronted with several landscapes of belief, some indigenous, others Muslim, transposed with their respective values from India and the Middle East. Although Mecca lies some eight thousand kilometres to the west of mosques in Java, it has a cosmopolitan value that compares favourably with the blatantly local village pantheons, who in fact usually put Allah in pride of place at the beginning of most invocations. If Islam arrived in Java as a transposable landscape of belief from so far away, Javanese beliefs also shifted their places and forms of expression as they were acculturated to Islam, and that in ways whose formal properties have great sociological interest. For instance the interpretations of the names of Allah above, displays a typically Javanese understanding of mystery, where secret signs (*sasmita*) deliberately conceal an inner meaning that the uninitiated cannot penetrate. As for the state itself, its institutions have usually had extra-Islamic historical roots, even if up until the nineteenth century Muslim societies sacralized their political forms of governance.

In Java the regional forms of culture, and the language which expresses them, were influenced by the Persian-Arabic culture that vehicled Islam in Malaysia and Indonesia. In Javanese the lexicon of religion is now mostly Arabic. These kinds of long-term changes in lexicon count more in social hierarchies of values than who won the last battle or election. In turn, Java influenced locally these Middle Eastern cultures as much as they influenced Southeast Asia (Malaysia, the Philippines and Indonesia): witness the pilgrimage of Nala Kirdha.

In Java, Islam encountered, in a way analogous to India, doctrines of immanence as sophisticated as its own doctrine of transcendence. The debate over the Sufi doctrine of the unity of being (*wahdat al-wūjud*) as it came out of Indian Islam to Sumatra, was an expression of this competition, and not just a critique of a given Sufi *tarékat*, the Naqshahbandiyya, originally from Turkistan. While in India, the four-part *varna* system was reproduced in a fourfold Muslim guise (Sayyid, descendants of 'Alī; Shaykh, from the Quraysh tribe; Mughals; and Afghan Parthan), the low caste Indian Muslims continued to practise Hindu *jati* or subcaste rules. In Java local customary law or *adat* also remained strong, although in Indonesia local customary law (*'urf*, more often *'āda*) was occasionally objectionable to Muslims' *fiqh*. Sometimes what was attacked were simply local variants of Islam, what Hefner (1997, p. 29) has called subaltern variants of Muslim practice. There existed in Java side by side an ancestral religion (*agama luri*), the so-called rural (*abangan*) peasant practices, and an ever-active Islamic élite which maintained an active network with major Muslim centres in the Middle East during the seventeenth and eighteenth centuries (Azyumardi Azra 1994).

The great watershed for the Javanese *umat* was decolonization and its transformation in the maelstrom of nationalism. The Dutch had not tried to eradicate Islam *per se*, so that

> the institutional infrastructure of Islam has allowed for both the social mobilization of the faithful and relative autonomy *vis-à-vis* the state, with pluralism and fragmentation characterizing the *umat* and its revered leaders. (Eva-Lotta E. Hedman 2001, p. 946)

In this context the hopes of the *umat* were very high on the eve of independence, and the unity of the *umat* quite lax. The imagined national community that finally prevailed was not a religious one, and even less an Islamic one. Just as the Dutch plantation system (*cultuurstelsel*) in the nineteenth century imagined a stereotyped Javanese village and only when their exploitation resulted in agricultural involution, did they realized such a village never existed, so Indonesian nationalists imagined the "unity (*bhinnéka*) of a religious diversity" contradicting the genuine unicity experienced by the Muslim *umat*, the only really unified religious community in the archipelago. After thirty years of the Soeharto New Order regime (1967–98) the danger for Islam is no longer posed by provincialism or regionalism containing non-Islamic faiths. The threats to Islam now come from Western individualism and materialism imported under the cover of nationalism, and that, despite an enormous revival of Islamic practice among Javanese Muslims. The demonization of Christians by Muslim fanatics is related to this climate. In order to consolidate a community in a situation where one cannot afford to call one's own into question too often, one needs an anti-community of pagans to bring one's own lacks into focus.

After the 1965–66 anti-Communist bloodbaths in Indonesia, the Muslims in Indonesia began again insisting on a famous phrase of seven words applying the *sharī'ah* to Indonesia. This unadopted 1945 Jakarta Charter would have made piety (*ibādāt*; Ind. *ibadat*) obligatory only for Muslims. Finally the Jakarta Charter, for not having gained any legal legitimacy, took on a spiritual one: the Indonesian nation's imagined destiny to be an Islamic republic. Nonetheless, at the beginning of the young Indonesian Republic (1950), the Nahdlatul Ulama (or NU; literally, the Rise of the Muslim Scholars) gained control of the Ministry of Religion and used its patronage to consolidate itself down till the early 1970s when it was evinced by the Pancasila ideology and the secularizing tendencies of the New Order regime. Subsequent efforts at renewal might be considered as efforts to reinvent their own tradition by laying claims to their capacity to encompass all of society. In the 1980s it was an NU scholar, Kyai Siddiq, who began promoting the notion of Islamic tolerance, seeking reconciliation with the modern state and nationalism (Feillard 1997, p. 137). This commitment to religious pluralism by the Nahdlatul Ulama revived the 1945 ethos that Muslims and non-Muslims had equal rights in the new Republic. The reference to the nation-state had become unavoidable. At the end of the colonial regime, the traditional Sunni tendency to consolidate the authority of a government had been reinforced by the nationalist sentiments of the NU officials. As the military New Order regime marginalized Islam, the ethical ethos of Islam looked more and more like the only source of *civilitas* available to Indonesians. This was to lead in the late 1980s to a massive movement to Islamicize Muslims from below, rather than from above through the state ministerial apparatus. After the efforts at Muslim political mobilization from above during the 1950s, the novelty of this approach was striking. To bring their lifestyles into conformity with Islamic norms, the *umat* was to be restructured by its own orthopraxis.

Traditional societies often refer to their social "whole" in terms of cosmogony. The deities created their world, and to think of this whole, it sufficed to recall this creation of mankind. The risk in using the notion of civil society is that it carries with it another, fragmented, segmentary notion of a societal whole corresponding to artificial political boundaries. The place ascribed to Islam in the post-colonial social morphology was dictated by the recent nationalism. While it is true that some nominal Muslims were alarmed by the Islamic renewal in the 1980s, certain of these fears have been overcome as the middle class have lived a more rational and, in that sense, more secularized Islam. On the other hand, throughout the 1980s the Muslims represented the only ethical alternative to the Soeharto military regime. In the early 1990s the NU leader Abdurrahman Wahid often reiterated his own nationalism, where it is Islam that guides the country through its moral authority and not through the imposition of the *Shafi'i shari'ah* as society's civil law (Feillard 1997, pp. 149–51).

Here lies a clear statement that part of society is distinct from its *umat*! Although there is an Iranian *umma* as opposed to an *umma* of the Arab world, the Indonesian *umat* recognized itself as separate from that of a non-Muslim Indonesian whole. During the 1990s, the future president of the Indonesian Republic Abdurrahman Wahid (1999–2000) fought against what he called the "re-confessionalization of society" by the Soeharto-sponsored ICMI (Association of Indonesian Muslim Intellectuals; Hefner 2000, ch. 6). For the moment (2004), it looks as though society expected too much of their first president in matters of Muslim leadership. After Soeharto's fall (May 1998), the idea that the *umat* should by itself have a major influence on the directions of political life, directing it towards Muslim values, seems difficult to achieve.

The political historian Azyumardi Azra recently published a collection of articles, entitled "Substantive Islam, so that the *umat* may not become sea foam" (*Islam Substantif: Agar Umat Tidak Jadi Buih*, 2000). He makes it sound as though the political élite of the two major Muslim parties, having gone beyond the borders of the *umat*, are operating like any élite, struggling to accumulate identity by using Muslim votes in the political arena of the capital city Jakarta. To make matters worse, the presence of a dozen party militias active today in Jakarta and elsewhere (*Prémanisme Politik 2000*, pp. 178–79), compromises the promise of a civil Islam, profiled during the 1990s resistance to the Soeharto military dictatorship. When and where did the *umat* lose its independence from the state and become the object of manipulation? When it tried to wield power inside the political arena. The perverse effect of these appeals to the community of Muslims, on this electoral constituency, seems now to be recognized by Muslim intellectuals. The dichotomy between the urban intelligentsia and the rural *ulama* in the Koranic boarding schools should not be exaggerated. They both felt responsible for the same *umat*. Ever since the 1920s, Muslim magazines and newspapers have been published whose titles included the reference to the *umat*. Azyumardi Azra's concern that secularization and hence fragmentation of the *umat* is a major current in twentieth century Indonesian Islamic life seems well-founded. Is the main constraint on the resurgence of Islam in Indonesia generally due, not to the upward pressure of *umat* as a social group, but to the downward effort at legitimization of the nation-state equipped with modern "infrastructural reach" (Hefner 1997, pp. 5–6)?

Certainly in the 1990s what lay outside the state in Indonesia was an independent Islam, and it felt it needed to channel and control Muslims. The *umat* was the conscious target of many actors' strategies. The new Muslim intellectuals addressed themselves to an urbanized educated *umat* through modern media. It is these educated Muslims who have opened up the vast question of what sort of Muslim society exists in Indonesia and how to influence its course or further development. Above and beyond personal piety and public rituals, some of these new Muslim leaders want to oppose secular nationalism and found an alternative Muslim city using "fresh" political models. Geertz and Hefner ask (1997, p. 19), whether most are alternative modernities, counter-modernities? But as I have asked above, can one reinvent a traditional, pure *umat*, without adopting some form of individualism? Given the massive recruitment of Muslims into the political élite, this may seem to be inevitable. One wonders what it means to the new Muslim élite to purify, say Java, of unacceptable innovations (*bid'a*; Ind. *bida'ah*) when it is certain that the greatest innovation has been the inexorable gestation of a nation-state over the last four centuries.

For certain Muslim intellectuals like Nurcholish Madjid the very quest for an "Islamic state" partakes of idolatry. The oneness of Allah (*tauhid*) means that Islam must not be identified with a state. But for the more sectarian Muslims, pluralism destroys the sovereignty of Allah, and society must be governed by the *sharī'ah* so as to reflect His unity. Both of these two positions seem to reflect the influence of Western Europe on the political history of Indonesia. This is not to say that it will take a similar course to that of European disenchantment, but that the role of individualism in Java in the twentieth century will influence any continued development of the Muslim community. A recently holistic society like Java is evolving in an unusual monotheistic (Pancasila), yet secular, nation-state and all religious communities will have to navigate between the earlier yet still influential social morphology, their awareness of the dangers of European style disenchantment and the risks of communalism, or hyperenchantment of the kind displayed by Indian and Pakistan. There are no other "Islamic" countries like Indonesia. As a window on the destiny of the twenty-first century Java has a lot to offer to those who would study it.

The slow disenchantment of the European feudal state with religious praxis was driven by the secularizing political philosophy of the incipient nation-state (Milbank 1990, chs. 1 and 2). In a complete discussion it would be necessary to acknowledge which qualities of the European nation-state have been adopted, *mutatis mutandis,* by Indonesian nationalists. In the Middle East, we understand that after the earliest expressions of Islam found in the society of Medina, there occurred an initial sacralization of a fundamentally secular state under the Ummayad caliphs (661–750). This substitution of human leadership for a divine prophetic and charismatic one would remain viable for more than a thousand years. A sacralization of Islamic cities and their society occurs once the five pillars are given socializing value (Boland 1982, pp. 159–60; Gardet 1981, p. 276). The sacred role of the caliph as defender of the faith is said to come directly from Allah and the uniform application of the *sharī'ah* to the *umma* is a programme for making whole the revelation to the prophet Muhammad on the social level. Inside this medieval Muslim holism there are nonetheless seeds of individualism that derive from their faith, and reorient their activities to the profane finalities of the city. The primacy of the spiritual, as soon as it is underwritten by the prince, elicits an expression of the autonomy of the temporal despite multiple denials of this secularization on the part of the lay theocracy. The rapid spatial expansion of Islam from the Medina polity initially implied not only an immense *jihad* to spread Islam, but also a compromise, the introduction of the agency of empire, rather than spontaneous conversion.

However, as Garth Fowden (1993, ch. 6) has shown, this empire was rapidly transformed into a commonwealth. Non-Arab converts (*mawali*) became less and less stigmatized intermediaries. Relations between the Sind (India) and Spain involved several *umma*, indispensable for propagating the faith, after the Abbasids made Baghdad the centre of the world (750), and once the Umayyad had fled to Spain. By the middle of the tenth century, Iran was already 90 per cent Muslim, and by the eleventh century Iraq, Syria, Egypt and North Africa were also almost entirely Muslim. What had changed of course was that these peoples' vested interest was in an Islamic monotheist commonwealth, rather than a unified Arab empire. In this sense monotheism was the pivot of the commonwealth, the new relation between the different *umma*. Between the seventh and the eleventh centuries, trade and migration brought into contact nomadic and agricultural peoples further east in northern India. Then between the eleventh and thirteenth centuries, Islamic conquest and political domination created new organizational forms for these Indo-Islamic states (Wink 1990, 1997). Ever since Alexander the Great, trade had opened the maritime silk route from China through Indonesia to the Persian gulf, and now for the second time after Hinduism and Buddhism, it would be used to transfer a religious landscape of belief to Java, that of Islam.

This first section has established that there are two parameters to Islamicization. One can be called historical: the spread of Islam from the past to the present with the gradual transposing of a Middle Eastern monotheism onto another geography of belief, that of Java. The second is political, best read in Indonesia by starting in the present and working backwards towards the nineteenth century roots of recent events. For example, the professionalization of Islamic cadres under the supervision of the Ministry of Religion is not only a phenomenon of bureaucratization by the supra-religious national ideology of Pancasila, but also the occasion for Islam political parties to advance (then later to pull back) from the postures of independence and distance *vis-à-vis* the government, that they had adopted after 1830 towards the Dutch colonial administration. By not being part of administration they could work directly with the faithful Muslims. The identity of Islam with the Javanese body social must now be addressed.

3. THE INCORPORATION OF ISLAM: THE UMAT A TRANSPOSABLE LANDSCAPE OF BELIEF

Even if the history of Islam is far from over, Java, for the moment, represents its major implantation in the Far East. It is useful to survey briefly the relation of South Asian Islam with that of Java since that is where it came through or from. Susan Bayly, in her book on the Indian sub-caste system (1999, p. 458) says that conversion is "the prosecution of claims to higher status by other and more militant means … in order to elevate their standing within a locally recognized scheme of ceremonial rank and precedence." Bayly rejects the issues of adherence to earlier "superstitions" as well as efforts to dissolve ritual relations in the interest of modernity, egalitarianism or social progress. In southern India the pre-colonial warrior culture had been syncretic. In the following colonial period legends of sacred competition taken out of context became rallying calls for political and other secularized competitive activities (1989, pp. 459–61). Bayly points out the paradox in the colonial period of growing hostility between religious groups accompanied by persistent or reinvented syncreticism. In the post-colonial period Arjun Appadurai calls this culturalization. For instance, he defines culture (1996, p. 13) as a "pervasive dimension of human discourse that exploits difference to generate diverse conceptions of group identity". And cultural as "only those differences that either express or set the ground work for the moblization of group identities".

Parts of these descriptions of southern India could be applied to Central Java if only because both until recently were tradition-bound societies. It is certain that Java is no longer a holistic society and not yet and individualistic one. Some twenty years ago Louis Dumont in his *Essais sur l'individualisme*

(1983) tried to encourage the study of these hybrid societies that he called pseudo-holisms. This anthropological perspective on modern ideology has indeed proved useful. Even where the holistic ideology subordinating the individual values to those of the society has lost it hold, traditional evaluation of social values in a horizon of transcendence remains and needs to be understood. The regular reappearance of juxtapositions surpassed by the encompassment on a higher order using a hierarchy of values has been our main example of this kind of mediation.

An example now belonging to the past was the traditional opposition of village and palace to be diagrammed at the end of Chapter 3. Another example, still valid despite the disappearance of the older cosmology, is the superiority of Islam as a religious value when the Javanese address the outside world. When the same person turns inwards toward his village, family and his ancestors, his ancestral Javanese religion often takes over. This sort of inversion of holism by a monotheistic Islamic individualism is motivated to the extent that Javanese ancestral religion can only survive in as much as it "admits" to the superiority of Islam whose religious vocabulary it has adopted, while reinterpreting much in terms of a traditional Javanese cosmos.

Can we put this level of sociology in the historical context of South Asian Islamization? Characteristically the history of Islam in South Asia is divided up into three periods:

- Following a Graeco-Roman penetration pattern, during the tenth till the twelfth centuries, Islam encircles the Indian coast through a network of Arabian Muslim traders.
- During the thirteenth and fourteenth centuries, Islam experiences an "imperial" expansion due to Muslim governance. A rupture with the past is occasioned by Moghul expansion.
- During the last phase of indigenization, Urdu, Gujarati, Bengali, and Tamil, and in Southeast Asia Malay and Chinese, become the languages of Islam's expression outside the mosque-based *salat* canonical prayers performed in Arabic.

Our presentation here involved using the history of the "Islamization" of Java to bring into focus the religious geography of Java once Islam has started to spread there. To show how two periods of Javanese history, the so-called Indianization and Islamization, are both written on the same substratum requires describing that third lense, local cosmologies. The difference between these two waves of acculturation coming from the West to insular Southeast Asia was that Islam eventually, very slowly, did become a mass religion in Java, while Hinduism and Buddhism never did. What determined their difference may have had as much to do with the evolution of social morphology under the impact of colonialism and contacts with the Middle East than with Islam itself. After the marginalization of the ancestral Javanese customs, Islam again permitted the Javanese to think in terms of a whole, that of the *umat*. One needs an overview of the first millennium to understand this. After the Gupta conquest of the Ganges valley, the Pallava kingdom based in Kanci began trading in Southeast Asia. In the first century AD once the Indian access to Siberian gold was cut off, and Indian traders went to Southeast Asia looking for other sources of it, Indonesia was first called the Land of Gold (Suvarnabhumi). The "Indianization" of Southeast Asia, if the concept has any meaning at all, can be seen as the continuation in diminished form of a much older process, the selective absorption of Indian culture by Southeast Asia, that began in north-west India itself and moved east and south across the subcontinent. The Indians did not colonize Southeast Asia; they were called in by monarchs attracted to the ideology of divine right rice culture. Hinduization was about placing the king and the divinities (*devata*) at the centre of their kingdoms on Mt Meru where the *lingga* of Siva rose (Hall 1985).

For Coedes (1949) the Chinese interest in Southeast Asia during the first millennium would not have been fundamentally different from the Indian one, except for the fact that Sinicization involved military annexation, while Indianization was peaceful, providing the "ritual dimensions" of governance or adaptation to local social structures. Furthermore until the late tenth century China was still using its continental overland silk route to the West and only beginning in the 980s did the Sung dynasty turn towards its Southern Sea (Nan Hai) where it dominated both trade and politics. Confucian traditions were much less accommodating to Southeast Asian folk traditions than were Indian ones.

In the second millennium, the one which concerns the expansion of Islam, one could say that while parts of India momentarily became an abode of Islam (*dār al-Islām*), continental and insular Southeast Asia remained a pagan (*dār al-harb*) in spite of important Muslim centres in Aceh, the Malay peninsula, Sulawesi (Celebes) and Java. The problem with generalizations about the second half of the second millennium, when Islam came on the scene in southern Asia is that amongst so many actors and decisive events, civilizational factors hadn't the time to mature. If we take the word modern in its etymological sense of "just now" (the Latin adverb, *modo*), modern history begins it breathtaking race here. The Ming were to leave the South China Sea (Nan Hai) in 1434; Vasco de Gama inaugurates the European trade route to the Indies in 1498, defeating off Gujarat a Mamaluke flotilla financed by the Ottomans, and in 1509 creating Goa and in 1511 conquering Malacca (Malay pensinsula). Only in 1561 did the Mughal empire begin to expand, to be followed, in 1756 a century later, by the British colonial effort in India. During this extremely busy period, Islam in Indonesia slowly, imperceptibly grew and spread. But what Islam was it?

In India, Turkey and central Asia spread the Hanafism of the Turks of Persian culture. Imam Abu Hanifi (700–+\–767) created this school of interpretation (*madhhab*) later used by the Abbasids, the Seldjukes, and the Ottomans. When the Koran and the *hadith* provided no clear-cut definition, Hanafism accepted personal opinion (*ra'y*) and rationality. On the east coast of Africa, parts of the south coast of India (Gaboriau 1995, p. 450) and in Indonesia the Shafi'ite school of interpretation used in jurisprudence tried to find a synthesis between divine will and human speculation, by tolerating human reasoning (*qiyas*) and the consensus of the doctors of the law (*idjma*). If we include the nineteenth and twentieth century in this sketch, we should also mention the influence of a third school, the Hanbalites. In their school of interpretation, all heresy (*bid'a*) was introduced by analogous reasoning. This literal school of interpretation popular in Iraq and Syria up until the fifteenth century; it gained renewed influence, thanks to the spread of Wahabite groups from what became Saudi Arabia.

The rise of Muslim kingdoms in India (eleventh century), in Sumatra (thirteenth century), and in Java (fifteenth century) provided protection for nascent Islam. This protection differed, however, depending on whether these polities were coastal sultanates or inland agrarian regimes. In contrast to Java's Muslim population in its north coastal ports, Hindu influence during the first millennium in the kingdom of the first Mataram had started in the very centre of Java (van Leur 1955), just as it had *mutatis mutandis* in Mon Dvaravati, Khmer Angkor and Pagan Burma. Beginning at the end of the thirteenth century coastal trading sultanates appear in Indonesia. Many artisans, for instance weavers working for Muslims sultanates, converted. But trade was not the exclusive vector.

Java took literary traditions from the west and exported them as oral traditions throughout Nusantara. Sanskrit literary creativity in Southeast Asia went no further east than Champa, and in Java no canon of sacred writings co-equal or superior to that of the king ever emerged before Islam and the Koran. This continued after the arrival of Islam. In India the place of the four founders of the Cishityya Sufi brotherhoods (Gaboriau 1995, p. 446) can be compared to the nine *wali* (friends) in the founding of Muslim north coast sultanates in Java. In northern India the brotherhoods tended to be central Asian in origin and syncretic, while in southern India the *tarekat* tended to be of Arabaic and Iranian origin, more "orthodox". In Java a network directly linked their Suf'i brotherhoods (*tarékat*) to India and Mecca beginning in the 1500s.

India with a current population of one billion is an entire subcontinent while Java is only an island, with a population today twice than that of Tamil Nadu. In India under the different inland Muslim sultanates, it was always more prestigious to be a first generation immigrant (Gaboriau 1995, p. 42). This was certainly not true of the Javanese aristocrats (*priyayi*). Nonetheless, the apanage system of Java resembled the non-hereditary *ikta* apanage system of the Muslim sultanates of northern India, because the fiefs were assigned only temporarily. Later the segmenting of the regional successor regimes of the Mughal polity (late 1600s and 1700s) proliferated competition between decentralized Indian kingdoms and chiefdoms. These polities resorted to caste symbols and language, which partially negated the integration of India taking place through pilgrimage and commercial exchange. Colonial rule separated out ritual relationships (with their schemes of honour) and their incorporations into kingdoms (Bayly 1999, p. 459). The result was more rigid communal boundaries. During the same period Java was succumbing to ever tighter control by the Dutch VOC due to internecine warfare amongst Javanese princes. In short, Javanese royal authority and the earlier social hierarchy began to disintegrate.

HISTORICAL PATTERNS

In East Asia (Buddhism), and in South and Southeast Asia, the clergy of Buddhism and Hinduism accompanied the spread of rice agriculture. They were imported by local rulers to consolidate their sphere of governance. On the other hand in India the Brahman priesthood and the ascetical corporations (*sangha*, etc.) maintained some independence *vis-à-vis* the courts of powerful rulers. This resulted in India in a diverse religious and political spectrum. Diversity which of course also exists in the archipelago of Indonesia is so great that the adjective "Indonesian" often has no cultural content compared to "Indian". Insularity remains the fundamental unavowed trait of Javanese sociology. Obviously, the typically Indonesian diversity of ecologies, languages, religions, modes of production, and political systems as well as the dichotomies between indigenous subsistence agriculture and commerce or between peasant agriculture and pastoralism, were all secured in a great variety of island bound ethno-linguistic, cultural, and ecological niches. In the Indian subcontinent on the other hand, the large subordinate populations were identified as distinct culturally, morally, and "biologically", so that these tribals or outcastes belonged to a societal outside that was still inside India. Although outside of India we find idealized social and moral orders composed of *varna* or their equivalent, no where else are found the *jati* like birth groups which order social plurality through sub-caste herarchies. All this is so unlike Java where until the nineteenth the population was small and the kings strove to keep them near their kingdoms. In Java outsiders and other "lesser" humans are ideally found overseas, *sabrang*.

Stratification, cultural diversity and religious charisma in Java were traditionally portrayed together in an inversion. The reversible figure of outer (Islamic)/inner Javanese ancestral traditions featured different levels of reality, a social outer one, and a monist's "inner one, the container/contained (*wadah*)", where later is deeper genealogically, chronologically and charismatically. It is here that we find the articulation of the Javanese construction of social stratification, cultural history and religious charisma. It was in this sociology that Islam was obliged to enter to penetrate Java and to emerge if it was to remain itself. The distinction of elder sister (autochthonous goddess) and younger brother (secular ruler) not only was the featured value of the hierarchy, but also permitted the colonized island to place Islam between itself and the Dutch the time it took to find independence. If Islam was not an administration, it did have an independent vision of Javanese society that left no place for the foreigners. The only problem lay that after independence Islam would have to find a new niche for itself in the multi-ethnic and multi-religious nation state.

One cannot situate Islam in monsoon Asia without a model of the social whole to account for the acculturation of an "imported" Muslim praxis and metaphysics. For as long as we have any written records (eighth century onwards, Damais 1990), Java has been a hierarchical society with a ritualized dimension to governance involving "divine right" rice agriculture (van Setten van der Meer 1979). When Islam arrived in Java on its north coast in the late 1400s, the Javanese notion of the "other", the foreigner, began a slow metamorphosis. Merle Ricklefs (in press, ch. 2) has suggested that from then up until the early 1600s on this *pasisir* (north coast), there was a two-way process of foreigners becoming Javanese and some Javanese becoming Muslim. To understand the status and the process of the Muslim community being grafted onto Javanese society, where does one begin? The *umat* that arrived on the north coast of Java in the fourteenth century was not the first foreign community to reach Indonesia before the appearance of the sixteenth century European colonialism. Like the colonizers that followed them, however, they kept open their lines of communication back to their point of origin (Mecca and Medina). Criteria for membership were constant and clear (the confession of faith, *salat*, fasting, circumcision, etc.).

Compared to northern Sumatra, the southern Celebes or the Malay peninsula, however, the adoption of Islam in Java turned out to be a slow process. How was the Muslim community grafted onto the pre-existing Javanese social morphology? In what sense can Islam be said to have become a local community? Starting from what we can know today, it is not always possible to reconstruct retrospectively the historical contours of the *umat*. Even contemporary facts blur the focus on the quite different contexts of the past. At the beginning of the twentieth century, the surpassing of local regional spiritual geographies was mainly due to anti-colonial nationalism; earlier it would have been due to commerce, and or, Islam. One may have been born Javanese, but during the twentieth century, after 1949, it has become possible to cease to be Javanese by becoming an "Indonesian" through personal choice. In so doing, one gains a certain cosmopolitan, inter-insular freedom to view the world in ways that are less embedded in the given insularity of any one society.

One consequence is that one can marry outside one's ethnic group. Choosing to leave one's family's social matrix raises the issue of what kind of community citizenship of the Indonesian Republic represents; the question is too massive to be addressed here (Watson 2000, ch. 4, 5, and 8). We will limit our inquiry here to the individualistic dimension that features in the Muslim *umat*. After four centuries, once Islam had become a thoroughly indigenous Javanese religious tradition, a part of village custom (*adat*), to what extent has it had to reinvent itself to fit into the new context, that of the Indonesian Republic?

This second question involves two issues. The distinction between public and private has been introduced to Indonesian social life, but at the same time, Pancasila ideology with its five tenets (belief in God, nationalism, humanitarianism, social justice, and democracy) professes that it is belief in Allah/God which ideologically permits the Republic to think of itself as a whole. From the point of view of Islam, this seems to me to be a pseudo-whole where the religion of Islam has been relegated to that of a just one among other religious persuasions. Is the Islamic *umat* itself a pseudo-whole, necessarily juxtaposed to other religious traditions in Indonesia, which are also obliged to reinvent themselves? The answer to these two fundamental questions will go a long way to understanding contemporary politicized Islam ravaging Aceh, Southern Kalimantan (Borneo), Ambon, and Java. Its nostalgia for a greater purity of intention (*niat*) has been translated more recently on the political level into militia actions against Christians. This should not hide the fact that recent weak governance in Indonesia has increased many Muslims' confidence in *sharī'ah*. But there is more to Islam than the Jakarta-centred, national level. It is to the rural world we shall now turn.

ISLAM IN THE VILLAGE

Here an ascribed status associated with the membership of a village-family cluster is an unavoidable given. The nature of irrigated wet rice agriculture in Southeast Asia favours villages staying put. Tax farmers formerly provided the link between village and palace. There existed no other hierarchy of values than those put forth by royal order and village custom. Thus ascribed social status did not depend initially on any individual qualifications. Villages today are composed of a minority of land-owning farmers and a large number of nearly or totally landless peasants working outside the villages for salaries. A second basic distinction is that between practising and non-practising "Muslims". In the Javanese villages to what extent does being a Muslim depend on individual qualifications? Very little. One can deepen one's commitment or neglect it, but one is born into the community. The Islam

FIGURE 1
**The birthday of Muhammad (*muladan*) at the Great Mosque on the
northern square (*alun-alun*) in Surakarta**

FIGURE 2
Arrival of the offerings from the Susuhunan's palace to the front of the porch of the Great Mosque for the birthday of Muhammad (*muladan*)

FIGURE 3
Women selling snacks in front of the Great Mosque for this holy day

FIGURE 4
**Ritual cleansing of the village of Krendawahana after the
rice harvest (1974); Young men bring over their family's platters
of food to be shared out. Each village fixed its own date according
to the Javanese calendar, while the Muslim festivals have invariable
dates deriving from urban calendars**

preaching (*dakwah*) movement of the 1980s and 1990s succeeded in making
some people more conscious of their commitment and occasionally converting
new members. A nominal or latent adherence that some Javanese individuals
display towards Islam does not require a conscious decision. As in Greece or
Italy, one does not need to be practising to be familiar with one's religious
culture. Islam can also be experienced as an ambient religious ecology. The
same can be said of the practice of Javanism, the indigenous polytheistic
beliefs (Beatty 1999). The cost of deliberately breaking up of social and
kinship ties in order to enter such a Muslim community from the sixteenth
and seventeenth centuries must have slowed down Islamization drastically.
Group conversions may well have been the norm. A strong religious identity
required sacrifices many non-Muslim Javanese were not prepared to make,
for individualism was not the dominant value of their society (Darrow 1987,
p. 123). Five hundred years after its arrival on the north coast of Java, one

FIGURE 5
After the ceremony, children bring home to their parents the shared remains

cannot say that Islam is in any way foreign to Java, neither has it effaced from the religious geography of that island its earlier spiritual heritage. Bipolar religious commitments (Islam for the outside world and Javanism for the inside world) are common and by many are not seen as syncretic, for as we have claimed above their ranking can be inverted. The Muslim *umma* has often been subsumed into local Javanese social networks. Islam was just attaining the status of "the" royal religion under Sultan Agung (r. 1613–46), when the Dutch landed in Batavia (West Java) at the beginning of the seventeenth century. In the remaining part of that century Islam remained as raja-centric as had the earlier synthesis of Buddhist and Hinduism. In south Central Java, however, over the subsequent centuries Islam was only partially court based. Up until the twentieth century one continued to get glimpses of this. Here is Nakamura's description of the venerable mosque of Mataram early in the twentieth century in the town of Kutha Gédhé south of Yogyakarta, a former court city, venerated as the burial site of the founder of the second Mataram dynasty, Panembahan Senapti Ingalaga (reigned *circa* 1584–1601):

(it) had been used for court rituals as well as for communal and personal rituals of the local Muslims. It was not only a royal property but also the mosque for the local *umat* Islam, community of Muslims. Traditionally, the local population accepted the leadership of court-appointed Mosque officials in community rituals. (Nakamura 1983, p. 93)

Here we have no Indian *sannyasi* or persons "outside the world". The *ulama* and the Muslim community claim to be part of society and even part of the royal hierarchy of this society. This is how one recognizes the superiority of the *umma*. Defining the Muslim community over and against non-Muslim Javanese, as in the earliest fifteenth and sixteenth century Javanese language texts, will gradually be suspended by the arrival of the Dutch. Henceforth (1600–1950) the infidel or *kafir* will be the VOC or the colonial government: the Javanese king is a Muslim when faced with the foreign invaders. When the Dutch and the Portuguese arrived in the archipelago in the early 1600s, they competed with the pre-existing international Islamic merchant class, composed of Chinese, Indians (mainly Gujerati's), and Arabs (Masselman 1963, ch. 10). During the Surabaya War (1717–23) a hundred years later, even Balinese, i.e. non-Muslim, soldiers were enrolled in a holy war against discredited Javanese kings, Pakubuwana I (died 1719) and Amangkurat IV (r. 1719–26; cf. Ricklefs 1993, chs. 10 and 11). Given the increasing dependence of these Central Javanese monarchs on the VOC (Dutch East India Company), the issue, Ricklefs says, is more about identity than orthodoxy.

After the Dutch subjugated and divided the Javanese (Muslim) aristocracy into four separate kingdoms in the 1750s, a last great *jihad* took place against the infidel colonialist: the Java War (1825–30). This Islamic rebellion mobilized both the *ulama* in the rural Koranic schools and disaffected aristocrats. One of these leaders, Kyai Maja played a major part in the Java War (died 1849; Carey 1981, p. 261, note 110). It was his family that was instrumental in the penetration of the first Muslim religious community and school (*pesantrèn*) into the Kaliasa/Krendawahana region in the early 1800s (cf. ch. 6 below). After the Java War, Dutch direct rule prevailed everywhere except the principalities (*vorstenlanden*) of south Central Java. During the nineteenth century this collaboration discredited the royal élites in Java, and the marginalized Muslim teachers in the countryside (Kartodirdjo 1972) began to represent the peasants as a Javanese identity resisting colonial rule. By definition this representation had to be discreet and localized. Too much notoriety brought a rapid military reaction from the Dutch. The *umat* who gathered for services for the Friday noon prayer in the early modern era benefited from an increasing, but not yet total, identification of Java as Muslim. Beyond the local village mosque, it clearest expression would have been the network of traditional Javanese religious communities led by Muslim teachers, *ulama* or *kyai*. However, these rural Muslim teachers could not refer to any overarching structuring principle other than the former sultanates.

Once Java lost its political independence to the Dutch, Muslims were respected, but remained fragmented. In this situation the "unreformed" rural Muslims could only be comforted by their participation in the classificatory schemas of the indigenous Javanese cosmology which rooted their microcosm in these local cosmological categories of peasant practice. All this would change radically at the beginning of the twentieth century. It was among the Muslim trading class that the first nationalist movement, the Sarekat Islam, would appear, in 1911. Without knowing it, under the influence of Wahabism, the most progressive Muslims would become the vectors of a secularizing urban culture of moral individualism. Initially a dimension of Muhammadiyah educational goals designed to disengage lukewarm Muslims from the ambient paganism, individualism emerged with a new conception of personal responsibility from itself inside Javanese society. This was no easy task. Hefner writes (2000, p. 33):

> The Europeans destroyed imperial Islam, undermined the authority of the native rulers, and unwittingly reinvigorated popular Islam. This new societally based Islam was different, of course, from the raja-centric traditions of the sixteenth and seventeenth centuries. European control of the state led Muslim leaders to develop a cautious and critical attitude toward government, and forced them to rely on their own resources to develop their institutions.

The development of the rural Koranic schools (*pesantrèn*) such as the one studied below in Chapter 6, is typical of the modest yet robust rural institutions of eighteenth and nineteenth century Javanese Islam (Dhofier 1982/1999). These Muslim centres were linked in a widespread commercial and *tarekat* network throughout Java, extending on to Sumatra and the Middle East (Dhofier 1982/1999, ch. 6). The distance the Muslims teachers, the *kyai,* took from the colonial regime did not however provide them with the ability to invent a new Muslim political culture. Even when anti-Dutch nationalism appeared it was initially Islamo-centric, based on an identity provided by the *umat*. Nonetheless, at the end of the nineteenth century the Javanese most attracted to individualistic Puritan Muslim nationalist sentiment were Muslim entrepreneurs, urban in orientation, not tied into the prestigious orthodoxy that came from the mastery of Islamic religious skills (recitation of the Koran, *fiqh* (Ind. *fikih*), and spiritual disciplines). As late as 1926 the conservative Nahdlatul Ulama would proclaim that there was nothing incompatible between colonial rule and Islam.

This was the time of the creation of many Islamic voluntary associations. The foundation by Javanese of the Muhammadiyah (12 November 1912) followed the creation of the Budi Utomo (1908) and the Sarekat Islam (1909), which initially involved overlapping membership. A Muhammadiyah newspaper was launched with the name *Umat Islam*. Later Muhammadiyah did much to promote the nationalist language, Indonesian (Malay). The period of pre-war nationalism was a difficult one for Javanese Muslims. In 1940 the newspaper *Berita Nadhlatoel Ulama* accused Sukarno of trying to put the *umat* to sleep, of killing its ideals. Politicians could not do without Islam, but repeatedly the problem lay in the fact that the Muslim community came equipped with its own internal law, the *shari'a*. If the *umat* had learned how to be a part of the greater Javanese social morphology, nothing in that earlier adaptation would equip it for dealing with the reduction of its hierarchy of values that Jakarta-based political life demanded.

One would have thought that with the departure of the Dutch, the identification of the *umat* with the archipelago-wide community of Muslims would have posed no problem, but parochial, provincial Javanese networks of *ulama* proved as strong as the broader bonds. During the anti-colonial revolution (1945–50) following the defeat of Japan, many organizations (Hizbullah, Sabillilah, Laskar Rakyat, etc.) were formed to defend the national independence and to defend Islam's place in that struggle. Islamic ideals were realized through these new groupings more than through the existing Muslim organizations. Feillard (1995, p. 46) remarks that the Nahdlatul Ulama in the revolutionary period was an organization dominated by a few charismatic *ulama* and activists, influential over local *ulama* and the *umma*, but lacked any real organizational strength. However, as Nakamura observes carefully (1983, pp. 104–105), if locally Muslims thought the nationalist revolution would produce a realization on earth of Islamic ideals, "The Indonesian Revolution ended as a national revolution and not as a social one." With the return of "normalcy", religion and politics, once merged in the revolutionary period were again separated out. This reveals the end of tendency which, at the end of the colonial era, sought to identify the social with Islam. Sukarno, in his speech of 1 June 1945, outlined religious neutrality and shored it up with the *Pancasila* or five principles of belief in God: belief in God, nationalism, humanitarianism, social justice, and democracy. Sukarno had captured the pulse of the nation, and especially Java, while it remained to the authors of the Jakarta Charter (*piagem*) to insist that Muslims follow Islamic law. There was no question of explicitly requiring that the president of the Republic be a Muslim, even if there was an unwritten law that he or she should nominally be so. If the *umat* is an inviolable (*haram*) community, the reformist Muslim programmes throughout the twentieth century nonetheless realistically envisaged the *umma* as composed of individuals with varying degrees of understanding.

Indeed their movement's programme was to eliminate the mixed (*gadho-gadho*) quality of the Muslim participation in this community. Reflecting this notion of inviolability (*haram*), Pak Ja'far from Kota Gedhé said sanguinely to Nakamura in 1971 (1983, p. 150), "It is true that the *umat* Islam has never been defeated from the outside, but only from within." The danger to the *umat* in the twentieth century came not so much from the fact that society that was polyvalent, that it had several hierarchies of values, and included non-practising Muslims and non-Muslims, as it was from local Muslims' desire to renegotiate the earlier conventions of its place in Javanese society. While they might be able to agree on what sort of Islam should be practised, there was no cohesive vision of the place of Islam in Indonesian society after colonialism (1949 onwards). In the post-war period, Indonesia, and the Muslim community in Java in particular, experienced an unravelling of socially ascribed roles and ranks. Kyai Haji Masjhudi from Kota Gedhé commented in 1971 (Nakamura 1983, p. 101), "Nowadays anybody can become any kind of person." (*Siapa-siapa bisa menjadi apa-apa saja.*) One wonders whether this member of Muhammadiyah is not reflecting on the competition of the state with its Islamic bureaucracy, the Ministry of Religion, the university and mosque intellectuals, a large Javanese Muslim organization, like the Nahdlatul Ulama, was losing its monopoly of the *umma*.

Did this prepare the Javanese Muslims to resign themselves to General Soeharto's regime? Not really. On the contrary, the development of Puritan Islam in the second half of the twentieth century in Java shows the ethical potential of the "occidental ideal of active behaviour (which) ... centrally fixes on the "personality" (Weber 1958, p. 199). Andrée Feillard wrote some five years before Soeharto's fall (May 1998) that since Indonesia lacked geographical unity and since Islam could not provide a substitute for it in an archipelago where the pre-Islamic traditions remained so strong, it was inevitable that a government ideology like the five principles of *Pancasila* would be elaborated as its lowest common denominator of national unity. For Feillard (1995, p. 313) the debate was no longer, as in 1945, *shari'a* or Pancasila, but monotheist *Pancasila* or polytheist *Pancasila*. Furthermore, would Pancasila protect Islam or protect Christians? And Feillard points out for the head of the Nahdlatul Ulama, Abdurrahman Wahid (who became President of the Republic in 1999) the question was not which *Pancasila*, but which Islam. Like the Catholic church in Western Europe, to survive in the modern world

Indonesian Islam had to act self-consciously, adapting itself to contemporary changing local conditions. The inhering community of mosque-based prayer was taken as a political token of Muslim coherence, but less by those who placed their confidence in reciting the supernumerary prayers and counting the invocations said on their prayer beads (*tasbih*), than by those gifted in public speaking and in astute judgements of the Jakarta political landscape.

In the 1970s a campaign was launched by Nurcholish Madjid to abolish the idolatry paid to the goal of the creation of an Islamic state. He argued against any absolutism on the part of Muslim political parties frustrated in their search for social prominence, denied them by the political power invested in the military regime in Jakarta at that time. By the next decade former Muslim political parties had withdrawn from the national electoral arena and "retreated" into social activism, to highlight the extent to which Java was not yet Muslim and its need for educational and revivalists programmes to make it so: bringing the Koran to the villages, constructing mosques in villages where they did not yet exist, and so on. Twenty years later (2002), one often heard that this had enabled lukewarm Muslims to deepen their faith, but that few non-practising Javanese had been converted. Clearly, the Islamization of Java is still ongoing.

The rise of Islam to social prominence in the last years of the Soeharto New Order regime was accompanied by the promotion of a Muslim ethic of inner conviction, vaguely comparable to German sociology's *Gesinnungsethik*, but at the same time there was a resurgence of Javanism in all its forms, reacting to the pressure of Islamic proselytism (*dakwah*; Arabic *da'wah*). Does that mean that Javanese society had broken up into factions? In a way it was the total dominance of Soeharto's New Order regime that gave the Muslims a chance to challenge it on ethical grounds. Since the Muslims were the only social group to have a vision of governance by civil as opposed to military dictate, this gave them the chance to promote civil Islam. The civility and tolerance promoted by the single largest political party in Java today (2002), the traditionalist Muslim movement, Nahdlatul Ulama (NU), encouraged at the highest level a tolerant secularized Islam. Yet immediately after Soeharto's fall from power, the value placed on the social harmonization of Javanese society as a whole, was seriously jeopardized by the conflicts on the archipelago's periphery (Aceh, Southwest Borneo, Moluccas, and East Timor). Even before the fall of that regime, public order was "privatized", and society was being encouraged to protect itself and even mobilize private armies to display the force of its members (van Dijk 2001). If the financing of the militias came from Jakarta, the local participants were not simply hired guns; they were trying to create a faction to fight with other imagined factions for the claim to be able to envisage the social whole that the collapse of Soeharto's dictatorship had finally unchained. The evolution of lawlessness meant that a special kind of individualism and gangsterism (*prémanisme*) associated with money and gun power terrorized society while pretending to be trying to restore it. The reform from within that occupied Islam in Jakarta during the 1980s, after defending itself against the danger of political recuperation, had to turn in the 1990s to another very different social ill, communal violence in East Java and other places. John Sidel (2001, pp. 58–59) has pointed that the violent horizontal competition for resources, recruitment and recognition that followed the fall of the New Order (May 1998) has resulted in the drawing of enduring boundaries between entire communities. From the factors sketched out in this section it seems that the morphology of Islamization of Java is experiencing a reduction of scale and a fragmentation of scope. As long as Islam was interwoven with tradition-bound Javanese culture and religious praxis, it was one with the public sphere, whereas now it is being privatized and finding itself inferior to a public order. Contrary to the Western European theory of civil society, cohabitation seems easier when religion is solidly part of the public sphere and not subject to private manipulation. This raises the whole issue of how the New Order privatized the public good for reasons of "security" and making matters that belonged in the public sphere into purely individual concerns. Java is not just a traditional society leaving behind it a hierarchy of values which had subordinated modern individual values to the relations of the social whole. It is a pseudo-democracy segregating social values rather than integrating them into the representations of society. This results in a lack of recognizable authority in the public sphere and an increase in violent competition for power.

4. A JAVANESE INDIVIDUALISM

Before attempting to sketch out further a description of the Muslim *umat*, it is first necessary to provide an outline of the nascent Javanese individualism *per se*. Peacock's (1978) study of the reformist psychology of Muslim Puritans in Yogyakarta suggests that, in Java at least, Muhammadiyah's movement towards rationalization and disenchantment was a slow one. The framework of communal meals (*slametan*) that ushers a baby into life and escorts an adult to beyond the grave, and that cosmic webbing that protects the central foetus sibling by associations with his surrounding cosmic elder foetus siblings (cf. ch. 1), is very much present among Muhammadiyah members also, even if the ritual forms are attenuated in some urban settings. Peacock found (1978, pp. 80–82) that the matrifocal Javanese house is as prevalent in puritan (*santri*) houses, as in those of conventional Muslims. Even more surprising, Peacock confirms that conjugality is subordinate to consanguinity in these houses and that relations apparently based on marriage are really bonds based on blood.

If biography is shaped into linear themes of mission, aspiration, and activism by strict Muslim commitments, rather than subsumed into a wider socio-cosmic order structured by myths of state (Peacock 1978, pp. 86–92), nonetheless Peacock's interviews (1978, p. 95) show almost no instances of personal conversion narratives.[6] By the late 1980s this would no longer have been the case. While adults' increased commitment to Islam is very common, the Central Javanese still celebrate the day after the end of the Ramadan fast called Lebaran, by asking, on bended knees, forgiveness of parents and respected elders. Eliminating the other-worldly status of ancestors from the fabric of Javanese life has been a goal of Islam for four hundred years in Central Java, and has yet to be accomplished! Javanese continue to pray on their family graves on important occasions in their private and public lives. There is a continually increasing scale of respect (*urmat*) and exalted, noble (*luhur*) starting with one's parents and running through one's ancestors right up to the prophet (*nabi*) and his companions (*sahabat*) in the long lists of witnesses recited in most village invocations. If many Javanese Muslims use the local prayer hall (*langgar*) or mosque for Friday noon prayer, the home still hosts many kinds of prayer, including of course, also, the five daily *salat* (Headley 2000).

This is significant to the extent that it is in front of the house that *wayang* is performed at marriages and circumcisions. The repertory of these shadow puppet plays does not present a literary development of character, but ritually reverses the upheaval (*gara-gara*) narrated down to the restoration of the social cosmic equilibrium. Although Islamic theatre used to exist, the even older Javanese plays (*wayang purwa*) are infinitely more popular with their classificatory play on male/female oppositions through the clown figures, the eldest of whom, the androgyne Semar, is himself a great and perhaps the oldest, Javanese god.

Let us now look at Javanese society without the somewhat articifial distinction of practising and non-practising Muslim. After all this is not the main distinction which obsesses Javanese as they go about their daily lives. If there is one, it is *duit* (money), as in the 1998 song *Goro-goro* (turmoil) of Sutjiwo Tejo. It is impossible to deal with post-"medieval" Javanese history and its changing social morphology without addressing the appearance of individualism in a society once characterized as holistic and hierarchical.

Clifford Geertz (1965, p. 144), commenting on the situation in East Java in the late 1950s, said that the peasant (*abangan*) mentality took the family as the smallest individual unit and imagined that the members of the village shared a similar fate. For the same period Hildred Geertz (1961) noted that marriage stabilized Javanese kin relations which in turn embodied the culture's structure, but that these were threatened by the appearance of individualism. What has changed since the Geertzs described Java of fifty years ago:

1. Pillarization (vertical solidarities) has been replaced by élite collusion at the expense of the social capital of Islam, aristocratic culture and ancestral religion (*agama luri*).
2. Their parallel hierarchies of values have been replaced by an evaluative indifference inspired by the monolithic and unique value of money for a plutocracy.
3. Integrated social spirals and networks have be superseded by the exploitation of cultural traits to create temporary political loyalties.
4. Social units such as the commune, sub-prefecture, and prefecture (*kalurahan, kacamatan* and *kabupatèn*) have little significance faced with the increasing presence of the scaleless topographies of the transient labourers whose only link with Java is often the phone booth (*wartel*).
5. Ascribed status as a facilitator for the articulation of morphologies with given social interests has been replaced by extra village individuation as a false portal towards freedom whereas in fact it only exports surplus families and their labour outside the village.
6. Upscaling for social patronage (*dipayungaké*) has been replaced in the current period of social disintegration by downscaling which now better assures local protection since patronage is exploitive.

Of course, social life has to continue to evolve. Immature individualism had always existed as a reaction against Javanese sociability, although resistance by urban adolescents against the traditional positioning of personality in a socio-cosmic order where self is structured by status and cosmology is nowadays more banal (Peacock 1978, p. 141). It is striking that in Javanese what traditionally is profoundly satisfying (*marem*) is what is close and intimate (*akrab*), that is to say family, the nucleus of which is the siblings. The conflation of basic categories like intimate (*akrab*) with refined (*alus*) and well-being (*slamet*) is all the more dramatic when one recalls that opposed to serenity (*katentreman*) are the coarse (*kasar*) passions (*hawa nafsu*) which are tamed by rationality (*akal*) even more thoroughly by patience (*sabar*) and acceptance (*nrima*). The summum of serene (*tentrem*) is termed *ikhlas*, an Arab term not easily distinguished from the harmony (*rukun*) typical of the socio-cosmic order. Multiplex and diffuse Javanese classifications of society have tried to achieve this state by pairing them with their cosmological counterparts. One's inner conscience (*hati nurani*) is open not only to the personal revelation (*wahyu*), but also to the subordination to one's superior (*atasan*) towards whom one practices self-effacement (*andhap-ansor*). Superiors display *noblesse oblige* (*parentah alus*), a kind of effortless command of inferiors by the charisma that inhabits them.

A convincing demonstration of the limits of Javanese holism has been worked out by George Quinn (1992, ch. 3), who studied the relationship between Javanese novelistic discourse and social reality. Here I would like to incorporate his conclusions in a model of Javanese society combining holism with nascent individualism. I propose that the Javanese may be individualistic in his construction of his inner self, i.e. how he tells himself his own biography, tests out his life projects, etc., but that his behaviour is holistic by the way it integrates and fits with his relationships with the outside social world. Using elements of ethics, metaphysics, mysticism and occult arts many Javanese still configure their interiority in terms of a common cosmology (Damarjati 1994). There is no reduction of an autonomous self in consequence.

S. Errington (1985, 1998) has argued that the Indonesian family may be best envisaged as a succession of sibling sets. In the case of the Bugis (South Celebes), they inhabit a house with cosmic dimensions. Quinn claimed (1992, pp. 131, 246) that in Java this embracing symmetrical unity of socio-cosmic origin becomes the common value of all members of a community. Already at birth, siblingship defines self in a relation where the Javanese makes contact with the macrocosm through his cult of "foetus sibling" (younger sibling placenta, older sibling amniotic fluid, etc.) whose physical trace disappears at his birth, but who act as his helpful sibling, guiding him throughout life. Individualistic consciousness is of only relative value in an integrated universe possessing a communal consciousness. This is not to say that very fragmented universes have not always existed in the consciousness of some Javanese. Indeed, this is a major theme in many Javanese novels, but it is described as the result of "forgetting (*lali*) who one is". Such common fragmenting of holistic sibling consciousness only serves to demonstrate that family and community guarantee a cohesive community. For the newly emergent middle class, whose numerous predicaments of parentage are described by Javanese novels (Quinn 1992, p. 162), such a coherent holistic order, extracted from an idealized peasant past, promises security. Community is paramount, though not invulnerable or infallible; identity and morality are founded in the Javanese communal cosmology. Leo Howe (2001) has just analysed a similar situation in Bali where colonialism and later Islam in the republican setting forced the Balinese to "name and claim" their religion. Where relations are given precedence over entities, what could be more logical than starting with siblingship. Siblingship defines all the kinds of interactions considered socially appropriate. It even contains the primordial taboo of incest, since "identicals" (brother and sisters) are deemed to repulse each other. As one might surmise, foregrounding incest with paradigms such as the myths about the rice goddess Sri and her younger brother Sadana (cf. ch. 2) supposes in-depth coherence. The nuclear family, based on siblingship, is an inviolable value, even when it is often not possible to make of a given marriage a viable relationship. Javanese novels, says Quinn (1999, pp. 185, 188), are essentially about domestic struggle and the return to the mythic male-female relationship epitomized by Sri-Sadana, the Javanese rice goddess and her younger brother king. Indeed this sister-brother intimacy is a primordial icon, but also a source of tension.

Quoting Yurij Lotman, Quinn (1992, pp. 242–43) argues that the Javanese novel is not about plots whose characters are driven to cross social boundaries. On the contrary in these *topoi* of domestic space, it is the house that structures the person in Javanese culture and prose. These are plotless texts where myth, ideology, and notions of order frame characters with inviolable binary semantic oppositions. In the European sense there can be no novels in Java. What then takes its place? The Javanese house (Quinn 1992, ch. 5) is also a complex space. The world-view found in these twentieth century novels is that of the front room or *pendhapa* which embodies myths of order. Javanese novels describe the violation of these *pendhapa* norms by an "outside" or exterior society. Behind, one finds the bedroom or *jromah* where all is laid bare. "(And) if a character attempts to disturb the honesty and the frankness of the bedroom by bearing into it the dissimulation of the *pendhapa,* the endeavour is bound to fail" (Quinn 1992, p. 212). Houses are about sharing spaces in predetermined ways.

Seno Sastroamidjojo (quoted by Quinn 1992, p. 123), says that "The different units within the totality ... certainly have their own identity and energy, but they are inseparable from the cosmic totality." So if randomness is unthinkable then the autonomous individual self looms very small next to the bonds of community. This is analysed by Quinn through his exploration of the Javanese concept of coincidence, the abundant use of which in Javanese narrative had always annoyed the Dutch scholars of Indonesian literature. In the world-view of the urban lower classes who read these novels, special significance is attached to coincidence since randomness is unthinkable. "Coincidence impels the reader away from critical reflection on justice and morality ... reconciling readers to a social order which limits the fulfilment of

individual aspirations." (Quinn 1992, p. 125) The important exception to
this is the modernist novel which accepts the larger space of the Indonesian
state as a higher level reality of which Javanese culture is only one element.
Indeed most novels written in this vein are in Indonesian, and they now
represent the vast majority of the total novels published in Java! By the
separation of Javanese from non-Javanese values, the modernist novel suggests
a way out. One can bridge these boundaries by individualistic struggle if one
is willing to "cease" being Javanese (Quinn 1992, p. 166). This often implies
leaving the most Javanese parts of the island and moving to the multi-ethnic
north coast cities. To some extent in the past adopting Islam meant taking
refuge in that part of the village where the practising or "white" Muslims
shared their quarters.

What remains for those who stay put? They are guaranteed integration
into a society, even if not in the slot they hoped for. Often the household
servants of an urban home or the young farm workers in a village house are
relatives needing support and providing labour for the family in exchange for
roof, food, and minimal social integration, but no salary. Not everyone is up
to founding a household. Even where there is social promotion for some
"successful" ones, just as in the rising Indian sub-castes, which create new
temple and lineage myths, the parvenus of the Javanese *priyayi* upper class do
not ruin it, but only diversify the criteria for membership in it.

At the foundation of this formerly holistic society therefore is the
morphology of the Javanese house. Initially the individual's body houses the
elder and younger foetus siblings with Ego's self at their centre. The ritual
enactment at birth of the relationship of these siblings (the burying of the
placenta, etc.) is only the first of several hierarchical levels of siblingship
(elder-younger) that will come into play and hopefully be consummated,
ideally by a marriage with a "sibling" and maintained by farming blessed by
the rice ancestor, elder sister Dewi Sri. Purification of the couple and
fertilization of the field are closely related. There is a special ritual alcove or
room for the rice goddess (Keeler 1983 and Quinn 1992, p. 233) at the
back of the house where offerings to Sri are made at the granary (*pedaringan*)
every Thursday night. On the other hand, uncontrollable younger siblings
called *kala* destroy self and crops (Headley 2000). These *topos* are strong
enough that in Javanese society even today the struggles of individual
Javanese to break free from them often result simply in their isolating
themselves from their own homes and spouses. In this sense a Javanese
household is the *topos* of one's own interiority, and one's "backroom friend"
(*kanca wingking*), is one's children's mother, i.e. one's wife. The only real
way to break free from these paradigms is to go outside Java where one has

no ancestors, no family graves to pray at when one is distressed, no siblings to protect one, in short no cohabitation. It is important to note at this point that in certain sense the Muslim community (*umat*) stands astride this frontier and can provide a link with the outside non-Javanese world for one trying to escape. Relationships are a given, not only a social construct; in this sense, the communion they provide is unique. Yet no one with whom one could construct another relationship and weave life can equal those provided by one's own house. Here the individual is clearly not an agent whose force of character is able to change any significant aspect of his biography. Human agency is rather located in the space of relationships that form a prior given and in which one is given the chance to play a passing role, on the condition of remain in the web. How then in such a society could one begin to convert to another religion?

5. THE MORPHOLOGIES OF THE JAVANESE MUSLIM COMMUNITY

Between the earlier enclosing cosmologies and the contemporary elective citizenship the following traits characterize the Javanese *umat* as a modern community:

1. Despite the multi-ethnic adherence to different cosmologies along the coastal trading routes of this archipelago, for several centuries Islam and Javanism shared a single cosmology, inland Java sheltering them both. What shattered this cosmology was colonialism and its correlate, nationalism. Henceforth Javanese could choose not to be Javanese anymore, and many did.

2. The passing of the single cosmology does not mean that the Javanese behave as individuals. They are still part of a finely articulated social framework that ascribes to them certain courses of action and techniques of evaluation.

3. Muslims were led to believe by the dismal course of nineteenth century history, that the twentieth would enable their community to realize its globalizing potential. This was an illusion of a Muslim modernity. What had just ended, colonial restrictions on the social mobilization, would be replaced in the new Republic by electoral politics and military regimes, neither of which wanted to adopt a hierarchy of Muslim values.

4. After the violence of May 1998, downscaling to the hamlet or neighbourhood (*kampung*) level proved indispensable for community survival, but it cannot be said that this is where the *umat* best expresses itself most completely.

5. In the post-colonial period neither the vestigial organizations of the *tarekat* nor the strong presence of Koranic schools had the authority to represent Islam nationally. It is well woven into local society, but unable to translate this strength into a vision of society not ridden with nationalism, and prey to political manipulation. As Muslim social institutions, schools, universities, hospitals, etc., grew in importance thanks to state subsidies and local organizational talents, so did social control over them. It seemed inevitable that the élite would operate out of the capital in Jakarta and become enmeshed in the secular networks of money politics that reigned there.

6. What appears as a two-tiered system of individualism at the national level and pseudo-holism on the local level emerges. Neither is genuinely Islamic. On the national level the Muslims are divided by supposed affiliation into a multitude of large and small parties. On the local level the *quartier* contains many who are only nominally Muslim or even not at all so.

7. The so-called "sweeping" in cities like Surakarta, the chasing away of all American or Europeans from hotels, or the banning of night life during the Ramadan fast, when the night fairs (*pasar malam*) used to flourish, are minor examples of the kind of symbolic expression of frustration and anger that is easily organized for political parties who hope to give themselves a front page slot in the Jakarta newspapers.

8. More deeply, the loss of control of urban life pushes many to seek to reinvent traditional cohesion, often before such efforts can be deployed, they are recuperated and exploited by the politicians who more than anyone are ejectable. Social solidarity is still a recent memory and certain of its more civil forms, legal aid, trade unions, inter-religious peace pacts, will surely play an important role. What is definitively post-modern however is a scepticism towards modernity, which has no more kept its promise than democracy.

Hefner poses the delicate issue of the historical fact that all world religions appeared only after the appearance of large kingdoms or even empires. "Having originated in empire, however, the world religions have not always been religions of empire." (1993, p. 29) If Javanese rulers were converted to Islam through commercial or diplomatic pressure, which history has sometimes recorded (Robson 1981), the average Javanese adopted Islam in the etymological sense of choosing it for themselves, when they were attracted to integration in *umat* of believers. If one cannot often objectify a person's motivations, one can try to understand what sort of community Islam represents in Central Java. Rather than speaking of conversion, as in the Greek *metanoia* (repentance), a term imbued with a Christian perspective of redemption, I prefer to use the sociological term of adoption or integration, and hence "Islamization" of individuals, families or communities by conforming to Islamic praxis (Watson 2000, p. 111). The objective of this book is to see how the configuration of values proposed by Islam becomes part of an earlier Javanese hierarchy of values, based on inclusive social integration. One cannot say that Javanese Muslims suffered very long from an identity crisis. A hundred and fifty years after the appearance of the first Muslims mosques on the north coast of Java, Sultan Agung (1613–45) laid the basis for a synthesis between Islam and Javanism (Ricklefs forthcoming, ch. 2). This synthesis was exceptional in Indonesia. For instance in northern Sumatra, during the same period, the peak of Islamic scriptural influence was already attained, although this included executions for apostasy (*murtad*) under Acehnese Sultan Iskandar Thani (ruled 1637–41; Reid 1993, pp. 175–86). The more recent ethnographic material presented in this volume suggests that in Java, while Islam was attributed its own prominent niche, the earlier hierarchy of values, peasant Javanese religiosity and the royal cults, incorporated Islam as a high value, but nonetheless subordinate to that whole.

As early as the end of eighth century, Javanese kings were building massive temples that proclaimed their paramount kingship and mapped the cosmos in such memorable structures as Borobudur (Mus 1935). This does not resemble Islam, at least in as much the imposition from the outside of a universal perspective was not historicized. The biographical where's and when's of Muhammad's life were not mapped out in a world history of a single chronological tenet. But the heretical massive stone temples projecting a vision of the world through the biography and enlightenment of a single person, Gautama Buddha, were not totally foreign to the Muslim notion of belief. The pattern of a biographical model to be imitated, Muhammad's gestures during the fivefold daily *salat*, were kept precisely in order to define the Muslims' relations with Allah. The recitation of the sacred text of the Koran can be compared to the formulaic usage of sacred syllables in the *saivasiddhānta* rites. The importance of a sacred language in both cases was appreciated in rural Java. Since one is not in Benares or Mecca, one must explore how systems of evaluation are woven into the local social fabric. As noted above, on the north coast of Java in the harbour trading centres the cosmos had become multi-ethnic, but did that mean the end to the quest for socio-cosmic fit? Perhaps yes, in the sense that locally society did not have deep roots in the inhabited space which was only transiently so. Social networks would be more inter-insular than rooted in family cemeteries located in historic village sites, where the mythological landscape was long-lasting and of some permanance. While Buddhism in mainland Southeast Asia has proved more malleable to indigenization than Islam in Java, local calendars, local ritual cycles, and local divinities were gradually to be abolished in favour of strict conformity to the monotheistic cult of Allah and the nourishing uniform word of the Koran. The distinctiveness of the "original" Javanese value system is stressed, but negatively so.

From the sociological point of view what is striking is that through the uniformity of a higher value system, earlier local cults are encompassed. For many Javanese what is original (*asli*) remained what is purely local. If the prestige of a geographical hierarchy is gauged by the breadth and expanse of one's cult, then their common reference is a greater horizontal spatial scale. But the older "local" traditions usually have more local genealogical depth. So it is that the Javanese had created two genealogies. They called the Muslim one "the right hand", and the Javanese one "the left". A systematic description, a modelization, of the introduction of Islam on the north coast of Java in the fifteenth century cannot be tied too closely nor separated out totally from the shorter term, more consciously engaged social, political and economic issues. Socio-religious change was clearly linked to those social networks serving other ends, for instance the commerce of Muslim traders. As such, adherence to Islam is often studied as an influence or barometer of socio-economic or political change. Lombard treated Islam as part of the Asiatic network that stimulated the emergence of the individual person and a new type of society based on geographical space and linear time (1990, vol. II). The notion of network is appropriate for certain kinds of comparison between societies, but it does not take into account the specific nature of social bonds in any given society. Java is nothing if it is not *sui generis* in this respect.

Here I have chosen to present the various types of religious behaviour embedded in everyday life as eminently social, juxtaposing public, royal invocations and prayer with another more private, personal praxis. Private, purely individual "religions" certainly do exist in traditional Southeast Asian societies, but mainly remain idiosyncratic. Only some became social movements. An example is the Javanese who participated in the quest for the "knowledge of the prophet Adam" (*èlmu nabi* Adam) of the Samin movement around Blora in north Central Java (Benda and Castles 1969). This study of the adoption of Islam *qua praxis* does provide a focus for the ongoing evolution of the earlier Javanese social morphology, for in the nineteenth century the best focus is the appearance of individualism through Islam.

This is not because the notion of soul (*nafs*) in Javanese Islam is an individualistic one. The Javanese frequentation of the tombs of their family members and saints in local cemeteries is ample proof that the souls of the dead are every bit as much a part of society as are the living (Lombard 1990, vol. II, p. 157). While *sūfī* like Hamzah Fansūrī (second half of the sixteenth century) would insist that all human souls are all constituted of the same light and thus founded in the same All (i.e. Allah), the earlier Javanese conception, as Lombard pointed out (1990, Vol. II, p. 162), is a social one where the quest is less for salvation than for a micro–macro-cosmic harmony. Just as geology, topography, and geography all provide different temporal scales for the study of human settlements and development of a natural environment, so in the chapters that follow we study the rituals, prayers, and myths of the Javanese less for what, than how they believe. Religious praxis is a richer vein than dogmatics for discovering forms of sociability and their changing realizations. Our engagement with these issues is a local, regional one. The issues raised by the entrance of Islam in to the region of Kaliasa-Krendawahana are multiple.

If rationality is to the forefront, is the Islamic cosmography a more ethical vision than the indigenous cosmologies? A ruler of Demak (Trenggana *c.* 1504–46) was the first Javanese king to assume the title of Sultan *c.* 1524, thanks to the authorization from Mecca that Sunan Gunung Jati had obtained for him. For three centuries, up until the Java War (1825–30), Javanese princes were tempted to exercise purely theocratic power. After the Java War the Netherlands Indies government recognized that local Islamic networks were able to challenge colonial rule in the name of both an indigenous and a universal order. Economic exploitation of the Javanese by the Dutch, by non-Muslims, did focus Javanese attention on their Islamic identity. Did Islam with its monotheist canons concerning Allah, the Muslim *umat* and the *sharī'ah* then provide a more inclusive religious institution than did the village cults? The study of the political parties that emerged at the beginning of the twentieth century indicates that sometimes Islam, by its critical distance from the colonial presence, facilitated a nascent nationalism (Ricklefs 1981, ch. 14). The period from 1900 to 1927 was a watershed for the rest of the twentieth century in terms of the emergence of national consciousness. At the beginning of the twentieth century, all the young national organizations were ethnically qualified. For instance, in 1908 the Budi Utomo was founded to pursue the transmission of knowledge in a traditional Javanese and non-Dutch manner, but the first pan-Indonesian organization was one of Muslim traders, the Sarekat Islam. It eventually spread from Central Java to other islands.

The wider Indonesian identity, as opposed to the various ethnic-linguistic groups that comprised it, would appear only with the stimulus of Islamic "modernism" brought back from Singapore and Cairo. This Wahabite movement encouraged breaking free from the four schools of Muslim law and returning to the Koran and *sunnah* (traditions of the prophet's life); this was its conservative aspect. By not closing the gate of reasoning (*bab al-ijtihād*), the thought of Muhammad 'Abduh (1849–1905) in particular, claimed that coming to terms with contemporary science required new legal interpretations which could pull Islam out of its backward ignorance. This was its progressive aspect. The Wahabite followed the Hanbalite legal school. It was the conservative aspect that provoked a negative reaction among the Central and East Javanese leaders of Shafi'i Koranic schools. Already in 1906 with the return from Mecca of the Minangkabau Haji Rasul (1879–1945), these Wahabite ideas spread in the Sumatran highlands. Soon schools became the vector for the variants on these reforms. In 1912 a religious teacher from the Yogyakarta palace (Central Java), who had studied in Mecca, Kyai Haji Ahmad Dahlan (1868–1923), founded the Way of Muhammad (Muhammadiyah) to counteract the advance of Christianity with Islamic education and social welfare programmes. Only after its founder's death, once its destiny was linked to that of the Mingangkabau, did it spread widely.

In 1905 the first colonial teaching decree (*guru odonnantie)* was promulgated requiring Koranic schools to have written permission from the colonial government to teach. It provoked little protest, but by the time of the second decree (1926), fervent Muslims were so miltant and politicized that the ordinance had to be revoked. During the First World War (1914–18), these Muslim political and educational movements were forced to dialogue with one another. Initially the issue was whether one could participate in militias to be created for the defence of the colonial government of the Dutch East Indies without being represented by the People's Council (Volksraad). Curiously, although in 1916 the Volkraad was finally created, the Indies militia bill failed to pass in the Dutch parliament itself. While the Budi Utomo continued to be Java-centric, the pan-Indonesian Sarekat Islam began to split into several factions.

In Central Java around Surakarta the leftist faction was led by Haji Misbach who proclaimed an Islamic Communism (Larson 1987, ch. 4). The orientation was very Javanese.[7] For instance, the local historic heroes of the PKI (Perserikatan Kommunist Indonesia, founded in 1920) were the leaders of the 1825–30 Java War against the Dutch, Prince Dipanagara and his religious advisor kyai Maja, both venerated in Krendawahana at the foot of Durga's shrine (cf. ch. 6). The PKI even harked back to the pre-Islamic kingdom of Majapahit (1294–*circa* 1527), as did Tjipto Mangoenkoesomo's Malay language newspaper, *Modjopait* (Semarang 1916+). Tensions between the Muslims of different persuasions came to a head after the publication on 11 January 1918 of an article in the Surakarta newspaper *Djawi Hisworo*, defaming the prophet for consuming alcohol and opium. Javanese mockery (*préeg*) had again taken Islam as its target (Headley 2002). The issue behind that blasphemy was whether the Javanese were going to adopt a Puritan Islam or not. For some traditionalists who did not want to be reformed by Middle Eastern norms, the founding of the Taman Siswa in 1922 by Ki Hadjar Dewantara (Suwardi) presented an acceptable alternative to the Persatuan Islam (Islamic Union) founded in Bandung in 1923. This later organization was animated by a half-Javanese, half-Tamil, A. Hassan, using its platform to attack all innovations (*bid'a*), and even nationalism, on the grounds that it divided the *umat* on the basis of citizenship. Formally speaking, he was correct in this, even if the actual effect was to further divide Javanese Muslims among themselves.

After the abolition of the Ottoman caliphate and Ibn Sa'ud's capture of Cairo in 1924, that fissure became open. In 1926 the Shafi'i Javanese teachers in the Koranic schools (*pesantrèn*) of East and Central Java, formally opposed the Hanbalite Wahabite reform. The founder of their movement, the Rise of the Ulama (old spelling: Nahdlatu'l-Oulamā) Kyai Haji Hasjim Asjari (1871–1947) was the leader of a Koranic school in Jombang, East Java. He was rapidly joined by other "orthodox" *kyai*, many being part of the larger family network that united this quasi-caste. While refusing the reformist position on the interpretation of the Koran which would incriminate the way their own teachers taught, these "orthodox" teachers and traders saw the need for setting up social welfare institutions concerned with educational improvement, poverty programmes, etc. The Nahdlatul Ulama became the largest Muslim movement on the island of Java, and has remained so to the present day.

The same dichotomy that had come to a head in Surakarta with the controversy surrounding the publication in the newly founded *Djawi Hisworo* (the Royal Javanese) newspaper, in these years created a split which down to the present day characterizes the distinction between the Muhammadiyah and the Nahdlatul Ulama. The puritanical or reformist Muslim reform movements themselves were beginning to split, not for the political reasons that were shattering the nascent nationalist parties, but on the issues of whether Islam was to be nationally or regionally rooted. This did not occur only in Java. Among the Minangkabau, the modernists qualified themselves as white, and the traditional Sufi-led Minangkabau as red, i.e. purely local. It is obvious that Islam was never local in the same sense as Javanese religious cults which could be limited to a single hamlet. Yet the fact that

Islam in Indonesia often had this strong regional focus eventually made it the object of suspicion by the nationalist political leaders and the armed forces after independence (1949).

Radicalism and communism in various forms would grow for a decade before being annihilated in the beginning of 1927 following the unsuccessful uprisings of late 1926. Although Islam had bifurcated in two main directions (Muhammadiyah and Nadhlatul Ulama), it maintained its central position in society through its capacity to critique Javanese society using its own hierarchy of values. It is true that since the sixteenth and seventeenth centuries, this orthodox Islamic exclusivism, a sort of *extra ecclesia nulla salutis*, had provided the leverage for a social critique of Javanism, both in the Javanese court and village society. Now it seemed that a large part of the *umat* identified with a Javanese expression of Islam and did not accept further purification of their so-called innovations. Yet Islam was not the unique expression of the destiny of the Javanese society. At the end of the nineteenth century, it was joined by local Javanese millenarian movements awaiting the appearance of the just king (*ratu adil*; Kartodirdjo 1973). These movements were able to challenge, at least ideologically, the political and economic order imposed by nineteenth century Dutch rule. Certainly the place given to Islam in the 1945 Constitution and its role in the subsequent republican era does not suggest a situation where Islam had a critical edge in political reflection. During the first half of the twentieth century this fall in leverage may have been due to the fact that for the *umat* to become a politicized religious community it would be forced to reinvent itself when faced with an increasingly secular nationalism.

But in other terms, do both Puritan Islamization and Westernization both favour individualism? The number of variable constraints one would have to take into consideration to answer these questions seems to preclude any ready answer. The urban Muslim neighbourhoods that read newspapers and attended meetings were more affected than the rural Muslims who occasionally refused to participate in "statuate labour" (*heerendienst*) and "communal labour" (*gemeentediensten*). A world religion like Islam disposes of rational criteria when it strictly defines the canon of receivable religious texts, leaving a role for hermeneutics, even personal interpretation (*ijtihād*; cf. Barton 1995; Abdullah Saeed 1996). But when the Koran stresses all men's equality before Allah, this surely operates, not directly as a means for justifying political action, but on a deeper level of "religious" individualism. The "emancipation" of the Javanese peasantry was going to take place there. The amorphous resistance of local Javanism (Beatty 1999, pp. 182–84) made the struggle against indifference to Islam a difficult one. Constant reinterpretation of Islam in terms of local religious philosophies was often not of the kind that permitted Puritans to distinguish themselves definitively from local cults. Here, the message of the prophet as the voice of anti-indigenous traditionalism meant something very different than in the cultural ecology of the Middle East or India where the Puritan thinkers like Muhammad 'Abduh and Abū l-A'lā al-Mawdūdī (1903–79) had emerged. The political economy of meaning tended to slip in and out of the border of authorized Islam as the social norm permitted Javanese to be part of Javanese society without being Muslim and without proposing syncretism.

Clearly after five centuries of Muslim presence on the island of Java, the society is not disenchanted in the Weberian sense and the cults of local or even island-wide spirits are still alive. Here a rationalized world religion has taken deep root in Javanese soil without it being exclusively identified with rationality. The local cults continued to enjoy a certain "religious freedom" and, paradoxically, Muslim "individualism" consolidated them in their margin of manoeuvre. The dynamic movements of reflection and philosophy associated with Javanism (*kejawèn*) and the interiority sects (*aliran kabathinan*) were even facilitated by the adoption of the lexicon of Islamic theology. Conversion seen through the eyes of the believers may mean adopting a new set of personal meanings, but from the outside, from the sociological point of view, it has to involve social markers by which one can identity oneself with Islam.

As a secular state, Indonesia is not formally a religious regime, but the Ministry of Religion can hardly be said to be indifferent to the promotion of Islam. At the same time, this ministry is realistic enough to recognize that more than 50 per cent of Indonesians have either no or only a partial self-identification with Islam. This is taken into account, not only in the New Order Pancasila ideology, but also in the importance accorded by that ideology to a fluent articulation of a seamless theism that characterizes most of Java, even if Christians are closer to Muslims than they are to interiority (*kabathinan*) groups. An authoritative Islamic religious institution is in place, but the authoritative cultural structure, what I have called a socio-cosmic morphology, is lacking. That two-tiered microcosm–macrocosm duality (*jagad alit–jagad gedhé*), that socio-cosmic dualism which characterizes many Javanese offerings and invocations had accommodated Islam over the centuries. It differs from what in Africa is sometimes referred to as local and higher level spiritual maps, the tier of higher divinities, as opposed to local spirits (Vincent, Dory and Verdier 1995; Masquelier 2001). In Java the higher sphere involves two pantheons and mythic cycles while the lower sphere refers that of the components of the Javanese persona (cf. chs. 1 and 2).

The formulation of the relationship between local spirits and Islamic figures is an extremely subtle one, as Beatty has shown (1999). Dual, left and right, Hindu and Islamic, genealogies do not adequately account for it. The philosophizing of Javanism does not lack sophistication, but like many such efforts is rarely accumulative. Since the distinction between subject and object is not maintained, this kind of thought is more mimetic than analytical (Lambek 2000). The exclusive religious affiliation that Islam has always claimed for itself had already been challenged in the Middle East by the admission of other monotheisms, the religious pluralism experienced around Mecca and Medina from Islam's inception in the seventh century. Society, thought of as part of a totality, a higher whole, including other monotheisms, was already the basis of the dhimmitude in the Middle East. Unlike Sumatra, where to be Acehnese or Minangkabau is to be Muslim, until recently in Java one did not find a clear opposition between localized pagan spirits and a universal hierarchy of Muslim prophets and Allah. Islam's centripedal role in Java stemmed most recently from the pillarizing (*verzuiling*) influence of political parties which cuts across social classes via religious adherence, while Islam provided a social identifier for the nascent anti-colonial movement at the beginning of the nineteenth century. This was to change on the local level in the second half of the twentieth century.

Even if Islamic networks in Central Java had always mixed commerce and teaching, during the Soeharto New Order, religion was professionalized for the first time and one could be a religious teacher and have a monthly salary. In the region of Kaliasa-Krendawahana the opportunities for new teaching positions (and salaries) in Islamic secondary schools date only from the 1970s. The entrance to a *kyai's* home is still often a maize of bails and crates. Nothing obliges him to separate his commercial activities from his role as a local teacher of orthodoxy. For the first time religion could be professed for financial gain, for a salary and eventually for a rising social status. It is in this context that *kyais* often separate their white (*putihan*) world from the workaday world where they have to deal with *kafir* with whom they are reluctant to marry or to cohabit in other than commercial ways. Their desire to promote Muslim ethics, theology and praxis has been a strong pole for many orthodox Muslims living in the plural society of Central Java and the focus of separate urban and village Islamic quartiers. Often as not, Islam was more surrounded than adapted to the earlier cultural mode. Its inherent content was recognized without exclusivism because an earlier holistic cosmology was still in place. As mentioned above, the exclusivistic monotheism of Islam and its thirst for social predominence have had to accommodate themselves in Java to a sophisticated indigenous society whose local adaptation of Indian Buddhism and Hinduism permitted it to maintain generally relaxed relations with Islam. Did the appearance of the Indonesian Republic deal a harder blow to Javanism than had Islam? By being citizens one is supposed to be equal before the laws of the republic. In this archipelago of religions and commerce, Java had reigned for centuries as the dominant political and cultural entity. Suddenly regions (Java, Bali, etc.) and religions were but the basis of equality and therefore their differences became less significant. Any discussion of the adoption of Islamic values has to take into account that today it is possible for a Javanese to step "outside" of Java and not necessarily to become a Muslim, but a generic Indonesian.

During the difficult years after the economic collapse during the summer of 1997 and since the fall of Soeharto, rogue elements in the army have managed to provoke religious hatreds *à la* Milosevic, but few Javanese subscribe to this politically and financially motivated *jihad*. Indeed Christianity, which in Central Java approaches 10 per cent of the population and is no longer demographically marginal has shown itself capable of making strong allies in the Muslim sphere precisely because they both represent a non-secularized, religious and citizen-oriented vision of democracy. Certain "interfidei" NGO's are of this type. Robert Hefner (1993, pp. 25–28) has discussed the moral economy of reference group theory emphasizes that self-identification is implicated in all choice. Yet in a society like that of the Javanese where the border between self and other is not as the same as in the individualistic societies of Europe, and where reflexive monitoring involves notions of group agency as well as different individual life worlds, the arrival of the larger outside world in the village sphere may disrupt, but also consolidate local society. The social construction of religious identity is multi-causal so that it often rises and subsides within the same individual depending on who he is, what he is doing and with whom. Successive conversions within a single lifetime are a common phenomena in Central Java. One often meets families where the children and the parents all have different religious affiliations (Headley ms. 1998). In such a society social morphology often explains more about behaviour than the study of individual commitments.

6. STRUCTURE OF THIS STUDY

The first part below concerns the early twentieth century rural sociology of religious territories in Krendawahan-Kaliasa. The social organization of village life is included in a broader social morphology whose hierarchy traditionally englobed the villages with a whole series of norms. This study begins with village households, their kindreds and their ritual links with palaces. Chapter 2 presents the founding myths of household and villages, and Chapter 3 analyses the kinds of embodiment that the cult of females divinities, especially the rice mother Sri, and their clienteles take in Central Java. In Chapter 4 a mid-nineteenth century regulation of landholding in Krendawahana is presented in the context of the final changes from apanage to sharecropping that occurred after the land reform beginning in 1909. Chapters 5 and 6 deal with two kinds of lineage's each identifying with Kaliasa in different ways. Chapter 5 presents urban aristocratic lineages attempting to rejuvenate themselves by refounding their own history of the Java War there. Chapter 6 analyses Muslim lineages encompassment of this area within the ever-expanding network of Islamic mosques and *pesantrèn*. This second part concludes that a comparative study of the transposable territories of Durga's clientele can be seen to be "losing ground" in a post-feudal and post-colonial milieu where Islam has attempted to reconstitute itself through a non-territorially community basis.

In Part Three on the varied ritual praxis, we look for the antecedents of the twentieth century patterns of the integrating Muslim and Javanese village cults. Chapters 7, 8 and 9 all concern the village level where Durga's cult in Krendawahana's clientele is both royal and peasant. Chapter 7 deals with Indian material from which Durga's cult was conceived, Chapter 8 with the sacrifice by the king of a buffalo in Durga's forest and Chapter 9 with the Muslim and Javanese mantra used for this sacrifice. Next the area of Kaliasa is left behind to broaden our description. In Chapter 10, the compiling of Javanese and Muslim cosmogonies is presented. Just as the corpus of prayers described in Chapter 8 contained both Arabic and Javanese formula, so beginning in the eighteenth century texts like the *Manikmaya* include both Islamic cosmographies and Javanese cosmogonies. These texts incarnate the kind of multiplicities that local religious territories display. Chapter 11 is an overview, from secondary sources, of the development of Javanese *salat* (mosque prayer). Islam, as we saw in the lineage networks of Chapter 4, proceeds by networks of religious officials who propagate codes of conduct and their rationales. Just as the cosmographies of Chapter 9 explain the appearance of Islamic space, so practice of *salat* submits the diversity of time to the invocation of the name of Allah through these five daily prayers.

In Part Four cosmology, conversion and community in Central Java are dealt with on the basis of very contemporary, post-1998, ethnography. The twelfth chapter attempts to understand the religious construction of this Central Javanese landscape as reinvented traditions challenged by the crisis (shattered social confidence and *jihad*) of the Muslim community today. Both Chapters 13 and 14 analyse hierarchies of values that predominated before village populations were de-territorialized and which are now deployed in urban landscapes, such as Surakarta, with some success. Inter-religious tolerance is invoked not by appeals to abstract principles but by ritual and theatre that portray the autonomy of these lost harmonies. The fifteenth and final chapter presents our concluding vision on the circulation of values exemplified the religious territory of Kaliasa-Krendawahana. How has modernity been appropriated by Islam? Certainly not by secularization *tel quel* but in large part by the accommodation to individualism. However individualism is in part curtailed by the centrality of custom (*adat*) in the process of putting back into circulation values and manners of evaluation of social ills that are indispensable for the cohabitation of ethnic and religious groups on the island of Java.

NOTES

1. Holism is here used as a general designation for any ideology that privileges the whole of society at the expense of, or by subordinating the individuals which go to make it up (Dumont 1983). It is obvious that a non-Arabic Muslim society does not form a whole in the same way that the Javanese cosmos did in Java until recently. The question as to whether Islamic monotheism in the Middle East, projected into the setting of Judeo-Christian monotheisms in the seventh century, was ever a holistic ideology, is a theological question which needs a sociological response society by society, century by century. Java clearly met its first monotheism in Islam, leading to a confrontation between its cosmology and Islam's soteriology.

2. By communalism we understand that when a society begins to be used its culture for a repertoire for identifying difference.

3. Cf. Hobsbawn and Ranger (1983).

4. Throughout this book the Javanese spelling (*umat*) will be retained, except when speaking about the Middle East.

5. Leiden Universiteit Bibliothek, Leiden Oriental ms. 6385, cf. ch. 8.

6. C. W. Watson in his study of autobiography and the representation of modern Indonesia (2000, pp. 109–10) found that religious experience was generally suppressed from the autobiographies of Muslim figures; he does not offer an explanation.

7. Cf. for another Muslim Communism, the Javanese area of Banten in West Java, Williams 2000.

PART I

THE SOCIOLOGY AND PRACTICE OF RELIGION IN CENTRAL JAVA

1

OF PALACES AND PLACENTA
The Praxis of Javanese Kindred

1.1 INTRODUCTION

The island of Java resembles Britain in possessing an unusual insularity. Situated at the crossroads of the maritime trade routes between China to the north and India and the Muslim and Mediterranean world to the west, this society has participated in international networks and absorbed foreign influences for over two thousand years. Nonetheless, once one leaves the cosmopolitan north coast, Java "Javanizes" into a "deep Asia". A new kind of cultural coherence emerged during 350 years of Dutch colonialism. What changed? Since the Dutch first sought spices in the archipelago in the 1590s, the majority of the Javanese population, more than a hundred million people today, have converted to Islam. This volume chronicles that conversion as seen from one region, just north of Surakarta in Central Java: the sacred forest of Krendawahana where Javanese kings from Surakarta offered blood sacrifices to the goddess Durga.

Why choose Durga's forest as an historical benchmark? From at least the eighteenth century the two rulers of Surakarta, the Susuhunan and the Mangkunagaran prince, invoked Durga at her *tertre* for the well being of their kingdoms. Most likely cults of this kind existed in other forests with the same or similar toponyms nearby earlier kingdoms elsewhere in Java. The invocations, and the mythology that accompanied the offerings made in that forest, created a richly woven fabric of belief that survived the arrival of Islam at the beginning of the nineteenth century. While elsewhere in the countryside the massive development of Islam has left few traces of its spread, the proximity of the cult of Durga in Krendawahana, simply because of its urban and royal patronage, and the mythological fame of its cultic site already found in the first book of the Indian epic, the Mahābhārata (*Ādiparva*[1]) of the shadow puppet theatre, permits a more detailed description of Islam's advance.

The construction of this new religious social space did not take place in an economic and political vacuum. Although the economic, political, and social changes that have swept through the region are not our focus here, they need to be sketched out.

In this area some fifteen kilometres north of the city of Surakarta where one can observe an interplay between the royal cult of Durga centred in the village of Krendawahana and the slow spread of Islam from the village of Kaliasa some two kilometres to the west, social influences are registered at different levels of the social structure. These urban-rural and rural-urban influences call into play the entire scale of Javanese social space, not just local provincial networks. The most obvious changes concern farming. Agricultural factors have framed the rural construction of this territory: the gradual disappearance of mutual aid in rice farming in the 1920s; the massive influx of sharecropping agreements in the 1930s; the recent spread of "green revolution" rice growing techniques in the 1970s; intensive capital investments in the 1980s and the flight of landless agricultural workers to the cities with their "better" salaries; the subsequent occasional improvements in agreements for the remaining sharecroppers due to labour shortages; and the massive unemployment which began in the summer of 1997 and led students and workers to return to their villages. In the meanwhile, the strictly religious construction continued evolving.

COMMERCIAL AGRICULTURE:
FROM SUBSISTENCE FARMING TO ITINERANT LABOUR

Comparing Javanese villages today with what we know of the Javanese countryside from the monographs of the first Dutchmen, such as L. Th. Mayer (published in 1897[2]), the last twenty-five years appears to have been a period of rapid social change around the village of Krendawahana. The land tenure system, and the crop rotation associated with it, were frequently changed and revolutionized by the introduction of high-yield varieties of rice. At the same time, the rapid rise of Koranic schools and improved Muslim "encadrement" at the level of hamlet mosque attendance, has curtailed the "mythological landscape"[3] of the countryside around Krendawahana.

By paying particular attention to the last twenty-five years of this process of change, one can gain a sense of the ethno-historical scale of the preceding two hundreds years' history, beginning some fifty years after the installation of the palace of Paku Buwana II (late 1745, early 1746) in Surakarta. Historical evidence permits us only to speak of Islamization in the area of Kaliasa-Krendawahana over the last two hundred years. Elsewhere in Java it began much earlier.

At the beginning of his reign (1613–1646), the Sultan Agung adopted his Islamic title, asking approval from Baghdad. Following the Treaty of Giyanti (13 February 1755) when the Kingdom of Mataram was divided into two parts, the *Susuhunan* (prince or king) of Surakarta did not bear the title Sultan as did the ruler in Yogyakarta, but the more "traditional" one of *Paku Buwana* ("Nail", i.e. pivot, of the World). This should not be interpreted as expressing indifference towards Islam in the newly founded palace of Surakarta: the Muslim quarter (*kauman*) was active here just as in Yogyakarta. Muslim religious feast days were the primary social, economic and religious link for the village of Krendawahana with the royal city of Surakarta, some fifteen kilometres to the south and home to the two palaces. Nonetheless, once a year "spearing" of buffalo (*maésa lawung*) for Durga took place in the Surakarta palaces from where these offerings were transported to a mound at the southern edge of the hamlet (cf. ch. 8). This was performed on the anniversary of the accession to the throne of the ruling monarch. The local agent (*bekel*) of the royal apanage holder (*patuh*) brought two-fifths of the paddy field produce or one-third of the dry field (*tegalan*) to the land owners, i.e. the apanage holders, on the occasion of the *Garebug Mulud* (third Muslim month) and the *Garebeg Puasa* (during the Ramadan fast; Houben 1994, pp. 331, 343–46). These visits, although costly to the peasants of Krendawahana, did not involve them personally. Furthermore, in areas where there were leaseholdings for commercial agriculture, the bond between the apanage[4] holder and the local agents[5] and the peasant households (*cacah*) they controlled was gradually severed. From the 1830s onwards the practice of Europeans renting out the apanages for commercial agriculture was increasingly common. Instead of having fixed revenues in kind, the land owners' monetary income became tied to the price of the Europeans' commercial crops on the world market. In a rain-fed irrigation area like Kaliasa these changes would have had little immediate effect, since little commercial agriculture was practised there.

As population density increased, however, the landless peasants began leaving their villages, since from the 1750s onwards Javanese rural economy was increasingly oriented to export trade (Houben 1994, pp. 315–33). In the area north of Surakarta roughly half the population was to become landless labourers (*glidhig*), as opposed to villagers who owned not only the gardens on which their houses were built but also wet and dry rice fields (*sikep*; Bremen 1983). This implies that half the population of the village were working as day-labourers at some distance from their homes. By the beginning of the nineteenth century, then, not only were many taxes paid in cash rather than in kind, but also the itinerant workers would often have been paid in cash. This was certainly the situation some 150 years later in the early 1970s, when transportation was still by foot or by bicycle.

THE COMING OF THE RAILWAY

When work began on the railroad linking Java's south-central two palace cities Surakarta and Yogyakarta to the north coast city of Semarang, there were ample opportunities for the inhabitants of the Kaliasa-Krendawahana area to find unskilled day labour. Throughout the period of the Cultivation System, the daily wage remained some twenty *duiten*, but the increased mass of copper coinage would have steadily devalued that sum. The overall effect of the arrival of the iron horse was to intensify commercial land use and to limit the arable land dedicated to rice fields (Houben 1994, p. 337). Certainly the forests of Kaliasa-Krendawahana had already been exploited, as Winter's book of Javanese dialogues testifies,[6] but from the 1830s onwards, the forests, and the wilderness as haunt of rebels and criminals, is increasingly an image in the shadow puppet theatre (*wayang*) stories, for the wilderness is henceforth an imagined landscape in myth and ritual. The upper Solo river basin had become the new domain of the European leaseholds found throughout the plains (indigo and sugar plantations) and mountains (tea and coffee plantations; Houben 1994, p. 337). Even if poor soil and lack of technical irrigation left the area to the east of Kaliasa relatively untouched, the area a few kilometers to the west of the Kaliasa-Surakarta road was exploited in this way. The stimulus of geographical mobility for tradesmen, who could henceforth ride third class on the railroad for two cents per kilometre, may have been an important factor, but rapidly the control of capital fell exclusively into the hands of the Europeans and the Chinese, creating a veritable dual economy first described by Boeke (1953). With the penetration of capitalist methods of production, a new form of control over land had become the primary means of social control. Houben concludes:

> Instead of the differentiated agrarian division of rights, which took the form of an extremely complicated network of personal relations, an impersonal relationship between the leaseholder and the people was established which

meant that the latter were not given access to products but only to undifferentiated purchasing power (money). (Houben 1994, pp. 347–48; Mayer 1897, vol. I, pp. 78–79).

1.2 ECONOMIC CHANGE AND RELIGIOUS IDENTITY

What are we to conclude from this résumé of mid-nineteenth century economics based on Houben's research on the principalities of Surakarta and Yogyakarta? There was, and still is, considerable variation from hamlet to hamlet. Krendawahana-Kaliasa was outside the areas of the Western enterprises (cf. Houben's map 1994, p. 294; reproduced on p. 168 of this volume), but next to the railroad going north to Semarang from Surakarta. The villages in this area were therefore largely living in a monetary economy. Even if, for instance, the weaving of local *lurik* cloth survived vestigially for another century (until the 1970s), a subsistence economy was increasingly a thing of the past for these peasants. The destruction of rural subsistence economy on the lands of the great plantations would have taken place more rapidly than in the Kaliasa area, but this does not mean that any autonomy was left to these villages regarding local agricultural practice. The study of neighbouring sub-prefectures (*kecamatan*) shows the same overall trends with regional variations (Headley 1979*a*, pp. 439–50).

While the agricultural autonomy of the villages diminished, then, as external constraints gradually came to dominate internal ones, the cultural autonomy of many villages survived much longer than their economic independence. For example, in a survey of the Islamic elements of hamlet life in the hamlet of Kolojongga (Sléman, D.I. Yogyakarta), Hyung-Jun Kim[7] found that only recently had the abolition of calendrical and communal *kendhuri* (communal meals) handed over the local ritual cycle to the urban Muslim religious sphere based well beyond the village. After some four hundred years of existence in central Java, the urban Islamic calendar had finally abolished the local village ritual cycle. What for centuries had been outside influences were definitively becoming inside constraints. On the level of the villages, one might have imagined this transformation as follows: the strictly Muslim meal involved no generalized reciprocity, while the traditional Javanese ones involved reciprocity not only among the peasant participants, but also with the spirits to whom they are offered, and with the neighbours, who shared in bearing the costs by bringing dishes.

So were the Muslim communal meals (*sadhekah* or *kendhuri*) becoming less reciprocal and more unilateral expressions of commensality oriented towards Allah, while the traditional Javanese ritual meal or *slametan* retained its socio-cosmic polyvalence? Andrew Beatty's study (1999) on the *slametan* in East Java indicates that what is developing is rather a ritual multi-vocality allowing each participant to express mutually exclusive views on Allah, the Koran and its revelation. The now internalized constraints of Muslim orthodoxy have yet to have the last word. In a recent analysis[8] of the anthropology of emotional practices in a Javanese village, Beatty proposes that public and private constructions of reality can be seen from the structuring role of emotion in loosely structured cognatic systems. In Java there is a fluid structure above the household; religious life is dependent on community life. For this level of the *slametan*, the likeness (*pada-pada*) of neighbours united by rituals, where physical proximity determines association, provides a temporary synthesis of diverse religious traditions by creating community and harmony (*rukun*). Feasting groups are supra-household and ritual constituencies are flexible. In this sense the microsocial structure is modular; place changes as houses are flexible units. The patterns of sociality are fluid and guided by emotion, where one feels "in place" (*pernah*) not shy (*isin*), hence not reluctant (*sungkan*) to visit. Although *pernah* means "located in space" and hence related by kinship, it is ritual *and* sentiment (where you can and can't go) that hold Javanese village society together. If domesticated emotions are elaborated inside the family, outside socialized sentiment is culturally framed. While inside the house equality is forbidden, outside the house it is *de rigueur*. *Rukun* is created by the way one enters a house. All this harmony is expensive, however, and each performance of it is in a sense a social challenge. The equality necessitates violent redistribution rituals (*rebutan*) and exorcising *dikalani*. According to Beatty's analysis summarized above, group sociality is defined not by internal organization but by relations with other groups.

Let us look at a few of their historical landmarks. How did the post-sixteenth century social and commercial mobility affect religious identity? Ricklefs has suggested that in the mid-seventeenth century Islam was primarily a social identifier. In the Koranic schools Islam certainly shaped its students' lives deeply, even if, elsewhere in society, and particularly in the *kraton*, Islam was apparently more powerful as a marker of cultural identity than as a guide to personal faith and behaviour (Ricklefs 1993, p. 11). In the seventeenth century, argues Ricklefs, the very notion of a Javanese people was a recent construct. It is possible that the idea of a Javanese identity came to be approximately conterminous with an Islamic identity as one of the fruits of the success of Islamization. This made membership of Javanese society less a matter of ancestry than of religion and culture (1993, pp. 12, 225). Social identity, concludes Ricklefs, was defined by religious belief.

During the *jihad* against Dutch colonialism called the Java War, the Sufi brotherhoods (*tarékat*) were to play a part in the network constituted by the Prince Dipanagara to confront the Dutch. By all accounts, the great watershed of recent Javanese history was the defeat of Prince Dipanagara during the Java War (1825–30), and the subsequent conversion of land tax into a system of forced deliveries of cash crops grown on village lands. The social and economic changes under the Cultivation System[9] (1830 to *circa* 1870; Ricklefs 1981, p. 118) obliging peasants to pay land rent in the form of land consecrated to cash crops, would be so drastic that throughout the second half of the nineteenth century the *tarékat* would provide the network for many of the peasant revolts throughout Java. From 1840 to 1875 there were peasant uprisings virtually every year (Kartodirdjo 1966: chs. 1, 2). This infamous Cultivation System (*cultuurstelsel*), would produce a net decline in the level of "welfare" in the villages, as S. van Deventer's three volume report (1865–66) amply demonstrated. This concerns our study to the extent that the old apanage system, already disrupted by the division of Mataram by the Giyanti Treaty (Houben 1994, pp. 41–49), would never recover from this brutal change in *faire valoir* on the part of the colonial authorities.

The Mangkunagaran principality, adjacent to that of the Susuhunan of Surakarta and including in its territory the village of Krendawahana (see Figure 1.1) would, in the subsequent "liberal" period, combine the practice of land tax (each field being attributed a grade according to its productivity; Headley 1980) with the setting up its own sugar mills at Tasikmadu and Colamadu at the end of the century (Pringgodigdo 1950). This exceptional introduction of Western commercial agriculture through a capitalistic venture on the part of a Javanese principality (cf. Houben 1994, chs. 5, 6) accounts for its considerable wealth up until 1949, when the newly created Republic of Indonesia abruptly nationalized its property. The pathetic descriptions by the newly impoverished aristocrats (interviews, ms. Headley 1995), gives a clear taste of *fin d'époque* as they are brutally forced to deal with twentieth century reality without the privilege of royal land tenure.

For the aristocrats, links to the religious past of Java would have been maintained through the Mangkunagaran, but for the peasants and minor officials of Kaliasa-Krendawahana, their networks of relationships were both more open (across the Cemara River several kilometers away was the territory of the Susuhunan) and more regional, depending on their families' place of origin. This can be seen in the fact that the nationalist revolution and departure from the political scene of many of the Javanese aristocrats,

FIGURE 1.1
Upper Solo River basin (Central Java)

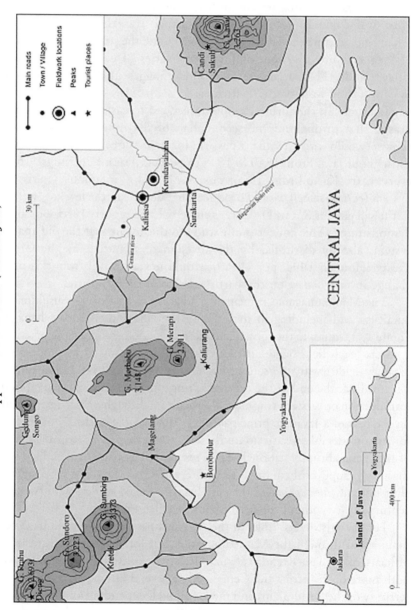

along with the Dutch, marks the end of the sacrifices on Durga's *tertre* at Krendawahana for almost thirty years. Then, in the claustrophobic cultural and political atmosphere prevalent in the late 1970s under Soeharto's New Order government, the lineage (*trah*) of the sixth Paku Buwana (reigned 1823–30) attempted a restoration of this cult. He had been deported to Ambon by the Dutch colonial authorities after Dipanagara's defeat in the Java War in 1830 where he wrote his *Babad Bangun Tapa* (cf. Wieringa 1994). The offerings in Krendawahana were recommenced with some of the same palace servants who had brought them thirty years earlier. One could think that neo-feudalism had returned though the back door, if it were not for the fact that this period of the late 1970s also corresponds to a period of great expansion of Islam and that not always under the surveillance of the New Order's Ministry of Religion.

It is this period of Soeharto's New Order regime (1967–98) which is our main concern here. Given our focus on hierarchies of religious values, we will begin by examining aspects of the social morphology capable of playing a part in the transmission of ritual and invocatory praxis rather than commercial networks and employment patterns which would imply a different description of social networks and kinship. Religious networks, often used by Muslims for trade, are not mistaken for the practice of their faith. Furthermore, the attempt to understand the last two hundred years of history in the Kaliasa-Krendawahana region, leads us to highlight features that are not always centrestage in the day-to-day world of strategies for economic survival among Javanese peasants in the 1990s. Being largely present unconsciously, these religious aspects have considerable capacity for endurance. Prayers to the goddess Durga were medieval Javanese creation hymns or cosmogonies (Headley 2000). Until the 1820s the mythology of this forest served to consolidate royal lineages. The idiom of siblingship is characteristic of both the foundation myths of the Javanese kingdoms and the customs for protecting peasant new-borns in the villages. After a discussion of this kind of siblingship, a sketch of the Javanese Muslims use of lineages will complete our description of Javanese kinship praxis.

1.3 FRIENDS AND ENEMIES: A PERSON'S FOUR "FOETUS SIBLINGS"

The Javanese possess a biographical, intimate dimension of "fictive" kinship. Already in the earliest observations by Muslims of Javanese kinship, dating from the sixteenth century, the "foetus sibling" attracted attention:

It is unbelief to say that among that which is born into the world together
with you, namely blood, the younger brother (placenta) and amniotic
fluid...[10] *An Early Code of Javanese Muslim Ethnics* (Drewes 1978, p. 39)

Throughout western Austronesia the foetus siblings play an important role in
the conception of a human being and his biographical existence.[11] For the
Javanese the most prominent are the umbilical cord and the amniotic fluid.
In the representation of birth held by Javanese, a baby is not alone, but is the
centre of a group made up of four "birth siblings" that is to say his placenta,
umbilical cord, amniotic fluid, and *vernix caseosa*: a creamy substance which
covers the body of a premature new-born (the closer the baby is to term, the
less thick is the cream, and it has totally disappeared from a baby carried
beyond term). Care is lavished not only on the new-born, but also on these
four partners in a baby's birth called its siblings (*sedulur*).[12] Their role does not
end at birth, but is prolonged by the ritual respect with which they are buried,
and the prayers addressed to them during the lifetime by the individual
(designated here by "Ego"), who is the visible centre of this invisible group of
siblings. In Bali these distinctions are taken several steps further. Each of the
four siblings is said to inhabit a specific part of the body and is said to have
helped in distinct and specific ways to have encouraged the foetus out of the
mother's womb into the world.

Javanese myths describe four enemies (*kala*[13]) as transformations of these
four siblings.[14] These are not only dangerous to a child at birth, but are also
the *kala* that pour from the slain body of Kala Gumerang, killed by Wisnu[15]
for attempting to carry off his wife Sri. These become the army of Pu(n)thut
Jantaka and attack the rice fields of the first Javanese village in animal form
(boar, monkey, etc).[16] In the case of the new-born child, the attackers can be
warded off by making offerings and by invoking their opposites or
permutations: the guardian spirits originating from the four quarters of the
cosmos at the creation of the universe who participate in the birth of each
baby. We see, then, that the life of the individual is closely connected with the
cosmos, and the birth of a baby with the birth of the universe. Thus, whether
it be the moment of birth of a mature foetus or the harvest of ripe rice,
fruition is fraught with danger, and requires ritual gifts.

Some of the Javanese-speaking population of this island, from farmers to
important government officials, are capable of relating their own individual
personal experiences with guardian angels, their *kanda,* their "birth siblings".
While your *kanda* give life, their opposites, *kala*, devour you. The "birth
siblings" can guide a human as he moves towards his destiny, through a
personal configuration of time and space. The biography of a child is either

FIGURE 1.2

The Help received from the four older brothers. The life companions suffering from neglect and closely watching the "me" in his state of contented mind (*lega-prana*)

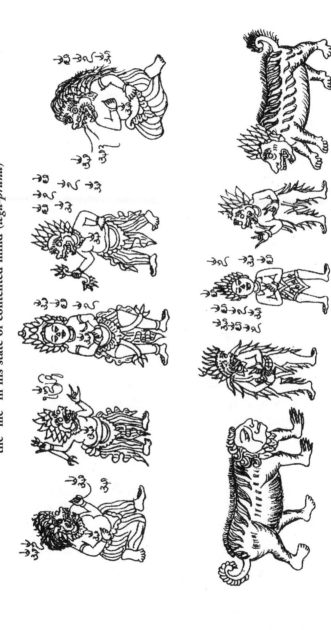

Source: Reproduced from C. Hooykaas, *Drawings of Balinese Sorcery* (Leiden: Brill, 1980), p. 30, by permission of the publisher.

enriched or endangered as he or she progresses across this landscape meeting these figures as friends or as enemies. The human prey of Lord Kala, as recounted in the myth, is said to be "soiled" (*reged* or *sukerta*). The term *sukerta*, meaning hexed, may derive from the Javanese *suker,* dirty.

From the beginning of the eighteenth century, Javanese creation myths were associated with Muslim cosmogonies (cf. Ch. 9). Together, they form an encompassing account of the creation of the universe. During the same period, Muslim holy sites appeared in the region north of Surakarta. The extended classifications of the birth siblings are used by Javanese, who were practising Muslims,[17] in the fourfold Muslim medical psychology. There the personality is considered to be composed of four "breaths" (humours or *napsu*):[18] accusing, approving, inspired, and quiescent. The different belief systems are synchronized by the pairing of the birth siblings with these four humours. They are considered by non-puritan Javanese Muslims to be expressions of the influence of the four siblings on "their" child. The multiplication of correspondences between the initial foursome of birth siblings and psychological humours is common, especially in the interiority sects (*kebathinan*) in Java.[19]

The four friends and enemies (*kanda* and *kala*) who accompany a person throughout his life are a reflection of the metamorphosis of the gods which takes place at the moment of the creation of the world: Siva (and his destructive permutation, *kala*) and his consort the goddess Uma (with her negative manifestation Durga). In an East Javanese creation myth (Smith-Hefner1996, pp. 271–300), the *Purvaka Bhumi*, it is made clear that to ensure that these demonic creators come down to earth return to heaven in the form of benevolent gods, a contract is established involving their departure as a recompense for prayers and offerings. In the more contemporary and better known birth of Kala stories, however, Kala, a spilt-seed son of Siva, marries his demonic extra-uterine mother Durga, and he is considered to be a man-eating demon who needs to be exorcized.

What the work of the Four Friends does make clear, although only in the creation myth, now more or less eclipsed in Javanese folklore, is the origin of one's skin, blood, bones, muscles, head and flesh.[20] The Four Friends were created out of the parts of Vidhi's body. Each has the capacity to forge the same element in mankind. Having been cursed for their reluctance to create the world, the Four Friends beg for forgiveness, and are exorcized by their father. This takes place prior to their participation in man's creation, yet the four *kalas* later attack mankind. The *kalas* keep their respective colours (white, yellow, red, and black), but the outstanding characteristic of the Four Friends is their capacity for a multi-variate classification of the four quarters, elements, days and colours. Their capacity to be protective or malevolent means that the rituals treating them not only expands a prior creation myth, but also places the endangered person under the protection of the Four Friends, thus estranging the four *kala* or enemies. Thus it is that through use, the creation myth has become an exorcism. The creation of man, in the shadow-puppet theatre exorcisms, is detached from the rest of the myth to purify man from an evil destiny (*sukerta*).

While in Java the Four Friends are not well known for their role in creating man, their role as his guardian angels is and can only be understood intellectually by invoking their role in this mythological past. The average midwife in Java is perfectly logical in insisting on the constituent parts of the multi-coloured offerings made to the attacking Kala, for thereby she recalls their inter-relationships. This is a shorthand for an eventually unknown or forgotten myth. The same is true of the offerings made to Kala at shadow-puppet theatre exorcisms, or of royal offerings by the ruler of Surakarta at the hillock of the goddess Durga. Kala and Durga "like" certain foods, and these offerings by their constituent elements, colours and names, correspond to what Kala and Durga are. There is little qualitative differences between the offerings to the Four Friends at birth and in the house-building rituals (Sastra 1924, pp. 110–11), or those to Kala at exorcisms or baby-protecting rituals. The offerings themselves do not suffice to evoke the name of the *persona* for whom they are destined, but in the ritual context, they do designate Kala or the Four Friends clearly. The difference in ritual contexts is much more pronounced than is the difference between the kinds of offerings.

How can one interpret that fact that the siblings, once cursed for their reluctance to create the world,[21] seem to play a role both in protecting and attacking the new creation, mankind? In terms of kinship, the ambiguities of man's relation with these demiurges may be visualized as shown in Figures 1.2 and 1.3 (the fifth position, here labelled androgyne, would normally be in the centre and correspond to Ego). The figures show the generational level of the first Javanese gods emerged from Viddhi or Wenang and how they are reconfigured concentrically around a centre (ego) as either friends or enemies in each generation.

The Javanese peasants do not sense this position as paradoxical, for the simple reason that they do not explicitly make the connection that is stated in the myth to the effect that "the *kala* are *kanda*", that the Bad Ones are the same siblings that become Friends.[22] For the adults with whom I talked, their relationship with the four foetus siblings was only a question of protective rituals to fend off the *kala* attacks at birth (older women knew much about these dangers) and the lullaby-prayers and offerings which are used against

FIGURE 1.3
Man's ambiguous relations with his demiurges

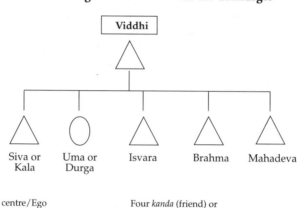

them. Often mention was made only of two, not four, siblings, playing a guardian angel role throughout one's adult life: the elder brother amniotic fluid (*kakang kawah*) and younger brother placenta (*adik ari-ari*). To these two siblings, brief prayers were made on going to sleep, on leaving the house to go on a journey, etc. There is no confusion between them and the bestiary that attacks new-borns under the direction of Kala, afflicting them with convulsions (*sawan sarap*).

Two ways exist to understand this opposition The first is to refer to a well-known Javanese myth treating lifecycle rituals recounted in the almanacs (*primbon*)[23] which are distributed throughout the island, explicitly stating that the gods become Kala's bestiary to attack new-born children. These pamphlets do not, however, connect the gods with the four friends or demiurges involved in the creation of the world and the first man, as did the myth recounted above, so the paradox I have singled out does not strike the Javanese.

The second way to understand the opposition between the Four Friends and Bad Ones is to distinguish the moments at which they take on roles in an individual's life. They become completely unrecognizable transformations of the same foursome. This is undertaken in Chapter 2 below where the chant or lullaby one's grandmother would sing to protect a grandchild from these four Kala's as the child sleeps is contrasted with the myth describing the birth of the child Raketan found in the almanac (*primbon*). This myth is used to explain how for the first time offerings were made to these demons to protect new-born children from illnesses.

Today, amongst the younger urban Javanese, less importance is given to the four enemies and the four friends as personae in Javanese representations of self. Nevertheless, Javanese generally recognize their importance in the outlook of older generations, whose values they may yet inherit. The most abstract level of opposition between the two roles played by the four or two symbolic siblings may yet be retained by the younger generation in terms of ecological concerns. The Bad Ones are *outside* dangers; they pollute the earth. The Four Friends are *inside*, interior protectors allowing one to orient, to position oneself *vis-à-vis* the outside world. The Four Friends or *kanda* derive from the cosmos, from the four cardinal directions, colours, elements, etc., to inhabit the centre of one's perceptions of these sets of correspondences. When this foursome have placed themselves in the microcosmic centre (i.e., the fifth position) creating me, bringing me out into the macrocosm, they not only position me in it, but also remain near me to orient me in the larger universe. This has an important consequence, for Javanese society and cosmos are inseparable. Javanese modernity, in whatever sense we take that term, has not yet succeeded in fracturing the Javanese society into compartmentalized individualities. Thus the significance of this mythology of Ego's coming into the cosmos in terms of Javanese social structure expresses itself in the Javanese attitudes towards ancestors and worship communities that form around them.

1.4 ANCESTORS AND SIBLINGS: TWO FOCI OF KINDRED IN INSULAR SOUTHEAST ASIAN SOCIETIES

In a system of cognatic descent where one traces one's common ancestor from all of both father and mother's families, one could be a member of as many virtual lineages as one has lineal ancestors. This means that cognatic descent groups cannot be residential groups, for what could the rules of residence be (Fox 1967, pp. 148–63)? One solution, found in insular Southeast Asia, is to use ancestors or their cemeteries as a focus for a non-residential worship community. Such ceremonial groups do exist: the Sagada Igorot in the central Luzon highlands (Eggan 1960); Bugis in southeastern Celebes (Chabot 1996) and the Javanese *trah or* lineage. Through restricted membership (by criteria other than sex) one could produce quasi-unilineal groups, giving them a patrilineal tinge. These keep a core of members together and compete with other "lineages" for the allegiance of absent ones. Goodenough (cf. Robin Fox 1967, p. 164) has distinguished between ancestor-focused and ego-focused groups (i.e., the kindred of a common relative, or of "Ego"). In Java, as elsewhere, there exists a division of responsibility: all Ego's kindred, however defined, have some duties towards him and some claims on him. In the northern Philippines, for example, descent groups may regulate ceremony and the use of land sites, while kindred deal in homicide payments and regulate exogamy. Thus the rights over land, possession of a parcel of it, and residence on it are separated out.

These descent groups are not always corporate, in the sense that corporate groups have an existence of their own, independent of the individuals composing them. Differences in possibilities for recruitment to a group depends on which focus is used, are shown in the Table 1.1 (Fox 1967, p. 172).

It is clear that within Southeast Asian societies there is as much scope for variation in these cognatic norms regarding the constitutions of households, as there is with the patrilineal societies in Africa (Murdock 1960, pp. 14, 40). What then is the spectrum for our comparison? In the centre of insular Southeast Asia, there exists a core of cognatic societies from Taiwan down through the Philippines to Borneo, Celebes, Java, and Lombok. To the west and east of this central column one finds unilineal social systems. Lebar's (1972) characterization of insular Southeast Asia does not separate out these two systems, suggesting that cognatic and the neighbouring unilineal systems share certain features central to our interests here. Two of these features are of particular relevance. The first is the near universal symbolic representation of "foetus siblings" that accompany Ego into the world at birth. As we have seen above, the most prominent are elder "brother/sister" amniotic fluid and younger "brother/sister" umbilical cord. The second is the existence of worship communities such as the Javanese corporate descent group called *trah*. As the title of this chapter suggests, these worship communities are potential or would be palaces, even if in Java they have little likelihood of being considered

TABLE 1.1
Groups of cognatic descendants

Recruitment	Focus	
	Ego	Ancestor
Unrestricted	Cognatic kindred	Unrestricted cognatic lineage
Restricted		
by sex	"Unilateral" kindred	Unilineal lineage
other	?	Restricted cognatic lineage

royal. The non-residential character of these corporate groups whose membership is voluntary although based on a genealogical criterion, contrasts with the ineluctably intimate dimension of the foetus sibling. There seems to be little more to Javanese kinship than these two highly contrasted features, which explains the recourse to an anthropology of emotion such as Andrew Beatty has developed.

The ceremonial groups or worship communities are variously construed. "Earlier settlers lineages" exist among the Minangkabau (Ok-Kyung Pak 1993). The Balinese *dadia* is an agnatic corporate group, that is, one which claims descent from a common male ancestor. Balinese consanguineal kinship is perfectly cognatic (Geertz 1975, p. 171) even though traced through the male line. Among the Bugis around Makassar, ceremonial kin groups, called worship communities by Chabot, designate participation in the worship of a common ancestor with one's own ritual specialist (*pinati*).

1.5 JAVANESE KINSHIP IN ITS AUSTRONESIAN CONTEXT

It is useful to bring Javanese social structure within this comparative Austronesian perspective in order to understand better its concept of foetus siblings and Javanese ancestral lineages or *trah*.

In a discussion of descent theories, Needham (1971, p. 10) insisted that different rights transmitted according to different modes give a system of rights and rules which do not necessarily correspond to any principle of descent. Clearly a common feature of saints, grandparents and ancestors is that they give focus to the group's elected identity using the perspective of an ascending genealogy, i.e., from us to them. An ancestor is a person to whom the group or the individual refers, both to distance him and to bring him closer to the group.[24] If death does not automatically transform someone into an ancestor, then a ritual or secondary burial may be required. The relation can then be construed as genealogical. As Fox and Sather (1996) point out, Austronesian social practice usually construes hierarchy and precedence in ways which are not always indicated from the perspective of descent theory. Table 1.2, made up on the basis of Lebar, displays some of this variety of these social features.

Lineages[25] (corporate or otherwise) in the Autronesian world are often variously described by anthropologists in terms of precedence and source (Fox and Sather 1996). Although in Java belonging to a *trah* may be optional, an individual does not make up community ancestors: society does. The difference between genealogically close ancestors and the more distant ones of

TABLE 1.2
Comparison of selected social features of several
western Austronesian societies

Ethnic Group	Selected Social Features

Sulawesi
  Eastern Toraja (Bare'e, etc.)
    (Lebar 1972, p. 132)
	• Bilateral descent;
	• Village membership defined by birth from mother (uterolateral);
	• Worship communities.

Southern Toraja (Lebar 1972, p. 133)	• Ambilineal descent; • Ramage (*pa'rapuan*) descent affiliated to several ancestor-oriented *tongkonan*.
Bugis (cf. Gibson 1995, p. 146)	• Optional affiliation with worship communities of relatives with authority; • Amongst the Ara (Bugis) there exist nested "houses".
Makassarese (Lebar 1972, p. 143)	• Endogamous localized segments of larger non-unilineal kin groups; • Bride price determines status.
Sasak of Lombok (Lebar 1972, p. 65)	• Bilateral descent with patrilineal emphasis provides bride wealth and ceremonial labour.
Balinese (Lebar 1972, p. 60)	• Patrilineal descent, virilocal residence (determined by the husband's family); • Village endogamy (marriage only within the residential community); • The household's courtyard divided by worship communities' (*dadia*) affiliations.

Sumatra
  Acehnese
    (Lebar 1972, p. 15)
	• Hawaiian terminology;
	• Bilateral descent with matrilineal preference (a recent development);
	• The four patrilineal *kawom* (siblings) have disappeared.

Minangkabau (Lebar 1972, p. 23)	• Matrilineal descent through *suku* (MoBr to sister's son); • "Earlier settler" lineages.

the worship communities is captured in Krausskopff's (1989, pp. 65–66) suggestion that close ancestors often assure the mode of transmission of rights, privileges and wealth, while distant ancestors transmit or guarantee norms and values. In either case, it is the descendants who make ancestors of the dead. In this sense ancestrality and filiation are two fundamental dimensions of social order and its reproduction. The extreme case is where the relationship between the living and the dead becomes visible during the funerals of the latter and may determine the rights of a society to the land it occupies.[26] Javanese princes are reported on at least four occasions to have swallowed the divine charisma of the deceased king in order to ensure their succession.[27] The charisma was visible in the form of a drop of sperm at the tip of the erect phallus of the deceased king.

Why in the central Indonesian "cognatic" societies are there are few *descending* genealogies from putative ancestors and mainly ascending ones? The kinship terminology distributes ascendants and descendants of collaterals (those who are descended from a common ancestor but through different lines) in such a way that family trees and distant siblings are unrecognizable. If personal names are forgotten, then the only thing left would be to identify where these nameless descendants from earlier ancestors lived and when. The reference terminology may occasionally ascend twelve generations (Headley 2001, p. 172), but the descending reference terminology is identical. This is even true for the patrilineal Balinese. Louis Berthe (1970, p. 709) called these terminologies "distributive nomenclatures". Koentjaraningrat notes (1985*b*, pp. 465–71) that Javanese contains some sixty-five kin terms. They mark an inner envelope distinguishing these close relatives from distant ones. The Javanese distinguish the first three collateral lines of Ego's generation. There is no preference for a given type of marriage even if there is a preferred direction based on birth order. A prospective male spouse should be born of parents older than wife's parents. There is no lineage input in such a system, since, as Berthe (1970, p. 710) pointed out, a given kind of marriage is never identified with a given relation of consanguinity. What is applicable to the Javanese on the basis of Berthe's observations on the Baduy is that the hierarchy derived from kinship appears exclusively through the categorical dichotomy of elder and younger.[28] This is often called a "diagonal" distinction in that it appears not between generations, but within the same generation.

Given the norm that a man will take a wife in his own generation with a comparable age to his younger brothers and sisters, a series of preferred marriages conforming with this obligation between first cousins (*misan*) could never constitute a cyclical arrangement. In effect, the eldest daughter at one end of the chain should not be married to a younger man at the other end of the chain, unless one claims that at the end of four generations elder and younger no longer counts. Nor can a cycle be constructed because the second generation will be composed exclusively of people who would be either of the immediate family or first cousins.[29] The direction preferred by Javanese marriage norms given below, acts to prevent the closure of the circle (Berthe 1965, pp. 202, 204). Six forms of marriage are commonly discouraged in rural Javanese society:

1. First degree cousins (*nak-sanak*)[30] should not marry, but often do, if related through the mother (*pancer wadon*) and provided the future husband's line is senior. Robson suspects that the prohibition at the first cousin level is a later insertion (1987, p. 515), as it is not found amongst the East Javanese and Baduy in West Java.

2. Marriage between second cousins (*misan*) is discouraged, yet does occur. We do not know what, if any, penalties are incurred.

3. The parents-in-law (*bésan*) relationship is the occasion of two prohibited patterns of marriage: The first is called *tumbak-tumbakan*,[31] meaning that parents become *bésan* twice over because the son of each side took the other's younger sister.

4. The second of the *bésan* prohibited marriages is called *dhadhung pinuntir*, or "rope given an extra twist" and involves the daughter of each side marrying the other's younger brother.

5. *Nunggal suson,* meaning "fed at the same breasts", corresponds to what Héritier (1994, pp. 309–25) calls incest of the second type .

6. *Nunggal welad* means that the prospective couple's umbilical cords were cut by the same bamboo knife. This may be metaphorical and mean to have the same mother, but a different father. It is difficult to see how the wielder of the bamboo knife, the midwife, could be the cause of the taboo.[32]

Opposite sex twins (*kembar dhampit*) are said to have been considered to be "spouses given by the Lord" (Robson 1987, p. 516). As an ideological trait left over from earlier royal strategies for accumulating identity, this will be explored in Chapter 2. Clearly it does not reflect practices that are encountered in everyday life, where the marriage between second degree cousins (*mindho*) is tolerated, in order to "bring back together the scattered bones" (*ngumpulaké balung pisah*). Thus the traditional saying, "first cousins become parents-in-law; second cousins become spouses" (*misan dadi bésan, mindho dadi bojo*). This is as close as one comes in Java to being able to construct any cycle that vaguely resembles "lineage" endogamy. Recently amongst the urban youth, of course, one is often free to marry with an "outsider", someone from another island and ethnic group. So while inter-ethnic and inter-religious marriages are less taboo than in the past they can only represent an individualistic ideal of "freed" love. Kin marriages remain a norm,[33] whether they be aristocratic and serve to maintain pure blood (a royal lineage, *trah ing kusuma*), or between peasants maintaining kindred ties identified by a family name (*sanak sedulur* or *golongan*) and hence often having an economic base. Having described the foetus sibling and what little there is to Javanese kinship, let us now turn to the more properly sociological dimensions of the Javanese culture of group formation.

"THEM AND US": JAVANESE UNDERSTANDING OF PERSONAL AND CORPORATE IDENTITY

To understand the role of lineage (*trah*) in the broader context of Javanese society, it is necessary to understand how "alterity" is perceived and represented. How individual is the Javanese concept of person? In one sense, self (*dhéwé*; *piyambak* can also mean alone, by oneself, *ijèn*) has a potential dimension of plurality from the very start. *Awak dhéwé* (oneself, one's own body) is already "one of us", opposed to "another" (*wong liya, liyan drayan* or *kebrayan*) designates someone else, but also any others.[34] Names and name-giving are the first important features of social identity.[35] A person is first given a little, or child's, name (*jeneng cilik*), then acquires a *paraban* or nickname during adolescence and finally on marrying receives a *jeneng tuwa* or adult name before being "known as" (*ketelah*) father or mother of a child named X (i.e., by a child's name). Gender differentiation in naming is also qualified by status, as in the practice of a woman using her husband's adult name, while only her immediate family, her siblings, continue to use her childhood name.[36] When a father gives a son a name on the occasion of his marriage, this may contain an element of his own name. Relatives (*sanak-sedulur*), include cousins out to and including the third degree, beyond which the distinction disappears between the elder generation (plus one) and the younger generation (minus one). In the peasant families genealogical amnesia often takes over beginning at the generation of grandfather or great-grandfather.

In village life, kindred is also extremely important in shaping the category of persons. If the concept of "shared poverty" has any meaning day-to-day, it is *vis-à-vis* these wide-flung networks of mutual aid that still pervade some areas of life (agriculture, health, cemetery rituals, marriages, house-building, etc.). One turns to the wife's family or the husband's family depending on the kinds of support each is capable of providing. The only competitor to these kin links is that of neighbours, but neighbours, though always on hand (next door), may be closer or more distant than nearby kin. To construe the morphology of the non-residential kindred groups one must understand that each family has several overlapping and often dissimilar sets of linkages depending on the means and size of the nuclear family involved.[37]

In Java today, perhaps for the first time, genealogies arising from Ego are being constructed that go well beyond the normal peasant genealogical amnesia or the claims of aristocratic descent (normally considered void after seven generations). These "new" genealogies or *trah* seem to be related to the loss of political power of the four Javanese royal houses which occurred in 1949 with the creation of the Republic of Indonesia. Prior to that only the king had a continuous genealogy back to the gods, while the aristocrats could only "genealogise" in terms of their descent from the king, or from a provincial governor (*bupati*) designated by him. Since the seventeenth century, the Javanese *pasisir* (north coast) historiography with its new Muslim view of time, has produced numerous volumes of "narrations" (*kandha*) of the Javanese past as they saw it (Lombard 1990, Vol. II, pp. 176–208). Incorporated into these seventeenth, eighteenth, and early nineteenth century histories are the Muslim (right-hand) and Indian-Javanese (left-hand) genealogies that lead back eventually to the cosmologies with which the world began (Pigeaud 1967, Vol. I, p. 130). There was a major literary effort to connect the major Muslim figures to the cosmogony through discussions of the "light of Mohammed" on the one hand, while preserving the role of the first Javanese kings and their purely Javanese cosmogonies on the other. Initially this gave rise to collections of genuine myths, but by the mid-nineteenth century one can speak of literary fabulations of which Ranggawarsita is the most famous author.

HIERARCHY AND BIRTH ORDER IN JAVANESE KINSHIP

This rest of this chapter will be concerned with the place of ancestors and foetus siblings in the Javanese social constructions, prior to the recent appearance of new uses of lineages to be discussed in Chapters 5 and 6. Only one of the four Central Javanese princes has retained political power in the contemporary republic, but their place in Javanese society is relevant to the ethnographic present, not only because they are still living in their palaces, but also because their place in the social landscape of south Central Java has yet to totally vanish with the coming of globalization, even though it has diminished dramatically.

Javanese kinship can be used to characterize traditional Javanese social structure. Behind the important distinction of elder and younger there exist foundation myths of hierarchy to which we will have to turn in order to be assured that the classification system is grounded in some social institution of meaning. In Java birth order theoretically determines whether one is the prey (*mangsa*) of hungry Kala, but in fact these birth order lists include everyone, making everyone a victim of Kala's hunger. Does this mean that birth order lists in some way represent a reconfiguration of the distinction of elder/ younger as it occurs in prescriptions concerning marriage described above? Berthe writing about the Baduy, a mountain group in West Java, has shown that hierarchy is derived from elder/younger distinction in kinship (translation S. C. Headley):

> We can, then, in all likelihood, consider that here [amongst the Baduy] the level of kinship and marriage on the one hand and power on the other, coincide, partially overlapping each other, or that a part of the one is projected on the other thanks to play of the birth order of the children ... functions are transmitted through the younger siblings, while the wealth is distributed (equally between all children) ... it is essential that the territory is embodied in one person, who in Indonesia is not a political leader, being principally charged with the partition and rotation of agricultural plots, as well as their development (1965, pp. 220–21).

As discussed below in Chapter 2, in Javanese mythology the dichotomy of priest and ruler was, *inter alia*, gendered. The elder sister Sri founded agriculture in the primordial village, while younger brother Sadana become its king.[38] This elder-younger dichotomy was replicated (without the sexual distinction) by the younger brother (*priyayi*)[39] aristocrats and eventually by administrators at all levels of the functioning of the realm. The hierarchy of a kinship system like that of the Javanese, when it functions inside a strong kingdom, embedded these categories in everyday life, insisting on a very rigid status system. An apanage kingdom like Mataram in Java was not a feudal system with fiefs. There were virtually no independent aristocratic houses near the palace. Landed aristocracy was only possible as long as one is assimilated to the classificatory status of "younger brother" of the king. *Vis-à-vis* the remaining Javanese you become an elder brother, *kakang* or *raka* (i.e., an aristocrat, a *priyayi*). Out of context, without knowing who is elder or younger, one cannot recognize if a person's status is high or low, if his qualities are good or bad. Javanese aristocratic names often used to indicate both their task (scribe, prosecutor, etc.) and their status within that function. The latter were initially temporary titles indicating at what distance they stood from the king either in terms of kinship or in function. These titles also might stand for the number of generations that separated a person from a preceding king from which they claimed descent (Koentjaraningrat 1985*b*, p. 237). Thus the importance of Javanese notions describing order and context that surround Ego. These classification systems locate areas of disorder:

- by the terms friend and enemy (*kanda* and *kala*) used in the birth-siblings terminology.
- by the terms designating ancestors during the bodily ablutions performed for Ego's twelve preceding generations (Headley 2000*a*, ch. 6).
- by the *sukerta* lists where this word for "soiled" indicates persons requiring *wayang* exorcisms.
- stemming from contact with incestuous elder sisters and underwater queens like Lara Kidul, the "ruler" of the southern ocean.

So far, the materials we have examined takes Ego as their focus, and the friendly and hostile virtual sibling surround this Ego. But are kings and queens subject to all these vicissitudes? James J. Fox, reconstructing the old Javanese kinship system, has written (1986, p. 324):

> A number of inferences may perhaps be drawn from this aspect of old Javanese kinship, especially in regard to the creation of generations. Possessing a long line of predecessors is as important as envisioning a long line of successors. Old Javanese kinship provides the categorical basis for such lines. What is interesting about Austronesian[40] — or perhaps even Southeast Asian — is that, in contrast to similar generational lines in India (…) this generational line is not an exclusive male line, but rather, after two generations, a line that is not denoted by sex at all. This is all the more striking since Hindu Javanese society recognised the category of *pitr* (pl. *pitaras*), "forefathers" (from the Sanskrit for "father") and the rites of *śraddha* performed in their honour.[41] Yet despite this Hindu model, ancestors, as indeed descendants, beyond the second generation, are categorically genderless. From this point of view it is possible to argue that were a dynasty to be perpetuated at some point through a female ancestor, this factor is only relevant for the immediate generations.

This affirmation seems contradicted by the myth of the founding of the Javanese primordial village by the siblings Sri and Sadana, the rice goddess and first Javanese king respectively. Their statues are placed in front of the sacred bed installed at the back of the princes' throne room. A few villagers have statues of this couple in front of their granaries, where in any case offerings are made to Sri. At the village level ancestors are often identified with the first masters of the land, as was Sadana.

Ruling in Java, emblematic in Sri's younger brother Sadana, is also represented by the junior line of the five Pandawa brothers of *Mahābhārata* cycle of the shadow puppet theatre. In Java more recently, younger, also means closer, for instance the more recent the noble's link to the king, the higher his rank. The king, the only person to have an uninterrupted genealogy, admitted a single ideal centre of power (Majapahit, Mataram, etc.). It was he who gave land grants to his family administrators. Before the introduction of Islam genealogies, kinship corresponded with nobility in the sense that they both proceed from the same social origin, the king, and both periodically become extinct. If all status emanated from the king himself, creating a cult of one's own ancestors was largely pointless. The older-younger distinction fixed their respective functions in terms of the Nail of the World (Paku Buwana) which was the title of the Surakarta monarch.

Where hierarchy is expressed in terms of elder and younger, a common feature of Austronesian societies, then the divinities and ancestors play the role of the elder. To adopt a comparative perspective, let us contrast the Javanese with two neighbouring societies, the Balinese to the east of Java and Baduy in the Sundanese region of West Java. A. Ottino (1994, p. 483) describes just such a hierarchy in Bali Age village of Trunyan where one is only ranked contextually, *vis-à-vis* either the first settlers or the rulers.[42] The relationship of genitors and progenitors is the idiom through which the entire village society is classified. The progenitor is at the origin of the group and has access to the source of life and the fertility of nature. The flow of life passes through this androgyne progenitor. Thus this male/female dyad takes precedence over all the other dyadic relationships and encompasses them. See Figure 1.4.

Amongst the Baduy, says Berthe: "… (we find) relationships between nature and culture where the first, represented by the elder, is redeemed by the second, manifested in the younger, in the form of the gods: divine ancestors, divinities of the sun" (1965, p. 222). In a later article speaking, not

FIGURE 1.4
Relationship of genitors and progenitors

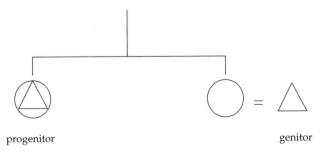

progenitor   genitor

about the central Indonesian cognatic societies, but about the western and
eastern Indonesian unilinear societies in general, Berthe reiterates this idea
which is the precursor of Levi Strauss' notion of "*sociétés à maison*":

> ... since we call these houses clans, lineages or branches, these are certainly
> then groups which, in entering into relationships defining the one over
> against the other, constituting society and giving it its shape, even more
> than the castes of the parents ... these groups always possess a name, equally
> inalienable as the landed property which belongs to them by right: just as
> much as the *suku* Minanngkabau, the Batak *marga*, the houses of Timor etc.
> (1970, p. 713)
>
> Such groups experience themselves as bound together by a profound
> solidarity; they are not only the products of a progressive segmentation, but
> above all of a genealogical continuity .... The stress is therefore placed on
> the continuity of the group, rather than on the membership of individuals.
> (Berthe 1970, p. 713)

If in the central cognatic core there are no permanent groups or lasting
alliances, Berthe (1970, pp. 716–18) asks what structures these societies. He
interprets all preferential forms of marriage as translations of considerations
of transmission of land wealth. In Central Java the social armature of the
kingdoms envisaged no marriage cycles outside of royalty. Where the king
exercised eminent domain for purposes of taxation, belonging to a lineage
was always limited by the nomenclature giving one's degree of kinship with
that king. Transposed onto Javanese society, the categories of Baduy (West
Java) and Javanese hierarchy would look as shown in Table 1.3.

In Sulawesi (Celebes) on the other hand, S. Errington describes the
nested houses of the Bugis in the kingdom of Luwu, each with their own
pusaka or heirloom:

> White blood's source is in the Upper World of the spirits and ancestors, and
> the Datu, a spirit in worldly form (*dewata mallino*), was the only complete

TABLE 1.3
Categories of Javanese and Baduy hierarchy

	Nature	Culture
Javanese	Elder sister Sri, the rice goddess	Younger brother Sadana, brother
Baduy	Divinities of the earth	Ancestors Master of the land; givers of apanage shares

being in the realm; everyone else, in lesser and lesser degrees as the hierarchy descended, was more partial, less complete. (1987, p. 425)

Later on Errington (1987, p. 437) states that:

> Eastern Indonesia begins with a House that has already fractured into multiple houses, and guarantees for itself that they can never be united into a single house again. The centrist societies of the Centrist Archipelago begin with a postulated single House and permit endogamy; their political problem is the danger of the centre's collapsing in on itself.

Indeed one way of formulating the weakness of the Mataram dynasty in Central Java (late sixteenth to twentieth century) lay just there. The Dutch colonialist practice of sponsoring dissident royal houses eventually broke that kingdom into four parts, after which it no longer threatened colonial sovereignty, but nor did society any longer have the form of an encompassing "house".

1.6 KINSHIP AND RITUAL IN PEASANT HOUSES AND PALACES

It was mentioned above that Javanese lists of soiled (*sukerta*) or hexed persons were inclusive and not exclusive. It is important to add that the faults selected concern only certain kinds of oppositions, namely those by which Javanese say how it is that some persons are born or become "incomplete". The explanatory value of the metaphorical categories of incompletion lies precisely in their capacity to express fault and incompletion as conceived on a higher paradigmatic level to which these metaphors' oppositions appeal, namely royal birth and sovereignty. Just as amongst the Bugis of Sulawesi, the Javanese king is the only really complete person. The data presented in Table 1.4 contrasts peasant and kingly "kin(g)ship" practice.

There are not only two kinds of houses, peasant and royal, that can be juxtaposed as in Java. Here again a comparison with a non-Javanese society proves useful. In the southern Celebes amongst the Ara, Gibson (1995, pp. 146–47) has described a "nesting" arrangement involving house and siblings. His diagram of the partial correspondence between body parts, house parts, members of the house and kin terms is shown in Table 1.5.

> Society is seen as a series of nested, relatively self-contained units which reproduce themselves without needing to exchange with other units. The basic unit is the human self, which is differentiated from birth into a set of spiritual "siblings". [*i.e Headley's foetus siblings*] This self is easily expanded into a household self conceived as a unit differentiated into sets of "siblings"

TABLE 1.4
Contrasts between peasant and kingly kinship practices

Peasant Kinship		
"Inside" Ego exist invisible siblings: umbilical cord, amniotic fluid, blood and *vernix caseosa*	Genealogical amnesia beyond generation +2 EGO Use of teknonyms to designate father and mother	Inclusive kin terms for Collaterals in Ego's generation and generation +1/–1.
Royal Kinship		
The King's body is the microcosm of his palace/kingdom	Link to female goddess, Ratu Kidul considered a classificatory elder sister through her visits to his palace. Terms for ascending aristocratic generation imply disintegration KING Lineage links (*trah*) to king and claims to an apanage disintegrate in seven generations	Exclusive categorization of same generation collaterals through apanage

of successive generations ... The deme itself can be thought of as a unit internally differentiated as a maximal sibling group of elders and juniors. Finally, spouses are ritually transformed into "siblings" through a series of rituals that equate them with their children, on the one hand and stress their descent from a common, anonymous household ancestor on the other. I interpret the metaphor of the house in Ara as solving a quite different symbolic problem, caused by the adoption of the idioms of siblingship and place as a means of conceiving the social order.

TABLE 1.5
House and sibling in Ara (Bugis)

Body parts at birth	Spirits in the house and their offerings	Members of house	Kin dimensions
Placenta/elder sibling	Odd and even offerings for anonymous female ancestor in attic.	Grandparents (elder sibling).	Undifferentiated unity of senior generation.
Muhammad/local saint	Odd and even offerings. Male and female house pillars. Elder brother and younger sister.	Brother, sister and younger sibling in initiation rituals.	Sexual duality of medial generation.
Caul	*Sarong* placed on pillars.		
Blood	Descendants. Base of peripheral pillars receive offerings by fours.	Grandchildren (younger sibling).	Undifferentiated multiplicity of junior generation.

Source: Gibson (1995).

The comparison of insular Southeast Asian social structures would certainly put Java at the weak end of the spectrum concerning those traits Levi-Strauss (1979, p. 177) has identified with *sociétés à maison*. That is to say:

> … a moral person holding a domain made up of both material and spiritual goods, which perpetuates itself by the passing on of his name, his fortune, titles, and lineage (real of fictive), held legitimately on the only condition that this continuity can express itself in parenthood or marriage, and most often the two together.

Java is skewed rather oddly in respect to this kind of social structure. Such lineages exist: the *trah*, which unite a considerable number of people through real or fictive kin ties (cf. Chs. 5 and 6). The notion of *société à maison*, however, sheds light on what we have just been discussing, namely the Javanese mythic and ritual representation of bodies and, their birth or well being. As sketched out above, human birth is a miniature creation of the world because accomplished by the same Four Friends who were its demiurges. The body, to be brought forth, must house these four symbolic siblings.

1.7 THE IDIOM OF SIBLINGSHIP: "HOUSE SOCIETIES" AND WORSHIP COMMUNITIES[43]

What are the similarities in Javanese representations between the constitution of a human foetus and that of a king. The constitution of the king differs *only* in that he is completed by divine ancestry. Even Islam did not initially challenge this pretension. Not only was the king a powerful human being in the military or economic sense, but because of the microcosmic process of his gestation, accompanied by the deities of the cardinal directions (a variation of the four symbolic siblings), the static image of the king in his palace, sustained and strengthened by this universal set of classificatory correspondences, was resplendent. This is why the same corpus of prayers was used by the king in his encounter with Durga on her hillock at Krendawahana as was used at the occasion of royal birth and coronation anniversary rituals. His house, and by implication the frontiers of his kingdom, are his incarnation, to such an extent that Behrend (1983) repeatedly insists on the fact that the king is present symbolically through the architecture of his palace even when he is absent physically.

If it were not for the relevance of the notion of *sociétés à maison* for neighbouring societies (Iban, Bugis, Batak, Balinese, and eastern Indonesian), no one would have thought to apply it to Java. But in fact the myths of both the creation of the world and of man set the stage for the Javanese treatment of their bodies as well as their kingdoms as houses. The body does not have the architecture of a house, but physically houses siblings during gestation. The similarity between the prayers and offerings used to exorcise and/or consolidate both body and royal household invite us to reach this conclusion.

The relevance of this claim is not purely ethnographic or intellectual. It explains how in the Javanese body social, the representation of the individual's links with the cosmos through the constituent symbolic siblings of his body was replicated at a higher level where the royal households claim to be a part of their universe. The palace/cosmos encompassed its territory from the "inside". Through macrocosmic symbolic siblings the king consolidates borders for his realm. For the peasantry, the royal kinship of these princely houses was anything but imaginary. The invisible meetings of the ruler of Surakarta with the evil demon Durga on her hillock plainly demonstrate his strength, as do his links with the royal ancestress and consort, the Queen of the Southern Seas. The king's ability to placate these powerful but ambiguous goddesses, and to accumulate identity as their consort and occupant of the palace, was based on the same mythology and similar invocations to those the peasant invoked when he requested an exorcism in the shadow-puppet theatre. The fact that neither recognized the structural homogeneity of their positions at opposite ends of the social scale, meant that the message was all the better embedded. It is the same house which the peasant represents as his body and which the king inhabits at the centre of the kingdom.

Their bodies, their houses, resemble each other because of their "housing", that is to say, because of their orientation (inside the corpus of Javanese mythology), where positioning is accomplished for the peasants by foetus siblings (the Four Friends) and for kings by propitious encounters with Kala's mother Durga, the metamorphosed ideal royal consort. The ancestral origin of kings is very important to the Javanese. If the rice goddess, Sri, and her brother Sadana attempted incest in order to give birth to the first Javanese rulers (cf. Chapter 2), the aid of the demonic goddesses Durga later serves to sweep aside those same obstacles (*wagel*) which the peasants by the prayers are hoping will be eliminated in *wayang* exorcisms. There is nothing static about the homogeneity of these commonly held representations. The peasants as well as the king are busy using them to deal with the world as befits their station. It is not by freezing them, but by seeing how the Javanese find a model for their actions in their customary traditional social institutions that one comes to see how for the Javanese the body is a kind of house. It is in this sense, and only in this sense, that the Javanese social structure may be better understood by comparing it with those social structures in Sumatra and eastern Indonesia which Levi-Strauss has baptized "*sociétés à maison*". Hopefully the distinction here has led to a clarification: Javanese peasants and kings hold distinct, but mutually inclusive visions of their bodies as houses. The lineages or *trah* as first practised by the Muslims outside the network of royal genealogy, announces a change of social morphology and the demise of an earlier form of governance.

When he investigated in the Indonesian archipelago, Lévi-Strauss (1977–78, pp. 494–95) observed that this notion of corporate group had given way to a new criterion, that of marriage, in which the married couple formed the nucleus of the kin group. This principle of unity he called the "house", because without any foundation in descent, property or residence (be it viri-, or uxorilocal), it is the objectivization of: "that unstable relation of marriage which, as an institution, the house has the role of immobilising, even if only in a phantasmatic form" (ibid.). Thus there are two types of analysis of the house: as an institution, and as a fetish.

Briefly stated the densely populated lowland societies of Java and peninsular Malaysia with their heavy state bureaucracies and, in Java, often landless peasants have carved out a considerable social space for the expression of "house" through the extensive use of the idiom of siblingship. This idiom expresses and maintains an identity, the intimacy of the family "house". At the same time, it is a technique or strategy for extending the idiom of the family, i.e. sibling-styled bonding, to distantly related or unrelated individuals.

In this sense it can be seen as a strategy for accumulating and establishing family identity even beyond the loosely classificatory family limits. However the extension of siblingship, of consanguinity, always assumes an implicit view of marriage and hence of incest.

The subtle and complex interrelation of a society's representations of these three realities, incest, marriage and siblingship, is the crux of our understanding of "house", for here "inside", "house", is containing, subsuming or encompassing the non-consanguineous "outside" world. Each society chooses its own definition of consanguinity. As Radcliffe-Brown has remarked (1952, p. 67), one can distinguish the internal solidarity of the sibling group from the unity of the group of siblings as they are perceived collectively from the outside.

Having understood the way in which kinship terms map out a given society's view of consanguinity, what is the identity[44] conveyed by such consanguinity? From one society to another this varies. In Africa, where filiation is often given priority over siblingship, the fundamental criterion for identity is identical sex. Thus the series mother/daughter and father/son is viewed as identical. However in cognatic kinship systems such as those of peninsular Malaysia and Java, it is the nuclear family that is taken as the unit of the identical. For being taken as identical one to another, husband/wife units (a nuclear family) preclude the transmission identity from one generation to another. Within a given generation, then, what is the identity that has been passed on from the preceding? None! Identity is that sense of belonging to a shared *persona* of the house, a *personne morale* one shares with one's fellow siblings. Beyond the culturally determined criterion for identity one can discern, irrespective of kinship system types, the building blocks of the notion of identity in the trait of siblings sharing the same sex.[45]

Having taken the brother/sister asymmetrical relationship as the finite unit in its reflection on difference, societies introduce a dynamic of potential finality into this relationship by characterizing its intra-sibling specificity *vis-à-vis* those "inherited" traits already received from parents. Incest is defined between those with whom one shares the same identity, taken here to mean womb. This has the effect of forcing on brother and sister the quest of a socially normative identity with another "sibling" of opposite sex. To quote Héritier (1979, p. 216):

> The symbolic beliefs of every human group concerning incest, its effects, taboos, are linked to beliefs concerning the relationship between the sexes, the organization and biological functioning and very likely other fields of representation, those of the relationship between the elements, the structure and operation of the world; the whole ethnic corpus of representations

concerning the structure of the body, of the world, of society and their manifold interrelationships...

If the notion of identical is at its strongest between siblings of the same sex (i.e. twin brothers or sisters), the prohibition of incest is culturally represented in Java as a barrier to the accumulation of brother/sister identity. This special sort of androgyne is conceived of as an excess which is only occasionally desirable. In traditional Java incest in the villages between whatever consanguineous members of the family was considered to provoke such great heat that the crops died of drought. Only kings could be imagined as marrying a classificatory mother or sister in order to perpetuate the royal household's line. The first Javanese queen according to the myths was appropriately called "Full of Heat" (*Tiksnawati*). Studies (Headley 1983; Jordaan and Josselin de Jong 1980) have shown how ideally in Java and certain parts of Sumatra and Malaysia the ultimate accumulation of identity is just this brother-sister marriage. According to many myths, this "disease" gave rise to the kings' and queens' ruling houses. The "house" of the kings, projected through this idiom of incestuous siblingship, becomes what Lévi-Strauss has described, referring to the Karo Batak and Atoni houses, as "that veritable microcosm which reflects, ..., an image of the universe and the whole system of social relations".

Comparing Java with eastern Indonesia, we find a similar preoccupation. For Traube (1979, p. 42) discussing the Mambai of East Timor, "The violent separation of the incestuous couple becomes a synecdoche for a new social order based on the obligatory distinction between the marital destinies of brothers and sister." In Java the prevention of the Sri and Sadana's incest is the occasion that allows for the founding of the first "village" kingdom. The fact that Mendhang Kamulan (literally, the origin of the rice chaff) is a village and not a state shows that this myth accounts for the origin of a whole social order.

McKinnon (1983, p. 45), discussing the Tanimbar totalizing god Ubila'a, shows he is both wife-giver and wife-taker, the greatest of nobles and the most lowly of thieves. Further she describes how (1995, p. 183):

> It is the ability to transform the impermanent pathways of sister and aunts into permanent rows of allied houses, to transform the movement of blood into the movement of valuables, to maintain a separate identity, and to become a fixed and enduring source of life for others that effects the generalization and objectification of relations that is the hallmark of named houses.

This sounds much like the transfer of royalty through the maintaining of royal heirlooms behind the ritual bed of Sri in Javanese places (cf. Ch. 2).

If cross-sex twins found house societies, then as Errington (1987, pp. 429–30) claims, to collapse their sexual difference is to return to a sort of primordial unity. Errington has constructed a useful table that plots the permission or prohibition of marrying any degree of sibling:

- The prohibition against marrying any degree of sibling (e.g., East Semai, Ifugao)
- The possibility of marrying a certain degree of siblings, but lack of knowledge of one's sibling beyond this first degree, making marriages "exogamous" by default (e.g., Luwu (Celebes) commoners).
- The allowance marriage of a sibling beyond a certain degree plus the knowledge of one's relatives before the prohibited degree (e.g., the Iban (Borneo), who prefer marriage to a first-, second-, or third-degree sibling).
- The allowance and strong desirability of marrying as close a sibling as possible (e.g., Luwu nobles at the top of the *kapolo*, who prefer to marry first degree siblings).
- The impulse to marry one's full sibling or opposite twin, but its prohibition (e.g., Luwu's founding myth).
- The desirability and legitimacy of marrying one full sibling or opposite-sex twin (e.g., Balinese foundation myths);
- The desirability of generating the world out of an unbroken unity, an act that would require no marriage at all.

The morphology of the Javanese "house" resembles Luwu social structure in differentiating between the peasant and the *kraton* (palace). The Javanese peasant "house" on the other hand is both similar to and different from the palace. Inside the real structure in which the nuclear family dwells, each family, the mother, makes offerings to the rice goddess, Sri, a victim of incest, who died and whose corpse gave rise to the first rice plants. The rice granary, the place where Thursday night offerings are made to her, occupies the same place in the peasants' house that the royal bed of the divine ancestress occupies in the Javanese king's palace. But clearly "house" has a cosmic meaning for the peasants beyond this resemblance of their homes with the king's palace. For the Javanese, the kin with whom one is linked via the idiom of siblingship includes not only the extended family classified as brothers and sisters, but also the foetus siblings that cohabited with Ego as placenta and amniotic fluid, and remain with Ego all through his or her life. His body "housed" them in the same way that the parents of the nuclear family house their children, who belong to one another as consanguineous brother and sister.

What I have called the body as a house is the earliest extension of Ego's relationships towards the surrounding world. It is through the idiom of the symbolic siblings that Ego orients himself or herself within the entire world. All use of Javanese almanacs for prediction is based on this correspondence. Ego's body as a house is a microcosm of the cosmos in inverse perspective, a self-contained and individual dwelling in the world for siblings. Ego and elder and younger siblings form a house by themselves, even if there is no physical roof over their heads, because of their link with the demiurges who created the world.

Foetus siblings are examples of the immobilizing of the marriage link through fictive kin. For if marriage founds the house, siblingship extends it. Why? McKinley (1975, p. 362) has shown for peninsular Malaysia how sibling terminologies have "a connective power of relatively structured siblingship which can be measured by the classificatory use of siblings terms". The tension between male and female lines and categories (cf. Laksono 1986, p. 43), prohibits the use of the husband's and wife's respective roles in creating children as an idiom of an initially horizontal and single generational bond (i.e., between cousins).

What makes the idiom of siblingship more suitable to express an outwardly extended bond is precisely that the ideally "strong" marriage (that of siblings, and especially twins) is between older sister and younger brother. Subsequently shielded from too direct expression, this model of wife and husband (Sri and Sadana for the Javanese) as older sister and younger brother is the objectivization of what is constantly reiterated amongst "classificatory" brothers and sisters, with the aim of enabling them to share in the common identity of the family's house. Peasant couples are hierarchized through the dichotomy elder/younger (wife is called younger sister), and the model also separates out what is appropriate for kings as opposed to his subjects. This is done without referring explicitly to the fact that each couple married in Java uses the metaphors of the first king and his elder sister, Sri. Sri and Sadana are the backdrop to marriage, and as often as not, their physical effigies are present to underline the similitude. Their Sanskritized forms designates them as Vishnu and Sri. Here we see how siblingship has become a metaphor for marriage, and, in the absence of any other corporate groups, the vehicle of inclusion in the nuclear family's house.

In Java, then, the human body through the process of birth becomes a "house" *vis-à-vis* the foetus siblings which accompany Ego into the world and orient him/her during the duration of his incarnate existence. The king's symbolic siblings do the same with the important difference that his "house" is a physical palace that reflects his role in creating the world. Carsten (1987) makes the interesting observation that in Langkawi (Malaysia) as the "house" is extended outward towards the village sphere through the idiom of siblingship, it acquires new meanings:

> ... having negated the individual ties which bind people of one house together, the community is constructed in an image which, although more powerful, is also based on the symbolism of the house.

A new kind of "phantasmagoric house" is created in which there are no strong dyadic ties between kin or bounded groups, only individual, separate men and women of the community, who consume food of a superior quality to that consumed in mere material houses. What connection is there between these two ideas of siblingship?

It is necessary to state precisely what is meant by the weak end of the scale or spectrum of "house" societies. These fetishised houses are usually small social groupings sharing property, regalia and a name through real or fictive kin ties. Those are the "houses" at the strong end of the scale and they may well exist side by side, so to speak, with the first kind as do the Javanese worship communities called *trah*, which in the final analysis are a remodelling of the palace-based family "house" in a post-colonial Javanese setting. What the Javanese are stressing is maintaining sibling-styled "closeness" (*krabatan*) as a model for extra-family social networks. The greater or lesser degree of generational depth and horizontal (i.e., Ego's generation) outreach characterizes these different "houses" as a society unto itself, for in every case they are based on a classificatory treatment of kin and non-kin as being consanguineous siblings of a single house. Recruitment is accomplished in the "kin-based social organization" by referring back to the visible social status of the "house", but in the case of these weaker "houses", the referent is a representation of the nuclear family's sibling group. This unusual treatment of the sibling group is only artificial because of the way the classificatory sibling terms are used to include even non-kin (i.e., not cousins), for in every other respect the representation of the "house" rests on very deep-rooted notions of marriage and incest as shown above.

The simplest classification of these different "houses" is by their capacity to include decreasing numbers of members of a society: the "house" at the strong end of the scale amongst the Kayan, Kenyah, and Modang in Borneo is a total social organization. The "house" of the Maranao and Maguindanao and the coastal Borneo sultanates fall in the middle of the spectrum by including all those associated with the princely power and its house, but no other social grouping. Finally at the weak end of the scale, by virtue of the idiom of siblingship, one finds some Malaysian peasant groups, and Central

Javanese peasants near the former centres of princely power, Yogyakarta and Surakarta. Here inclusion is total, concerning all individuals, but fragile because the idiom of siblingship is based not on a permanent social organization but on the temporary inclusion through marriage in the nuclear family, into a phantasmagoric "house", which is only represented by the king through his ritual marriage with the divine ancestress of the royal line, the queen of the southern seas.

Paradoxically the less the "house" is founded on kin-based social organization of an objective sort, the greater its capacity for inclusion. The extension of the idiom of siblingship, whether it be from the peasants' real or foetus siblings, seems to have a potential for inclusion that socially prominent élite families are hard put to rival. For, as in Marcel Pagnol's play *César* (1976, p. 241), when Marius confronts the perpetrators of his exile, he says they have all lost their closeness with him by betraying their friendships:

> And of us four, none of us has a house, which is truly his house....

The kin-based "house" must take into account the biographical vicissitudes of real life. The idiom of siblingship provides the occasion for an axiomatic "house" to appeal to a principle. It is an imagined community where siblingship nostalgically conveys the bonds of a partially imaginary family "house" wherein siblings are an extension of one's own identity.

NOTES

1. Javanese version *Kitab Ādiparva*, vol. II (1958): 122–22; Sanskrit version (Poona edition no. 214–25 (1933): 837–77.
2. Cf. bibliography of Koentjariningrat 1975 for an overview of these early studies.
3. The cosmogenesis of the world has it that the world of dead and the living is one. Any landscape has the possibility of revealing the past to those who know it through the myths. The definition of mythological landscape is given in Maurice Leenhaardt (1943) *Do Kamo. personne et mythe dans le monde mélanésien*, especially chapters 4 and 12.
4. The verbal form of this noun in French meant simply to endow someone with a mean of subsistence, and in Java this means a form of tax farming. Apanage is concerned not only with the royal extended family, but more generally with anyone whom the king wanted to provide for (in Latin *ad panis,* "for bread"). On the practice of renting/selling these apanages to the highest bidder, increasingly common after the 1840s, cf. Houben (1994, pp. 260–61).
5. Locally the *bekel* were often related to one another; on the different types of *bekel*; cf. Houben (1994, pp. 344–46). Under the European leaseholders the more independent *bekel majegan* or *maron* gradually disappeared or were reduced

to something approaching plantation foremen (*mandhor*). However on the unleased *kejawèn* estates the position of the *bekel* was increased and strengthened through his role in recruiting new workers.

6. 1848; Dutch translation in Poerbatjaraka (1940, pp. 291–92).

7. In his 1996 Ph.D. thesis at ANU, Canberra: "Reformist Muslims in a Yogyakarta Village. The Islamic Transformation of contemporary Socio-Religious Life", pp. 154 and 164.

8. Lecture at the Ecole Hautes Etudes en Sciences Sociales, Paris 11.VI.02.

9. The region of the principalities was exempt from the direct application of the Cultivation System because they had semi-autonomous status, but suffered from the effects of this economic polity to the extent that it completely dominated the Javanese economy as such.

10. (13b) "…iya barengira metu ika, getih ari-ari kakawah ika ari-ari kang aniksa ing sira lumumpat, nora bisa, kang angucap iku kupur."

11. For instance, in the Central Sulawesi (Celebes), cf. the recent ethnography *Conceiving Spirits*, by Jennifer W. Norse (1999).

12. This section is adapted from S. C. Headley, "The Body as a house in Javanese society" (1987*a*): 133–52.

13. Kala is a proper name designating the most notorious of the *kala* or enemies.

14. Cf. S. C. Headley, "Le lit-grenier et la déesse de la fécondité à Java: rites nuptiaux?", (1983, pp. 77–86).

15. Throughout, the names of Javanese "Hindu" gods will be spelt as in Java and not as in India.

16. Canto 15 of the *Manikmaya* (1981). A transposition of this is found in the Bunginese myth from Ujung Pandang where Sri's thousands of grandchildren all want to marry her and become the driving rain.

17. As in peninsular Malaysia where the ethnic Malay Muslims have similar beliefs to those of the Javanese concerning birth siblings. Cf. McKinley (1975).

18. In Javanese these originally Arabic terms are written: *mutmainah, amarah, sufiyah and lawwamah*. These must be distinguished from another set of four (intention, soul, mentality and spirit) which are functions not humours.

19. Cf. R. Wiryapanitra, *Serat Kidungan Kawedhar* (reprinted 1979), pp. 124–28; cf. Jerome Weiss, *Folk Psychology of the Javanese of Ponorogo.* (1977).

20. Throughout this book myths are of course cited not as canonical texts to justify a given argument, but as texts proving the existence of certain kinds of associations and correspondences.

21. For their refusal to create cf. the Tengger cosmology, cf. Smith Hefner (1996, pp. 271–72).

22. The trace of the four demiurges from the cosmology above is found in an exorcism tale, the *Sri Tanjung* (edition Prijono 1938) from the sixteenth century. They have been interpolated later with *pawukon*-style almanac texts which describe the associations of birds, colours, etc., with the four cardinal directions found in Javanese calendars.

23. Cf. Tiknopranoto (1962, pp. 27–33).

24. Cf. Metcalf's 1982 study on Berawan (Borneo) genealogical funeral chants and Errington (1989, ch. 7) on forgetting genealogies among the Bugis of Luwu (Sulawesi/Celebes).

25. As Geertz (1975, p. 5) remarks on the Balinese *dadia*, neither lineage, clan, sib, kindred, ramage or ambilateral descent group translate the idea of an agnatic highly corporate group of persons who believe that they are all descendents of one common ancestor. For this reason the Javanese term *trah* is best used in the original and without translation.

26. Cf. the case in Ghana described by J. Goody in *Death Property and Ancestors* (1962).

27. Cf. Senapati (reinged *circa* 1584–1601), son of Kyai Gedhé Pamanahan, Pangeran Puger (Paku Buwana I, reigned 1704–19) and Paku Buwana III (1749–88).

28. Cf. Berthe (1965, p. 200) describing the Baduy in West Java: "… la prohibition du mariage, pour un Ego masculin, avec toute la parenté sur sa gauche (les aînés)."

29. For longer description, cf. Geertz (1961, p. 160); Koentjaraningrat (1985*b*, p. 271); Robson (1987).

30. *Nak* here means a member of a group (as in Proto Malayo-Polynesian, cf. Blust (1993, pp. 62–63), thus a member of that *sanak* (niece or nephew) group. Synonyms of *nak sanak; nak (n)dulur; nak sedulur*.

31. This literally means to spear one another; but has the secondary meaning of taboo.

32. There are a group of relatively universal prohibitions that concern illicit accumulations of the "identical", for instance the Christian prohibition against marriage of babies baptised in the same water. This sixth prohibition against marriage may be of this type.

33. Cf. Koentjaraningrat (1968, pp. 53–58). For a Balinese comparison, cf. Alit Kertaraharja, "Srimben, Balinese woman behind presidents", *Jakarta Post*, 10 January 2002, where family and communal banishment for marrying an "outsider", i.e., a lower caste male, entailed being banned for life from entering the family house, and praying at pura (temple).

34. Cf. Robson (1987, p. 515). Note that the closeness of the family is indicated by the term *krabatan*. *Somah* is used in statistics to designate the nuclear "family" and its head (equivalent to the Indonesian expression *kepala keluarga*). *Brayat* the nuclear or the close extended family, depending on context, is the locus of all that is *brayan*.

35. Cf. Louwerier (1905, pp. 251–57); Poensen (1870, pp. 304–21).

36. When speaking about a spouse the choice involves some sixteen possibilities. Cf. Koentjaraningrat 1985, p. 265.

37. Murdock (1960) suggested that the following questions be asked in order to understand the structure of each family:

1. What is the centre of the orientation of kindred (e.g. common ancestor or common relative)?
2. Who is the initiator of kindred activities?
3. What are the boundaries of the collateral extension of kindred?
4. What affinities are included or excluded?
5. What is the conceptualization of absentees in kindred activities?
6. What resolutions are there for conflicting obligations?

38. On the north coast and in certain rural regions of Java, no reference to the two blessed ones (*loro blonya*) is normative. In the Sunda area and on the north coast one often finds two pots (*klemuk*) one with unhusked rice and the other filled with coins related to Sadana, associated with wealth more than kingship. Communication of Rens Heringa. Cf. B. P. H. Poeroebaya, "Rondom de huwelijken in de Kraton te Jogyakarta" (1939).

39. The compound *pri-yayi* is made up of a Sanskrit prefix for beloved which came to mean male/man in Javanese and *yayi* which means younger sibling or relative and is cognate with *ari*, *rari* and *rayi*.

40. (Note added by author) Austronesian designates a language family stretching from Taiwan (its non-Chinese speakers) through the Philippines, Indonesia, Micronesia, Melanesia and Polynesia, and including some languages in Madagascar.

41. Cf. the citations in Zoetmulder's dictionary (1982, pp. 1372–73) of the litanies of rising ancestral generations: "bapa, kaki, buyut, pitung, anggas, muning, krepek" as opposed to litanies of descending generations: "anak, putu, buyut, cicik, muning, pitung, anggas". Despite what Fox claims (1986, p. 324), it is only when these terms are cited as a litany that it is possible to distinguish ancestors from descendants.

42. Cf. also the monograph of J. Danandjaja (1980).

43. This section is adapted from Headley (1987, pp. 209–18).

44. By identity I designate a subjective Ego constructed notion of person. Later by "identical" I understand a two-faced epistemological criterion for retaining sameness and difference as relevant in the domain of kinship. Just as not all phonetic difference is pertinent neither is all similarity retained as criterion for identical in kinship.

45. As Héritier has written: "The strongest identical is that of same sex twins, the same sex sibling, amongst the cousins the parallel cousin of the same sex...With the possible negation of the difference of sexes, that fundamental mark of alterity, one seems to touch on the nucleus of the reflection of human groups about themselves, beginning with which is constituted all social organization and all ideology." (Héritier 1979, p. 227). The culturally determined notion of identity may rest on variable representations of consanguinity, but the notion of identical vehiculed by kinship terms necessarily reposes on the notion of differences between sexes whose most elementary expression is the asymetric relation of brother and sister. Héritier describes it as ..."The basic element of any kinship

structure, for all is included there and not only the simple difference of sex for it is pregnant with the other features: the necessary marriage with other similar units, procreation which comes from the former and the procreations that are to come, the choice between principles of filiation, the crossing of collateral lines which emerge, the relative relationship of elder." (Héritier 1981, p. 47).

2

THE VILLAGE "KINGDOM"
The Bed of Sri and the Realm of Sadana

This chapter[1] poses the issue of origin myths of social order in Java, mentioned in passing in Chapter 1. In traditional Indonesian societies origin myths often formed a charter of social morphology. Whether they remain there after the arrival of modern ideologies is, of course, another question. Despite the enormous evolution of Javanese villages through peasantry and beyond, and *non obstant* post-modernism, the role of these founding myths is still evident. The premise of this myth is that the first kingdom was a primordial village, Mendhang Kamulan. The meaning of the name of this village, "the origin of the rice chaff", implies that rice has its origin in the same inhabited space as this first human social organization. There are not many ways to conceptualize the whole of a society like Java and these origin myths have not been sufficiently explored for our purposes. Rape is presented in the best known myth as the reason for the death of the rice goddess from whose fertile body rice and children come. In the other major variant, her younger brother, whom she has attempted to marry, returns to heaven but is reduplicated into the first king of Java, just as she is reduplicated as a rice field python repatriated by peasants to a village granary. Copulation related to rape or incest, rice cultivation and granary rituals are rendered in these myths homologous with the basic configuration of siblingship which orients the peasants in the cosmos and leaves the kingdom with privileged access to this founding princess.

2.1 THE BIRTH OF A JAVANESE

If as H.W. Scheffler (1977) has said, "Kinship is a locally elaborated theory to account for how children are born", then the conceptualization and rituals surrounding birth are indications not only of the Javanese notion of physiology but also of personality formation and psychology. This vein has been mined by Jerome Weiss in his *Folk Psychology of the Javanese of Ponorogo* (1977, ch. 4). While in the islands to the east and the west of Java, lineage ancestors are often important members of kin groups, on Java these forefathers "are" those unsual older and younger brothers or sisters to Ego, I call "foetus siblings", which remaining intimate guides throughout life (cf. Ch. 1), even after their former physical "bodies", the amniotic fluid and placenta respectively, are buried in the ground at birth. Also called "symbolic siblings" (Koentjaraningrat 1960, p. 95) or birth spirits (Norse 1999), they tell us about the initial socio-cosmic orientation a Javanese person was given.

As was claimed in Chapter 1, what the Javanese "cognatic" person may lack in the way of kin ties through his "Hawaïan" classificatory kindred (cousins called by same terms as siblings), he may try to make up through the cosmological pentads to which his symbolic older and younger siblings unite him. This involvement with spirits in the womb can continue throughout life. The family adopts a watchful (*prihatin*) attitude after the sixth month of pregnancy of the mother. *Prihatin* obviates anxieties and makes the family aware of the possibility of disturbing events surrounding the entrance of this new member into the family circle. The *slametan* held during the ninth month to honour the older sibling amniotic fluid (*kakang kawah*) and younger sibling placenta (*adik ari-ari*) reinforces the vigilance that *prihatin* represents. In fact some informants mention the blood and the *vernix caseosa* as two additional siblings, which would make a total of four (C. Geertz 1960, pp. 38–50, 85–128). This suggests that in Java as on Bali today (Hooykaas 1974, pp. 85–128), there were once two elder and two younger symbolic siblings, which would have constituted a fivefold siblingship (*panca sanak*).

From its mother the foetus receives the red elements (skin, blood, and the internal organs), from the father the white ones (bone, marrow, and brain), and from God life (*nyawa*), character (*budi*), and the five senses (*pancadriya*). During pregnancy the foetus is often addressed by the mother who encourages it to imitate the good qualities she sees in people surrounding her. The ancient Austronesian taboo concerning the mockery of animals (cf. Blust 1981, pp. 296–97; Weiss 1977, pp. 142–44) is observed during pregnancy lest the child be born resembling the very trait one scorned.

When the foetus is physically completely assembled, i.e. after the third *lapan* (thirty-five day period), when the celestial light (*nur*) is joined with it in an appropriate balance of the four essences (*sari papat*: fire, water, earth, and air), the foetus constitutes a microcosm (*jagad alit*) of the greater cosmos (*jagad gedhé*) from which it was drawn, and to which it will return after birth and death. Nonetheless the hour of its birth having drawn near, it does not want to leave the womb and it will do so only because its elder and younger siblings (amniotic fluid and placenta) "force" their sibling "Ego" out into the macrocosm.

Today some Javanese *kabathinan* sect, have built on this apparent paradox of a foetus composed of the four cosmic elements that have been brought in to form its body, which is then "born" into the very cosmos of which it was formerly a part and from which it is now temporarily individualized in a "human" body.[2] The subsequent relations of Ego's elder and younger siblings with the different macro-cosmological pentads to which Ego as a microcosmic incarnation (*titisan*) is linked, should not obscure the fact that the intimacy of these prenatal siblings is never really lost. These birth spirits may continue to protect one, but they are only one facet of the forces of creation. For instance, in the Banyumas region (southwest Central Java; Bertling 1936, p. 121) at the marriage of the oldest daughter there used to be a ritual mock robbery (called *bégalan*)[3] of the household utensils being transported by the groom's men (Pemberton 1994, pp. 214–15). Pemberton describes the disappearance of this custom in south Central Java in the 1970s and 80s. This may well be part of what Pemberton (1994, p. 214) calls the "fragmenting of Sri's world" which began in the late colonial period and was "preserved" in an idealized version of Javanese "manners", by Padmasoesastra, in his book of customs (*Tatatjara*[4]). What is surprising is that Pemberton does not so much invoke the influence of Islam on Javanese culture as he does a colonial influence that pushes the Javanese to posturing as something that it never was. The *bégalan* used to embody excesses associated with violent dissemination (production and fertility). In Javanese these rites are called *rebutan* (literally, tearing apart). These, says Pemberton, were replaced with scenes of orderly customary law or *adat*. Little comparative fieldwork on these conception and rituals has been done in Central and East Java, nor between the numerous ethno-linguistic areas of the archipelago where these representations are quasi-universal in one form or another.[5] The common traits between the Balinese and Javanese classificatory value of the pentad are summarized below. The important differences in the number of the foetus siblings, largely derived from literary erudition, are not rooted in the rural landscape that concerns us here.

In Java the importance of the rituals surrounding the burial of the younger brother placenta (or sister if Ego is female) underground (*pendhem*) and the "evacuation" of the amniotic fluid towards the ground (it falls of its own accord through the air) is everywhere acknowledged. Every family household in Krendawahana north of Surakarta observed these rites in the 1970s. Geertz stressed their gravity in the region of Paré (East Java) in the mid-1950s although his explanation does not convince me. Geertz claims (1961, p. 89)

> Cutting the child free from his "younger brother placenta" is a magically delicate task performed only by a midwife ... designed to make the burial permanent so that the spirit of the afterbirth will be kept under control and not cause sickness to the infant.

The symbolic siblings have malevolent as well as benevolent forms as seen in Chapter 1, but, as the prayer that accompanies the burial (Geertz 1960, p. 46) of the umbilical cord stresses, Father and Mother earth become the guardians of the umbilical cord (and of the placenta with which it is buried, presumably in a common pot). It is they and not the younger symbolic sibling which might threaten the new-born child. The nuance is not insignificant, as here we see the dimension of sibling generation beginning to open out towards generations plus one and two which is eventually expanded into a full genealogical body "of royal authority" as was seen in Chapter 1.

In fact, although the *setan* are numerous, much of the medical lore explaining illness identifies its causes with the actions of the spirit "grandparents" of humanity, *kaki among* and *nini among*. *Among* means to protect, but, if these spirits are neglected, they don't always do so. Although the actual burial sites of the umbilical cord and the placenta vary, they are usually in the ground under the eaves of the roof of the front or back door of the house, to the left or the right depending on the sex. Such domestic household rites are notoriously discreet, banal, and take place almost unnoticed, yet few families forget them, for they represent the physiology of human reproduction. Many of the more ostentatious, refined (*alus*) rituals are optional and related to prestige and wealth. All this leads me to think that the siblings and Ego are being incorporated into the household and not being "cut free" from one another. The imagined phenomenon of foetal transfer (*anak pujan*), as well as various beliefs concerning the conception of twins, implies (Weiss 1977, pp. 159–60, 177–78) that the issue of separating out real and false siblings lies elsewhere. The choice of marriage partners not surprisingly gives the clearest indication of Javanese notions of the need for clarifying sibling intimacy.

2.2 BUILDING A HOUSE FOR A FAMILY

Families are like waves. They are always on the surface of the water, rising and falling in place. The house, like the ocean, is swept by a succession of waves who have in common that they belong not only to the same family, whose members grow up and leave, but also to the same house. When a society such as the Javanese does not have great genealogical depth, one can see that the siblings symbolizing one's macrocosmic origins recall another kind of forefather. These ancestral beings in the form of symbolic siblings accompany Ego into the house, lie buried under its eaves and guard the person until death takes him back out of the house. Let us see if this is borne out in the rituals surrounding the building of the house.

The following ritual was observed by Poensen (1875, p. 131) near Kediri more than a hundred years ago, in 1874. The officiant (*pujannga*) comes to the site prior to the erection of the four main pillars (*saka guru*) which will support the roof and does this on a propitious day called the "guiding" day (*guru dinten*). The celebrant has the first pothole dug in the southeast corner and the other three proceeding west, north, and east. In the first hole a common offering for the house's raw materials is made: the *cok bakal*. The order observed in erecting the pillars is called going round the stable (*mubang kandang*). Starting with the southeast pillar, the officiant directs the men to stabilize them by attaching a piece of blue cloth, some stalks of rice and a pair of jasmine flowers near the joint of the first pillar with the horizontal rectangular frame that will support the roof. This offering is called the "arousing of protection" (*bangun tulak*). Next the celebrant offers incense and foodstuffs in the centre of the site before the raising of the roof-frame (*empyak*) when he prays:

> Come friends let us now raise the roof-frame. First that of the front side of the house, so that the master of the house may receive many guests.

And addressing a prayer to the titulary deity (*dhanyang*) of the site, the celebrant says:

> Dhanyang, may this site be under your protection. I offer you sweet-smelling cooked rice and budding jasmine flowers.

> May I succeed in raising this house and have no bad luck as we go further up.

Then the four main pillars, as well as a fifth, are wrapped in strips of coloured cloth or *lètrèk*.[6] The fifth beam, the *pengeret*, is a timber superimposed on the rectangular frame *empyak* from the ends of which two uprights called *tuwuh* (literally, sprout) extend to support the ridgepole. So it is the upper rectangular part of the house that is colour co-ordinated by these *lètrèk* cloths. Javanese basic colours are uniquely Austronesian (Damais 1967, pp. 75– 118). Their associations are shown in Table 2.1.

Not only does the house have a north-south orientation, a propitious day for its raising and a *genus loci* to bless its construction, but also the colours of the four directions are permanently attached to its pillars which support its roof. The house will lodge the family "better" if its identification with the macrocosm is recalled. In this it is like a man, made in the image of a cosmos, yet it is more than a man, larger than the members of its family who temporarily drawn into being, move about the earth, form families, build houses and then disappear again into the ground. For this reason the house finds itself on the side of the macrocosm, even if it has to be regularly rebuilt.

The structural parallel of palace offerings with the peasant's cult to his virtual siblings can be seen in peasant offerings for the construction of their houses. These parallel palace offerings are made every Thursday night by the royal servants for the well-being of the kingdom and its king.[7] There exist peasant offerings which are made once and for all when the peasants builds his house (Table 2.2). For how long have these food offerings included ones which ask for Muhammad's blessing? These include the householder's offerings, or rather his wife's, which are restricted to modest and discreet ones in the granary to Dewi Sri, the rice godess, once a week, on the same Thursday nights that the king's servants are elaborately placing dozens of offerings around the cardinal points of his palace, which inside its walls constitutes a sort of forbidden city.

If peasants lack a "body of authority" (*raga wisésa*) of the generational depth that aristocrats may possess (ch. 1), they do have their own pantheon with a less profound genealogical depth as we can see in the right-hand

TABLE 2.1
Colour co-ordinates in house building

Red (female blood)	**Black** (*langgeng*, peace during building)
	Red (and white) (female blood–white seed = unity of the family)
Yellow (*wening*, purity of heart)	**Blue-green** (*subur*, prosperity of the family)

TABLE 2.2
Offerings for the construction of a Javanese peasant's house

Food Offerings	Foetus Sibling	Offerings' Destination
rice cooked in coconut milk (*sekul kebuli*)		for Muhammad's blessing
rice balls (*sekul golong*)		honouring the village guardian spirit (*dhanyang*)
rice cone (*tumpeng*)		honouring the prophets from Adam to Muhammad and his companions
rice meal pancake (*apam*)		honours the deceased and the ancestors
porridge (*jenang mahkota* or *sengkala*)	placenta	Kaki and Nini Among, or Sang Marmati/Mahamarti (*memetri*, to cherish)
white porridge	amniotic fluid	invisible sibling
black or blue porridge	afterbirth	invisible sibling
rose porridge	umbilical cord	invisible sibling
red porridge	blood	invisible sibling

Source: Sastra Amidjaja (1924), pp. 110–11.

column in Table 2.2. Another kind of genealogy, a prophetic one, is slowly being introduced here from Islam.

In Krendawahana in early 1974 Pak Musli rebuilt his house with freshly-cut timbers on a site only a few yards from its former one. He called a village elder, Damsuri, to pronounce the mantra while a full set new offerings were made. Clearly the construction, whose elements were laid out on the ground around his yard, needed to be "bound up" anew, in short become vertical. But there was also concern for the horizontal plane. A yellow *tumbal* or hex was fixed on the front door to prevent dangerous people from entering it. In the same vein, after the birth of a child, one puts on the door lintels the "thousand obstacles" (*perdhang séwu*), which is an amulet (or a simple drawing) resembling a quiver of black and white strips bounds with rattan and a red cloth to ward off the *kala* that might harm the new-born.

Since the house is an institution and not just a structure,[8] its "horizontal" perspective is not only that of the geometry of space. One symbol carved on the underside of the cross-beam (or short purlin; *pengeret*), mentioned above, is a pair of young climbing (*tuwuh*) plants (*paré enom*). These are symbolized by the colours green and yellow, and converge in the centre of the cross-beam where, as often as not, an oil lamp is suspended. In the more elaborate decorations of nobles this may be replaced by a white lotus (*kumudawati*) with the colours of the eight cardinal directions. All these motifs serve to orient the house in the cosmos.

In certain areas north of Surakarta, but not exclusively, the cloths wrapped around the pillars are red and white (like the Indonesian national flag which is a distant cousin of these *sindur* cloth motifs), the same as that worn by a bride's mother the night of her wedding. This use of coloured clothing is connected to her redeeming (*tebus*) one of the pair of blossoms of the areca palm (*kembar mayang*; sometimes they are only leaf cut-outs), called "twins", placed on either side of the ritual bed of Sri (*k(r)obongan*) in front of which sit the bride and groom during a marriage ceremony.[9] The sculptures on the short purlin and the two vertical beams called sprouts (*tuwuh*) are the *kembar mayang* continued onto the rafters, as it were. Identified as a tree of life by J. Hooykaas-van Leeuwen Boumkamp (1957, p. 118), they may well recall the tree of life (*kayon*) often sculpted on the screen *warana* that bars access to the evil spirits and persons into the inner room (*dalem*) in Figure 2.1. If this is the case, then the fifth of the cloth offerings is for the tree of life embodied in this part of the house.

However this may be, it is clear that the colour motifs used in the ritual clothing of members of families and in building houses show some parallels. This stands to reason, for according to Koji Miyazaki (1979, p. 32), "It is the relations of the sets and not the association of the elements that conveys the message." Whatever variation exists amongst the pairs of colours used in the *lètrèk* cloths in different parts of Java, their relation with the house's protection of its inhabitants is undeniable. In the same way whatever plants one may decide to have sculpted on one's cross-beam, their relation with the pair of areca blossoms (*kembar mayang*) used in marriage ceremonies is clear. All these are elements in a chain of rituals designed to make the house a home, in the sense of a microcosm (*jagad alit*): *domus mundus est.*

2.3 THE JAVANESE HOUSE

If one entered a Javanese peasant's house at mealtime (cf. Figure 2.1), one could find the male members grouped in the central room (no. 3, *dalem*) if there are guests to feed; if not, they would eat in the back half of the house. In any case the women wait their turn in the kitchen. In the back of this front room a partition (4a) composed of sculpted wood, slightly recessed *vis-à-vis* the rest of the wall, resembles the screen (no. 2, *warana*) around which one had to walk to enter this room from the outside. Not all recent houses have a full screen, but there is usually some trace of it in the panelling that

FIGURE 2.1
Layout of a house in Central Java

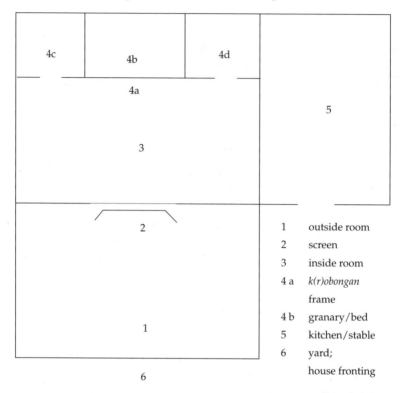

1	outside room
2	screen
3	inside room
4 a	*k(r)obongan*
	frame
4 b	granary/bed
5	kitchen/stable
6	yard;
	house fronting

separates the inside from the outside rooms. The name (*k(r)obongan*) of the room (4b) which lies behind carved panels at the back of the *dalem* (4a) may refer to the burning (*obong*) of incense there. Although, as on the screen (2), they may be reduced to very modest decorations, every peasant will tell you that the "inner" (*krobong*) room is the *krobongan*, where rice and heirlooms are shut away. If one sleeps in the neighbouring rooms (4c and 4d), the central section usually contains a chest that serves as a rice granary, and it is there that any heirlooms the family possesses are deposited.

But what explains the wood carving on the front of the *kobongon* wall? Compare the simple peasant house with a princely one. For anyone who has ever been in the main back room (or *dalem*, no. 3) of an aristocratic house or been allowed to visit the *dalem* of a palace (which is rarely possible), the transformation of these panels from what we have described of a peasant's house is revealing.[10] Flanked by two statues of a handsome seated prince (Sadana) and a beautiful seated princess (Sri), the carving is elaborated on several different levels framing the opening of a luxurious nuptial bed! The bed and its multitude of cushions are covered in ornate silk *cindhé*. Peering in, one can distinguish on the back pillows a pair of woven flower ear-rings laid on either side of an invisible head. The women responsible for changing the ear-rings every Thursday night, say that the lady represented just outside the *k(r)obongon* in sculpture is the one who is deemed to be invisibly resting on the bed: the rice goddess Sri (the shining one).

It is in front of this wedding bed, even if in a poor peasant's house it only exists in the minimal form of a frieze of wood carvings, that most marriages in Java are still celebrated. If it does not exist even in vestigial form it can be created by the owner of the house out of his imagination using, for instance, gold paper cut-outs, displaying shadow puppet style chariots carrying the divinized newly married couple aloft. This means that most couples are married in a parents' home as if they were Sri and Sadana, often glossed as Uma and Wisnu. Even when people have moved into suburban Javanese style — "*perumnas*" (subsidized housing) which would not permit such a wedding — they rent a marriage hall garishly reproducing all the features of the traditional *dalem* and *kobongan*.

J. Hooykaas (1957) found that in some undefinable "past" the bride and groom on their wedding day are actually presented as being inhabited by the god and goddess of love. The middle Javanese prose text *Tantri Kamandika* (cf. C. Hooykaas 1931, pp. 48–49) describes this "real" nature in the following terms:

FIGURE 2.2
Statues of Sri and Sadana in a pick-up truck going to a wedding

At the exact moment of the consummation of the marriage the God Iswara and his spouse Ardhanari incarnate themselves in the bridal couple when they are on their couch. Batari Wisnu and his Spouse, Batari Sri — all the gods are there. This is the result of the marriage: the daily worship of the gods. Do not forget that. What is the result? The whole country is prosperous, the rainy seasons are long, all the plants grow lusciously on the earth and so there is plenty of food. That is why I want to marry daily.

The link between the true nature of the Lord and Lady on earth, the exorcism of the evil spirits (*kala*) that attack new-born children and the "essence" of marriage is now within our grasp. J. Hooykaas' demonstration, which up to this point was exemplary, surprisingly misses the mark.[11] She insists (1961, p. 278) that Uma/Sri should be understood here as Visnu's, not Iswara's (Siwa/Guru), spouse and that the tantric view of sexual union of the god and goddess in an androgyne form (*ardhanaresvara*) subsumes the old Indonesian concept of the union of Father sky and Mother earth. The myth of Sri and Sadana presented below, however, presents an elder sister/younger brother incestuous marriage and the consequences it entails in terms of excessive heat: a heat which would annihilate all the prosperity invoked in the Javanese passage translated above were it not that what is not possible for humans is possible for gods.[12]

Clearly there is a cosmological dimension to marriage. We should look for its expression in myth, not because we wish to turn our back on the social constraints of village society,[13] but because, as Augé (1982, pp. 45–47) has stated, religion cannot be treated simultaneously as both an expression of a system of knowledge and as a socially effective system. He elaborates this saying,

> … all physical or physiological disorders refer to a social disorder, not only in the sense that one reflects the other … but in the sense that both of them refer to the same interpretational grid and contribute to the gradual and problematical definition of a logic of practice …. It is the whole social order that may be read in a "trial" of this sort …

In Java, and especially in the myth to be presented below, the prohibition of incest arbitrates between marriage, the "birth" of children and rice, and the unspoken foundation of social order in the kingdom, in the institution of its first kings in an imaginary primordial village. Historical kingdoms may have come and gone, and been superseded by the present Republic of Indonesia, but the rural Javanese do not seem to be in a hurry to undertake any ideological palace-cleaning in order to replace these foundations with new and "better" ones. In the nineteenth century principalities of Central Java, the Surakarta aristocrats (*priyayi*) postured to make their Dutch colonial masters' tutelage "respectable" (Pemberton 1994). They lost the respect of their subjects and the ability to represent Javanese society. However, the threat currently posed by communalism to the unity and coherence of the Republic of Indonesia is inherited from the experience of the 1965–66 "anti-communist" massacres initiated by the "new order" which then came to power. All these very twentieth century dimensions of power relations and strategies are secularizations of nationalism and not the ways of living and fitting into Javanese society discussed here.

2.4 CHILDBIRTH AND THE RICE HARVEST IN THE MYTH OF SRI: THE FIRST SOCIAL LEVEL

The eliding of the representation of a "royal" bed with that of a peasant's granary displays the uniformity in the layout of all *traditional* Javanese houses, peasant or royal. This means that none of the differences in the practical use of space in an urban prince's palace and a rural peasant's dwelling were allowed to interfere with the minimum ritual layout of the *kobongan* inside the *dalem*. The peasants know that the granary is the place of Sri, even without her statue, for the rice of which she is the fertility is stocked there and even if the nobles may not stock their rice in this place they know that it is often done in the villages. Where rice is, Sri is. The co-penetration of this link between Sri and rice does not yet, however, explain that of peasant marriage and the bond between an elder sister, Sri, and her younger brother Sadana. Why was this conformity possible? For an understanding of this, we will initially take a narrative approach, using the myths that lay behind these architectural representations. Who is Sri? Who is Sadana? Javanese myths speak abundantly of them, and even books for grade school age children reproduce their tales. Clearly all these text are pitched at different levels of evaluation.

There are a multitude of variants and here I will use a long one (seventy pages) collected in Central Java by Jumeiri Siti Ramadjah and published in Jakarta (no date) in an Indonesian translation without the Javanese original. What follows is a paraphrase and condensation with my own comments in brackets, unless otherwise indicated by quotation marks and italics marking direct translation:

In a kingdom at the beginning of the history of Java, there was a king Mahapunggung ("the big fool") who wanted to marry his son to a certain Panitra, and this despite his opposition; for this son, Sadana, was completely devoted to his older sister (or in some versions his twin sister) Sri. Faced with his father's command, Sadana fled the palace in the middle of the night, followed the next day by his sister Sri, who was distraught at his disappearance.

Then it was that the ogre king of the forest Medangkumuwung (=? shining rice chaff) asked for the hand of Sri. Bewildered by the disappearance of his daughter Sri, Mahapunggung replied to the delegate of the ogre king that the person who could find her could marry her. [Thus unwittingly opening to Sadana the possibility to marry his own sister.]

Across the fields and the forests of Java, Sri is pursued by the demon army of Pulasva, the ogre king, whose leader, Kalandaru, is gifted with supernatural scent. Multiple battles follow when this horde encircles successive villages where Sri is hidden, while she continues to search for her brother. She meets a certain father Bawadha on her way, at the place where his younger brother was killed by the ogre Kalandaru. Then in his company she arrives in the village of the Perfume of Rice chaff (Medhangwangi).

"In the village of father Bawadha, was his wife named Patani (place of repose). When this respected old man and the goddess Sri arrived in the village, Patani was in the midst of cleaning her house. Only then did the goddess ask the wife of the respected elder:

'Patani where is your inner room (pajangan = *decorated place). I feel tired, I feel like sleeping a moment. Clean this place, appoint it with a mattress, cross cushions and pillows. Don't forget to prepare the lamp, a pitcher of water, nice chews of betel, powdered yellow leaves and flowers (used for marriages and rituals) and burning incense. These are offering for my own person. May I not be disappointed when I want to drink or to chew betel.'"*

Patani provided all that was asked of her. When all was ready, the goddess Sri entered into this central room. There she experienced a very strong feeling. In that place the holy girl slept. She only closed her eyes an instant, then she awoke, drank water and chewed betel. The goddess Sri said:

"I am not yet hungry. You had better put this cone of rice with its four side dishes inside the k(r)obongan. *I feel satisfied after having drunk the water from this pitcher* (kendi) *and my nap was agreeable. I cannot thank you enough. Every time you prepare food, do as you have just done. But also dispose a* sisik-milik *mat and* baraban *cushions as protection. All that will help my nap. Every Thursday evening, I would like to have this room cleaned, the water pitcher changed, and that offerings of powdered yellows leaves and flowers be laid out and that incense be burned. Whoever follows these instructions will receive his whole life through an abundance of clothes and food. What is more, I forbid that a sarong be shaken out at night, or that one sweeps or cleans the bed after sunset. Each time, clean it in the morning, before the sun rises, sweep the yard and clean up well your bed*

place. As for you father Bawadha, you must never open the pantry cupboard (simpènan) *of you wife for that will cause frequent losses."*

Such were the ritual councils given by the shining (*sri*) goddess to the wife and husband concerning the central room. They vowed to obey.

"Following the path in the pursuit of the goddess Sri, the ogre Kalandaru was always able to know which way she was headed thanks to the power he possessed. Therefore when she was in Medangwangi, he encircled the hamlet with all his band of ogres. Their (man-eating) voices made the sound of a hurricane when they found the human scent and discovered the girl. Father Bawadha was indeed startled on realising that the ogres had encircled the village…"

This brief extract of Javanese oral literature (*Dewi Sri* pp. 6–9) illustrates the representation of the Javanese inner room called *k(r)obongan*, but also the reasons which Javanese give to justify their beliefs. On the one hand Sri finds a bed to rest on while seeking her younger brother Sadana, and on the other a person who welcomes Sri risks being devoured if he does not provide himself with proper ritual protection in the form of the offerings for Sri. Sri will be faithful to her promise and those who guard her bed will have food and clothes, which is the Javanese expression for abundance.

VARIATIONS: OTHER SISTERS, OTHER KINGDOMS

It is in the logic of these myths' recursive motifs that they cannot be extracted one from another and isolated. Their hearing or reading always refers one on to other permutations which have no clear beginning or ending. One must be aware that Javanese have multiple metaphors and tropes surrounding rice, its first planting and first preparation (steaming, boiling, etc.) involving father-daughter incest (Guru rapes and buries Sri; Guru drops his seed which becomes the rice field parasites and the illnesses which attack infants) and brother-sister incest (Sadana and Sri's destinies to be recounted below). These myths correspond only in a general way to the ritual prescriptions (offerings, auspicious and nefarious times, and directions, etc.) which preserve the specifically unexpected and apparently irrational systemic links between them. For instance, the stating of a taboo that against shaking out a *sarong* at night, can be related to the reciting of such a myth.

An example: the accumulation of identity which is represented by brother-sister incest is deemed to produce heat. "Full of Heat" (Tiksnawati) is one of the names of Sri (*Dewi Sri*, p. 50). In certain versions of the myth this "incestuous" heat provokes the death of Sri and Sadana from whose cadavers come plants and animals. A close variation in the *Manikmaya* (1981, vol. I) involves the incestuous passion of Sri's father for a prohibited woman provoking the fall of his seed, called *kala*(s), who eat men and ripe rice before its planters can harvest it. One could well ask whether the bed and the granary presented in a single myth, that of Dewi Sri, do not epitomize the symmetrical superpositioning of a whole series of variations. Or are they instead simply comparable ritual apparatus related to fields and homes? While dealing with this corpus of variations[14] available in the Javanese oral lore, I will try to answer this question below.

In the middle of the myth we find the role of the bed sufficiently developed to permit its juxtaposition *vis-à-vis* the granary. Having given advice on how to protect their rice store in the granary to the peasants of the village of Boga, the goddess Sri is finally united with her brother Sadana, but only after she has been killed by the ogres and revivified by Narada, the elder brother of the master of the world Jagadnata (i.e. Guru/Siwa). With his peasant friends Sadana erects a village named Sri Ngawanti. This village is attacked by the king of the ogres, Pulasva. But Sadana incarnates himself in a hurricane and kills Pulasva. Then, with the aid of an ascetic, a minister of the king Mahapunggung recuperates the couple, who do not want to return to their father's palace. They remain in the village and the king's delegation returns. The elder brother Narada is furious at their refusal and menaces: "If that is how it is, albeit you are brother and sister, you can just become husband and wife." They then feel guilty and can't undertake this act. Narada surmises that, although they are only mortals, that they wish to become god and goddess, but warns them all that they must suffer.

WIFE AND HUSBAND, SNAKE AND BIRD, BABIES AND RICE

Following the threat to be forced to remain on earth, Sri and Sadana's heavenly "connections" play an increasing role in the story. After Sri and Sadana have suffered their father's condemnation, during the night Sri first becomes a snake in the rice field and her younger brother, a swallow. The next morning at dawn the village has been metamorphosed into a jungle and all its inhabitants have become animals. What is more, Sri and Sadana have been separated, each having gone their separate ways.

Having become a paddy field snake, Sri with difficulty reached a village, where there lived a sterile wife Ken Sanggi and her husband Kyai Wrigu. The husband had consulted an ascetic who told her that they would have an incarnation of the goddess "Full of Heat" (Tiksnawati) as their child if they drank "yoga" water from four sources: the earth, the sky, plants and the soul. He advised his wife of this. After several months of pregnancy, the couple returned to visit the ascetic who instructed them how to capture and raise a paddy field snake by providing it with precisely those offerings prescribed by Sri to be placed in the "decorated" (*pajangan*) central room. It was on this bed that they were to place the snake after its capture. Then the wife gave birth to a child. In a dream the husband heard the snake give his daughter a name: Raketan (the intimate one).

At the same time a cosmic disturbance occurs in the sky coinciding with the incarnation of the goddess Tiksnawati, who had disappeared from heaven without leaving any trace. In four different forms four gods are successively sent to destroy this incarnation. First of all the master of the world (Jagadnata, i.e. Guru) sends Kala, disguised as a jackal (*srigala*). But the snake (Sri) appears to the husband Kyai Wrigu in a dream, indicating what ritual defences would protect the baby: rice coloured yellow. Then Brahma arrives in the form of the bull Gumarang, and in the same manner, in a dream, the serpent counsels the father to place an offering of red-coloured rice to drive away the steer.

The third God, Wisnu, in the form of a wild boar, is repulsed by propitiatory offerings of black coloured rice. And finally the master of the world (Jagadnata) himself travels with fourteen gods, all incarnate in animals preceded by Kala disguised as the king of the fish, attacking at three successive moments of the night in three different manifestations, each provoking nocturnal convulsions (*sawan sarap*). And again by following the magical indications of the snake Sri, the father of the child is able to repulse the celestial army.

Listening to this story the Javanese will spontaneously associate the four colours in which the gods appear with the foursome that attack the ripe rice in the paddy fields and who are led by Puntut Jantaka, the primordial enemy of rice, this other fruit of Sri's body. In almanacs sold in urban kiosks, this myth is told in abridged form and the ritual offerings are specified for those who are outside of the oral transmissions of this lore.

THE FIRST JAVANESE VILLAGE BETWEEN HEAVEN AND EARTH

Let us skip to the end of the myth (pp. 57–68): The master of the world (Jagadnata) returned to heaven and sent the fairies to convince Sri to come back to heaven becoming a fairy herself (p. 57). The fairies said that Sadana had already done so, becoming a deity after a ritual of exorcism. Hearing this,

FIGURE 2.3
Kala and his army of convulsion-bearing animals

Source: *Pawukon Ageng*, Radyapustaka Museum, Surakarta. (Cf. Table 3.3, p. 158.)

Sri immediately asked that one be performed for her. Thus it was that the paddy field snake returned as Sri, not the human Sri, daughter of Mahapunggung, but the fairy Sri, granddaughter of Wisnu (p. 66). In fact Sri and Sadana were persuaded to return to heaven through the belief that the other was there already, whereas in reality they were both exorcized the same day before either had returned.

For on his side, Sadana, the younger brother, convinced that Sri had already left for heaven transformed into a fairy, let himself be persuaded by an ascetic to marry his daughter Subadha. She became pregnant by him and Sadana awaited the birth of his child. He had consented to this union more out of docility than enthusiasm. On her side, Sri had wanted to remain with the new-born child of Kyai Wrigu and Sanngi, concerned as she was about a new attack by the heavenly horde. But the fairies explained to Sri that the celestial animosity against the little girl was due to the fact that the goddess Tiksnawati was incarnate in her, and had left heaven without forewarning the master of the world, Jagadnata. (In other versions, the father of Tiksnawati has committed incest with her thus creating the great heat for which she is named.)

Sri then responds: *"Sang Hyang Jagadnata is loving and kind, his power decides all things, but one cannot be so forced without causing suffering. Such generosity is without love, for how does he exercise his power as just now with Tiksnawati, if it is not by constraint? Constraint on constraint in order to rule over all! Why does he deploy such force over people? If Hyang Jagadnata is characterized by such molestation, the human community will certainly revolt more and more."*

Not knowing what to answer, the fairies return to the sky. The husband, Kyai Wrigu, and his wife enter the *k(r)obongan* to clean it and find not a serpent but a woman fairy, the goddess Sri. She tells them her entire story and destiny (in "Javanese" Arabic, *tekdir*). They discover their genealogy, for Kyai Wrigu, the husband, is a fifth generation descendant of the god Guru (=Jagadnata), whereas Sri is the granddaughter of Guru's brother Wisnu. Finally there is a meal with the standard offerings and Sri receives the fairies returned from heaven to announce to her that (p. 61):

FIGURE 2.4
Potential incest provoking reduplication

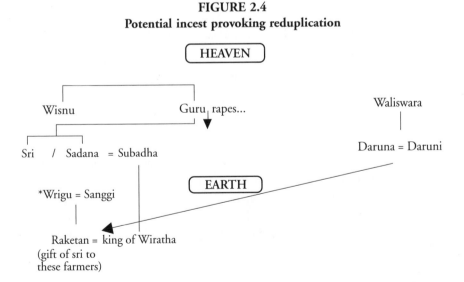

*(Sri is said to be the third generation descendant of Wisnu and Wrigu the fifth.)

"*Know that the children of the god Waliswara named the god Daruna and the goddess Daruni have soiled heaven, committing sister-brother incest. They have both been chased from heaven and have descended to earth. The god Daruna is incarnate in the new-born child Subadha. The goddess Daruni has become incarnate in the child Wrigu as an incarnation of the goddess Tiksnawati. Later when they are adult, the child Wrigu will marry the child Subadha. They will have an only child who will become the queen of the king Wiratha. Later it is from him that the kings of Java will descend.*" And Sri replies, "*If that is the case I will give myself over, I will obey all that the gods want.*" She is then ordered to mount up to heaven in a chariot shining with red light pulled by the bull Gumarang,[15] and using as a driving whip the snake Serang. The fairies go to heaven to look for it.

Still in their central room, Kyai Wrigu and his wife worry about the fever their baby has contracted. Sri explains that it is due to the "full of heat's" (Tiknsawti's) possession of the child. As soon as she says these words, Tiksnawati speaks, and Daruni replaces Tiksnawati's in the body of the baby. Then the heavenly chariot arrives, and Sri and Tiksnawati take their places in it to leave for heaven. The serpent Serang possesses a fecundity sack and when the whip snaps[16] he scatters in the sky seminal liquid, which falls to the earth, seeding it. In the same vein: before harvesting the rice, one makes offerings to Sri so that it will be a rich harvest; when a child is about to be born, one makes rice offerings to rice to protect it.

THE PERMANENCE OF THE MYTHOLOGICAL LANDSCAPE

The variations on the theme of the rice goddess in the minds of the Javanese are relatively fixed compared to the numerous schemata in the cultural corpus of Austronesian mythologies, numbering certainly in the thousands of variants.[17] Nowadays *wayang kulit* (shadow play theatre) does much to preserve the pertinence of myths during specific ritual occasions, but at the same time wayang has slowly moved towards secularized entertainment (Sers 1996, ch. 1; Mrazek 2003). Javanese who do not risk being involved in planting rice or making earring offerings to the invisible Sri stretched out on her bed, have their own reading. Mythology stretches our critical reason, trying to seize "unseizable" objects by writing them down (cf. M. Detienne 1981). This bed in the *k(r)obongan* defies our conceptions about the procreation of plants and babies. At most our translation of it is a tribute to the fascination with the power of this myth, but it is not yet a Javanese listening to it. If scientific, rational satisfaction is the oxygen of much of Western culture, one must admit another oxygen to other cultural social spaces. Without this latitude, we would not be able to approach the object of our inquiry, the myth of Sri and Sadana.

What then is the relationship between the granary and the bed? The symmetry we thought we perceived between the peasants giving rest and a food offering to Sri and the protection against the demons that pursue her and cause convulsions in young babies, seems confirmed at the end of the myth when Sri is said to assure the fecundity of rice harvest and the health of new-born children. Yet this juxtaposition is still too narrow. If instead of basing our interpretation only on the granary or the rice, we realize that the location of the bed is the same as that of the granary, the myth becomes coherent, for it is on "on the bed" that the most important incidents in the story turn.

The binary oppositions of this myth are easy to identify: the pursuing ogres are distinguished from the refugee in the peasants' inner room. The refusal of the father's will is opposed to the consent of the older sister and the younger brother one for another.[18] And again, there is the refusal of the marriage to the stranger and foreigner Pulasva, as opposed to the marriage of the sibling who has fled to a foreign country. Royalty as instituted by doubles of the gods is contrasted to sterile peasants who cannot even reproduce their own kind. Other binary oppositions serve to draw closer the juxtaposed members. The agents of royalty from the sky descend into a village on earth. An exile paradoxically brings the siblings back to the family house. Incestuous marriages (Guru/Tiksnawati; Daruna/Daruni; Sri/Sadana) produce too much heat, yet make fertile the otherwise sterile unions of peasant couples. The cleaning of beds (the place of sperm) fills the granary with rice.

Instead of developing further a structural exegesis of these traits, it seems to me preferable here to refer to certain ritual gestures congruent to these myths, even if sometimes the myth is not invoked directly to justify them. On Thursday night as the sun sets, one lights a lamp for Sri, places a small bowl of water in which floats some petals, and burns incense whose smoke one can barely see. This tradition assures benefits for lives which otherwise have little margin of manoeuvre. For it is Sri who asked for these offerings, and few families are unaware of this, even if after emigrating to the urban centres they do not offer them themselves.

If the daily life of the Javanese, which has nothing exotic about it, finds a place of convergence in the mythical bed which their ancestors claim was frequented by a goddess, must we conclude that their history, which they know but which for us is just legend, cannot be the place where they purify themselves from danger by gifts and supplication? It is we who are asking questions about their bed; they pose none about ours. One doesn't deconstruct another's bed so easily, for it is the place of an intimacy which would be lost in the process (cf. A. Giddens 1992; Augé 1982, p. 92 on G. Bataille).

This myth shuffles through several kinds of sexual deficiencies. By explaining how incest might take place between gods in the world of men, it establishes the concept of an anti-incestuous order. By offerings Javanese purify the risk incest poses to fertility. Between the bed and the granary no incest occurred. What the incest did produce was the cadaver of the rice goddess and the lineage of the first kings of Java, which the peasants "conjure up" by nuptial rites of fecundity. Their concern is clearly rice and children. Among them the incarnation (*jalma*) of the a god in the uterus of a woman does not transform the surrogate womb or necessitate exorcism. The resting place of the goddesses, the successive incarnations through human wombs of the doubles of Sri and Sadana, seem quite indifferent to their contact with peasant humanity. Visitations by the gods to peasants is sometimes beneficial and sometimes not, just as rice field harvests are sometimes good and sometimes bad. The order of the kings instituted by the gods is almost the opposite of the peasant world. While kings accumulate royal and divine identity by the attraction of the siblings for one another, sexuality/fertility for the peasants is often as not sterile or blatantly dangerous. One needs protection from fertility of the wrong sort. This is poetically typified by a seeding prayer recorded from the village elder Damsuri in Krendawahana in 1974:

> Allah, Uma (Siwa's consort), Gendrayana (grandson of Arjuna). The fruits of the forest of Ladhayang are seven great bees: the god of the wind, the goddess of the wind. In the barn yard, look there are many chicken, great granaries, much riches. Look at the water buffalo and the cow, look at the pasture land and the fly bird; praying. Look at the flow of the river, look at the plough, look at the stable. In the forest of Caruban when it is day, the family is together. When it is night, there are many demons.

In the hierarchical kingdoms insular Southeast Asia with their cognatic kinship, problems of recruitment are endemic. For instance, the princely houses in the southern Philippines analysed by Loyre (1989), have recourse to lineagelike bilateral descent groups, less in order to attain an apical ancestor than to bring down to Ego the legitimizing claim of belonging to the princely house. The problem of collateral branches is resolved by stressing the "family" ties that bind followers to leaders, by making this entourage face the king as the centre. As S. Errington (1989) has explained, many insular Southeast Asian kings are inside as much as they are above their subjects. This is reflected in the terminologies for the king's house or palace. In Javanese, for instance, an exalted person in a throne room during an audience is typically addressed as *panjenengan dalem* (you nobles, i.e. the "interior" honoured ones). As we saw above, *dalem* is also one of the names for that part of a peasants' house where rice is stored. Both king and peasants displayed statues or other motifs indicating the presence of Sri (the older sister, queen and rice goddess) and Sadana (the younger brother, and king) on either side of this part of the house, and in the palace, the regalia, the legitimizing heirlooms, were kept behind this royal bed/rice closet.

The Javanese example should not be overstressed because of its appealing clarity. Janet Carsten (1995, pp. 105–28) has shown, in the fishing village of Langkawi (Malaysia), that what appears to be an extreme opposition between inside female domestic domains and outside male public domains is equally "representative" of the objectivization of the tension between male and female roles in perpetuating their common house. In princely houses the problem of inclusion, this dependency of the house's clients, is in each case expressed in the metaphor of kinship which overcomes social and horizontal distance by recourse to an illusion, an objectivisation of classificatory ties between them. Their "house", expressed in the idiom of siblingship, is otherwise fraught with the tension of elder/younger, male and female (cf. Héritier 1981, pp. 53–66). That the lord/servant relationship appears in due course out of these siblingship metaphors is due to the genealogical bricolage to which sibling terms lend themselves. As McKinley (1975, p. 361) has shown, relative age, i.e. elder/younger, gives siblingship multi-generational importance.

The Muslim "houses" in the coastal sultanates of Borneo and southern Philippines, remain quite limited groups, not reaching out to embrace the whole of society as do those stratified societies of Borneo (Kayan, Kenyah) which ascribe status to all members of their ethno-linguistic group. They are also unlike the royal Javanese and Malay "minimal" house which, although resting on the nuclear family, can, through the idiom of siblingship, include other *kampung* residents and entire hamlets. Here, at least in Java, the representation of the gestation of the foetus with its placenta and amniotic fluid, made each individual a "house" in a way that was "capitalized" on by the princes, by representation of their palace as centre of the creation of both man and the world. In this respect the Malay sultanates may have been half-way between the great Javanese kingdoms and the lesser coastal sultanates of the southern Philippines and Borneo (cf. Benjamin 1980).

2.5 RITUAL DOMESTICATION OF HIERARCHY

What Pemberton has called the complusion of cultural recovery (1994, p. 197) has, in the 1970s to 90s, made the south Central Javanese marriage

more "traditional" than it ever was in the 1920s and 30s. The spartan
republican spirit apparent after Indonesia's independence (1949) had vanished
by the late 60s. What had been a cultural form of political domination (for
example, certain umbrellas were reserved to given ranks of Javanese nobles,
etc.) has now become the object of a dubious aesthetic (such as exclusive
aristocratic weddings) and a blatantly conspicuous spending by the bourgeois
of all origins: king for a day (*ratu sadina*) and proud of it. If the *krobongan* in
the rented marriage hall is fake, that is not new. This was seen in the villages
even between the wars. For Pemberton (1994, p. 200, note 5, p. 204) the fact
that the "site of authenticity (can) never again be replicated" in no way
jeopardizes the "awareness (*kasadaran*)" of this authenticity. So if marriage
adat (custom) is counterfeit, and, many features of the rice rituals (*methik*) for
Dewi Sri have disappeared subsequent to the green revolution, what is there
left as a touchstone? This reduces the Javanese topos to fable (*mythos*) and it
is as such, as a weakened legend that Pemberton takes up the myth of Sri.

First he describes the harvest rituals in which, after an offering and a
mantra, a bride and rice goddess made out of flowers and rice stalk, is taken
back to the *krobongan* in the house as Sri, also indicated as "mother" by her
rice child. This inflates the rice goddess into three generations: mother, bride,
and child. Pemberton comments (1994, pp. 209–10):

> Juxtaposed in practice are two generative logics: one works by substitution
> and reserves seeds for transformation into a sign of surplus, the other works
> through the unbridled (one is tempted to say unbridal-ed) process of
> dissemination inherent in *rebutan* [the children's tearing apart of the offerings
> after the weaving of the bride and child] contestation whose scattering
> impulse gives rise to the very preconditions of reproduction. Sri's world,
> thus, is motivated not so much by the mutual incorporation of these two
> logics into a singular source of generation as by their periodic juxtaposition.
> Rather than ritually representing the origins of rice as if they were mythically
> contained in Sri(*lowati*) stories, *methik* practices reproduce the disseminative
> implications of those stories where the issue of ultimate origin is itself
> scattered. In the process, *methik* practices reproduce, moreover, not only
> rice but the means by which humans, too, may be reproduced. For so to
> speak of weddings, as the *dhukun* demonstrated, is to speak of rice-stalk
> weddings and thus, to speak of practices of surplus and rebutan contestation
> in which the groom may not, in fact reign as king.

For Pemberton (1994, pp. 210–16), scattered origins are concomitant
with surplus, contestation, and domestication. If the bride passes the eve of
her marriage in Sri's inner room, it is because she will there be transformed by
the fairies (*widadari*) thanks to the lustre of Sri. One activates the signs of

increment, says Pemberton, by scattering the marriage offering on the public road in the four cardinal directions. But in the myth of Sri and Sadana, the bride goes into the k(r)obongan the night before the wedding (midadarèni) for the process of substitution. The contact with the widadari that night leaves her glowing (with pamor). On the wedding day the more terrestrial meeting takes place. These so-called temu (meeting) practices (reduced to six by Pemberton 1994, pp. 212–14) are seen to be the centre of the authentically traditional reproductive ritual, as opposed to the newly contructed "colonial" model stressing subservience:

1. Pairs of areca blossoms (kembar mayang) are exchanged on behalf of the young couple whereby the bride and groom are "planted", to make them fertile. After the wedding these plants are thrown in the road and their flowering is scattered by children tearing them apart.
2. On the threshold a bridal couple steps over a water buffalo yoke (or another basic tool), relating this marriage to agricultural or artisan productivity.
3. A betel nut fight presents their sexual play.
4. The "seed of life" egg crushed conjointly under the feet of the bride and groom.
5. Seeds and money (kacar kucur) poured by groom on bride's lap by the groom are a figure of insemination and livelihood. In certain parts of Java jars of the same represent Sri and Sadana.
6. Finally bride and groom spoon-feed (dulangan) each other; this may be preceded by a struggle (rebutan) over a whole cooked chicken as in the harvest ritual.

But for Pemberton these figures of increment have lost ground to stronger figures of subservience. He claims:

> ... the logics that would regenerate a fertile rural world in contemporary Java — what one is tempted to call, almost nostalgically a world of Sri — have themselves fragmented and become scattered by the very force of the "tradition" that would appear to frame them. That is, the disseminative implications of Sri's origins-implications that render the issue of origins itself highly problematic — seem to have exceeded the possiblities contained by a cultural renaissance articulated within a framework of explicitly "ritual" [cf. Asad 1993, ch. 3] representation and interpretation. What remains are isloated traces of agricultural and social reproductive practices activated by periodically juxtaposing signs of increment with rebutan struggles of dispersal and supplementary acts of dissemination, traces lying at the edges of New Order discursive comprehension, traces of

surplus thus most liable to recuperation for the sake of "Beautiful Indonesia" diversity or to ritual circumvention of their unlicensed difference. (Pemberton 1994, p. 214)

The only fundamental element of the myth that is not moving in the direction which Pemberton describes is the dimension of kinship. Sri-Sadana's elder sister-younger brother "wedding", never celebrated, is nonetheless pregnant with three dimensions of intimacy: same generation, elder-younger, senior-junior. The "cosmetics" of the substitution of the bride for Sri, the obtaining of the glow resulting from the passage in the *k(r)obongan,* is still there in the village houses and in palace. They represent the highest level of possible proximity. Their intimacy is tantamount to attempting reproduction by the same womb and the same sperm. There could not be a more centripedal marriage reproduced in Raketan and the king of Wiratha, without alterity. This may be the archetypal union between the gods for royalty, who need not marry as humans do by going "outside" the nucelar family. Sri and Sadana's very flight from the father's kingdom suffices to institute the prohibition of incest in the primordial human village by its excess of heat or danger. Yet elder sister and younger brother reduplicate themselves in separate species, a snake and a bird, who then give birth to the first king and queen of Java. The village they founded may return to jungle but their passage on earth has both created cereal agriculture and founded a kingdom.

In the generation of the gods' children three possible relations are sketched out: separation (Sri and Sadana), rape (Tiksnawati) and incest (Daruna and Daruni). All three have beneficial effects on earth. In any human marriage these involve risks which remain unspoken, for they need not be evoked unless one is trying to overstep the established boundaries. For instance traditionally in Java, first cousins may marry only if the female line (*pancer wadon*) is junior to the male's. The same rule applies to third degree cousins; second degree cousins (called first degree ones, *misan*) may not marry. What is preserved from the myth's treatment of incestuous sibling relations is the elder/younger taboo.

To return to the contemporary sociology of Javanese marriage at the beginning of the twenty-first century, Pemberton's conclusion is that:

> The history of the vanishing Sri in Java reveals a certain shift ... the domesticating potential of "Java" that enframes and contains practices within a singular figure of cultural identity, a figure that would eventually, express itself through "ritual".... Focusing its gaze on the wedding ritual as a dominant image of cultural authority, the subject of "Java" would produce so many kings-for-a-day and transform the possibilities of Sri into newly

domesticated ideals of obedience, loyalty, virginal purity, cooperation and other everyday expression of a replicable order of things. (1994, p. 215)

What Pemberton describes as the increasing use of marriage to express subservience instead of meeting and blessing (1994, p. 218) is well demonstated by his analysis of the binding of the marriage by the groom before a Muslim official. This *ijab* in colonial times included the *sungkem*.[19] But now the crawling forward (*dhodhok*) to touch another's knees with one's forehead while prostrating before him or her (*sungkem*) of several elders including parents is the climactic moment in the meeting ceremonies and takes place at "home". Respect to the elders is stressed, but not their blessing. Everything has become traditional moral duty (*kewajiban moral tradisional*), says Pemberton — everything, that is, except the unconscious grammar of elder/younger marriage taboos which are still at work. Not only is Sri's siblingship still a mechanism of substitution in the *k(r)obongan* through which all Javanese brides pass, but the two other principal female divinities of Java, Durga and Lara Kidul, still occupy the place in the pantheon of Javanese spirits that they have in the past. The virtual siblings of one's birth, the *kanda*,[20] still threaten as *kala* in their nefarious form. The Javanese kings still make offerings to them and if all these kings, except the Hamengku Buwana of Yogyakarta, have lost all power in the secular realm, their relationship to these spirit queens is still unique and can be pre-empted by no one. What remains to be explained is how the myth of Sri incarnating herself in the bride was translated in the past into the unconscious respect of the elder/younger marriage taboo whereby the grooms parent's generation must be elder to that of the bride's. We will attempt to unravel this in Chapter 3. After that, in Chapters 5 and 6, two contemporary manifestations of cultural recovery by Javanese lineages (aristocratic and Muslim) will be studied in order to complete our sketch of the mythological landscape at the end of the twentieth century.

EGO'S FOUR SIBLINGS IN BALI AND JAVA

In Java the afterbirth is one's younger sibling and the amniotic fluid one's elder. Since ours is a historical investigation of the social morphology of an area of Central Java, certain cultural comparisons with Bali are useful, presenting the Javanese data against a "clearer" background. In Bali the amniotic fluid, blood, and *vernix caseosa* along with the afterbirth are also considered to be elder brothers (or sisters, depending on one's own sex). To the extent that they are one with Ego they never differ from one's own sex. The first three being liquidlike disappear after birth, but the afterbirth, as in

Java, is the main recipient of the attention bestowed on the four siblings during the successive name-giving/changing ceremonies that the Balinese observe during adolescence (C. Hooykaas 1974, pp. 1–4).

As in Java, the afterbirth is buried either side of the doorway leading into the house where one sleeps, and that according to sex (Hooykaas 1974, pp. 97–98; for Java male on the right, female on the left). The Balinese five elder siblings and the Javanese younger and older siblings accompany everyone throughout life and are independent of descent and marriage. Yet, paradoxically, they are kin and important kin at that. It is through them that one relates to space and time. For just as there are the five siblings (*panca sanak*), there are the gods of the five directions (cardinal, plus center or Ego) and the five days of the week. Hooykaas stressed that (1974, p. 2):

> This unity of macrocosm and microcosm is a basic and beloved piece of Balinese philosophy.

During the annual Balinese day of *nyepi* (practice of silence and inactivity), the exorcist priest (*sengguhu*) expels the evil force (*bhuta*) from the island. To do this they recite a litany of three hundred eight-syllable lines describing the creation of the world in which the refusal of the first four sons of the primordial being who were ordered to create the world results in their being transfomed into beasts of prey. After Pretanjala, the fifth son, learns the mantra, he is capable of creating the world. The other four sons are then forgiven and named the gods of the four cardinal directions. This resembles very closely the Javanese exorcisms (*ruwatan*), and especially the Tengger liberation of souls (*entas-entas*) ritual.

The advent of Indian religions to the archipelago brought the nomenclature of a pantheon, but as in the case of the five seers (Hooykaas 1974, pp. 129–70) little more. With the four siblings an Austronesian myth and polythetic classification are at work here. The classificatory siblingship used in western Austronesian is well attested through the central section of the archipelago and has resisted "Indianization" and Islamization. The anthropomorphic identification of parts of the world with parts of the body or of siblingship did not await the advent of Samkhya philosophy from India to be used in Java and Bali. All personhood is relational and the society is built out of such relationships and not individuals. One's body is not the innermost point in one's identity, for an invisible world inhabits it and has relationships from the oriented cosmos in which it moves.

Weck's study of Balinese medical texts (ms. 1.113)[21] illustrates how the four elder siblings enter and leave their younger brother. While residing in him, they inhabit the heart liver, kidneys, and bile. Weck's text (ms. 1.220 summarized by Hooykaas) states:

All people have visible and invisible body; visible and invisible parents, visible and invisible brothes and sisters.

As Hooykaas has shown (1974, pp. 107–109), these four elder siblings are transformed during the foetus's growth, and, just as the foetus changes name each month during ten months, so also does the cosmos represented by the four elder siblings evolve. Being both demi-gods and demons, the four siblings initially identified with the amniotic fluid, blood, *vernix caseosa*, and foetus, later correspond with:

- the skin, sinews, bones, and bone marrow;
- white, red, yellow, black (Ego is multi-coloured as are the central Kala);
- the directional and planetary gods: Isvara, Brahman, Maha-deva, Visnu, and Siwa/Guru in the middle;
- feeling, hearing, seeing, taste, and smell; and
- the five elements.

Katherane Mershon (1971) described seven rituals held for a growing child. For instance, a mother nursing her new-born, begins by letting four drops of milk fall from her breast onto the floor, thus nourishing the four elder siblings. Hooykaas showed (1974, p. 135) that such pentads, called in Java the five seers (*panca kosika*), are identified first with the foetus but also with the infant as it grows. They are very much a preoccupation of medieval Javanese popular "medical" booklets,[22] which have influenced contemporary Balinese treatises. Hooykaas claims (1974, p. 98):

This reasoning explains why Kanda Mpat (the four friends; or *catur sanak*) is the same as *panca sanak* (the five sibling) … Whether we speak of *Catur Kanda* or of *Kanda Mpat*, what is meant is *Panca Sanak*, which the Javanese and the Balinese mind is inclined to link with the numerous, if not innumerable other pentads filling the minds of the educated.

One could add that these pentads are just as present in a numeroloigcal form, that of prognostics, in the Javanese *primbon-pawukon* booklets[23] widely available today in kiosks in Java as well as in much of the *kabathinan* (interiority) sects' discourse. Prognostics uses these pentads, but ignores their agents, the four siblings. They only speak of Ego, i.e., younger sibling; the others in a sense disappear. But one treats them as if they were still part of the cosmos (*buvana agung*). The erudite Balinese and Javanese conceptions of the role of mother and father tend to vary in their respective texts.

Weck (cf. Hooykaas 1974, p. 105) found Balinese texts stating that the amniotic fluid and the placenta originate from the father, but that the blood and *vernix caseosa* were from the mother. However the same manuscript *Bhagavan Aṅggstya Parva*, goes on to say that both the male and female see each containing their respective *bayu* (male) and *rasa* (female) parts and that these are each fivefold, at least in name: *pañca-bāyu* and *pañca-āksara*. The fourteenth century Javanese Buddhist text, the *Kuñjara Karna* (Teeuw and Robson 1981), says that the foetus, three months after conception, is an imperfect egg called *Si Lalaca*, but that seven days later the five gross elements (*pañca-maha bhuta*: earth, water, fire, air and aether) endow the foetus with the fivefold soul (*pañcatma*).

The four elder siblings have remained in popular consciousness down to the present day in Javanese psychology (cf. Weiss 1977, chs. 4 and 10). The fivefold soul (*atman*) in Java had been related to the five mythological seers (*kusika*) who have since disappeared from the Javanese scene, but who once reigned over the above fivefold extensions of the person by their classifications of the cosmos. Hooykaas's discovery (1974, p. 136) needs to be brought forward to these contemporary popular Javanese notions of classificatory psychology, for even if the daily rituals consecrated to the five elder siblings (Hooykaas 1974, p. 96) and the devotions to the malevolent siblings at the five village shrines only survive in Bali, nonetheless both in Java and as well as Bali, the *dhalang* remains their exorcist and Durga/Rangda their queen.

In their positive benevolent form, the Balinese *Tutur Kuranata Bolon* (Hooykaas 1974, p. 121) reminds us that:

> These are the seats of the Heavenly gods and of the nine (terrestrial) gods in your body, and those of the four brothers who are born at the same time.

The elder brother's duty is to be with their younger brother all the time, in all places. One might wonder how it could be otherwise for the four siblings: skin, blood, flesh and muscle are as intimate to one's self as it is possible to be. Only here, the self has a cosmological dimension that relates it by fivefold correspondences to the very creation of the universe it inhabits, and in which it is called to discern its relations, as well as its place and role.

In the myth of the beginning of the world (*purvaka bhumi*; Hooykaas 1974, pp. 10–51) the Balinese (more precisely, the villages that produced the six texts he cites) express another vision of these sibling relationships. From his bones the Void created the Brass Waxpot named Umā and then five boys, the fifth being the combination of the colours of the first four. He was called Pretañjala. The first four sons refused the Void's wish that they create the world together. They were changed into animals and banished as the gods of the four directions. Umā and Pretañjala, now called Grandmother and Grandfather Patuk, are taught the mantras and then each produce a Gaṅgā river. After the gods fell into the dried-up rivers, they became an ocean and the earth appeared. Then the two gods united and had four children. Immediately there appeared the four banished brothers (tiger, ogre, snake, and crocodile) saying, "Elder brother and sister, bestow forgiveness upon the younger brothers…" (Hooykaas 1974, p. 23) The two gods go to heaven and ask the Void to exorcise the four brothers, to which he acquiesces on the condition that Umā and Pretañjala marry and become an androgyne god. Their disfigurement removed, the four siblings return to the north, south, east and west. Later Umā and Pretañjala change into Durga and Kala from which emanate all things evil. Kala has as many names as he has forms: in the woods, in the sky, on the roads, in the house beams, in the mattress, in the rain, in the market place, in stone, etc. The four brothers each also become Kala with one of his four colours.

2.6 CONCLUSION

This myth, the litany of the *resi Bhujangga* (Hooykaas 1974, pp. 52–84), used by the exorcist priest during the annual purifications by *nyepi* (keeping silence) presents much of the same material as is found in the East Javanese Tengger creation myth. The Central Javanese birth of Kala myth also derives from it (Headley 2000). In both the Balinese (Hooykaas 1974, p. 75, verses 32à–332) and the Central Javanese Murwa Kala myths, man may be eaten by his co-creators, Umā and Pretañjala transformed into Durga and Kala:

And then a covenant they made:

That mankind in the Middle Sphere,
At the full moon and when at new,
Should not by Kāla be accursed,
Should not by Durgā be accursed.

God Kāla shall not eat him,
The Goddess Durgā eat him not;
From his Ten Evils he be freed.
The High God said: "Let it be so."

Gone is the form that they then had.
To their first form they returned;
God Kāla, Guru has become
And Durgā, Umā has become.

This may in fact be at the origin of Sri's protection of human children that we studied in her myth above. The elder-younger opposition would then be considered auspicious when correlated to male-female while the younger-elder in correlation to female-male nefarious and destructive.

In the first chapter we saw that the articulation of Javanese social morphology through the dimensions of cognatic kinship was limited to the structural features of elective ancestral lineages and the foetus siblings, all relatively weak features until assumed into the total social organization of a hierarchical kingdom with divine right rice agriculture and elaborate court rituals. In this chapter, we see that myth and ritual to bind together a person through the flow of life from his/her foetus siblings with cosmic links has the same role that prescriptive features of eastern Indonesian kinship occupy in their exchange system. The comparative study of Austronesian siblings terms by Blust (1993) and the semantics of Ego's generation in Austronesian kinship classifications by Fox (1994, pp. 127–39) clarifies the symbolic expressions of elder sister-younger brother marriage presented in the myths studied here. Fox (1994, p. 136) has analysed the diversity of possibilities offered by elder brother/younger sister. In Javanese and Malay spouses are assimilated to the category of intimate cross-sibling.

This particular use of elder/younger which in some sense assimilates loving spouses to the category of intimate cross-sibling occurs in languages that use the elder/younger terms between same sex siblings … Some societies give systematic expression to this feature of lingusitic usage and make it the basis for designating the "prescribed spouse".[24]

As Fox points out in his article, we need to discover the diversity of the semantics of the Austronesian terminological systems on the basis of sets of terms that partially resemble one another. What are the features that are most likely to permutate from one alternative to another? The relational universe of the Austronesians, says Fox, is established by varying the number of kinship terms used (from ten to forty) and the kinds of relationships that are signalled by using the same terms which in each system can take on different meanings. The first dimension (relatedness) Fox calls completeness, and second dimension (kinds of relations) are designated determinants of reference. For Ego's generation there are eight proto Malayo-Polynesian kinship terms that can be used as benchmarks for comparison: two describe relative age (elder/younger); two gender (male/female); and two gender between related individuals. The last two are not paired: *hipar* (affine) denoting affinity and *qasawa* (spouse), marriage. As Fox writes (1994, p. 135):

> Comparative evidence, however, would suggest the opposite: that prescriptive rules have been "invented" in different parts of the Austronesian world —

and even in near neighbouring societies — using different parts of a related lexicon. From this perspective, "prescription" is not a thing-in-itself, but a possible organisational component of some systems that can be structured in different ways using different linguistic resources.

The fact that the Javanese terminologies for Ego's generation and that of Ego's parents distinguish between the gender of elder siblings rather than younger sibling (when Ego is speaking) is clearly the precondition for discouraging a male from marrying a spouse from an elder line or a female from taking a spouse from a junior line. What the Javanese terminological systems do *not* do, is to develop the feature of the gender of the speaker which Fox has shown "is often elaborated as a major semantic resource in the creation of systems of directed marriage" (Fox 1994, p. 139). Nonetheless, while displaying strongly bilateral features, the myth of Sri, studied in this chapter, illustrates how the distinction between elder sister and younger brother comes to have symbolic importance in the direction in which spouses should be sought.

What about the substitution that Robson surmised for the Javanese term for first cousin (*nak-sanak*), which pushed the original term *misanan* (which means "first") out to second cousin, an evolution which never seems to have taken place in east Javanese? Is this in any way related to the elder/younger dichotomy that is reflected in the shallow Javanese descent group hierarchy? The debate stimulated by Blust's discussion of what he calls "cross-sibling substitution drifts" (1994, pp. 60–68) should soon throw light on this:

> … surely this correspondence of morphologically transparent terminology for affinal groups involved in asymmetric alliance and of morphologically opaque terminology for cross-siblings cannot be accidental. (Blust 1994, p. 61)

Notes

1. Part of this chapter was published as "Le lit-grenier et la déesse de la fécondité à Java: rites nuptiaux?", in *Dialogue* "Le Lit" (no. 82, 4è trimester, 1983): 77–86.
2. Cf. Harun Hadiwijono (1967) on *nukat gaib* and *roh* or *suksma* spirits.
3. Mangunwiryatmo's *Kawruh bubak Kawah-Langkahan Tingkeban* (Cendrawasih Surakarta 1990), pp. 1–2, describes quite a different marriage ritual going by the name of *bubak kawah*, namely a ritual refeshment served first of all to the groom in front of the grainery or *krobongan*: "…*klenthing kaisenan Parutaning Dewegan, sasampunipun dipun sigar-tengah. Tinutupan suwekan mori-pethak. … Sasampunipun, lajeng ngecakaken mantra, sarwi mbibak tutuping klenthing wau*".
4. Cf. Ki Padmasoesastra, *Serat Tatatjara ngadat sarta kalakoewanipoen titijang Djawi, ingkang taksih loemèngkèt dhateng goegontoehon*. Batawi 1907, 391 pp.

5. C. Hooykaas (1980, p. 30) has presented some interesting illustrations of the four older life companion suffering from neglect while Ego is in a state of contented mind (*lega prana*). Since the word *prana* has three semantic fields: attraction (of people), yogic control of breathing and clitoris, these Balinese *prana* merit further investigation. For symbolic sibling amongst the Gayo Batak, cf. Bowen (1993, ch. 9).

6. *Lètrèk* defined in Poerwardarminta's Javanese-Javanese dictionary (1930, p. 366) as: *krama/ngoko araning lurik kang panewuné arang warnané abang, kuning lan sapanggalané kang lumrah nganngo mung wong kang tingkeb*. C. Geertz (1960, p. 40) suggests that these offerings are to the spirits who live in the rafters, in Central Java (around Surakarta) they are put on their four columns before they are put upright and stabilize, as Poensen suggests, the dwelling. The same cloth is used for the seventh month *slamentan* or *tinkeban* of the foetus, although I am not sure here it is always the loosely-woven red *lurik* material described by Poerwadarminta above. What is certain is that some aspects of the birth rituals and house-building ceremonies are the homologous.

7. Cf. *Le Buffle et la Reine quatre rituels à Java central* (1984, 50 minutes). My film shows the preparation and the changing of the offerings as occurs every Thursday night in the Mangkunagaran palace in Surakarta.

8. Cf. A. Rapoport, *House Form and Culture* (Englewood Cliffs: Prentice Hall, 1969), pp. 46; Izikowitz and Sorensen (1982) and A. M. Viaro (1980).

9. Pairs of plants are frequent in Javanese rituals and are often interpreted in terms of one another. For instance in a ten-page booklet entitled *Tata Upacara Mantu* published by the Mangkunagaran's Reksa Pustaka (no date) the visit the night before the marraige (*midodarèni*) by the groom, is accompanied by the gods and goddesses as well as these two trees with golden leaves. They are identified by K.R.T. Jurumartani (*Tuwuhan Manten in Pura Pakualaman*, Gajah Mada Press, 1981?, p. 4) as identical in name at least (Déwandaru and Jayandaru) with the two *waringin* (banyan) in the middle of the northen *alun-alun* in Yogyakarta. These are in turn identified (p. 31) with the tree of deliverance (Tārayāna) which if upside-down (i.e., downward growing) is the *waringin sungsang* or Siva's hanging linga. This is a symbol of fertility while the ithyphallic linga is raised and seed retaining. Cf. Pemberton (1994), p. 211 and notes.

10. Cf. the photographs presented by Maclaine Pont (1924), especially plate IV: photos 11 & 12 (two Surakarta *kobongan* dated 1650–1750), plate V (photo 16) a merchant's house from Kota Gédhé and plate VII (photo 20) a Malang house, *circa* 1900, and photo 21 from Ploso near Pacitan.

11. Yet in her 1957 article on pre-muslim religious background of marriage in Java and Bali, in *Indonésie* vol. X.2, pp. 109–36 her conclusion was much closer to ours.

12. J. J. Ras has shown in Java the literary forms royal marriage try to imitate the divine marriage between Uma and Siva (1973, pp. 411–56). Royal marriage is conceived of as an incarnation (*titisan/jalma*) of the heavenly one. The tales

that propound this most clearly are Panji texts where the incest and marriage between Kala Surya (King Jayalengkara) and his older sister Candra Swara and his wife Candra Lata (a snake) are paralleled by both Panji's and Panji's father marriages thus:

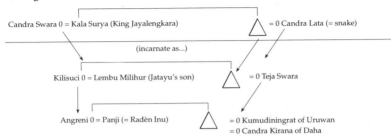

13. Among others, Muslim networks some of which are highly economic. The nexus of village-based wholesalers in rice, hamlet functionaries and landlords and local Muslim *kyai* created networks of powerful interests relying on kin links locally in order to better dominate rural life. These could last over several generations as F. Hüsken's (1988; 2001*b*) treatment of the area of Pati shows.

14. Cl. Lévi-Strauss first presented this notion of permutation in the *Journal of American Folklore* (no. 270) in 1955.

15. In the Sundanese Dewi Sri myth called Nyi Pohatji (Hidding 1929), she has two older brothers, the bull Gumarang and the dog Badug Basu, who protect the rice field for her.

16. The practice during the *sekatèn* festival of Javanese peasant buying whips in front of the palaces and taking them back to their villages reflects their association with fertility.

17. Cf. T. Mabuchi, "Tales concerning the origins of grains in Insular Southeast Asia", *Asian Folklore Studies* vol. 23, no. 1 (1964): 1–91. The bibliography and a discussion of the broken grain myths is contained in Headley, (à paraître 2003) "Les moitiés d'homme à Java: leur reproduction, nourriture et mise à mort." *Les Moitiés d'Homme.* (forthcoming, L'Homme #174); "Les Moitiés d'Homme et les Sociétés Complètes. une ébauche austronésienne." (2004 L'Homme #172).

18. Pemberton (1994, p. 207) cites a Banyumas variation of the myth where Guru murders Sadana out of jealousy and a Sundanese version where it is clearly Guru's amorous advances that kill Sri.

19. Or *ngaras* (krama inggil for *ambung*) = to kiss.

20. The word *kanda* is best known from the titles of Balinese texts discussing their composition in the human person (Hooykaas 1974). It may derive from the Sanskrit word for "cluster (*kāṇḍa*)" (Gonda 1972, p. 179) and later came to designate the siblings who are "sections" of Ego. It is widely used in Bali and in *kejawèn* literature. When I have not used the more descriptive paraphrase of "foetus siblings", I have paraphrased *kanda* as "friends" (in Javanese literally *kanca*, related to companion *manca*; Pigeaud 1983, p. 68).

21. I have worked from an English translation to be found in the Mead archives of the Library of Congress, and not the original German edition.
22. Cf. Kuntara Wiryamartana in *Bijdragen* no. 149-III (1993): 503–10. The seventeenth century Merbabu *lontar* collection housed in the National Library in Jakarta and catalogued by Kartika Setyawati, I. Kuntara Wiryamartanna, and W. van den Mollen (2002).
23. Cf. Headley, "The Javanese *wuku* weeks: icons of good and bad time", (forthcoming).
24. Fox (1994, p. 136) gives as an example: "This is precisely what occurs in the Tana 'Ai system (central east Flores). In Tana 'Ai, the elder category, *wué*, is used by a woman to refer to her sister and her parallel cousin, but also to refer to her male cross-cousins (MBS, FZS) from among whom she is enjoined to find a husband. Similarly, the younger category, *wari*, is used by a man to refer to his brothers and parallel cousins, but also to his female cross-cousins (MBD, FZD) from among whom he must find a wife. Unlike *ipar* which is used reciprocally in Sikka, *wué/wari* are cross-sex reciprocal in Tana 'Ai.

3

VILLAGE GODDESSES, THEIR HIERARCHY, AND CLIENTELE

3.1 INTRODUCTION

In the first chapter we isolated two features of Javanese social morphology — lineages and the foetus siblings — which favoured the creation of worship communities and the articulation of the Javanese society within the cosmos. Despite the strength of the Asiatic commercial networks and a limited occidentalization of this Javanese "crossroads", the particularity of the cognatic societies in the centre of the Nusantara archipelago was that the social organization of Java (Lombard 1990), the social inheritance of the concentric medieval kingdoms, and the divine right rice agriculture with its strict social hierarchy founded economically on an apanage system, were to be harmonized as a *whole*, so that cohesion and equilibrium were constant preoccupations.

In Chapter 2, we saw that during the life of a person, myth and ritual bind him/her through a web of correspondences together with his/her foetus siblings' cosmic dimensions. These two levels, micro and macrocosmic (*jagad alit; jagad gedhé*), refer to one another at the same time as the greater envelops the lesser. The conclusion of Chapter 2 concerned the semantics of Ego's generation in Austronesian kinship classifications where the symbolic expressions of elder sister-younger brother marriage appeared in Javanese myths defining kingship in terms of marriage with an elder female goddess. In Javanese and Malay, spouses are classified by a distinctive use of elder/younger and are assimilated to the category of intimate cross-sibling. In eastern Indonesian this linguistic feature can become the basis for designating the prescribed spouse.

Whereas in Chapter 2 we sketched out the relationship of village cults of the rice goddess Sri to those at the centre of the Javanese kingdoms in the palace, here we shall explore other provincial cults of female divinities, and how they relate. The rice goddess (*dewi*) Sri is not the only female divinity worshipped in the palace complexes (*kraton*) of the Javanese kings (*ratu*) or venerated in shrines in the countryside. The cult of Durga in Krendawahana, for example, belongs to the type of rural cults and to that of royal cults. Only the emissaries of the king are entitled to celebrate the annual buffalo spearing (*maésa lawung*) ceremony, even if peasants from Central Java and beyond regularly come year round to Durga's tertre to fast, pray and make "personal" offerings. Although much has been written about the character of individual Javanese goddesses (Wessing 1997*b*), the place of these cults in Javanese society *as a whole* needs investigation. Though female divinities have roles in myths, one cannot expect to identify them as "persons" providing different kinds of biographical evidence for their "selves". They are better defined by the institutional features of their cult and by their clientele. So then who is Sri?

Inside the palace the name Sri can designate the divine consort of the Vishnu, a prototypical queen.[1] The word *Sri* may also designate the radiance of the *sakti* (power) of a king, incarnate in his consort. Written on the lintels of certain doorways of the Surakarta Susuhunan's palace, it designates the ruler, Sri (Sunan). Closely related is *Sri*, as an epithet, indicating good fortune and prosperity and so it is that an honorific prefix or title, *sri*, is placed in front of the names of gods or aristocrats. Furthermore, as we have seen in the previous chapter, this goddess is the object of parallel cults in the palace complexes and the village rice granaries. In rural classifications, deities are placed in a taxonomy of spirits. Thus one can compare Sri with the entire taxonomy of immaterial beings (cf. analysis of Koentjaraningrat 1985*b*). Once this is done, one can approach divinities sociologically, i.e., by examining the spheres of influence which they are believed to possess. This will be attempted here, even if it is difficult to be precise about the recent changes these cults have undergone.

There are two kinds of data available for the study of the female divinities in Java. The contemporary evidence is abundant, but the roles of the goddesses have been reinterpreted in highly contradictory ways by the Javanese (cf. Beatty 1999 and Pemberton 1994). The data from preceding centuries, on the other hand, is so fragmentary that it is more difficult to evaluate.

For the contemporary period, evidence is of five main kinds:

1. Ancient Javanese *myths* (Sri and Sadana, Mikukuhan, etc.) and historical legends (*Manikmaya, Babad Tanah Jawi*, etc.) still circulating in oral and written form.
2. Customary (*adat*) *invocations* of indeterminate age used during offerings (Headley 1996*a*, pp. 212–15; Soedjijono et al. 1987; for Bali, Goudriaan and Hooykaas 1971).
3. The related *architecture* of palaces and village houses centred on the middle compartment (*senthong tengah*). (Maijer 1894; Maclaine Pont 1923–24; Frick 1991, 1994; Brontodiningrat 1975; Keeler 1983; Headley 1989).
4. The *rituals* for other female divinities worshipped in or by the palace which can clarify our understanding of Sri (Brakel 1997).
5. Recent *village ethnographies* of the cult of Sri (R. Heringa 1997; V.A. Asmussen 1999).

Understanding "who" Sri is will help us understand where Durga lies in the Javanese mythological landscape. We will begin by (1) identifying the relationship of the mythology of Sri to Javanese kingship; (2) examining access and hierarchy in her cult; (3) comparing the cult's social space with that of two other goddesses, Lara Kidul and Durga; and (4) analysing the circulation of values associated with these cults.

3.2 SRI IN JAVANESE KINGSHIP

Durga, as a female divinity, is an exceptional figure in rural Javanese cults. An advantage in studying Sri's position in the Javanese palace at Surakarta where no rice is actually grown, and her counterpart in the rural peasants' cult, is that we get a perspective on Java's social and religious hierarchy. Although peasant rice cultivators are at the bottom of the social pyramid, it is they who maintained the widely known myths about Sri, and the origin myths of the first Javanese kingdom. The peasant and palace world are deeply estranged nowadays, but four hundred years ago, when the second Mataram dynasty was founded in Central Java, their links were stronger. In those years the peasants constituted a central concern of the king, whose tax base relied on their ability to grow rice and his ability to tax it in kind (Hagesteijn 1989; van Setten van der Meer 1979; Suhartono 1991). Historically the kings' taxation rested on apanage, "farming" out the villages to royal tax collectors (*demang; bekel*), but also on the shared perception that the rice goddess came to the aid of the peasants and of kings in different ways. The implications of this will be explored in Chapter 4.

As we have seen in Chapter 2, the Javanese myth, Sri and Sadana,[2] known in numerous local variants,[3] portrays Sri as the source (*kamulan*) of rice and of its chaff (*medhang* or *mendhang*) when hulled. These two Javanese terms, source and (rice) chaff, are used in the name of the primordial Javanese village Medhang Kamulan. In Javanese myths, rice is usually given by the gods, as are the first king and kingdom. However the transfer of rice and kingship from heaven to earth only occurs with difficulty. It often involves Sri being raped and killed by her father and subsequently buried on earth (cf. *Manikmaya*; Headley 2000*a*). It is from her corpse that all the comestible plants first sprout. These origin myths leave little doubt that humanity has become indebted to the gods on account of these gifts, although this unilaterality is not emphasized. The version presented in the previous chapter does not include the rape episode, although it does retain the motif of incest.

In some versions of the myth, when Sri and Sadana flee heaven in order to unite on earth, their (older sister-younger brother) incestuous union is consummated indirectly by a double proxy. Once on earth, they are separated. Sadana becomes a bird and has a boy named Subadha with Laksmitawahni. At the same time another couple, Daruna and Daruni, commit incest in the heavens. Their daughter, Tiksnawati, is transferred to earth under the name of Raketan (intimate). This is the baby given to the childless peasant Wrigu by Sri, who protects it from the attacks of the gods by telling the parents what kind of offerings will deter these divinities turned demonic. The time of Sri and Sadana's separation corresponds to the period when they accomplished the foundation on earth of rice agriculture (Sri) and kingship (Sadana) respectively. Table 3.1 outlines the relations between heavenly and earthly events in this myth. Providing the village where Sri resides with a female child, destined to marry the recently born child of Sadana, Subadha, is equivalent to providing the conditions for another incest between an indefinite number of Javanese kings and the ancestral goddess. By tracing ritual descent through their maternal lines and having a ritual annual meeting with the queen of the southern seas, Solonese kings maintained their royal identity. "Civilizing humanity" occurred on the island of Java through the reinstitution of such a primordial first hierarchy.

As we have seen above, Sri is equally at home in both the modest village granaries (*pedaringan*) and in the celestial royal palaces. But how can Sadana and Sri found Javanese society by an incestuous elopement to earth? The shift from divine siblingship to royal parentage occurs subsequent to their incest. A divine couple founds human society: hence the statues of Sri and Sadana as

TABLE 3.1
Episodic table of Sri and Sadana's descent to earth

Sri, the older sister	Sadana, the younger brother	Daruna and Daruni (Sri and Sadana's double)
Sri flees her father Mahapunggung's palace in Purawcarita (in a heaven) to reunite with Sadana who beforehand had fled to earth.	Sadana is banished from heaven after refusing marriage to a bride chosen by his father-king.	
Pulasva, the demon king of Medangkamulan, seeks to marry Sri. After her flight from heaven, he pursues her on earth.		
In return for her protection, a woman farmer, Petani, grants food and shelter in her bed/granary to the fleeing goddess in the village of Medangwangi.		
The bird Wilmuka helps Sri, still pursued by Pulasva, in her flight through Medangwantu, Medanggowong, etc.		
Sri is reunited with Sadana and they found the village of Sri Ngawanti.		
	Sadana kills the demon king Pulasva, in Medhangkamulan.	
⟶		
Rukmawati advises Mahapunggung of the imminence of Sri's marriage.		
Narada is sent to find Sri and Sadana on earth, and threatens the couple with a curse if they marry.		
Sri changes into a snake and goes off to the village of Wasutira.	Sadana, become a *sriti* bird, flies off, and later marries Lakmitawahni in the village of Ngatasangin.	
Sri, now a snake, warns Wrigu that their new baby Raketan (= Tiksnawati) will be attacked on the order of Jagadnata (Siwa) by Kala incarnate as a jackal. See also Table 3.3.	Sadana and Lakmitawahni expect a child.	In heaven Daruna and Daruni's incest leads to the incarnation of their infant Tiksnawati (full of fire) on earth as Raketan.
⟵	◆	
Sri leaves her form as a snake in the paddy field to become the rice goddess in the granary.	Sadana returns to heaven as a god.	
Sri (and Tiksnawati) return to heaven to find Sadana.	From Niketan and Subadha (children of Sri and Sadana respectively) will descend the future kings of Java.	

a couple in the throne rooms of palaces in Central Java. During the second Mataram realm, however, that is since the seventeenth century, another origin myth takes as its named apical figure a different female ancestress, the goddess of the southern ocean, Lara Kidul. Sri has not been totally eclipsed, since she continues to lie in state behind the throne, but Lara Kidul appears to each ruling king during annual palace rituals. And in any case Sri and Sadana in the form of jars of rice seed and coins continue to hold their own in Javanese peasant houses (R. Heringa 1997, 2003).

The elder sister-younger brother relationship of Sri and Sadana described in Chapter 2 has bifurcated into a rice ritual in the village where Sri is addressed as mother (*(em-)bok*), and a palace ritual where Sri, the elder sister of the first Javanese king, is reduplicated by Sri the Consort of Visnu. Village prayers to Sri stress locality (granary), while palace prayers to both Lara Kidul and Sri stress royal descent and genealogy.

For the second Mataram, however, a young maiden reincarnating (*manjing*) the ancestral consort of all the preceding kings bears the name of queen (*kanjeng ratu*) of the south (Kidul), because her realm and palace lie under the southern ocean. Lara Kidul, then, is a creature of the oceanic underworld and has a very different origin from Sri the rice goddess. Nevertheless, these two "distinct" goddesses exist on a second level of observation, and analysis which suggests that they are permutations one of the other. Lara Kidul's cult hardly extends beyond the palaces and a number of villages on the southern coast (Wessing 1997*a*). Sri's permeates the entire island of Java. In the rural areas Sri combats adverse spirits, and is less ambiguous than the dangerous goddess Durga in her sacred forests scattered around Java or Lara Kidul in her ocean who commands armies of ambivalent spirits. As the main rice goddess, Sri seems to have lost her consort. How can we understand this?

The layers of rural mythological geography contain permutations of these deities' roles. In the prayer for bringing in the rice to the granary of Pak Danuri cited in Chapter 2, there was no mention of Sri at all, although the prayer is said to her and Sadana. The "spiritual geography" there implies a familiarity with the holy forests and their spiritual inhabitants throughout the upper Solo river basin from Ngawi all the way up to Wonogiri. The couple at the centre of this formula is the wind gods. Its benevolent attention is invoked not only on the rice, but also on the entire livelihood of the peasant farm. The mention of helpers (*réwang*) suggest that there are also enemies; in Javanese the existence of spirit friends (*kanda*) implies their transformation in less favourable circumstances into parasites or aggressive spirits (*kala*) as was shown in relation to the foetus siblings. The female goddess is acknowledged by the presence of her helpers, even where she is not mentioned.

How a "*Sri*" is to be invoked in a given location thus depends on who one is and where one is in a social hierarchy, as is clear if we contrast the village invocation and palace prayers. Every Thursday in the royal palace of the Susuhunan of Surakarta during the 1980s, it was Bok Rengga and her four assistants (*abdi dalem*) who spent four hours laying out offerings and praying over them.[4] These prayers take place in the same time-frame as those to Sri in the village granaries. In the palace, no special invocations need be said out loud, but are simply laid down at doorways, etc., while kneeling, and with a *sembah* (the Indian *anjali*) saying *sotto voce* "For the well-being of Sri Susuhunan and that of the kingdom ...". Given the number of offerings in the large palace complex, oversights may occur and for that reason the *abdi-dalem* often excuse themselves for their faults (*luput*, letting go, losing).

There is an exception to this pattern. At the palace the lady in charge of prayers to Lara Kidul, *tumenggung* Saka (Headley 1996a, pp. 212–15) comes out with the four women who have previously laid out the other offerings, and ascends the three floors of the Sanggabuwana (pillar of the world) tower to the north of the the throne pavilion (Prabasuyasa). There she prays aloud over the offerings her companions have brought up there. She is the only one to pray in this way, not because the recto-tonic recitative technique is a difficult one, but because this prayer has been ordered by the king for the welfare of his kingdom, so she is repeating what it is her duty to accomplish and this should be done in a performative mode, that is to say, out loud. The same vocal technique is used when she brings out the offering to the Muslim *modin* (his Javanese title is *abdi dalem juru suranata*) who also says *buda* (Javanese) prayers at the Marakata pavilion palace on the twenty-first night of Ramadan or at the tertre of Durga in Krendawahana when mantra are said by the assistant of the *abdi dalem juru suranata* over the even more elaborate offerings (*sajèn*) laid out there.[5] The other people present witness the offerings and the audible prayers said over them, which would not be the case if it were a private offering when *sotto voce* invocations are always used. Thus it is not Tumenggung Saka who prays, but the king, who prays reflexively through her voice. A translation of the Javanese prayer at the top of the tower where the king may once a year encounter his consort and ancestress, the queen of the southern seas, Lara Kidul, is as follows:

> I implore you. I, the servant *nyai mas tumenggung* Saka, for an offering. All the servants visiting here invoke the royal blessing to present food, flowers, betel chew, cigarettes, blue glutinous rice and sugar to your lord highness sovereign Kencana Wungga (purple gold) with Nyai Lara Kidul in the palace of the pavilion Saka Duman (hibiscus of felicity). The servant has

accomplished the action of presenting this royal food. The servant implores blessing and well-being.

What kind of disposition is being displayed here? One of the palace's former bedaya dancers explained this to me as follows. One can make a *sembah* and present offerings (literally prepare food, *caos dhahar*) at any time. The force (*daya*) of the palace *regalia* in all its manifestations (doorways, tower, carriages, ritual bed of the *kobongan*, etc.) was there at any moment so that one who sincerely (*sejatos*) asked for blessing could do so for he, by introspection, would be responsible (bear the answer, *tanggung jawab*) for his personal private faults, and not just the ceremonial ones (*luput*). That is why one does not ritualize one's voice, but addresses the divinity with faith and confidence. Self correction and asking for forgiveness may precede these invocations. Introduced by a *sembah* (reverence), using concentration (*rasa*) engendered by fasting from food and sleep which promotes attentiveness, even the solitude of an individual act has a quasi-royal authority. Arjuna, the *ksatriya* warrior named Mintaraga in meditation in the depths of the forest, is the model of this behaviour.

The profoundly personal *topos* of this search for well-being is not very different from the requests for the well-being of the kingdom or the rice harvest. What is clearly very different is the circuit through which these similar values are passed. In one case the blessing is for the one invoking, in the other two cases (village or kingdom), society is taken as a whole and the ecology of the welfare is global.

3.3 ADDRESSING SRI: ACCESS AND HIERARCHY

In the myth of Sri the older sister provides the first Javanese human "community"[6] in the primordial realm of Medhang Kamulan with its hierarchy. Once the child Raketan is separated from her protectress and "mother", Sri returns to heaven whence she had come.[7] The continuation of the first village "kingdom" is then dependent on the accomplishment of the rice rituals in village fields and granaries,[8] and those performed by the Javanese kings descending from this separated, then reunited sibling couple. Kingship (the *karatwan* of the *ratu*, in old Javanese) arises from the incestuous relationship. In Javanese mythology kingship is the perogative of the male-dominated palace, while the female deities Durga and Lara Kidul have a special place on its boundaries. By moving the "goal posts" on the kingdom, certain villages play on the installation of female deities on newly created boundaries of which their villages are the centre.

Just what is to be found on the boundaries? A "just" king (*ratu adil* or *erucakra, i.e. Vairocana*) may emerge from the periphery to inaugurate a new reign (Lombard 1990, vol. III, pp. 143–50). If a gendered geography places the cults of the female goddesses Lara Kidul and Durga on the periphery and male kingship in the centre, this should be understood as an encompassed opposition not a dyadic one. To make this claim clear, we will present it in diagrammatic form in Figures 3.1 to 3.3. Figure 3.1 reproduced the ideal plan

FIGURE 3.1
The palace microcosm

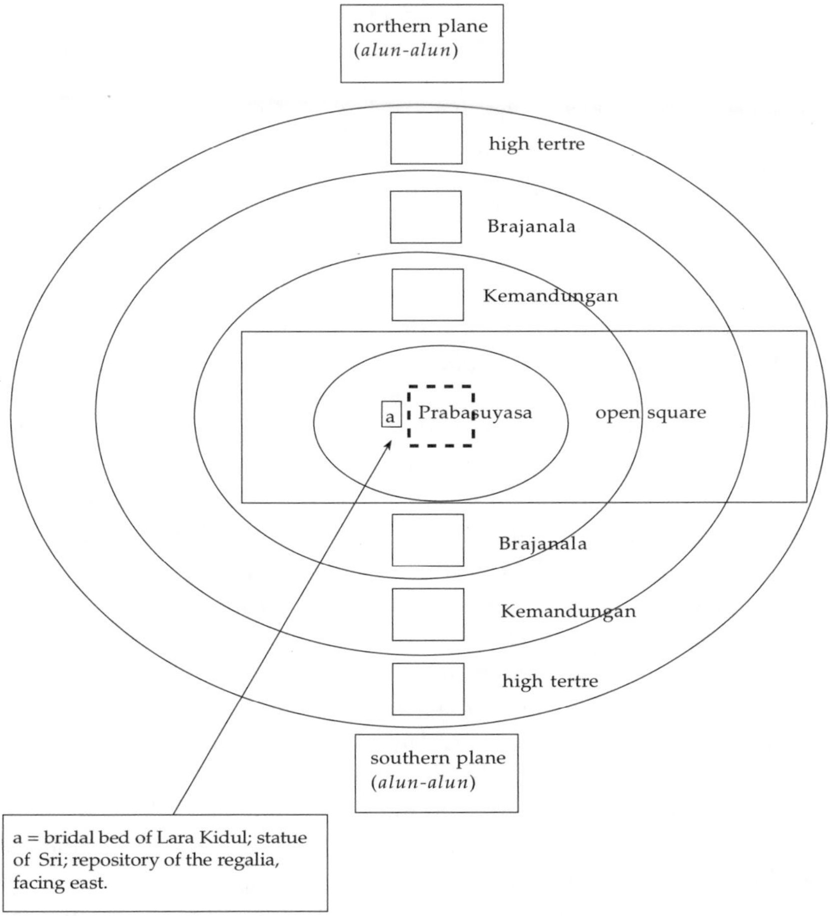

Source: Adapted from T. E. Behrend (1983).

of the Surakarta Susuhunan's palace as *imago mundi*,[9] a miniature mirror image of the macrocosmos. Durga to the north of the palace and Lara Kidul to the south are the objects of important annual royal offerings because, if propitiated, they consolidate the kingdom. These two demon "queens" lord over and lead spirit armies.[10]

As the royal centre of the kingdom, the palace is greater than the village but the unity of cosmos itself embraces them both as in the recursive relationship shown in Figure 3.1. On the bottom line we see that palace and village are opposed in a binary manner, but as the palace claims exclusive access to the cosmos via its microcosmic form (*jagad alit*), it alone can be directly opposed to the macrocosmic (*jagad ageng* or *buwana agung*).

Whether the village–palace relationship occasionally takes the form of a double recursion (Figures 3.2 and 3.3) is a question that should be answered case by case. That would imply that a village or town had pretensions to independence *vis-à-vis* the political and ritual capital and was affirming it by cultic practices linking it directly to the macrocosmos.

North of Solo at the offering tertre to Durga in Krendawahana, few local villagers were implicated in the cult other than the local guardian's family, whereas in Dlepih (south of Surakarta near Wonogiri), Brakel reports that the cult of the royal consort was actively encouraged by its village patrons. The royal offerings consolidated this local cultic practice.[11] Usually their aim is not to surplant the king outright, but implicitly to bypass his ritual precedence, his palace's greater proximity in the macro–microcosmic nexus, by addressing other "divinities" (cf. Figure 3.3). Under certain conditions, as we have seen in the harvest prayers above, village prayers refer to a reduced local spiritual geography that does not place the royal palace in its centre. This is due more to a change of scale, than to any refusal of a higher scale. Village titulary deities (*dhanyang dhusun*) express villagers' desire for a direct access of their own to the macrocosmos in a non-challenging way. The scale of inhabited space (old Javanese *wanwa* or *wanua*) is a constant constraint making rural ritual more limited in scope and yet more varied in content than the royal one.

In the past, certain Muslim cults claimed to provide just such independent access of the cosmos and this directly challenged the monopoly of the king (cf. Figure 3.3). Revolt demonstrated the maximum independence from the palace cult, of which the prime example was the Java War (1825–30) led by the Muslim prince Dipanagara. This sort of claim could not be tolerated by Javanese kings. But in lesser ways, *ulama* who left the court and set up rural Islamic centres with Koranic schools made a clear statement of independence

FIGURE 3.2
Recursive encompassment

Recursive encompassment, i.e. on the lower level A is opposed to B and on the higher level A represents B.

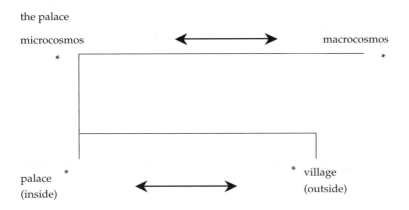

FIGURE 3.3
Recursive inclusion

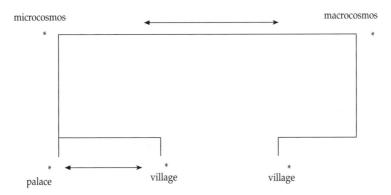

that could not always be bought off by royal decrees creating tax free holdings (*perdikan*).[12]

Local village cosmologies situate Sri differently than palace conceptions, as is illustrated by Rens Heringa (1997), discussing an area some twenty-five kilometres southwest of Tuban in East Java. She describes two phases in a yearly ritual cycle: the harmonious cycle (October to March) and the violent one, which begins with the rice harvest from March to May. During this period, the village wives, personifying (em)Mbok Sri, make food offerings (*maganan*) at the ancestral graves to married men, and then the young unmarried men fight (*kroyok*; *ngrebut*) for their share, enacting a rape of Mother Ipit. This is said to recall the rape of the rice goddess, "an outsider from the cosmic realm, who voluntarily allows herself to be 'eaten'". Just as "planted" (*ditanemi*) can mean "buried" (the body of the raped alien female), so "eaten" (*mangan*) can mean "sexual devouring" (Heringa 1997, pp. 364, 368.) This rape, clearly described in the eighteenth century poem *Manikmaya*,[13] here takes in a very local context in the village of Kerek, owing little to the palace portrayals of Sri. The royal siblings Sri and Sadana's "longing to mingle" (*kepingin campur*) incestuously is assiduously encouraged by the farmer's care of their individual ripening paddy fields (Heringa 1997, p. 367).[14]

Developing recursive inclusion (Figure 3.3) permitted a limited independence from the centre where the rice goddess Sri is perceived to belong "officially" in the palace ritual cycle. This claim could never be complete while thousands of villagers far and wide continued to perform their own rice couple marriages with straw figurines as they harvested rice from their paddy fields.

From the eighth to the eighteenth century Javanese social hierarchy was dominated in changing ways by Javanese kings. Their independence, if not their status, was first compromised by the victory of Dutch colonialism (a policy of divide and rule ending in 1756 with Treaty of Giyanti), yet their palaces are still there and the rites accomplished inside them continue. Even as the conflict of interpretations surrounding the place of female deities in Javanese court culture has grown more confusing in the ethnographic and historical literature, the humble cult of the villagers' rice goddess Sri in a country largely populated by Muslims has discreetly survived. This perhaps reflects the stability of Sri's village clientele in contrast to the disappearance of the palaces as centres of real political leverage. Although the authority of the Javanese kings over collective rituals since the fall of Majapahit has never stopped disintegrating, the city of Solo is still taken by it populace as a ritual unit for purification rites. The urban exorcisms (*ruwatan kota*, June 2000[15]) witness to this fact (Headley 2002). Solo has the reputation of being radical (the strength of its labour movements and Communist party prior to 1965; the violence of its anti-Soeharto/GOLKAR manifestations), but nonetheless it continues to shelter two former royal palaces which remain ritual as much as tourist attractions.

3.4 ASSESSING SRI: ACCESS AND HIERARCHY

Jordaan wrote (1997, p. 296) that Dewi Sri represents welfare and Durga, warfare. Thus they "encompass" the goddess of the southern ocean, Nyai Lara Kidul, who ambiguously represents both. It is not clear whether Jordaan uses the term "encompass" in the technical sense it possesses in social science discussions (Forth 1998: ch. 14). It is worth pursuing this question, since its pertinence has not been justified here. To encompass means to envelop hierarchically (cf. Dumont's appendix to *Homo Hierarchicus*, 1979). A becomes superior hierarchically to B by surrounding and enveloping it. This scope or scale is experienced socially, so it is not simply a category of logical opposition.

For instance, Francine Brinkgreve (1997) has used the notion of encompassment to describe the fact that Durga, the Great Goddess in Bali, encompasses two other goddesses, Durga the goddess of death and Pritiwi the goddess of germinating life. This she deduced from the fact that the Balinese *bebangkit* offerings, a general category, encompassed *bebangkit* offerings (for the death goddess Durga) and *pulagembal* offerings (for the goddess of germinating life, Pritiwi).

To return to Java, the effort by Brakel (1997) to compare the cult of Durga at Krendwahana and Lara Kidul on the south coast on the basis of the similarity of offerings is only partially conclusive. On the one hand she *has* shown that there were occasions for offerings to other queens of demon armies. These rites were associated with the Surakarta Susuhunan, Mangkunagaran's and the Yogyanese Sultan's coronation rituals, and their anniversaries, or rulers' birthdays (Brakel 1997, pp. 260, 262, 266, 267, 272). These are royal *slametan* for the benefit of the entire kingdom, and should contain offerings, both raw and cooked, animal and vegetable. The significance of the recent additional offerings of a sunflower bridegroom (*pengantèn kakung bunga*) and male and female rice flour human figures (*bekakak*; 1997, pp. 258, 267) still eludes us, despite of many parallels elsewhere. These couples made of rice flour dough contain imitation blood, suggesting there had been human sacrifices. Should one stress that this pair is a couple, even a royal couple? Their use in an annual sacrifice in Sleman, Yogyakarta involves the beheading of a pair of couples with coconut sugar blood pouring forth (Harmanto Bratasiswara vol. I, 1994, p. 52).

Southwest of the palace city of Surakarta, the pre-eminent offering to the goddess of the southern ocean at Parang Tritis is cloth, while Durga at Krendawahana (Headley 1979*b*) to the north of Solo receives food, both raw and cooked, animal and vegetable. Brakel concludes (1997, pp. 277–79) that in popular mentality Durga, as the demonic form of Uma/Paravatī, Siva's consort, in her forest sanctuary north of Surakarta represents the unreceptive female, the sperm that is wasted, while inside the palace Nyai Lara Kidul is ritually received, representing the womb (the *tunjung bang*, red lotus) and the process of reunion. For Brakel both are connected to death and to marriage, just as both represent the function of the female rulers of the spirits. Brakel implies, but does not say, that Durga and Nyai Lara Kidul are manifestations of a polymorph goddess, presumably a generic *sri*, which may take several forms.[16] The problem with any notion of polymorph is that so many different spirits are capable of appearing in so many different forms that this quality *by itself* is insufficient to distinguish the three goddesses in question. The extent and nature of their clientele, however, may allow us to compare them in a sociological context, especially through the notion of social space. Geography is indispensable to this task.

We have stressed the locality of these cults since Sri's is both a rural and royal cult; while those of Durga and Lara Kidul have mainly royal sponsorship. Clienteles make differences in their scales of social status. Let us briefly look at the Indian precedent. The existence of the Durga/Mahadevī cults in India[17] is well known and, although the Indian *geste* of *Devimāhātmaya* does not have seemed to have reached Java, except in a few stava still found in Bali, the iconography of Durga's victory over Mahīsa (*mahisāsuramardanī*) certainly did (cf. fifty-six Javanese sculptures studied by Ratnaesih 1979). Durga's influence historically in Java cannot be underestimated in situating Sri in the palace context. Price (1996, pp. 136–39) has stressed that in India celebrations of monarchy involving the Goddess Durga bifurcated between palace and temple. The annual *navaratri* or "nine nights" associated Durga with the protection of ruling lineages throughout India. But villagers also chose Durga (called Kalī or Badhrakalī)[18] for protection. For instance in the area of Madurai (Tamilnadu), she alone among the orthodox pantheon received offerings with animal blood. For the villagers, these offerings had to involve shedding of blood which could then represent the violence that provided protection. In Java since Sri lies in state along side the king's holiest weapons (*pusaka*) in their room behind the throne, one can only wonder if she also was not also once associated with a protective violence, not along the Indian model, just mentioned, but in line with some Javanese permutation. If so, cults on the borders of the realm (the southern seas for Lara Kidul or in the Krendawahana forest for Durga) would be symmetrical to a cult taking place in the very centre of the palace.

Brakel's investigation of the offshoots of Nyai Lara Kidul cult at the waterfall at Dlepih near Wonogiri is particularly useful in understanding the tensions that existed between village and palace cults. The Senapati

(r. 1584–1601) here mentioned is the founding figure of the second Mataram dynasty. Quoting and translating from the early nineteenth century version of the encyclopaedic *Serat Centhini*[19] reveals the existence of yet another spirit queen:

Ratu Dlepih and Ratu Kidul	Ratu Dlēpih Ratu Kidul,
were [both] taken as wives by	kagarwa (n)Jēng Senapati,
Kangjeng Sénapati,	
so mother and daughter are co-wives;	dadya bu maru lan putra,
they protect the king's divine power	rumēksa wahyuning aji,
all over the island of Java,	tah-tēlatah nungsa Jawa,
Ratu Dlepih on the land,	ing dhartan Ratu Dlēpih
Ratu Kidul in the ocean	Ing samodra Ratu Kidul,
Both guard the King	samya remēksèng narpati
Sénapati Ingalaga	Sénapati ing alaga,
who is married to spirits and nymphs;	awayuh prayangan pēri.
[they are] the rulers of the spirits	ratu-ratuning lēlēmbut,
on the land and in the ocean.	dharatan ing jēladri.

This is a big claim on behalf of the relatively minor offering site of Dlepih. Many such offering sites (*pundhèn*) exist. Whom do these local female deities protect? They do not all have royal clientele, and some local offering sites do not even locate the palace as the centre of the kingdom. There was, however, competition between local shrines for royal sponsorship in the veneration of these deities. An independent local shrine, especially a Muslim one, was often interpreted by the royal centre as a potential pivot for revolt. A rural clientele was capable of frequent devotions for local purposes and the king's annual offerings would have had to encompass this. The way to bring about encompassment was generally the famous Javanese *mancapat* classificatory system whose broad outlines are well studied. For Ossenbruggen (1916/1983 English translation) *spatial* distinction by four/five patterns (called *prapat* or *mancapat*, cf. J. D. Hunger 1910; Rouffaer 1905/1931) was primordial. These settlement patterns, where four villages oriented by the four points of the compass were related to a fifth village in the centre with their headman's residence, were complemented by a temporal distinction in time between the five market days of the Javanese five-day week. This provides us with a Javanese way to integrate the rice goddess Sri into a complex of female warrior godesses,[20] including Durga and Nyai Lara Kidul. Durga's role as a border (*wates*) guardian is especially clear.

Further distinctions existed between right and left, deriving from a dualistic preoccupation with high and low, young (associated with West and North[21]) and old (East and South, cf. Pigeaud 1983, pp. 75–76). Pigeaud reconfirms that the term *mancapat* designates the four "companion" villages. The classificatory social power of such distinctions are well known, but as Pigeaud is at pains to point out:

> The few times in Java a classification is applied to the whole of human society (the sons of Kandihawan), it is the Four-Five division. It is difficult to find anything in Javanese thought that refers directly to bipartition of the entire human society,... (Pigeaud 1928/1983, p. 78).

Pigeaud (1928) stressed that the Javanese sense of socio-cosmic community, shared by all, was expressed in these shared correspondences relating colours, the directions of the compass, numerology, animals, plants, and divinities. Do these relate frames of mind or social structures to celestial phenomena? The binary oppositions whose rarity Pigeaud insisted upon the so-called left/right (*kiwa/tengen*) oppositions are a polythetic classification since the members of this "family" resemble each other in dissimilar ways (cf. Table 3.2). Both resemblance and encompassment are at work here.

Why should Lara Kidul be present both off the south coast in her oceanic kingdom and in the tower in the palace? Her role as a perpetually refounding ancestor of the Mataram kingdom who at the same time is the ritual consort of its king, has often been studied, usually using the account of her meeting

TABLE 3.2
Left/right oppositions

Left and Older	Right and Younger oppositions
1. The Goddess Sri, in the form of a statue before the *k(r)obongan*	Her younger brother Sadana representing secular power
2. The immobile older king	Younger brother minister (secular power)
3. The elder cousins Kurawa	Younger cousins Pandawa (recovering rule)
4. Androgyne Semar and elder brother Narada	Younger brother Guru (Siwa) (exercising dominion)
5. Older, Javanese pantheon	Younger Muslim *wali*, and caliph; defenders of the faith.
6. Older northern, southern and central temple palaces	Younger eastern and western outlying provinces

with Senapati Ingalaga found in the *Babad Tanah Djawi* (1941, pp. 77–80). She became or always was (it is impossible to know which) a regalia like the weapons revered behind her royal bedroom in the centre of the palace which are royal insignia. The cult of these weapons has never been linked with a Javanese Durga, yet in India the autumn goddess festival described in the *Purāna* gives ample evidence for this.[22] If we envisage that the martial aspects of a Durga, the commander of a demon army, were attenuated in urban Java, one would have a goddess, a sort of generic *sri*, characterized by her feminine youth and sexuality. This would leave a savage Durga to rule over jungles, a sort of female lord of the forests (*banaspati* or *Agni*). The problem with such speculative analysis, however suggestive, is that there is no proof of any kind to support it.

Taking a different approach, can we detect any fundamental shift in the Javanese pantheon of goddesses since the arrrival of Islam? Allah and his *nabi*, *wali* and saints with unambiguous monotheism as their primary value, have competed for prestige with the polyvalent Javanese deities who both create, harmonize and destroy human society. The soteriological dimension of Islam is at odds with the socio-cosmic one of the Javanese divinities who guarantee the cohesion of the whole. We have suggested that the location of Sri gives a key to her interpretation, since that is where one finds her clientele. The long-standing Javanese propensity for classifying places puts Sri in the peasant house or in the centre of the palace of a former kingdom. Although feudal power and its apanage system disappeared, the spatial matrix of the palace(s), despite this loss of status, are still reproduced today in the Javanese rice farmers' houses. These classifications remain primary. Although we have no trace of the Dewi Sri myth in medieval Javanese literature, Sri could be said to be the model of a queen like the consort of Krtawijaya (reigned as Wijayaparākramawardhana 1447–1451) described Waringin Pitu Charter (Dam D. 1447) in these terms:

> She who is the living image of the daughter of the Lord of the mountains
> (Umā), and whose body was created by Lokesha, Keshava and Maheshvara
> (= Brahmā, Vishnu and Shiva), to be embraced by the king, the Lord of
> Java, to increase the prosperity of mankind to every one's delight.

It is important to realize that what is permanent in the cult of these goddesses is that they allowed the values that structured social networks to articulate Java's changing social morphology. The values may acquire different properties in the course of their circulation within a given social formation, i.e. synchronically. In this epistomological sense, a goddess can be treated as a means of evaluating the morphology of society; worshipping a goddess allows one to get "around" in the society. The presence of different goddesses within the palace is only one illustration of this. To complicate matters further, we are dealing today with a society whose palaces are politically powerless and whose countryside is experiencing the end of peasantry (Elson 1997).

3.5 GODDESSES AND THE CIRCULATION OF VALUES: PAST AND PRESENT

By values I understand different relations and elements evalued in terms of an opposition as seen by the Javanese. Their evaluation hierarchized their society as a whole producing different levels. When I say that values circulate I mean that the society, by evaluating these oppositions between relations and elements, constructs a hierarchy which contributes to the articulation of that social morphology. In the case of Durga, she both protects the kingdom from its enemies both far away and near at hand, and creates a social scale and space with ascribed status and access to her cult.

Kenneth Hall (1996) has explored relations between personal status and ritualized exchange in the kingdoms of Singasari (1222–92) and Majapahit (1292–1519/27?). The great royal feast that converted wealth into status was the new year celebration of Caitra-Phalguna. According to Hall, displays of public grandeur during the earlier Singasari dynasty were replaced during the dynasty of Majapahit with consumption of private luxuries by a rising élite. Under the Singasari kings, temples centralized competition, while during the Majapahit kingdom the Caitra-Phalguna and Rajapatnī ritual feasts converted material wealth into symbolic capital. Visits to the king's palace and the shared activities with this ruler and his royal family during their annual tours through the countryside were also sources of status. The personalized redistribution of Singasari by the king to his rural aristocrats became rare during the Majapahit kingdom. However, as the Ferry Charter (dated 1358) shows, rural rituals to honour the king imitating those held in the capital were encouraged in the provinces. The wearing of textiles whose use confirmed social rank reinforced competition for status. The advent of wealth derived from foreign commerce expanded the reciprocity networks as more goods became available for redistribution. However too much social rivalry and competition encouraged links to the north coast (*pasisir*) trading communities or the creation of local independent enclaves. From the point of view of the inland court, this was to be prevented.

In the middle Javanese literature of great Majapahit kingdom, Sri the rice goddess was not important. Unknown in the *Pararaton* or *Deśawarṇana* (*Nāgarakertāgama*), in the compendium of Javanese mythology the *Tantu*

Panggelaran, Sri's cult is limited to her role as the consort of Wisnu who descends to earth to found the first kingdom in Medhang-gana (Pigeaud 1924, p. 60). Wisnu here clearly reduplicates Sadana. But already the introduction to the *Tantu Panggelaran* quoted below smacks of the kind of Hesiodic alienation that occurs when compiling diverse mythological sources, when one is "committed" to none. The compiler was not of palace origin (Poerbatjaraka 1952, p. 60), and yet his tone expresses an urban distaste for the boorishness of rural life; the myths he compiles are well on their way to becoming mere legends and lore:

> Ah the pleasure of hearing it told, the story of the island of Java in ancient times … [here there were initially no humans until Brahma and Wisnu made them, then] the actions of the human-born increased and extended. Yet without homes were male and female, naked in the forest, seeking shelter for their bodies. They produced nothing, there were no societal traditions (*tinirūtirūnya*). They were without cloth: loincloths, sarong scarves, sashes, courtly robes, headpieces, and headbands. They uttered sound not knowing emotional essence. Only leaves and fruits were eaten by them. Such was the human condition in ancient times.[23]

The repetition of the comment "according to the tales of old …" in the *Tantu Panggelaran* reveals the distance the author has taken from the myths he is compiling as he describes different rural communities (*mandala*) in Java. For our study, one episode at the beginning of this work is interesting. The sons of Guru descend from heaven to teach men how to be human: Içvara teaches men ethics (*daśaśīla* and *pancaiksā*); Mahadeva descends as a goldsmith; Wisnu, called Kandyawan and Sri (Kanyawan), descend creating the first kingdom in Medhang-gana. They teach weaving to mankind. They have five sons: Mangukuhan, Sandhang-garba, Katung-malaras, Karung-kalah, Wrtti-kandayun, the youngest.

> [**Tantu Panggelaran § 61**] There came the mounts of Dame Sri, four birds, namely: the turtle dove, the wood dove, the red dove and the black dove. The five youths [sons of Kandyawan] charged at them, after which the birds took refuge in a *wareng* tree. Wrtti-kandaywan threw [a stone] at them with his slingshot and the birds' crop was cut off. In the turtle doves were white seeds, the black [dove] were black ones, in the red dove were red ones, and in the forest dove were yellow ones. The odour of them spread its scent abroad. The five boys rejoiced and ate them [= the yellow seeds] all up. That is why up till now there are no yellow (curcuma) seeds for they were all devoured by the five boys. Mangukuhan seeded the white, red and black ones. That is how rice has comes down to the present day. But the chaff of the yellow seeds which he planted, that was the curcuma. Such were the

total number of the four seeds such as there are up till now .... Now shall be discussed concerning Kandyawan, who left behind him five sons to succeed him, but none was willing. Finally he had them draw straws of *alang-alang* grass. He who drew the one rolled up on itself was to be the one who would replace him as king. The four drew straws, but the rolled up one was not pulled out. The last to draw was Wrtti-kandyawan who got the rolled up one. So it was Wrtti-kandyawan who was made king. In what concerns Mangukuhan, his lot was to be a farmer, the source of the foodstuffs of the king. Sandhang-garbha lot was to be a merchant, the source of the king's gold [money], Katung-malaras's lot was to be a palm wine taper, the source of the kings palm wine (*tuwak*). Karung-kalah's lot was to be a butcher, the source of the king's meat.

Given the innumerable myths found throughout western Indonesia which link the origin of rice with Sri, Dutch scholars such as Pigeaud have assumed that she was a figure in indigenous mythologies and was later given a Sanskrit epithet or name. But in the myth above, five births are part of a classificatory system and the sacrifice of Sri and her burial has vanished from the literary explanation of the origin of rice. Sri is an element of a five-four (*mancapat*) manner of classifying colours, food stuffs, the five brothers. All this centred on fulfilling the requirements of the king with his position in the central matrix. Surplus, redistribution and status are well integrated here in a cosmological model that is freely arranged using different mythic episodes. The world of the gods, the role of the jewel Dumilah, the rape of Tiksnawati (full of heat), which make up the core of *Manikmaya* myth, a more recent eighteenth century compendium, are absent here. In the *Tanti Panggelaran*, we seem to be dealing with a mythological corpus that has been domesticated by a strong well-functioning kingdom. It is impossible to anticipate any contest for the central position of the state in this classification system.

To conclude our study of the myth of Sri, let us return to the place of this widely known myth in the Javanese countryside today. Against an approach stressing the continuities in rice goddess traditions, some authors have recently stressed the fragmenting effect of conflicting interpretations on the Javanese belief system. This allows them to speak, for instance, of Sri's "disappearance" by which is meant that she has lost her position in an encompassing hierarchy to become the object of conscious cultural manipulation on the part of a disenchanted populace. Pemberton illustrates this point of view, as does Beatty in a quite different way, forming his interpretation in terms of multi-vocality.

The history of the vanishing of Sri in Java reveals a certain shift, ..., through which a form of domestication inherent in weddings and related practices coincides with the domesticating potential of "Java" that inframes and contains practices with a singular figures of cultural identity, a figure that would, eventually, express itself through "ritual". (Pemberton 1994, pp. 204–16)

> Whereas Muslim Javanese have tended, in recent years, to perform agricultural rituals in a perfunctory manner, knowing they are "old fashioned" and disapproved by pious youth and it is no doubt sensible that industrial fertilisers, pesticides and rice goddesses don't really belong together; in contrast Hindus, have actually expanded the range of rituals. Thus Muslims allow Dewi Sri to languish unattended in the rice fields, while the Krajan [= fictive name for a village in the East Javanese area of Banyuwangi, south of the town of Rogojampi] temple priest invites her to his orange picking along with Mother Earth and the *danyang* (place spirit). (Beatty 1999, p. 229)

Even if post-colonial deconstruction is necessary to understand contemporary Java, are the Javanese of the colonial period always to be "blamed"? Writing on the Maravar kingdom in Tamilnadu, nearby to the famous "hollow crown" principality of the Pudokkatai Kallar (cf. N. Dirks 1987), Pamela Price wrote:

> The embedded nature of symbols of worship with notions of power, honour and authority helped to mitigate the potential of colonial hegemony for radical disruption in local political cultures. (P. Price 1996, p. 4)

Not all evidence is to be weighed equally. A sociological comparison of rural and urban Javanese cults must be addressed through the issue of clienteles. The royal polity totally vanished fifty years ago, but the pantheon and its cosmology refuses to do so. The evidence of personal testimony is not always available, but one way to capture of the voice of these participants in rituals is through their invocations, mantra, etc. On the other hand the evidence of myth, completely devoid of biographical data, is best interpreted as logical variants within a given socio-cultural area. That would exclude the use of Indian models for Javanese rites unless there was germane iconographic or textual evidence. As mentioned above, in the case of Durga we have no Javanese translations of the Sanskrit *Mārkandeya Purāna* nor the *Devimāhātmaya* to draw from. Furthermore the whole Indian based opposition of clean and unclean, pure and impure offerings giving social classes a specific access to deities is irrelevant to Java.

From the viewpoint of ritualized kinship, the decisive issue is: who is allowed to enshrine as consort which goddess, with what sort of womb (flaming, etc.) and giving what kind of descendants? Peasants cannot approach a goddess as formidable as Durga with her flaming womb, nor Lara Kidul.

While peasant farmers have no children with Sri, the rice goddess Sri protects their children and she is also "eaten" (and in this sense "married") by everyone. Durga, on the other hand, "snatches" princes and devotees into her invisible palace at Krendawahana, the so-called field of the odour of cadavers (*gandamayit*). Death, violence, and sexuality so associated create a field requiring hierarchical encompassment to which one can appeal for protection; the ambiguity of Durga is that she is both danger and protection. Her role inversions recall those of the deities attacking babies with convulsions. Contact with the cosmos, circulating both life and death, requires a hierarchizing these values, that also traces out a pattern of circulation.

It is also important to remember that these figures whom the Javanese venerate also have intrinsic relations among *themselves*. For Muslims, valued relations (i.e. *wali* and Mohammad) are licit and others illicit from the monotheistic point of view. Nonetheless, for the average Javanese, religious pluralism does exist. Until recently, it did not even pose a problem for the village *modin* (Islamic officiant) to celebrate Muslim and non-Muslim rituals inclusively. In Figure 3.4 we have plotted out not what the Javanese see as the realm of possible relations with spirits available to them, for these have more narrow regional and sociological constraints, but what to the non-Javanese observer seems possible when comparing several villagers and palaces in the Surakarta and Yogyakarta regions of Central Java. In Figure 3.5 encompassment is contrasted to protection, which indicates that the social whole is beginning to fissure. This is plotted onto a simple geography of the Surakarta lowlands and mountains.

If spirits stand in some way between villages and palaces, protecting and separating, why are some spirits profoundly ambivalent, becoming demons on occasion? The myth of Sri's incest explained this transformation of foetus siblings into Kala (Headley 2000*a*, ch. 6). What kind of protection do these ambiguous beings provide? In everyday speech the image of the

FIGURE 3.4

Network of encompassment (1) and protection (2) available

FIGURE 3.5
The articulation of the inclusive relationships between Durga, Sri and Ratu Lara Kidul's three palaces (Krendawahana, Surakarta and the Southern Ocean)

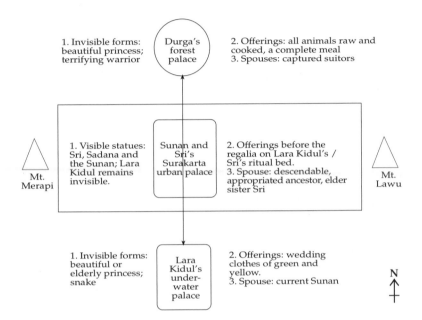

shelter of an umbrella is sometimes used (*dipayungaké*). If there are room for several people under a large umbrella held high enough, when shifting focus from one's own person to a larger social space, this metaphor expressed the relation of hierarchy to the scale of social space. Ritually and politically protection is composed of a more than horizontal, spatial sociological focus. The dimension of encompassment of which the centre, the king "inside" his kingdom is capable of, is then associated with invisibility. Such sacred enchantment (*angker*) in the Javanese sense is both dangerous and valued. If one dares to approach them, spirits incarnate, subject to metamorphoses, both desirable proximity (protecting gods) or preferred distance (demons). In both cases it is only by offerings that the necessary protection can be put in place and maintained.

Protection varies in kind. Village protective "founding" spirits (*cikal-bakal* or *dhanyang dhusun*) protect smaller areas than Javanese divinities or the friends of Allah (*wali*) who helped to found certain Javanese (Muslim) kingdoms. Their vertical hierarchical encompassment may also be differentiated. Personal piety provides individual protection. Javanese daily use of the verb "protect" may involve a defensive sacrifice (*mbélani*) for someone or something, caring (*ngopèni*), shelter (*nyeyub/mlindhungi*), or watchfulness (*njaga/ngreksa*). Some terms are specific to ritual vocabulary. Thus one maintains (*rukti*) one's ritual defences of the household rice granary; one frees (*lukat/ngruwat*) one's house from attacks through mantra and offerings; one destroys (*nyirnaken*) the parasites (*kala*) that bring sickness to persons and rice fields. The entire list of habitual expresssions would be very long, but it is sometimes summarized in brief ejaculations like "well-being" (*rahayu*), repeated three times in ritual formula. The performative aspect of these interventions is clearly inseparable from the representations that lie behind them. Invocations are latent to almost any need, no matter how trivial or unusal.[24]

Large Javanese families often include Christians, Muslims and Javanists. Beatty (1999) has discussed at length how Javanese villagers' respective discourses are reinterpreted and tolerated on the village level. He focuses on the self-conscious strategies of Javanese peasants when defining their religion *vis-à-vis* that of their neighbours. The semblance of totality that the *slametan* meal provides in its variant morphologies is achieved by defining no distinct community of commensality. Thus local sanctuaries are frequented by the entire village, but each in its own distinctive way. Widely shared frameworks protect the more specific, exclusive ones. Many tropes of experience are thus exteriorly cast in the language of Islam. As Beatty says (1999, p. 5) "... style and manner register important factors such as authority, censorship, indeterminancy and compromise." The Sentolo (Kebumen) Muslim *sedakah* for the ricefield exorcism using wooden replicas of Bima's phallus carried around in processions at night, showed that this sort of juxtaposition. It existed already in the 1930s (Headley 2003). Much of the *slametan* was Muslim, while the ritual's myths and cultic tools were purely Javanese. Beatty's point is that variant religious forms are not to be identified with distinct groups before they are understood as reflecting relationships with these other practices. Their values bear the mark of the peasants' observations of the entire village religious arena.

Our concern is how the social protection speaks to all parties involved, the protected, the protecting, and those in whose interest it is that such a network exist. Both human and spirit beings participate in the same cosmic and social frame, even if Sri and the peasants may at first seem at opposite ends of a spectrum. The feature of encompassment generally remains unremarkable during the invocation of the relationship, which concentrates on the ritual efficacy of such verbal appeals. The "high" powers are given pride of place; the offerings are also present as a witness to their sphere (*wilayah*) of influence to which the orant makes his appeal. In this sense the spirit world is formally similar to the kings' sphere of influence. Having made this observation, one should at once say that both kings and peasants recognize the same cosmology (Headley 2000*a*, ch. 7).

The rejection of authoritive narratives by postmodernism has become so common that it has become difficult for some anthropologists to imagine the parameters of belief. For such masters of suspicion, religious culture is only a feature of politics which has recently dissimulated the modern transformation of Javanese beliefs into "truly ancient practice" in order to hide new political strategies behind such falsely embedded traditions.

Encompassment is not the same thing as shared interests, mutual recognition, and confirmation of status, all qualities we recognize in systems of exchange. To make this point clearer, let us look at the offerings proposed by Sri to Wrigu and Petani to protect rice, Sri herself and the baby Niketan from the attack of the demonized deities. Subsequent to the gods' failure to prevent the consummation of Sri and Sadana's incest, these benevolent deities are transformed into killers, reminiscent of the transformation of Siwa and Uma into Kala and Durga at the end of the creation myth of the *resi* Bhujangga (Hooykaas 1974, pp. 66–72). In myths, these awe-inspiring protectors of self in this world will become its destroyers if not appeased (Headley 1983, p. 82). Their dominion would humanly-speaking be catastrophic: a rampage of wild animals who attack peasant houses and attempt to kill their new-born babies. The recommendations given by Sri in dreams to the peasant Wrigu show him how to protect their new-born child from this destructive attack of Kala the jackal and his fourteen companions led by Jagadnata (the world ruler). Their malevolent metamorphoses are listed in Table 3.3.

The ritual and offerings defending new-born children against these "animal" attacks giving babies fatal convulsions (*sawan sarap*) are described in almanacs sold all over Java.[25] Tanaya (1897–1980) (see Figure 3.6), Central Java's most productive almanac writer, borrowed material from the *Pustakaraja Purwa*[26] of *radèn ngabèhi* Ranggawarsita (1802–73). Much of this kind of data is still found orally in Central Javanese villages. This mythology of divine metamorphoses, then, is widespread. It is important for our understanding of encompassment, for it presents massive reversal of roles. Here the goddess Sri defends humanity; the attacking divinities include no female figures whatsoever. The opposition of a benevolent (*sri*) female ricefield python (*sawer sawa*) to destructive male animals/gods shows that both have capacities for metamorphosis, but of differing types. The estrangement of heaven and earth

TABLE 3.3
Malevolent metamorphoses

Javanese Divinity	Attacking Animals
Kala	jackal/wolf (*segawon ajag*) or, during the second wave, the dog Wiyunghyang
Brahma	bull, Kala Gumarang
Wisnu	boar, *cèlèng* Demalung
During the second wave, the above animals attack collectively, along with the following:	
Jagadnata	monkey Kukila
Maheswara	sheep (*wedhus*) Parucul
Yama	deer Ujung
Kuwera	rat, Jinada
Prit-anjala	the bird Emprit (meliphagides)
Siwah	the *manjangan* (tiger?) Randhi
Rudra	the bull Andini
Surya (the sun)	the locust Anggas
Bayu (the wind)	the water buffalo Andhanu
Naradha	the frog Pas
Candra (the moon)	the cat Candramawa
Basuki	a male snake

is not yet complete in these origins myths, and that can partially explain these hostilities. The divinities are chasing the new-born child to prevent the establishment of an earthly kingdom. Later, propitiation comes to mean keeping the gods as gods, sending them back to their heaven. In the *Manikmaya*, the primordial attack during the first rice harvest at Mendhang Kamulan involved the same cast of demonic gods, but, significantly, without Sri to defend the ricefields.

In the myth, Sri defends new-born babies against the first attack of animals or accidents (*sambékala*). One uses the mantra: "Om, Kala honour (to) Siwa" (*Om, Kala nama siwayeh*; translation?). The short and corrupted Old Javanese mantra used in villages are secondary in Javanese practice to the ritual offerings laid around the house at night. Peasants would have manipulated the offerings more dexterously than these, for them, archaic formula. Far from the villages, in the Surakarta palace, the text read to protect new-born royal children (*putra-putri dalem*) are not these short mantra of rural birth rituals, but a long creation myth[27] in which there is no mention of Sri

FIGURE 3.6
Portrait of Raden Tanaya

whatsoever. The beginning of the institution of offerings by Javanese "makes sense" in the context of the myth in which it is told. In the Ranggawarsita's nineteenth century literary compilation of mythologicial history, the *Pustakaraja Purwa*, it is said to become "custom".

> It is said that the behaviour which the ancestors showed towards Dewi Sri as well the actions of Kyai Wrigu followed the instructions of Dewi Sri which then spread throughout the island of Java. Javanese likewise apply yellow powder to their bodies down to the present day. Just as in the past at the free standing granary, the hulling log (*lesung*), the indoor granary, the *petanèn* (indoor granary) every Thursday night are offered powdered *borèh* (ground from flowers) with burning incense. The *petanèn* is set in order, the pillows (for Sri's head) are set up and enclosed in netting with an offering of a jar (*kendhi*) of water. Beginning in the past people began to harvest rice with offerings of *ayu* bananas and *ayu* betel, (and) *borèh* flower powder, laid out freshly with a white cotton cloth, in order to make Sri come. Beginning in that past there were also gifts of chicken boiled in spiced coconut milk,

pounded grain porridge offered for people had children, along with vigils (*melèk*) during which the house was decorated with (protective ornaments of) pineapple leaves, thorn tree (*widara*) leaves, and other kinds of means. (Serat Pustakaraja Purwa, vol. 3, 1994, pp. 82–83).

Gods who kill your children belong to a hierarchy that is not a domestic one, but a wider cosmology involving creation and destruction. The role of kings is elided with that of gods, by their centrality in ritual space, but this cannot go too far or the phenomenon of encompassment of the social by the cosmic will not raise the king's palace above the status of every and any village. Appeasing them or rendering their forms benevolent involves one not only in ritual action, but in a social space that extends well beyond that of the rural farmer ken. In this mythological landscape, the first "human" player was a king. These customary patterns of nurturing of life at birth, and marriage are now followed by Muslim death rituals. This is a marked historical change. Death rituals are now uniquely the domain of Islam, while birth and marriage along with harvest have continued to be the realm of Sri, long after the Javanese kings' realms have collapsed and Islam has spread far and wide.

In that sense, at the beginning of the twenty-first century, Sri is the last "goddess", that is to say value, with a full sweep of clients and hence a nearly total social network, left over from the second Mataram dynasty (1613–1755). She has left the palace and returned to the primordial Javanese village of Medhang Kamulan whence she came. As a few Indonesian rice farmers return to organic farming (*Far Eastern Economic Review*, 17 May 2000), we may yet see a post-Green Revolution appoach to Sri that fits in none of the categories described above. As long as her myths and the dangers she protects against are spoken of, it seems unlikely that her place in the Javanese hierarchy of spirits will disappear. Indeed the Javanese have been caring (*ngopèni*) for her invisible body for so long that to speak of her disappearance might well seem to them obtuse. She disappeared into the rice granary with the *beginning* of society. The same cannot be said for the cult of Durga and Lara Kidul, whose political base has been eroded, while that of Islam's has been strengthened throughout the last century. After examining in Chapter 4 the erosion of the economic foundation of the royal apanage system, in Part II (Chapters 6 and 7), we will present the restructuring of the religious landscape of Krendawahana-Kaliasa by Islamic lineages and aristocratic.

NOTES

1. In this paper Wishnu will not be discussed, although he figures frequently in shadow puppet theatre as the spouse of Sri. The consort of Sri dealt with here is

the mythical first Javanese king Sadana, the younger brother of Sri found in Javanese myths.

2. As in the preceding chapter, the version used here and analysed in Headley 1983 is taken from *Dewi Sri, Ceritera Rakyat dari daerah Surakarta, Jawa Tengah*, Proyek Pengembangan Media Kebudyaan, Ditjen. Kebudayaan Departemen Pendidikan dan Kebudayaan, R. I., 69 pp. No author or translator given.

3. A. C. Kruijt 1903; J. Kats 1916; *Tjerita Rakyat*, 1963; Danandjaja 1972.

4. Cf. My documentary film, *Le Buffle et la Reine quatre rituels à Java central* (1984; 50 minutes). This film shows the preparation and the changing of the offerings as occurs every Thursday night in the Mangkunagaran palace in Surakarta.

5. The offerings are recorded in my film: *La Prière à Java, trois styles sur le corps, avec des offrandes et dans la mosquée* 1989, 50 minutes; co-production CNRS/ ORSTOM.

6. Cf. *Serat Pustakaraja Purwa* 3 (1994): 81–82, "Jabangbayi Raketan wineca anurunaken para ratu tanah Jawi".

7. Ibid., pp. 80–81.

8. Ibid., pp. 82–83.

9. Adapted from T. E. Behrend, "Kraton and Cosmos in Traditional Java" (M.A. thesis, Univeristy of Wisconsin at Madison, 1983).

10. To my knowledge, there are no links between Sri and the female palace *garde de corps* nor with the female servants (*ampilan semara*) who bore during royal ceremonies the insignia or regalia of the kings.

11. Robert Wessing (1997*a*, pp. 97–120) gives another example of local cults in his study of the area of Puger (near Pacitan) along the south coast of Java.

12. Clearly what is said here only applies to Central Java. The Sasak case (Lombok, cf. E. Budiwanti 2000), in southern Sumatra around Palembang (Gadjahnata and Swasono 1986) and in the Banjar areas of southern Borneo (Alfani Daud 1997) is quite different.

13. Cf. Canto 13: 1 (1981, p. 103) for the rape of Uma and the appearance of the fallen seed (Kala). A second female figure is also raped in canto 15: 48 (1981, p. 131) was called the Dumilah jewel and later Tiksnawati (full of heat).

14. Cf. Jay (1969, p. 214).

15. This was recently celebrated following on the burning ot the Solo's "great market" (Pasar Gedhé). An earlier shopping mall *ruwatan* in Solo is examined in Chapter 13. Cf. for the evolution of the role the rulers of the kingdom of Klungkung (Bali) in collective rituals, cf. Wierner (1995, p. 56).

16. Brakel (1997, p. 279). "The offerings and myths show that Javanese concepts of the spirit world are diverse enough to allow for more than one female ruler, with different places of worship and complementary functions and shapes."

17. On the eventual visit of Mpu Tanakung to Vijayanagara in the middle of the fifteenth century cf. *Siwarātrikalpa* (1969, pp. 19–25).

18. Cf. the DurgāStava in Goudriaan and Hooykaas (1970, pp. 196–207), where Durgā is called Bhadra-kālī in stanza 15. Stanza 10 contains a reference to

holding the horns of Yama's servant Mhisha and the last three stanzas are a hymn to the goddess Nārāyanī from the *Mārkandeya Purāna*.

19. Vol. 8, 1998, pp. 18–19 [Kinanthi meter 416: 4–5]), Brakel (1997, p. 277).

20. Cf. Burton Stein's study of the Mahanavami (1984). Yokochi (1999, pp. 73–74 and 87–88) discusses the historical evolution of Durga as a warrior goddess in India.

21. But in old Javanese *purwa* means north.

22. The most important references in the classic Sanskrit texts are: *Skanda Purāna* 7.1.83.39–60; *Nārada Purāna* 1.11817cd–22; *Agni Purāna* 268.13cd–16ab; *Visnudharmottara Purāna* 2.158.1–8; *Bhavisya Purāna* 4.138.1–115.

23. Translation, Zurbuchen (1976, pp. 70–76); cf. Pigeaud (1924, p. 58) for Javanese text.

24. I once attended at midnight the sacrifice of a black duck behind Durga's shrine in Krendawahana to increase the sales of a shishkebab (*saté*) stall in a nearby urban food stand.

25. i.e. Tiknoparnoto (1962).

26. On the displacement of *pujangga* like Ranggawarsita by Javanologists, cf, Kenji Tsuchiya (1990).

27. Cf. Headley (2000*a*, pp. 143–55) which presents a translation and a commentary of a Javanese palace cosmogony: ms. 547Ka "Mengeti Kuwajiban Abdi Dalem Juru Suranata: Maésa Lawung, Donga-donga Nglabuh, …", *transcribed by Nancy K. Florida in 1985. It is available through the Cornell Univ. Surakarta Ms. Project (KS #189; reel:118/9).* Ms. p. 8.

4

DETERRITORIALIZATION
The End of Peasant Livelihood

4.1 HISTORICAL OVERVIEW

In the preceding chapter, it was claimed that the profoundly village-centred *topos* of the search for well-being was homologous to a larger, whole society, the difference lying in the circuit through which these similar values are passed. In the rural situation, a blessing is invoked for that particular place, whereas in the palace invocation society, incarnated in the ruler, is taken as a whole. Since the village perspective is so strongly rooted in an inhabited space, it is important to understand the evolution of the village communities in terms of their land tenure and taxation procedures. Without this, it is difficult to understand the transformation from membership in a village to a non-territorial community like the Javanese Muslim *umat*. Membership in the village involved many constraints. One could not leave the village and settle in another one since all able-bodied family heads and farmers, called *cacah*, were indebted to the ruler. The relationship of servant to master (*kawula-gusti*) was thus also economic. The king measured his resources in terms of numbers of these *cacah*. On the other hand the destiny of the village was perceived in large part as a communal one; local spirits protected the frontiers of that particular space and the residents who honoured its deities (*dhanyang*) at offering sites, sacred trees and wells, etc. The local ritual calendar involved the annual farming cycle as it related to these local deities. Communal meals were held, and communal labour was necessary for rebuilding houses and restoring bridges and wells. The king held no royal eminent domain (*vorstelijk eigendomsrecht*[1]) over the village land; the local Javanese princes did not even measure these lands; what they did count was the number of farming families on them. They were preoccupied by sociology, not by territory measured in square metres of rice fields.

The apanage system in the central (*nagaragung*) lands, those closest to the king's palace, was controlled by the extended royal family. Relatives of the current and preceding kings parleyed their kinship relation as best they could into tax farming settlements (*lungguh*) and the *cacah* accorded them by the raja. The king, on the other hand, did not content himself with distributing rights to tax farming. He also exercised a monopoly on ritual genealogies leading back to the founders, both divine and human, of his dynasty. The offerings (*labuhan*) he made annually in the four cardinal directions of his kingdom (Krendawahana was the site of the offerings in northerly direction) were his exclusive prerogative; through his dynastic and mythological ancestors the king's lineage could enable him to protect the frontiers and the well-being inside his kingdom.[2] Thus territory concerned not only military frontiers, but also "genealogical" landscapes. The whole notion of a transposable landscape of belief, such as Islam conveyed, was to prove an innovation here in the sense that traditionally integration was achieved through orientation to the central palace, whereas Islam provided an exterior focus: Mecca, where the historical traces of the origin of Islam could be visited during the hajj.[3]

As we will see again in Chapter 12 dealing with the reconstruction of social confidence after the fall of the Soeharto dictatorship, when Javanese society is in its greatest difficulty, it is also at its most legible. The construction of this new religious landscape did not take place in an economic, social, and political vacuum, any more than the shifts in village kindred discussed in Chapter 1. The initial fissuring of the earlier social morphology, its cosmology and its reproduction in time and space by the Dutch during the seventeenth and eighteenth centuries, directly put into question the place of the Javanese king as the linchpin not only of the older apanage system, but also of the economy of Java generally.

Ultimately the foundations of the Javanese apanage system go back to the beginning of the second Mataram dynasty, to the early seventeenth century. Here we see the traditional *faire valoir* and Islamic religion side by side, having little influence on one another. Although Sultan Agung (r. 1613–46) adopted the Islamic title, sultan, with approval from Bagdad, there was nothing Islamic about the form of "divine right" rice agriculture and taxation then practised, which was still based on the centrality of the king in what was envisaged as a single and unique kingdom. In this sense the adoption of Islam did not initially decentralize the Javanese vision of their place in Southeast

Asia or in the world. The apanage system was a system of distribution: in the central provinces (*nagaragung*) the largest shares were accorded to those closest to the king depending on their degree of kinship; in the outlying provinces (*mancanagara*) a patrimonial bureaucracy allotted functionaries appointed by the king these rights to farm taxes (Rouffaer 1905, p. 619). The important differences in the distribution of land settlements (*lungguh*) depended on other factors as well which varied over time. Commerce had been important until the arrival of the Europeans, who in a sense forced the Javanese back into their own hinterlands. It was Sultan Agung who, considering himself a "prince and a soldier, not a merchant like the other princes of Java", centralized his power in the commercial backwater of south-central Java away from the commercial trading cities of the north coast. His monopoly of rice was continued by his successor Amangkurat I (r. 1646–1677). When the Dutch emissary R. van Goens asked why his subjects could not sail and engage in trading ventures, Amangkurat replied, "My people have nothing of their own as you have, but everything of theirs comes to me, and without strong government I would not be king for a day." (A. Reid 1980, p. 449) Roughly a century later, the Javanese war that ended with the treaty of Giyanti (13 February 1755), by which Nicholas Harting, "the Pacificator", succeeded in dividing Mataram in two halves: Surakarta and Yogyakarta. Both cities had active Muslim quarters.

In the nineteenth century a new land leasehold system apparently permitted the aristocrats (*priyayi*) to augment their income by renting directly to foreigners transformed certain village lands into plantations (Houben 1994, chs. 1 and 6). This evolution instead came into conflict with a deeply rooted aspect of Javanese sociology: the notion of inhabited (*wanua*) space. By stressing the imagined role of the royal right of eminent domain, the Dutch during the mid-nineteenth century sought to prove that the notion of private property had never existed among the Javanese peasants.

The Dutch ethical policy at the end of the nineteenth century tried in vain, to lessen the social tensions engendered by the extreme exploitation of the forced delivery system (1830–60s). This was not lost on the Javanese. At the beginning of the twentieth century, the Javanese were able to take stock of the history of the preceding century. The ten years between 1917 and 1927 saw the appearance of communism and radical political movements, challenging a colonial reform of taxation on agricultural land. The context was volatile. From mid-1918 until mid-1920, the price of daily necessities rose, while wages did not increase. Famines broke out as food supplies dwindled (Wonogiri 1917; Kedhiri 1918); sugar cane fields were put to the torch in protest. What Savitri Scherer[4] describes as the most significant criticism of Javanese social structure ever delivered during the colonial period was made by a native member of the Volksraad (Peoples' Council) on 26 June 1919:

> In his speech, Tjipto [Dr. Tjipto Mangoenkoesomo, 1885–1943] made it clear to his audience who and what was causing the suffering of the people. It was not due to the simplistic reason, the evil of foreign subjugation *per se*; no, he went further to probe the cause, to spell out to his audience that their own ruling heads, the members of the Javanese ruling class, were not blameless in conducing the worsening of the living conditions of the people. His attack on the Sunan for the Sunan's exploitation of his people was not only a direct affront to the sacred symbols of Javanese rulership and the ruling class in general, by which the ruler supposedly represents and protects the interests of his subjects, in a *gusti-kawula* agreement … colonial exploitation could not function effectively on Javanese soil without the backing of their own ruling heads. The threat implied by Tjipto's argument was that he destroyed the sanctity of the remaining symbol of the highest authority which was still intact, as it had been before Java was subjugated by foreign rule. He destroyed what was the fundamental basis of how Javanese society had been governed.

What to do when it was no longer possible to conceive of the whole of Javanese society in terms of an articulated hierarchy of values and the king's centrality in that ritual and economic hierarchy? The problem was institutional rather than epistemological. Not surprisingly, in this unstable context, efforts to establish new religions increased in frequency during the second half of the nineteenth century and the beginning of the twentieth. For example, at the end of September 1919 in the village of Karangwungu (Klaten) a collaborator of Haji Misbach (cf. below), Mangoenatmodjo, founded a radical new religious movement called Red Islam (Islam Abangan), later designated as the Red League (Sarekat Abang). It quickly gained twelve thousand members, and would have continued to spread had the colonial government not clamped down on the freedom of assembly in May 1920 (Larson 1987, pp. 113–14).

Paradoxically Larson claims that in the area of Surakarta, the Communism which emerged in Central Java in Surakarta in these same years was so weakened by strong tendencies towards anarchism and nihilism that it could not produce coherent programmes for social change. Haji Misbach (called the red *haji*) typified the beginnings of Communism in Surakarta by his mixing of traditional religion and radical politics. Larson (1987, p. 123), commenting on his conversion to communism, says that it is "… a typical example of the Javanese bent for syncreticism, as his adherence to communism was no stricter than his adherence to Islam."

It is well known that from the mid-1970s, the land tenure system and the crop rotation associated with it were revolutionized by the introduction of the high-yield varieties, at a time when there was a rapid rise of Koranic schools and improved Muslim "encadrement" at the level of hamlet mosque attendance, resulting in a change in the "mythological landscape"[5] of the countryside around Krendawahana. Of course these changes in agriculture began after the Java War (1825–30), with the introduction of a plantation-driven agricultural export economy and, later, a tax on the quality of land rather than the number of families occupying it.[6] By the beginning of the twentieth century, Central Java had already become an agricultural "peasant society", and its land tenure system, the *faire valoir*, collapsed under the dual pressure of international depressions and the desperation of peasant poverty.[7] The changes that took place throughout the twentieth century, outlined in Chapter 1, led, according to R. E. Elson (1997), to a passage from community to citizenry with social and spatial mobility so great that peasant livelihood had come to an end. After the age of commerce in the sixteenth and seventeenth centuries, the commercialism of large scale exports and demography in the nineteenth and twentieth created larger scales of economy (national, regional, and global) that would completely dominate how families raised crops, and forcing them to rely respond rapidly to changes in market prices and increasingly on off-farm income.

Locally one can trace the history of these socio-economic changes to well before the Java War, with the period after the installation of the palace of Paku Buwana II (1745–46) in Surakarta. It was then that the Javanese principalities, having lost to the Dutch their provinces on the north coast and the eastern salient (*oosthoek*) of Java (Pringgodigdo 1950, appendix map 5), experienced a crisis in the traditional taxing mechanism, the apanage system. Their revenues were so diminished by the loss of their outlying provinces, that they stopped collecting taxes themselves through their tax farmers (*bekel*), and began subletting their lands settlements in land (*lungguh*) to others ready to use them for commercial cropping. In 1781 the Susuhunan of Surakarta had to limit the renting of apanage lands by Javanese aristocrats to three years, because of their recent imprudent contracts with Chinese and European *rentmeesters* (Soepomo 1927, p. 39). The ultimate dangers of these "modernizing" approaches to agriculture were political. This would become fully apparent in the reign of Mangkunagarna V (1881–96). Mangkunagaran IV (r. 1853–81) was the ruler who established his own "royal plantations". During the reign of his successor, there occurred a period of such financial turbulence that the Dutch took control of them at the same time as refloating them financially (Pringgodigdo 1950, pp. 60–70).

FIGURE 4.1
Western Enterprises in the Principalities

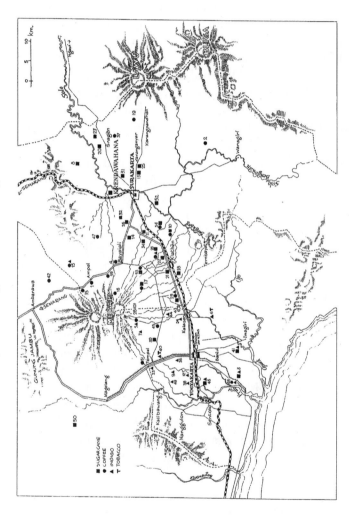

Source: Adapted from J. H. Houben, *Kraton and Kumpeni: Surakarta and Yogyakarta, 1830–1870*, Verhandelingen 164. (Leiden: KITLV Press, 1994), p. 294, with permission of the author and publisher.

As already noted, the watershed of modern Javanese history was the defeat of Prince Dipanagara at the end of the Java War (1825–30), and the subsequent Dutch Culture System (*cultuurstelsel* 1830–60), which resulted in a net decline in the level of "welfare" in the villages. After 1830, rather than paying a land tax in kind, the land rent in Java was made to correspond to turning over 20 per cent (later 33 per cent) of their land to the forced cultivation of commercial crops for exportation by the colonial government. This concerns our study to the extent that the old apanage system, already disrupted by the division in two of Mataram by the Giyanti Treaty (Houben 1994, pp. 41–49), was destroyed by this brutal change in *faire valoir* on the part of the colonial authorities. With the apanage system went the graduated hierarchical relationship between Javanese, which without incarnating any atomistic individualism, was more personalized than their bureaucratic and economic replacement.

In a longer historical perspective, it is difficult to describe Central Java in all its diversity. Peter Carey (1981, 1992) has presented a wealth of historical data on the Java War and its causes. Perhaps what is best documented since the collapse of the uprising led by Prince Dipanagara in March 1830 was the rural *economic* history of Java. The Dutch colonial regime took a crucial economic interest in the countryside after their introduction of the Cultivation System, and there is abundant documentation on the social transformation it brought about.

Immediately after the Java War, in 1832, a certain Sadita (Houben 1994, p. 221) circulated a petition in the Solo region warning the Susuhunan of Surakarta, and the Sultan of Yogyakarta, as well as the Dutch, that the curse of Allah would be upon them for their compromises and greed. For the next fifty years the aristocracy itself also continued to plot the overthrow of the Dutch. As Kumar concludes (1982, p. 274),

> The other characteristic of the later Suryengalagan movements [1883+] and others like them which is immediately striking is their reliance on supernatural assistance and their extreme voluntarism. That they were so soon surpressed is not entirely attributable to the increasingly effective control of the colonial government, but also to the wistful and already-disarmed nature of the movements themselves. They seem rarely to move beyond the tactics of prophecy, claims to supernatural powers and sometimes a joint pilgrimage to a location traditionally associated with the coming of the just king.

The memories of such revolts did not fade away quickly. *A posteriori*, Krendawahana was conceived of as such a place when the lineage of Paku Buwana VI created a memorial for his meeting with Prince Diapanagara there in 1979.

FIGURE 4.2
Selling cooking pots in Kaliasa on market day

For the village of Krendawahana, which produced no cash crops, the primary urban link for all matters social and economic (i.e. taxation) was through the nearby Mangkunagaran palace in Surakarta, some fifteen kilometres to the south. This was not true of matters Islamic, for which the village outreach was quite diffuse. For instance in the Jamsaren Koranic school (*pesantrèn*) in Surakarta, one could study Muslim jurisprudence (*fikh*), or in the village of Popongan to the east of Surakarta be initiated into the Naqsyabandiyah Sufi brotherhood (*tarékat*).

The largest city between Yogyakarta to the southwest and Semarang to the north, Surakarta lying in a vast rice plain between the twin great volcanoes of Merapi and Merbabu in the west, and Lawu in the east, was shared by two princes' palaces with their retinues. In the northern square (*alun-alun*) at the

FIGURE 4.3
Selling fried *tofu* in Kaliasa on market day

larger of these two kingdoms, the annual Muslim religious feast days, the three so-called celebrations or *garebeg*,[8] took place in a uniquely royal form. The apanage holders and their tax farmers were obliged to be present and pay certain of their taxes at these dates as will be detailed in the village ordinance from the 1850s translated below. These festivals mixed royal subservience to Allah with the people's dependence on the king for certain kinds of intervention to the divine on their behalf, as well as popular night fairs. At the same time, even though the offering site to Durga was in Mangkunagaran territory, both palaces collaborated in a yearly "spearing" of buffalo (*maésa lawung*) offered by the Solo kings for Durga's tertre in the Krendawahana (cf. Ch. 8). This was performed on the occasion of the anniversary of the accession to the throne of their respective ruling monarchs.

FIGURE 4.4
Bringing home rice harvest in June 1974 before the introduction of
mechanical threshing and electrical hulling

Breman has shown that during the nineteenth century the colonial organization of production necessitated redefining the nature of peasant access to land. From the 1750s and continuing down to the twentieth century the colonial authorities saw what they wanted to see in the Javanese village, invoking different historical justifications according to their changing perspectives. Initially, when land was abundant and the population scarce, the colonial government demanded forced cultivation of export crops and infrastructural forced labour, both poorly paid or even unpaid. The institution of taxation on villages lands *as a whole* through a local tax farmer (*bekel*), the so-called *admodiatie* system introduced by Raffles at the beginning of the nineteenth century, explains why the Dutch imagined agrarian land ownership to be communal. Free access to land would have prevented control over labour. As Breman (1983, ch. 1) says communal property was a euphemism for the negation of private property. Only at the beginning of the twentieth century when land became scarce did the Dutch actually survey the existing surfaces. It would be several more decades before peasants began to buy and sell their "heirlooms", i.e. their rice fields.

There was also a rapid evolution in the demographic pressure and mobility, especially after the railway was built (cf. Ch. 1). The overall effect of the arrival of the iron horse was to intensify commercial land use by facilitating exportation of produce to Java's north coast city of Semarang and to limit the arable land consecrated to rice fields (Houben 1994, p. 337). An obvious fact can be mentioned in passing here. The installation of plantation agriculture in Java took only a few decades, while the "cultivation" of Islam required centuries. We will see below that this is because of the differences in the types of community at stake. The *cultuurstelsel* created forced labour gangs and

FIGURE 4.5
Danuri (seventy years old in 1974 and very alert), elder (*mancakaki*) of Krendawahana, was often consulted for his knowledge of ritual. His son Slamet Sujaka made a prosperous career teaching Islam catechism in Tawan Manggu (Karanganyar), while his wife taught grade school in Krendawahana

FIGURE 4.6
Damsiri (fifty-eight years old in 1974), small landholder owning
a quarter of a hectare of poor quality *sawah* (rice field)

necessitated the handing over of whole sections of village lands to the colonial
plantations, destroying, once and for all, village economic autarchy. At the
same time, Muslims were "enlarging" the village in a very different way,
creating an *umat*, a community of people sharing a common faith (*iman*;
Koran II, 177), which led to defined behaviour to which the village could add
little of its own cultural patrimony. There could not be two more divergent
social evolutions.

In general in Central Java, the causes of further social differentiation in
the twentieth century were agrarian (White and Gunawan Wiradi 1989).
Hüsken (1988) has provided us with a detailed historical survey from 1850
to 1980 of the region of Tayu near Pati, where he also elucidated the
twentieth century cycles of commercialization and accumulation in the Javanese
village he calls Gondosari. In the period of economic innovation, the green
revolution, less labour was required in the fields because of the use of sickles
and threshing machines. The village élite practised rural capitalism:
sharecropping, wholesale buying of rice still growing, and more recently

capital investment in fertilizers, pesticides, and so on. This did not necessarily involve proletarization, but renewed strategies involving land tenure and sharecropping, using informally bonded labour who are also political dependants guaranteed long-term contracts with their patron (Hüsken 1989).

Political change, especially the development of nationalistic values and the appearance of the first political parties, has been carefully examined. For Surakarta, Larson (1987) provides a description of the thirty years prior to the Japanese occupation. The Javanese aristocrats, and the Dutch efforts at reform and modernization of the Susuhunan's palace administration, were unwelcome since they were not accompanied by any greater political autonomy. This impasse would eventually lead to the demise of the palace as a political force (Larson 1987, p. 189). Paku Buwana X, who died in 1938, had had strong links with the Sarékat Islam from its inception in 1912 during his lengthy attempt to become a great Javanese king.

The *terminus ad quem* of our study is the final period corresponding to Soeharto's New Order regime (1967–98). Given our focus on the introduction of Muslim social values[9] we must begin retrospectively, spanning the previous two hundred years in the Kaliasa-Krendawahana region, highlighting the long-term features of land tenure more than the day-to-day world of strategies for economic survival among Javanese peasants. *Faire valoir* as a social form, like features of language, often presents itself unconsciously, partially surviving tenaciously in the well-grounded praxis. The payment of the village administration using "communal" lands rather than government salaries is one example of the holderovers from the age of apanage.

In studying, however briefly, the land tenure system of Krendawahana, it is important to stress how slowly things changed. When I worked on the village land cadastre in 1973, it was completely out of date. It had been and still needed to be corrected many times over due to deaths, inheritance and undeclared sales of all kinds. Titles of the bureaucrats that supposedly administered the laws governing village land tenure dated from 1939 (*Mangkoenagaran Rijksblad* no. 2 and 3) needed to be revised and brought up to date. On 10 November 1956, the Bupati of Karanganyar, R. Soekarto Singolodro, issued a guide of twenty-five pages to the village headmen (*lurah*) and farmers in general to guide them through the maze of laws written in Dutch, Javanese and Indonesian.

The earliest document that I have located concerning apanage taxation in the Mangkunagaran dates from 1855.[10] It demonstrates the situation immediately after the Java War. As its reading is quite clear, it suffices to provide a translation. It will give us a benchmark from which to judge the drastic changes we have just sketched out above and which we will continue to describe in the third section below. My comments are in brackets following certain articles.

4.2 MANGKUNAGARAN VILLAGE ORDINANCE OF 3 MARCH 1855

The following ordinance is fixed by myself, Pangeran Adipati Aria Prangwedana IV, Lientenant Colonel of my Legion in Surakarta concerning the Ngabehi, Demang, Rangga and Bekel who are to deliver the products of the royal lands (*perembé*) and the allocated lands (*pamajegan*) in the domain of the Prangwedana.

Article 1

Those who aspire to the posts of *ngabèhi* (*radèn bei*: inferior rank of functionaries), *demang*, *rangga* and *bekel* should not obtain these ranks by gifts of valuables or money. Only those serving as military (*prajurit*) or in another service of the Pangeran Adipati Aria can fill these posts. It is not permitted for them to ask for *duwit pangunjung*[11] or *panganyaranyar*.[12] He who is guilty of this fault cannot fill that position, and he who receives a gift or *pangunjung* or *panganyarpanyar* monies will be punished in proportion to the gravity of the circumstances.

Article 2

The hierarchy whose positions are included in this decree, are designated by the title of *mantri* (functionaries), enumerated from *kliwon* down to *demang*. That classification of *mantri*, outside the capital (the seat of the Mangkunagaran principality of Surakarta), will be the following.

1. Those who have the position of *kliwon* will have the title of *ngabèhi*.
2. Those who have the position of *panéwu* will have the title of *ngabèhi*.
3. Those who have the position of *panatas* will have the title of *demang-panèkar*.
4. Those who have the position of *panèket* will have the title of *demang-panèkar*.
5. Those who have the position of *panglawé* will have the title of *rangga*.
6. A *bekel* who owns a hamlet will receive the title of *patingkah* if beforehand he was the chief of the others (*bekel*) in neigbouring hamlets.
7. An apanage holder (*bekel*) who is not the chief (*bekel*) among the others will be considered an ordinary *bekel*.
   A police officer is not an (administrative) function, but police officers receive official duties from those in charge of these affairs.

Article 3

For the maintenance of the functionaries mentioned above, there exist the *bengkok* (rice fields designated for the administration; Dutch, *ambtsveld*), whose size will be calculated according to their position as well as according to the fertility and the amount of fields under their management, or according to the quantity of the crops or seeds that these fields require, or according to the size of apanage (*lungguh*, settlement given a servant of the king) of the *bekel*, and to the extent that that is just and where local customs are respected.

- The *bengkok* of the *rangga* are 1¹/₂ what the *bekel* receive.
- The *bengkok* of the *demang* are four times what the *bekel* receive.
- The *bengkok* of the *demang panékar* are 4¹/₂ times what the *bekel* receive.
- The *bengkok* of the *ngabèhi* are six times what the *bekel* receive, while the *bengkok* of the (rural) *kliwon* are equivalent those those of the capital

[The titles *panéwu, panatas, paneket* and *panglawé* etymologically imply the control over a thousand, a hundred, fifty and twenty-five *cacah* respectively. A *cacah* or a *panguwala* (a person in debt bondage; Hoadley 1994, p. 41) is an individual with or without family whose relationship with the sovereign is characterized by indebtedness. Comparing articles three and four, one notices that the proportions of *cacah* assigned to these ranks are one to six and not that proportion which their titles imply. This suggests a flattening of the hierarchy, requiring this redefinition of their titles.]

Article 4

The village (*desa*) on which the *ngabèhi* or the *demang* are settled belongs to their *bengkok*, but if there are two or several village united, their *bengkok* comprises only one of these villages, while for the other village(s) a rent should be paid. Thus an exceptionally large village is, or should be divided, as long is *bengkok* is sufficiently large. The rice fields (*sawah*) near the villages should be included in their *bengkok*, and it is not legal to choose other rice fields.

The *bengkok* of the Rangga and the *bekel* should include their (villages') gardens and fruit trees and the rice fields near the villages on which they are settled; and they are not permitted to take other rice fields.

Article 5

The dependants (*sentana*) of the *ngabèhi* and down to and including those of the *bekel*, do not receive government *bengkok*. Nonetheless they are allowed to have dependants (*sentana*) as long as they renounce giving them any part of their *bengkok*.

(Among those below the rank of *bekel*) only, the *kabayan* and the *kahum* receive a *bengkok* whose size is fixed by the administration. The *bengkok* of the taxable inhabitants of the village (*sikep*) are now annulled, their responsibilities must be accomplished by the service personnel.[13]

Article 6
In every royal (*karajan*) village, hamlet (*dukuh*), agglomeration (*grumbul*, literally thicket), there should not be more than one *bekel*, who should always be named by the *ngabèhi* or the *demang* under whose management the village falls.

[Articles four, five and six show that kinship bonds (*sedulur* or *sentana*) posed difficulties for the royal kingdom, together with other kinds of dependants who tended to devour the livelihood of their patron. Palmier (1960, ch. 8) shows that during the nineteenth century kinship ties continued to furnish means of access to power for the *affines*, the families of the mother and wife. The prerogatives of the royal lineages of all the preceding kings was supposedly totally extinguished after seven generations. On the non-royal village level one sees in article nine that the *sikep*, the villagers owning rice fields and benefiting from full rights in the village sphere also had their own clientele (*numpang*, their "passengers") as in the eighteenth century. Article nine reinforces their hold on their dependants who might try to flee to another village by punishing the apanage holder (*bekel*) who attempt to receive them.]

Article 7
The rank of *bekel* under the *demang* is calculated according to the size of the villages, the *bekel* of the largest being named for the *rangga*; below them follow those of the *demang*. The rank of the villages remains calculated according to their size.

Article 8
The number of the rice fields under a *demang* whose rent is to be paid, should be divided (and) established their with their houses. It is not permitted to any one to establish themselves in a village as a *ngindung* or a *nyagak kapat*.[14] There also may be persons who refuse to farm, and the *bekel* who pays the lease should impose on his subordinates to do so. There are also people who, infirm because of their great age, have to have the farming done by their children, their grandchildren or the *batih* (servants) of *bekel*. To the persons who are infirm and have no family, no rice fields are granted and no tax is levied on their gardens (*kebun*). Nevertheless they are authorized to stay and

live there. It may be that the number of healthy men is greater than that of the rice fields. The men who have no share in the rice fields are called *ngindung* (villagers without rights, usually living in the house belonging to someone else and situated in someone else's garden). They must pay the administrations tax, which is separate from the lease of the village, from the rents from the village rice fields, which each time is paid by the mid-year, that is to say during the month of Sapar and Pasa, at which time their corvée for the administration will be noted by writing.

Article 9

The men who are already established in the village are not allowed to move out without a *layang padang*,[15] from the *ngabèhi* of the *demang* under whom they fall.

These chiefs can without difficulty oppose the giving of such a *layang padang* when there is no justification. In the case when a villager does this (without permission) and he must pay a fine, this should not be more than four florens. If a villager who falls under the Prangwedana wants to move to another village under the authority of the Prangwedana, the villagers should not be adopted. If they have no *layang padang* and belong to men in the territory of the Susuhunan, then their village headman (*lurah*) or *bekel* should be informed (of their intentions). If they belong to the territory of the (Dutch) Government or of that of Yogyakarta, then they should be told to ask for a *layang padang* from their head man so that no further question will remain. If ever a headman takes the risk of accepting men from the territory of the Prangwedana who do not have a *layang padang*, the respective headmen of these men must inform the administration who will fine such a chief. Nevertheless such a chief should not be fined more than eight florens, for the men were not of the territory of the Prangwedana and had no *layang padang*.

Article 10

The *rangga* and the *bekel* of villages who renounce their *bengkok* must appear in their turn in the palace in order to be inspected by the *demang*.

At this time they are obliged to submit for inspection the stallions and geldings so as to determine who are their owners and to what use they will now serve.

The *ngabèhi* and the *demang* who are competent will take the horses in the *bekel's* possession and will determine the worth of each one of these.

The presence and activities of the *rangga* and the *bekel* will be determined by their *ngabèhi* and *demang* in the manner described below.

Article 11

As for the untilled (*berran*) and newly-opened mountain rice terrace, not taxable for the first three years, (*petalan*) rice fields, the dry rice (*pagagan*) fields, the river bank (*setrèn*) rice fields, the eroded (*padas pèrèng*) rice fields (where gravel has replaced the original soil), etc. as well as the uncultivated orchards (*kitren hirengan*), these will not be taxed, nor pay rent, but will later be organized in the same way as the *babok* (principal apanage) rice fields.

In the same way, if a person has just been settled with a new hamlet where they are beginning to cultivate irrigated rice fields and dry fields, etc., they should not be subject to any tax for three harvests (*ajot*), nor should (their cultivators) be subject to any corvée (*heeren diensten*), but they should be totally free of all of that. The *bekel* will have their lands assigned them later. And in order for that to be so, their chief must ask for written permission from the administration. If that is not done as is here provided for, the *bekel* will be punished according to the (gravity) of the circumstances.

[Article 11 shows the interest the Mangkunagaran has in extending the surface of cultivated lands, and Article 12 shows how this translated into the need to have a cadastre of all the cultivated and untilled rice fields, as well as the fields rendered "bald" by erosion.]

Article 12

Each time there are lands known as "bald" (*gundul*; rice fields not explicitly belonging to the village but to its farmers), these must be inscribed by the chief, if such spaces exist. Otherwise such rice fields mentioned above must be united to those of the neighbouring village; these rice fields nonetheless remain under the authority of the same *demang* to whom their usufruct goes. Thus there was a village Karang Kapek which possessed an incalculable number of neighbouring rice fields, which nonetheless was still under the management (*beheer*) of the Demang to whom their usufruct should have returned.

All this should take place with the accord of the native administrator (*Inlandsch bestuur*). It might be that the village of Karang Kapek lies far from its rice fields, and then they should not be attributed to it.

Article 13

The taxes *taker turun* (taxes paid in money by the *bekel* to those on whom the king has settled them) and *baceran* (money reserved for daily use, hence costs exterior to those of the household, i.e. exceptional taxes on the farmers) are now revalidated while the sums previously demanded for the taxes *krigaji pagerdon* (service tax to be paid in money to the king by the person who holds the apanage), *paduguhan* (cost of hospitality), *penaiban* and *gugur gunung* can no longer be fixed. On the other hand the money from rents must be justified in terms of the productivity of the fields.

It is not permitted for *ngabèhi* and for the *demang* under them to increase the rents (on the fields) without first informing the native administration. If ever this is done, they will be suspended for a hundred days from the royal dignity (*kaprabon*) and their subordinates will be informed of this. Thus they risk at the end of the time of their mandate to be withdrawn from their posts.

The rents must be paid four times a year, as follows:

* on the second of the month of Sapar;
* on the eighth of the month of Juadilakir;
* on the twenty-second of the month of Pasa; and
* on the eighth of the month of Besar.

Since the rent is paid in four instalments, it is one fourth that is paid each time with the help of the chief mentioned above, the entire (rent) to be received in the ten days after the day that he himself comes to the capital. Five days after the expiration of this date, if it is not done, they will be penalized in order that the above be paid. The rents should not be in money but delivered as is the present custom.

[In Article 13 we find that certain *bekel* had taken the initiative to maximalize their personal profits by increasing rents. The Mangkunagaran administration, by doubling the number of times payments were made per year, hoped to limit these abuses. These were also ritual events of importance but the fiscal link to these *garebeg* seems to be fading from sight. On the other hand, in Article 15, the need to respect and celebrate the village level feasts (*bersih desa, dhayang dusun* offerings) is kept centre stage. A. Reid has pointed out (1988, pp. 137–46) that while in Burma and Siam, all legal suits had to be in writing, in insular Southeast Asia judicial procedures were based on oral law. This implied confidence in a divine order that would punish those who lied, but also highly local oral sources for these customs. Hence the need to respect *adat* (custom) in all its regional particularities. Javanese written law codes did exist in the urban palaces, but they were never followed to the letter but served as literary heirlooms like their Indian forebears, the *Manava-dharmasastra*.]

Article 14

The headmen of the villages mentioned above do not have the right to have their subordinates work (without pay) in the rice fields. Nonetheless they may, in this respect, ask for help from their subordinates to whom they must give food and payment according to the local customs.

In the same way the authorities have no control over, nor can they take over the fruit trees and untilled fields of the population, for these must be shared out among their owners.

Article 15

The headmen should as far as is possible try to use for the population the local traditions or customs, and try themselves to solve the problems of expenditures. They (should) try to facilitate the organization of the ritual cleansing of the village after the rice harvest (*bersih desa*), the ceremony at the end of the fasting month of Pasa (Maleman), the festival contributions (*susubangan*), and the gifts of food offerings (on a flat woven bamboo basket or *tampah*). In these matters local customs must always be followed with care. Someone who would innovate in these matters will be fined a floren. In general one must watch over the tranquillity and the security of the local population.

Article 16

From the *ngabèhi* down to the *demang*, it is not permitted to rent rice fields or dry fields (*tegalan*) cultivated once the village population's crops are no longer there, or to rent these lands to villagers other than those already on this territory. It is also forbidden to rent rice fields, etc. in fourths (*prapat*) or fifths (*mancalima*), in the event that there is sufficient land under their jurisdiction (for that). In the opposite case, this must take place with the prior permission of the Native Administration.

[In Article 16 the five-four proportionality of the Javanese *faire valoir*, the famous *mancapat* (Ossenbruggen 1916; Pigeaud 1928), here called *prapat* or *mancalima*, is invoked to claim that only the king can alienate the fifth or foreign part (*manca*) of the product of village lands to those he names as apanage holders (*bekel*).]

Article 17

It is forbidden as follows:

1. to abuse the population or to destroy a village;
2. to inflict damage on the Native Administration;

3. to fine or punish without prior permission of the Native Administration;
4. for *bekel* or those below them to fire or appoint any one without prior permission of the Native Administration;
5. to avail oneself of the property of one's subordinates;
6. to assume two positions;
7. to open a gambling house; and
8. to shelter evil doers and to oneself commit a guilty act.

Those who undertake to commit one of the forbidden acts listed above will be punished.

Article 18
The causes for suspension or banishment (from one's position) are the following:

1. counterfeiting money;
2. making or selling explosives;
3. clandestine selling of opium;
4. selling bird's nests;
5. distilling or selling rice alcohol (*arak*);
6. making salt; and
7. selling stolen coffee.

[Article 18 shows that certain luxury product but also certain vital ones remained a royal monopoly. Probably only gunpowder and opium eventually passed into the hands of the colonial government, whereas the others remained with the local principalities.]

Promulgated on Saturday the 14th,
of Jamaliladir of the Dal year 1783 (=1854).

This document cannot be precisely situated in the complex evolution of *faire valoir* in Central Java as a whole. A considerable historical literature continues to struggle with the application of certain basic notions (*cacah-kawula*) which ultimately deprive the older cadastres of any historical value. Hoadley has written.[16]

> For the bulk of the *nagara agung*, the apppointment letters grant compensation for office. These vary in quantity from four to ten thousand labour units (*cacah gawéning wong*) each living in villages listed in the document. As pointed out by Crawfurd in 1813, the term *cacah* "... is of

no practical use in the ordinary details of agriculture or Revenue, but it is by this denomination solely that the Registers of the lands are kept." (Mackenzie Private Collection No. 21, f. 216). In the phrase *cacah gawéning wong*, *cacah* simply means number. *Gawéning wong* (in ngoko the terms mean "work" and "person") signifies the labour of human beings. Within the context of the Sultan bestowing *gawéning wong* on newly elevated officials in compensation for services rendered or expected this means that the units of work were part of the realm's material resources at the sovereign's disposal …."

4.3 PRE-COLONIAL BONDAGE

The general picture of this rural agricultural organization can, however, be brought into focus and this is, in itself, a big step towards situating the notion of dependency in these Central Javanese principalities. As A. Reid (1988, pp. 120–72) has shown, many of its characteristics which are so foreign to European society were common to Southeast Asian ones. I will summarize below Reid's sketch of this social organization. Their basic motif in Western Austronesia is one of descent groups competing for power. Power here is calculated by the capacity to recruit dependants. Sacred descent from a divine ancestress, for instance the queen of the southern seas in Central Java, is totally restrictive, since there is only one candidate for such position, while adoption of children and marriage into quasi lineages and houses are loosely structured. Another feature, inflexible by definition, is the vertical obligation between a patron, one's master, and the bondsmen, who were usually held through indebtedness. The pretexts for bondage were debts acquired in trading, in paying bride-price, gambling and, of course, bad harvests.

Bondage underlies many types of dependency. It was so widespread that the first European traders arriving in the archipelago in the north coast cities of Java and Sumatra in the sixteenth century were surprised to find that no free wage labour was available. No natives would work for wages and they could only be rented from their owners at very high rates. Manual labour was associated with servitude. Since wages did not attract labourers, local "lords" often used advances in the place of salaries to obtain work force. This immediately led their workers into debt. When people sold themselves into debt bondage, they thought of themselves as becoming subjects and not slaves; such bondage was the only way of securing labour mobility. For Reid (1988, p. 135) the production system using this bondage system was not very different from the European feudal household system. In ancient and medieval Europe, however, both the kingdom and the church recognized legal conditions of freedom which, says Reid (1988, p. 136) also led to recognizing the freedom to accumulate capital. In Southeast Asia it was not capital that was the traditional value, but people as dependants.

Sharī'ah, however, placed a constraint on this since it was forbidden to enslave a Muslim or sell a Muslim who had already been enslaved. Reid (1988, p. 133) claims that Java, which up until *circa* 1500 had been the most important importer of slaves, tended to import from non-Muslim islands after Islamization. Islam has a precise set of rules governing the destiny of slaves. With the rise of the coastal sultanates and their urban ports, which lacked the shared cultural bonds of the smaller societies or the autocratic centrality of the agrarian principalities, another set of private laws for the merchant class who were not exclusively Muslim was needed.

It is hard for us to imagine how this system functioned because it was both more personal and more pecuniary, that is, money was required to buy men into debt. But once they were in debt that relationship was characterized by loyalty and not the legal character of the dependency. As Reid wrote (1988, p. 129), "Maritime commerce had for so many centuries penetrated their region that Southeast Asians appeared accustomed to thinking of themselves as assets having a cash values." This is equally reflected in the nature of warfare where one sought not to kill one's adversaries but to "enslave" them, i.e., to bring them back to populate one's own territory. Since land was abundant in Central Java until the nineteenth century, one sought to populate the lands and not to increase productivity. War captives were distributed to powerful courtiers in order to better protect oneself and one's highest ranking subjects.

Thus in lowland Southeast Asia, and sometimes in the highlands, farming frontiers were often opened up by bondmen pioneers (cf. article 11 above). Often sailors, miners, and builders were bondsmen, and so were artisans. All these dependants worked only part-time in order that they could earn their livings in the remaining time at their disposal. The ruler never paid out of his treasury, but settled villages on his courtiers through the appropriate headmen and intermediaries, giving them the right to manpower, to dependants. Although a ruler claimed the right of the labour of all his subjects, all bondsmen were "settled" in self-financing niches. None of this involved counting lands in hectares or squares metres. For the first time in the nineteenth century, the rise in demographic density in Central Java and the consequent appearance of land scarcity justified that the control of manpower be converted into measurement of land. But even then, to keep the rural population on the land, the dependency of debt bondage was translated into a deliberate confusion concerning communal ownership (*gemeen bezit*) of their village lands. This was applied in various ways, but there was a certain continuity between the apanage system in pre-1757 Central Java and the period leading up to the culture system introduced in the 1830s. Frans Husken has written (2001, pp. 77–78):

> Unequal shares partly reflected the pre-communal social differentiation as well as population density, but these tendencies might have been strengthened in the nineteenth century by the indebtedness of shareholders who, being unable to pay their debts, were forced to cede their share to better-off villagers. A major difference in land tenure, however, was brought about by the land rights accruing to the members of the village administration…

> (from Note 4) A process of accumulation which seems only possible in villages which used a system of "fixed shares". In other cases differential access to land was probably the consequence of good relations with the village officials who had to redistribute the land periodically or of managing to be entitled to more than one share, for example, by accumulating shares through parents and parents-in-law.

4.4 LAND TENURE AFTER THE CULTIVATION SYSTEM (1830–70)[17]

After the Java War the Dutch colonial government adopted a system of indirect administration of all villages by the Javanese aristocrats (*pamong praja*) paired at the district (regency in Dutch) and subdistrict level by Dutch counterparts. Village level administration cost the Dutch nothing as it was self-financed by giving the village headman a large share of its best rice fields. At the end of the Java War (1830), colonial government made general the land tenure arrangements in the village to allow for the spread of services and *corvée* labour among its inhabitants. Those to whom the communally "owned" rice fields were periodically distributed would have to pay land tax and *corvée* obligation, but those who only owned home plots would only have to perform *corvée* services. Changing the number of communal landholdings risked diminishing the rights of villagers to this communally held agricultural land, the *sikep*, or share in the ricefields. To justify how this kind of village "autonomy" could be transferred to the needs of the sugar mills, van Moll and 's Jacob stated (Huskens' translation 2001, p. 103):

> … the communal nature of the village is at the same time a safety belt for its inhabitants in that it tries to maintain a status quo and a barrier to improvements in their economic well-being, in that it keeps alive a collective focus at the expense of individual progress.

Such a profitable colonial administration concealed itself behind the pretence of respecting the inviolability of the "primordial" community of the peasants.

The land tax paid in kind (rice) was to be replaced by land tax paid in profitable export crops (sugar, coffee, indigo, etc.). For the peasants, of course, growing rice had been much more profitable, but the colonial regime attempted to remodel the villages by force, with varying success throughout Java.

Once the infamous cultivation system (*cultuurstelsel*), had been abandoned, what sort of land tenure system was left? A detailed answer to this question was attempted in the three volumes of W.B. Bergsma's *Eindrésumé* (The Final Résumé), an inquiry launched in 1866.[18] According to Kano's (1977, p. 16) summary of W.B. Bergsma's work, during this period (1830–70), three kinds of property (*bezit*) emerged:

1. Inheritable ownership. *Yasa* was not individual property but could be inherited (*erfelijk* individual *bezit*) subject to three restrictions:
   - who could become an owner;
   - on the sale of the land to anyone outside the village even one's own family;
   - on the recognition of these rights once the "owner" was no longer the person farming these fields.
2. Communal ownership. Four conditions existed in order to qualify. The considerable variations that existed are noted by Kano (1977, pp. 15–21):
   - be able to accomplish the *corvée* that accompanied this right;
   - be married;
   - own a house surrounded by a garden;
   - be accepted by all the other members (*kerndorpers*).
3. The lands held in guise of payment of village office-holders:
   These lands bore two names: in the central provinces (*nagaragung*), *lungguh* (settlements, i.e. apanage lands) and in the outlying provinces (*mancanagara*), *bengkok*. Abolished in 1819 (law no. II), this system was renewed in 1832 and 1866. These lands represented usually less than seven hectacres and in 50 per cent of the village studied less that five hectacres, in general occupying some 5–15 per cent of the communal lands, although they were often the very best.

Taxation followed the penetration of money into the village economy at the same time as it encouraged it. As early as around 1618 Jan Pieterszoon Coen, founder and first Governor General of Batavia, notes that Chinese junks brought whole shiploads of small copper coins (*cassies*) to the north coast of Java where they disappeared into the villages without a trace (Boeke

1842, p. 61). Nevertheless one cannot say that the monetization of village economy was that rapid, since two hundred years later, as van den Bosch said in 1818 (Boeke 1942, p. 66), "To have the right to collect land rent a Javanese will give anything, but to get money nothing." The development of taxation did become one of the bases for the recruitment of work force in the mid-nineteenth century. Beginning in the 1850s the hand of the Dutch administration in the principalities could be felt even more strongly in this domain. Along the lines of the growing industrialization of Holland itself, the newly empowered "liberals" of the States General Dutch Parliament sought definitively to abandon anything resembling the fixed quotas of exportable crops (*contingenten*) initially practised by the V.O.C. between 1690 and 1790 and later continued through the policy of forced deliveries (*gedwongen liveringen*) of the cultivation system. Willem Wolters (1994, pp. 173, 175),[19] points out that final abandonment of this older V.O.C. policy in Java represented a final abandonment of the Javanese rulers' "feudal" control of people rather than land:

> The cultivation system involved land rent and corvée labour which were replaced by modern taxes (import duties, excise tax, income tax, business tax). The state began protecting private business and no longer directly managed resources. Although the colonial sate tended to view the village as unchanging community ruled by *adat*, between 1874–1921 arable and was expanded, commercial agriculture with its native exports adopted and trade relations changed property rights and labour relationships.

In general the move was from one of bureaucratic rights over people towards individual rights over land. The Dutch colonization of Java was to continue henceforth by private enterprise, but these private planters needed access to land they could not acquire through buying. Already in 1830 the regime of communal lands had been imposed from outside in a situation where the peasants preferred the regime of lands held in individual inheritance (*yasa* or *lanyah*) to the *pusaka* or communal lands that were redistributed annually or every few years. The Dutch "liberal" reformers thought that by declaring private property (*eigendom*) the lands held by Javanese, all other lands could be declared property of the colonial state and later rented out by them to Dutch planters. These long-term leases of "state" lands at cheap rents were called *erfpacht*, and involved leases from eighteen to ninety-nine years. The conservatives retorted by saying that the Javanese communal customary bond to the earth would not permit treating the land through the Western notion of property. The purpose of the *Eindrésumé* inquiry was to provide an empirical answer to this question.

We know that the percentage of rice fields held as the common property of the village (*pusaka* or *bengkok* fields) varied widely from village to village, reflecting the history of local land tenure (date of clearing, migration, fission, proximity of sugar mills, erosion/fertility, etc.). What did characterize almost all Javanese villages, however, was that the peasants' home plots, even those of farmers (*penumpang* and *mondok*) without paddy fields or dry fields were not taxed while they brought in twice as much as did a *sawah* (Husken 2001, pp. 88–89). This distinction between taxable cultivated space and untaxable residential space (*pekarangan*) may be the ultimate foundation of the autonomy of a village, between living in a village and living in an urban *kampung*. As Husken states (2001, p. 98) what made the village a community was its right to *elect* its own headman or *lurah*, who, although he acted on behalf of the district government, also defended with the other members of the village élite the ability of this rural institution to make sense of its shared space through the application of its own autonomous customs. By the end of the twentieth century the village élite would no longer see any advantage for them to protect the village from outside influences. Already during the nineteenth century, this autonomy was of a patron–client order linked to other nearby villages; Huskens translates several interesting passages from the Moll and 's Jacob's[20] study begun in 1903 and published in 1913. Coming some eighty years after the introduction of the culture system and some forty years after its progressive abolition, these remarks show the resilience of certain mistaken assumptions about village life, but also a shrewd understanding of the retrograde effect of village communities on outside capital investments.

> There the native can find his own identity as well as a sanctuary because he can live according to the values and beliefs which are dear to him .... In the *desa* [village], however, the threads of his individual life are interwoven with those of his fellow villagers and there the individual dissolves himself in the community .... The *desa* has made him into a pack animal, liable predominantly to collective psychological stimuli and expressing itself in collective moods and turns. (cited in Husken 2001, p. 99)

Equally interesting is the role that van Moll and 's Jacob ascribe to the collective fetters of sociability that tie the peasant to his community. That their vision of the role of individualism could be a deliberate colonial illusion was impossible for these authors to imagine, so deeply was that premise embedded in their discourse. Here is the passage they wrote concerning the prospect for greater prosperity:

> The survey also shows that a process of capital formation is gradually on its way in the *desa*. As far as this merely consists of an accumulation of land in a few hands, it does not mean much: it is a movement of capital only, but

no creation of new resources, ... an egalitarian distribution of incomes among villagers is gradually giving way to more differentiation ... In order for this nucleus to grow, the forces which arise out of economic differentiation have to be strong, healthy and permanent. In other words, they have to be indicative of a striving for individual advancement .... First of all individual life has to be become disentangled from the community and has to acquire a broader and unbiased world view. In other words, the *desa* will have to transform itself from a barrier into a driving force to the individualization of its inhabitants. (Husken's translation 2001, pp. 106–107):

Is that all there is to the story of the deterritorialization of Javanese villages? Unfortunately, the most recent period, since the total economic collapse of mid-1997, has stripped away the last vestiges of community life left in these rural agglomerations.

4.5 JAVANESE VILLAGES AFTER *KRISMON* (1997+)

In a recent study with Gunawan Wiradi, Jan Breman[21] analysed two rural coastal villages, one near Cirebon and another south of Pamanukan, half-way from Cirebon to Jakarta. Four traits characterized them: the pressure caused by demographic growth on the rural means of subsistence; a highly unequal distribution of the ownership of agricultural land; the declining importance of agriculture; migration to the urban economy. Some 170 years beforehand, in 1833, the causes of peasant unrest described by Peter Boomgaard (2001, p. 23)[22] following the forced introduction of cultivation of sugar in Comal (Pemalang district between Tegal and Pekalongan on the north coast of Java) were surprisingly similar to the post-1997 situation described by Breman and Wiradi to the west of Comal. With the forced cultivation of sugar introduced in 1833, there began a migration, called in the Dutch colonial parlance *verhuizingen*, or (*volks*) *verloop*. Wage labour began to take over from cultivation of rice fields. Four sources of the unrest and dissatisfaction (*kurang marem* or *ontevredenheid*) are cited:

1. the limited extent of arable land remaining;
2. the burden of forced services (*corvées*);
3. the distance of certain cane fields from the villages; and
4. the proportion of land rent to crop payments. Rice cultivation for those who had access to land was often twice as profitable to them than renting their fields for eighteen months to the Dutch.

As Boomgaard points (2001, p. 17) in some areas of the north coast of Java this situation had been a long time in the making, since as far back as 1719 thirty-seven sugar mills were listed along Pasisir or north coast.

The combination of the total economic crisis and the fall of Soeharto and his New Order dictatorship have openly revealed the development strategy of "betting on the strong". Monetization of the village economy was so total that at the height of the crisis (1998) some village shops *stopped* selling rice altogether in order to avoid having to sell it on credit! If the depression of 1929 had led to a demonetization of the rural Javanese economy, the 1997 crash did not do so. Again and again, Breman and Wiradi insist that "the communal-oriented social based on patronage and reciprocity between the strong and the weak" had been replaced by polarization and exclusion organized by the local agents of the Soeharto regime, the enriched village élite: the so-called *orang kayu baru*. How does polarization translate into labour relations and land tenure? Some eight out of ten families owned no farm land! Either they worked in the closed field (*ceblokan*) system where agro-industry managers paid them one-fifth of the harvest against performance of all pre-harvest tasks and notably planting; or, in the open field or *bawon* system, all harvesters were given one-tenth of the rice as wages in kind, while pre-harvest labour is paid in cash.

In fact, of course, most villagers are no longer famers but migrant labourers who, without giving up their village identity, leave this rural setting to work near or in Jakarta, with all the negative effects that the separation between home and work brings on the family and household. The village élites, clients of the district (*kabupatèn*) and subdistrict (*kacamatan*) authorities, have expanded their economic network well beyond the village borders and abandoned interest in running these villages as headmen (*lurah*) had in the past. In the area of Comal, kinship ties which had been strong enough in some cases to protect family members associated with the PKI (Indonesian Communist Party) from slaughter in 1965–66, were now being used by the landed gentry to control supra-village resources as far away as Jakarta and Sumatra, writes Husken (2001, p. 235[23]). To them the village as the realm of patron–clients relations has often ceased to be "advantageous". For five or six generations, up to the twentieth century, the lineages, or *trah*, to be discussed in the next two chapters, traced themselves back to the village founder and his charisma (*wahyu*), and had been used in the areas studied by Husken to control land and labour. Now (since 1970) descent and affinity are less and less needed to reinforce the political power and economic wealth that once thrived on village social cohesion. The dimension of the entire village community is no longer critical to the élite families who have been busy strengthening the outside alliances which their earlier trading alliances had afforded them and which in a milieu of increased commercialization were now their social capital.

What kind of community is left? It is a bitter irony that after thirty years of Soeharto's regime which deliberately shut down any social land political space in which the landless and near landless could have expressed their common cause (Breman and Wiradi 2002, p. 307), that now even the poor have lost their traditional Javanese sociability. It is replaced by monetization and contractual labour networks. Kinship and neighbourhood relations do unite the village poor allowing them to share or redistribute income and employment, but there is so little to pool. Ritual events are increasingly avoided with the result that the landless peasants downscale the very social capital that kept alive networks which could have mobilized these resources. The young, having been raised with the belief that their livelihood lies outside the village in contractual labour, now find that both the informal sector and the formal sector has shrunk disastrously. As Breman and Wiradi point out (2002, p. 25), the very village spirit of living together on the same shared territory which has bound Javanese villages together for centuries is disavowed. The World Bank,[24] having endorsed the old colonial vision of the village as the ultimate sanctuary of social solidarity during the entire Soeharto regime, now proclaims that these rural communities are without structure and not units of social affiliation. As will be shown in Chapter 12, paradoxically this is not true of those peasants who have reached the extremity of exclusion, those who have lost their villages. These vagrants maintain a deep aspiration towards the recreation of these bonds created by sharing social space and aiding one another through elementary acts of social solidarity. The most basic notion of livelihood amongst the squatter villages on the edge of large cities is not individualistic.

Lea Jellinek wrote of Jakarta slum-dwellers (1991, p. 51), "As in most societies, crisis brought out a sense of unity among the *kampung* dwellers." On the contrary, the recent crisis in Javanese villages has also brought out a feeling of mistrust of the poor on the part of the village élite, who on occasion have refused to allow special distributions of inexpensive rice set aside by the government's social safety net programme during "Special Market Operations". It is here that the memory of strict village reciprocity takes a perverse turn and community pretensions are shown to be hollow. As Breman and Wiradi conclude (2002, p. 308): "The crisis in Indonesia has stopped being a purely monetary-economic recession and has escalated into a far-reaching disruption of society as a whole." It is this whole, society at large and the place of a Javanese within it, that is being shown to be untenable where individualism is allowed free rein.

NOTES

1. On the Dutch misunderstandings on this question, cf. critique of P. Roo de la Faille,'s *Over het Grandenrecht onder Javaansch Vorstenbestuur* by B. Schrieke (1919–20).
2. The case of intermediary deities, between village and kingdom, taken up in Chapter 3, smacks of attempt to revolt against the central ruler.
3. The *ka'ba* in Mecca had initially been constructed by Seth, but was destroyed by the flood, and had to be reconstructed by Abraham and Ismael (Koran 2.127).
4. "Harmony and Dissonance: Early Nationalist thought in Java" (M. A. thesis, Cornell University, 1975, pp. 161–63), quoted in Larson (1987, pp. 111–12).
5. The definition of this useful concept is given in Maurice Leenhaardt's *Do Kamo* (1947).
6. Cf. Robert van Neil (1981). On the question of forced labour (*herendienst*) and the image of the Javanese native, cf. Syed Husein Alatas (1977). The best general survey of the *faire valoir* is: Hiroyoshi Kano, *Land Tenure System and the Desa Community in Nineteenth-century Java*, (1977). Cf. also his critique of C. Geertz's agriculgtural involution theory (1979).
7. Cf. A. J. S. Reid (1980).
8. On the Yogyakarta *garebeg*, cf. Soedjono Tirtokoesoemo (1931); and Marcel Bonneff (1974).
9. The question to be posed in this study is to what extent values in Javanese culture have become less hierarchical and have become more individualistic. And to what extent can Java be characterized as having adopted a pseudo individualism still partially characterized by holistic values. Cf. L. Dumont (1983) and for a socio-linguistic perspective, J. Errington (1998).
10. This village decree comes from a collection of typescripts translated from the Javanese (here no. 13) into Dutch by G. R. Rouffaer for his history of the Javanese principalities (Carey 1978, p. 125). Initially, I was not able to locate the Javanese original and worked from the Dutch translation made in 1889–90 by G. P. Rouffaer (1860–1928). It figures in the Koninklijk Instituut for Land-, Taal- en Volkenkunde under H699 (*cf.* H. J. de Graaf, *Catalogue van de Westerse Handschriften* (1963, p. 23). Notes were composed by Rouffaer, while the remarks in parentheses and in brackets are my own. An earlier transcribed *aksara* text, *Pranatan ing bab laku-lakuné amajegaké bumi désa*, of 1837 is found in the Leiden Univ. Bibl. Cod. Or. 10,735 (12 pp.), concerning the Dutch in Surakarta and Yogyakarta.
11. A gift of money for nomination and elevation of someone to a post; from *pangunjung*, to elevate some one to a dignity.
12. A gift of money by someone who installs someone in a new position.
13. Those who "belong" to these families. What is a servant for the aristocratic (*priyayi*) families is treated as a member of the family (*batih*) for a village headman (*bekel*).

14. *Nyajak* (pillar) or *nyajak kapat* (erect a fourth pillar in a house), that is to say set oneself up somewhere as a villager with full rights to a share in the communal ricefields (*sikep* or *baku kenceng*).
15. Written permission. From *padang*, light, hence a letter giving a light or *layang katrangan*, i.e., which furnishes an explanation.
16. From Hoadley's essay "The Archive of Yogyakarta and Javanese Administrative History", (2000).
17. The cultivation system was dismantled piecemeal. In 1869 the Suez Canal was opened and in 1870 an Agrarian Law was passed allowing private enterprise to invest in commercial agriculture but restricting land ownership (but not the leasing of land) to Indonesians.
18. For later reports, cf. Frans Husken (1994).
19. Willem Wolters "From Corvée to contract labour. Institutional innovatio ina Central Javanese village around the turn of the century", (1994).
20. J. F. A. C. Moll and H. 's Jacob, *De Desa-Volkshuishouding in Cijfers*, (1913).
21. Jan Breman and Gunawan Wiradi (2002).
22. Peter Boomgaard, "A bird's-eye view of Economic and Social Development in the District of Comal, 1740–1940", (2001).
23. Frans Huskens "Continuity and Change in Local Politics. The village Administration and Control of Land and Labour", (2001). Cf. also *Jakarta Post*, "Culture of sharing undermines local property rights", 25 April 2001.
24. Cited in Breman and Wiradi (2002, p. 33, note 8).

PART II

RECONSTRUCTION OF LOCAL RELIGIOUS HISTORY

5

VILLAGE MUSLIM LINEAGES
New Genealogies in the
Forest "Guardian of Death"

5.1 THE QUESTION OF THE CONTEXT:
JAVANESE AND INDIAN ISLAM

Islamization in Java has been ongoing for some five hundred years and, in other parts of Indonesia, for even longer. Should a historian study this as a process of conversion or as suggested in the Introduction as an acculturation, that is to say, a cultural "adoption" involving both deliberate and involuntary adaptations by successive generations of Muslims?

Given the paucity of data this choice is often not left open. The biographies of individuals converted have usually vanished with the death of those concerned. Furthermore the conversion perspective, whether individual or aggregate, leaves little role for the ethno-historian who seeks to introduce a diachronic dimension. For that it is also useful to look for comparative data from other countries. A brief comparison with the Islamization of India,[1] whose history lasted more than a thousand years, heightens the specific character of Javanese Islam.

Assayag (1995, p. 29) claims that, in India, Muslims generally preferred commerce over proselytism, which pushed them to adopt both local culture and languages. That is equally the case in Java (Pigeaud and de Graaf 1976), where is impossible to consider Islam as a foreign or imported religion, to speak as if the customs and the usages of both Javanese Muslims and non-Muslims were not cut from the same cultural cloth. What explains the lack of similitude between Java and India in this comparison is that the Javanese Hindu-Buddhist tradition disappeared as a state-supported, if not an organized religion in the seventeenth century after the fall of the kingdom of Majapahit (*circa* AD 1527), while 90 per cent of the Indian population continued in the Hindu tradition. Factors such as nineteenth century Dutch colonial distrust of Islamic movements or in the twentieth century nationalists' combat against the Darul Islam separatists Muslim movements of the 1950s provoked distinction and isolation that had not existed since the arrival of Islam on the Javanese political scene in the late sixteenth century.

Eaton (1993, pp. 219, 305) has discussed the relation between the Islamization of Bengal and pioneering Muslim agricultural communities clearing forests (= suffix -*kāthi* in Bengali place names). In Java, research on rural Islamization before the twentieth century,[2] shows that these new religious communities sometimes by necessity pioneering agricultural communities as well. In Java the extent to which agricultural expansion was linked to the spread of Islam in the countryside through the foundation of new *pesantrèn* (Muslim schools), although not the main factor, for reclaiming land for cultivation, certainly did exist.

Everywhere religions are practised contextually. Assayag says that in the state of Karnataka, the differences between Islam and Hinduism are most pronounced in their respective devotions to their god(s), while the ecstatic approach found in the cults for liberation from demons attenuates these differences considerably.

> Whenever it is necessary to combat illness or affliction, the religious affiliations only superficially modify the cognitive universe common to evil, its aetiology and its therapy; ... (Assayag 1995, pp. 77–76).

The cults practised around the graves of Javanese Muslim holy men, the friends (*wali*) of God who possess a spiritual jurisdiction (Arabic, *walāya*; Javanese, *wilayah*) differ exteriorly through the rituals practised at other pilgrimage sites, bearing traces (*patilasan*) of sacred powers (*kramat, sakti*) found in holy trees, rocks, etc. (Chambert-Loir and Guillot 1995, pp. 235–66). Nonetheless in general the hagiography of Javanese holy men, Muslim and non-Muslim, show mutual influences: great Javanese heroes borrowing from Muslim hagiography and Javanese Muslim saints displaying the traits of the pre-Muslim figures. Since there is only one language to describe such holiness and since the Arabic vocabulary has completely impregnated these semantic fields in Javanese displacing most of the older Sanskrit words, it could hardly be otherwise.

In India the grave of a holy person is served by his followers or family, but venerated locally by a broader clientele. The cemetery and the nearby mosque is owned by their descendants and, or dependants. It serves as an identity pole for the guild or community that maintains it (Assayag 1995, p. 110), but is frequented by a larger greater public. The management of certain kinds of holy graves in India does not resemble that of the *trah* lineages administration of Javanese graveyards who are clearly more restricted to the descendants of the families buried there. In Indonesia such organizations have been called "worship communities" (Chabot 1950); their morphology will be described below.

What of the rural shrines not related to a Muslim saint? These could nonetheless be poles of attraction for Muslims. For instance in India, demons only exist in as much as they are opposed to the gods (often their younger siblings). Assayag (1995, p. 100) found that in Karnataka this juxtaposition had been taken over by Islam:

> As the goddess, symbol the centrality of the king, needs her troop of demons, the axis (Arabic, *quṭb*) of holiness has meaning only to the extent that a cohort of *djinns* lays siege to her and continually menaces the order of the world.

And the difference in their organization of social space according to Assayag lay in the fact that:

> ... the sanctuaries of the universal goddess singularises the place names while the mausoleums of the saints are valued as so many intercessions to a God who for being one is indeed far away.

In Java two cults of the "royal" goddesses, Durga at Krendawahana where she is both queen of the demons and an aid to the king, and that of the queen, *kangjeng ratu* Lara Kidul on the southern coast, may be interpreted by shadow puppet theatre (*wayang*) as the ultimate Purānic opposition of the warring gods and the demons transposed to the continuing struggle for sovereignty between the Pandawa and the Kurawa. While the Javanese king dealt with only a limited higher pantheon (one or two goddesses, Wisnu, Siva, or Buddha) and the popular shadow puppet theatre mythology brought on stage hundred of mythological courtiers and knights, demons and ogres, while the Javanese countryside was filled with little "insignificant" shrines where the common people dealt with spirits in their own manner.

These rural sites, with little history, some mythology and ambiguous identities (benevolent or malevolent manifestations), often played a creative and evolutive role in the negotiation of relations between Islamic and indigenous religious traditions. The mythological landscape of both Java and India was shaped both by the creation of biographies for the grave sites of local little-known heroes, holy men, or Muslims saints. Sometimes these played a thoroughly partisan role. As Assayag says of the Muslim witnesses in India (1995, p. 207):

> The work of memory which gave the saints the attributes of soldiers of God, clothed in the sacrificial garment of the martyr, took charge of the defence of this internal frontier — indifferent to any physical boundary of the territory — by which the community symbolised both its social cohesion and its religious identity.

The transformation from a pagan to a Muslim land (*dār al-harb; dār al-Islām*) took at least two forms in Karnataka. "Memory-places" existed where a full historical tradition forces the present to repeat the past (Assayag 1995, p. 208). These differ from sites where the absence of any permanent historical memory permits, during the passage of significant events, the creation of a manner of rememorization dictated by those present events and needs. The heavy anchor linking the *litterati* to the past is an obstacle to manipulations of recent events, while the warrior, marabout, or sufi can be drawn, indeed redrawn, by recent events. For Assayag (1995, pp. 172, 213) a biographical *topos* can become affirmation of identity despite borrowings from neighbours of "a different religion". Devereux (1975, p. 283), cited by Assayag, claimed fifty years ago that there exists a dissociative acculturation, operating by differentiation. In a dissociative acculturation, the adaptation of a segment of a culture does not involve the adoption of the underlying culture. These ulamic or maraboutic approaches negotiate social textures between differing lineages and social solidarity. The saint is a mirror of the prophet who is a mirror of God and brings heaven closer to earth. While scriptural exoteric religion is interiorized (*bāthin*) and universal (sanctifying a local figure), popular religion remained exoteric (*zāhir*) with its own form of particular devotion, limited by its frontiers. For Assayag (1995, p. 212), there are two stylizations of the collective memory of groups; one is less historical than semiological, less chronological than genealogical. In either case the relationship between Hinduism and Islam in India has, and in southern India still does, constitute a cultural system.

If tradition is not an inheritance, patrimony, or ethnicity, but a rivalry or competition between social partners, as Assayag claims, then at many different levels of society, agents will debate over what constitutes the links that unite them, their shared identity. The intensity of their interaction is a tribute to the agents' ability to attribute meaning to these interactions: thus there exists a dialectic of reciprocal assignations. The symbolic apparatus produced by their social life is a relatively coherent system, even if over time it proves to be profoundly unstable. The variability of the interactions creates free spaces for inventiveness or at least normal dissent. For Assayag (1995, p. 220):

everyone lives ... from compromises which he invents and contradictions which he manages ... For these are the ways we reuse for our own ends the imposed order ... guaranteeing ... the "fragile flowers of difference" (Lévi-Strauss).

This brief discussion of Islamization in India opens perspectives on Islamization in Java. In the introduction of this volume we adopted the position that the process of adopting Islam in Java which occurred over the last five hundred years, involved a historical break-up of a single cosmology that sheltered both Javanese ancestral religion and Islam. Recently interrupted, as in India, by violent political battles which have separated the religious communities in Indonesia, yet even in this context, Javanese Islam is, more than ever, the principle metaphor for a universal hierarchy of values of this society. When the politically-motivated *jihad* against Christians broke out following Soeharto's downfall (1998), mainstream Javanese Muslims today often suggested that Islam in Java cannot move forward by imitating fanatic Middle Eastern practices.

5.2 THE "GENEALOGY OF THE NOBLE ANCESTORS OF KALIASA"[3]

Indonesian day tourists to the Palaeolithic site of Sangiran on the north side of the Cemara river, or Javanese going to meditate (*ziarah*) at Durga's offering site (*pundhèn*) at the sacred forest of Krendawahana on the south side of this same eastward flowing tributary of the Solo River, do not notice that this area contains a significant and well-orchestrated recent history, that of the introduction of Islam into this region. The local Muslim lineages representing important local Muslim cemeteries here are responsible for its development. Although in 1973 I had met Pak Digdo who lived near the grave and mosque of Kyai Yahya, which we visited together, it was only some twenty yeras later when Haji Abdullah Usman from the Solo *kauman*, was overseeing in 1995 the construction of a minaret at the Kaliasa mosque on behalf of its lineage (*trah*) that I realized its importance. It was also then that I was shown their lineage in written form, composed by Kyai Haji Idris (alias Suratmo), former headman or *lurah* of Sambiredjo and now a locally famous ulama of the Sufi brotherhood, Syadziliyah.[4] This vast genealogy was composed by Kyai Idris on behalf of a Kaliasa Muslim lineage or *trah*. The importance of a Muslim reading of the sacred landscape of this area better known to some for its cult of Bhatari Durga was now apparent.

Muslims have another map for the religious geography of this area, it is initially because their founders are buried there. As the lineage book containing

FIGURE 5.1
Map of the Surakarta/Kaliasa region

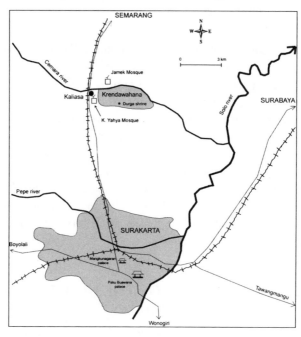

Source: Adapted by Remy Delage from a 1972 Indonesian Department of Forestry map (Province of Central Java); original scale 1:100,000.

FIGURE 5.2
Kyai Digdo in the graveyard of *kyai haji* Muhammad Korib (alias Murtojo) in 1974

FIGURE 5.3
The grave of *kyai haji* Muhammad Korib (alias Murtojo)

FIGURE 5.4
The minaret of the Jamek Mosque (completed in 1995) in Jaga Patèn, north of the Cemara River near Kaliasa

the genealogy of the "Great Family of the Descendants of Nitimenggolo" (*Silsilah Keluarga Besar Kaliasa Trah Nitimenggolo*) indicates, some three thousand members are identified today with these graves and mosques. There are six such cemeteries in the Kaliasa area.[5] This genealogy, published by the *trah* of Kaliasa sometime in the early 1970s, and the oral data assembled in this book from people associated with the *trah*, provides an essentially oral history of Islamization of Kaliasa. Summarized thanks to the intricate genealogical lists used in the 400-page book, the data represents a history from the contemporary perspective of a large Javanese worship community. Shortly before the book's publication, in 1969, Badruddin Hongowongso founded a *pondhok pesantrèn* (Islamic boarding school) in Kaliasa Jetis Karangpung.[6] By 1983 it claimed to have 38 teachers and 655 students (*santri*). Kyai Haji Badruddin Hongowongso is the first name mentioned in the publication's list of advisors (*penaséhat*) and he perhaps more than anyone had a vested interest in developing Kaliasa's reputation for his school was located there.

Over a period of two hundred years (1790–1990) in three suburban villages near Surakarta, to wit Mondongan, Lawéyan,[7] and Prabon, numerous Muslims maintained lineage ties to the cemeteries of Kaliasa. This apparently began with *pangéran* Hadipati Monduroredjo, the *bupati* (district chief) of Grobogan later became preacher (*ketib*) in Pathi, and who finally died in Lawéyan, Surakarta. His son, R. M. Tumenggung Kartonagoro, was Kyai Ageng Ketib (preacher) in Lawéyan and his grandson Kyai Gulu (i.e., *penghulu*) buried next to his grandfather and father on the banks of the same stream in Mondongan (Surakarta).

The grandson of Kyai Gulu was Kyai Nitimenggolo (or Kerti Manggolo; several spellings are used). He is considered the apical figure of the Kaliasa *trah*. Most of his ten children by his three successive wives are buried in Kaliasa. His name, perhaps means the "ordering of auspiciousness"; it resembles that of a pre-Islamic religious functionary, but the dictionaries do not confirm the existence of any such title. Our genealogy considers him to be an eleventh generation descendent of the last king of Majapahit, Prabu Brawijaya V, a very common claim in such genealogical texts. He also in the sixth generation said to be descended from Kyai Ageng Jurumartani (uncle of Senapati Mataram (reigned *circa* 1584–1601); cf. de Graaf and Pigeaud 1974, p. 156), alias Mondoroko I (a prime minister and confident of Mangkurat II (r. 1677–1703). There seems to be some confusion as to generation here so the identification remains to be confirmed. In any case, Kyai Nitimenggolo is at a half-way point between the next ten generations of descendants and the previous ten generations which separate him from the last king of Majapahit Brawijaya V. This last king of Majapahit is commonly the apical source for these Central Javanese lineages. One notices immediately that although they are Muslims, their connections with the aristocratic courts are very strong. Although no one claims to be a royal descendent, having a *trah ing kusuma*, before their implantation in Kaliasa as court officials they must have behaved as such.

It is with the third child (and second son) of this Nitimenggolo, Kyai Abdul Jalal I (alias Turmudi), that the Muslim history of Kaliasa began.[8] Abdul Jalal I's elder brother Kartotaruno is said to have left Mondongan, Surakarta for Gathak Padan near Klathèn. Then his younger brother, Abdul Jalal I, followed him, before going to study at a Muslim boarding school (*pondhok pesantrèn*) in Surabaya. From there Abdul Jalal I went to study at the *pondhok* of Maja Badheran[9] (to the west of Tegalgondo), presumably identifiable with the father of the famous Kyai Maja. At the end of the eighteenth century, a *kyai's* tasks were:

* to pray for the welfare of Surakarta;
* to hold religious services on Friday;
* to instruct the *santri* of the village (de Steurs 1833, p. 15 claims there was large library of Arabic books in this village); and
* to go to Surakarta whenever the *penghulu* called a meeting there.

The introduction to the genealogy claims that it was this teacher that sent him to "spread Islam" in the area some fourteen kilometres north of Surakarta straddling the Cemara River. Since 1757 this area lay directly on the border drawn by the Cemara River between the lands of the Kasusunan to the north and those of the Mangkunagaran to the south.

Although the "Nitimenggolo" version of the spreading of Islam in the area of Kaliasa may ignore even earlier events unrelated to their lineage, the facts provided are precious. Indeed some of the dates may be earlier than is acknowledged in the genealogy.[10] For instance, there do seem to have been ties between the descendants of Nitimenggolo and these two *perdikan* (tax-free) villages to the north of Delanggu. Abdul Ngarip (alias Kyai Badheran the senior) was made *ketib imam* of the freehold of Badheran by Paku Buwana IV (r. 1788–1820). Was this just some ten years before the Java War broke out (cf. Carey 1981, pp. 261–62[11]), i.e. at the end of the reign of Paku Buwana IV or much earlier? One imagines that the *perdikan* of Badheran would have needed several decades to develop its reputation.

Kyai Badheran (according to Sagimun 1981) was married to R.A. Mursilah, a daughter of Adipati Murtodiningrat, himself married to a daughter of Hamengku Buwana (H.B.) II, R.A. Mursiah, sister of H.B.III, and aunt of Dipanagara. The family of Kyai Badheran had numerous contacts in both the Surakarta and Yogyakarta courts. Carey (1981, p. 262) explains that this is why many of them followed Dipanagara in the Java *jihad* war against the Dutch.

Kyai Badheran's son, Kyai Maja, was the main religious advisor to Prince Dipanagara during the first part of the anti-Dutch *jihad*, until the battle of Gowok (15 October 1826). Kyai Maja is supposed to have married R.A. Mangkubumi, the divorced wife of Dipanagara's uncle (Sagimun 1981). The Nitimenggolo genealogy claims that Abdul Jalal (III)'s wife was from Maja. Several other children according to the Kaliasa genealogy were married to a close relatives of Kyai Maja. Thus Mangu Rejo, son of Haji Moh. Korib (Kyai Murtodho), was married to a daughter of Kyai Maja, and Kyai Maja's elder brother Wirapatih (alias Kyai Baheran II) would have married his daughter to Abdul Jalal II from Kaliasa.

The excursus just now concerning the milieu of Kyai Maja[12] to the southwest of Kaliasa is justified by the publicity given in the early 1980s to the so-called national hero Sinuhun Banguntapa (P.B.VI) who is connected both to Kyai Maja and to Kaliasa. This will be presented in Chapter 6 below. The meeting of P.B. VI in 1824 with Pangeran Dipanagara and Radèn Ayu Sumirah in order to give them the Surakarta *pusaka* (heirloom) with Kyai Maja as witness only came to light in the late 1970s precisely the same decade when Badruddin Hongowongso founded his *pondhok pesantrèn* (Islamic boarding school) in Kaliasa Jetis Karangpung. Are these two histories conscious of each other's existence? The Durga's tertre (i.e., the one at Krendawahana near Kaliasa) must have known many different locations over the centuries; indeed a ninth century temple dedicated to Durga and Siwa was excavated at Nusukan just to the north of Solo. The invisible kingdom of Kalayuwati, of *bathari* Durga,[13] supposedly followed the historical kingdoms of Javanese kings throughout Central and Eastern Java for more than a thousand years.[14] At the point in history at which Kaliasa first appears to us, at the end of the eighteenth century, the pre-eminence of Durga seems to be challenged by being paired with another cult, an Islamic one.[15] The twin forests border the north and south banks of the Cemara river. The one to the north of the river becomes Muslim once the mosque supported by P.B. IV is installed in that forest named Jaga Patèn (= ? the guardian of death[16]). To the south of the river lie other mosques and cemeteries, slightly to the east the haunted forest of the Odour of Cadavers (Gandamayit) wherein in Krendawahana one finds Durga's offering ground. The northern most position is usurped by the mosque in the

Susuhunan's domain and Durga to the south of it cannot move further north without leaving the domain of the Mangkunagaran whose territory ends there.

To step back from the village level perspective, and look at Java as a whole permits one to realize that the milieu of the Muslim tax-empt villages territory with their rural officials (*kyai perdikan* or *pradikan*) was not the same as that of the *kyai* or *santri kraton*. Carey (1981, p. 248 note 51) translating *santri* as a collective plural, as "religious communities" describes three kinds:

- *kraton santri* "… members of Islamic hierarchy in the palace towns, mosque officials" (*pengulu, ketib, marbot* and *modin*).
- *pradikan santri* "… religious teachers and caretakers (*juru kunci*) who lived in the tax-free villages".
- independent religious teachers (*kyai, guru*) who thrived as local teachers of spiritual disciplines and mysticism in country areas.

Their instruction was heterogeneous and could vary from bestowing magical charms (*jimat*) to orthodox instruction in Koranic exegesis. Often there was bitter rivalry between the last group and the *kraton santris*, those with official positions. Thus when they migrated to the area north of Surakarta, the children of Nitimenggolo came with a whole network of links to the varied urban and rural world of the Javanese Muslim leaders. They would have maintained these links to further their project for the new Kaliasa mosques. Although their may never have been an institutional school before 1969, that seems unlikely and certainly each *kyai* would have informally dispensed his own teaching to train his *santri*.

So to now return to the our genealogy, the *Silsilah Leluhur Kaliasa*, Abdul Jalal I arrived at the Cemara River and began to pray (? the five *sholat*) on a rock, *watu soye*,[17] in the middle of that river. At the level of Kaliasa the Cemara River bed occupies the bottom of a gorge. It was there that Abdul Jalal I received the revelation that Allah would have him implant a mosque at Grasak on the north bank of the stream. This forest, still called by what is probably its pre-Muslim name, Jaga Patèn, was to be cleared by Abdul Jalal I, i.e., by his students. He continued to receive infused knowledge (*ilmu*) from his communion (*munajat*) with Allah. Through his prayers and ascetic feats, not the least of which was simply to enter this evil area dominated by devils and other invisible evil spirits, Abdul Jalal I furthered his Islamic pioneering.

The tradition of clearing (*mbabad*) new lands in forests, sacred or otherwise for Muslim schools seems to have been widespread from the end of the sixteenth century to the end of the nineteenth century. It followed older

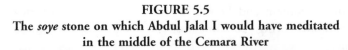

FIGURE 5.5
The *soye* stone on which Abdul Jalal I would have meditated
in the middle of the Cemara River

patterns of settlement by the Hindu-Buddhist *mandala* communities. As late as 1880, K.H. Muhammad Hadi, for instance, shortly after returning from Mecca, opened up for cultivation an *angker* forest at Girikusumo, 25 kilometres south of Semarang.[18]

The next event widely recounted in oral tradition and reproduced in writing by the genealogy, "occurred" sometime during the reign of Paku Buwana IV (reigned 1788–1820). This king went hunting at Krendawahana for the deer meat, venison, which his pregnant consort craved in Durga's sacred forest. There he totally disappeared,[19] as if swallowed by the forest. None of his suite could find any trace of him and they finally turned to the local Muslim leader, Kyai Abdul Jalal, who suggested that his elder sister's third son, Bagus Murtojo (or Murtolo/Murtodho;[20] later Haji Mohammad Korib) would be able to force the hand of the evil spirits from this haunted forest (*alas angker*). It should be added that the forest's fame is not only local but also due to the Javanese *wayang* where it is also known for being the centre of Durga's invisible kingdom. Murtojo's mission was successful, he returned the lost king to his courtiers, and so began the link between the palace of P.B. IV and the area of Kaliasa that gave it, for the first time, a Muslim cachet for the outside world.

The grateful king then named this area Kaliasa.[21] The tale above may form the background for its etymology, linking the river (*kali*) Cemara to another name of Durga, Kali, but to date this toponym has defied convincing explanation.[22]

The Susuhunan of Surakarta is then said to have given Abdul Jalal the land north of the river as a freehold (*perdikan*) for a mosque to be built there. For this he supplied both the hand-carved doors and the *mimbar* (preaching pulpit) which are still there today, as a well as a sacred *kris* and a spear (the *tombak kyai* Ronda) conserved as precious heirlooms (*pusaka*). Finally he took Bagus Murtojo as an adoptive son.

FIGURE 5.6
Kyai haji Abdullah Usman, from the Kauman in Surakarta and co-ordinator of the construction of the minaret, in front of the original early nineteenth century doors of Jamek Mosque. Usman gave the author his last copy of the genealogy of the Nitimenggolo *trah* in Kaliasa

This last association of Haji Muhammad Korib (alias Murtojo, Murtolo, or Murtodho) with P.B. IV raises the question, for the while unanswerable, if he is not the same personage as the one who served as *penghulu* by P.B. IV and by whose hand three letters have come down to us dated *circa* 1783 (cf. Fokkens 1886, pp. 489–97). The contradiction of the sources is one of dating, which seems to lie in the fact that a *penghulu* of this name is from Surakarta seven years before our Kaliasa documents would have him receive his appointment to do so. Although Fokken's chronology is uncontroversial, for these manscript letters are dated, their signatory's name is written Murtolohojo which is ambiguous. Is this the same figure as our modern Kaliasa documents refer to? This could explain the hesitations in its spelling where the consonant combination (in Latin letters: vowel+L+H+vowel) is unstable. Guillot (1985, p. 144) in a recent article on the Panaraga *perdikan* villages does not identify this figure, designated by his court title as *kyai* Tapsir Anom Adiningrat. The three letters we have of him concern the appointment of the eldest son of Ilyas (died *circa* 1800), head of the Surakarta *perdikan* of Tegalsari, south of Panaraga.[23]

What remains of this nineteenth-century implantation of a group of Muslims from Surakarta and the Maja region? Around Kaliasa today there are several mosques and graveyards that bear the names of these founding fathers and above all the *trah* that unites this lineage into worshipping community focused on the burial grounds.

5.3 ISLAMIZATION, KORANIC SCHOOLS, AND JAVANESE *TRAH*

On the level of its sub-prefectures (*kecamatan*), the history of the Islamization of Central Java is often difficult to construct. It seems to have taken place in many different ways. In the subdistrict of Gondongrejo, north of the palace city of Surakarta, the introduction of Muslim lineages around mosques, cemeteries, and later Koranic schools (i.e., *pondhok pesantrèn*) was coterminous with the opening of a *pesantrèn* and indeed with the very settlement of this forested land. The spiritual geography of this area, with its historically important offering site (*pundhèn*) to Bathari Durga, provides data on the potential for lateral expansion using networks founded on grave place, Islamic school (*pondhok*) and genealogy (*trah*). How are they cadastred or bounded (*wates*)? We will begin by describing the Javanese form of social organization translated here as lineage (*trah*). Our presentation here in large part summarizes the research of Sjafri Sairin.[24]

FIGURE 5.7
Original pulpit (*mimbar*) of the Jamek Mosque in the Jaga Patèn "forest"

Koentjaraningrat established forty years ago that Javanese have two kinds of bilateral kinship groups:

1. *golongan*, i.e., kindred, based on nuclear family; and
2. *alur waris*, Javanese lineage-based and ancestor-oriented ambilineal occasional kin group.

It is important to note that this ambilineal kin group is strictly genealogical, whereas the corporate groups called *trah* are open to spouses and non-kin.[25] Sjafri Sairin (1982) considered the *trah* as an association and a corporate group, rather than as a kinship group, characterized by common ownership of property, common system of authority, perpetuity, and collective responsibility. It might also be qualified as a "house" for religious communities.

After the Dutch V.O.C. policy of "forced deliveries" was discarded at the end of the eighteenth century, the "Cultivation System" (1830–70) effectively redefined the bases of Javanese social organization. In the principalities this had been grounded on the apanage system in the eighteenth century; henceforth during the nineteenth century the conditions were gradually assembled for the appearance, at the end of the nineteenth century, of modern political and social organizations administered like the Budi Utomo (1908) and Muhammadiyah (1912). In the twentieth century a further evolution allowing the traditional aristocratic palace *trah* to appear outside the palace enabling their members to develop social identity and gain prestige. This was due to downward mobility of the aristocrats (*priyayi*) following independence in 1949, the upward mobility of the common people (*wong cilik*) and the continuing horizontal mobility of the *santri* or migrating *priyayi* (cf. Sjafri Sairin 1982, p. 86). The relation of organizational structures and symbols to those of the *kabathinan* groups developing in the 1950s and earlier political groups remains to be explored in detail.

A "naive" definition of the the lineages or *trah*[26] would claim that they: (1) maintain kinship feeling; (2) enhance status through social and economic interaction. In Javanese one encounters expressions such as:

trah ing kusuma rembesing madu = descend from a royal family (literally: descend from a flower seeping with honey);

X trah-tumerah manggon ing desa = X lived in the village generation after generation.

One also uses the metaphor of ashes (*awu*) to establish one's generational ranking in a lineage. Thus *tuwané awu*, family ranking by age of parent's generation, as in the expression "Whose ashes are the older ones?"(*awuné tuwa sapa?*). More simply one can ask: "Do you have a lineage?"(*sampéyan gadhah trah?*). However amongst *santri* (strict or puritan Muslims) the Arabic word *bani* (= sons or children) is often used instead of *trah*. *Bani* includes "near and far siblings" (*sedulur cedhak lan adoh*). One can say that so and so is still "consanguineous" (*isih muhrim*; from the Arabic word *mahram*).

To describe these groupings, educated *priyayi* use the Indonesian term *ikatan keluarga* or *keluarga*, whereas the *santri*, affiliated with religious schools, tend to use *wong putihan*, *wong sudagar* (Muslim traders), or simply *wong santri*. Marriage alliances between nobles (*ndara* and *priyayi*) in the past pushed descendants to consolidate their positions as "near nobles" by establishing these *trah* lineages. Tracing of genealogies is a tradition among *ndara* and *priyayi* groups, so recruitment is obvious. Even if you don't want to participate you are registered.[27] Surprisingly enough now that the palaces no longer have any political power, these aristocratic *trah* are still flourishing. Note that in the subdistrict of Gondongrejo, Kaliasa *trah* uses the same written system of notation for descent as the palace genealogy (*silsilah*) of the

Mangkunagaran in Surakarta.[28] So far no Christian *trah* have been documented, although Muslim Chinese *trah* are known.[29]

More *priyayi trah* and *santri trah* have been established since independence than ever before. Sjafri Sairin (1982, p. 34) asks the question whether a "religious" leader is necessary for the apical ancestor of a *santri trah*? His answer is that to found a *trah* one needs: (1) an "appropriate" ancestor, with a prestigious name or one liked to a famous place; (2) to formulate a common interest for the members; and (3) an active group of founders. This contrasts very clearly with the limited genealogical knowledge of commoners (*wong cilik*). The peasants tend to pray to their guardian spirits, the fictive kin placenta and amniotic fluid[30] or at their parents' graves since they have no *trah* graveyard.

Distant kin are recruited as close kin through marriage. If you marry a *nak-sanak* (first cousin), it is hard to change it into an in-law relationship for it is already so close. Whereas a *misanan* (second cousin) or a *mindoan* (third cousin) is ideal. In reality all members of the nuclear *kulawarga* ("my *warga*") are lumped together and three kinds of membership allows for extraordinary and honorary members to be included.

"To bring together the separated bones" (*balung pisah*) is usually done through monthly meetings. For instance in the *trah* Sinduprojo, they hold mutual forgiveness meetings after *puasa* (*halal bi(l) halal* or *syawalan*[31]) and friendship or reconciliation meetings (*silahturahmi*). These annual meetings after the fast (*puasa*) usually bring thirty to fifty people together. What is the relation between these and the *saranan slametan* held in the month of Sadran (eighth month) in the mosque or on the grave the last Friday before the fasting month of Puwasa?

It is specific to the Muslim lineages, sometimes called *bani*, to make *qabilah*, a first generation segmentary group, which branches in the form of descent groupings from the children of the founder often corresponding to different regions. Some *bani* hold monthly recitation and prayer sessions (*pengajian*). Santri *trah* sometimes state as their goal intermarriage through a Lajnah Munakahah, or councils for marriage set up to resolve quarrels and encourage arranged marriages.

5.4 HOLY SITES AND THEIR CLIENTELE

Muslim *kyai* regard the family as the fundamental institution of the Muslim community.[32] It transmits a certain knowledge called *ilmu laduni*. Hopefully one's *gus* (from *si bagus*), admired sons (or grandsons), will be recognized as having inherited your inspiration or *ilmu laduni* and thus the *pesantrèn*, which is your private property, will continue to be recognized as fulfilling a public interest.

Most *kyai* are interrelated. There is a stratification system among the *kyai* of major *pesantrèn*, distinguishing them from those of secondary *pesantrèn*. This means that organizing a lineage became the interest of particular, but not unrelated kin groups. So *kyai ulama* are only a part of the *santri* community, their distinguished members (*wong mulya*) and leaders. Under the Javanese sultans they had exclusive authority to decide on property, marriage, divorce, and inheritance. Their reputation before the bureaucratization of their posts under colonial palace control was very good. Thus the *Serat Cabolèk* (1975, p. 42), composed around the beginning of the nineteenth century, says, "In their hearts, ... the *ulama* are the best people of the world." The most famous and powerful associations (*krabatan*) of Muslim leaders come from the seventeenth and eighteenth century networks of *ulama* linking Indonesia and the Middle East. They practised strategic intermarriages.[33] Kuntowijoyo states that by the beginning of the nineteenth century the Surakarta court had incorporated the *penghulu* and the *naib* (*pengulu's* assistants) into the class of *priyayi*.[34] By the Dutch colonial government's 1882 decree, the Priesterraad (a kind of Majelis Ulama) was made part of the Landraad. This is well into the period of the secularization of the aristocrats and the palace Islamic officials. It is because of this bureaucratization that Pijper remarks that the rural religious teachers had more prestige than the urban, palace-based *penghulu*.[35] The topological reflection of these networks still is partially visible in the cemeteries of these families to which their descendants regularly go to pray.

The practice of pilgrimage (*ziarah*), usually to a tomb, was Javanized over the centuries, when holy sites used as offering grounds (*pundhèn*), some very ancient like that of Durga in Krendawahana, qualified as tombs.[36] In this particular case, the steps leading up to the tree led to the invisible door opening onto her spirit kingdom. Resting places (*pasaréan*) near sacred trees, etc., houses (*pasanggrahan*) of important personages is where one makes an offering at a family grave (*nyekar* or *nyadran*) during the month of Sadran (or Saban, i.e., the eighth month, also called *arwah* = soul). These chosen sites in traditional Javanese spiritual geography are often found on top of hills or on the coast, at sites providing water: springs for ablutions and holy water. Because night is day for the dead, one often went there to pray at the beginning of the night.

Sometimes these cemeteries and/or *pesantrèn* were to be found in freehold (*perdikan*) villages of which there were three kinds: those for the care of graves, of mosques and/or of *pesantren*.[37] Villages with important Muslim figures would sometimes solicit privileges certified by the king. These differed from the Muslim quarters (*kauman*) that surrounded the urban mosques where the *bupati* or king settled what were called favoured (literally "selected") individuals (*mijèn*).

Karel Steenbrink (1984, p. 168) claims that by far the most common *perdikan* were those in charge of graves, for instance the grave of Senapati at Kota Gedhé. This small town had a formal "feudal" social hierarchy, according to Van Mook,[38] yet many cottage industries sprung up in Kota Gedhé which later became a nursery of Muhammadiyah leaders, opposed to feudal customs. In fact only a very few *perdikan* freeholds were there to care for *pesantrèn*, while many were in charge of the graveyard that lay behind or to the side of a *mesjid*. Kaliasa conforms to this pattern for the prior existence of mosques and graves of the descendants of the original *kyai* which predated by around a century and a half the establishment of the first Koranic school.

5.5 "WORSHIP COMMUNITIES" AND LINEAGES: A COMPARATIVE PERSPECTIVE FROM SULAWESI TO SUMATRA, VIA JAVA[39]

The term, which we have been using here, "worship communities" was invented to describe the Bugis organization of ancestor worship in southern Sulawesi (Celebes). That area has been the object of several studies concerning lineages and religious practice which can put the Javanese *trah* in comparative perspective. Starting out from the Bugis, Shelley Errington has concluded that the "(h)ouses of insular South-East Asia are better regarded as worship communities unified around the *pusaka* (heirlooms) they hold rather than as kinship groupings".[40]

Chabot, the first to use this nomenclature (1950, p. 81) defines a "worship community" as a group of relatives whose members worship their ancestors at places and times designated for this purpose. He links ancestor worship to kinship in the following manner: "In practice an individual participates primarily in the worship of the group with which he lives." One's choice of worship community is determined to a great deal by the social standing of one's kinsmen. There is a demonstrable preference among people to turn to prominent members of the related group in ritual matters.

Our conclusion is of the same order, namely that the Javanese *trah* in Kaliasa does for Muslim descendants of famous *kyai*, what the ruler of the former Javanese kingdoms used to do for their own extended family:[41] unite them around a single apical ancestor. By uniting a large group of descendants who thus participate in a corporate centre of local Islam, the *trah* provides a social axis for giving regional Islam local roots and influence.

As J. J. Fox has shown,[42] sharing of origins is socially-defined and always circumscribed in the Austronesian world. A shattering of initial unity as in the myth of the origin of man: destruction of cosmic tree; breaking of the universal egg; separation of a primary couple. The introduction of new origins (Christian, Muslim or Buddhist, and Hindu) have enhanced rather than obliterated this preoccupation. Marshall Salhins in *Islands of History* (1985) has described the stranger king, or Muslim saint, or Brahman in the Austronesian world who often appears as the main figure in the origin myth of man from a shattered primordial unity. In much the same way, in the Javanese myth of Jaka Samodra (founder of a Muslim principality of the apostle saints of Gresik on the north coast of Java), he is washed ashore in a box and raised by a pious widow.[43]

If source, root, base, or trunk are metaphors for specific ascent groups, they are often accompanied by myths of origin, narrative, and journey. Fox claims (1995, p. 221) that "path" is a common Austronesian metaphor for social relationships. Descent and marriage, he says, are not the principle criterion for typifying Austronesian societies. Origins are a prime marker for social identity. Fox identifies:

1. Systems of lateral expansion: found from Hawaii to Madagascar, these societies are bilateral, usually on large islands that have areas for potential expansion (Luzon, Mindoro, Borneo, Madagascar, early Maori, historical Hawaiians). There the principle mode of social differentiation was relative age (older/younger). Younger often moves away to establish a new centre for local precedence.

2. Systems of "apical demotion": a more exclusive mode of predatory expulsion found initially on smaller islands, and coastal margins (trading and raiding). The appearance of apical demotion is dependent on demographic density (i.e., pressure on land and water) as in Java. It displays a single source in their narrative of origin and exclusive genealogies. In any given generation only one line retains status and ultimately one individual. This is a dynastic device of an élite (rulers, kings, raja, sultans, sacred chiefs). Here genealogies preserved the names of both marriage partners; for status derives from both sides. In the central eastern part of Austronesia the brother/sister pair is stressed, the cultural ideal being that this pair or their lines of sibling differentiation should be united in their offspring (Fox 1995, p. 224). In the eastern part of Austronesia this is also stressed to the extent that father's sister's line are important to the calculation of status.

Systems of lateral expansion have narratives of origin which focus on place. Systems of apical demotion have narratives of origin that focus on person (genealogies, relations of high persons and the transmission of status).

Thomas Reuter (1992, p. 514) poses for Sumatra, with its systems of lateral expansion, a general question. Is there greater emphasis on territorial origin and genealogical openness in groups when there is a shift towards uxorilocal marriage and genetrix derivation of membership? In Rejang, Gayo and especially Minangkabau, matrifocal genealogical origin groups are less exclusive than their patrifocal counterparts elsewhere.

For Reuter (1992, p. 516) genealogical origin and territorial origin are two closely interwoven forms of precedence; both are based on a common ideology of precedence and origin upstream from any distinction between patri-/matri-lineal. These questions of precedence and origin are at the centre of Sumatran ideas of status and identity, which is what concerns the Javanese *trah*. In Sumatra, place, "post-marital residence of a couple within a particular social unit (is considered as) more crucial in determining the membership status of children than the gender through which ancestry is normally traced." So also in Java the members of a *trah* rely on ancestry to create a social unit in one place where the pathways to that place are the construction of their historical migration. They form a metaphoric tracer for the expansion both of Islam and habitable space at the expense of forests.

The importance of topogeny in Sumatra (Reuter 1992, p. 516) is to be linked to the expansiveness of the societies. A series of foundation events produces an order of topological precedence. Such a socially constructed "topogeny" is often, but not necessarily, interwoven with tales of ancestral origins. Thus Reuter writes (1992, p. 490):

> "Lineages" were regarded as things rather than as a way of constructing identity by focusing on ancestry.

This is born out by topogeny. Among the Batak one has "historical sequences of affinal ties, conceptualized as a "flow of life" (cf. Fox 1980, pp. 12–13) and embodied in a chain of women."

> The ideology of precedence not only serves to interpret, but also to produce events ... to maximise status. (1992, p. 493)

Here status is construed as precedence in terms of ancestry and topogeny.

Reuter asks (1992, p. 493): Does the concept of precedence fail to distinguish between the levels of ideological principles and social structure?

> A necessary distinction is one between a "principle of precedence" and an "order of precedence" ... While there is a set of logical principles (asymmetry, recursiveness, transitivity) which is summarised by the term "precedence", there are several categories of socially defined events to which it can be related in order to construct different "orders of precedence".

So here what people do is not treated as individual acts incorporated into a series of events, but as processes structured from their very onset by a higher social logic. This resembles the notion of hierarchy used to described the socio-cosmological fit of the values structuring traditional Javanese village described in Chapter 3 above.

The reactivation of the cult of Durga in Krendawahana in 1979,[44] did nothing to raise the prestige of the palace aristocrats among the Muslims of the nearby villages and probably very little to raise their own status as the palace no longer ruled as a kingdom. In Kaliasa the *trah* now has deep local roots; it represents more than four thousand people, both present locally and linked to Kaliasa from afar. Although some middle-class Javanese are willing to participate in the Surakarta palaces' efforts to propogate neo-feudalism on the basis of an ancient cult to Durga, they could not reverse local networks of Muslims. To say that the sociology of Islam has escaped the *priyayi* aristocrats vision of social hierarchy, is really to say that there is no longer a global hierarchy recognized by all Javanese. Now there are several kinds of *trah* in Java. Other lineages have been written in the landscape of the area's graves and mosques, and over Durga's tertre. Despite the continuing annual pilgrimages on the occasion of the buffalo sacrifice (*maésa lawung*) for the anniversary of the king's coronation, the invisible kingdom of Durga meant less to the local inhabitants than the assembling of the bones of their ancestors buried there. The force behind this was as much the sociological work of the *trah* as the preaching (*dakwah*) of the Muslims.

5.6 APPENDICES: GENEALOGIES CITED

Source: *Silsilah Leluhur Kaliasa* (Keluarga Besar/Trah Nitimenggolo), by K.H. Muhammad Idris alias Suratmo (former village headman of Sambirejo)

GENEALOGY OF ABDUL JALAL I

1. Raja Pajang Sultan Hadiwijoyo: Jaka Tingkir
2. Adipati Joyowongso
3. Adiapti Honggowongso
4. Adiapti Kyai Gulu
5. Adiapti Kyai Sekar Petak (Pedan)
6. Adipati Nitimenggolo (fallen in the field of battle in Purwokerta during the reign of Untung Suropati)
7. Kyai Abdul Jalal I (*merdikan* Kaliasa)
8. Kyai Abdul Jalal II

9. Kyai Abdul Jalal IV
10. Kyai Abdul Jalal III (Kyai Minhad)

GENEALOGY OF KYAI HAJI RADÈN BAGUS MURTOJO (K.H. MOH. KORIB)

1. Prabu Browijoyo V raja Majapahit Berputera (Bondan Dedjawan (K. Ageng Tarub II))
2. Kyai ageng Wonosobo
3. Kyai ageng Madepandan (I)
4. Kyai ageng Pekeringan (kyai ageng Sobo)
5. Kyai Ageng Jurumartani (uncle of Senapati Mataram, cf. de Graaf & Pigeaud 1974, p. 156) (Pageran Mondoroko(I) = *patih* & confidant of Mangkurat II)
6. Kyai Ageng Pangeran Mandurorejo (Patih Sultan Agung Mataram) = in Silsilah Pangeran Hadipati M. (= Djuru Wiroprobo) buried in Kaliwungu (Kendal)
7. R.M. Tumenggung Kartonagoro, *bupati* Grobogan, later in Pati became *ketib*; later to Lawéyan after buried in Mondongan (not in List) on the banks of the stream) (=? Kyai Ageng Radèn Tumenggeng Maduranegoro)
8. Kyai Ageng Gulu (*pengulu*; buried on banks of stream in Mondongan)
9. Kyai Ageng Honggowongso
10. Kyai Ageng Niti Manggolo (Kyai Kerti Manggolo I; has ten children called: "Leluhur kita Keluaraga besar Kaliasa")
11. Kyai Haji Radèn Bagus Murtojo (cf. history of Kaliasa above and identification in note 2).

GENEALOGY OF NITIMENGGOLO I (TEN CHILDREN)

1. Nyai Somenggolo (Solo Lawéyan)
2. Nyai Kartotaruno (Kyai Kartotaruno dari Pajang; son of Nitimenggolo?)
3. Kayi Abdul Jalal
4. Nyai Suro Taruno
5. Nyai Reso Setiko
6. Kyai Ismail
7. Kyai Nuryodi
8. Kyai Niti Menggolo II (Lawéyan)
9. Kyai Somodrono
10. Kyai Khamdani (Pasuruhan, East Java; grave Rujak Gadung (Kyai Solo))

Genealogy of Kyai Kartotaruna (Son of Mandurorejo Above)

1. Kyai Abu Bakar
2. Kyai Abdul Kadir
3. Kyai Mohammed Qorib (kyai Murtojo)
4. Nyai Surodrono
5. Kyai Zakariya (Nujum Dipanagoro)
6. Kyai Mustahal
7. Kyai Abdulrahman (died in Saudia Arabia where his body was buried, however, it kept coming back from the sea onto shore there until it was buried in Kaliasa.)

Genealogy of Kyai Mohammed Qorib (Kyai R. Bagus Murtojo)

1. Kyai Kertoyudo
2. Nyai Honggodipo Kaliasa (menantu Kyai Maja)
3. Kyai Kliwon Wiroprojo (bupati)
4. Kyai Ketip Sememi (Pengulu Yogya)
5. Kyai haji Yahyo
6. Nyai Kasan Mohamad
7. Nyai Mangunrejo
8. Nyai Imanraji
9. Kyai Muhamad

Genealogy of Kyai Haji Yahyo

(they would have all died in the early 1900s)
1. Kyai Haji Umar Ngijo
2. Kliwon Tumengngn Gitodipuro (Bupati Karangéde di Kacangan, Gemolong)
3. Nyai Martowijoyo
4. Radèn Rangga Mangun Sudiro I
5. Radèn Ngabei Citroyahyono
6. Radèn Somo Atmojo
7. Radèn Marto Atmojo
8. Haji Abdul Kanan
9. Nyai Joyosuroyo
10. Radèn Ngabei Mangunsutomo
11. Nyai Joyo Suhardo
12. Nyai Gito Kartolo

13. Nyai Sastro Atmojo
14. Nyai Giti Panuksmo
15. Nyai Gitominardo
16. Nyai Mandrosastro
17. Radèn Ngabei Wrekso Suyahyo (Jogomandero)

GENEALOGY OF KYAI MAJA

(Cf. source: Sagimun M.D., Kyai Maja (Jakarta, Proyek Inventarisasi dan Dokumentasi Sejarah Nasional, Dept. P.&K., 1981, 108 pp.)

GENEALOGY OF SECOND KYAI MAJA

(Source: pp. 8–9, in "Kisah Ringkas perjuangan R.A.Sumirah, R.A. Khadiyah, R.A. Marwiyah dan kyai Suhudo Som membantu Pengran Diponegoro perang melawan Penjajahan Belanda" disusun oleh Soekro Djogosarkoro, Karanganyar, 23. VII.1976).

NOTES

1. For an up-to-date bibliography, cf. Wink (1990/1997); Jackie Assayag (1995).
2. Cf. Steenbrink (1984); Kuntowijoyo (1991); Azyumardi Azra (1994); van Bruinessen (1992, ch. 12 and 1995).
3. *Silsilah Lelhur Kaliasa*. The word translated here as "genealogy" is the Malay-Javanese word derived from the Arabic, *silsila*. It is used in Sūfi' brotherhoods or *tarèkat* for the "chain" of transmission of spiritual authority and may derive from the classical Greek word for "chain", '*alusida*, where in religious literature, it has the same meaning.
4. In the Surakarta newspaper *Solo Pos* (27 December 2001), Heru Ismantoro reported on the 829th anniversary of the Al Imamu Syeikh Ali Abil Hasan As Syadzili ra that took place on 26 December in the mosque of Muqorrobin in the village of Kacangan, Andong, Boyolali. The article was entitled "Our Task is to return to the roots of humanity"and in the first paragraph he mentions Kyai Haji Muhammad Idris, the teacher and *ulama* of the *ṭariqa* Syadziliyah.
5. To wit: Ngrukun Kaliasa (commemoration or *sadranan* day 23 in the month of Ruwah); Kaliasa South bank (i.e., *Sabrang Kidul*; 23 Ruwah); Kaliasa Sabrang Tengah Koriban (24 Ruwah); Kaliasa North bank (*Sabrang Lor*; 25 Ruwah); Kaliasa Ngoro-oro (25 Ruwah); Kacangan Ngandong (26 Ruwah).
6. Cf. *Nama dan alamat Pondok Pesantren Indonesia* (Proyek Pembinaan dan Bantuan Kepada Pondok Pesantren; Direktorat Jendral Pembinaan Kelembagaan Agama Islam; Dept. Agama R.I., 1982/83).

In the province of Central Java there are, according to this list, 609 *pondhok*: more than thirty each are found in the *kabupatèn* (prefectures) of Semarang, Kendal, Demak, Pathi, Cilacap, Wonosobo. Boyolali has 9, Sragen 5 , Karanganyar 4, Sukoharjo 3, and Surakarta 7. In the *kabupatèn* of Sragen one finds:

Kaliasa Jetis Karangpung Kalijambé Sragen: founded by K.H. Badruddin Hongowoso in 1969 with (in 1983) 38 teachers (*guru/ustadz*) and 655 *santri*. This village is the fourth going east from Purwadadi road on the north side of the river Cemara.

Karangmojo Andong Boyolali: founded 1906 by Haji Djumeri HS.; 10 *guru/ustadz* and 150 santri. It has a big new white two-storey mosque and is now called Pondhok Al-Quran.

7. Lawi(/é)yan is mentioned in the *Serat Centhini* (late eighteenth century) during some fifty pages. In vol. 3 (1988, *pupuh* 254) Cebolang goes there to perfom *ziarah* on the tomb of Ki Ageng Enis. In the Lawiyan mosque Ki Sali explains the prophecy of Jayabaya with its trichotomic time periods of seven hundred years. In vol. 4 (*pupuh* 257 passim) this discussion continues until Ki Atyanta begins his exposition concerning Kayamatkobra according to the Hadis and Seh Markaban's reign in Egypt.

8. Kyai Kartotaruno is said to be from Pajang, but in the genealogy of the *Silsilah* the second child of Nitimenggolo I is listed as Nyai Kartotaruno, i.e. a woman.

9. In fact there are two separate *pondhok*, here elided into one; cf. Carey (1981, pp. 261–62).

10. The most obvious problem with this history of the creation of freehold by the Susuhunan is that at this period (1820s) the area around Kaliasa has been in Mangkunagaran territory for some sixty years. The Islamic court milieu in the mid-nineteenth century in Surakarta are little studied, but cf. Simuh, *Mistik Islam Kejawèn. Radèn Ngabehi Ranggawarsita. Suatu Studi Terhadap Serat Wirid Hidayat Jati.* (Jakarta: Penerbit Universitas Indonesia, 1988); and Moh. Ardani, *Al-Qur'an dan Sufisme Mangkunagaran IV (Studi Serat-serat Piwulang)* (Dana Bhakti, Surakarta, n.d.). Sumarsam says (*Gamelan. Cultural Interaction and Musical Development in Central Java* (Chicago: University of Chicago Press, 1995), pp. 91–93, cf. also pp. 50–53; 58–59) that on the basis of the rare data on "Islamic" musical performances in the court of the Mangkunagaran that the mid-nineteenth century was considerably less developed than the earlier period of Mas Said (Mangkunagaran I, 1725–95); cf. Zainuddin Fananie, *Restrukturisasi Budaya Jawa. Perspektif KGPAA Mangkunagara I* (Surakarta: Muhallaidyah Univerity Press, 2000). How the Islamic reformism of the second half of the nineteenth century relates to court culture has yet to be studied with any precision, but in the Mankunagaran Dutch cultural influences grew stronger and this cannot have been favourable to Islam.

11. Cf. P.B.R. Carey, *Babad Dipanagara. An account of the outbreak of the Java War* (Kuala Lumpur: Malaysian Branch of the Royal Asiatic Society, monograph

no. 9, 1981.) Cf. also Tim G. Babcock, *Kampung Jawa Tondano* (Yogyakarta: Gadjah Mada Univ. Press, 1988).

12. Maja is a place name that here designates a famous *kyai* from that place.

13. Sunar Tri Suyanto, *Pahlawan Kemerdekaan Nasional RI Sinuhun Banguntapa* (Solo: Tiga Serangkai 1984), pp. 66; cf. also Headley (1980).

14. Cf. the B.A. thesis (Fakultas Sastra Universitas Indonesia, Jakarta) by Ratnaesih on the Museum Pusat collection of fifty-six Durgāmahishāuramardinī statues. Four are from the Sunda area, twenty-three from Central Java and twenty-six from East Java.

15. Ricklefs (1974, p. 243, note 46) gives a Javanese text of the revelation to Sultan Ngrun (folio 3 verso) "Java has become a deep forest; let people be planted there!" The first and second expeditions of the Sultan met with catastrophic defeat as both the spirits and the forces of nature opposed his expedition. The Sultan then told his religious advisors to pray for a *jimat tumbal* to defeat these Javanese spirits. Upon its reception it was buried in different places in Java and Bali. They were then brought under control. They were ordered by a voice sent from Allah to fear the Prophet and the king of Java, and to submit to the authority of the queen who rules in the Southern Ocean. The voice forewarned though that in the final age of unrest that the spirits will again move among men (Ricklefs 1974, p. 243).

16. The word *patèn* usually means "permanent, fixed, shut", but if *jaga* here means the "the guarding or guardian of", what could an adjective *patèn* mean in that compound? Provisionally I translate it as above. Horne gives "sacrificial offering", not found in Pigeaud (1994, p. 452). Cf. Gericke and Roorda (1901, vol. II, p. 263 ff).

17. This seems to be a reference to the same place (*ingkang sakinten lebet Soyanipun*) that the bowels and some of the blood of the buffalo offered to Durga were abandoned, according to R.T. Pujodipura in Kraemers notes Leiden COr. 10.846(4).

18. Cf. Martin van Bruinessen, *Tarékat Naqsybandiyah di Indonesia* (Bandung: Mizan, 1992), p. 156.

19. On the disappearance of P.B. VI (reigned 1823–30) from the middle of the Krendawahana forest, cf. Sunar 1984, p. 68. Cf. also *Serat Rajaweddha* where it is Pangéran Natakusuma, a son of P.B. IV, who disappears. However the late local headman, Sastrodiwiryo and Kyai Digdo both tell of the disappearance of the king P.B. VI. This is probably a confusion with P.B. IV due to the recent proclamation of P.B. VI as a national hero.

20. Cf. for possible identification the letters circa 1800 from the *penghulu* Moertolhojo to the brother of Kyai Maja (?; cf. genealogy above in note 2), Kyai Hasan Basri, cited p. 497 by F. Fokkens "Vrije desa's op Java en Madoera" (1886). The *Silsilah Leluhur Kaliasa*, pp. 8–9, hesitates between Bagus Murtojo and Murtolo under P.B. IV. The rapprochement of both date and name is not conclusive, but highly suggestive of an historical identification.

21. Adiwidjaja, *Pustaka Jawi*, no. 6 (1927) p. 55, "Tegesipoen Kalijasa angsal-angsaling pemanggih dalemipoen sang wadya Bathari Durga. Krendawahana namung kanggé prabat ngantosaken ing bab angen kula negesi Kaliyasa: mila irahipoen harangan(?) mungel tegesipoen Kaliyasa, boten Krendawahana."

22. Cf. Natawidjaja (1927, pp. 21–25); P. A. Adiwidjaja (1927, p. 55); and R. Ng. Poerbatjaraka (1940, pp. 291–93).

23. The only other descendant from Kaliasa itself, to have occupied a notable place in the Solo court was Kyai Haji Yahya who was the advisor (*penaséhat*) and director of the Association of Indonesian Haji under P.B. X (private conversation with Radèn Ibnu Pradigdo 56 years old, Sambireja, Kaliasa; 27 May 1995).

24. *Javanese Trah. Kin-Based Social Organisation* (Yogyakarta: UGM Press, 1982), passim.

25. Wife's membership ends with divorce, but not with death, unless she marries a non-*trah* member. Some *trah* have youth organizations whose members are not yet full *trah* members. Adoptive children may also qualify, but not a step-child. The term for pseudo member is *anggota cangkokan*.

26. Cf. Sjafri Sairin (1982). According to the dictionary of Gericke & Roorda 1901, the word *truh* (rain, water or blood: flowing from high to low) is related to the word, *trah*, through these meanings:
    1. to descend, cf. *tedhak*, (krama inggil) *turun*.
    2. blood relatives; social group, (*krama inggil*) *asli* or *gotrah*.
    3. descent (Dutch *afkomst, afstameling*).
    Other related words:
    – *truh* = fine rain, i.e. (*ngoko*) *udan riwis*;
    – convalesce, *tirah*;
    – remaining, *turuh*;
    – small flow of water (*turuh*);
    – to pour water over hands, wash a kris with arsenic, infect with a disease (*nuruh*).

27. Cf. *Pratélan Para Dalem Soewargi Kangdjeng Goeti Pangeran Adipati Arja Mangoennagar I hing Soerakarta Hadiningrat*, 1973 edition, privately published, Surakarta, 280pp.

28. Ibid.

29. Cf. *Pangunuban Trah R. Tumenggung Secodiningrat Yogyakarta, Buku Riwayat dan Silsilah*, edited by Purwosugiyanto (2nd edition 1985), 41pp.

30. Cf. S.C. Headley "The Body as a house in Javanese Society" (1987*a*); and "The Idiom of Siblingship", (1987*b*).

31. *Syawal* is the tenth Arabic month, the month of fasting not to be confused with the eighth month *ruwah* or *Saban* (or in Arabic *Sya'ban*), when one *nyadran*, i.e., makes an offering. The main annual pilgrimage to the grave of one's ancestor for the Javanese just before and after the ninth month of *Puwasa*. The word *sadran* comes from the Sanskrit *śhrāddha* which for Pigeaud is basically a Tantric Buddhist ritual, cf. *Nāgarakertāgama* ch. 9 and Pigeaud's reflections (vol. IV, 1960–63, p. 424).

32. The following is based on Zamakhsyari Dhofier, "Kinship and Marriage among the Javanese Kyai" (1980).

33. For the nineteenth century background, see Zamakhsyari Dhofier's *Tradisi Pesantren; studi tentang kepandangan hidup Kyai* (1982), pp. 64, 86.

34. Kuntowijoyo, "Serat Cabolek dan Mitos Pembangkangan Islam: Melacak Asal-Usul Ketegangan antara Islam dan Birokrasi" (1991).

35. G.F. Pijper (1985, p. 72), *Studi tentang Islam Indonesia 1900–1950* (Jakarta: Universiti Indonesia 1985), cited by Kuntowijoyo (1991, p. 126).

36. James J. Fox, "Ziarah. Visits to the Tombs of the Wali, the Founders of Islam on Java" (1991).

37. C. Snouck Hurgronje (1991) advisiezen dated 7 March 1895, which criticizes Fokkens' 1886 study. Cf. also Karel A. Steenbrink "Lembaga Perdikan dan Fungsinya dalam Pengembangan Islam" (1984). The Dutch historian and sociologist B.J.O. Schrieke (1975) had attacked the Dutch view that the Javanese king had immanent domain on all land. Although villages like the one in the deed (*piagem*) of the year A.D. 939 became *perdikan* villages directly dependent on the king, even these were eventually taken by their headmen as their own lands. In any event Schrieke did not consider such village freeholds had any important function in the spreading of Islam. For the ritual networks of the Majapahit period, cf. K.R. Hall 1996.

38. H.J. van Mook, "Koeta Gede", 1926.

39. The term in Dutch is "*vererings gemeenschap*" (cult from *vereren* = honour, venerate). Cf. H. Th. Chabot, *Verwantschap, Stand en Sexe in Zuid-Celebes* (1950); the chapter on "Worship Communities" (pp. 61–66) and the chapter on "ornament" or worship communities, pp. 67–77.

40. Shelly Errington, "Incestuous Twins and the House Societies of Insular Southeast Asia" (1987).

41. Cf. the 1994 journalistic account of *Mangkunagaran. Apa yang Terjadi?* (Solo 1994) which describes what happened when the M.N. *krabatan keluarga besar* tried to make their association into a foundation (*yayasan*).

42. James J. Fox "Austronesian Societies and their Transformations" (1995).

43. Perhaps to be identified with Pinatih, foster mother of Iskak of Blambangan, first Sunan Giri (near Gresik, East Java). In the beginning of the sixteenth century there were two Sunan Giri (Pigeaud and de Graaf 1976, p. 15).

44. Cf. S. C. Headley "The Ritual Lancing of Durga's Buffalo in Surakarta and the Offering of its Blood in the Krendawahana forest." 1979; also "Recyclage Rituel au Centre de Java: Le "re-lancement" du Buffle de Durga", *1980*.

6

VILLAGE MAPS FOR ROYAL LINEAGES
Paku Buwana VI in Durga's Forest

In Chapter 4 on the deterritorialization of the Javanese village communities it was shown that the Javanese village headman, the *bekel*, was first and foremost a tax farmer and that his role was often in blatant contradiction to the territorial integrity of the village (Elson 1997, pp. 28–30). To begin with, the function of tax farmer was usually bought. Where the village settlement was at a certain distance from the palace administration, the *bekel* and his followers could develop their common interests at the margin of the stratified centralization of the divine right rice agriculture. As discussed in Chapter 3, between the village cults and the royal cults there existed a massive gap that was sometimes filled by regional cults, although these always risked royal censure. The appearance of a supra-village sphere often took the form of networks animated by lineages. These "new" genealogies manifested the partial marginalization of communities based on the "sharing" of a common village space, and the deployment of worship communities in a patchwork of kin-based networks whose activities could lie dormant for shorter or longer periods of time.

Javanese religious praxis in local territorial communities such as the village or the urban *quartier* (cf. Chapter 13) mostly involves either mosque-based worship or family life passage events with prayer meals (*slametan*) organized at a home, which then serves as the site of the invocations. It is also possible, however, for a person to go away, alone or with his family, on a pilgrimage, to pray at a particular shrine in the mountains or on the tomb of a king or Muslim saint in the valleys. Leaving Java aside, throughout western

Austronesia, a third praxis which is not rooted in a place, such as a mosque or a household, takes as its focus kinship ties in the form of lineages worship communities. In Java, these cults are usually voluntary associations. In Part II we are describing two lineages, one aristocratic and the other Muslim, each one constituting a community of worship "centred" in the Kaliasa region. While their centre is territorial, their members are scattered. Each of these lineages also represented an historical stage in the development of individuation in the Javanese social morphology. The aristocratic lineage harks back to the time when only the king, through his kingdom, could embrace the entire society and align it with the macrocosm through his role as the ritual centre of society. It was through proximity to such a royal cognatic genealogy that the responsibility for tax farming was distributed. This praxis led to paramount lineages being defined in terms of a royal person or that of his predecessors. The Muslim lineages, on the other hand, represent not a raja-centric ritual praxis, but a series of worship communities linked to graveyards of earlier Muslim leaders who opened up new, often rural, Muslim centres, and developed mosques and Muslims schools (*pesantrèn*) there. In due course (Ch. 15) these two phenomena will be tied together in the perspective of a pseudo-individualistic social-morphology, but here we present the ethnographic data.

6.1 FOR THE BLESSING OF THE GODDESS

In 1949 the food offerings (*caos dhahar*) by the royal houses of Surakarta of buffalo's flesh, etc., on the tertre of Durga in the sacred forest of Krendawahana came to an end. The republican spirit of the newly independent Indonesian Government displaced the legitimacy of the two palaces of Surakarta in many ways. The sacrifice of a buffalo had originally been offered by the Susuhunan of Surakarta and derived from the famous poem *Devimāhātmaya* (the magnanimous goddess), celebrating an Indian Puranic myth of the victory of Durga over the attacks of the buffalo, *maésa*, general of the demon (*asura*) armies. This victory was often depicted in the iconography of Central and Eastern Java between the tenth and the fifteenth centuries. After the Islamization of the newly established kingdoms of south Central Java in the sixteenth century, this "Hindu" ritual had nonetheless continued.

Despite a promising prelude in the first third of the twentieth century (cf. Larson 1987), during the "physical" revolution against the Dutch colonialists (1945–50), the role of the Surakarta royal houses waned in comparison to that of Yogyakarta, whose sultan was to become the vice-president of the new republic (cf. Kahin 1952, p. 194, note 4). If in 1949 the courts of Susuhunan and the junior palace of the Mangkunagaran, in whose territory Krendawahana lay, abandoned their annual offerings, what led them to recommence this ritual some thirty years later?[1] A journalist, Moch Nursjahid P., present at this occasion, wrote an article in the Semarang newspaper *Suara Merdéka's* Sunday supplement, *Minggu Ini* (no. 59: I & VII), sections of which we have translated at length below:

> The twenty-sixth of March 1979, the day of Monday Kliwon (in other terms the twenty-seventh day of the month of Rabingulakir, 1979, or the year Dal 1911) a prayer ceremony (*hajad*) was held to celebrate "the ritual offering of the royal *slametan* (collective meal) for the Spearing of the buffalo (*Maésa Lawung*) by the palace of Surakarta Hadiningrat."
>
> In the past, when the palace was still powerful, the offerings were done on a great scale (up to forty water buffalo were offered), but the ritual has now taken on much more modest proportions. It suffices to sacrifice one buffalo, a few ducks and several chickens. The official in charge of the ceremony, the *abdi dalem* Juru Suranata, was accompanied by many personalities of high rank (*priyagung*) belonging to the court, including R.T. Purwodipuro, K.R.M.H. Banuingrat, R.T. Brotonagoro and K.R.T. Kusumatanoyo, constituted the palace's delegation.
>
> **The blessing (*berkah*) of the goddess Bathari Durga**
> According to the explanations given by K.R.T. Kusumatanoyo, the ritual offerings for the *Maésa Lawung* had been uninterrupted since the period of the sang *Prabu* Jayabaya, king of Kediri. His son, sang Prabu Jayahamijoyo, replaced him after his death. When a flood destroyed Kediri and the palace had to be reconstructed in Pagedongan, Batari Durga granted her assistance. She also helped sang *Prabu* Jayahamijoyo when he fought against the king of the *djinn* to the west of the Solo River (i.e. in the area of Surakarta) and also to sang *Prabu* Kusumowicitro and sang *Prabu* Citrokusumo when they created the kingdom of Pengging Witaradya (end of the XVth century). So she did down to the period of the kingdoms of Demak, Pajang and Kartasura. Batari Durga has been considered as the protector of the kings of Java and their people since the transfer of the kingdom to Surakarta [1745–46]. It is in remembrance of this protection and to give thanks to Batari Durga that each year the sacrifice of *Maésa Lawung* is made at the end of the month of Rabingulakir [Bakda Mulud, end of the third Muslim month]. By these sacrifices, Batari Durga's blessing is solicited so that the family of the king and all the people enjoy lasting good health, happiness, security and peace.
>
> The word *Maésa Lawung* comes from *mahisa*, which means buffalo, and *lawung*, which means lance. That seems to mean that the offering in question is a buffalo killed by lancing. In military terminology, *liwung* means "wild, primitive or illegal", or "in the fullness of his strength". What

will be offered is therefore literally a wild buffalo in the fullness of his strength, that is to say a buffalo that has never been worked in a rice field.

The most important elements of this sacrifice are: the raw pounded/ground up meat (gecok), the head of the buffalo, and different varieties of cooked porridge and rice. The expense of all these elements is such that they are often replaced by pieces of meat bought at the butcher's. The prayers pronounced by the *abdi dalem* Juru Suranata are still the ancient Javanese Hindu-Buddhist ones. Their meaning is based on the mantra the King of the Wheel of Time (*kalacakra*), which was composed, they said, by Sri Batara Wisnu, and then inscribed, on the chest of Batara Kala, the son of Durga Kala . This is the interpretation made by K.R.T. Kusumatanoyo.

The forest of Krendawahana is, according to legend, the invisible kingdom of Batari Durga, queen of the djinn and the demons, and is extremely dangerous for it is haunted. "The man who draws near is a dead man (*jalma mara, jalma mati*)": such is the saying of the venerable *dhalang* (shadow puppeteer). In the past the forest stretched from the deer park of Kartasura called Banalaya [now located just to the north of Surakarta] to Purwadadi, Grobangan [some fifty kilometres to the north of Surakarta in the Kendeng hills].

Today what is called the forest (*alas*) of Krendawahana is reduced to a village bearing the same name and included in the sub-district of Gondangrejo, district of Karanganyar. This village is situated about 2.5 kilometres to the east of Kaliyoso and some seventeen kilometres to the north of Solo.

The ritual sacrifice takes place on the outskirts of the village, on a small tertre of stones surrounded by white ficus and other shade trees. Two ramshackle houses with bamboo walls serve as shelters for those who ask (of Durga) her blessing (*berkah*).

According to the scribe (*carik*) of Krendawahana who occupies the function of guardian of this holy place, people come in crowds to ask for (Durga's) blessing on the evening of Tuesday Kliwon and Friday Kliwon. Many are Chinese from Malang, Surabaya and other east Javanese towns. Besides the white ficus one finds another vestiges of the past, the shining stone named "the stone for performing meditation" (*sela ambangun tapa*), and the army pool (*sendang séna*[2]). Here, the traders request the magic formula (*palarisan*[3]) permitting them to sell rapidly all their goods and take a prolonged bath (*karamas*[4]) during the night. The stone called "shining" evokes historical events, for it is there that the prince Dipanagara, *kyai* Maja, Sentot Prawirodirjo, Raden Sumirah and their followers met to prepare Dipanagara's war (1825–1830).

This place of the "shining stone" is where the prince Dipanagara received as an inheritance/gift from Paku Buwana VI (Sinuhun Bangun Tapa) the dagger *kyai* Sandang Lawé [Black Stork; Ardeola bacchus, or

Egretta garzetta?]. Afterwards, the heroine *Raden Ayu* Sumirah (later called *Nyai* Kedunggubeh because she married the ulama of Kedunggubeh) also received an inheritance from Paku Buwana VI, Susuhunan of Surakarta [reigned 1823–1830, then exiled to Ambon by the Dutch]. Amongst the heirlooms (*pusaka*) received, figure the sabre *kyai* Sabuk Janur (Light Green Sash), the lance *kyai* Tundung Mungsuh (Dispersing Enemies), the arrowhead Surwendo, saddles and cropped whips. On the order of the court transmitted by G. R. Ay. Sosronagoro, R. Satibi Mulyosaputera, great-great-grand-daughter of R. Ay. Soemirah, the site of the so-called shining stone has recently been renovated. That restoration, which cost almost half a million rupees, was finished on Wednesday Wagé, the second day of March 1978.

Portrait of Bathari Durga

About a year ago, an incredible, but nonetheless authentic, miracle occurred. During the ceremony of sacrifice, Mochtarsom, son of R. Satibi Mulyosaputra, took a colour photograph. When the film was developed, what did one see? Amongst the white ficus trees one could see the silhouette of a beautiful young woman of Indian type. She wore a red sari and had a crown on her head.

Mochtarsom affirmed convincingly to us that this did not derive from any fault in the film or error in development. Many copies of the photograph were made, and sent as proofs to the sub-district of Gondangrejo. Furthermore one can examine an enlargement of the photograph at the house of Mochtarsom in Notoningrat in Solo. Believe it or not, but his silhouette of the beautiful young woman is in reality according to the elders, that of Bathari Durga, incarnation (*jalma*) of Dewi Uma, wife of Betara Guru, who was willing to appear to us.

6.2 THE NEEDS OF A HERO

This newspaper account of Durga's cult in Krendawahana only reflects a part of the traditions surrounding this goddess which Javanese oral tradition brings down to the present. It is nonetheless precious for being the first written account after her cult recommenced on this tertre in 1979. The palace officials replied carefully to the questions of the journalist. The presentation made of the background of the reinstatement of this ceremony established two brand new "facts": the appearance of Durga in a colour photograph during this first performance in thirty years of an abandoned ritual; and, more importantly, the use of this iconography to establish Durga's tertre as the meeting place of Paku Buwana VI (r. 1823–30) and Prince Dipanagara to prepare the Java War. The new avatar of Durga is therefore linked to an

FIGURE 6.1
Imagined portrait of Paku Buwana VI, proclaimed national hero in 1964.
He is known as the Awakening of Ascetical Powers or Bangun Tapa, which is
traditionally what he is said to have been doing when he was arrested by
the Dutch on the south coast of Java on 6 June 1830

Source: Reproduced from Sunar Tri Suyanto, *Pahlawan Kemerdékaan Nasional RI Sinuhun Banguntapa* (Solo: Tiga Serangkai, 1984), p. 5, with permission of the publisher.

updating of the ritual, but with new historical input. It is this second element — the participation of the Susuhunan of Surakarta in the Java War — which will retain our attention.

Carey has shown that the wavering attitude of this ruler, Paku Buwana VI, at the beginning of the war, was caused initially by the influence of the

Surakarta *Patih* Sasradiningrat and later by the sojourn at court (30 July 1825) of the Dutch diplomat, De Kock. Yet Carey writes (1981, p. 292, note 241), "It is certain that he secretly sympathised with Dipanagara, and in another passage in the *Buku* (written 1842–3 by Cakranagara) he is cast in the role of Prabu Baladewa, the ruler of Madura in the wayang theatre, who was strongly sympathetic to the Kurawa cause yet was tricked by Prabu Kresna into meditating at the Grojogan Sewu, and thus missed taking part in the Bratayuda, the final contest between the Kurawa and the Pandhawa."[5]

Could this recently attested meeting between Dipanagara and Paku Buwana VI be the expression of considerable regret on the part of the descendants of Paku Buwana VI that he did not take any meaningful part in the five-year-long struggle of Dipanagara against the Dutch? Later on, the resistance of the Surakarta palaces from 1945 to 1950 towards the Japanese and Dutch, was judged to be much less progressive than that of the Yogyakarta sultan (cf. Soejatno 1974, pp. 105–10; Larson 1987). The museum of the "physical revolution" commemorating the ousting of the Dutch was therefore built in the nationalist and progressive Yogyakarta and not in Surakarta, due to the "wait-and-see" strategies of both the latter's aristocrats (*priyayi*) and the outspoken rivalry with the Solo-based Communist Persatuan Perjuangan (Unified Struggle). It seems that the loss of prestige felt by the Surakarta aristocratic lineages as a result of twice missing their chance to play a significant role in the two great revolutions of modern Javanese history, might explain why the descendants of Paku Buwana VI here displayed a previously little known tradition concerning the rebellious fervour of the sixth Susuhunan of Surakarta. The question is not, did the meeting really take place, but what treatment is such a meeting being given? As Nancy Florida has remarked (1995, p. 52), the Javanese (re-)writing of history is already a historical event.

Some eight years before the renewal of the *Maésa Lawung* ceremony we see Paku Buwana's VI's memory being reconstituted, beginning on 3 October 1971 with a lecture by G.P.H. Djatikusumo entitled the "Political History of Paku Buwana VI".[6] The lecture took place under the patronage of a committee, Kol-Dalem Paku Buwana VI, representing his descendants. According to the palace history of Paku Buwana VI written in 1906 he died of a horse-cart accident in February 1849, or as recounted by his daughter, Radèn Ayu Timur, to her brother, he died of a lung infection (Florida 1995, p. 57 note 12). In his 1971 lecture, G.P.H. Djatikusumo held that Paku Buwana VI died of a gunshot wound inflicted by a Dutch rifle. Nancy Florida, who spent eight years in the Surakarta palace in the 1980s, sketches a portrait of Paku Buwana VI that not only reflects her familiarity with the palace literary traditions (1995, pp. 53–57), but also the interest the *kraton* more recently had been taking in this tragic figure who died in exile.

Florida (1995, p. 54) begins by quoting a contemporary of the Surakarta monarch, Lieutenant General H. M. de Kock. He complained that Paku Buwana VI "... frequently goes off fishing and hunting ... A Mohammedan despot (...) must, if he is to inspire honour and respect, show himself little outside his *Kraton* ... The Emperor has little natural intellect, and yet he has picked up an extensive knowledge of Javanese historical traditions (...); he writes fluently/smartly (*vlug*) and he has read extensively." For Florida (1995, p. 55), "Although ostensibly supporting his Dutch overlords against the rebels, Surakarta's king was known to have sympathized with, and likely to have secretly assisted, the rebellious Dipanagara." After the defeat of Dipanagara and the annexation of all the outlying (*mancanagara*) lands of both the Yogyakarta and Surakarta courts in 1830, for Florida there is no doubt what Paku Buwana VI was attempting when he left for Mancingan: "This act provoked the young Paku Buwana to action; he protested the annexation by withdrawing secretly to the tombs of his ancestors and to the magical embrace of his spiritual consort. Almost certainly preparing for armed rebellion, the twenty-three-year-old Paku Buwana VI was arrested in June 1830 on Java's southern coast..."(Florida 1995, pp. 55–56). If we take Florida's version for fact, then, our contemporary descendants of Paku Buwana VI were simply projecting a few years into the recent past a sentiment that the ruler entertained after the defeat of Dipanagara, by conjuring up a hypothetical meeting with Dipanagara in Krendawahana during the course of the rebellion of 1825–30. Sunar Tri Suyanto's biography of this king (1984, pp. 64–72) claims it took place on the 10 of Sura 1751 (AD 1824).

The Surakarta descendants of Paku Buwana VI were clearly interested in his memory and belatedly received governmental encouragement in the context of the campaign to memorialize provincial "national heroes" (Taufik Abdullah 1976, pp. 59–65). This seems to be the source of a much longer written account (some 256 pages) corresponding to the newly refurbished *Maésa Lawung* published in 1984 in a Solonese secondary school textbook publishing house, Tiga Serangkai: Sunar Tri Suyanto: *Pahlawan Kemerdékaan Nasional RI, Sinuhun Banguntapa*. The least one can say about this text is that it is not at pains to justify historically the sources of its very detailed chronology.

The movement to create provincial and national heroes (cf. Leclerc 1973), born out the military's respect for its own predecessors and heroes in the anti-colonial struggle, took on a renewed momentum during the Soeharto regime, when the provincial governors were in vast majority drawn from the military. Regional committees were named to permit each province to designate its own heroes. In Jakarta the Ministries of Education and Cultural Affairs and the Ministry of Defence and Security then submitted their recommendations to the President.

In the provinces, the aristocratic (*priyayi*) families still enjoyed an elevated social rank, positions which they wanted to protect, (cf. Sutherland 1975, pp. 74–76). These committees were sometimes influenced by the desire of the *priyayi* to attribute to their recent ancestors a glory that would enhance their entire family line. The most prominent example of this of course was the wife of President Soeharto, Ibu Tien, who began the Mangadeg foundation for the development of the Mangkunagaran house to which until the 1970s she had marginal ties. The Soeharto mausoleum which now houses her body near Matesih is of monumental proportions and is further enhanced by its proximity to the graves of Mangkunagaran kings.

The renewal of the annual *Maésa Lawung* ritual was certainly achieved by the palace of the Susuhunan of Surakarta, but in conjunction with a group of several lineages (*trah*) as can be surmised from Sunar Tri Suyanto's expression of thanks (1984, pp. 8–9) to the following individuals and *trah* they represent at the end of his preface to his biography of Sinuhun Banguntapa (Paku Buwana VI):

- K.R.M.H. Yosodipuro (fourth generation descendant of Paku Buwana VI). Sunar Tri Suyanto himself is the grandson of R.M. Haryo Yosodipuro;
- G.P.H.A. Jatikusumo, Letjen TNI Purniwirawan;
- Panitia Sub Muda-Mudi Trah Kraton Surakarta;
- The lineages of the descendants of participants in the struggle against the Dutch;
- *Trah R.A.* Soemirah;
- *Trah R.A.* Akhadiyah;
- *Trah R. Tumenggung* Prawirodigdoyo (cf. Suyanto 1984, p. 87);
- *Trah Kyai* Mojo (the representative in the Surakarta Kauman must have been Haji Bilal whom I interviewed in June 1995); and
- *Trah Kyai* Soehodo Som (cf. Suyanto 1984, p. 91)

These families provided information, monies, and moral support for the effort to commemmorate Paku Buwana VI and their own ancestors at the tertre in the Krendawahana's former forest.

The glorification of ancestors and the establishment of mausoleums has always been an important activity in Java, but since Independence in 1949 has been taken on by a rapidly increasing number of new lineages.[7] The 1965 military take-over by Soeharto provided certain aristocratic families, especially those with important members in the military, with renewed prestige, and this sought expression in marriage rituals.[8] But the nobility no longer had a monopoly here. For Anderson (1973), Leclerc (1973, p. 423) and S.T. Alisjahbana (1949, p. 390) the evolution of Indonesian vocabulary reflects the decline of the democratic ideology and the rise of a class of professional managers who, like Ibnu Sutowo, the former director of Pertamina, can celebrate his daughter's marriage with all the pomp of Hamengku Buwana IX. Something has changed since Leslie Palmier wrote these lines (1960, p. 158):

> ... it may be said that high position in the social-status system, though it enabled the holder to raise his position in the class-status system, at the same time limited the means by which it was raised and therefore the extent to which it was raised. It is pertinent here to add that this was only possible since the values of the traditional social-status system, in the field of costume at least, were accepted by those who held high position in the modern social-status system (though perhaps a low one in the traditional) and were concerned to maintain (or, in the latter case, to raise) their position in the traditional.

The Javanese attitude of moderation in consumption, still valued by the leaders of the first governments after independence, was unashamedly forsaken. Although they were in a strong position both *vis-à-vis* the foreign companies trying to invest in Indonesia and their poor cousins back in Central Java, they were nonetheless plagued by the issue of the legitimacy of their succession as rulers succeeding the Dutch colonialists and its *priyayi* bureaucracy. For Anderson (1973, pp. 74–78) the problem of the legitimacy of the succession of Soeharto generation which linked foreign capital to aristocratic neo-feudal provincial biographical backgrounds was real. The generation born in the cosmopolitan capital of Jakarta did not share their nineteenth century *vorstenlanden* (principalities) values. The élite of the new generation belonged to a broadly Indonesian society; they no longer thought in terms of a Central Javanese one.

In this context it may well be that the effort to establish the historical role of Paku Buwana VI was the initiative of several lineages trying to capture a prestige that they had not gained either by their participation in the 1945–49 struggle for independence or during the earlier Java War (1825–30). The minimal case to be made here is that once the Javanese military and their aristocratic relatives had immoderately and ostentatiously flouted any adherence to the official government ideology (*Pancasila*) founded on mutual aid (*gotong-royong*); it was the past that had become a limited good. It is in this sense that the aristocratic descendants of the past who had exclusive access not to current status but to a former prestige, began to manipulate it as a matter of course.

6.3 REWRITING HISTORY

Arjun Appadurai (1981, pp. 201–19) has analysed the cultural limits of the past as a symbolic resource in the South Asian countries. Their written historical charters (like the Javanese copper-plate *prasasti* from the eighth century onwards) began to sever the politics of discourse from myth. Especially after the arrival of European colonialists in Java, in the early seventeenth century the role of myth in appealing to a social whole was gradually fragmented by the Dutch values. Like Hindu India, Muslim Java displayed until recently the traits of pre-modern societies in its treatment of rank, ritual, and kinship, at the same time as it showed large-scale social organization, temporal depth, literacy, and civilizational complexity (cf. Appadurai 1981, p. 204). The code of norms by which a society is able to talk about its past, says Appadurai (1981, p. 218), tells us how they can talk about themselves and their present.

Having been proclaimed a national hero in 1964,[9] Paku Buwana VI momentarily emerged from obscurity along with other nineteenth century heroes such as *Pangéran* Antasari of Banjarmasin (Borneo). The Java War received little substantive help from Susuhunan's court, but it might have. According to Carey (1979, p. 72) the court of Surakarta was on the point of joining Dipanagara's cause when the Dutch General Kock arrived in Surakarta on 30 July 1825. Owing, perhaps, to the youth of the Sunan, the policy of the court seems to have been to rally to the side of the winners.

When Paku Buwana V died on 5 September 1823, his eldest illegitimate son, Raden Mas Saperdan (the future Paku Buwana VI) who had been cared for by the Prime Minister (*patih*), was accepted reluctantly by the court at the beginning of the war since he was too young to be held responsible for the decisions taken at the court of Surakarta. Between 1788 and 1820, Paku Buwana IV had done all that was in his power to drag the court of Yogyakarta under Hamengku Buwana (H.B.) II (1792–1810; 1811–12) into struggles against the English, their sepoys, the Muslim *santri* and the Dutch, all the while maintaining a façade of amicable relations through marriages and agreements concluded by his Prime Minister (Carey, no date, p. 102). When Paku Buwana VI did accede to the throne, the Dutch resident took over control of the seals of state, the prime minister of Surakarta became responsible for the administration of the country and the members of the royal family took responsibility for the education of the young Sunan who was still a minor (Carey 1975, p. 200).

When Dipanagara's rebel army neared Delanggu (some twenty kilometres to the west of Solo), the Sunan's army were ordered to let him pass through, but the Sunan's troops later went on to fight on the Dutch side during the battle of Gowok (15 October 1826) where Dipanagara met with defeat. Carey (1974, pp. 19–21; 1979, p. 74) describes how *kyai* Maja, the principal Muslim ally of Dipanagara in the Surakarta region, refused to become his Muslim adviser (*pengulu*) because the title Dipanagara really aspired to was that of *imam*, leader of all the Muslims. *Kyai* Maja hoped that the main military effort would be directed not against Yogyakarta, Dipanagara's own court of origin (Carey 1979, pp. 74–75), but against Surakarta, so that *kyai* Maja's own sphere of influence would be increased. In fact Gowok, where Dipanagara was not only defeated but also gravely injured, was the last major confrontation of the war. Henceforth the initiative passed to the Dutch side, while the relationship between Dipanagara and *kyai* Maja soured. The Muslim leader was criticized for having imprudently encouraged an attack on Surakarta in his own interest and thus precipitated this defeat at Gowok. If, then, Dipanagara was aided by the presence of a major Muslim leader like *kyai* Maja and certain members of his entourage, he paid a high price for this backing.

In the period just before the outbreak of the Java War, the issue of leasing agricultural land was already so delicate that Van der Capellen, Governor General 1816–26, dared not raise it despite being encouraged to do so by the Baron de Salis', resident of Surakarta. After the war, however, in 1830, reflecting the general bitterness over Dutch annexation of part of his territory and the impact of the new colonial policy of forced deliveries of agricultural products for export, the young Susuhunan Paku Buwana VI began thinking about these questions quite independently. Nonetheless, neither forms of exploitation, estate leasing or forced deliveries were able to unite the principalities of Yogyakarta and Surakarta into a common front *vis-à-vis* the Dutch. Carey comments:

> Surakarta specially had the feeling of having suffered unjustly by the annexation of its territories, for it had rested faithful to the Dutch during the entire war and had even provided reinforcements. (Carey 1979, p. 88)

To return to the twentieth century, why did members of the court of Surakarta bring back the body of Paku Buwana VI and have it buried in the royal cemetery common to both royal houses at Imogiri (cf. Ricklefs 1974, p. 237)? Had an ancient yet little known historical tradition pushed this group of aristocrats towards a biographical re-evaluation? Whatever the case may be, fourteen years after his reburial at Imogiri, Djatikusumo in 1971 stated that the autopsy of the exhumed body of Paku Buwana VI showed that he had been killed by a bullet shot from a Bakker rifle, the issue of the Dutch soldiers in the 1820s. This clearly follows up on the 1966 claim of Hadiwidjojo (1966, pp. 4–5), two years after the proclamation of Paku Buwana VI as national hero (nine years after the transfer of the contents of his tomb from Ambon to Imogiri) that he had been accused by General de Kock of collaborating (*sekutu*) with *Pangéran* Dipanagara. According to *G.P.H.* Hadiwidjojo (1966, p. 5), Paku Buwana VI was accused of this conspiracy against the Dutch on the basis of a fake letter,

> judging from the Royal stamp in a wax seal already used to seal the fake letter before it was loosened. The General was astonished, at a loss. In spite of that, Grandfather (i.e. Paku Buwana VI) was banished (G.P.H. Hadiwidjojo 1966, p. 4).

Between 1966 and 1971 there is thus already considerable discrepancy in local traditions concerning Paku Buwana VI. Peter Carey, an Oxford University historian of nineteenth-century Java, nevertheless provoked another kind of unanimity. In 1976 certain members of these lineages in Surakarta prevented Carey from giving a lecture on this topic from yet another point of view, that of a non-Javanese historian.

Let us now look at the claims of Djatikusumo expressed in 1971 in his lecture in Javanese on the actual meeting of Paku Buwana VI and Dipanagara. His comparisons between the Krendawahana meeting with that of Yalta have been left out.

6.4 TALKING UP "POLITICAL" HISTORY

One day his Highness Sinuhun Kanjeng Susuhunan Pakubuwana VI arrived near the forest of Krendawahana. According to myth, this forest in Krendawahana was the palace (*dhaton*) of Sang Batari Durga, so it is hallowed and haunted (*angker*). As the proverb says, "A man who approaches it is a dead man." Nonetheless His Majesty approached it, accompanied by his parents and courtesans as well as a troop of Dutch dragoons and their officers. Having come to the outskirts of the woods, those who accompanied him saluted him respectfully. His Highness and several courtiers then entered deep into the forest. His Majesty quickly managed to break away from the others. He continued to a small village in the centre of the forest to speak with *kyai* Maja and Raden Sentot Alibasah [son of Raden Rangga and leader of the rebel cavalry who will eclipse *kyai* Maja after the latter broke with Dipanagara following the battle of Gowok]. The next morning, when His Majesty returns to his palace, he explained that he disappeared (*kalap*) while looking for *sam-sam* water,[10] but met Batari Durga instead. Who is this Batari Durga? In the stories of Indian mythology, Batari Durga is a goddess who has the power to give death. So His Highness explained that his meeting with Batari Durga in the depths of forest of Krendawahana permitted him to reflect on the strategy of the war, on how to exterminate the Dutch army. That is why the password Krendawahana is used as a password to designate this encounter.

Just as in the ravines (or crater) of Mt Merapi (April–May, 1825 cf. Suyanto 1984, pp. 80–84) an allusion to the earlier meeting at Muntilan whose password was Candradimuka?) there had been a consultation on the policy and tactics of the war, in the forest of Krendawahana a discussion had been held on the strategy of the war. Thus those who went to the forest of Krendawahana were called *war wadana* (sub-district leaders).

They say that the "bandit" Dipanagara had already been able to enter the town of Surakarta, and that he had even penetrated the hamlets of Telukana and Slompratan, which would mean that he had almost reached the palace. In reality prince Dipanagara was going alone to the palace to speak with His Highness. In the course of this meeting the Dutch resident suspected the loyalty of the court and reinforced the guard. His Majesty ordered the palace soldiers to open fire at Slompratan. The chariot of prince Dipanagara which had been left along the way was quickly hidden (in the carriage stables?) of Baluwarti to the north-west of the palace. After these deliberations what was the attitude of K.G.P.A.H. Mangkunagaran II and the Sultan Cakraningrat of Madura?

With these final ambiguous insinuations the author seems to manifest the desire to compare those who openly collaborated with the Dutch from the beginning of the war (the neighbouring palace of the Mangkunagaran and the Madurese), with Paku Buwana VI whose attitude was more nuanced. It is not so sure that historians would find an enormous difference between the two. What interests the anthropologist in these recitations of supposed historical facts is the way in which myth and mythic palaces are brought in to shore up newly restored "events", rather than what factual foundation underlies these narratives. Nowhere else is any meeting between Paku Buwana VI actually described. It is insinuated as possible, however, and as Djatikusumo says Krendawahana is the "password" (*pasemon*) for such a meeting.

6.5 MEETING DURGA

"Thick, deep, secret or hard" forests are described by the Javanese word *werit* (*writ*). This term also means "inhabited by spirits", "lying in wait for prey". In the Asmara Supi story, there is a forest called Siluman (meaning "evil spirit"), where there exists a medicine which can cure the princess of Ngesam (cf. Ricklefs 1974, pp. 238–39 for all that follows). The queen of the spirits there, named Genawati (the Genukwatu in of the *Kidung Lelembut* of the *Serat Sakondhar*) shows that Asmara Supi is identified with the place where this medicine is found. Ricklefs suggests that Genawati, like other female spirits, may be simply a manifestation of the central deity Ratu Kidul, queen of the southern ocean. But, unlike the Yogyakarta region where the northern cult site is the male deity, Sapa Jagat, on the volcano Merapi, in the Surakarta region further east there are two symmetrical spirit queens, Durga to the north and the queen of the southern seas on the south coast. Indeed, as stated in Chapter 3, there are a multitude of forests all over Java each with its own spirit queen, only some of these being identified with the more important goddesses, geographical "pairs" of the same kind as Durga and Ratu Lara Kidul. Certainly as in the case of mystical teachers (*pandhita/pendeta*) "single pine" (Cemara Tunggal; Ricklefs 1974. p. 240, note 26), the queen of the south constantly takes on proper names as she has none of her own. This is generally not the case with Durga, however, except when she is the cursed form of Uma. There she is called the goddess "who is not" (*tan ana*; i.e. "comparable" to any other). As was discussed in Chapter 3, the fact that Ratu Kidul especially aids kings (Ricklefs 1974:, p. 240) is a basic dimension of Javanese spiritual and social geography. In this respect Durga is more dangerous.

Stories of visits to Durga can also be found locally in the hamlets around Krendawahana (cf. Ch. 8), but they belong to another framework with its own motivations. The overlap between all these narratives, with multiple personages and transposable places, lends itself to their retelling. For instance in the *Babad Serong* (1941, pp. 102–108; cf. Ch. 8, note 57)) we read that K.P.A. Soerjataningrat (son of Mangkunagaran II; former name, P.M. Panji Manguningrat) came to meditate at Durga's tertre with its nine ficus trees.

Finally, in another text, the *Serat Rajaweda* (cf. Ch. 8) describing the "disappearance in Gandamayu (charnel field, i.e. Krendawahana)", relates how prince Natakusuma, son of Paku Buwana IV and son-in-law of M.N. II. was lured into the invisible palace of Durga by the appearance of two purple does. Subjugated by the charms of Durga, the prince never returned. What is interesting about these two Javanese narratives is that they are primarily concerned about the possibility of meeting with Durga, while the Dutch concern was solely whether Paku Buwana VI was maintaining secret contacts with Dipanagara and his entourage, and therefore who went where and when. The recent cult of Paku Buwana VI as a national hero is in fact looking at the events of the 1820s with just this "Dutch" perspective at the same time as claiming a new appearance of Durga at her shrine. This narrative is at the same time both completely traditional and new.

To describe these divergent viewpoints, let us return to the details of the newspaper article in *Suara Merdéka*. The shining stone near Durga's tertre called the stone "for performing meditation" (*bangun tapa*) has been designated as marking the spot where Dipanagara received the Black Stork "kris" from Paku Buwana VI. The large stone there had always been described as shining (*gilang*), but it was also considered to be recipient or *kenthing* for the blood of sacrificed animals. This refers to the offering to Durga originally conceived to commemorate her victory over the general of the demon armies, *Mahisha* in Sanskrit, corrupted into high Javanese meaning buffalo (*maésa*). During the first half of this century, however, the villagers referred to this stone as the place where the demon Burisrawa had meditated prior to his attempt to win over the Black Lady (Lara Ireng), Sembadra the wife of Arjuna. This story is well known from shadow puppet theatre (cf. Kodiron 1962, pp. 28–34). Beginning in 1979 with the construction of the new sanctuary around this stone, the peasants in Krendawahana were being told that it had another history, another patron than the well-known ogre. Was the rapprochement between the name of the stone and the name of Paku Buwana VI "Bangun Tapa" coincidental?

The king's title, Bangun Tapa, derives from his visit on 6 June 1830 to Mancingan (Houben 1994, pp. 33–38) near the south coast, "close" to the invisible realm of Ratu Lara Kidul and not that of Durga, far to the north. His trip to Mancingan occurred at the end of Java War when all was lost. Paku Buwana VI was about to be forced to accept a humiliating settlement which his loyalty to the Dutch throughout most of the war should have permitted him to avoid. He was trying to impregnate himself with new spiritual force. He needed the kind of cosmic renewal that Sénapati Ingalaga, the founder of the dynasty, had received there on the south coast. Meditation on the graves of the kings from Sultan Agung onwards provided Javanese rulers with new *cahya*, the light of power. It is assumed that he went to a cave called Langsé, described in the *Serat Saloka Dharma* as a place for tapa or meditation (cf. Houben 1994, p. 35, note 48). In fact, all he got for his troubles was being accused by the Dutch of sedition and taken to Semarang and eventually to Ambon. What is clear from the Dutch accounts (Houben 1994, p. 34) is that already in 1828 Van den Bosch had considered Paku Buwana VI's loyalty dubious and that he seized on the unauthorized trip to Mancingan as the pretext for immediate exile.

Dipanagara himself had visited and meditated at eight holy places prior to undertaking his jihad. Ricklefs (1974, p. 247), reviewing the references to Lipura in the Pandak region south of Yogyakarta in the *Babad Tanah Djawi* and the *Baron Sakendar*, says that this was the site of the sacred black and yet shining stone, Séla Gilang. This was where, at the end of the sixteenth century, a shooting star fell next to the sleeping Sénapati. Both motifs are clearly being overlaid on the meditation stone of the ogre Burisrawa at Krendawahana on the occasion of the renewal of the offerings to Durga there.

It is easy to understand the presence of a kris amongst the regalia (*pusaka*) offered by Paku Buwana VI to Dipanagara: it personifies the support that the lineages of certain contemporaries of Paku Buwana VI wished to recall in 1979. What causes all these motifs to come together in Krendawahana today is the palpable trace of these events. In the 1983 film I made of the *Maésa Lawung* there, one sees the elderly aristocrats touching with their fingers the stone "for performing meditation" (*bangun tapa*) which the walls of the new sanctuary now surrounded. There were between ten and fifteen old men, and they spent fifteen minutes discovering the contours of the boulder with their aged fingers, commenting to each other on the various traces (*patilasan*) of this significant moment in Javanese history. Subtle traces indeed.

Starting from a newspaper article describing the renewal of a ritual, we have focused our attention on two innovations, two new meetings. The first is supposed to be of historical import, that between Dipanagara and Paku Buwana VI. Oddly enough it is the defeated rebel who has a solid historical reputation, while in the middle of the twentieth century the descendants of Paku Buwana VI are still trying to restore his honour. Their task is all the more difficult as the territory of Krendawahana is now in the hands of a subdistrict government. It has been two hundred years since the apanage system vanished. Today any "aristocrats" have the right to visit Krendawahana and pray there, but little more than that. Krendawahana has ceased to be the territory of either the Mangkunagarnan or Susuhunan's royal domain. The naming of Paku Buwana VI as a national hero some forty years ago does not seem to have improved his reputation in the mind of the average Javanese, for whom the landless lineages of Surkarta's aristocrats are irrelevant. The second encounter is accompanied by a photographic proof that a Hindu-Javanese spirit queen, Durga, traditional ally of the kings of Surakarta, still appears at the doors of her invisible realm. Why has the renewal of the *maésa lawung* offering at Krendawahana been seized upon to project these two encounters?

First consider the means of this renewal. We see the use of oral traditions of obscure origin consolidated by the written word (newspaper articles, and books, but also lectures and radio broadcasts) and photographic iconography for use in newspapers. Henceforth the national hero has a portrait and the goddess, a luminous avatar.

What of the political-military patronage which enabled the lineages of the various personages who Dipanagara was supposed to have met, at Krendawahana and elsewhere? We do not have the details of these relationships, but the kind of oral and genealogical history the different lineages were able to provide them with was not in and of itself suspect. As we saw in Chapter 5 the *trah* are in fact good sources for local history and their genealogies are relatively reliable. The fact that during the Java War (1825–30), the Dutch always suspected Paku Buwana VI of limited loyalty to their cause was enough to build up the password (*pasemon*) out of the place name Krendawahana, which allowed for the development of an ancillary cult near the tertre of Durga in this village.

I went back to interview *R. M.* Riya Jasadipura in May 1995, some twelve years after his radio broadcasts on the subject and eleven years after the publication of the 250-page "historical biography" on Paku Buwana VI's participation in the Java War. To suggest that his effort to renew Paku Buwana VI's reputation had not succeeded, he used the Javanese adage, "You cannot make a good walking cane out of old wood". That indeed seems to have been so. The walls surrounding the shining stone, where Dipanagara and Paku Buwana VI might have met, were cracked and leaning outwards towards the rice fields into which they were shortly to fall. Only a few old aristrocrats come out there once a year to touch with their fingers the nondescript contours of the boulder and talk to each other about a past meeting that has been forgotten, but more simply may never have happened.

The basis of that narrative had been other meetings, for instance that of Durga with Natakusuma. It was more traditionally Javanese to vanish as did Natakusuma than to be captured and exiled by the Dutch as was Paku Buwana VI. When he did leave his palace, to go to Mancingan to consult his deity (*déwa*, as the princes in his palace explained, Houben 1994, p. 36, note 51), or to seek the Queen of the Southern Seas as Nahuys later wrote (1852, p. 164), he met instead the resident of Yogyakarta, J.F.W. Nes and Lieutenant-Colonel B. Sollewijn (Houben 1994, p. 33, note 43; 34, note 44). They immediately arrested him and took him to the fort at Kotha Gedhé, near Yogyakarta. From there he was taken to Semarang and exiled to Ambon where he wrote his *Babad Bangun Tapa* (Wieringa 1994). What was accomplished in 1979 was a recycling of the *Maésa Lawung* ritual. The restoration of the tarnished reputation of Paku Buwana VI's lineage was quite unsuccessful, but the revival of an important and ancient ritual showed it to be no worse for having been in storage. Durga was certainly still present in Krendawahana, and now the princely cult could pursue its various interests there.

The exclusivity of royal lineages paralleled the exclusivity of their tax farmers in the royal apanage system. Once this system had been abolished, their mode of calculating proximity to a ruling or former king interested only themselves, while the Muslim lineages, on the other hand, based on continuing residence in the Kaliasa-Krendawahana area, or contacts through worship community networks around the graves there, were able to draw together large numbers of people living throughout the island. These worship communities would construct a number of mosques and constituted a means of uniting religious endeavour via a large network of common ancestors. Clearly the prestige that came from descending from such a lineage was as valuable, if not more so, than calculating one's descent from Paku Buwana VI.

6.6 APPENDIX: RECENT CHRONOLOGY OF TEXTS ON PAKU BUWANA VI

(1) Due to the intervention of Letjen G.P.H. Jatikusuma, Paku Buwana VI was reburied from Batugajah, Ambon to Imogiri arriving 13 March 1957; by 19 November 1958 the grave was finished and the *maéjan* or tombstone was placed on 19 December 1958 (Hadiwidjojo 1966, p. 13). This seems to imply that a building of the above ground was added to the grave a full year and a half later.

(2) Proclamation of Paku Buwana VI as "pahlawan kemerdekaan nasional Republik Indonesia" on 17 November 1964, announced at Balai Kota Surakarta on 10 December 1964.

(3) Two years later G.P.H. Hadiwidjojo in a lecture (in Javanese) in Solo (25 November 1966, pp. 4–5) claims that Paku Buwana VI had been unjustly accused of collaborating with the Dutch.

(4) G.P.H. Djatikusomo's lecture of 3 October 1971, some five years later, entitled the "Sejarah Politik: Sinuhun Kandjeng Susuhunan Paku Buwana VI" (mimeographed, 20pp. (in Javanese); patronized by a committee, "Kol-Dalem Paku Buwana VI" representing Paku Buwana VI's descendants.

(5) Soekro Djagosarkoro in Karanganyar (23 July 1976) privately publishes an eleven-page article "Kisah ringkas perjuangan R.A. Sumirah, R.A. Khadiyah, R.A. Marwiyah and Kyai Suhodo Som membantu Pangéran Diponegoro perang melawan penjajahan Belanda (1825–1830)." His sources are five history books (H.F. Aukes, Sulistyo Wiromandoko; Sanusi Pane; Dr. Sukamto; L. Yama) and the oral testimony of descendants of the "heros" figuring in the title above.

(6) Raden Mas Riyo Yosodipuro's eleven-page mimeogaphed article (July 1980) "Sejarahdalem Sampéyandalem Ingkang Sinihun Kangjeng Susuhunan Pakubuwono VI Pahlawan Kemerdekaan Nasional Republik Indonesia". The author is the *santana canggahdalem* (=fourth generation descendant of) Paku Buwana VI.

(7) Newspaper article "Sesaji 'Mahesa Lawung' untuk Memperingati Kembalinya P. Sambernyawa", *Suara Merdéka*, 31 March 1982, pp. 12, 20.

(8) Below follows a résumé of the very inventive newspaper article by Murhono Hs., "Sunan Paku Buwana VI Berperan Perang Diponagoro" in *Sinar Harapan* (12 January 1983):

If Paku Buwana VI met Pangeran Dipanagara but only really helped the Dutch, why was he banished to Ambon, just as Pangeran Dipanagaran was to Menado? The author throws suspicion on Dutch sources, and puts forward instead the *Sejarah Negari Dalem Surakarta* (cf. Museum Radya Püstaka no. 341) a text used by K.P.H. Jatikusomo. The Surakarta *kraton* was supposed to have used the "*kekuatan mistik kebathinan Islam*" in this war during which the main concern of Paku Buwana VI was to reunite the two halves of the kingdom.

R.M. Supardan, the future Paku Buwana VI, at the age of ten would have been inspired by the sight of his grandfather Paku Buwana IV fighting the British. Appearance of a mysterious *syekh arab* comparing the three sons of Paku Buwana IV with three *kurma* or fruit dates; he claimed that all three would reign. Paku Buwana VI was seventeen years old when he acceded to the throne in 1822. Paku Buwana VI had the legality to conduct a war as opposed to a revolt, while Dipanagara could only conduct a *pemberontakan* (revolt), were it not for the fact that as an ulama he could lead the people in a jihad against the *kafir*. But as Murhono explains:

"*Tetapi Sunan Paku Buwana VI terikat dengan perjanjian tentang bantuan yang harus dikerahkan apabila Belanda mendapat perlawanan. Untuk melakasanakan dua maksud yang saling bertentangan, Paku Buwana VI menyerahkan bala bantuan yang dipimpin oleh K.P.H. Kusumoyudo* [on this prince, cf. Carey 1981, XXVI], *dan memberikan bantuan kepada P. Diponegoro.*"

"This kind of behaviour is not like that of a chameleon but a tactic." Paku Buwana VI did everything secretly, using "sandi sastra". It is said that Paku Buwana VI disappeared into the forest of Krendawahana meeting with Batari Durga. What really happened was an officialisation of the Bulkiyo troop (the core division of Prince Dipanagara), named after an aid of Batari Durga who disposed of the power of death ..." So Paku Buwana VI confided the *pusaka* weapons to R.A. Sumirah: a saddle called Kyai Sabukangin (sash of the wind), a sword called Kyai Janur (light green coconut leaf), a lance, Kyai Tundhungmunggsuh, an arrow Kyai Sirwinda and a package Kyai Karumbo. To Dipanagara he gave a kris Sandhanglawé, the match of Yogyakarta kris called Kyai Wisobontulu.

Paku Buwana VI let it be known that, riding on the back of the fish Kyai

Kutuk, he entered the crater of Candrodimuko, the crater of Mt Merapi. What is true is that he went to the cave of the King (Gua Raja) above the country estate at Sela with his messenger, Kyai Imam Rosyi or Kyai Kuthuk Singomanjat to meet and discuss with Pangeran Dipanagara.

During the battle of Tanjung Anom (Gawok, Kartasura) was Pangeran Dipanagara shot with a golden bullet by Paku Buwana VI? Of course not. What really happened was that at the country estate of Jatiroga, he gave Pangeran Dipanagara gold to cover the cost of the war.

Everything Paku Buwana VI did was done in secret. It was said that he went to the south coast to pray for a son, but a man of his spiritual strength didn't need to.

Paku Buwana VI was making a war and Pangeran Dipanagara was executing it. Pangeran Dipanagara reported to Paku Buwana VI regularly, even in the palace at Surakarta.

When Paku Buwana VI met Pangeran Dipanagara in Jatimon in November 1829 he was ready to declare total war. Pangeran Dipanagara was to attack the fortress in Magelang on Christmas 1829. But his capture at Klaten in December 1829 stopped this plan and it is attributed to someone's treason. He was banished to Ambon and later shot.

Pangeran Dipanagara and Paku Buwanan VI's joint effort failed because of feudalism; it was not yet a people's war.

(9) Notes on S.C. Headley's interview with R.M. Riyo Yosodipuro, after his Surakarta Radio broadcast on local history (3 March 1983) entitled "Pembacaan Buku Sejarah" (8 March 1983).

(10) Newspaper article "'Caos Dahar' di patisasan Krendowahono dari Kraton Surakarta", *Buana Minggu*, 13 March 1983, pp. 4, 10. R.M. Riyo Yosodipuro is the source of most of the journalist's reporting which highlights Paku Buwanan's meeting there.

(11) Film by S.C. Headley on the 1983 Maesa Lawung: *le Buffle et la Reine quatre rituels à Java central* (1984; 50 minutes)

(12) Sunar Tri Suyanto, *Pahlawan Kemerdékaan Nasional RI Sinuhun Banguntapa*, (1984).

(13) Pak Ton's article "Sesaji Wiludjengan Nagari Mahésa Lawung", *Jayabaya*, 9 December 1990, p. 8; an enlarged version of the author's same article is recyled in Jayabaya in December 1993, pp. 40, 51) containing a reference to Paku Buwanan VI's meeting with Dipanagara. It also describes the guardians (*jurukunci*) of Krendawahana as being important Muslim figures: Kyai Yahya (Sambirejo, Kaliasa) and Kyai Martaya (=Murtaja) mentioned above as the person who retreived Paku Buwanan VI (or in other versions Paku Buwanan IV) from the forest.

(14) S. C. Headley's interview with R.M. Riyo Yosodipuro in May 1995, in which he described this reconstituted history as "a walking cane made from old wood", that is to say a useless object. For another aspect of Radèn Ngabéhi Yasadipura's activities in Surakarta, cf. Pemberton (1994, p. 235).

NOTES

1. An initial revival of this ritual occurred on 17 February 1975, but it was only fully celebrated in 1979.
2. *Séna* in Javanese means army; here one should probably read *sana*, i.e. place.
3. This is probably a misunderstanding on the journalist's part. What one finds on the stone are divine traces (*patilasan*, not magic formula *palarisan*).
4. Hadiwidjoyo (1972, p. 120). "A deep purification of the soul ... necessary because one is about to confront the presence of invisible spirits."
5. LOr 2163, XXI.24-9, p. 277
6. P. Carey of Trinity Collge Oxford graciously gave me a copy of this lecture.
7. Cf. Ch. 1.4. Also, Anderson on Sukarno's grave (1973, pp. 61–72); Pemberton (1994, ch. 4); and S. Sidamukti (1928) on Mangkunagaran VI's grave in Banalaya.
8. Cf. the coverage of Hamengku Buwana's son marriage in *Parikesit*, 20 May 1974 and *Suara Merdéka*, 21 May 1996.
9. Declaration no. 294, signed by the President of the Indonesian Republic on 17 November 1964.
10. I.e. *janjam* the name of a sacred well in Mecca and hence the water taken from that well. The parallel between the quest of Dewa Ruci for the water of immortality (*banyu urip*) in the underwater palace of Ratu Lara Kidul and the use of the well in Krendawahana used for more banal ablutions seems unjustified.

PART III

INVOKING THE COSMOS, MAGNIFYING ALLAH: STRUCTURING A LANDSCAPE IN THE SEVENTEENTH AND EIGHTEENTH CENTURIES

7

THE KHANDAVA FOREST IN INDIA
AND ITS JAVANESE DEMON QUEEN

The passage of time has left its mark on the structure of inhabited space around Kaliasa but nowhere more than in the former forest of Krendawahana. A once free-floating toponym, now attached to the south back of the Cemara River, evokes in the minds of the Javanese peasant a whole series of associations deriving from oral literature and the wayang. Denys Lombard has summarized the aura of Javanese sacred forests (*alas angker*) and the typically Javanese vision of the forest found in literature (1974, p. 478; translation S.C. Headley):

> ... the echo of a society in the process of change which seeks to disengage itself from its ecological context felt to have become outmoded, a society which is elaborating its own notion of "savagery". The opposition between a cleared, cultivated and domesticated space as opposed to savage, primitive, dangerous space. Yet at the same time the ambivalence of the forest where there continue to live in front line position constituted by hermitages, those replaceable supernatural forces which only the *resi* (seers) know how to reconcile, and which any true hero must provoke and dominate if he wants to profit in the valleys from the esteem of his fellows.

On the other hand the forest as a school of nature, the inspiration of the poet, so important in India, gained wide favour in the Javanese court literature known as *kawi* (Zoetmulder 1974, pp. 163–64). This explains how the toponym of Khāndava (i.e., Krendawahana) appeared in the Javanese late tenth-century prose translation of the *Ādiparwa*, the first volume of the immense Indian epic of the *Mahābhārata*. This old Javanese text, with a dedication (*manggala*) to Siwa, derives from one north Indian version of the Mahābhārata. In Javanese it has been reduced to about 36 per cent of its original length in Sanskrit. Each part (*parva*) translated individually into Javanese varies in different proportions from its Sanskit original.

The date of the translation implies the prior existence of palace culture which is amply attested in Central Java at this period. As if to tease our imaginations, there was once a temple (*candi*) dedicated to Siwa and Durga some seven kilometres to the south of Krendawahana in what is now the village of Nusukan, on the northern outskirts of Surakarta, or city of the eighteenth century. The eight-armed Durga statue there (75 centimetres high) is indeed a Mahishāsuramardanī.[1] The *Oudheidkundig Verslag* (1917, p. 74) dates this site by its bricks to the period of Dieng (eighth century). It lay close to the recent royal Mangkunagaran cemetery in Banalaya.

Thus the north-south ritual axis[2] of Surakarta has been given importance in a number of ways over a millennium. Obviously, by the time renewal of palace culture in south Central Java took place in the sixteenth century, the flowering of old Javanese literature had past, but the renown of this famous forest, whose apocalyptic destruction in the Mahābhārata epic, presented below, remained.

It is tempting to pass over these old literary traces of Indian culture and go directly on to the "Javanese" forest of Gandamayit (odour of cadavers), as the forest of Krendawahana is known in the shadow puppet theatre. Yet the giving of a Sanskrit toponym, Krendawahana, to this particular forest even if it is recent (eighteenth century?), cannot have been innocent. The court centre (no peasant would have come up with such a *lieu-dit*) was making an explicit appeal for the protection of the palace/kingdom to its south on behalf of "Javanized" Durga, who was known as the queen of the demon armies inhabiting a forest with such a name. Earlier, the creation of old Javanese literary works dedicated to deities like Siwa was to "promote the invincibility of the king and the prosperity of the world", as mpu Panulah says in the epilogue of the *Hariwangsa* (Zoetmulder 1974, pp. 173–85). Dedications (*manggala*) describe literary works as if they were temples for the chosen deity (*iṣṭadewatā*). There is a generic Tantric culture at work here, which is neither specifically Hindu nor Buddhist, but involves establishing the god in one's heart as if it were a statue by means of *yantra* (hymns, flowers, mudra, and mantra).

Political anthropology may be used as an introduction to historical anthroplogy, as Maurice Bloch remarked. One could study the *maesa lawung* in the same perspective as John Pemberton (1994), that is to say as the use of ritual as a way of escaping the colonial authority by repeating a Javanese past, deemed by the Dutch to be harmless. It fitted in with the use of the category of customary law (*adat*) by the colonial authorities, a fence around natives, while in the late 1970s its revival used Javanism to restore lineages. The cult of Durga in the forest of Krendawahana has kept alive the last vestiges of this cultural ecology through the annual royal offerings made there and the people's use of the shrine for their own private concerns. The myths of the *Ādiparwa* (1958, pp. 112–22) may not have directly inspired any very famous play of the contemporary *wayang* theatre, but it did put this forest "on the map". This is not to say that any peasant identified the forest near the Kuruksetra in the *Mahābhārata*. with a forest in Java. The Javanese forest on the south bank of the Cemara River disappeared two hundred years ago, but not the vision of the forest that their ancestors had. Only the myths remain. Below we have summarized the myth as it appears in the first book of the old Javanese *Ādiparwa*.[3]

7.1 THE BURNING OF THE KHANDAVA FOREST

Krsna and Arjuna are strolling along the banks of the Yamunā river during the visit of Krsna to the forest of Khāndhava near the Kuru-ksetra. Abhimanyu the son of Sambadra and Arjuna has just been born. During a banquet a Brahmin arrives, who is none other than the god of fire, Agni. He has come to burn the forest of Khāndhava, which is protected by the storm god Indra whose friend the snake Taksaka lives there. In the Sanskrit version it is explained that Agni is ill and that the total destruction by fire of this forest will cure him. Other divinities bring Arjuna and Krnsa the necessary magic arms to fight Indra.

The conflagration is identical to that of the end of an epoch (*yuga*) with its eschatological fire. The animals all run amok trying to escape as they are shot down by Arjuna's arrows. The aquatic animals are burned alive. Indra arrives with his mountainous black clouds. Thunder rang out sounding like the end of the world (in old Javanese, *mahapralaya*). Indra dropped a first ocean on the forest. Arjuna raised a roof of magic arrows to protect the fire.

The flight of the snake Taksaka's spouse ends when its head is severed by Arjuna's arrow, but its child Asvasena flies off to Indra. Finally Indra ceases throwing oceans on the blazing forest when he hears that its father, the snake Taksaka, has escaped the blaze. Arjuna and Krsna then continue unimpeded their destruction.

Several titans, notably Maya their leader, rather than burn to death, take service as slaves of Krsna. Four quail (*puyuh*) also escaped and later populated the extinct forest. Why they were allowed to escape is explained. One of the quail, Mandapāla, had been a monk (*pendeta brahmacari*) but on returning from the realm of *dharmaraja*, became incarnate in a quail. He supplicates Agni to spare his children to continue in the dharma of the brahmin. The sacrifices of their father and the devotion of their mother faced with the encroaching blaze moved Agni to compassion.

This résumé of a ten-page myth from the Sanskrit *Mahābhārata* about an apocalyptic fire is the last episode the Javanese *Ādiparwa*. I have condensed it here by leaving aside its literary developments. It will be commented on at the end of this chapter, once we have plotted out other purely local myths that have replaced it in Java. So *kārandha* (kind of duck, cf. the Javanese *Ramayana* VII, 31.21 and the *Ādiparwa* above) while it was translated as *puyuh*, gave the modern Javanese toponym Krenda.[4]

On the other hand the Sanskrit toponym *khāndava* could not to be translated into Javanese. It was simply the place name for a forest in the *kuruksetra* (the "clearing of the Kuru clan") near to the town of Khāndhava-prastha, in other words the region of modern Delhi. Already used in the *Tāndya-Brahmana* XXV.3 and the *Taittirīya Aranyaka*, the root of this place name is obviously *khand*, to destroy, as in *khanda-pralaya*, a partial destruction of the universe up to the third heaven. The antithesis creation-destruction which structures the whole *Māhabhārata* (Biardeau 1971, *passim*) does not seem to have struck the Javanese mythological imagination. So abetted by the confusion between *k* and *kh*, the first term of the toponym, *kāranda*, became *krenda* while *dahana* (the burning of) was taken over as *wahana*. *Vāna*, forest in Sanskrit (*wana* in Javanese) was lost in the sense that it translated independently of the original Sanskrit compound as *alas*, giving *alas Krendawahana* (the Krendawhana forest), from the Sanskrit, Khāndavavānadahana (the burning of the Khāndhava forest).

We have seen that the *Ādiparva* apocalypsis has been lost in translation; it remains to be seen how Durga came to be associated with this new Javanese forest with its foreign name. The presence of the quail next to Durga's son Kala in the Javanese iconography of the thirty weeks cannot be sufficient. One might have thought that the burning of this forest, being called explicitly a *mahapralaya*, displays the essential traits of character of Siva whose immanent energy or *sakti* is Umā/Kalī/Durgā. But clearly we have no proof yet that the word *dahana* (burning) connoted to the Javanese *pralaya*. In fact while meaning "death" and "epidemic" in Javanese, this term *pralaya* (Pigeaud's dictionary 1938, p. 479) associated with the vocabulary of the *wayang*, came to mean the day of resurrection, i.e. judgement (Arabic, *qiyāma*; Prawiroatmojo 1975, p. 108).

None of this Sanskrit data gives any clues why Durga should have come to be associated with the Krendawahana forest. Yet the alternative name for Krendawhana is Gandamayit (the odour of cadavers) which in the *Sri Tanjung*[5] (Prijono 1938) and later *wayang* is a cemetery or charnal ground where a witch, a form of Durga may be found (Headley 1991). This means the toponym Gandamayit or Gandamayu has been associated to the place name Krendawahana.

7.2 DURGA'S VENERATION IN JAVA: FROM INDIAN MYTHS TO JAVANESE ICONOGRAPHY

If the burning of the Krenda forest could not have been understood in Java in the same way as by the Indians, how did the Javanese, great connoisseurs of the *Mahābhārata*, understand it? There exists a recent "classical" Javano-Balinese poem, the *Khāndavavānadahana*; inside Java however (as opposed to Bali where this poem "survived"), it probably remained unknown. Why in Java is it Durga who is associated with Krendawahana and not Agni and Indra, Arjuna and Krsna? The Javanese repertory of the shadow puppet theatre, the principal means of popularizing the *Mahābhārata* outside the palace literati, can not explain the *Ādiparva*'s reading of this toponym. The Javanese *wayang* plays that refer to the toponym of Krendawahana,[6] do so only in terms of the invisible kingdom of Durga that lies in this forest and not in terms of any apocalyptic fire. It is with Javanese myths that it is connected, not Indian.

Is the Durga so often portrayed in Javanese stone iconography[7] the one associated with Krendawahana, where her statue was taken away some sixty years ago? No! Certainly this iconography[8] derived from the widely known Indian poem as the *Devī-Māhātmyam*, found in the *Mārkandeya-Purāna*, and the *Devī-bhāgavata* (fifth *skandha*).[9] In India the *Devī-Māhātmyam* rivals the *Gītā* for popularity, as the iconography of Durga's victory over the giant buffalo rivals the iconography of Siva. But although this iconography of Durga is widespread, no text, no play in Java provides a source for it. It seems that this iconography travelled to Java in stone or bronze but not in writing.[10]

What "installed" Durgā in the forest of Krendawahana was no particular myth, but the apanage system and the ritual offerings of the palace in the four cardinal directions of its kingdom. The king placed Durga there for protection, as the general of her demon armies could protect him. Durga, the "slender lady" is already found in the Central Javanese temple of Prambanan (Lara Jongrang; 856 A.D.), in the northern niche of the Siwa temple, associated with Visnu as Srī (one name for the goddess) and she "remains" there today.[11] Possibly she is no longer playing a role in the same myth in the massive thirteenth century Durga of Singasari (now in the Leiden Museum), but her northern orientation remains the same, as does her colour association (black). This total social canvas of the palace in the centre and the protective offering sites with their divinities in the four cardinal directions, is new or foreign to

Java only in the sense that before there were kingdoms it would have had no meaning. Durga enters Java along with kingship. Nevertheless, the indigenous Javanese disposition of the five colours gradually takes over from the Indian one.[12] The kinship links between the king and his Javanese predecessor-kings motivates the construction of temples for ancestors and divinities to protect the royal lineage. Once there is a kingdom, this articulation takes on a cultural expression whose forms, beauty and permanence (these monuments remain in place after the dynasty has vanished) tempt us into thinking that we can appreciate the belief systems or ideology that underlay them in their time. Really all that is possible is to specify very partial fragments of such mentalities (Jordaan and Wessing 1996).

Two facts initially strike the Western ethnographer. One is that Agni's burning the forest of Krendawahana in the end of the *Ādiparwa* is not one of the tales translated into modern verse (*tembang cilik*) in the eighteenth century when the *Mahābhārata* in old Javanese had become incomprehensible. This story is hardly known either in writing or through the *wayang* shadow puppet theatre. Secondly Durga is venerated in a village once surrounded by a forest with a "Sanskrit" toponym. Until 1949 and then again beginning in 1979 the two palaces of Surakarta shared, through an alternating schedule, the offering of the blood of a buffalo. In the case of the Susuhunan it was transferred from the palace kitchen where *tumenggung* Gandarasa was in charge of preparing the offerings for the tertre of Durga. After the rebellion of Prince Dipanagara (1825–30) the advance of Islam in this region went unchallenged, but nor did it challenge the continuation of this older cult. Rather Islam was part and parcel of the same royal political cosmology. The *abdi dalem* Suranata used Muslim prayers over the buffalo's blood before it left the palace and again as it was offered to Durga in her cult (translation in Chapter 9). What has survived through the centuries is this cohesion, enriched certainly in the seventeenth century by Islam, but nonetheless possessed of its own coherence. If anything has jeopardized it, it was the appearance of the Indonesian Republic which led to the suspension of the offerings for thirty years. Their renewal in 1979 may yet prove to be abortive.

During my first stay in the village of Krendawahana (1973–74) I asked the village *lurah* (headman) if there was not a *pundhèn* (place of worship, from *mundhi*, to honour or venerate) in the village. He said that Batari Durga was the queen of an invisible kingdom, centred on the tertre of their *pundhèn* which was in the centre of the last vestiges of a sacred forest called Krendawahana. No one else in the village had much to add to this brief account and for several months that was all there was to be known. A search in the palace archives, on the basis that they might have been constituted during the annual organization of their offering, revealed that the accounting department of the Mangkunagaran palace had indeed kept such records. This left me in the awkward position of knowing more about Durga's cult and the later mantra used than the villagers did.

When I gave the village headman a transcription of these prayers which I had found along with the accounts of the costs of these offerings, this stimulated his *kejawèn* (Javanese religious) leanings, and henceforth we had much to talk about. Sastrodiwiryo had been using another *pundhèn* nearby that of Durga, created in his garden some thirty years before by the "Resident", Bapak Sudiro, who had encountered Visnu Trimurti while trying to find the exact spot of Durga's kingdom. At least that is how the village tradition described the foundation of this secondary *pundhèn*. This shrine has since crumbled beyond recognition. The old lurah often spent his nights in a hut in this garden.

Pilgrimages to Durga's shrine immediately to the west involved spending the night there, but not without appropriate preparation for the spirits and especially those of the dead which can be seen at night. What is more, the villagers of Krendawahana, the *lurah* excluded, tended to avoid Durga's shrine. The only normal reason to pass by there would have been to reach the village secretary's rice fields: the path led nowhere except to Durga.

A concrete effect of the presence of Durga's tertre in their village was to make any performance of shadow puppet theatre taboo. In the past the *lurah* used to organize *tayuban* dances for entertainment during circumcision and marriage ceremonies, but eventually these were frowned upon as occasions for drinking and light debauchery. The village Muslims did not try to exterminate Durga's cult, but the more strict amongst them said all one would find there were little devils (*sétan*).

If I have taken the time to describe my informants, it should now be clear why; much of the background on this cult came from the milieu of the palace and its aristocrats. Even the village headman in Krendawahana was a *radèn* (low-ranking nobility) from Bekonang to the east of Surakarta, appointed by the last prince of the Mangkunagaran house just after the Second World War and therefore in some sense inheritor of their royal ideology.

The pilgrims came from the towns and cities of central and east Java on the eves of Selasa-Kliwon or Jemuwah-Legi (propitious days in the Javanese thirty-five-day "month"). In the early 1970s about a hundred and fifty people a year took the trouble to sign the guest book. Their contact with the villagers was limited. At the time there was not a single shop in the village, so they had to bring their food with them and were allowed to take water from a public well built there. One small pavilion (*balai*) just to the west of the tree growing out of the summit of Durga's tertre provided them with rest and a place to prepare offerings, before going to sit at the foot of her tertre, that is at the south end facing north just as one would find a statue of Durga in a early Javanese temple complex like Prambanan. To the rule that most of the pilgrims to this shrine where from outside the area, there was one exception which the *lurah* impressed upon me, that of *radèn* Pradigdo, member of the nearby Kaliasa Muslim lineage and local eccentric recluse. He came for three days and three nights on one occasion, fasting strictly and meditating at this favourable source. Leaving aside the restaurant owners who come to Krendawahana to get blessed with quick riches, the clientele of Durga's shrine can be divided into those who practise meditation (Muslim or otherwise), and those who confine their religious devotions to brief formulaic prayers with all the conventions that it entails. One should not be completely taken in by reforming Muslims polemics against ritual offerings at this kind of *pundèn*. Some people, including Muslims, come here to meditate for hours on end and do not use black magic.

By way of conclusion, it is impossible to find in the contemporary praxis at the shrine any trace of the burning of the Khāndhavavana described in the *Ādiparwa*. In East Java, where Durga's son Kala is associated nominally with the god of fire Agni, one might find some role for her son in the making of this conflagration. It might be that in Central Java Durga's ambiguous role as queen of the demons, making her both *deva* and *asura*, indicates why her victory over the demon buffalo Mahisha has been remembered at this tertre. Those who remember it, of course, are the palace officials who have the task of annually preparing the water buffalo's blood offerings and bringing them out to the *pundhèn*. But there is more history here than they are aware of.

7.3 INDIAN AND JAVANESE FORESTS FROM THE MAHĀBHĀRATA

In India the passage of Durga into the camp of the gods, indeed as Siva's consort, seems to date roughly from the period of the first contacts between the Aryans and the Dravidians. It is useful to pause over this momentarily, for we are looking in Java for a link between Durga and Agni, the fire god. In the *Rig Veda*, Varuna and Indra fought in the camp of the demon *asura*, until the storm god Indra killed the dragon (*ahi*), who had encircled the mountain thus barring the descent of the waters, and became Vrtrahan (the Vrtra killer). This ambiguity in early Indo-European mythology is so profound that in Iran the *ahura* (=*asura*) became the gods and the *daiva* (=*deva*) became the demons, the reverse of their nomenclature in India.

The attacks of the *asura* against the gods continued well beyond the Vedic period to characterize Indian Purānic cosmogony and the famous victory of Durga over the giant buffalo Mahisha is nothing more than an expression of this. In certain rural cults one even finds traces that this enemy was a kind of Siwa, known to have been horned in the pre-Aryan Harappa culture. Damodar D. Kosambi traces the pre-Vedic origins of Durga in this way (1970, p. 62; translation S.C. Headley):

> ... but it is not to the pastoral populations (*gavali*) that one should attribute the construction of the original megaliths; they contented themselves with reusing megaliths and carved stones for altars and funerary tumuli. Their masculine god, the one who was going to become Mhasoba, had no consort originally and was for a time in conflict with the original mother goddess of the gatherers. Sometimes one finds primitive altars where one sees the mother goddess doing in the demon buffalo Mhasoba and then four hundred metres further along one finds her married to the same Mhasoba, whose name is only slightly modified. The reflection of this situation in Brahmanism is Parvatī [Durgā] consort of Siva but crushing Mahishāsura. Parvatī sometimes returns to her origins by trampling down Siva as well. It is significant that the tricephalous prototype of Siva represented in an Indus valley seal shows him with a head-dress of buffalo horns.

And concerning the masking of the rural origin of some cults of many of these cults, Kosambi adds (1970, pp. 71–72):

> When a cult spreads and becomes popular, the god is often identified with Siva or Visnu, the goddess becoming Parvatī, Laksmī or some other Brahmanized divinity. The most interesting are the goddesses who are the object of an intense cult, but in a very limited area and whose name has no etymology: Mengai, Mandhrai, Udalai, Songjai, Kumbhalja, Jhanjhani, etc. The final "-ai" signifies mother.

For some thousand years the Javanese kings used the motif of the goddess killing the demonic buffalo in their major temple constructions. From the sixteenth century, they started making offerings to the four cardinal directions in a less grandiose manner, of the kind which has survived down to the present day at the modest shrine to Durga. The dating of the texts and iconographic motifs does not answer problems posed by this evolution, but will provide a useful cadre to frame our comparative data. This initial cadre is Indian.

Malamoud[13] recalls the definition of man in the Brāhmana: a sacrificial victim capable of sacrificing:

> If it is true that certain sacrifices need be made in the forest, nonetheless sacrifices are basically the work of the *grama* [the village as opposed to the forest, *aranya*] or rather the *gramya* man, not only because the victim (or the vegetable offering) necessarily belonged to the village sphere, except for the soma plant, but also because the sacrificer could only be a married householder, possessing fire and disposing of the necessary riches to procure the material of the oblation and what to pay the celebrants.

A *vānapratha*, that is to say an *asrama*, is therefore a mixture of village and forest unless it is inhabited exclusively by ascetics (*samyāsin*) using only stone or wood tool or who, having even abandoned these as well as the use of their hands, use solely their mouths as do the beast of the forest.

The ambience of a forest residence (*vānapratha*) in Java took on another allure by defining itself against the palace with its grass-free foreground, *alun-alun*.[14] Denys Lombard (1974, p. 478) has qualified this space as a memorial to the original effort that founded the social group as well as the authority which has power over it. The virgin forest where man dares to enter is beyond human boundaries.

> Nonetheless the forest, domain of the spirits and the effluvium remains ambivalent. It is always in some hermitage on an isolated mountainside that the *resi* reside, ascetics who have learnt the secrets of plants and things, who will heal a wounded hero with his balms and confide to him finally absolute knowledge (*ilmu*). (Lombard 1974, p. 482)

The Indian version of this dual vision dominates the Indian myth of the *Mahābhārata* epic where the descendants of Pandu, having lost their kingdom in a game of dice to those of Kuru, are exiled in a forest. Their attempt to leave the forest and join battle with their opponents is a combat latent with the destruction of the world (Renou and Filliozat 1947, vol. I, p. 386).

One must admit that the tissue of the epic contains some incoherence, for instance the place of the burning of the Khāṇḍava forest at the end of the *Ādiparva*. Recapitulating the overture to the eighteen-day battle between the Kurava and the Pandava, this episode is present in the quasi-totality of the manuscripts cited by the Poona critical edition. The narrative evokes dramatic war-like gestures, and is reluctant to disclose its source in the cosmogonies, so that when it comes to an event like the apocalyptic burning of this forest, it is hardly able to make a smooth transition. The sequence of episodes preceding it are the following:

— Kidnapping of Subadrā, the sister of Krsna by Arjuna during the eleventh year of his exile.

— At the end of the twelfth year Arjuna returns to the Khāndhavaprastha and to Draupadī who inhabits its capital, Indraprastha.

— Birth of Abhimanyu, child of Subadrā and Arjuna.

— Birth of Sutasoma, child of Draupadī and Bhimasena.

— [Beginning of the Khāndava Parva, the chapter of the burning of the Khāndava forest.]

— The golden age under the reign of Yudhisthira

— During a feast on the banks of the Yamunā discord breaks out.

— Arjuna and Vaudeva (Krsna) separate themselves from the drunken women and meet a brahmin of golden colouring;

— The king Janamejaya asks the epic-teller Vaiśampāyana to explain why Agni wants to devour the Khāndava forest. In the B.O.R.I. (Poona) edition (cf. note vol. 1.215.11) this incident is relegated to appendix I(118).

— Vaiśampāyana says she will only repeat the story of the conflagration as it is told by the resi in the Purāna.

— Thus begins the story of the king Svetaki who after meditating on mount Kailasa asks Rudra-Siva to help him make a hundred-year-long sacrifice. Rudra-Siva replies by demanding a twelve-year-long libation of ghee (cf. note to vol. I. 217, Poona edition).

— Having drunk these continual libations, Agni begins to lose his colour and strength and ceases to shine. Brahma tells him he can return to normal by eating the fat of the inhabitants of the Khāndava forest which Agni had already burnt once, but which had become the haunt of the enemies of the gods, the *asura*. The excerpt from the Purāna ends here.

— With the aid of Vayu (the wind god), Agni is going to burn the forest seven times over, but to do so asks Brahma to take care of the impediments that Indra will create. Brahma promises to incarnate himself in Nara and Narayana (Arjuna and Vasudeva) to whom the necessary magic weapons will be given.

— Seeing the ritual massacre of the inhabitants of the forest beginning as they flee from the fire of Agni and are slaughtered by Arjuna and Krsna's weapons, the gods ask Indra, that enemy of the demons (*asura*): "Has the time come for the end of the world (*pralaya*)?" He does not answer, but rains down the great deluge which is unable to stop the fire. A battle is engaged next between Indra on the one side and Agni, Arjuna and Krsna on the other, whose literary style is clearly epic.

— Indra killer of Vrta (Vedic demon who held back the waters; I.219) understood that the victory of Nara and Narayana (Arjuna and Krsna) is ordained by destiny. The gods leave the field of battle and with Indra retired to heaven.

— Agni swallows all the inhabitants of the forest, who fleeing the forest were struck down by the arms of Krsna and Arjuna. For fifteen days the destruction of the forest continues unimpeded by any intervention of the gods.

— Agni spares six inhabitants: the snake Asvasena, the demon Maya and the four quail. Their story evokes the compassion of Agni;

— The four quail hymn the glory of Agni who saved them.

— That is how the god of fire with the aid of Arjuna and Krsna consumed the forest of Khāṇḍava for the well-being of the world.

In her *Etudes Mythologiques Hindoue* (III), Madelaine Biardeau (1971, p. 75) comments that any *pralaya* or apocalyptic destruction of the world, even if not inserted in a cosmogony, "… can be considered as a cosmic funeral where the cremation is followed by the immersion of the ashes in the water". A major incoherence of our narration is identified by Biardeau's comparative study of *pralaya* from which she concludes that: "… the phase of burning is placed under the aegis of Rudra or Kalāgni or Kalāgnirudra or Kala,[15] whereas the flood cast Nārāyana in the main role." The entire theme of Nārāyana (Visnu) who sleeps on the 'single wave' (*ekārnava*), that is to say the 'remainder' (*sesha*), the coiled serpent, seems absent from the end of the *Ādiparva*. But one can ask what role the rains of Indra played earlier in the narrative. As Biardeau remarks (1971, p. 74; cf. 212), "Everything happens as if the flood, by putting an end to the destruction of the fire, was transforming the ruins of the old world into a fertile chaos, pregnant with the world to come, where Brahma will have his creatures reborn."

Notice the indifference of the epic tradition to the basic themes here. In the Sanskrit as well as the Javanese version what is evoked is simply a massacre. This terrible destructive power, according to Biardeau (1976, p. 127) serves as a trope for sacrifice in the Purāna since "… the cosmic fire of the Purāna was conceived of as a sacrifice of a particular kind, for one is to see in it a funerary sacrifice, but whose 'remainder' (*śeṣa*) was nonetheless important for the ulterior destiny of the individual and the world." Biardeau's study of Purānic *yuga* (ages) and *kalpa* (eras) is useful here (1976, pp. 121–35).[16]

Having established the deeper structure of the *avatara* myths, Biardeau shows how the epic myth makes the *avatāra* the model for the king (1976, pp. 203–17). The myth of Parsurama finds its prolongation by passing from one *yuga* to another via the *avatāra* of Visnu. Almost immediately the *asura* take over and the earth complains to Brahma. Then Visnu's *avatāra* are given two unusual turns. The gods are initally asked by Brahma to incarnate themselves on earth and ask Visnu to aid them. He immediately accepts. Biardeau comments (1976, p. 204; translation S.C. Headley):

This is indeed an *avatāra* myth: a destruction is envisaged in order to destroy the *asura* and for the good of the world, but the *avatāra* in the strict sense, Krsna, incarnation of Visnu and his brahmin double Vyasa, passes onto the second level. This change in accent is calculated, since the birth of the Pandava and their hundred cousins is then described in detail: we know Pandu, condemned to absolute continence by a malediction, must count on his wife, who has received the power to call on the god of her choice to conceive a son. Already before her marriage she had already secretly had a son by Surya, whom she abandoned and who reappeared next to Duryodhana. Yudhistira, the elder and official son, is thus the son of dharma, Bhima of Vayu, Arjuna of Indra and the two twins Nakula and Sahadeva of the Asvins [cf. Dumézil, *Mythe et Epopée* I, p. 53 sq.]. Confronting the Pandava and rivalling them from their birth on via their mother, the hundred children of Dhṛtarāṣṭra are born. In this monstrous birth Siva and Vyasa had a hand. The elder Duryodhana is the *asura* Kali, while all the others are *raksasa* [demons]. What is being prepared on earth is thus a combat between the *deva* and the *asura*, where the later seem initially assured of victory, as is usual in the myths of *avatāra*.

The marriage of the Pāndava with Draupadī is also an instance of *avatāra* since she was born when her father, the king Draupada, made a sacrifice to have a son who could combat the brahmin Drona. The son Dhṛṣṭadyumna was born of fire, avatar of the god Agni while his sister was born of the altar, *vedi*. Biardeau (1976, p. 205) remarks that she is an incarnation of the prosperous, shining Srī, the shining earth, inseparable companion of Agni, for there is no prosperity without sacrifice. At the same time she is inseparable from Visnu, who ever since the Veda was identified with sacrifice. This dual identification is found in Java in the following formula: Durga (Umā-Srī) with Kala-Agni and Srī with Visnu (the Autronesian Sri and Sadana).

Then Krsna and his elder brother Baladeva enter the scene for the first time. Krsna encourages the companions of Arjuna to marry with "Srī" and then his own sister Subadrā. In the same way as the sacrifice for the crowning of a king (*rājasūya*; cf. Javanese *wayang* play discussed in ch. 14, p. 505[17]) Yudhistira, the king of the *dharma*, prepares the great sacrifice which will be the war of the *Mahābhārata*, so Krsna and Arjuna must make an invisible fire (*ajeyanalam*, cf. MBh. X.123.14; 125.14). As Biardeau has said (1976, p. 211; translation S.C. Headley):

We have seen how the destruction of the world (*pralaya*) once dominated by Rudra-Siva (or his form Kalāgni) then passed under the responsibility of Nārāyana with the flood and the preparation for a re-creation … However as in the *pralaya*, the action of Siva (and of Asvatthāman) must be contained. Krsna-Nārāyana watches that there be left a "remainder" …

It is in this sense that one can say that the epic is a not, first of all, a vehicle for the myth of an *avātara*, but only a mythic model for the terrestrial king who makes his own the gestures of the incarnate figure. Biardeau says (1976, pp. 213–14) that when Siva's murderous power, the fire and the flood, are over, life begins again, Krsna reigns to the exclusion of any earthly power. That is, he prefers to delegate his power to his devotee (*bhakta*). The king in this epic becomes an emanation, an *avatāra* of the god. So logically as soon as Krsna dies, the Pandava lose all power, Arjuna can no longer string his bow. In the fifth book of the *Mahābhārata* (48.20–21; 49.20–21) one reads:

> It is said that Krsna is Nārāyana and Phalguna (=Arjuna). Nārāyana and Nara are a single and same being doubled. Both by their acts win imperishable and stable worlds. Here and there they are always born again when the time of war comes.

These conclusions of Biardeau concerning the structure of the epic of the *Mahābhārata* are indeed surprising. Not only does the strange incident at the end of the Javanese *Ādiparva*, the burning of the Krenda forest, turn out to be a leitmotif throughout this enormous Indian myth, but also the personages Krsna and Arjuna, at the centre of the Javanese as well as Indian understandings of the epic, are accomplishing archetypal actions in the Khāndava forest. The burning of this forest thus already presents the structure of the entire *Mahābhārata* epic. As Biardeau (1976, p. 216) concludes, this is a near cosmic war framed by two great royal sacrifices, an interruption of the world whose continuity is at stake crystallized by the dynastic conflict, for the continuity of the royal *dharma* alone assures the coherence of the cosmos. The *avatāra* show how the *dharma* operates as destiny to guide the toy figures which are men. The roles played by the duty of the king and the divine are complementary in a structure that accounts both for the world's lot and the norms which should preside over its government.

Having seen the ideological and philosophical role of the burning of the forest, we can now return to the Javanese versions and poetic adaptations of the *Mahābhārata* to see how the stories found in the Javanese *Ādiparwa* (Wedyamanta 1958, vol. II, pp. 96–102) were disseminated in that island, beginning with Sunda and Upasunda episode and continuing on to the great conflagration.

A late classical poem (*kakawin* in Javanese but using Sanskrit meters) entitled the *Ratnawijaya* (the victory of the (girl made of jewels), tells of the battle between the ogres Sunda and Upasunda for Tilottamā discussed below. Another *kakawin* the "Burning of the Khāṇḍava forest" (*Khāṇḍhavavanadahana*) contains all these episodes from that of the ogres down to the conflagration: Sunda-Upasunda's death in battle for Tilottamā; the visit of the shining brahmin; the cause of Arjuna's exile; the marriage of Arjuna with Ulupuy and Citragandha; the liberation of these fairies from their malediction; the drunken feast on mount Raiwataka; the kidnapping of Subadrā; and the burning of the forest of Khāndawa. This poem was certainly composed in Bali using the prose version of the *Adiparva* (Juynböll 1909, sections 192–214; Zoetmulder 1974, p. 384). A late composition with many neologisms, according to Zoetmulder, it is interesting for its shows that even after the fall of Majapahit (*circa* 1527) the interest for the *Adiparwa* was still great, at least in Bali, such that selected episodes from its last section could be grouped together in new poetic composition. Here is a succinct résumé of the Sunda-Upasunda episode from the Javanese prose *Ādiparva* section 17 (1958, vol. 2, pp. 96–102)

> In Indraprastha Narada explains to Yuddhistira the danger represented by the meditation of Sunda and Upsaunda designed to submit the three continents under their power with the acquiescence of Brahma. Attacking the world the two ogres (*raksasa*) burnt all the mantra. At Brahma's suggestion the sage Wiśmakarmā made a goddess, Tilottamā, of small grains to conquer the ogres. On seeing her the two brothers were so subjugated by her beauty that they began fighting over her. The moral of the story for Yuddhistira is that if his five brothers ever dispute with each other over their common wife Draupadī, they should practice asceticism for twelve years in the forest.

What was the logic of this recomposition? The structure of the narrative of the *Khāṇḍhavavanadahana* is the same as the one that Biardeau permitted us to find in the *Mahābhārata* as a whole. The heaven is attacked and conquered by the *asura*. Then these titans are overcome by the intervention of the gods. Sometimes this victory is accomplished by Devī, in other words an Indian-styled Durga. The Javanese Sunda and Upasunda illustrate this (cf. Brahmānda Purāna section IV.25.75–88 in Gonda's edition), whereas in the Sanskrit texts Sumbha and Nisumbha are only one amongst a host of enemies. Javanese texts, like the *Ratnawijaya* expand this considerably from the succinct *Brahmānda Purāna* version.

7.4 THE BURNING OF THE FOREST AND THE GODDESS' VICTORY OVER THE DEMON BUFFALO

The extremely large number of so-called Mahishamardanī statues or goddess dominating the demon buffalo, found in Java makes this form of Devī, *the*

Javanese goddess, the archetypal form is that of a set of nine Durgā just as in Nepal. As Pott has shown (1966, p. 86), the *purāna* present other versions of this victory not known apparently in Java. For instance the *Vāmanapurāna* where the goddess Kātyāyanī (a form of Durga with eighteen arms) slays the buffalo Mahishāsura on the Vindhya mountains. In the *Padmāpurāna* the Vindhya mountains are said to personify ignorance

Even if the popular non-Brahmanic origins of the buffalo-slaying goddess are affirmed (cf. Varenne 1975, pp. XI & XII), the "best" place to study the iconography of the victory the goddess for Java is therefore the Devī-*Māhātmya* (Agrawala 1963), which having been incorporated into the *Mārkandeya Purāna* (MP) in India, remained vastly popular as an independent work and has dominated Javanese iconography. Sanskrit texts like the *Hari Wangsa* contain long prayers to Durgā celebrating her victory, but the Javanese mpu Panuluh's *Hari Wangsa* (Teeuw 1950) is a much shorter and poorer translation from the twelfth century Kediri East Javanese court and has no invocations to Durgā, but the same author's, *Kakawin Ghatotkacāsraya* (Sutjipto Wirjosuparto 1960) does have prayers for Durga's victory. They seem to be our only written Javanese source for a description of Durga's victory over a titan buffalo. No translation of the Devī-Māhātmya is known in Java (Boeles 1942[18]). After Siva's the most popular iconography in Java was that of Durga's slaying of the titan buffalo and this according to the canon's of Indian sculpture.[19]

The key episodes of the *Devī-Māhātmya* (the Glorification of the goddess) are as follows:

* The conflict between Visnu and the demons Madhu and Kaitabha at the creation (*sisrkṣā*) of the world. The creation and the first praise (*stotra*) of the great goddess; the death of the two demons (MP, ch. 81).
* The battle between the titan (*asura*) buffalo Mahisha; the second praise of the goddess by the gods (MP, chs. 82–84).
* The gods on Mt. Himavat invoke Candikā after the *asura* Sumbha and Nisumbha have conquered them. Parvatī arrives and Candikā comes out of her body. The third praise of the goddess. Sumba wants to marry Candikā and in order to do so most vanquish her in combat (MP, chs. 85–86) Candikā successively destroys the general Dhumra-locana, then Canda and Munda.
* The great *asura* Rakta-vija's blood is drunk by Kalī (MP, ch. 88).
* Despite Sumbha's aid, Nisumbha is killed (MP, ch. 89).
* Ambikā absorbs all the other goddesses to combat and kill Sumbha. Fourth and final praise of the goddess (MP, chs. 91–9).

One notices that despite its recursiveness, there is also a progression in the narration. From the goddess Devī comes first Candikā then Kalī and finally Ambikā. The goddess created by the gods first attracts the twin *asura* and in the battles that follow the expansion of her *sakti* (divine power) assures the final victory of the gods.[20]

The menace (re-)presented is the same, domination by the *asura*. It provides the frame of this myth and resembles episodes from the *Mahābhārata*: the burning of the Khāṇḍava forest by Agni; the attack by Sunda-Upasunda. The attacks enumerated by the *Devī-mahātmya* above, by Madhu and Kaitabha, by Mahisha, by Chanda and Munda,[21] by Rakta-vija and by Sumbha and Nisumbha, all present the same danger and are suppressed by the same person (Durgā/Camundā) in the same manner. In this sense the

FIGURE 7.1
Stone bas-relief of Durga's victory over the titan buffalo Mahishā in the Mahishāsuramardanī *mandapa* of the temple complex (seventh to eighth centuries) at Mahabalipuram. During the Indian Pallava (third to ninth centuries) dynasty, it is from such ports that trading boats sailed to and from Sumatra and Java (Srīvijaya/Sailaendra dynasties, seventh to ninth centuries). This iconography spread throughout Java but the text of the famous poem *Devī Māhātmya* which recounts the victory of the goddess over the evil buffalo apparently was never read in the archipelago

FIGURE 7.2
Three contemporary concrete painted statues of Durga's victory over the titan
buffalo Mahishā atop modern temples in the environs of Pondichery

FIGURE 7.3
Processional plastic statues of Durga's victory over Mahishā stored in the
eaves of a temple staircase between outings

iconography of the victory over the titan buffalo (*mahishāsuramardanī*)
represents a digest of them all. All these manifestations of *sakti* (divine power)
have the same source, the goddess. However identified, these Javanese
transpositions leave us with uncomfortable ambiguities.

7.5 A SKETCH OF THE ICONOGRAPHY OF DURGA'S VICTORY IN INDIA AND JAVA

Certain "saktic" elements of the narrative of the victory over the buffalo are
very old. Even before looking at the local Javanese additions to this myth, the

Indian composition is highly disparate, composed of Indo-European and Dravidians elements. According to Beythan (Renou and Filliozat 1947, p. 1058) the Dravidian source is the red war god Ceyyōn, son of the goddess Korravei (the victorious one). This hunter uses a spear and roams the hills and savannah before later being absorbed into Siva.

Even the Tantric elements are not that recent. If Durgā had a non-Aryan substratum of greater importance than any other divinity in the Brahmanic pantheon (Renou and Filliozat 1947, p. 1074), she is integrated and elevated in Tantrism in such a way as to lose this Dravidian personality.[22]

Turning to Tantrism in Java, the oldest text there of Siva-Siddhanta is the *Bhuvanasamkṣepa*, which is in between pre-sectarian Saivism and Siva-Siddhanta. Here Siva is already posited as the identity between microcosm and macrocosm. He is the original phenomenon. In the Javanese *Bhuvanasamkṣepa* one finds the ritual of imposition (*nyāsa*) founded on both a cosmography and a graphogony (ritual writing on the cosmos). The five initials of the name of Siva are placed on the essential parts of the body of the devotee such that he is filled with the divine essence. The cosmic co-ordinates are clearly of a Purānic origin: seven worlds, five elements, the *manas* (mind as opposed to soul) etc. (Renou and Filliozat 1947, p. 1295).

The Javanese practised the inner "construction" (*sādhana*) of *liṅgga* (phallus) called *ātma-liṅga-liṅgōdbhava* as is testified by texts like the *Jnānasiddhānta* (cf. Soebadio's edition 1971 and Headley 1996, pp. 324–25). In contemporary Javanese exorcism the application of letters or syllables (*nyāsa*) is practised in the exorcism of Durga's son, turned husband, Kala. The Letters on the Chest (*sastra ing dhadha*) mantra (cf. Ch. 9) used to purify Kala, for instance, contains the same cosmogonic and graphogony references as the prayers used in the *maésa lawung* invocations at the foot of Durga's tertre. In fact it comes from the same corpus of prayers (Headley, 2000*a*, ch. 5). So although this corpus is now used for exorcisms (that of people afflicted by Kala Durga's son) and basically derive from a creation myth, what has remained from the earlier Javanese practices are these rituals of imposition (*nyāsa*) of letters. The *bija-mantra* of Indian cosmogonic ("seed syllables" from which the world is created) are called *sastra-jendra* in contemporary Java and are less associated with cosmogony than with different parts of the human body (microcosm) and the exorcisms mentioned above. They are nonetheless important for they provide an historical link with the tenth century Javanese Saivism that in a certain sense took over from the sort of saktism that explained in India the myth of Durga's victory over the buffalo. Stated differently, the *yantra* or receptacle of the royal protective rituals became these blood offerings to the queen of the demon armies who in return protected the Javanese kings of the second Mataram from the very real *asura* who were their enemies. What was lost in the Javanization of the Durga was the connection with the three strands (*guṇa*: goodness, passion, and darkness) of Samkya philosophy which was conceived of as a coherent whole in the *Mārkandeya-Purāna* (Rao 1914, p. 337):

Goddess Mahalaksmī		
Sattva-gunātmika: (having the quality of goodness)	Rajasa-gunātmika: (having the quality of passion)	Tamasa-gunātmika: (having the quality of darkness)
Gaurī Visnu	Laksmī Hiranyagarbha	Sarasvati Rudra

coupled deities

The eclecticism which characterized the tantric movement in general (Renou and Filliozat 1947, para. 848) meant that in practice, the producing (*sādhana*) of a female deity took precedence over the philosophical background that underlay it. None of the Mīmāmsa postulates that explain the imposition of syllables on the different parts of the body seem to have come to Java (Biardeau 1964). What one finds in Java, for instance, in the dedication (*manggala*) of the "recent" classical poem *Khāndhawawanadahana* (Zoetmulder 1974, p. 495) is the presence of the god "seated on a hidden lotus" evoked in *sakala-niṣkala* (material-immaterial) form through a "praise of victory".[23] In tantric Saivaite yoga, the mode of the divinity in the heart (*anandakandapadma*) is still evoked in Bali and in Java well after the arrival of Islam. As Zoetmulder says (1974, pp. 184–85) the manner of installing (*pratiśtha*) the divinity in the body, the temple, a statue, or a literary composition for the erection of a temple (*manggala*) consists in evoking the receptacle of the divinity:

> This union is of a transitory nature, lasting no longer than the brief moment of ecstatic rapture experienced in surrendering oneself to the overwhelming power of the aesthetic experience. But it is also a foretaste of and a preparation for the union with the deity that is *kalepasan* or liberation, and the definitive release from the snares in which the world keeps man trapped, from the cycle of recurrent rebirths. This is the ultimate aim of every yogi.

This practice was known in Java from the tenth century on through texts like the *Vṛhaspati tattwa* (Sudarshana Dewi 1957), *Bhuvanakośa*, and the *Bhuvanasamkṣépa*. On the one hand they belong to the Saivitic Purāna, says Gonda (1965, p. 279; translation S.C. Headley):

> They treat of the nature and the manifestations of Siva, who is the first cause of the constitutive principles of the world (*guṇa* as in *samkhya*) and the point of departure of the emanation and present its five forms [ether, air, fire, water and earth] and its five hierarchical aspects; they present a double form between immanence and transcendence (sometimes primarily all theist, sometimes primarily philosophical). They contain the theories known from *samkhya*, Puranic cosmogonies, Vedanta cosmogonies, a doctrine obtained by the absorption in a Vedantic manner of the absolute in the divinity. The soteriology particularly is characterised by advice with a view to union with the supreme principle based on the foundation of a literal correspondence between the macrocosm and the microcosm. Unity is obtained by means of a technique of ecstasy, usually simplified by using a ritual of the "imposition by meditation"; one carries over to the essential parts of the body the sacred syllables incarnating certain aspects of the god.

If the early Javanese temples of the eighth to the tenth century used such notions of installation in the receptacle (*yantra*), what place could the *geste* of the victory over the buffalo from the Purana have had? These Javanese texts, unknown in India, show that Java had known a Purānic, pre-sectarian Saivaism (pre-second millennium?). The great number of statues of this very particular iconography suggests one interpretation: the rituals of the great temples Durga occupied a prominent place by protecting the king.

At Prambanan, according to the recent work of Roy Jordaan (1991),[24] it seems that the churning of the ocean myth was realized ritually by flooding the temple grounds, thus producing holy water. There is no mention of buffalo sacrifices to Durga. Pigeaud's comments (1960, vol. 4, p. 313) on the fourteenth century Javanese new year celebrations comparing them to the *maésa lawung* celebrated in the first month of the Muslim year and resembling the Tenggerese Karo celebrations in the month of *bhādra* (August–September) seem based only on the common features of large amounts of liquor and food consumed at these festivals. The bridge between Prambanan and the second Mataram of Central Java (seventeenth to twentieth centuries) is more likely to be found in the continuous Tantric undercurrents associated with the cult of Durga that stretched from the Pallava Kingdom (250–910 A.D.) in south India and reached the Malay peninsula by the sixth century.

This kind of Tantric data comes mainly from eastern Java. Much has been written about the meaning of these temples-tombs erected by kings like Krtanagara.[25] It is partially illuminated by replacing the Siva *linga* in this context as van Akkeren (1951, p. 13) has done.

> ... this *linga* and *stupa* ... are rooted in very old convictions and traditions commonly held in India and South-East Asia. Both are in nature a new body which people took as a substitute for a dead ancestor, king or teacher. They were used as a means to come into contact with the deceased and his cosmic beneficial powers, his royal authority and dharma. In this substitute both the deity and the deceased become one. In the *linga* and the *stupa* people have a focal point of supernatural power, on which the prosperity of the country depends.

What separates Prambanan in Central Java from the later East Javanese Purwapatapan temple is thus a partial (*vis-à-vis* India) evolution towards saktism and tantrism, and of course a syncretism between Buddhism and Saivism. In early Central Java, for instance, Pott (1966, pp. 104–15) finds no trace of the influence of the feminine principle nor the demonization of certain divinities that will later characterize Javanese tantra. In Java this will only go so far. Durga will be integrated into the Saivitic-Buddhist pantheons of East Java. Although Guhyeçsvarī is known, the full complement of the Tantric nine Durga's never imposed itself.[26]

In his *Yoga and Yantra* (1966), P.H. Pott provides a thorough exploration of the Javanese Tantric pantheon. Here is the evolution he uncovers. Whereas in Prambanan (Central Java; AD 856), Durga, Ganesa and Guru surround Siwa respectively on the north, west and south, in the East Javanese Bhairawa cults that at Purwapatapan (candi "B", Singasari), one finds a statue of Camundā (a from of Durga) in the northern cell, Parvatī in the southern and Mahakala between them. As Aichele (1959) had demonstrated the Austronesian north-south axis, a metaphor for totality, is in the process of imposing itself.

To conclude, Durga as the slayer of the demon buffalo, Mahishāsuramardanī, remains in Java the form *par excellence* of the goddess (Pott 1966, pp. 86–87). Durga is associated by the Javanese with her combat against Agni the destroyer of the universe in as much as they assimilate her victory over demons like the buffalo Mahisha with the repulsing of the demon armies that would destroy the world order, finally making *asura* into *deva*. Paradoxically in East Java Durga's son Kala is assimilated to Kalāgni, this same destructive fire. How this assimilation took place in detail still escapes us, but in the course of this chapter we have seen at least the elements that produced the assimilation: the iconographic canon of the Durgā's victory over the buffalo, at royal cults in temples. At obscure forest shrines, like Krendawahana, outside the palace city, Hindu philosophy and its domestication in the forms of Javanese cosmology were carefully and durably reduced to oral traditions not textual canons.

NOTES

1. Stutterheim (1937), pp. 72–79; this statue of Durga (B10) is available in Leiden under the number (Oudkundige Dienst., no. 8749).
2. Aichele (1959) has shown how the expression "north-south" came to express the idea of totality in ancient Javanese literature.
3. *Kitab Adiparwa* (1958, vol. II, pp. 112–22). This corresponds to the *parva* numbered 214–25 in the Poona Sanskrit critical edition of Vishnu S. Sukthankar (Bhandarkar Oriental Research Institute, 1933). S. Sorenson, *An Index to the Names of the Mahābhārata* (1904; reprint 1963 Motilal Barnasidas, Delhi) gives a concordance to the divisions of the Bombay, and Calcutta editions, and English translation of Roy. The shorter Javanese translation/adaptation is sometimes hard to understand due to its condensation and the longer Sanskrit version clarifies these passages.
4. One can unravel the etymology of the name of Krendawahana by examining the word for quail (the only bird to survive the conflagration). *Puyuh* means quail in old and modern Javanese as well as in Indonesian. In popular culture the Javanese notice that while the male (*bencé*) is known for resting passively on the nest, the female goes forth to work and eventually to fight. It is the popular etymology proposed by *Ādiparwa* above which provides our clues. In Sanskrit *kārandava* (duck; *bèbèk* in Javanese) was translated as *puyuh* in Javanese, a bird known in the horoscope iconography where it figures along with Durga's son Kala in the thirteenth week of the Javanese thirty week year. But the Sanskrit *kārandava* (duck) was transcribed into old Javanese as *karandawa*, then *krenda*, becoming a literary variant for the word duck (Poerwardarminta 1930, p. 320), but which regionally also means a covered stretcher for the deceased (modern Javanese *bandhosa*). On the other hand the Javanese toponym *alas* (forest) Krendawahana translated the Sanskrit Kārandāvahana, which as we saw above is the name of a forest in the *Mahābhārata*. The Javanese-Javanese dictionary of Poerwardarminta (1930) seems to take into account a discussion of these questions that appeared in three articles in the Javanese magazine *Pustaka Jawi* (no. V–VI, pp. 21, 55, 151).

   I propose to simplify that discussion in the following manner: the opposition between *k* and *kh* in Sanskrit not being recognized in old or modern Javanese, two distinct Sanskrit words (*kārandha* and *khāndhava*) were confounded after the *Ādiparwa* was translated. This can be seen in the understanding the toponym given to Durga's sacred forest.

5. Kown from Majapahit bas-reliefs, this old story, the sequel to the *Sudamala*, comes down to us in an East Javanese version. There Uma, in the form of the demon Ra Nini, lives in the cemetery of Gandamayu.

6. For example: *Sembadra Larung* (Kodiron 1968); Bima Bungkus (tape recording in six casettes, Lokanata 1973, Surakarta); and the exorcism *Murwa Kala* edited by R. Tanojo (1964).

7. Cf. *passim*, Ratnaesih, "Durgāmahishāsuramardini".

8. For the evolution of this iconography in India and Java, cf. Ratnaesih's B.A. thesis "Durgāmahisāsuramardinī". Satyawati Suleiman (*Monuments of Ancient Indonesia*, no date, p. 7 and plate 14) shows a Mahisamardanī statue from Tenjolaya (Cicalengka; now in the Jakarta museum) which is dated by the jewelry to the eight century. It has a Cham girdle with short ends; by the end of the Majapahit these ends will hang down to the feet.

9. On an introduction to Indian sources for Durgā's killing of the giant buffalo described in this geste cf. David Kinsley (1987); Berkson (1994) *passim* and above all the ethnographic study of Biardeau (1989). David J. Stuart-Fox," Pura Besakih: Temple-State Relations from Precolonial to Modern Times" (1991, pp. 11–42) shows that a connection between the Indian traditions and the Balinese have been stretched but not to the point of breaking entirely.

   p. 20: To be a state temple one has to have state contribution towards maintenance and enactment of rituals. Each kingdom had several in different regions (several hundred for all of Bali). These ensure regional order and prosperity. Some regional temple are Temples of the Realm, Sadkahyangan. These are usually located on the mountains and by the sea. "Save perhaps for the early Mataram period in Java, in Java and Bali political and religious spheres of life have distinct centers, which differs from the Indian norm."

   pp. 17–18: Hierarchical levels of ritual: *pedanda* rituals (only six out of seventy-three at Besakih's public temples) and *pemangku* rituals. "This hierarchical level of ritual is directly related to organization of the enactment of ritual, which in turn is related to social and political organisation. These call upon different sets of social relations. An examination of the mean of funding, preparation and performance at different periods of the temple's history reveals a great deal about the structure of Balinese society and how it has been transformed, and about the changing relationship between state and temple." Here the people paying are not those preparing the ritual.

   p. 21: on the Rsi Markandeya oral tradition recently written down which accounts for "… Pura Besakih (more specifically, the temple called Pura Basukihan) the location of the first Hindu ritual on Bali, and so serves as a charter of Besakih's status as the oldest and paramount centre of Hindus worship in Bali." cf. Goris *Bali Further Studies* (1969); Korn (1932, p. 189).

10. *Devī-mahātmaya* has no history (cf. J. Varenne: XIII) "de la préhistoire de ces oeuvres, nous ne pouvons rien connaître comme si les auteurs avaient systématiquement éliminé ce qu'ils considéraient sans doute comme de mauvaises

approximations de la Somme qu'ils rédigiaient. Par voie de conséquences les oeuvres ultérieures sont dans leur grande majorité de simples commentaires." Already in the *Devi-mahātmaya* (13, 10) Suranatha and Samādhi decide to worship the goddess and install themselves on the banks of a river (13, 9) where they venerate a statue of her they have made of clay.

11. Cf. Marijke J. Klokke (1994, p. 76), "On the Orientation of Ancient Javanese Temples: the Example of Candi Surowono". Klokke (1994, p. 82) points out that the Indian sequence of directions (*purwa, daksina, paścima, uttara*) stresses the movement of the sun in a day, while the Javanese Austronesian one stresses bi-polarity (*lor-kidul; kulwan-wetan*).

12. Cf. Louis-Chalres Damais (1969) on the symbolic colours of the four cardinal points in Indonesia.

13. (1975, p. 119), citing Oldenburg, *Die Weltanschaung der Brāhmana-Texte* (1919, p. 41 sq).

14. Levelled and grassless fields to the north and the south of the palace (*kraton*) of the king or the sultan. Two *waringin* (*ficus benjamina*) are planted in the middle of these planes.

15. On Kala, cf. Biardeau (1971, p. 69).

16. The passage from one age (*yuga*) to another is not analogous to that of one epoch (*kalpa*) to another. This is first of all because the golden age of the Krtayuga, dominated by heat (*tapas*), is not equivalent to the Purānic *pratisarga* or recreation, but also because the Tretayuga, dominated by knowledge, the Dvaparayuga, dominated by sacrifice, and the Kaliyuga, where the supreme value is the gift, express primarily the logic of individual renaissances which depend on the cycle of dharma. As Biardeau says, the holism of this Indian cosmology is overarching (1976, p. 123; translation S.C. Headley):

> One then notices that in fact one can describe the succession of *yuga* without any reference to an *avatāra*. It is impossible to describe the genesis or the end of a world without introducing the corresponding forms of the divinity. Homologous with the temporal cycles, are the cosmic spheres and the levels of manifestation of the divinity. With a *yuga*, the harmony is broken: one describes the state of the earth, but what is at stake is in fact a triple world since the dharma does not permit dissociation between the earth, heaven or hell. The supreme divinity can simply be absent. That means that its presence is not absolutely necessary to the structure of time in the *yuga* or to the conception of the progressive degradation of the *dharma*. It is true that the latter is often related to time which plays above a destructive role, but this reference only makes the play of individual karma and the process of the socio-cosmic cycle more difficult.

Biardeau continues (1976, pp. 123–33) by showing how many times the end of *yuga* does take on Purānic allure; in *Mahābhārata* (III.272.31–32) the Purūsha of *Rgveda* hymn X.90 is cited. The bed provided by the coiled serpent is literally the white ashes, that "remainder" (*śeṣa*, the name of the serpent), symbolizing the origin of recreation (*pratisarga*), the passage from renouncing the world to sacrifice, i.e. the recreation of the new world. In this passage, Siva does not explain to Jayadratha the Purānic cosmogony, but instead tells the myths of the sacrificial boar down to the man-lion and the midget (Vāmana), thus evoking these *avatāra* by the narrative of the installation of the *vārāhakalpa* (era of Vishu as a wild boar). Biardeau concludes that although the Purānic cosmogonies do not disappear, they are transformed into *avātara*.

But even if the end of a *kalpa* is not necessarily accompanied by a decline in *dharma*, the *Mahābhārata* offers us numerous examples of that. In the *Vanaparvan* of the *Mahābhārata*, Mārkandeya attributes to the end of a *yuga*, all the habitual characteristics of a *pralaya*. It is above all this cosmic fire that the epic authors retain to characterize the end of a *mahāyuga*. A comparative study of these, however, convinced Biardeau (1976, pp. 133, 136); that the end of a *yuga* was nonetheless distinguished from the end of a *kalpa*.

> In other words it is most important to respect this symbolism if one wants to understand the overall outline of the epic. And if it is true that the central event of the narrative is the end of a *yuga* (or its semblance), it is startling to realize that we risk misunderstanding the meaning of the entire story if we don't already understand the referential context which is essential to it: the alternation between Purānic creations and re-absorbings. If there is a point of view from which it is true to say that the epic is earlier that the Purāna, it is certainly not that of its doctrinal content. (Biardeau 1976, p. 135; translation S.C. Headley)

17. Cf. Dumézil, *Mythe et Epopée. Types Epiques Indo-Européens* (1995, ch. 4). This myth exists in the Javanese wayang theatre repertory, cf. Ki Sarwanto, *Sesaji Raja Suyo* (1991) and analysed in Chapter 14 below.

18. It is dangerous to be categorically affirmative in these matters. For instance invocation no. 324 in Goudriaan and Hooykaas *Stuti and Stava* (1971, pp. 196–207) contains a *stotra* to Durgā. Verses one to eight (Asthaka-mantra with much sound play using kernel (*bīja*) syllables) are separate; in verses nine to eighteen, seven out ten have Sanskrit counterparts. Verses nine to eighteen refer to Durgā as Kālī or Bhadra-Kalī, Kāla-rātrī, Cāmundhā and other names.

   The last three *slokas* dedicated to Durgā's favourable aspect, where she is called Narāyanī derive from the *Mārkandheya-Purāna*, ch. 91, although the order is scrambled. A full translation taken from Goudriaan and Hooykaas is presented in Chapter 9 below.

19. Obviously one often finds sculptures of Parvatī/Umā/Durga associated with those of Siva in the same place since she is his *sakti* or consort. Cf. Juynböll 1909, vol. V, 15–19. In the Jakarta National Museum alone there are some 195 specimens. Few are from West Java and the rest are half from Central Java and half from East Java, but nothing says that this collection is representative. On the

role of Durga in such exorcisms as the Sudamala, Calon Arang, and the Murwakala, cf. Headley (2000*a*). We will not deal with the obscure questions surrounding Javanese Tantrism here.
20. In the first chapter (Agrawala 1963, pp. 37–38) there is also an Purānic cosmic vision.

> 1.49. When the universe was converted into an Infinite Ocean and the Lord Vishnu having entered Yoginadra became asleep on the couch of the cosmic serpent Sesa, then at the end of the Kalpa (*pralaya*).
> 1.50. Two terrible Asuras, the well-known Madhu and Kaitabha, sprang from the impurity of the two ears of Visnu and attacked Brahma to slay him.
> 1.51. Prajapati Brahma, seated on the lotus rising from the navel of Visnu, saw those violent *asuras*, also noticing Narayana in dream state.
> 1.52. Began to invoke with a concentrated mind the Goddess Yoganindra dwelling in the eyes of Hari with a view to bring the Lord in a conscious state.
> 1.53. The resplendent Lord Brahma praised the Goddess of Sleep, the incomparable power of Visnu, the queen of the cosmos, supporter of the world and the cause of its maintenance and dissolution.

Next begins the first praise (*stotra*) by Brahma of Ratrī (that is to say the goddess Durgā called Devī). We see that in the Sivaite milieu this goddess plays a similar destructive role to that of Agni in the burning of the Khāṇḍava forest. Is this any more that a superficial similarity? The only Javanese texts we have identified so far as a source for this myth are as poor in iconographic details as the Sanskrit original (*Brahmānda Purāna*; cf. Poona Sanskrit 1895, edition IV.27.75 and 88). Even if the *Devī-Māhātmya* has reached Java in iconography alone, we are obliged to look at the text that inspired these canonical motifs. The main episodes are found in chapters two and four presented below in Agrawala's translation (1963, pp. 45–75; the author has modified some of the translator's punctuation to make the reading more fluid):

> 2.1. In former times the battle between the Deva and the Asura raged for a full hundred years, when Indra was the king of the Gods and Mahisha of the Demons.
> 2.2. There the divine army was defeated by the powerful Asuras. Having defeated all the gods Mahishāsura became Indra.
> 2.3. Then the vanquished Devas making the lotus born Prajāpati (Brahmā) their leader approached Siva and Visnu.
> 2.4. The gods described to them in detail all that had happened in the form of the defeat of the gods brought about by Mahishāsura.
> 2.8. Having thus heard the words of the Devas, Visnu and Siva both became angry with frowning eye-brows on their faces.

2.9. From the face of Visnu, filled with intense indignation, as well as from that of Brahmā and Siva, sprang forth fierce heat.

2.10. From the bodies of other Devas also headed by Indra issued forth a resplendent lustre (çaktadinām). All this light (tejas) became unified into one.

2.11. Then that matchless light born from the bodies of all the gods gathered into a single corpus and turned into a woman enveloping the three worlds by her lustre.

[Then just as in the Javanese Murwa Kala myth where the body of Kala is made from the weapons thrown down at him by the gods, so here (2.12–38) each god gives the woman a weapon which becomes a part of her body (and not a weapon in her hand). The battle enflames the four quarters of the universe (2.39–3.19) and during the course of the ensuing battle Devī's name becomes successively Candikā (2.49), Ambikā (2.66), Parameçwarī (3.18).]

3.20. As his army was thus being destroyed, Mahishāsura assuming his buffalo form terrified the Ganas of the goddess.

3.28. She threw her noose over him and bound the great *asura*. Thus caught in battle he gave up his buffalo form.

[Having become a lion, then an elephant, he finally becomes a buffalo again.]

3.33. Then the world-mother enraged as Candikā quaffed and quaffed again and again the best of drinks and laughed boisterously with reddened eyes.

3.37. ... she jumped and landed herself on the great *asura* and pressing her foot on this throat struck him with a spear (çūla).

3.38. Thereupon trampled under her foot, the *asura* half-issued forth from his buffalo mouth in his real human form,

[Here begins the second *stotra* of the *Devī-māhātmya*.]

4.1. When the most valorous but evil-natured *asura* together with the demon army was vanquished by the goddess, Indra and the hosts of other gods began to praise her with their words, bending in humility their necks, and shoulders, while their bodies looked by the hair horripilated with ecstasy.

4.2. The goddess, who stretched out this world by her power, whose body comprises the entire powers of all the hosts of gods, her, Ambikā, worthy of worship by all gods and great Rshi. We bow before in faith. May she ordain blessings for us!

4.3. May she, whose peerless majesty and power Ananta adorable, Brahmā and Hara cannot in soothe declare, may she, Candikā, to protect the entire world and to destroy the fear of evil turn her mind.

4.4. Her, who is Good-Fortune (Lakshmī) herself in the dwellings of men of good deeds, — Fortune in those men of sinful souls; whose intelligence (*buddhi*) in the hearts of the prudent, who is faith (*sraddhā*) in those of the good, and modesty (*lajjā*) in that of high-born men; Her, even thee, we bow before; protect the universe, of goddess! Can we describe this they thought-transcending form (*rupācintya*)?

4.6. Thou art the cause of all the worlds. Thou characterised by three qualities (*guṇa*), by faults Thou art not known. Even by Hari, Hara and the other gods thou art incomprehensible art the resort of all. Thou art the entire world which is composed of parts.

4.9. Sound is thy soul, thou art the repository of the most spotless Rk and Yajus hymns. And of the Sāmans, which have the charming-worded texts of the Udjitha as Goddess art the triple Veda, the adorable, and for the existence and production of all the worlds art active. Thou art the supreme destroyer of pains.

4.10. Art mental vigour, O Goddess! hast comprehended the essence of all the scriptures. Art Durgā, the boat to cross the difficult ocean of existence, devoid of all attachments. Art Srī, who has planted her dominion alone in the heart of Kaitabha's foe. Indeed art Gaurī, who has fixed her dwelling in the moon-crested god.

4.23. With thy spear (*çūla*) protect us, O Goddess. Protect us with they sword also, O Ambikā. By the clanging of thy bell protect us, and by the twanging of the thong of thy bow.

4.24. In the east guard us, and in the west! O Chandikā, guard us in the south by the brandishing of thy spear, and also in the north, O Goddess.

4.25. Whatever gentle forms (*saumya rupa*) of thee wander about in the three worlds and whatever exceeding terrible forms wander, by means of them guard us and the earth.

This, of course, is the gesture that is captured in the majority of the statues of the Mahishāsuramardanī. One should notice that the tantric qualities: emanation (*sadhana*) instead of incarnation (*avatāra*), violent and gory victory after drinking, etc., of Durgā's victory which come over clearly in the poem's account are less clearly rendered in Javanese sculpture. On the development of the tantric elements in Indian iconography cf.: P. Gururaja Bhatt, *Studies in Tuluva History and Culture* (1975) which gives four clear stages in the evolution of her sculpture (pp. 306ff.); D. R. Rajeshwari, *Sakti Iconography* (no date) gives some early Tamil literary data on the self-sacrifices, usually by self-decapitation, at Durga's temples (pp. 53–58); R. Nagaswamy *Tantric Cult of South India* (no date; pp. 145–54) gives description of the tantric cult to Durga at Mamallapuram (=Mahābalipuram), the great Pallava port city known to have been in contact with Sumatra and Java from early on and especially in the eight-tenth centuries; K.N. Srinivasan, *Cave-Temples of the Pallavas* (1964, ch. 2) gives a good chronology of the different lines of kings in terms of the cave sculpture. The famous Mahishamardanī *mandapam* cave temple at Mahābalipuram is described at pp. 148–55. On the earliest period, cf. Odile Divakaran "Durgā the Great

Goddess: Meanings and Forms in the Early Period" (1985). P.K. Agrawala, *Goddesses in Ancient India* (1984) gives proto-historical materials the goddess from the Indus valley Harappa seals (pp. 30–38) and a classification of the Rgvedic goddesses (pp. 48–56); numismatic material on proto-types of Durgā can be found in Bandana Saraswati "Ambā-Nana-Durgā" (1965); while B.N. Mukherjee, *Nana on Lion, a study in Kushāna numismatic art* (no date) pp. 18–20, 119–20 explains the origins of Durgā lion-riding (*simhavāhinī*) from numismatic evidence.

21. *Mārkandeya Purāna* (ch. 7) with stronger Tantric overtones: Thus when Sumbha and Chanda attack the goddess is enraged and Kalī appears from her brow: 7.6. "Carrying a strange Khatvanga (skull-topped staff) decorated with a garland of human heads, clad in a tiger's skin looking terrible owing to her emaciated flesh."

22. In the cadre of a saktism still close to Samkhya and the epic cosmogonies of the *Mahābhārata* she (Narayanī, i.e., Tilottamā) declares in a hymn after slaying Sumbha (*Devī-māhātmya*, Agrawala translation 1963, pp. 140–41):

> 11.38. When the twenty-eighth *yuga* has arrived in the Vaivasvata Manu (the current era, *manvantara*, of four million years), two other great *asura* named Sumbha and Nisumbha will be born.
> 11.39. Then from the womb of Yosoda in the house of the cow-herd king Nanda, dwelling on the Vindhya mountain, I shall destroy those two *asura*.
> 11.42. Thenceforth the gods in heaven and mortal men on this earth praising me shall always refer to me as the red-toothed one.
> 11.43. And again when rain and water will fall for a hundred years, propitiated by the Munis, I shall be born on the earth but not from a womb.
> 11.45. At that time, O gods, I shall support the whole world with life-sustaining vegetables, born out of my own body, until the rains set in again. Then I shall be famed on earth as Sakambari.
> 11.51. Thus whenever trouble shall arise on account of Danavas, I shall become incarnate and destroy the enemies.

23. "*lilālungguh i guhyapdma gelaren stuti jayajaya murti niskala*", Zoetmulder (1974, p. 183 and fn 244).

24. Roy Jordaan and Robert Wessing "Human Sacrifice at Prambanan" (1996).

25. Cf. *Nagarakertāgama* 43.5; Pott (1966, pp. 128–31); Santoso (1975, pp. 54–55, 70–71, 103, 17, 115, 126, 127); Soekomo (1975, passim).

26. Cf. M. S. Slusser (1982, vol. II, p. 322) for its Nepalese appearances. Cf. plate XIII, which looks like a buffalo-killing goddess, but in reconstructions it is hard to tell. Pott's discussion (1966, pp. 86–89, 131) of Camundai of Ardimulya at Krtanagara's Purwapatapan mentions that she is called Guhyeçvara i.e. one of the nine Durgā who is also described in the *Svayambhu Purāna* as Khagānanā.

8

THE SPEARING OF DURGA'S BUFFALO

In Chapter 7 we saw how the toponym of Krendawahana, scene of an apocalyptic destruction of that forest, was gradually replaced by a different religious geography in Java. On the one hand the battle over duty undertaken by Krsna and Arjuna, although it remained the central theme in the *wayang* lore of the *Mahābhārata,* was replaced with royal rituals where practices in which Javanese creation myths associate with the offering for Durga's victory over the demon buffalo. This *sakti* cult of female sacred force was accompanied by evocations of Siva's *linga* using syllables placed on different parts of the body. These same syllables, used in Indian cosmogonies, the *bija mantra*, were often replaced by typically Javanese cosmologies. In the *Purwa Bumi* myth found in East Java (Tengger), Guru's and the Goddesses' (Bhattari) yoga produced the deities established in the cardinal directions in the form of animals. From her subsequent yoga were produced the elements making up the cosmos corresponding to the parts of her body. As we will see in this chapter this kind of genesis narrative is preserved in the mantra offered to Durga during the *Maésa Lawung* buffalo sacrifice.

The theme of the burning of Krenda forest, however, does not disappear immediately. The fourteenth century *Nagarakertāgama* (cantos 50–52) describe a royal hunt in the environs of Singasari which is compared to the massacre of the animals in the Krendawahana forest. C.C. Berg (1953, p. 143) describes this as a metaphor for the conquest of the archipelago, but Pigeaud dismisses it (1962, vol. IV, p. 145) as a "light literary description" in the style of the *Pancatantra.*

FIGURE 8.1

The famous Sinagari dynasty (thirteenth century: East Java) statue of the
victory of Durga over the titan buffalo Mahishā. Now located in the
Rijksvolkenkunde Museum in Leiden; cf. H.H. Juynböll, *Katalog des
Ethnographischen Reichmuseums*, Band V
(Leiden: E.J. Brill, 1909), pp. 15–16

The evolution of Durga's victory over the buffalo on the other hand, as
we saw in Chapter 7, continues to develop. Even though the myth never
really became established, Durga's cult and its ritual took solid root in Java.
The very Sanskrit word for buffalo, *mahisha*, often took the form *maésa* in the
Nusantara (van der Tuuk, vol. IV, 1898, pp. 575–76). Damais (1957) tries to
show that the Persian term *nisan* is not the origin of the word *maésan* or
sacrifice post, but rather the Sanskrit word for buffalo:

FIGURE 8.2

Durgāmahishāmardanī (slayer of Mashisha) from the north cellar of the main
temple of Prambanan (ninth century), Central Java. The sculpture may be of
a later date; cf. Roy Jordaan (1996), pp. 79–81

FIGURE 8.3

Durgāmahishāmardanī (slayer of Mashisha) from the
Radyapustaka Museum, Surakarta, Central Java

FIGURE 8.4
Wayang **sketch of Durga**

Source: Reksopustaka, Mangkunagaran Palace, Surakarta.

A pre-Hindu custom in certain regions of the archipelago attached buffalo to rough stone pillars (a sort of menhir) which were sacrificed at the feasts of the dead. After the ceremony the sacrificial pillar remained in place. ... in this respect it is not without importance to remark that the most ancient inscriptions in Indonesia are found in the eastern part of Kalimantan (Borneo) on stone pillars .... called *yupa* which is the Sanskrit term for a sacrificial pillar. It therefore seems to us not impossible that the word *maésan* might be the Indonesian equivalent (even if its origin is Sanskrit) of what is called technically in Sanskrit as *yupa*.

If today *maésan* means a stone placed at the head of a grave (Mayer 1897, p. 531 gives several of the possible forms), the word *maésa* (*krama* for *kebo* or buffalo) is still used in ritual invocations to describe the buffalo killed for, in lieu of, by Durga. For instance the sacrifice of the *maésa lawung,* refers to slaughtering by lance (*lawung*).[1] The buffalo meat should come from a beast that has never pulled a plow. What is designated by the causative form (*di-aké*) of the verb *lawung* indicates that the beast is sacrificed by being "speared" (i.e. behind the front shoulder) and not sacrificed by having its throat cut (*sembelih,* as in Muslim goat sacrifices at Idul Adha).

The Jesuit anthropologist Baker (1976, pp. 119–26), in his synthesis on indigenous Indonesian religions, classifies the *maésa lawung* ritual with the famous *bedhaya ketawang* dance because both express the sacred cosmic order by reuniting a dichotomy. Baker did not provide an adequate description of the ritual, referring only to Hadiwijoyo (1972). Besides our own fieldwork in Krendawahana itself, there are useful written sources:

1. In 1973 the Javanese literati *radèn* Tanoyo, a well-known compiler of almanacs (*primbon* and *pawukon*), lent me his fifteen-page adaptation of a transcription of the manuscript by *Radèn tumenggung* Pujadipura (R. M. T. Bratadiningrat), the Surakarta palace *abdi-dalem bupati anom juru* Suranata (official responsible for the *maésa lawung*) in the 1940s.[2] Whether Tanoyo was the one who in 1937 encouraged Bratadiningrat and the officials around him to write up the full manuscript described below (no. 3) is not clear.

2. In April 1974 I obtained a seven-page transcription of a Mangkunagaran Palace (*askara* (Javanese script) ms; from the "*bundel slametan Maésa Lawung*"). It contained some ten prayers and a brief history of the rite probably derived from Bratadiningrat's text.

3. By far the oldest and fullest version of the description of this ritual is ms. 547 Ka entitled *Kraton Surakarta Kuwajiban Abdidalem Juru Suranata.* This dates from 1941 to 1945. It contains some forty prayers and the destination for various *labuhan* ("abandonings", i.e. offerings), as well as an intriguing description of the qualifications necessary for the officiant. Nancy K. Florida's 1985 transcription, which was deposited in the Sasana Pustaka (library) of the Surakarta Palace, runs to 130 pages of typescript. This will be used principally in Chapter 9.

All the secondary witnesses for the *maésa lawung* mentioned below are precious, for even in Pigeaud's nearly exhaustive four volume catalogue of Javanese 1968 manuscript below, there is to be found only one small reference, in an eight page ms. of notes made by Kraemer (Leiden Codex Or. 10.846 §4). Dr. Singgih Wibisono (1972, pp. 6–7, 10–12, 16–17) in a booklet on displaying of the heirlooms (*kirap pusaka*) ritual still held on the first of Sura, the Javanese new year, mentions a "golden buffalo" (*kangjeng kyai kebo mas*) lance and the albino buffalo (*kyai* Slamet) used in the Javanese new year late night procession around the palace, but these seem to have no direct relation to the ritual held in Krendawahana.

8.1 DESCRIPTION OF THE BUFFALO SACRIFICE IN THE *MAÉSA LAWUNG*

We give here a description of the Rajawedda or *Maésa lawung* entitled "Duties of the palace official"[3] (*abdhi dalem juru*):

> The functions of the *abdhi dalem bekel juru*[4] consist in presenting on the first of each Rabingulakir month [the fourth Muslim month, also called Bakda Mulud] a report to the palace on the ritual meal (*slametan*) of the buffalo sacrificed by lancing (*maésa lawung*). In other words, he must come out before seven in the morning to the Sokalanggèn ["pillars of pleasure" hall] wearing a *dodot* batik of varied colour but without winged motifs, in a black fez, bearing a cleaver-like kris, a *sikepan* vest, or a kind of *beskap cita* vest (buttoned down the middle), etc., he makes his report to his Highness (*Saméyan Dalem*), inviting the higher officials (*priyagung wedana*) to go to the Srimanganti at seven o'clock. After this he returns to present himself to the *panéwu kabayan nagari*.
>
> 4. [...enumerates the ten kinds of (*abdi dalem juru*) and the 4,3 ha. (1, 5 jung) appanage which accompanies their office.]
>
> 5. [...describes the ritual held at the mosque and the procession in the evening with the heirloom (*pusaka*) buffalo Kangjeng Kyai Slamet.]

FIGURE 8.5
Decorated sacrificial buffalo in 1996

Source: Reksopustaka, Mangkunagaran Palace, Surakarta.

FIGURE 8.6
Procession of the *Maésa Lawung* offerings in 1996 from the Mangkunagaran
Palace to Durga's tertre (*pundhèn*) in Krendawahana

Source: Reksopustaka, Mangkunagaran Palace, Surakarta.

FIGURE 8.7
Severed buffalo head

Source: Reksopustaka, Mangkunagaran Palace, Surakarta.

FIGURE 8.8
Two *abdi dalem* from the palace of Paku Buwana XII
addressing the assembly at foot of Durga's tertre

FIGURE 8.9
Four *abdi dalem* at the base of *pundhèn* praying

FIGURE 8.10
Woman reaching towards effigy of human sacrifice (*bekakak*)

6. The Ceremony of the royal well-being [=*wilujengan nagari*] (the Rajawedda) or Lancing of the buffalo (*maésa lawung*).

Compiled by Radèn Tumengung Pudjadipura, the *abdi dalem bupati anom juru* Suranata, in Surkarta. It happened that the royal *slametan* (=ritual meal) has become part of custom (*adat*) beginning in the Buddhist period under the name of Rajawedda. The King Jaya Nata Binatara accomplished this same royal *slametan*, that is to say that the venerable King Binatara offered this *slametan* at the beginning of each year, coming out of the Pancaniti (room in the high tertre (Sitinggil) where the throne was placed) to pronounce the Rajawedda *slametan* (occurrence) and to pray for the welfare of the kingdom and all its inhabitants, wishing for the reign of peace in the palace and in all the provinces. This (occurred) until the great King Sri Prabu Ajipamasa[5] of the kingdom of Pengging called this *slametan* a Rajawedda, a buffalo lancing. It is said that at the time of Sang Prabu Sitawaka of Gilingaja there occurred various troubles, epidemics, etc. such that there was no longer any peace in the capital nor in the provinces in the *candrasangkala* 387 (=?465 A.D.) year indicated by the words *pujaning brahmana guna*. With the permission of Sri Prabu Sitawaka, the brahman Raddi of Andongdadapan [said to be near Salatiga] was ordained to make a sacrifice [*tumbal* may mean here an animal replacement for a human victim] for the palace and all the provinces. The brahman replied, "According to your wish," and effectuated the sacrifice required, a royal sacrifice which the population of all the hamlets received the order to offer at the beginning of the year, that is to say a *grama wedda* (literally, a fire knowledge; probably a *rasulan*, a *slametan*) a ritual meal for the *rajawedda* (royal wisdom), and only a little time passed before the epidemics diminished, the troubles calmed down and a peaceful order established itself in the capital and prosperity reigned over all the earth. That is why the inhabitants of the villages celebrated these *slametan* [i.e. annual prufications rites or *bersih dusun*] to purify their hamlets from that time till now.

In the time of the venerable King sri prabu Ajipamasa who had his palace at Pengging, there appeared an enemy monster from Ngimaimantaka from over the seas. Sang prabu Ajipamasa called the *gandarwa*,[6] King Karawu and said to him, "Oh elder brother King Karawu, how can we make this enemy disappear? And the *gandarwa*, King Karawu replied, "Your excellence, later this enemy will become very large, so it would be good to ask from Batari (Durga) the aid of the demon army from Krendawahana. Sang Prabu was very pleased and ordered the *gandarwa*, the King Karawu, to go to Krendawahana to ask Batari Kalayuwati (=Durga) to do the necessary. Then the goddess Kalayuwati replied: "Oh sang Sampatisuta (other name of Kuruwa) I consider that it is a negligence that our king demands courageous behaviour, but how much time has gone by since he ascended the throne of Pengging without ever offering a sacrificial buffalo in the charnel field (Setra Gangamayu, i.e. odour of cadavers). And now you come for help! The King Karawu said he only asked for forgiveness, and the king of the *gandarwa* returned to Pengging to beg Sri Prabu Ajipamasa to make his response known to Batari Kalayuwati.

Sri Prabu Ajipamasa was alarmed and summoned the *patih* (minister) Tambakbaya to prepare a *maésa lawung* on behalf of the king and all the dignitaries. As soon as the requisites were ready for the sacrifice the order to leave for Krendawahana was given. The army of the hunters started marching and once they were received (by Durga), she furnished in aid an army of ogres (*ditya*), as many as were necessary. Henceforth the *slametan* Rajawedda was called *maésa lawung* (buffalo spearing) because it referred to a buffalo from the forest (*maésa wanan*) who lived from one generation to another wild in the forest, never domesticated by man for the plow. Buffaloes of this sort are called *maésa lawung*. It is said that in the kingdom of Demak, the one who ascended the throne under the name Sinuhun Kangjeng Sultan Sah Ngalam Akbar in 1439[7] who spread Islam in Java during his reign, esteemed that the *slametan* Rajawedda and the customs and ceremonies associated with it did not agree with the Muslim religion. Thus it was that often the ritual was no longer authorised. Beginning with the period when the capital was in Demak, the provinces experienced sickness, and pillage was such that there was no security or peace. The country was divided when during the propagation of Islam whose merits where no longer evident, the august king ordered the minister Tumenggung Mangkurat, to enjoin all the functionaries to consult with the counsellors and nine *wali* (literally, friends of God). The discussions were to begin by a meditation (*tapa brata*) on the *darmastuti* (hymn to dharma; perhaps the name of a room in the palace). The arrows of this meditation were clear-seeing ideas whose perspective was knowledge. These arrows were unceasingly shot to implore the mercy of God Almighty. After the proclamation of this order, half of the palace functionaries continued to pursue their habitual tasks while the other half practised meditation accomplishing diverse sacrifices. The *wali* were also organised in like manner, and even the king himself considered that the fact of worshipping (*pitre puja*, literally honouring the fathers) constituted an authentic security and assured the prosperity of the kingdom of Demak. The next month Sunan Kalijaga received a revelation, a sign whose interior meaning was as follows: in order that the kingdom of Demak might truly be peaceful, his majesty Kangjeng Sultan Sah Ngalam Akbar must command from his throne instruction to benefit by their salutary effects the entire country by defending it magically against dangers.

The functionaries of the palace and the nine *wali* were advised of the situation, that is to say that the royal customs of Majapahit [the preceding Hindu-Buddhist dynasty] were to be maintained because they were considered as still necessary to the kingdom of Demak, susceptible of being used to favour by their "captivating" action the development of the Muslim religion. It is said that beginning with the period that he became king, five years passed before he ordered a *raja wedda*. Beginning in 1442 (=1520 A.D.)[8] his majesty Kangjeng Sultan Sah Ngalam Akbar decreed the ordering of a *slametan raja wedda*, a *maésa lawung*, according to the customary law (*adat*) of Majapahit, which he ordered Sunan Bonang and Sunan Giri to codify with its rituals and the prayers by consulting the officials who knew the ordo of the *raja wedda* in the palace of Majapahit. The prayers were given form by Sunan Bonang beginning in that period, the invocations of the *raja wedda* being written out mixing Arabic, Javanese and Buddhist (Sanskrit), following a higher revelation. Hardly a month passed before the kingdom of Demak (as well as) the provinces, having received these instructions, became peaceful and prosperous (both) in the capital and in the provinces.

Until the period when the kingdom's palace was at Kartasura,[9] under the reign of his majesty Kangjeng Susuhunan Pakubuwana II, the traditional rite (*wijos*) of the royal *slametan* of the *maésa lawung* continued to be performed regularly during the first month of the year.

It was precisely the eighteenth, Rebo Wagé of the month of Sura, the year Jé, numbered 1670 (=1748 A.D.) that his majesty Sinuhun Kangjeng Pakubuwana II transferred the palace of Kartasura to the town of Surakarta Adiningrat. One hundred days (before the day of) Kemis Legi, the twenty-sixth of the month of Rabingulakir of the year Jé. Then there was no longer any obstacle to the perpetuation of the *slametan*. The permission to observe the *maésa lawung* was changed in the month of Rabingulakir, being fixed on the last "visiting" day (*pasowanan*) of the month. Henceforth the *adat* for its performance was as follows:

(1) The apanage officer (*abdi dalem pamajegan*) ordered that a free-range (i.e. "lancing") buffalo be found. The "field hunter" officer (*abdi dalem Tuwaburu Palawija*) was the one to receive orders to procure game from the forest, deer, tigers, dwarf deer, flying squirrels (*walangkapa*), etc. Several days passed in order to arrange for the *slametan*, all those charged with the *maésa lawung* prepared the game that was supposed to be offered. Here are the properties of the buffalo for lancing: its eyes *anjait* (=?smallish), a white collar around its neck that is more or less complete, a regular coat around the shoulders. It must be a male buffalo, handsome and without fault. After an interval of several days for the needs of the organisers of the ceremony, the officials responsible must inspect the slaughter house, examine the buffalo; that is to say they are required to equip the slaughter house for the butcher (*abdi dalem jagal gudel*) who does the slaughtering.[10]

(2) The attendant to the throne room (*abdi dalem marbot paramasana*) must prepare the high tertre (*siti inggil*). Two recipients are to be prepared for the blood; the lot is taken to be cooked without spices; as for the flesh

it is cooked for the *slametan* the night before the celebration of the royal ceremony (*ajad dalem*). The *abdi dalem juru* takes care of the execution of the Javanese prayers; usually the *abdi dalem* Reksa-Sugata and the *abdi dalem nyai lurah* Gandarasa prepare the rice with accompanying dishes (*sekul langgi*) which will be served for this sort of *slametan*. The same day as the royal *slametan* of the *maésa lawung*, in the morning, the *abdi dalem* Juru Suranata with the *abdi dalem nyai lurah* Gandarasa, together, appear with the accessories necessary for the dedication (*labuh*) of the offering prepared at the Maligé (in front of the palace). The two cups of blood (placed) in a single box, will be offered once prepared by the *abdi dalem* Juru who reads the Javanese (Buddhist) prayer *Sastra Pedati* ("wagon of letters"[11]). Next the king leaves to give an audience. The *abdi dalem bupati* Estri[12] presents a report on the celebration of the royal *slametan* of the *maésa lawung* and repeats the order of the king to the *abdi dalem bupati anom* Damel Gandek (executor of king's orders) who transmits the royal order to the Papatih Dalem (interior minister). Those attending next move to the reception hall (Séwayana at the Siti Inggil) while the Pepatih Dalem with all the prefects (*abdi dalem bupati*) celebrate a royal *slametan*, making sure that all is in place in the reception hall Séwayana. The Papatih Dalem next transmits the royal order to begin the royal *slametan* with all that that entails to the *abdi dalem bupati anom juru* Suranata, ordering him to proclaim the Arabic, Buddhist and Javanese prayers. Once the royal *slametan* is completed, the offerings (*labuh*), that is to say the blood of the buffalo to be lanced in two boxes,[13] equipped to contain the vases in which they are brought into the depths of the Krendawahana forest (setra Gandamayu). The blood is brought by the *abdi dalem* Marbot Paramasana. As to the *abdi dalem* who attend this royal *slametan*, they eat their food together, brought individually, in woven round trays. But nowadays the individual trays have been replaced, following the King's request, by tables no longer having the form of round trays (*ancak*) but that of the low tables used at evening receptions. [The remainder of the text concerns the colours of these offerings.]

It is not easy to situate this text critically. The historical reconstruction the author undertakes seems to owe something to the mid-nineteenth century works of Ranggawarsita, himself reacting to the Dutch interest in historical periodization (Kenchi Tschiya 1990). His sense of the evolution of the customary sacrifice is heightened not only by a veneration of its antiquity but also by a real recognition that it is in some sense "out of time". His dates are necessarily wrong but his sense that although capital cities change there is a real continuity between Javanese kingdoms is quite accurate. Although he had no ambition to write a history in the Dutch sense, he did a fair job of it, providing *radèn* Tanoyo in 1937 with the only account we have available. Is he the same author who in 1941 (re-)composed the lengthy palace ms (Sasana

Pustaka 547 Ka, pp. 25–46 in transcription) under Paku Buwana XI? It seems likely, but in the days of Paku Buwana X, there was a whole corps of officials for the performance of invocations: *abdi dalem Bupati Anom Juru Suranata Radèn Tumenggung Pujadiningrat* for the Islamic prayers (a sort of palace *modin* for the *masjid* Pudyasana); *abdi dalem mantri Juru Suranata Radèn Ngabèhi Pujastaruna* for the Buddhist prayers, one *lurah* and nine *jajar* (subordinate bearers) to accompany the offerings.[14] It seems that the officials involved in Islam had come to have the higher rank. It should be possible to gather more data on the evolution of this group of palace officials from late nineteenth century Dutch descriptions. Did the Suranata originally outrank the other Suranata, who did the Arabic prayers and if so when was the hierarchy reversed?

The folder (*bundel*) on the *maésa lawung* offerings made by the neighbouring and junior palace of the Mangkunagaran contains the same prayers given by the Susuhanan (Paku Buwana's) palace manuscript, although it is dated 1918, thus predating by twenty-three years the more complete text from the Sasana Pustaka. At the time of writing there seems no way of establishing when the two palaces started collaborating or alternating in the delivery of these offerings to the forest of Krendawahana.

It is possible, however, to sketch the relationship of the two palaces over the last 250 years. The territory of the princedom of the Mangkunagaran (including the then forest of Krendawahana) was created after what is called the "third succession war" (1757), third referring to the ascension to the throne of Paku Buwana III with such carefully applied Dutch V.O.C. support that they managed to split the kingdom of Mataram into two, then into four. Paku Buwana II's elder brother, Pangéran Ario Mangkunegara, had been exiled to Ceylon in 1728 and eventually to South Africa (de Kaap). For the better part of seven years, his son, Mas Said, kept up an armed struggle, long after the other contestant Pangéran Mangkubumi (the other brother of Paku Buwana II) had been persuaded to lay down his arms by the offer of approximately half the kingdom centred on Yogyakarta.

Once the Treaty of Giyanti was signed with Mangkubumi (13 February 1755), Mas Said continued his fight. The new Dutch commander Hartingh was more inclined to diplomatic methods than to military ones, and having a good command of Javanese, was quite skilful. Finally on 17 March 1757,[15] in Salatiga to the west of the capital in Surakarta, Mas Said was made Pangéran Miji (chosen prince) with the title of Pangéran Adipati Mangkunegara.

Several times his small kingdom was increased in size. In 1788–90 the hostilities between the Yogyakarta and Surakarta major palaces began again over seizure of territories and questions of title (the Susuhunan in Surakarta persisted in refusing that of the Mangkubumi). Paku Buwana IV's newfound opposition to the V.O.C.[16] had apparently also been fuelled by Muslim *ulama* (a certain Kyai Santri and Kyai Bakhman) who encouraged resistance to the V.O.C. At this stage the small principality of the Mangkunagaran was more tightly bound to the V.O.C. through the signing of an Act of Assurance, which also partially released him from his submission to the Susuhunan. Yet after 1792 certain of the Mangkunagaran princes continued to be in the service of the Sunan. It was only in this period that the apanage (*lungguh*) lands of the Mangkunagaran consisting of 4,000 *cacah* were described as vassal's fief (*leengebied*). The Mangkunagaran was decreed henceforth to be loyal to both the Susuhuan and the V.O.C.

The size of the vassal lands of the Mangkunagaran were increased in 1813, when the British gave it another 1,000 *cacah*[17] for its help in defeating the rebellion of the Yogyakarta sultan. After the Java War in 1830 an additional 500 *cacah* were given, bringing the total to 5,500. Thereafter the number of *cacah* was not augmented.

The legion of the Mangkunagaran continued to be supported with varying subsidies by the V.O.C. and later Daendals; it was re-established by Raffles in 1812 during the English interregnum in Java. The Mangkunagaran legion fought against the Javanese national hero Dipanagara in the Java War (1825–30) and again at the end of the century during the second expedition against the Acehnese (1873–74). The end of the nineteenth century (1888–98) was to see the Mangkunagaran become heavily indebted and three successive Dutch residents manage their plantations and the running of their "own" sugar factories.[18]

This brief outline makes it clear that relations between the two Surakarta palaces were always fraught with difficulties, but apparently none so great as to merit the creation of a new Krendawahana forest once the old one (after the founding of the new capital in Surakarta in 1745–46; Soepomo and Ricklefs 1967) was established. Had their relations been totally unmanageable, the transfer of the offering to the Krendawahana forest to the north of both Surakarta palaces but still in Mangkunagaran territory might have been so difficult as to justify situating it even further north. This would have brought it inside the Paku Buwana's lands. This did not take place, however, nor did the difficulties of transporting the offerings lead to the establishment of one of the other cardinal points as the place of celebrating the new year or Rabingulakir month festival. From around early 1746, when the new capital city was first occupied in Surakarta, the political situation was so unstable for the next seventy-five years (till after the Java War) that other preoccupations were perhaps more pressing.

8.2 THE RESPONSIBILITIES OF THE SURANATA: SACRIFICE VIA COSMOGONY

In any event, an evolution took place among the officials responsible for the *maésa lawung* and other ceremonies. In the fifteenth century there were armed guards called *suranata* who surrounded the Sunan Kudus and whose function was half military and half religious (de Graaf and Pigeaud 1974, p. 68 (note 66, p. 257), 100 (note 103, p. 268)). These soldier-believers gradually evolved into court chaplains with their own *penghulu* whose mosque (*mesjid suranatan*) lay inside the inner court and was the private Muslim place of worship for the family. It is not known exactly how it was used. What we do know is that both the Surakarta and Yogyakarta (Taman Sari) courts maintained underground or underwater meditation halls for their sovereigns where the religious practice seems far from canonical mosque *salat* (cf. Behrend 1983). A dual mosque disposition (one inside the personal compound of the king and one on the northern square) dates from Sunan Giri, reflecting a pre-Muslim practice according to de Graaf and Pigeaud (1974, p. 100 (268 note 103)). Whatever that might have been, there most certainly was a duality between these mosques and the high tertre facing the northern *alun-alun* around which most of the important juridical and ritual events took place. Worship there featured the position of the king as paramount while the great mosque placed the *umma'* in a more egalitarian position before the higher being. In those equal ranks the king had no place. In that spectrum the *suranata* seem to have lost their military function but gained an "in-house" function where they bridged past and present religious roles. The higher *suranata* eventually limited themselves to Muslim prayer, leaving the Buddhist invocations for the lower "clergy". Table 8.1 are compares the lists of prayers for the *maésa lawung* ritual from the respective Surakarta palaces.

Clearly the prayers from the Susuhunan's Sasanapustaka manuscript are quite dissimilar from the Mangkunagaran's corpus. The latter is much closer to the "pan-Javanese" corpus for exorcisms (*ruwatan*; cf. Table 5.1, Headley 2000a, p. 143 comparing this palace collection with two corpus of exorcism mantra). In the second and Arabic half of the more recent Paku Buwana palace collection many well-known Javanese prayers with Javanese names have been given new Arabic contents, indicating that the *abdi dalem suranata* have replaced many of the Javanese invocations at a recent date (1940s?). This

TABLE 8.1
Prayers for the *Maésa Lawung* from the Surakarta palaces
(// means same text as that in the first column)

Sasana (Paku Buwana)	Reksopustaka (Mangkunagaran)
1. Bubuka	//donga Sanga Buwono (some Arabic)
2. donga Mangkurat	//donga Bumi
3. donga Mangkurat bis	donga Jejeg
4. donga Songga Buwana	donga lungguh (B)*
5. donga Rubung	donga Tulak Bilahi (some Arabic)
6. donga Burung Kapala	//donga Nurbuwat (some Arabic)
7. donga Sida Lungguh	

Buddhists prayers

8. donga Tetep Pelungguhané/donga Hakeng	
9. donga Lungguhing Badan	//Kalacakra (B)*
10. donga Jejeg Jumeneng (puji buda)	Sastrapedati
11. donga mas Kumambang	Banyak Dhalang
12. donga Bumi	Gumbala Geni
13. donga Cipta rasa	Puji Banyu
14. donga Cipta Ratu	Mandala Giri
15. donga Iman (arabic)	
16. donga Hadi Mulya	
17. donga Turun Sih	
18. donga Rajah Kalacakra	
19. donga Gendrayana	
20. donga Tulak	
21. donga Tulak Tanggul	

Arabic prayers

22. donga Karaton (arabic)
23. donga Nurbuwat (arabic)
24. donga Suleman (arabic)
25. donga Mulya (arabic)
26. donga Sayuta (arabic)
27. donga Hadimulya (arabic)
28. donga Bala Serewu (arabic)
29. donga Sakethi (arabic)
30. donga Tulak Bilahi (arabic)
31. donga Slamet (arabic)
32. donga Mulya (arabic)
33. donga Tawil ngumur (arabic)
34. donga Kabulla
35. donga Panutupipun

*The Reksapustaka manuscript reproduces the same list of prayers three times and "B" indicates the difference between the first and second of these lists.

indicates quite a rapid evolution of the Javanese prayer corpus (cf. Arps 1996, pp. 94–103). The *kidungan* (protective songs used as lullabies, etc., cf. Arps 1996 and Wiryapanitra 1979) once used some of the same invocations with the corpus of prayers used in the *wayang* exorcisms. The comparative Table 8.2 shows how the 1937 collection of Wiryapanitra and Probohardjono's 1960s collection taken from a Surakarta palace collection compare.

TABLE 8.2
Protective songs from Wiryapanitra (1937/1979) and Probohardjono (1965)

Wiryapanitra 1937/1979	Probohardjono 1965
Kidung weksa ing wengi, p. 103+ (stanza 1–8 in *dhandhanggula* meter)	*Kikidung weksa ing wengi* pp. 5–6 (stanza 1–9 in *dhandhanggula*)
(stanza 10–16 in *dhandhanggula*)	Kikidung Hartati pp. 6–7 (10 stanzas in *dhandhanggula*)
(stanza 17–26 in *dhandhanggula*)	Kidung Hartadaja pp. 7–8 (10 stanzas in *dhandhanggula*)
(stanza 17–37 in *dhandhanggula*)	Kikidung Jatimulya pp. 8–10 (11 stanzas in *dhandhanggula*))
(stanza 38–40 in *dhandhanggula*)	Kikidung Sagara Rab p. 10 (3 stanzas in in *dhandhanggula*)
(stanza 41–45 in *dhandhanggula*)	Kidung Akadang Premati p. 11 (6 stanzas in *dhandhanggula*)
Pujiyan, pp. 151–53 (stanza 1–26 in *sinom*)	Kidung Padhayangan Tanah Jawa pp. 12–15 (26 stanzas in *sinom*)
Pujiyan, pp. 153–54 (stanzas in *asmaradana*)	Kidung Padhayangan Surakarta (11 stanzas in *asmaradana*)
Pujiyan, pp. 154–57 (24 stanzas in *kinanti*)	Kidung Pangléla-léla pp. 17–20 (29 stanzas in Kinanti)
Pujiyan, pp. 159–63 (10 stanzas in *durma*)	Kidung Waringin Sungsang (11 stanzas in *durma*)
Pujiyan pp. 164–70 (11 stanzas 77–83 in *durma*)	Kikidung Balé Anyar pp. 27–28 (12 stanzas in *durma*) (partially identical to mantra Banyak Dhalang. cf. ch. 9)

The last two cosmogonic invocations in the right-hand column are used by the Mangkunagaran at the *maésa lawung*. It is useful to compare the invocations used by the *abdi dalem juru* Suranata on the occasion of the birth of a prince or princess in the palace as described in the Surakarta Palace Sasana Pustaka manuscript,[19] with the invocations used in a *wayang* creation myth and a *wayang* exorcism (*ruwatan* using the birth of Kala myth). Here, as opposed to the *méasa lawung*, one finds a more ancient and less Islamicized corpus, reflecting a preoccupation with cosmogony. If one were to speculate about the date of its origin, its composite and partially corrupt texts would suggest post-Majapahit, but the relatively rapid evolution of these texts could allow for a much more recent date.

In conclusion, the list of diverse qualifications to become *principal* officiant (*bupati anom juru* Suranata: manuscript Sasana Pustaka pp. 1–24) for certain rituals in the Surakarta palace illustrates a period and a place where palace traditional beliefs and Islam co-existed in tolerance. Astrology, numerology, traditional week- and month-based divination, the Koran, Dutch letters, and Malay language are listed side by side as necessary qualifications along with required memorization of the prayers to be discussed Chapter 9. There is no explicit indication of the relative importance of the diverse invocations in this Susuhunan Palace manual "Responsibilities of the Palace Official *Suranata* (… prayers, mantra and songs)" so we can surmise that each year the respective accents in the ceremony may have varied.

8.3 KRENDAWAHANA AS SEEN BY THE MANGKUNAGARAN

We have four testimonies giving a glimpse of a non-aristocratic vision of the forest of Batari Durga as seen from outside the palace:

- my conversation with the village headman or *lurah* of Krendawahana recorded in 1974;
- a 1915 article from the Solo newspaper *Djawi Hisworo*;
- Kraemer's notes on a conversation with R.T. Pujodipura who may have been the compiler of Mangkunagaran *Bundel Slametan*;
- Kraemer's summary of the ten most important *slametans*, which contextualizes the *maésa lawung* (Leiden University OrO 10,846 §2).

In March 1974 I gave the headman (*lurah*) of Krendawahana the fourteen-page text on the *maésa lawung* that *radèn* Tanoyo had written in 1937, which he had recently passed on to me. For the previous few months I had spent several hours a day in the company of this elderly village headman, Sastrodiwiryo, but he had never divulged his thoughts on the tertre of Durga. On reading Tanaya's text, however, he told me how happy he was to have read the "real" history of this offering ground and asked me if I wanted him to tell me another local history, certainly less authentic, but the way the village elders there told the story:

> "All this took place a long time ago, perhaps two hundred years before…"

As he told his story of how Paku Buwana VI became lost in the Krendawahana forest before being found (cf. Ch. 3 and 6 *supra*), I was reminded of another disappearance, not of Paku Buwana VI, but of the prince Natakusuma, son of Mangkunagaran VI who in fact lived during the reign of Paku Buwana VI. This also came from Tanoyo's Serat *Raja wedda* and relates how prince Natakusuma, son of Paku Buwana IV and son-in-law of Mangkunagaran II[20] was lured into the invisible palace of Durga by the appearance of two purple does. The prince, subjugated by the charms of Durga, never returned. What is interesting about these two Javanese narratives is that they are primarily concerned with the possibility of meeting with Durga, not, as in the local Kalioso Muslim versions, with a *kyai* who rescued the king or prince.

A *Djawi Hisworo*[21] article, dated 15 March 1916, insists that the date of the *maésa lawung* must be the first Senen Kemis of the month Rabingulakir. The king receives while still in the Pangelaran (open pavilion on top of the Siti Inggil),[22] all the high and low officials including what it calls the "Muslim officials", *hamba ulama Djuru,* who say the prayers before the sharing of the meat and other offerings. A piece of each animal sacrificed is also taken to the forest of Krendawahana. Nowadays (1990s) the prayers are said in a much smaller pavilion to the west of the Smarakata in the inner palace, and a meal is shared at the tertre of Durga by all who have accompanied the offering to Durga's tertre.

The interest of Kraemer's notes, besides that of his impeccable transcription of the Arabic words, resides in the details that Radèn Tumenggung Pujadipura confided to him. There is, for instance, a *kalang* (=? itinerant group) of butchers (*jagal*) employed in the forest to sacrifice the three or four young buffalo (*gudèl*) which are left to roam free in the Krendawahana forest in order that the animals sacrificed might never have been yoked to a plough. The bowels of the sacrificed animals are thrown in the *cinet* (?) well there. In this connection the mention of the seven *Ficus Benjamina* (*waringin*) indicates that the well is probably the one now called the well of the ogre Burisrawa.[23]

In any event Pujadipura says the seven *waringin* have now died according to
the proverb: "Every ground that is holy possesses a large tree, once it dies the
ground becomes neutral" (*tawar lemah sangar kayu ageng, ojod mimang*), and
that the site is not longer *angker* or *kramat* (sacred). Kraemer also notes that
R.T. Pujadipura insists that all that flies, walks, or swims (*kutu walang ataga*)
must be present on the offering tray. The list of offerings for 4 July 1949
shows that Kalioso provided the buffalo, Slagaima (=?) and various kinds of
birds (nine in total) as did the prefecture of Wonogiri (nineteen items
including birds), and Selogiri a lesser number, while the *kapanéwon* of the
palace in Surakarta provided six birds bought presumably at the market. Birds
outnumber all other offerings.

Next is given the seating of each of the officials at the high tertre, here
called Sewayana. R.T. Pujidipura was responsible for seating them and it was
also he, of course, who said the prayers for the palace *slametan*.

This Bupati ends with the interesting remark that on the same day a
similar ceremony takes place on the anniversary of the sultan of Yogyakarta
but that he does not know its name and that no buffalo sacrifice is involved.
Kraemer's list of prayers includes a number of variants: the *donga* Songga
Buwana Mangkurat Sari is longer and has more Arabic formulas than the one
found in the Mangkunagaran *bundel slametan*. Four *donga*, Tulak Bilahi,
Bumi, Jerjer and Lungguh are almost entirely in Arabic but have kept their
Javanese names, belying an earlier Javanese text.

In Kraemer's list of *slametan*[24] there is one group, the fundamental (*baku*)
slametan, where the common people (*tiyang alit*) are not admitted, and this
includes the *maésa lawung*. It is said that the village people's equivalent is the
annual purification of their hamlets (*bersih dusun* or *rasulan*). The *bersih
dusun* are for the well-being of the hamlets, while the Arab and Buddhist
prayers addressed to Batari Durga are for the glory (*mulya*) of the king
(*Dalem*; literally inside). In conclusion the three *garebeg* by their Muslim
motifs and the collection of taxes which took place conjointly, distinguish
themselves quite readily from the *maésa lawung* devoted to the ruler (*Dalem*)
and hence to the kingdom's well-being. Nonetheless the *maésa lawung* share
one of the traits of the *garebeg*, the obligatory presence of certain categories of
high officials and the exclusion of commoners. The villagers have their own
local protective deity, *dhanyang baureksa dusun*, to whom a *slametan* is offered
after the May/June rice harvest. At each end of the social scale there are
protective boundaries, and these do not coincide. In fact the correspondence
between the Muslim feasts and the *garebeg* leaves the *maésa lawung* aside. The
division of time, that of the twelve months of the lunar year, might be
represented as follows:

Birth (*mawlid*) and End (*ba'da*) of the year
1. beginning of the year; Garebeg Besar (tenth of the twelfth month)
2. slametan of the *garebeg* of the fourth month (*ba'da Mulud*)
3. *lebaran* or end of the fast (*ba'da Puasa* twenty-first to twenty-ninth of the ninth month); coincides with the third and minor *garebeg*.

Outside the two principalities of Yogyakarta and Surakarta where the great *garebeg* were held, one could speak of two Muslim feasts: the birth of the prophet and *Lebaran* at the end of Ramadan. The *garebeg* of the fourth month disappears as soon as there is no popular fair[25] (*sekaten*) to support them. Does this mean that the Muslim calendar has replaced the Hindu-Buddhist one? According to Pigeaud (1962, p. 1208), these two Muslim feasts might well be the transposition of the Saiva-Buddhists festivals known in the court and the countryside during the dynasty of Majapahit. To support this speculation, he cites the fourteenth century *Nāgarakertāgama* (canto 69.3.1) where the cult of Rājapatnī is celebrated everywhere during the months of July to September (Shrāwana-Bhadra). So according to Pigeaud the religious feast of Rājapatnī would have been replaced by the feast of *Lebaran* as follows:

- One visits the graves of one's ancestors specially during the month of Ruwah (*arwāh* in Arabic means spirits)
- Pigeaud citing R.A.A. Kromo Jaya Adinegara (*Oudheidkundig Verslag* 1923, p. 53), accepts that the ritual of *lebaran* came from the *shraddha* festivals, even etymologically, for to go to the tombs at that time of the year is called *nadran*, which for Pigeaud is a corruption of the word *shraddha*.
- On the other hand, during the west monsoon there existed in the fourteenth century an annual harvest festival during the month of Phalguna-Caitra (February–March). It is the traces of this that we find in the seven-day *sekaten*[26] of the contemporary *garebeg* Mulud: minor fertility rites, the snapping of whips and the sharing of betel chews; with every eight years a Mulud Dal (actually the fifth or Dal year of the eight year *windu* cycle) consisting of the cooking of a mammoth pot of rice by the king and queen in person.

Pigeaud closes his discussion of the correspondences between the Majapahit and Muslim Mataram calendar by identifying the chthonic goddess who is reborn after the June harvest and at the end of every dry season (end of September or Bhadra) with the goddess of death Durga, the spirit grandmother (*hyang nini*) as she was known. As suggestive as Pigeaud's (1962, vol. IV, pp. 209–11) ideas are, this can hardly be called a proof. Yet since no one else has explored the culture of the Javanese fourteenth century so thoroughly, he merits being quoted in full. His argument runs as follows:

The cult during the months of Shrāwana-Bhadra in Majapahit took the form of new year ceremonies in honour of Rājapatnī during the month of Shrāwana: the passage of the old period to the new by the resurrection of this goddess. She is called Prajñapāramitā (the perfection of intelligence), or Maya, the name given to Rājapatnī, for she, like Nature, comes back to life at the beginning of each year.

The title of Mahārājapatnī, the great Royal Dame, is exceptional and seems to refer to the divine nature of Rājapatnī, who in canto 2.1.2 is referred to as Parama-Bhagavatī, a name of Uma-Durga, the supreme Sivaite goddess. Both these facts seem to justify an hypothesis of an ancient rural cult of a chthonic Javanese goddess being identified in the Mahapahit period with the cult of the royal ancestress.

In the old mythological poems of the *Sudamala* and the *Sri Tanjung,* Ra Nini or Hyang Nini were perhaps the names given to goddesses in the rural sanctuaries (*caitya*).

Pigeaud's suggestion that the goddess of the southern seas well known in contemporary Java for being the royal ancestress of the second Mataram dynasty can be identified with Rājapatnī is justified to the extent that they are both royal ancestress. Having ignored the role of Durga in the contemporary *maésa lawung* cult, however, that author has failed to realize that the goddess is a double at either end of the north-south axis stretching between the southern ocean and the forest at Krendawahana and symbolising the totality of the kingdom.

8.4 THE ABANDONING OF OFFERINGS (*LABUHAN*) IN DURGA'S FOREST

As suggested before, the sacred forest of Durga is not one but a multiple toponym that moved across Java as the cult of the goddess went from kingdom to kingdom. What is most obscure is the influence of popular peasant cults on *hyang nini*, obscurely relating to the raped and buried rice goddess from whose corpse the edible plants first grew (cf. Headley 2004). Many offerings were made to Durga in addition to the buffaloes offered by kings. That is, the pan-western Austronesian use of buffalo in sacrifices[27] whether at harvest rituals (Tunjung (Kalimantan), etc.) or at death rituals (Toraja (Sulawesi), etc.), has in Java become the privilege of the king by the use of an Indian derived iconographic motif and an identification of Durga with the lineage ancestress of the kingdom.

A former sub-prefecture official (*panéwu*) of the village of Kalioso, Ng. Hardjopandojo described the dedication of the offerings (*Djawa* 1941, pp. 109–11). Although his contribution was published in Dutch many of his Javanese terms were retained (translation S.C. Headley):

About twelve kilometres north of Solo to the east of the Kalioso train stop of the N.I.S. (Dutch East Indies Railroads) lie the woods of Kalioso. The name of this forest is famous especially in the *wayang*, for it is in that forest that Dewi Uma resides, better known under the name of Batari Durgam, god of the spirits and other invisible beings.

This place is famous because they always pray there to Batari Durga for her good favour towards those who come there to plead and invoke her for their destiny. She will not refuse even mean requests and she fulfils all the prayers addressed to her. Thus it is that Durga is a source for black magic.

Such are the legend and the character (of that goddess) in the shadow puppet theatre which still today are part of the beliefs of the large majority of the population.

We cannot say to what extent these beliefs exist in the court of the Mangkunagaran. On the other hand it is a fact that once a year, that is to say the last Thursday or Monday evening in the before the fourth of Sapar (the second month), date of the birthday of the current autonomous governor (*Zelfbestuurder*) offerings are made at the tertre (*sanggaran*) by this governor.

The tertre is situated on a large flat plot of land or around 1,4 hectares (four *bau*). This is broken in the middle by a hillock slightly to the west of the centre on which grows a large *rau* tree (variety of *cemara* or Podocarpus imbricata) which is called the throne of sang hyang Kalayuwati (= hyang Pramuni or batari Durga in *wayang* parlance).

The offerings which the current autonomous governor (i.e. the Mangkunagaran prince) has brought every year for his anniversary consist in the following elements:
(1) *sekul weduk* (rice cooked in coconut milk)
(2) *sekul asahan* (regular rice with meat and fish side dishes)
(3) *tubesan peken* or *jajan pasar* (diverse purées or *jegang*). ...

All the ingredients of fourth item are prepared in the house of the *panéwu* of Gondangreja (name of the sub-prefecture whose seat was in Kalioso[28]) according to precise rules of which a few are cited: one does not have the right to taste the dishes; the odour of the dishes should not be sniffed, nor that of the slaughtered goat. The costs of the offerings is seventeen florens.

When everything is ready, they bring the offerings in procession to the tertre about a kilometre from the house of the *panéwu*. This procession,[29] besides the offering bearers, includes the *panghulu naib* (regional Muslim officials who do marriages, etc.), a village headman with the rank of *rangga* (an aristocrat, or *priyayi*), one of the *mantri* of the indigenous administration (*Inlandsch Bestuur*), one of whom wears the clothing of the "autonmous governor" and that of his consort. When the other village officials have arrived at the tertre, a *slametan* is held, after which the exquisite dishes are distributed to the villagers, this of course only after the shrine guardian (*juru kunci*) has pronounced the *balasréwu* prayer (= *carakan balik*, or backwards alphabet;[30] cf. Ch. 9) and had announced the purpose for which the slametan was being held.

The articles of clothing to be consecrated for the Prince are:

(1) a sarong (*nyamping*) of any pattern whatsoever;

(2) a vest (*rasukan*);

(3) a headcloth (*destar*) of any pattern whatsoever;

For the consort:

(4) a *sarong* of any pattern whatsoever;

(5) a vest;

(6) a scarf (*semeken*; chest wrap) without any motif.

This clothing is placed in the shadow of the *rau* tree, to be reclaimed only after the goat has been put to death and its blood offered to the goddess.

The sacrifice of the goat takes place to the south of the great stone[31] and to the west of the old well[32] near the rau tree mentioned above.

After the ceremony described above, the men transport the clothes to the house of the *panéwu*. The next day they are taken to the palace by them or other officials who have the rank of aristocrats (*priyayi*).

Having arrived, they are stored, and the night before the birthday of the autonomous ruler (the fourth of Sapar), the clothing is again taken out and brought forth by the servants responsible to the queen consort.

What is interesting about this low-ranking official's account dating from 1940, is the role of the clothing and the sacrifice of the goat on the occasion of the celebration of the Mangkunagaran's ruler's birthday (*wiyosan dalem*). The cosmogonic is less to the centre of this ritual than the one put on by the Susuhunan; even the villagers go to partake of the *slametan*. According to a letter found in the archives of the Mangkunagaran, the *slametan* was fixed for 5 March 1940 so that the clothing would be returned one month before the prince's anniversary. This flexibility concerning the date of the *slametan* in Krendawahana can be better understood if we imagine that originally the anniversary commemorated was not the birth, but the date of accession to the throne of the prince. Most principalities in Central Java have maintained at least part of these practices.[33]

Another way to configure the cult of Durga in her forest of Krendawahana, which keeps in focus the predominance of the north-south axis, is to consider just two of four offerings made annually to the four cardinal points. Clearly the fifth synthetic point in the cross-like pattern (*mancapat*) was the palace itself in the centre. On Mt Lawu to the west (inside Mangkunagaran realm), it was again they who had the responsibility of delivering other kingdom's offerings. To bring the offerings of the Susuhunan and the Yogyakarta sultan up the four-thousand-metre volcanic mountain, was not only difficult; its "indirectness" (the multiplicity of intermediaries) also resulted in a gradual diminishment of its importance. It was usually in those directions where the kingdom had direct access that they placed the greatest importance on a given direction. And this usually meant the north-south axis.

Just as Krendawahana has been located in several sites, the offerings to the south, to the queen of the southern sea, are still done at Parang Tritis but have also been performed at other sites depending on who was offering, i.e. which prince or which village(r). The Yogyakarta sultan gave equal importance to the offerings to the north, to Empu Rama Permadi (or Sapu Jagat), on the very active volcano of Merapi. This site, which is to the west for the two Surakarta realms, attracted little attention from them. And the offering site to the west of Yogyakarta was also of lesser importance. There is a curious mixture of permanence and indifference in the placing of these orientations, which is highlighted by the fragmentation of Mataram into four kingdoms after the 1755 Giyanti Treaty. Clearly after this date no one kingdom had the total mastery of all four of the traditional offering sites. It is important to note that just before that division, when the capital was moved from Kartasura to Surakarta in 1745, the description of this transfer given by the *Babad Giyanti*,[34] written at the end of the eighteenth century by Yadadipura the elder (1729–1803), gives no mention of the north-south ritual orientation (Durga/Lara Ratu Kidul) other than that of the planting of the pairs of *ficus* (*waringin*) on the northern and southern squares (*alun-alun*) that frame the palace compound and which bring the palace peace and prosperity.

This presents us with a three formulation of hierarchy, sometimes called by the Javanese their spiritual geography for offerings and worship:

1. The major north-south axis, i.e. Krendawahana to the north of Surakarta or Merapi to the north of Yogyakarta and the southern ocean to the south of both.[35]
2. A cruciform axis with the palace (Surakarta or Yogyakarta) in the centre.
3. A multitude of doubles (Dlepih, near Wonogiri to the south of Surakarta), as a substitute for the southern ocean; the grotto of Kewadusan to east in the village of Kay Apak on the slopes of Lawu, each having their own specific local *raison d'être*.[36]

There exists some overlap between the second and the third configurations. In 1890 *radèn ngabèhi* Hardjapradata from Klaten gave a list of six principal *labuhan* or sites for dedicating offerings. He distinguishes these by the fact that instead of being normal offerings (*sadranan*) placed on the ground (for which he gives a list of sixty-six sites), these are places where the offerings are carried off by water, salt or fresh. So here, *labuh* is understood in the same sense as *larung* (to abandon to the waves whether of the sea or in a river). The common feature of all these shrines is that they are presented as a place where an encounter, a contact, has taken place, and still can, between a spirit, protecting or menacing, and a community or individual.

Clearly the greater the individual, noble or king and the more widely known the spirit (the consort of Siwa or the queen of the southern seas), the greater the importance of the encounter. Thus the tree growing in the middle of a stream that one day permitted the Mangkunagaran prince to escape from his enemies gives birth to its own legend,[37] but does not necessarily give rise to a cult or ritual of any permanence.

The permanence of these "contacts" rituals is apparent from two texts given here. The first is an extract from the Buddhist treatise, the *Sutosoma*,[38] that dates from the fourteenth century (translation of Soewito Santoso 1975, pp. 551–20):

> The king Dasabahu was intrepid and delighted to see so many powerful enemies. Arrows and axes were thrown in ever increasing number. The king went into meditation by means of yoga for a moment, remembering the holy Durga, and the goddess Mahabherawi (another form of Durga) appeared. Immediately she cried with a high voice and became visible to all the giants in her four-armed form. The arrows of the giants were destroyed and disappeared instantly when they returned to her tongue and were made to disappear for all the giants have their origin in her…
>
> The (ogre) king Porusāda was overwhelmed when all the arrows of the giants were destroyed and disappeared. He recited a hymn to pacify the goddess Durga in order to destroy the spell cast on her.

The second example is the famous foundational encounter already mentioned between the first ruler of the second Mataram dynasty Senapati (reigned 1575–1601) with the queen of the southern sea. Since then every subsequent king has her as his "consort". The text is from the abridged prose version of the *Babad Tanah Djawi* (Olthoff's Dutch translation 1941, pp. 79–82).[39] At the time of their meeting Senapati has not yet founded his kingdom:

> While Kyai Djuru went to Merapi, Senapati left towards the East, letting himself float down[40] the Umpak River. At the mouth he met in a rice field

ditch a Tunggal Wulung fish (purple banner[41]) who kindly offered him his back as a seat. Senapati thanked him and returned to land ... then there was a violent storm that tore up the trees. The fish were thrown on the dry land and the water became so hot that one would have said it was boiling.

These natural phenomena attracted the attention of Rara Kidul (the virgin of the South). She came out (of the ocean) and saw Senapati in prayer. She surmised his thoughts. And when he approached her, she made a *sembah* (like the Indian *anjali*) enchanted by his beauty. All the Javanese spirits serve her.[42] Then she pacified Senapati and calm returned to nature and the dead fish returned to life.

After that Senapati went with the princess to the underwater palace where they caressed each other for three days and three nights and he received teachings in the art of governing, particularly in the art of invoking the spirits... (pp. 82–83) Senapati returned from the palace of the queen walking on the water.[43] At Parang Tritis (where he came onto dry land) he met Sunan Kalijaga[44] sitting in a cave of stalactites, plunged into meditation. Senapati immediately received from him the advice not to put is trust in sakti (magical powers), not to be proud, etc. ..."Come we will go to Mataram. I want to see your residence". At Mataram the saint saw that the residence of Senapati still had no walls.

What approach will enable us to link the daily experiences at the village shrines and the literary monument to traditional Javanese ideology such as the one translated above? The answer, we believe, is to find a spiritual geography that is comparative and regional. We need to be able to juxtapose different versions of the use of the same shrine in order to get a vision of the changes of the use of a given site over one or two centuries.

If on the occasion of the foundation of the new palace of Surakarata in 1745, the Susuhunan's ritual specialists baptized a forest to the north of the newly constructed capital Krendawahana or Kalioso in the hope that it would flourish as had Indraprastha in the Mahābhārata,[45] how did the Mangkunagaran principality, which took it over only a few years later (1757?), manage this spiritual patrimony?

8.5 THE MANGKUNAGARAN FOREST TERTRE: ROYAL RITUAL AND VILLAGE LORE

We will start by citing a selection from the most banal of our witnesses, extracted from the first book of Javanese conversations (1848) ever published. A Eurasian working in Surakarta as a translator for the Dutch beginning in 1825, C.F. Winter Sr was asked by the Institute for the Javanese Language to elaborate a first manual for the Javanese spoken language. He included as his second example of spoken Javanese the following explanation of Krendawahana.[46]

— "Where does this path lead to?
— To the woods of Krendawahana;
— To whom does that woods belong?
— To the kingdom of the Mangkunagaran.
— Is it a vast forest?
— No it is a miserable little thicket.
— Is this woods *angker* (haunted or sacred) like they say?
— According to what is said, that is so.
— Were you ever in the area of the woods of Krendawahana?
— Yes!
— If the woods are haunted, are there still any hunters who dare to go hunting there?
— If they are Javanese, few dare go hunting there. Only the Dutch and other foreigners dare to enter therein.
— Why is the woods of Krendawhana sacred?
— According to what is said, its being haunted is because the goddess Durga has her residence there.
— It is still not clear why this woods is *angker*. What happens to people who go hunting there;
— They say this, that if one doesn't come back crazy, one disappears altogether;
— By disappear do you mean die?
— No, one disappears because one is carried away by the spirits.
— Do you believe that?
— How can I not believe it? These are well known facts. Either you return crazy from being in the woods or you disappear without leaving any trace.

Paradoxically, this disingenuous bit of dialogue is the earliest completely European testimony we have of the Krendawahana forest lying to the north of Surakarta. It seems that "real" history only begins when a European tourist visited a Javanese holy site. Witnesses before Winter's "imagined" dialogue of a European with a Javanese (but impossible to date), stress the disappearance of those who come to close to Durga. Whereas those who go unprepared to the southern seas are swallowed up by the waves covering an underwater palace, those who go too close to Durga's realm are swept away by its beauty. But this is only one dimension of the spiritual geography. Until quite recently it represented the northern boundary of the Mangkunagaran realm after which one entered the territory of the Susuhunan. As late as 1971, when the eighth Mangkunagaran went campaigning for the government's GOLKAR party, he followed the conquest route (*overingstocht*) which Mas Sahid, the founder of the principality, used when he took possession of his territory in 1755–56. Five years later the Semarang newpaper, *Suara Merdéka*, began reporting that there was a project afoot to restore the *maésa lawung* offerings (*labuhan*) on the part of the Mangkunagaran. As shown in Chapter 6, this was primarily a Susuhunan initiative stemming from the lineage of Paku Buwana VI. That it had been Paku Buwana XII and Sukarno who had brought back the body of Paku Buwana VI from Ambon in March 1957 generated considerable interest in the court circles about Paku Buwana VI's eventual contacts with the rebel Prince Dipanagara (Jatikusumo 1971, pp. 12–15) Nonetheless, even the journalist knew that the forest of Durga was a strong geographical marker lying within the former kingdom of the Mangkunagaran. And this occurred when the Mangedeg foundation had just built a tourist hotel inside its palace walls; this hotel prospered briefly and then fell into disrepair in the early nineties whereas the renewal of the *labuhan* offerings to Durga still continues apace. Who could have predicted this?

For the common people, however, the forest remains a place where one disappears (*kelap*). The last village headman appointed by the Mangkunagaran principality in the late forties, *radèn* Sastrodiwiryo, knew from oral sources the tale of the disappearance of the Susuhunan Paku Buwana VI which Radèn Tanoyo put into writing in his *Serat Raja Weddha* (Treatise on the Wisdom of Kings), a section of which was translated in section 8.1. It is interesting to note that the closer one gets to the palace milieu the less important the personage who disappears into the forest becomes. In Radèn Tanoyo's version it is no longer Paku Buwana VI who disappears but the son of the second wife (*mantu-dalem*) of Mangkunagarana II, a certain Pangéran Natakusuma.[47] We will compare these two versions below.

Radèn Tanoyo must have received his version both from the milieu of the Mangkunagaran palace and that of the Susuhunan. It was written in *sinom* meter:

> Next is told what Mangkunagaran II [reigned 1796–1825]. There was a prince Pangeran Natakusuma,[48] son of the second wife of the king, who at that time had two children: a daughter and an older son Pangéran Prangwédana who became the son-in-law of Sri Bupati [Paku Buwana V, r. 1788–1820], whose daughter married Adipati Trebaya.
>
> Adipati Natadiningrat, in fact the grandfather of the family, at that time had seven sisters. Pangéran Natasumeki (=Natakusuma) went out to hunt in the forest of Lapan, accompanied by only a single person, a hunter who never left him, following him step by step.
>
> (*Pucing* meter) Once in the forest, he descended from his horse in order to penetrate the jungle (*wanawasa*). First he went to the north, while his

attendant sang a poem. There only this servant remained who followed him. They went north to Blemben, to the hamlet of Ngumbulpring, then on the path to Watuburik to the West.[49]

(They next arrived) at a dark and horrible ravine [the river Cemara; near Krendawahana flows through this sort of canyon] and when they were getting ready to traverse it [this would mean entering the forest of Jagapatèn to the north of the river], the hunter calmly said, "Aduh Majesty, do not cross over here! This is the sacred,[50] formidable and deep place of hyang Batari Durga. This place is called the field of the odour of corpses (Setra Gandamayi) and is in the centre of the Lapan forest".

But the prince wanted to continue to see this sacred site (*kabuyutan*) and at that instant the hunter had the illusion that he saw a deer to the south [i.e., in the direction of the Krendawahana woods].

Once the hunter had parted, (the Prince) entered into (the centre of) the Lapan forest and had the sudden vision of twin purple deer.

They were Jaramaya and Rinumaya attracting him. When the prince saw them, his heart was enchanted in every way and he fell into the ravine where these two dark deer stood.

For a moment the prince was dumbfounded and then he saw a beautiful palace and a magnificent park. He entered therein.

Thus it was that he perceived two attractive girls coming towards him, who politely said to him these sweet words, "O Sire, follow us. Our grandmother, Nata Setra Gandamayu, hyang Batari Durga asks that we escort you Sire."

And soon they entered into a room shining with light where one saw hyang Pramuni (Durga) sitting on a throne.

Rays shone from her as from the sun. She made a sign with her hand to the prince to approach her and not to be intimidated by her for she was his very own grandmother.[51]

The prince seated himself respectfully by making a *sembah*. Hyang Pramuni said, "In truth I have called you (here) to make you a king. I command on the spirits (*lelembut*) who surround me (like a screen, *warana*): djins, nymphs, titulary protecting spirits (*dhanyang prayangan*) of this Sunyaruri world which is not separate from the ephemeral world."

"Certainly my child is Hyang Agungmuni (the great ascetic) Dagel (the clown) whom I command like all the other spirits of the invisible world."

The prince did not hesitate in abandoning all to enter into sang hyang Pramuni's (palace). He had already renounced his (earthly) palace without any ado.

What happened next? The hunter, who was separated from the prince, had already killed several deer. Coming back to the place where the prince had been, he only found his horse waiting tied to a tree. The prince was not there.

The hunter thought that his majesty the prince had been seduced, for that was hyang Durga Dewi's sort of trick; she often called to the inhabitants of the villages;

The village headmen (*bekel*) of Blemben and Watuburik came armed, but when they heard (what had happened) they were aghast and wanted to flee, saying, "In a formidable ravine, in a cave on the thorny slope, we will all be buried. It is certain that he left no traces. Let's decide among ourselves how to let the news be known."

The hunter and the armed men went back shortly thereafter and told the Sovereign what had happened to his son from the beginning till the end.

Very surprised, the king reflected. As to the prince's wife, it was as if she had died, but without any wounds, and finally her heart ceased to beat.

An order coming from the almighty power of God cannot be rejected. Humanity can only follow after the power of the Kyai Dhalang Wayang (the puppeteer).

Compared with the oral version in village "high" language *(krama desa)* which Sastrodiwiryo, the village headman, gave me of the same tale, the written text of *radèn* Tanoyo has a certain literary panache. Another oral version came to me via the following circuitous route. A retired official of the palace lived in Sambirejo (Kalioso), a few kilometres to the west of Durga's tertre. He died around 1972, but his son Pradigdo lived nearby in semi-retirement in a garden near the tombs of his ancestors (see Figure 5.2). He once came and spent three days fasting and meditating at Durga's tertre and on that occasion had several conversations with Sastrodiwiryo, the headman at that time, on whom he made a favourable impression. Sastrodiwiryo's version of the disappearance (*kelap*) of a prince stems from the scion of prominent Muslim local families from Kalioso. Although the village headman had himself witnessed the last *maésa lawung* sacrifices in the late 1940s, he had no access to the type of documents that *radèn* Tanoyo was collating. So I went to see "kyai" Digdo myself in 1974 and he quickly launched into an edifying tale to the honour of his Muslim ancestors, of which the following is a partial transcription and translation. It clearly reflects the local traditions that the court lineages were about to mobilize for their renewal of the *maésa lawung*.

In 1825 when Paku Buwana [VI] was sultan of Surakarta under the name of Sinuhun Bangun Tapa, the forest of Krendawahana was known to be haunted by the sacred (*angker*), wild animals, *djin* and many kinds of satans. According to the shadow puppet theatre this forest, whose other name is Gandamayit (odour of cadavers), is the kingdom of Batari Durga or Sang

Hyang Pramuni. In these plays [i.e. the Birth of Kala] it is said that Durga had been rejected by her husband, the king of the gods Batari Guru, after he had lost his seed. That is how Batari Durga came to be the forest's queen of the spirits and wild animals. In fact the forest is divided in two by the river Cemara, and the northern part is called the forest Jagapatèn but it is no (longer) haunted.

My ancestor kyai Murtaja, originally from Pajang, was the son of kyai Kartataruna, *bupati* (prefect) at the court of Pajang[52] until this was transferred to Mataram. At that time Kyai Kartataruna became a *kyai* of the Muslim religion. He was descended from the sultan of Pajang whose name was Hadiwijaya or Jaka Tingkir. Towards 1820 his wife and her younger brother departed for the north of the Cemara River and built a house in village of Kalioso. The son of Nyai Kartataruna built a house to the south of the Cemara River on the edge of the forest. He was called Radèn Bagus Murtaja. One day at the time of the Dipanagara war [1825–1830], Paku Buwana VI went to a house in the forest of Krendawahana because his consort Permaisuri Raja Mengandung wanted to eat fowl.

Perhaps also because he was troubled by the presence of the Dutch governor general in Java and was looking for an opportunity (to give) Dipanagara's permission to start a holy war against the Dutch. Having arrived at the centre of the forest with two men, the king disappeared. The two reported the matter to the palace. A (search) group was constituted, guided by men from the Mangkunagaran, but they could not find the king. They then asked Kyai Murtaja for help, (for) he was living on the edge of the forest. Shortly thereafter he brought the king back to the people assembled there. As a gift, the king gave the forest of Krendawahana to Kyai Murtaja in apanage (*lungguh*) and this *kyai* became the teacher of the king.

Later in 1830 at the end of the Dipanagara war, Kyai Murtaja and his son Kyai Yahya[53] brought calm to the sultanate of Yogyakarta. In gratitude the sultan of Yogyakarta offered to Kyai Murtaja the possibility of making the *haj* with his son. On returning from the *haj*, Kyai Murtaja took the name of Kyai Haji Mohammad Korib and built a mosque in Kalioso.[54]

On 14 June 1830 Paku Buwana VI was exiled to Menado by the Dutch Governor General because of his links with Dipanagara. But it had been agreed that the younger brother of Paku Buwana VI would become Paku Buwana VII and that after that the son of Paku Buwana VI would become Paku Buwana VIII. Kyai Haji Mohammad Korib and his son were regretted thus [delay in succession]. At the death of his father Paku Buwana VII (1858), the son of Paku Buwana VII claimed the title of sultan. It was only in 1861 that the son of Paku Buwana VI became Paku Buwana IX after having been heir apparent under Paku Buwana VIII. As a consequence of that (entitlement), Haji Yahya was named counsellor (*panaséhat*) and director of the Association of Indonesian Haji. He kept these functions under Paku Buwana X.

If the historical sequence is occasionally scrambled in this story, it is nevertheless obvious that *kyai* Murtaja is neither *kyai* Mojo (Maja), the great leader of Dipanagara's jihad, nor Murtalhajab[55] who figures as a *penghulu* in Surakarta just before the beginning of the nineteenth century.

Digdo, the man who recounted this oral history of the disappearance of Paku Buwana VI, also said that the columns of the mosque that now bore the name of *kyai* Yahya were built from the last great trees cut in the Krendawahana forest. The horror inspired by Durga's sylvan residence is clearly described as in decline. A king gives the shrine of Durga to a Muslim, Murtaja, and its trees are cut down to build a mosque. Even a Eurasian like Winter (1848, pp. 1–2) can speak of a "miserable thicket" (*grumbul*).

Even if, however, its sacredness as well as its dimension were shrunk by an increasingly ambient Muslim context, the site itself was never completely neutralized (*nawar*). Paradoxically, after telling its story in such a way as to describe the Islamization of the area, it is *kyai* Digdo, the great grandson of *kyai* Murtaja, who spent three days meditating and fasting at the *pundhèn* (offering site) of Batari. This shows that the spiritual geography has been expanded to include Muslim tombs and mosques in the Kaliasa area, but that adjustment did not require the destruction of shrines to demon queens like Durga. One proof of this is that alongside the old protective songs (*kidungan*) describing the sacred shrines of the upper Solo river basin, a modern magazine, *Tjundaka* (no. 3, 1972?), published an article on the most *kramat* (sacredly powerful) sites in the Surakarta area, giving explanations of their individual *genus loci* (*dhanyang baureksa*). Krendawahana figured in this list with a photograph of Durga's tertre and the admission that the forest was now reduced to a few trees surrounding this mound.

The forest of Krendawahana, like many others having a religious reputation, are homes to the spirits. *Radèn* Tanoyo in 1971 even wrote a five-page "Councils to the Elders" (*Fatwa-fatwané para Pinituwa*) which gives the prayers and lists the sprits to be addressed when one is cutting down a forest. The short list already contains twenty-eight names. This artificial resuscitation of old traditions (Javanese forests are now run by army-controlled plantation-styled companies) has only an antiquarian value. These local "garden-variety" spirits are rarely spoken of in writing, unlike famous myths concerning the 'Just King' (*ratu adil*), Erucakra who will establish his kingdom in the mythical forest of Katangga.[56] Even twentieth century messianic figures claimed to have invisible armies (Kartodirdjo Sartono 1973, pp. 98–99). The exile of the most prominent "just king" Prince Dipanagara did nothing to diminish the messianic movements in the middle and late twentieth centuries, but reading Sartono (1966, 1972, 1973) one has the impression that the palaces of these messianic leader were not deeply rooted in any particular local geography. Genealogy and healing powers established their credibility more than territoriality. But these flesh and blood would-be leaders can be seen, whereas the spirits and divinities whose contact is sought in a specific location are invisible. The attempt to attach a messianic or *jihad* connotation to the site of Krendawahana by the lineage of Paku Buwana VI, some one hundred and fifty years after he arranged a meeting there with Dipanagara, failed miserably. What does still seem possible is the recycling of detached motifs in written texts like that of Tantrik Mataram (1966, pp. 61–68; 4th ed.) where the albino buffalo (*kebo bulé*) reminds the reader of *kyai* Slamet brought out for the displaying (*kirap*) of the heirlooms (*pusaka*) every Javanese new year around the palace walls of Surakarta.

Rather than speak of renewed representation, it seems that one should speak of a certain permanence of the Javanese spiritual geography. The great wandering *ulama* encyclopaedia, the *Serat Centhini*, finished in the beginning of the nineteenth century, but representing an eighteenth-century outlook, has Mas Cebolang (1986, vol. 2, §157) attend an exorcism, the Partadewa. The scene of the action is the primeval Javanese village Mendhangkawit. Certain places require certain kinds of behaviour, and if one cannot, for whatever reason, go back there, one imports the toponym into the play. What is unusual about Krendawahana is that it is a royal boundary that once recapitulated the north-south axis, the totality of the kingdom, along with the offering site overlooking the southern ocean. The variety of ways in which one can write about or tell stories about Gandamayit/Krendawahana does not displace the fact that the Indian Durga's victory over the titan buffalo was incorporated into the very foundations of the Javanese kingdom through the cosmology analysed in the next chapter.

Two more witnesses will be cited, this time from Javanese historical (*babad*) treatises. The first dates from 1941 and pretends to describe the forest in 1820. The authors of the *Babad Serong*,[57] the Pangujuban Handanawarih (=Andana Warih, the Theosophical Society of the Mangkunagaran; Nugraha 2001, ch. 3) wrote it during the 1930s. They meet in the palace which had belonged to Soerjataningrat, whose ghost they felt still haunted it. This "history" of some nine hundred pages with a summary in two hundred and four pages, concerns the life of a son of Mangkunagaran II, K.P.A. Soerjataningrat, in his youth called Radèn Mas Panji Manguningrat. The authors found their title by using the name of area to the east of Sragen called Serong. In the *Babad Serong* (1941, pp. 102–108) one reads that K.P.A. Soerjataningrat (son of Mangkunagaran II; his former name had been P.M. Panji Manguningrat) meditated at the foot of Durga's tertre with its nine ficus. This prince had fought during the Java War on the side of the Dutch with the rest of the Mangkunagaran troops at the battle of Ngendu to the north of Sragen.

Radèn Mas Panji Manguningrat is speaking with Mangunyuda (p. 100). He is discouraged by his sins, by the idea that the Lord does not hear his prayers and does not grant him mercy. He wonders whether he should not go and pray at Krendawahana, for he has heard that in that holy place, the Lord grants the demands of those who pray there and perhaps he will be permitted to enter into that forbidden kingdom. If not, "...I will be eaten by the formidable devils that inhabit that forest there." What follows is my résumé of this section:

> (p. 102) On their way to the forest, on arriving in the village of Titang, Manguningrat and Maungunyuda ask a peasant if there is a sacred forest where prayers are granted. The peasant replies that there is a great tree with many leaves, but for the rest they had better ask the inhabitants of the neighbouring village of Kalioso.
>
> (p. 106) There they meet a peasant by the name of Danakrama, to whom Mangunyuda asks if it is really in this forest that the kingdom of the palace of Batari Durga, the dark thicket (grumbul gelap) there and many wild animals but no one enters there...
>
> (p. 108) Next Danakrama gives a long series of etymological explanations.[58] *Krenda* means coffin (*trebela*), and *wahana* chariot (*tempakan*). But wahana also means to burn (i.e. *dahana*). Then Danakrama adds that there are also lots of *mliwis* birds, a variety of quail (*karandawa*). And from the above he concludes that Krendawahana forest means a forest with lots of quail. To explain this Danakrama continues: the Hindu legend, told by the descendants of the Bharata, speaks of Batara Mahadewa, enamoured of Dewi Uma, who descended to meditate on the mountain of Himawat. The place where he meditated was called Kailasa[59] and was the heavenly residence (*kayangan*) of Dewi Uma who on earth was called Batari Durga. It is from this name Kailasa that the village of Kaliasa gets its name.
>
> Then Raden Mas Panji and Mangunyuda are, led by Danakrama, penetrated into Krendawahana, the residence of Batari Durga who takes the form of a white banyan tree, with nine other trees planted around it.[60] The two men meditated all night there without meeting anything[61] and in the morning they left."

This recent witness presents the tertre of Durga as not always equal to its reputation. *Radèn* Tanoyo's claims in the *Serat Raja Wedda* dates from only a few years before this *Babad Serong*, but represent a strong palace tradition, whereas here the quests of aristocrats are not always so easily fulfilled.

Another witness is Yasadipura the elder, writing his *Babad Giyanti* (1937–39, 8th vol., pp. 8–9) around 1820. He provides a kind of follow up to the *Babad Tanah Jawi* in which we read of Senapati's meeting with the queen of the southern seas. Here, some one hundred and twenty years earlier, the sacredness of the site is presented as attenuated A brief scene depicts the son of the king Hadiwijaya (=? Jaka Tingkir). Somewhat in the manner of Arjuna in the *Bhagavadgītā*, this king hesitates to go to battle at Pagelen (to the south of Borobudur). He speaks of his scruples to an old man near the woods of Krendawahana. Several difficulties of translation remain:

> Both prince Harya Purbajeki and prince Mangkukusuma are frightened, lowering their eyes in shame, intimidated by their elder brother Sri Nara Pati Pangéran Hadiwijaya. He (then) spoke slowly, "I am not like (?) the Susunan, I want to go to the extraordinary forest of Krendawahana."
>
> In the village there was an old man, who as a child was called Nalasuta, and after his circumcision, Pak Gambreng the tenth child (?). The name of this village is Banyurip, Susunan, (but) later it disappeared (?) Nalasuta …had five children.
>
> He seated himself next to the prince. "Who are you? I wanted to know whose child you are." "I am the son of the king, named Hadiwijaya. My father is Sunan Prabu." The old man sat next to him for a long while. "Duh Sire, I want to speak to you. I know that you are of the caste of the warriors (*satriya*). Never be attached to anything, Lord. If you covet women or horses you will lose the strength of your courage (*prawira*). You descend from soldier king, grow in wisdom. Attachments are no good, they turn us away from salvation."

This story continues with a veiled admission on the part of the prince that the old man has touched on the core of his problem, but the two companions of the king find the old man's advice absurd and laugh a great deal at him. The old man ends by being annoyed that his advice for going straight into battle has been ridiculed and he refuses to accompany them further on their path. On separating from them he says to the prince: "Don't ever be divided, the land of Java has only two lords. Be confident like the Dutch." It is strange that his advice should end on such a note. He is hardly a Krisna. The style of this story is quite different from the others, treating Krendawahana only as a place for quest into the science of life. The identity of the old man is kept quite discreet as well as his relation with the sacred forest. There is only a vague resemblance to the figure of the old man who gives Ki Ageng Solo the heavenly fire (*wahyu*) and which every year is brought back from his tomb to the palace of Surakarata (cf. Schrieke 1924, pp. 290–

91 quoted by Lind 1975, p. 17). In general Yasadipura seems to let the description of the "historical" events take over from any spiritual problematics. But stories, if not events, continue to proliferate, until in the 1970s writing about them is perhaps a greater form of authority than retelling them. I say this because now villagers always qualify their oral tales with claims of deference to the authority of written ones. The *mancakaki*, the village elders, feel in a position of inferiority *vis-à-vis* the urban user of the printed culture. But interference from outside narratives does not date from the 1970s. The following newspaper account from the *Djawi Hiswaro* (15 March 1915) shows how even at the beginning of this century local cults were controlled and on occasion suppressed by the county police on orders from the provincial capital.[62] The village referred to as Sambirejo is in fact the site of more than a hundred tombs of different branches (Haji Murtaja, etc.) of the Nitimenggala lineage discussed in Chapter 4. The article is entitled "Destruction".

> As we reported recently, to the north of the village of Nusukan (in the principality of the Mangkunagaran) there exists a tomb named "*buruj*" (Arabic word meaning "distinguished by destiny"). People recently deceased and already decomposed are buried in this thicket near the tomb of the (former) village headman of the village of Sambirejo "distinguished by destiny". Since the time (when the village chief was buried there) until now, it is surprising to see how this tomb has become a place favourable for asceticism (*petirakatan*), to such an extent that every Friday people come by the hundreds in order to get pregnant (etc.), practising *en masse* meditation in this place.
>
> Once the situation was known to the authorities, they were determined to make it return to normal. The morning after they learnt of the matter, the government of the Mangkunagaran had it (the tomb) removed. On Monday 27th March 1915, the tomb was opened by several workers under the direction of the head of police (*panéwu gunung*) and several low-ranking officials. The *buruj* corpse and the earth surrounding it were placed in a white *mori* cloth, and thrown in the waters of the "Blessed" (Begawan) Solo river. All trace of the tomb was removed and the earth was leveled.
>
> Whatever the cause (of this phenomenon), it is clear that henceforth there will be no one to meditate in this place.

Why was this cult so objectionable to the authorities? We will probably never know, but it is interesting that, already at the beginning of the twentieth century, as a counterweight to the pole of attraction represented by Durga's tertre in the Krendawhana woods, the lineage cemeteries of Sambirejo and Kaliasa in general were for whatever reason developing clientele.

8.6 LEVELS AND LANDSCAPES IN THE DURGA CULTS

Despite reviewing the twenty witnesses to the spiritual geography of Krendawahana/Kaliasa above, we have still left aside one major source for the representation of Durga and her forest: that of the Javanese shadow puppet theatre, the *wayang*. These stories are in a certain sense atemporal because set elsewhere, even where they are used to comment on the here and now. Two plays, the *Death of Semar* and the *Abandoning Sembadra to the Waves* provided as examples of this mythical geography.

One might begin this résumé of witnesses by asking why one comes to such a dangerous *werit* (inhabited by spirits) forest. The answer is that it enables one to meditate and the body is inordinately heated by the mystery of the nearby presence. Already at the beginning of the twentieth century, Snouck Hurgronje (1906, vol. I, p. 305) had remarked that the quality of well-being was conveyed in western Austronesian languages by the quality of freshness or cool, while the powers of evil are represented by the quality of heat. Simply asking how this affects the frequentation of the forest shrine provides a preliminary synthesis.

The capital of a kingdom as opposed to the wilderness of forest is a well-known contrast to spectators of the *wayang*. This is not simply an opposition of civilized and uncivilized. In the shadow puppet play, *Abandoning Sembadra to the Waves,* there is a scene (Kodiran 1968, pp. 28–34) where Borisrawa, the ogre king of Mandraka (Salya) abandons the palace for the forest having fallen in love with Sembadra the wife of Arjuna. The forest is thus the place of unsatisfied desires. E. Lind (1975, p. 40), citing a poetic text the *Serat Rama,* shows that there is a link between Banaspati (the lord of the forests) and the *waringin* (*Ficus benjamina*) also called by that name. A third party also bears that name in Java: that is Agni whose lion head adorns the lintels of many east Javanese temples. Finally in old Javanese Kala, the god of death and destruction, is considered an aspect of Agni or Rudra, the fire that destroys the world (cf. *sub voce*: Zoetmulder 1982). At that period the cycle of the destruction of the world (*kaliyuga*) and its reconstruction by Wisnu or Buddha were well known even if there was a tendency to reduce them from five to two (*jaman edan, jaman mas* = the mad and golden periods[63]). So Banaspati, the lord of the forest, has become a name of Agni and Kala: one of his manifestations. Finally this provides us with a link between the Krendawahana of Durga and the Kandavawanadahana of the *Ādiparva* studied in Chapter 7.

To understand the opposition between palace and forest, one must remember the myth of the creation of the world in the *Manikmaya* (Made of Jewels) myth and its purification in the Birth of Kala (*Murwa Kala*) or the Praying with the Body (*Mintaraga*) play. All are known to Javanese who are fond of *wayang*. They would therefore be familiar with the notion of a menace which can turn a society into a savage desert whose lord is Banaspati or Kala.

In Java, however there are two sorts of wilderness, one in the forest and the other on the sea, especially the southern sea. When she treats of the processions that distance dangers, Lind (1975, p. 60) concludes that the Javanese conceive of epidemics, the pest and death in general, as coming from the spirits of the southern sea where Lara Kidul is queen, or from the north, from a forest/desert where there lurks a demon (whose mother is Durga) who eats man.[64] The attacks from the south seem more significant in some royal cults than others.

We have, then, two deserts and two queens. But in the Javanese mythological landscape of the *wayang* there is a third party whom seems to have disappeared from the landscape of popular rural piety, a male god, Guru or Siwa. Lind, translating from a Birth of Kala myth (Leiden Univ. Cod. Or. 5593), presents Guru as exasperated by a female ascetic whose exploits cause a cosmic upheaval (*gara-gara*). This situation reverses the roles we saw when Senapati went to meditate on the south coast. There the upheaval was caused by a male.

> (stanza 8–10) The goddess Tanana (incomparable) was practising ascetics in a grotto in a forest. She asked herself if there was a man virile enough to marry her, for she was hot (from meditation). "If I am not liberated (from this heat), how will he who would have me for his spouse be virile enough to marry me, for I am an only daughter. I have no brother, I have no sister. If I was male I would be an *ugal-ugil* (only son). Since I am female I am called *unting-unting*, an only child which is hot."
>
> (stanza 56–68) Only Batara Guru is a true man (*lanang sejati*) and has the magical virility become her husband ... [Guru is unable to contain his desire, which falls on the ocean in the form of seed producing a monster divinity called "Fallen Seed"]. The saliva of the wind deity (Bayu) finally gave life to the fallen seed rolled up on the beach and the baby grew....This being (then) met with the goddess Tanana [i. e. Durga, exiled on earth and deformed for having refused the advances of Guru.] who explains his origin and tells him that because of his strange birth he is called Kama Salah (fallen seed). He asks if she accepts to be her mother; she consents and provides him with a suite of servants, forty "west wind" spirits (*bayu barat*)...

Lind remarks that this quality of heat, *panas*, is also attributed to royalty. Schrieke (1955, vol. II, pp. 70–72) has shown that the attribute of flaming vulva characterizes the literary and mythological description of certain Javanese queens. There is a famous description of the queen of the Sundanese (West Java) realm of Pajajaran[65] cited by Brandes (1897, pp. 54–55) who was too sexually demanding for the sultan of Banten, the ruler of Cirebon, and even for the king of Mataram, who because she was good for nothing (*wong wdon iki wus ora nana gawé*) sold her for three guns to the Dutch who, by possessing her, became rulers of the island.

C.C. Berg (1965, pp. 93–115) has analysed this data and denies that the Javanese queens were in any sense incarnations of Durga. But Durga's particularity, that of having an enormous and powerful sexual organ, leads Schrieke and Lind to insist on the fact that the man who can master her becomes king. If we accept this point of view, then Senapati's relation with the queen of the southern seas and the *maésa lawung* point of contact to the north become manifestations of the north-south expression of totality found in the old Javanese metaphor of *lor-kidul*. This metaphor encompasses the polarity in the sense that Lind speaks of a symbolic absorption of the extremities (especially the menaces from abroad, *sabrang*) toward the centre, the palace, the seat of the king. It is interesting that the two dimensional opposition of north-south, regularly expanded to 4/5 and 8/9 by used of the cardinal direction and the centre, is ambiguously expressed in the notion of crosswise dimension (*alang*). This term is expanded to mean a hindrance, obstacle (*alangan*), from which one can be purified in a *ruwatan* exorcism after having been pursued by Durga's son Kala. The crosswise position (*malang*) is unlucky. But in its causative forms "to block", "impede" (*dialangaké*), one is protected. Bad luck can be returned towards its perpetrator, that foreigner who comes from rolling over the wilderness of the seas,[66] like the ogre Kala.

In order to begin to understand what the Javanese call "heat" (*panas*), and especially that heat of Durga-Lara Kidul existing to the north and the south of the palaces, we have no better witness than their respective cults. It is interesting to note that in the 1859 map of the *residentie* of Surakarta compiled by W.J. Versteg, the Mangkunagaran is shown having its own *alun-alun* (cleared field) to the north of its palace over the Pépé river on the land now occupied by Pasar Legi whose streets in the forms of crosses are unique in Surakarta. It would be interesting to know the rationalization behinds its transformation in the minds of the Mangkunagaran palace officials.

The preponderance noted above of Lara Kidul over Durga is evident in the ritual activities in the palace. The *bedhaya ketawang* dances[67] and the weekly offering to the queen of the south at the summit of the Sangga Buwana tower (Headley 1996, pp. 212–15) both indicate that she is someone whom it is desirable to receive inside the palace, whereas Durga remains a wild (*dhèdhès*) divinity who attracts people into her palace where they disappear forever.

Clearly there has been an evolution since Mahendradatta, the mother of Erlanga (eleventh-century East Javanese king)), himself the great-grandson of the first king of East Java, Sindok, was enshrined in a statue having the form of Mahishamardanī (Durga killing the titan buffalo) and the meeting between Senapati and the queen of the southern seas purported to have taken place in the early seventeenth century. The Javanese have not changed goddess here but they certainly have changed myth. And in a similar manner between Agni (the Lord of the forest, Banaspati) who burns with an apocalyptic blaze the forest of Khandavawana in the book of the *Mahābhārata* and Kala the "hot" son of the spilt seed of his father Siwa pursuing victims aided by Durga's demon army, the danger has become personalized, even if to some extent it can be argued that Kala is a Javanese equivalent of Agni.

The *mise en scène* of the myth of Mahishamardanī by the Javanese royalty, their adaptation and indigenous evolution displays the power concentrated in the king variously called *andaru, pulung, wahyu kedaton,* or *teja.* This translated what in the Indian world was conceived of as royal fortune (*raja laksmi*). Each respective variant of this value maintained its own semantic fields (Lind 1975, p. 69). So Durga on the royal level and her son Kala on the personal level (both emerged from the same cosmogonic myth in the *Manikmaya*) incarnated the destructive forces outside the control of the kingdom or the individual. Durga/Kala were opposed to Sri-Uma/Wisnu as "soiled" was to well-being (*sukerta/slamet*), as the wild forces of nature are to well being, being free from danger (*slamet = luput ing bebaya*). E. Lind states (1975, ch. 2) that where there are no obstacles (*ora ana sakara-kara*), there is *slamet*: her point is that since in the Javanese perspective the centre may be opposed to the periphery, and at the same time absorb it and represent the totality, so *slamet* represents both the order opposed to destruction and a state of equilibrium.

The grafting of the myth from the *Adiparva* onto the Indian iconography of Durga's victory over the titan buffalo was given a geographical polyvalence from the moment that Durga's son Kala became the object of *individualistic* exorcism rites. For though Durga's cult was always centred round the forest of Krendawahana, the depredations of Kala could take place anywhere in Java, in any one's house. Rather than the king sending buffalo blood or his clothes to Durga's forest, in the case of the Birth of Kala exorcisms the *dhalang* goes to the home of the afflicted to perform the myth of Kala's birth in shadow puppet theatre. The ritual boundaries are quite different (Headley 2000*a*, ch. 7.6). Collective cosmologies now serve private needs. The same corpus of invocations used in the royal rituals will be found in the personal family-based exorcisms. It is to these mantra that we must now turn.

NOTES

1. Note that here *dilawungaké* means speared, but that this verb also means "to let a buffalo roam freely, and not work before the plow". Indeed the sacrificial buffalo is supposed to be one that has never been attached for farm work.
2. *Karaton-dalem Surakarta Hadiningrat Sasana Pustaka*, no. 547 Ka. Cf. Nancy Florida's catalogue (1993, p. 128), and her 1985 transcription of the complete text.
3. Florida's transcription (1985, pp. 25–34) corresponds to folios 17–23 of the Javanese original.
4. This is a lesser functionary (a *bekel*) serving under the *abdi-dalem bupati anom juru* Suranata.
5. Cf. de Graaf and Pigeaud (1974, p. 306) who ascribe this king of the very real kingdom of Pengging to the pseudo-historiography of Ranggawarsita in the mid-nineteenth century.
6. *Gandarwa* are flying messengers of the Indian gods where they play an important role in literature and mythology. They are found from Japan to Java vehiculed in large part in north Asia by Buddhism.
7. This date is far too early. Sah Ngalam Akbar III, alias for sultan (after *circa* 1524) Tranggana of Demak (reigned probably 1504–46); was the last strong sultan of Demak. His successor, sunan Prawata was murdered, but avenged by Jaka Tingkir, later sultan of Pajang. Cf. de Graaf and Pigeaud (1976, pp. 6–9).
8. The description here may well be a nineteenth century literary recomposition, some of whose traditions nonetheless date from the early sixteenth century.
9. N.B. the author writes as if the kingdom(s), all being Javanese, differ only in the location of their capitals.
10. The term *mragad* (not to be confused with *wragad*) indicates a Muslim style of slaughter (cf. krama, *sembelèh*): killing by sliting the throat and not by lancing. This may suggest why the term *maésa lawung* could come to mean not the spearing of the buffalo but a "free-range" buffalo.
11. Cf. translation and analysis Chapter 9.
12. Perhaps equivalent in function to the tasks now executed by Tumenggung Saka, a sort of female major-domo, cf. Headley (1996*a*, pp. 212–15).
13. These *kandaga* (Poerwardaminta 1930, p. 256) hang from rings from poles and are brought forth, shaded by a ritual parasol and accompanied by high officials, princes and ministers.
14. The first page of the palace manuscript gives a certain number of details concerning its composition.
15. This treaty has been lost according to a twenty-eight-page manuscript of the Mangkunagaran history deposited in the Reksapustaka dated 24 June 1977

(written by N. Florida and/or J. Pemberton?) and written in English from which this account is taken. For the period leading up to Pangéran Ario Mangkunegara's exile, cf. M.C. Ricklefs, *War, Culture and Economy in Java 1677–1726* (1993).

16. For this period, cf. de Jonge, *De Opkomst van het Nederlandsch gezag in Oost-Indie* (vol. XII, pp. 194–234) cited by the ms. history in note 12.

17. =240 jung; one jung = +/− 28.400 sq. metres. There are as many *cacah* as *bau* or *karya*, but if there are five *bau* in each *jung*, one of them was for the tax collector appointed to that apanage. The king received one half of the produce of the four *bau* i.e. two-fifths of a *jung*. As a sort of *terminas ad quem* for deforestation, by 1947 the village of Krendawahana had 139 ha. (?*sawah*) under cultivation and was paying an annual tax to the Mangkunagaran of 300 guilders (Mangkunagaran Archives box 5.256), whereas in 1915 the population of 127 cultivated only 26 *bau* of rice fields all classes combined (Mangkunagaran Archives M.N.VI box 31).

18. Cf. Pringgodigdo, *De Mangkoenegorosche Onderneemingen*, ch. 4 (1950).

19. Given in the first section of the ms. pp. 1–24 in transcription; the ones above in Table 8.1 found on pp. 25–46 were specifically for the *maésa lawung*.

20. According to the genealogy of Soemahatmaka graciously lent to me by P.B.R. Carey of Oxford University. The Dutch military archives do apparently confirm that Natakusuma participated actively in the war against Dipanagara.

21. This article was kindly referred to me by P.B.R. Carey of Trinity College, Oxford as well as the notes in Javanese (Leiden OrC. 8652 F) of which Rinkes is the probable author.

22. Also called the *balairung Sitinggil lan Sanasuméwa*. This Suméwa is where the Pati dalem or first minister is seated in the Pangelaran.

23. Is this the river Beton or the water hole Kopi which the Bundel Slametan at the Mangkunagaran refers to as the destination of certain offerings? "…*panglabuhipun dumateng ing banawi Beton utawi kedung Kopi, ingkang sakinten lebet Soyanipun* [ch. 4, note 9], *ingkang nyemplungaken abdi dalem Chatib, sarampungipun abdi dalem Chatib ingkang nglabuh wau sowan wadana caos, nglapuskaen anggènipun anglabuh.*"(transcription p. 5) It seems that this is not the well near Durga's tertre, but the nearby Cemara River and more precisely the rock called *soya* in the account of Abdul Jalal I exploits in establishing the first mosque in the region.

24. Leiden Or. 10.846§2: These are the *slametan* of the eighth of Sura (the first Javanese month); the *slametan* of the twelfth of Mulud (third month); the *maésa lawung* or *rajawedda slametan* of the fifteenth of Ruwah (eighth month); the *punggahan slametan* (beginning of the fast on the thirtieth of Ruwah); the *maleman* or night *slametan* on the 21, 23, 25, 27, and 29th of the ninth or fasting month, Puasa; the minor (*andap-andapan slametan* the night before the Puasa Garebeg), the Idul Fitri (end of the fast); the *syawalan slametan* in the tenth month of Sawal; the tenth and last "great" *slametan* falls on the tenth of Sawal and that *garebeg* is called Besar or great.

25. Until the Second World War the *sekaten* were the *royal* festivals taking place on the north *alun-alun* of the palace enclosure. Cf *Suluh Sekaten* by Chronos (1940) in the Reksapustaka of the Mangkunagaran palace.

26. Cf. Darsiti Soeratman (2000, ch. 4).

27. Cf. Kreemer (1956, sections 27–35).

28. The former seat of the sub-prefecture of Gondangrejo had been in the village of the same name in the middle of that district. But with the opening of the Surakarta-Semarang railroad in 1863 marking the western boundary of that sub-prefecture it was judged opportune to move the district seat to Kaliasa in the north-west corner of this territory. The *Babad Mangkunagaran* (Leiden Cod. Or. 6781:100) states it was the terrible explosion of the Merapi volcano that marked that period as much as the opening of the railroad with the new opportunities for coolie labour involved in its construction.

29. Beginning in 1979 when the ritual was recommenced after a thirty-year interval, the offerings were prepared at the Mangkunagaran and brought directly by minibus to the village of Krendawahana. This can be explained as much by the fact that the *panéwu*, now called *camat*, was a provincial appointee as by the facilities of automotive transportation.

30. The text of the version given here is as follows:
    "Hong wilaheng awegena mastuti jagat dewa betara,
    ya jagat pramudita, sang yang Pikulun.
    Hong wilaheng tata winanci,
    hong wilaheng mastuna masidem,
    hong hyang sri batari Klayuwati, yugané hulun."
    (Then begins the backwards recitation of the alphabet. Comparison with Pink's version (1995, p. 238) reveals more than average corruption.)
    "Ya maha raja jara maya
    yamarami rinumaya,
    yamiduru duru rudu maya,
    ya silipa pala sija
    ya sijaka kya sija
    ya hama maha sija
    yada yuda daju ja."

31. Now enclosed by a wall and rededicated to a meeting between the rebel prince Dipanagara and the Susuhunan Paku Buwana VI, cf. ch. 3.

32. This area is now a rice field.

33. On the *labuhan* to the east at the summit of Mt Lawu, cf. Adam (1940, pp. 107–18) for whom Sunan Lawu is the elder lineage, being that the younger lineage of the reigning kings of Mataram. *Serba-serbi di Gunung Lawu* by Djogosarkoro (1973, pp. 45–62) gives an image of what a Javanese might know of these traditions in the 1970's.

34. Cf. the edition of Buning (1937, vol. 1, pp. 7–15); translation Soepomo and Ricklefs (1967, pp. 88–108).

35. The sites on the south coast vary. For instance Hardjapranata (archives KITLV J240), in 1890 cites the island of Nusa Kembangan near Cilacap, as well as Brasot on the Praga river to the south of Yogykakarta.

36. Certain of the kiosk almanacs list all the the local protecting spirits to be found in these sacred shrines and give protective song texts whch can be sung to evoke their aid either on the spot itself or at the centre, i.e. the capital. Cf. Soetardi Soeryohoedoyo, *Pepali Ki Ageng Solo* (1980).

37. *Tjarijosipun Benawi Sala ingkang inggil* (1940, pp. 36–37); and M. Hardjadisastra and M. Jasasoeparta, *Tjarijos Redi Lawoe* (1936).

38. The other name of this poem by Mpu Tantular who wrote under the Majapahit king Rājasangara (Hayam Wuruk; reigned 1350–89) is Porusādasuta or "The eater of defeated men". These man-eating demons in contemporary Java are represented by the figure of Kala, Durga's son.

39. For Sultan Agung's (reigned 1613–45) encounter with the queen of the south, cf. Jan Hostetler's translation of extracts of the *Babad Serat Nitik* in *Archipel* no. 24 (1982, pp. 127–42): "Bedhaya Semang: the Sacred Danse of Yogyakarta".

40. By consigning oneself to the waves and the current, one makes one's body an offering like the trays of offerings that are left to float away; this *tapa ngeli* is one of the eight forms of Javanese meditation.

41. On Tunggal Wulung, cf. Lind (1975, pp. 44–60, especially p. 55).

42. This claim is made of both Durga and the queen of the southern seas and it is thus that they are doubles of one another.

43. The "porch of cliffs"; offering site on the southern coast near the mouth of the Umpak.

44. One of the nine *wali* or friends of Allah who implanted Islam in Java in the seventeenth century.

45. This is what Poerbatjaraka suggests (1940, p. 293) apparently not on the basis of the *Babad Giyanti*, which says nothing of the kind, but on the basis of discussions which appeared in the *Pustoko Djawi* (1927, no. V, p. 151 and no. VI, pp. 21, 55) between that author, Natawidjaja, and P.A. Adiwidjaja concerning the etymology of Kaliasa. For Adiwidjaja Kaliasa meant the house of the army (of Durga: *dalemipun sang sadya batari Durga* (1927, p. 55). Poerbatjaraka was unable to accept the idea that this original name for the forest had been displaced by the toponym Krendawahana borrowed from the shadow puppet theatre. The question remains open.

46. In the earliest maps I have consulted at the KITLV in Leiden, those of 1859 (compiled by W. J. Westeg) and 1861–66 (Topgraphische Kaart der Residentie published in 1876(?) by Beijerinck and Ockerse) Kaliasa figures prominently because of its railroad station but Krendawahana doesn't appear. Several nearby villages do so that its absence may be a result of the cartography not of ignorance.

47. Not to be confused with Pangéran Natakusuma the son of an unofficial wife of Paku Buwana IV (1788–1820) who was favoured by Paku Buwana VI. He

commanded the troops of the Susuhuan at Pajung in Auguest–September 1826 when Diapanagaran was defeated at Gawok (16 October 1826). He behaved quite badly during the battle and was relieved of his functions.

48. There is a personage of the same name in the *Babad Mangkunagaran* (LUB, MS lor 6781, pp. 39–45), but is it the same?

49. Neither the map of 1859 nor that of 1861–63 available in the KITLV map room in Leiden, permit us to localize any of these toponyms.

50. *Kabuyutan* from the root *buyut*, or great-grandparents.

51. This description reminds one of the relationship that holds between the Susuhunan of Surakarta and the queen of the southern seas; it will be analysed below in some detail.

52. We will let pass the obvious incoherence in the historical side of his account which was clarified in Chapter 5.

53. According to the *Silsilah Leluhur Kalioso*, pp. 12 and 14, Kartataruna's first son married the daughter of the Pengulu Mertolojo of Surakarta; his third son Murtaja (alias Haji Muhammad Korib) was married twice; his first son by his second wife was Haji Yahya.

54. There is one that nowadays bears the name of Kyai Yahya, but I was told that although the mosque is old, its name is recent.

55. Cf. Chapter 5 and the documents Fokkens published (1887, p. 497) on Murtalhaja.

56. Cf; Kartodirdjo Sartono (1972, pp. 94–96).

57. Since pages 1–4 are missing, it is not possible to give the publisher or the printer, nor the date of the edition which was probably printed in very few copies. In Surakarta already the book is rare. Two portraits of the prince Soerjanataningrat are found between pages 14–15 and 15–16. After p. 397 one finds a facsimile of a letter dated 3 September 1826 from the resident Mac Gillavry describing the behaviour of the prince during the battle at the village of Ngendu north of Sragen. The exterior dimensions of the book are 13.5 by 20 cm and the written page occupies 9.5 by 14.5 with eighteen lines per page.

58. One wonders if these were not partially borrowed from the *Pustaka Djawi* articles cites above.

59. By inversion of the *il* it is an easy step from Kailasa to Kaliasa. This gives rise to the assimilation of Kaliasa to the heavenly Kailasa in popular lore.

60. Even today there is a semi-circle of trees planted there; the number nine suggests the nine *bhairawa* (terrifying nymphes) known in the cult of Durga's collective manifestations (Slusser 1982, pp. 322, 344), often associated with the nine points of the compass.

61. At night one can meet with spirits, especially if one is meditating, naked, etc.

62. This article can be found in Leiden Univ. Cod. Or. 8652, no. 15; cf. many more examples in Kartodirdjo Sartono's 1973 study of Javanese messianic movements in the nineteenth and twentieth centuries.

63. Cf. Anderson (1972, p. 20); Schrieke (1955, pp. 76–86).

64. Cf. Headley 2000*a* for the Indian treatments of the different magical powers (*sakti*) of Durga cf. Sircar (1967); Bhattacharrya (1971); Kooij (1972), and Beane (1977).

65. Hadiwidjojo (no date, pp. 1–6) explains that the Queen of the South (Ratu Kidul) was the daughter of the last king of Pajajaran, but also the granddaughter of the king of the spirits Sagaluh. Having gone to meditate on Mt Kumbang she became a spirit herself. She sometimes appears as a woman and sometimes as a man. Although on several occasion she asked Senapati and Sultan Agung to stay and rule with her in her kingdom, they managed to refuse by promising that every subsequent king of Mataram would marry her.

66. Curiously enough the word for wave (*alun*) is the same word reduplicated that designates the fields to the north or the south of the palaces of the provincial regents or kings. Were these grassless fields, which could hardly have undulated (*ngalun*), ever thought of as oceans? It seems unlikely.

67. This most sacred of Javanese dances involves a choreography with nine virgins and is executed on the day on the accession of the ruler to the throne and in subsequent years celebrates the ruler's continuing relation with the queen of the southern seas. It has been suggested that, besides the planetary symbolism (Saturn, Venus, Mars, Jupiter, Mercury, the sun, the moon and Râhu and Ketu, the moon's ascending and descending nodes), that the nine female dancers may have been thought of as the Bhairava that are the regents of space (*mātṛkās*) as Navadurgā. Cf. C. Brakel (1992).

9

INVOKING THE GODDESS DURGA; WORSHIPPING ALLAH

9.1 THE CORPUS OF THE MANTRA

The value of studying the different collections of invocation used for Durga in Krendawhana and elsewhere is to see, before this cult became *haram* (forbidden) for Muslims, the extent to which these prayer had begun to absorb Islamic terminology. Praying at graves of holy men to gain merit (*pahala* from the Sanskrit *phala*) is common among Javanese; Muslims and non-Muslim alike "send their prayers" (*ngirim donga*) in repetitive waves from the foot of the tertre (Pradjarta Dirdjosanjoto 1999, p. 89). However, few people have had access to the collections of mantras used in Krendawahana. The mantra for the *maésa lawung*, those used for the accession to the throne of the king and the birth of princes and outside the palace for the so-called Birth of Kala or exorcism (*ruwatan*) of, as well as some protective songs (*kidungan*), overlap, producing their present patchwork quality. Only the protective songs had some diffusion in the population. The *dhalang* kept his as heirlooms to be given only to those few puppeteers who were deemed by their masters to be strong enough to perform the exorcisms. In order to perform exorcisms, contemporary *dhalang* are usually required to be descended through seven or more generations from the court *dhalang* Panjang Mas or Cremaganda (van Groenendael 1985, pp. 58–65). The *maésa lawung* mantra were by definition a palace possession. We have seen in the preceding chapter the list of qualifications required to present oneself for the post of *abdi dalem juru* Suranata.

These mantras are "polyvalent"; they have multiple uses and may be sung on very different occasions. Furthermore there is an important historical dimension in the case of one mantra, the Tata Winanci for it is found in Bali and among the East Javanese Tengger. That having been said, Nancy Smith-Hefner (1992) for the Tengger *pembaron* ritual of renewal gives a seven-prayer corpus that seems to be older than other known cosmogonies.

The fact that these various mantras used in the buffalo sacrifices to Durga by the Susuhunan or Mangkunagaran palace officials[1] on the anniversaries of coronation, are also used for exorcistic lullabies, and in the *wayang* purification ceremonies certainly sugggests that they are heterogeneous not only in usage but also probably in origin. There is as no proof that they diversified from an earlier common palace corpus some three centuries ago. The first and longest invocation unique to the palace corpus, *Tata Winanci* tells in mantra form the first half of the wayang *Birth of Kala* myth. This mantra begins earlier on in the story, the very moment of the creation of the world may be told. Paradoxically their present position is at the end of this *wayang* play. The "beginning of becoming" (*Purwaning Dumadi*), the another name for the *Tata Winanci*, is not indispensable to "retelling" this exorcistic myth said over the victim of Kala's hunger. This may explain why this mantra in now only heard at palace rituals. The changing number of mantras in a corpus varies with their ritual usage but not in any regular way. Scrambling their order poses a problem for those who are not yet familiar with purifications by *wayang*, but not for those who are (Headley 2000*a*, ch. 5). In this study foregrounding Islam, we will concentrate on the creation of the body of the cosmic giant in two mantra, Wagon of Letters (section 9.3) and the Dhalang's Goose (section 9.4), which are clearly the continuation of the first mantra's (*Tata Winanci*) original creation myth; the second mantra is understood in the light of the first. These two mantras have alternate names (respectively, Letter on the Chest and New Pavilion) and varying contents reflecting their different uses in the context of *wayang* purification rituals or the sacrifices on Durga's tertre, etc.

The comparison of different collections of mantra shows that four mantras are stable members of the rituals enumerated above. These are all in Javanese and are longer than the Arabic ones. They also have a narrative if formulaic content that the Muslim prayers lack. The first mantra we have already mentioned is the *Tata Winanci* "Let there be no disturbance" (Sasana Pustaka ms. 547 Ka, p. 49). It is rare and yet sets the stage for all the others. This first invocation is explicitly called "the beginning of becoming", i.e. creation

(*Purwaning Dumadi*) in Probohardjono's corpus. It is the cosmology that contextualizes the other mantras.

Context is "a set of *pragmatic indices, co-ordinates*, or *reference points* (as they are variously called) for speakers, addressees, times of utterance, place of utterance, indicated objects and whatever else." (Levinson 1983, p. 58). Despite a good deal of fragmentation and corruption in the other mantras, their context is sufficiently clear to distinguish a meaningful arrangement in the corpus. No indigenous cosmogonies set in a mantra genre in contemporary Java outside the *Tata Winanci* are known to me. This leads me to believe that these cosmogonic mantras appended to the *Birth of Kala* purification are a reiteration of its theme: purification is achieved by renewal as exemplified in the first creation. Said another way, the *Tata Winanci* is the *Birth of Kala* exorcism is an invocation couched in terms a genesis myth of which the birth of Kala was once a part.

Does that order necessarily represent in any sense a later form? In a compilation of creation of myths, the *Manikmaya* (vol. 1, 1981), this cosmogony is found, albeit in epic not in mantra form. In the Pancot Kidul purification (Headley 2000a, ch. 4), the cosmogony, used on Mt Lawu, comes at the beginning, "where it belongs". This lead me to think that when the myth is being resaid as mantra for purification, it is detached and recited at the end of the play. The original cosmogony is read off Kala's body as a real *dénouement*, a true unravelling of evil.

9.2 THE ISLAMIZATION OF THE INVOCATIONS TO DURGA

In Chapter 8 (Table 8.1) it was said that the second half of the more recent Paku Buwana palace collection of mantras (nos 22–35) is in Arabic. However corrupt, they still have their original Javanese names even if they have been given new Arabic contents. We surmised that certain *abdi dalem* Suranata have replaced many of the Javanese invocations at a recent date (?1941) with Muslim ones. If this were true it would indicate a rapid evolution of the Javanese prayer corpus. In the Mangkunagaran prayer corpus, the one used for Durga's offerings when the Mangkunagaran was in charge, there are only a few prayers with a Muslim veneer consisting of the introduction of terms like Allah, Allahumma; "kun faya kun" (the divine fiat), etc. Essentially Islam remains foreign to these Mangkunagaran *Maésa Lawung* invocations; it has made much greater inroads in the Susuhunan palace corpus.

Below, the prayers having parallels in the Susuhunan's Sasana Pustaka collection of prayers said in the palace chamber called *Dalem Prabasuyasa* by the *abdi dalem juru* during the night vigil for the birth of a royal prince are marked with an asterisk. Even if according to the palace collection they suggest that were not used for other occasions, in fact the Susuhunan used a similar collection of prayers as did the Mangkunagaran for the *Maésa Lawung* buffalo sacrifice. And most these prayers are best well known from the *Birth of Kala* exorcisms.

The Mangkunagaran manuscript (*Bundel Maésa Lawung*, no number) gives three versions of its shorter collection of prayers, while the Susuhunan Sasana Pustaka (ms. 547 Ka) gives a single version. The penmanship of both manuscripts suggests they were all executed by the same hand, but that does not necessarily mean they were written by the same author. Two prayers given by the *bundel maésa lawung* in the Mangkunagaran are sometimes sufficiently different to merit being included for comparison, which we have done in sections 9.3 and 9.4.

SELECTED "TRANSLATION" OF MANGKUNAGARAN CORPUS

I have put in italics the copyist's comments. My own comments, mainly about manuscript variations, are in parentheses. The prayers themselves are unitalicized. The titles of prayers are in bold font:

Here are the prayers for the maésa lawung meal (slametan) *for entire kingdom of Surakarta. This slametan falls on the last Thursday of the month of Rabingulakir:*

"In the name of the Lord most merciful and compassionate (Bismillah hirochman hirochim) O Lord, O Allah, O Allah, O Allah, O Lord most merciful and compassionate. Be gracious unto us (3× = three times). O Lord in the highest (3×), exalt us (3×). O greatly clement Lord (3×), pardon us (3×). Glorify us (3×), exalt us (3×). O Lord who are rich in mercy, omniscient Lord, instruct us. O Lord king of all, guide us (3×). O omniscient Lord (3×), convert us. O Lord be our God, of Lord Muhammad, Lord Mangkuratsari, for all that is in the world, we pray you, always grant us your salvation."

"O Lord Mangkuratsari, who commands the entire umat (community), who gives force, who hears prayers, who grants well-being, who gives serenity and who gives salvation (salam)."

This is the Support of the World prayer:
"O Lord who is great above all, there is no other God but Allah and Mohammad is his prophet (*rasul*). O Lord to you we give thanks and in you we put our trust. O Lord some have sinned, come to us whom you welcome. Of all the community throughout the world have mercy of Lord Sanggabuwana, who touches what is cut (idiom?), who walks afar (idiom?) because of your mercy. Receive every man in the world and by the prayers

of the prophets, by the prayers of the *wali* (friends of God), by the *pandita* (teachers) and by the prayers of ordinary communities, by the prayers of those who meditate, by the prayers of the Muslims,[2] Lord, may well-being be received by everyone. And may all praise Allah, Allah the all-powerful."

This is the Earth prayer:
"O august Lord
(? the Sasanapustaka ms.: Allahuma anta pa'ini),
earth who proffers homage (bekti),
world that proffers blessings,
(?faanta/waanta) the earth free from all temptations (the five dangers),
(?waanta) the earth free from all bad luck,
(?waanta) the earth free from all bad luck,
(?waanta) the earth free from all suffering,
(?waanta) the earth free from all sickness,
(?faanta/waanta) the earth free from all poison,
Rohilapi, king of the all men,
blessed are you forever* slamet tulak Amin.

(*Mangkunagaran ms. can be corrected here by Sasana Pustaka ms. Donga Jejeg Jumeneng to read, "iya kanak buduwa iya kanas tangin", a phrase which appears in several prayers. What this means on the other hand is not yet clear.)

"This is the Jejeg prayer;
"Lord, installed, installed on the earth of (?huallah).
The Lord, noble jewel, installed over all the earth's world (?huallah)
The lord installed over the earth (by his) fiat."

(The *donga Jejeg Jumeneng* (=?'elevated standing upright') from the Sasana Pustaka ms. is different in content, and already the two Mangkunagaran versions of this prayer were dissimilar. We have not tried to translate the second of these.)

Halahuma jejeg,	Allahumma lungguh
nabi Adam hu Allah,	halungguh hing
	siti pratala huallah
halahuma jejeg.	Allahhumma retna
	mulya
nabiku nabi Suleman,	halungguh king
hu Allah	sabumi ngalam huallah
Halahuma jejeg,	Allahumma.
jejegku nabi Allah	Halungguh king bumi
rohmat olah, jejeg	kun payakun
saking,	
Allah hu akbar.	

"Lord (Allahuma) residing, residing on the Pratala land Lord. Lord noble jewel, residing in all the lands, Lord residing in the land, 'I am who I am' (=the divine fiat)"

"This is the prayer for **Tulak Bilahi** *(repulsing bad luck):*
Allahumma (lord) repulse bad luck (coming from) the east.
Allahumma (lord) repulse bad luck (coming from) the south
Allahumma (lord) repulse bad luck (coming from) the north.
Allahumma (lord) repulse bad luck (coming from) the west.
Allahumma (lord) repulse bad luck (coming from) the zenith.
Allahumma (lord) repulse bad luck (coming from) the nadir.

"This is the **Nurbuwat** *(radiance of the prophet)*[3] *prayer:*
O loving lord, radiance (*nurbuwat*), guide of the Lord. There is no other god than Allah and Muhammad is his prophet. Lord estrange from us all the attacks of the evil one and brings us closer to the signs of goodness. May salvation and prosperity come (upon us) thanks to the Mohammad. Estrange from us the destiny of the heathen and bring us close to you Lord."

*"Here ends the above prayers which are continued by Arabic prayers as needed or useful (*mikantuki*). Below are found the Hakeng or Buddhist worship (prayers): The ritual of the abdi dalem juru Suranata when there is a birth or when a member of the royal family is sick. Prayers for when someone has sinned or asks for a benediction for the Sampéyan dalem hingkang Sinuhun Kangjeng Susuhunan IXth.*[4] *The melody is ngentrung.*[5] *"*
(Then follow the prayers:) *Sastrapedati; Banyak Dhalang; Gumbala Geni; Puji Banyu; Mandala Giri* (and finally a dismissal).

After presenting the initial group of shorter mantras, I have translated and analysed the two most commonly used longer mantras:

1. Wagon of Letters (*Sastra Pedhati*, variant of the Letters on the Chest (*Sastra ing Dhadha*) mantra.)
2. *Banyak Dhalang* and its variant the New Pavilion or *Balé Anyar*.

9.3 TRANSLATION OF THE WAGON OF LETTERS OR LETTERS ON THE CHEST MANTRA

These mantras continue the cosmogonic genre found in the *Tata Winanci* prayer without really being a genesis narrative. In the case of Letters on the Chest (*Sastra ing Dhadha*) the formula are imagined to be written on and read from Kala's body, thus they are proper to an exorcism (*ruwatan*) ritual. The contents of other mantra, not dealt with here are less context-specific, being simply prayers accompanying the setting down of the offerings in front of

Durga's tree in Krendawahana or in the case of *wayang*, invocations the *dhalang* uses for the exorcism. These remaining mantras are summarized in the footnote.[6] A final mantra in the *wayang*, The Purification of the Platform (*Ruwat Panggung*) describes the "world sweeper" who will use his iron broom to sweep away the followers of Kala that remain. It underscores the element of reiteration that pervades the entire corpus of mantras. This reiteration can also explain how individual mantras comes to change place with others. They are all in some sense repetitions of what has gone before, i.e., the creation of the world.

Sastra Binedhati is translated here as "Wagon of Letters". Wagon, as a translation of *p/bedhati*, is tentative. This mantra has two different titles, *Sastra Binedati*[7] or *Sastra ing Dhadha* (Letters on the Chest) which cannot always be explained by the context in which they are to be used. Depending on the corpus, this can designate the same or slightly different mantras. These variants permit comparison of the texts themselves. The two below represent the state of maximum dissimilarity between the versions I have found. Used in the context of the *Maésa Lawung*, the *Sastra Binedati* recounts the creation of the earth. The *Sastra ing Dhadha* (Letters on the Chest) used in the context of a *wayang* purification recounts the creation of the theatre and its props.

The contents of the second mantra, however, are clear. The world is described as made up by the parts of Ego's body (a deity is speaking through the empirical reciter) or *wayang* theatre props. The cosmogony of the *Tata Winanci* mantra is definitely continued in this second one. The constitution of this cosmic body in the second mantra started in the first mantra when the *jawata* attacked the fallen seed (Kala) and their weapons were absorbed by the formless blob that is blown across the ocean. Eventually they becoming Kala's limbs. The same episode is also recounted in the beginning of the *Birth of Kala*, the falling of the seed into the ocean is set in the broader context of a creation myth.

FIRST VERSION: WAGON OF LETTERS MANTRA

The *Sastra Binedhati* during the *maésa lawung* lasts some two minutes. This prayer was for the well-being of the kingdom during the buffalo sacrifice on the tertre of Batari Durga by Pak Puja, the *abdi dalem juru* Suranata, officiating for the palace of the Susuhunan of Surakarta in the village of Krendawahana (10 February 1983). It is available on film: S.C. Headley, *le Buffle et la Reine quatre rituels à Java central*, 50 minutes; (CNRS Audio-Visuel & CeDRASEMI-1984). The mantra had been memorized by Pak Puja from a transcription of the Sasana Pustaka palace text (p. 10), the same text contains the *Tata Winanci*. It is the second prayer in that collection. The mantra at the tertre in Krendawahana is always recited out loud.

In 1985 I went to visit Pak Puja in his house in Solo after filming the ceremonies for Durga in Krendawahana. Showing him the film I had made of the ritual, at which he celebrated, did not in any way encourage him to show me the text of the prayers. Later in the same year, I was able to get a copy of the manuscript directly from the palace library. At that point Pak Puja was willing to go over with me another version that I had found in the Mangkunagaran palace library in 1974. Pak Puja had memorized the mantra from transcribed, latinized versions. He was not very fluent in reading *aksara* (the Javanese alphabet). When I asked him whether the differences from the texts he was used to reciting were significant, it became apparent that he never tried to understand what he recited, but concentrated exclusively on their memorization and enunciation. Nonetheless he occasionally changed words: it sounded as though he sometimes mistook an archaic word in the special vocabulary of the prayers for a similar sounding everyday word, even if the latter made no sense in that particular context. This is of interest since it shows that the identification of the parts of the speaker's body with the parts of the universe has a reality which is not only conceptual and linguistic, but in this case actually belongs also to the ethnographic description of the performance. The propositions of this mantra have been numbered by myself in order to refer back to them in the subsequent analysis.

1. Om is appropriate! (The chorus after each line uses the refrain: "well-being", three times).
2. Sire world is by body.
3. My stature is as high as a silk cotton tree (some 30 m.).
4. My hair is the sire Rumaya (from *kurumayan?*[28]).
5. My face is the earth around the sacrificial post.
6. My eyes are the eyes of a bird.
7. My ear is sire "sign".
8. My nose is the whistling of the wind.
9. My mouth is the sire human cave.
10. My mouth is Lady Saraswati.[9]
11. My teeth are sire ravine[10] stone.
12. My tongue is sire tillable earth.
13. My chin is sire *sumong* (?) stone.

15. My clavicle is sire king of the Darma (=? Yama).
16. My arm is the *nerajung* (=?) earth
17. My backbone is the earth sloping like the back of a cow.
18. My armpit is the folded earth.
19. My chest is the hardened clay.
20. My abdomen is the sloping earth.
21. My feet are sire twin mountains.
22. My buttocks are sire *menje* fruit.
23. My anus is the burrow (?) of the porcupine.
24. My bed is the spilled earth.
25. My urine is spring water.
26. My thigh is the shaded earth.
27. The flat of my foot is the field earth.
28. My gait is the earthquake during the cyclone,
29. like thunder and lightning is my gait.
30. Fear! Be gone all monsters!
31. Durga and Kala be gone!
32. O Giver descends to me in the middle world!
33. Together with the gods I pray.
34. Amahraja (= ?King Yama) that I say.
35. Amahraja is my prayer. (*The Kalacakra mantra follows*)[11]
36. Let all evil doers be gone!
37. Let all who approach lose their magic!
38. Let those who cause hunger, give fullness!
39. Let those who make poor, give riches!
40. Let those who cause suffering give well-being!
41. May those who attack lose their power!
42. Evil-doers, be loyal!
43. Well-being, well-being, well-being!

(Followed by the declaration that the kingdom's
slametan was completed.)

Second version: "Letters on the Chest" mantra

During the *wayang* purification *Sastra ing Dhadha* last some 2:30 minutes.
During live *wayang* performances, it is rare to be allowed to transcribe the
dhalang's sotto voce recitation of the mantras. Usually one must rely on
written versions from the plot (*pakem*) summaries. The fact that the *dhalang's*
voice is no longer audible (the microphone has been cut off) reduces the

attention of the audience. They quickly begin their own private conversations, creating an overall "grey noise" that prevents hearing anything that the *dhalang* might be saying. The Writing on the Chest mantra, as its title might suggest, only concerns the *dhalang*, Guru, Kala and the victim, who can hear what the *dhalang* is saying from his place behind the puppet screen. An exception to this norm of sotto voce recitation was *dhalang* Suyatna Wiknyasarana's performance for the exorcism of the two sons of Ing. Mohammed Santasa in the Mangkunagaran palace on 28 December 1982. The mantras were pronounced aloud and easily transcribed from the cassettes.

1. "Om, the taboo is appropriate!
2. Before the heavens existed,
3. Who is *Kunfayakun* (= I say and it is[12]).
4. *Kun* ("am") means my (puppets') chest.
5. to spread out (the heavens) means
   to spread out my wayang (screen).
6. My platform is the foundation of the world.
7. The unfurling of the world takes the form
   of my cloth screen.
8. Drizzle takes the form of my foot tapping
   (on the cymbals hanging from the puppet chest).
9. My puppet is Sire "rusted bone".
10. My banana trunk and platform are
    Sire Pejo (?=*pejuh*; male seed) the king.
11. Sire "flaming light of life" is my shadow lamp.
12. My shadow lamp is the unique jewel
13. My wick is the prophet Moses.[13]
14. My oil is the god of the wind.
15. Sire Brahma illumines by pincers.
16. The fairies do not pinch the lamp black.
17. rather they repel bodily illnesses,
    ills of hindrance and the three impurities.
18. Like the trail of a shooting star,
19. madness is destroyed,
    disappearing without a trace!

(This was directly followed by the mantras *Balé Anyar* and *Banyak Dhalang*.)

These two invocations are summarized here phrase by phrase; P. here stands for "proposition".

Letters on the Chest	*Wagons of Letters*
BIRTH OF KALA	MAÉSA LAWUNG
P1: Om is fitting	P1: Om is fitting.
P2: Before there was the universe.	P2: The world is my body.
P3: There was the divine *fiat.*	P3–29: The "x" is my "y", etc.
P4–14: The "x" is my "y".	
P15: Brahma light my pincers!	
P16: Fairies do not pinch the flame	
of the wayang lamp.	
P17–18: but reject illnesses!	P30: Be gone all monsters.
P19: The ills disappear.	P31: Kala and Durga be gone.
	P32: O Giver descend!
	P33: I'll pray with the gods.
	P34–35: Amahraja is my prayer.
	P36–42: Kalacakra mantra
	P43: (Chorus) Well-being!
	(repeated three times)

On the anniversaries of coronations, at the royal buffalo sacrifice, the parties representing kings are silent and all face the tree that marks the place of the doors to Batari Durga's invisible kingdom. The celebrant reciting the prayers speaks out loud. The obscurity of many of the words, combined with the empirical speaker's lack of understanding of them and the apparent lack of pertinence and fit with the context of the buffalo sacrifice renders these invocations difficult to comprehend.

What *is* understood by the empirical speaker, the *abdi dalem juru* Suranata, as well as by the audience, is *Om*. The *minimal* meaning of Om at the beginning of a mantra is not really qualitatively different from saying "Greetings" (*nuwun*) at the threshold of a house to inaugurate a visit and begin a dialogue. According to the convention of enunciating these invocations, *Om* is usually whispered. Whether it is *sotto voce* as in the Birth of Kala play, or cantilating (*ura-ura*) out loud as in the *Maésa Lawung*, both these presentations claim and are understood to claim that communication is possible. Mantras, which are difficult to understand using only a written text, are rendered "comprehensible" in the context of the use of *om* which opens up the channels of communication, just as *nuwun* does.

The party to this dialogue, the invisible *Om*, is a syllable which secretly (*sandhi*) reveals the transcendence of the divine word (*sabda*). The *Sastra Binedhati* begins *Hong wilaheng*[14] *prayoganira*, which I have freely paraphrased as "Om, the taboo is appropriate". The appropriateness (=*prayoga*) of taboo is a self-explanatory statement of a consensus behind which the Javanese place themselves the sacred phoneme "Om".

Just as all public meetings begin with an Islamic invocation of God's blessing, the use of the introductory sound "*hong*" (*Om* in Sanskrit) defines insight of the divine presence and is identical to the divinity; it brings power to the man who uses it appropriately.[15]

The first verses of both *Sastra Binedhati* and *Sastra ing Dhadha* indicate an epiphany. In religious language epiphanies are a manifestation of what one normally assumed could not be manifest. In the words of Ricoeur: "...il faut laisser être ce qui se montre..." ("... one must let be what appears..."; 1981, pp. 348–49). In the Solonese palace, Sanskrit and Arabic formulae are quoted to manifest creation.

Before the heavens existed,	*dhèk durung awang-awang uwung-uwung*
Who is was *Kunfayakun* (the divine fiat, = "I am who I am")	*sing ana kunfayakun*
Kun ("am") means my (puppets') chest	*Kun maknaning kotakku.*

As Sperber and Wilson say (1986, p. 228), "Direct quotations are the most obvious examples of utterances used to represent not what they describe, but what they resemble." Thus it makes sense that the third party's voice is used as an icon. What is surprising is that to imitate the moment of creation, the Sanskrit *Om* pronounces an Arabic fiat. Islamic theology has come in to reinforce a totally Javanese Hindu cosmogony. This process is not uncommon for scriptural citation in Javanese mosques. The preacher's (*modin*) personal language is subordinate to an intensification of the dialogue which lets the "other" voice continue, through the listening of the public. In such recontextualization, the descriptive function is replaced by a poetic revelation.

The Letters on the Chest mantra continues by identifying various parts of the body and the personage of the true *dhalang* with the diverse props of the shadow puppet theatre. The mantra used in the royal buffalo sacrifices identifies the parts of the Ego's body with parts of the earth or kinds of stone. In either case, the mantra speaks out with elocutionary force to identify the parts of the body of a mysterious "I" with the parts of the well-known earth or theatre. What is familiar, that is the earth and the *wayang* props, serves to reveal what is mysterious, the creator.

After the opening verse, the Letters on the Chest and Wagon of Letters mantras contain a series of repetitive syntaxes on the pattern: "the revered world is my body", i.e. the "x" is my "y", etc. The deity addressed remains unnamed, but immediately this predicative syntax in the Wagon of Letters mantra begins to assemble an "I" made possible by applying the syllable Hong /Om in the following manner:

Om is the best way!	*Hong prayoganira;*
Sire world is by body.	*Sang buwana sariraku.*
My stature is that of the silk	*Randhu kepuh pangadegku.*
cotton tree (some 45 m.).	
My hair is the sire *Rumaya*	*Rambutku sang kurumeyan.*
My face is the sire earth	*Raiku sang lemah paesan.*
around the sacrificial pillar.	
My eyes are the eyes of a bird.	*Mataku socaning manuk.*

These are in fact superimposed voices, hierarchically arranged, and independent one from another. Thus it is that the *dhalang* in the Birth of Kala may recite from a written text in a *sotto voce* mode that reserves the text for his "other" self, Wisnu, Guru's delegate. Wisnu, "speaker of the world" (*kandabuwana*) in the *ruwatan*, listens, so to speak, to what Guru the father wrote on Kala's body.

In the *maésa lawung* Pak Puja sits at the foot of Durga's *tertre* after the jars of blood have been placed before the invisible doors of her kingdom, saying that the cosmic man has a body shaped like a human one, but made out of the constituent elements of the terrestrial globe. This identification is obtained by superimposed voices as above.

This distinction is presented by O. Ducrot (1972) as one between two different kinds of speaker. Ducrot designates "L" as belonging to the commentary on the enunciation; and "lamda" as belonging inside the sense, to the description of the world. This corresponds to the distinction we have made above. The minimal unit for the comprehension of these obscure Javanese mantra is not the sentence, but the performance of a given kind of speech act. The study of the corpus of mantra provides us with the sequence of the types of speech acts taking place.

A succinct résumé the two versions of the *Sastra Bindhati* and the *Sastra ing Dhadha* mantra proposition by proposition brings out their illocutionary dimension. The persons taking part in this proposition by proposition *mise en scène* can be treated as parties to a common prayer. Each series of propositions can then be attributed according to who said it to whom.

These texts are recited in the *maésa lawung* or read silently as in the Birth of Kala or sung as in *kidungan* to protect babies from illness,[16] addressing the people and spirits at hand. The *dhalang, abdi dalem juru* Suranata, and the singer of lullabies saying the mantra knows who is there, i.e. whom Kala is chasing, the young man collectively designated as Jathusmati ("nearly dead").

FIGURE 9.1
Diagram by destination/recipient of the propositions

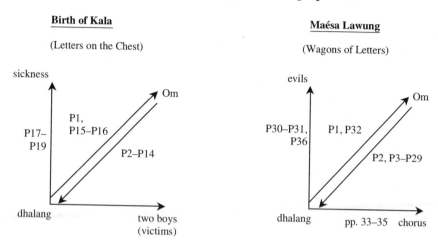

Birth of Kala

(Letters on the Chest)

Maésa Lawung

(Wagons of Letters)

The spirits, the invisible audience before whom the performance is mounted, need to be informed who it is that needs protection. The victim requesting the prayer need not be named, unless it is to identify himself with someone more powerful than himself. In the Birth of Kala exorcisms, it is common for the *dhalang* to identify himself with Wisnu, the true (*sejati*) *dhalang*. The family that has solicited the prayer has been personalized by puppets. The human victims will be tonsured at the end of the performance. Those in need are made clear to the spirits by the special language, prayer melodies and gestures. *Om, the taboo is appropriate*, or *There is a song that protects....* signals to the spirits to begin listening.

TATA WINANCI AND SASTRA BINEDHATI/SASTRA ING DHADHA

Although, the *Tata Winanci* mantra is not recited for the buffalo sacrifice at the foot of Durga's tertre, the name of that mantra is mentioned at the very beginning of these invocations. In 1983, the first mantra recited by Pak Puja at the foot of Durga's tertre began with a short prayer explaining why he was burning incense. In the first verse of this prayer he says "*tata winanci*", which is a garbled, shortened form of "*Let there be no disturbance (Awignam astu namas sidem)*"[17] as if to acknowledge that although he was not reciting that mantra in full. Its initial benediction was nevertheless the backdrop for all that followed.

The *Tata Winanci* ends with the statement that Kala has no body, but we have seen in the Birth of Kala and the *Manikmaya* how the gods' weapons hurled at the amorphous blob on the ocean are incorporated to constitute his limbs. In the second mantra, the recitation of the mantra has built up a full "body" for its cosmic man. In the second proposition, one can see a logic of invoking, building up a deity, limb by limb, out of the chthonic elements that go to make up the earth. This seems to be a way of repossessing the demon-invested "hot" earth which really belongs to the deity Kartidara (=the giver). In the other version, *Sastra ing Dhadha*, that mantra performs the same sort of assemblage by identifying the props of the *wayang* with the constituent elements of the earth to be purified.

In *wayang* purifications the *dhalang* is Wisnu. The title of the palace officiant, "king of the gods" (*suranata*),[18] indicates that he speaks for the heavenly pantheon. The transformation of creation occurs during the passage from ordinary language to special communication with the divine: *Om* of P1, P54 in *Tata Winanci*; and the *Om* P1, as well as the *aji* prayer of P32 and 33 in *Sastra Binedhati* and the P1 of the *Sastra ing Dhadhi*.) The dhalang can also speak as a god via the syntax, "My 'X' is my 'Y' ". He can speak the other powerful mantra which ordinary men can only use after fasting and by much repetition. The *Sastra Binedhati* concludes with the Kalacakra mantra, a well-known alphabetic recitation in the form of a wheel with eight spokes in eight directions on which are written the syllables. The research of Soedjijono et al. in East Java (1987: 118–80) shows that this conception of the danger of reciting such powerful mantra is still held today.

In more normal conversational contexts, we cannot only identify the speakers, but also process the information they give us. Here, the identity of the speakers is ambiguous, while what they say is more or less clear. The bulk of P3–29 in the *Maésa Lawung*, the *Sastra Binedhati*, is composed of readily identifiable noun propositions (=NP) such as hair, face, earth, and stone. What is not clear is P2: "My body is the world". Whose body, which world? The distinction between givenness and definiteness is useful here, for while the hair, face, earth, and stone are definite they are not given. We do not know to whom they belong.

This predicament is commonly found in other creation myths (cf. Gibert 1986, pp. 28–42). A creation event is described using elements of our knowledge of known history, but the primordial, original scene itself is ineffable, as no one was there observing it. The fascination with origins is due to the elusive nature of one's own beginnings, which can only be known second-hand. In this mantra corpus the anaphoric (=backwards and upwards) reference to parts of the great body is set in motion. Thus, even if the language is obscure and not well understood, the Javanese who attend feel implicated by the present-past, present-future movement of the recitations and the concerns (*prakara*) which they treat. The participants spontaneously come forward at the end of the official prayer to add their own invocations at the foot of Durga's shrine.

This suggests that the earlier dialogue continues to be operative. Today they accept the mantras as an account of the mysterious beginnings of the world. They situate themselves by their relationship with the deity whose body is described as responsible for the beginning of the world. Their cataphoric relations with this deity (=forward reference, i.e. prayers for good health of the new-born, purifications of adults) reify the anaphoric one of the myth. Reciting a creation myth has direct effects on those who now inhabit the earth.

"May those who attack lose their power"(P41) in the *Sastra Binedhati* resembles the battle against Kala (P52–53) in the *Tata Winanci* mantra where a struggle is going on between Guru's army and Kala. The scenario of the *Tata Winanci* mantra is creation, and provides the stage for an initial conflict between Guru, along with Durga the creator, and Kala, the unsuccessful creation (Headley 2000, pp. 143–55). The outcome of the conflict is precluded by the fact that the creator of all will renew his creation by being the subject of the myth.

9.4 THE *DHALANG'S* GOOSE MANTRA AND THE NEW PAVILION SONG

I have chosen to use exceptionally clear recording of these mantras from a *wayang* performance rather than from the *maésa lawung* at Krendawahana. In fact it is fortunate that the corpus of these prayers permits comparisons from one usage to another for they are corrupt and hard to translate without some recourse to the context of enunciation and usage. During the performance of Birth of Kala by the *dhalang* Suyatna Wiknyasarana (Mangkunagaran palace, 28 December 1982), the recitation (*ura-ura*) of the mantra lasted some ten minutes. There was a hushed accompaniment by a female voice in the background. A third mantra, the *Dhalang's* Goose, was preceded by an abbreviated *Sastra Binedhati* (2:30 minutes) and a shortened *Balé Anyar* (1:10 minutes) mantra, and followed by the *Kumbula Geni* (1:45 minutes). The *Dhalang's* Goose was the longest of the four mantras (3:30 minutes), even though it was sung more rapidly than the others. The translation, as the question marks below indicate, is especially problematic. The same mantra text is used in the *Maésa Lawung* ritual when it is performed by the Mangkunagaran:

Translation: New Pavilion mantra
1. Om, the taboo is appropriate.
My intention is to stand aright in the middle of the world,
a handsome knight not devious.
My behaviour is without twists.
5. Located in the centre of the heart,
in fact I am the true *dhalang*,
perfectly pure.
Om, the taboo is appropriate
Sire fluttering King, spinning

Dhalang's Goose mantra
1. Om, the taboo is appropriate
Sire king, fluttering emblems[19]
He immediately flies off from the throne,
moving towards the south.
5. Looking for a quiet place,
once he arrives in this hamlet.
Beyond the eight ogres appears a new pavilion
At a large well the bloody water sparkles
Drawn up by a castrated guardian
10. with the umbilical cord of a thief
Wash with care
Its behaviour is like the wind (*maruta?*)
The ills of passion, sicknesses of the three stains
are perfected by the true dhalang.

15. Om, the taboo is appropriate
Sire King fluttering
My child is sire *dhalang's* goose
(?) that which is able to be protected
is in this village, in the new pavilion
20. Without spreading the contents of the great well
whose bloody water sparkles
drawn up by a castrated guardian
with the umbilical cord of a thief
The aerial roots of a banyan tree
25. A carved wooden spear handle
Graceful appeared its behaviour, father (?)
Om, the taboo is appropriate
ills of passion, obstacles ills are cast away on the waves

sickness of the three stains, all the afflictions
30. curses of same generation elders (=? *kakang kawah*, etc.)
There is a young unmarried man if a flower (*hanga* =?)
then there is a young woman moving forward
Its(=?) beam of light is called the earth
If indeed (You?) are wearing the ills of passion,
                    the sickness of the three stains
35. hurry to observe sire frog the ascetic
"Plop, plop!"
He cried out when he made this noise
moving around *anauta* (?).
Most vows of penance,
40. curses of elders if they follow
The song of the true *dhalang* produces health
There are old men and old women
suitable for the strength of the *dhalang's* goose
but it is advisable to marry quickly
45. Who is it that has bad advice,
(*muyang* =?) tenfold then observe
Sire (?goose) is carried on the waves, spinning in the river
There is a *garuda* with an iron beak
Do not eat my child, my grandchild
50. Peck away at passion ills, three impurities sickness
all the vows of penance
The curse (*upata*) of same generation relatives
the curse (*upata*) of the true *dhalang*
effectively produce well-being

55. Om, the taboo is appropriate
more than a thousand armed men
not one is left
I indeed disperse the enemy
sick with coughing and dizziness
60. These are dispersed by the force
of penance, by curses of fire
They are dispersed by the force
of penance, by the earth curse
They are dispersed by the force
65. of penance, by the wind curse
and then return to their own location.

Then the *gamelan* takes up the next melody and the *dhalang*, laying his mantra booklet aside, picks up the marionettes, and respectfully addresses the marionette which represents the father of the two sons being exorcised, saying:

> *Dhalang*: I request now that you give me permission to purify your two sons. Beginning now may your will be done, perfected my effort to purify from impurities (*sukerta*) the sons.

The hair-cutting and ablutions conclude the Birth of Kala purification.

New Pavilion Protective Song

The Banyak Dhalang (*Dhalang's* Goose) mantra translated above is similar to the New Pavilion mantra from the *kidungan* (protective song) collection used traditionally to protect new-born babies. This equivalent mantra from the *kidungan* collection is used for protection against illnesses, but is slightly shorter and develops more thoroughly the ritual orientations of the cardinal directions. For this chanted version the commentary published in Surakarta in 1937 by R. Wiryapanitra is available. Occasionally this author elucidates difficult terms, but for the better part of his commentary he interprets the meaning of this obscure mantra using sexual imagery familiar in the earlier *suluk* literary texts such as *Darma Gandul* and *Gatholoco*.[20] The footnotes here contain certain comments of R. Wiryapanitra (1937/1979, pp. 164–70). This *kidungan* is written in *durma* meter.[21]

This translation is certainly not definitive. It was based simply on whatever stanza in a given version made some sense, when other readings were quite incomprehensible.[22] To claim that this translation was based on a diplomatic compilation of the variants available would be pretentious so the references have been left out.

1. Here is my song sung for the new pavilion,[23]
without (anything) laid out, all quiet,
refreshing, shaded sombre.
The flowering bamboo is dead.[24]
The scoop (for the well?) has a hole, without a lock.
The wood is a trident.

2. (At) the great well with at its head a shimmering pond,
falling on (her) chest, it is mixed in
Its sides and head are spotted.
Whirling, it turns around,

tied by thief's cord.
The chest caves in,
rolled up and squeezed.

3. The serpent king is the guardian of the flowered jewels (=seed);[25]
the jewels which adhere have an odour;
they are sharp in the uterus
impatient and moving constantly,
insisting,
inciting and coming back.

4. Falling downwards, they are beckoned and greeted;
Soon they are covered over;
There a girl arrives;
the couple knows each other.
Wherever there is betel nut, the couple is promised to each other;
The couple throws it away;
Never dare (prolong it).

5. Dame Old Maid shelters with a parasol the writing
[="wheel of Time or Kalacakra" mantra].
Her mount is the Ji snake.
Her whip a male snake;
whipping to the east,
sweeping all the illnesses to the side,
shoved back to the east,
she whips (them) again.

6. The illnesses from the east are whipped and shoved back,
returning once again to the south.
Coming up from the south,
they are then whipped away,
returning again to the south,
whipped they have already returned

7. The illnesses from above (once) whipped are repulsed,
returning above again.
The illnesses from below
whipped are shoved away.
The dangers and the enemies

from the right arrive,
from the pale white east.

8.   The silver city called Ki Tarulata (=?)
bringing an army of hundreds of thousands
His guard is unharmed
totally free of illnesses;
My sibling[26] from the south arrives
Sire "awakened Tara"
red[27] is (this) city of copper.

9.   (with) an army of 900,000 guardians.
repulsing all the illnesses,
effacing all dangers
My sibling arrives from the west.
Sire Manguntara is yellow;
its city is of gold,
(and) its army 700,000.

10. The guards are unharmed free from schemes,
hexes, aims, and devils.
My sibling from the north arrives,
black is his colour.
(This city) is named Sire pavilion of secret lore (=*supi*).
Its city is in iron;
its carries with it an army of hundreds of thousands.

11. The guards are safe, free from any plans
Oh, Allah take witness!
Earth take witness!
In the four directions of the heavens,
the angels fly in circles;
Ten thousand prophets
protect (both) night and day.

12. Come closer four thousand angels!
All in birdlike form,
they peck away a the illnesses
and the nightmares.
The curses are all vanquished,
devoured, destroyed,
pecked, cut, and ground up.

COMMENTARY ON THE *DHALANG*'S GOOSE AND THE NEW PAVILION

There is no longer any question of cosmogony here such as was found in the first and second mantras, *Tata Winanci* and *Sastra Binedhati*. The last part of the New Pavailion mantra recalls the exorcistic invocation of the *Sri Tanjung* with its references to the four cardinal directions and the "cities" of different metals and colours. The invocation provides no preliminary notion to the listener of who is speaking. As confusing as they are, the New Pavilion and *Dhalang*'s Goose invocations are nonetheless clearly made up of agents effecting a purifying mission *vis-à-vis* specific ills. This makes some sense in the Birth of Kala exorcism and the protective songs for new-born children. It should be recalled that the *maésa lawung* also is a sort of *ruwatan* for the royal family and the kingdom. In five propositions (P3, 6, 14, 41, 53, and 58) the handsome knight, the True *Dhalang*, and the "I" are put forward as the "agent" of the ritual. Evil and the two boys (the objects of that particular exorcism in the Mangkunagaran palace) are only dealt with through the monologic intervention of this *dhalang*. The True *Dhalang* is placed in the centre and speaks for the terrestrial *dhalang* and the celestial *Om*. This institutes a vertical dimension (heaven-earth) to which are joined the horizontal dimensions where the ills will later be relegated. The empirical officiant has the True *Dhalang* descend to the middle of the earth to speak on his own behalf and that of the person to be cured and protected.

I was able to record only once these protective songs in actual use; they are better known from kiosk penny pamphlets which one still finds in abundance. The New Pavilion (*Balai Anyar*) from the *kidungan* corpus has a polyphony that is apparent in the *wayang* versions. The tension deployed in the conversation with the spirits during the protective song New Pavilion is evident thanks to the use of the cardinal directions. The interlocutory dimension in this song protecting children, is expressed on two levels: when sung by the mothers or grandmothers for children who are sick or simply as lullabies to protect them during the coming night. When the true *dhalang*, supposedly located in the centre of the heart, speaks through the voice of the reciter, the latter is formally identified with this true *dhalang*, who is addressing dangers personified as siblings from the four horizontal directions, the reciter opens up a vertical dimension using the *Om* formulas. He institutes an earthly dimension with a description of events which are centred around an eerie village with its calm pavilion and its well of blood, finally expelling passions and illnesses to the four quarters this world. Installed in the middle of the world, the "virgin Wudhu shelters with the parasol (of writing,) the *Kalacakra* mantra" ("*Rara Wudhu apepayung Kalacakra*").

The *Dhalang's Goose* prayer as translated above seems at first reading all but incomprehensible, not only because of the problems posed by translation, but also because the anthropology of its recitation provides no indication of what it might mean. Nor did the presence of a recipient bearing the name *Dhalang's Goose* among the regalia (*pusaka*) the south-central Javanese palaces prove to be much help.

However some useful information about the meaning of its title, The *Dhalang's Goose*, can be found amongst the Tengger of the Bromo highlands of East Java (N. Smith-Hefner 1983, ch. 5 & 6 and R. Hefner 1985, pp. 8, 9). There, the "dhalang's goose" appears both as a sacred cooking container and as a live duck. This vessel, the object of the attentions of the Tengger priest's wife, has vanished from the lowland Javanese ritual usage. It is the priest who describes what is cooking when he says:

> Hong! I describe the worship of the Sire Dhalang's Goose (*ki banyak dhalang*) container. The clay pot is cooking. The skeleton of the dish is the evil spirit Dustodurjana. The fire wood is that spirit's bones. The tinder is the hair. The fire is the evil of his desire; the water his urine; the cooking pot his body; the rice-steaming basket (*kukusan*) is his anus; the rice itself his teeth.[28]

Clearly this mantra uses the same system of corporeal identifications as the *Sastra Binedhati* and the *Sastra ing Dhadha* mantra. The context in which this prayer is said is the following. During the *entas-entas* ceremony, Tenggerese ritual purification for the ascent (*entas*) to heaven of the souls of the deceased, the creation of the world is described in a long prayer entitled "The Beginning of the World" (*Purwabumi*[29]). The exorcism is accomplished after reading this Javanese genesis by separating out Kala and Durga. As R. Hefner points out (1985, p. 180) there are no references to lineage ties to guardian ancestors. Local popular Tengger tradition has given way to a world cosmology. This is accomplished by transforming, by "cooking", by offering food to evil divinities that become the good gods they once were in the original cosmogony. R. Hefner gives the following description of the Tengger purification (1985, p. 181):

> Here again, as in the *purwabumi* (creation myth), evil is personified in the form of yet another spirit Durstodurjono, and the priest's labour is in effect to transform and push back the threat of that spirit's evil. Here the labour of transformation is not only described in prayer, it is symbolically represented in the cooking by the priest's wife. This symbolic mimesis will be the basis for the rite's purification. As his wife cooks, the priest announces his challenge to evil:

"You have finished preparing your soup. In what does your work consist? It has pushed Dustodurjono back to the east, and with him have gone all the impurities of the body. Let them return to their places."

The priest repeats this prayer for each of the four directions of the wind. Having made his challenge to the forces of evil, the priest in prayer becomes more defiant, addressing each of the winds with the same challenge: "Although you would (falsely) call yourself the god Suworo, or Brahma, Mahadewa, or Wisnu, you are not! The priest's power is awesome indeed; he turns back evil by denying the very name that evil would give itself."

R. Hefner has described a different culinary operation accomplished by the priest's wife following the ritual above (Hefner 1985, pp. 169–70). The actual purification of the souls of the dead consists in "sewing" the cloth above each man's head to the father (*petra*) figure representing the departed and placed in front of the member of his family. After this is accomplished the priest...

> ...returns again to the first man, this time with a small mandrake (*bèbèk*) in hand, its feet bound with a string to which is attached a cloth purse containing coins and betel leaf. The priest's wife stands next to him, placing a few grains of the rice she cooked moments earlier on the cloth cover over the head of the seated representative of the dead. The priests immediately steps in and moves the mandrake over the cloth in a scraping fashion, allowing the animal to peck at the rice.

This is done over each pair, man and father effigy, and then the duck is hurled across the room to an assistant, at which point the priest's wife begins the same operation all over again with a hen. Now if one rereads the lowland Javanese *Dhalang's Goose* mantra, the comparison with this Tengger ritual is quite obvious. The *Dhalang's* goose is a bird that pecks away sins either in the form of a cooking utensil (as such it is still part of the Central Javanese palace regalia), or in the form of a live bird which is still used only by these highland Javanese in the Tengger region.

9.5 IMPLICATED PERFORMANCE

In the introduction to this chapter, the discussion of the behaviour of the participants in these purification rituals was (paradoxically) laid aside just at the moment when the pragmatic dimension of the mantra was presented for analysis. If the participation of the family or the princes of a kingdom, asking for the liberation of one of their members from evil does not, necessarily, take place through listening to, and or understanding the inaudible and incomprehensible mantra, what are they doing?

It might seem that without being able to hear and understand the mantra, the notion of graphogony and writing on the body of demons and humans, would remain quite inaccessible to the average Javanese. In fact the offerings they make at each *ruwatan* or at *maésa lawung* suffice to render the notion self-evident for them. An offering of fruit, of cooked food, of batik, or of money, in Javanese and Indonesian parlance "redeems" (*tebus*) the situation it is destined for. During the recitation by the *dhalang* of this complex mixture of myth and invocation, the family are usually praying and concentrating on the issue at hand, healing one of their members. Durga protects those who honour her. Anaphora from the afflicted body via the body of Kala to the body of creator is a more complex notion but is not qualitatively a different relationship. This will be discussed in Chapter 10.

Deliverance from illness involving mortal danger, in even the simplest conception, requires agency and the whole preceding drama enacted on the screen with puppets has made it clear to the viewers that the *dhalang* Kandabuwana, "Speak the world" is that speaker of healing anaphoras. The very fact that evil Kala has a history makes it possible through narrative to untie the knot of malevolence called *sukerta* with which he ties his victim to his own hungry destiny.

The notion of *ana-phoros*, "carrying forward", has been recently transferred from classical rhetoric to semantics to semiotics in the last hundred years, but can here to used quite simply to describe the Javanese attitude towards precedents. Metaphor is already anaphoric and was used throughout these invocations. It was nowhere said that the body of human being can be used to imagine how the cosmos was created; nor was it necessary to define the primordial role of lightning and thunder in the first mantra, the *Tata Winanci*, for they are *prima facie* cataclysmic moments preceding an event in light and sound. Thus if the human body is the creation *par excellence*, if the divine creator had a body, it would be both similar to and yet greater than and different from our own.

But the "redeeming" quality of anaphora requires a sacrifice on the part of the intercessor; one has to "give up" an offering, as well as one's attention in prayer while awaiting the response of the deity addressed. There exists a socially instituted precedent and convention that if one implicates oneself this way, one can redeem and prevent the evil obstacles from arising. Even if the dialogic aspect of invocation is formally absent in their oral ritual, one is obliged to describe the prayer performed by the participants in a pragmatic way. The presence of the chorus chanting "well-being" at the foot of Durga's tree after every verse of the *Sastra Bedhati* mantra at the *maésa lawung* ritual reinstates the dialogic ambiance on the part of the royal family's delegates.

This chapter, although it tells us a great deal about how the Javanese prayed in front of Durga's shrine in Krendawahana, has revealed little about the influence of Javanese prayer on Islamic invocation. After examining the general evolution of Muslim prayer in the Javanese cultural ecology in Chapter 10, we will return to a comparison of Muslim genesis narratives as they were compilated with Javanese cosmogonies in Chapter 11.

NOTES

1. *abdi dalem juru* Suranata = literally: "(servant responsible for) the king of the gods".
2. This strongly resembles the Donga Turun Sih ("Making Love Descend") prayer of the Sasana Pustaka ms. 547 Ka, p. 40 of N. Florida's transliterated version.
3. Entirely in Arabic, there exist three versions of this prayer: two longer ones in the Sasana Pustaka ms., and one shorter one in the Mangkunagaran ms. The translation of the shorter one that follows is certainly highly speculative and represents the interpetation of a director of the Surakarta Academy of Arts (STSI), Dr Soetarno, who was not especially familiar with Muslim prayer.
4. Elsewhere in the historical section on the *maésa lawung raja wedda*, the author(s) do mention the sixth Mangkunagaran and his kingdom as the destination of the their prayers, and even give the date of 1918 as the year of the celebration, which makes one think that the manuscript is a composite of a Susuhunan text and a Mangkunagaran one.
5. Songs accompanied by a small drum, often using Middle Eastern rhythms.
6. Before studying in detail three mantras, a résumé of the contents of a whole mantra corpus is useful. E. Lind (1975, pp. 134–51) has done a translation of a Yogyakarta prose manuscript of the Birth of Kala with its mantras which will serve this purpose. I have summarized below the mantras in the order in which they are found in her translation of that Yogyakarta manuscript (Leiden Oriental ms. 6525/1). The numbers and titles in parentheses, added to the Yogya mantra in the list below, refer to Table 8.1.

   (1) Towards the end of the *wayang kulit* play told in this prose text, Kala claiming to be older than the *dhalang* challenges him (ms. 27.1; Lind 1975, p. 140). Then the *dhalang* begins to read the letters on his own body describing the planets and stars located on what we must suppose is a body of cosmic proportions (ms. 27.3–28.5). Then the *dhalang* continues saying, "My eyes existed first, the earth also is in me; my name is the 'inverted banyan' (a heavenly tree)." A description follows of the parts of his body composed of various metals and their alloys (ms. 29.1–31.8; name of this mantra *waringin sungsang*).

   (2) In turn the *dhalang* then reads the letters written on Kala's body beginning with his forehead. These compose a Javanese alphabet written backwards. (*Caraka Balik*; no. 3 in Table 8.1)

(3) Continuing on Kala's throat (or shoulder blades), the *dhalang* reads: "Kala withdraws because he is feeling ill, cured by Wisnu. Wisnu falls ill, the illness sits on his veins and in his gall bladder, he is cured by Brama; Brama falls ill, he is cured by Guru; Guru falls ill and he is cured by Wenang. The Powerful One (Wenang) does not fall ill, but unites with Sang Hyang Tunggal (the unified One), and the two become one feeling. Then the true feeling is purified by the Omnipotent. (*Sastra Telak*; no. 4 Table 8.1)

(4) The *dhalang* then reads the letters on Kala's chest. This mantra is analysed in detail later on (section 9.3). Kala emerges from Guru's spilt seed. His mother is earth, and he is called *sang* Kemale (Arabic for "perfect") for he resembles a jewel. The ocean he floats on, turns in turmoil. Sun and moon are thrown at Kala only to become his flesh and blood; rocks become his eyelashes; bells become his head and tongue; two caves become his nostrils, a jagged rock becomes his mouth; weapons become his neck and teeth; lightning becomes his hair and beard; hollow stones become his glance; faulty seed calls out: "I am Kala and the gods are afraid to look at me."(*Sastra ing Dhadha* ms. 33.2–34.8 or *Sastra Bedhati*; no. 5 in Table 8.1)

(5) The *dhalang* then recites a spell to drive away the upside-down Papag saying that he, the dhalang, has becomes the king Destroyer (*pamunah*) with the power to exorcize stains (*sukerta*): "My wrath is that of Nata Buwana (world order). My voice fills the heaven with a clamorous noise. My wrath is thunder and darkness. I descend this moment guarded by the five holy beings (=the demiurges): Kusika, Gagra, Kurusa, Pritanjala all guard my body" (ms. 37.6–39.1; Lind 1975, p. 143).

(6) Another list referring to the celestial exorcist describes how his body is composed of two snakes and the weapons thrown at him, as was the case with Kala. He is called the "quivering or fluttering" king of the New Pavilion (=*Balé Anyar*; is no. 8 above, translated in §4 below), whose ultimate power resides in the non-Existent one's ability to destroy evil. The great communal well (*bendhung*) is used to exorcize illness, not through the quality of its water, but through its metaphorical surging (cf. Wiryapanitra 1979, pp. 164–67). Birds with iron beaks remove all impurities and leave only Sri and Sadana (no. 8 in Table 8.1, the *Banyak Dhalang* or *dhalang's goose* mantra is usually found with the *Balé Anyar*).

(7) The shadow of the sacred tree-like shape is evoked (*kayon* or *gunungan*), repelling all the illnesses by the *dhalang's* naming of Durga and Kala, the demon leaders.

(8) The fluttering king at the great well of blood meets with the *dhalang's* goose and the *dukun ki Empu*. The fragmentation of the text here, due to omissions and corruptions, makes it hard to follow mantra 7 and 8 closely.

(9) Dazzling Gana (=Ganesa, a brother of Kala) is described limb by limb. The evil spirits are enumerated whom Iswara's child (Gana) conquers by his storms (ms. 51.1).

(10) The flaming beard (*Gumabala Geni*; no. 12 in Table 8.1) mantra: fires and colours from the four directions are described as victorious over curses (ms. 51.2).

(11) The majesty of creation is "coming out from the saying of the mantras". This veritable definition of mantra recitation implies that its effect is not guaranteed. Placed on Mt Meru, this is the holy elixir of immortality (*amarta*). A list of illnesses exorcized by the non-Existent is given (ms. 51.11).

(12) At a golden pavilion bringing welfare (*sangkar welang*), the five sages (cf. mantra no. 5 in Table 8.1) are exorcized by this prayer (ms. 52.10).

(13) *Wayang* puppets corresponding to the thirteen categories of *sukerta* (stained or polluted) children, are brought out of the *dhalang's* box to be exorcized. Once Kala is purified, he returns to his form as Siwa, and Durga becomes Uma again. Then Kala is bathed and the *dhalang* whispers in his ear, "Kala remember you must return to Jati Sorangan (the true Sorangan=?). You come from nothing, you return to nothing."

(14) Next those to be purified ask for a prayer, called Kurameyan (=?jolly child): "my jolly child, you are chubby, rolling around like a jewel" (ms. 59.3).

(15) Kala is then driven away by the *Gumbala Geni* spell. All are given provision for their leave taking. The *dhalang's* final speech concludes: "I am the true *dhalang*, I am able to stand without legs, to reach for things without hands, to see without eyes, to hear without ears, to speak without a mouth, to think without a mind." (ms. 59.5–6).

(16) Next the child to be purified is bathed and the mantra ends: "The diseases are exorcized; that which is true is left over".

(17) The dhalang "speak the world" (*kandha buwana*) finishes by bathing himself, calling in the "world sweeper" (*sapu jagat*) to use his iron broom to sweep away the followers of Kala who may still remain.

7. *Binedhati/pinedhati* poses the following problem of translation *Pedhati* is a *grobak*, i.e., a bullock-drawn wagon with a roof. With the verbal infix -*in*-, one could interpret it as footsoldier as in Old Javanese; thus "letters acting as infantry".

8. Cf. Peter Pink (1996, p. 236).

9. Written *sang saraseti*, it was pronounced as *sangsaya sekti*. Because it is question of the mouth, it may refers to sang Saraswati, the goddess of eloquence and learning, sometimes identified with Durga. Cf. Zoetmulder (1982, p. 1691).

10. Each term for earth designates a different kind of soil.

11. Cf. Pink's analysis in Headley 1996c. Ranggawarsita's "translation" (Pink 1996, pp. 238–39) in some vague sense corresponds to this section.

12. The glosses on *Kunfayakun* are voluminous; cf. ch 10, pp. 380–81. Here it suffices to say that it is taken from the Koran where it represents the divine fiat or *firman* and is used quite freely in Javanese to designate the creative power of the word of Allah.

13. Example of a recent intrusion into this prayer of a Muslim element not found in other versions.

14. The term *wilaheng* poses a problem. Padmosoetkotjo (1960, vol. II, p. 123) identifies *hèng* with *hyang*. If one understands *ila* as interdiction, although *wilang*=number could be understood, one would translate the term as a sacred taboo, a divine interdiction. In old Javanese (Zoetmulder 1982, vol. I, pp. 624–25) *ila* was what was against the *dharma*. *Mila*, the verbal form meant "it is forbidden", which suggested the translation attempted here. A freer paraphrase would run "Om (observing) the taboos is proper". Has the modern Javanese word for "proper" (*prayoga*) completely displaced the meaning of "applying" (*yoga*) a mantra here? As yet, none of the translations for this formula are satisfactory.

15. That having been said, in the Javanese corpus of mantra which we are examining, one is admittedly a long way away from the Hinduism, the "application" (*prayoga*) cannot be explained by the psychological alchemy found in Tantric rites once known in Java, cf. Gonda (1952, pp. 160–62 and Padoux 1980, p. 19).

16. B. Arps (1996) has given a thorough description of what he calls the "cogency" of these protective songs.

17. "*Hong Wilaheng mawigena tata winanci*/refrain: *Rahayu / mas tuna masidem /* refrain / *niyatingsun nyekel menyang /* refrain /....".

18. *Suranata* = *suranatha* in Sanskrit = king of the gods.

19. In the Tengger region these are made out of woven bamboo strips; cf. Hefner (1985, p. 326).

20. Cf. translation of *Gatholoco* by B. Anderson in *Indonesia*, no. 32: 109–50; no. 33: 31–88, April 1981–82. Headley (2002) analyses the anti-Islamic sentiments of this genre.

21. A stanza consists of six verses having the following number of feet and final vowels respectively: 12a, 7i, 6a, 8i, 5a, 7i.

22. In fact, printed editons were consulted and used for their variant readings which explains an occasional deviation from Wiryapanitra text. Cf. Mangkunagaran Palace Library ms. F48, p. 18; *Serat Kidungan*, edited by Proboharjono (Solo: Ratna, 1965), pp. 26–28; *Serat Kidungan*, edited by Soebarno (Solo, no date), pp. 25–28; *Kidungan*, edited by Tanoyo (Solo: Sadu-Budi, 1965 & 1975), pp. 22–23; *Serat Kidungan* (Indo-Jaya, no author, no date;), pp. 19–20; *Serat Kidungan*, edited by Tanoyo (Solo: Sri-Mulja, 1964), pp. 21–23; 160 *Kidungan Djangkep*, edited by Para Pudjangga Kraton Mataram lan Surakarta (Solo: Tjahja, 1961), pp. 17–19; *Kidungan Purwadjati*, edited by Tanojo (Surkarta: Tri-Jas 1966), pp. 53–54. For the genre of *kidung* songs, cf. B. Arps (1996).

23. Identified with Jerusalem (Baitul-muqaddas) by Wiryapanitra (1979, pp. 90; 164).

24. Sign of an extraordinary village for this bamboo flowers only once in each century.

25. =head of the penis, Wiryapanitra (1979, p. 91), for whom the rest of stanza 2 describes the movements of the male sex in the female vagina.
26. Tanoyo (1966, p. 53) reads here *sanaku prapta* = my siblings arrive.
27. Identified by Wiryapanitra (1976, p. 95) with a woman's psyché at rest (*nafsu mutmainah*).
28. This translation is taken from Hefner's 1982 Michigan Ph.D. dissertation, p. 338 and differs slightly from the version in the published book (1985, pp. 180–81).
29. Cf. text in Smith-Hefner (1996); R. Hefner (1985, ch. 8 *passim*); and Headley (1985) for comparisons with Central Java and Bali.

10

THE JAVANIZATION OF ISLAMIC PRAYER; THE ISLAMIZATION OF JAVANESE PRAYER

The role of Muslim prayer in the corpus of mantras used during the *maésa lawung* ritual at Krendawahana was a superficial one. It was also a temporary one in as much as eventually (1979+) the highest ranking *abdi dalem juru* Suranata one would confine himself to Muslim prayers in Muslim settings and no longer attend the offering of sacrifice buffalo meat at Durga's tertre. Constantly changing with each generation, it needs to be envisaged against a much broader historical and geographical backdrop which is what this chapter sketches out. Most of the material presented here comes from Central Java but the earliest witnesses are found on its north coast.

The Javanese were in a way colonized theologically by their way of defending their own traditions. We give examples from over four centuries of how Islamic prayer took root in Javanese soil. Perhaps the real test for the progress of Islamization is the increasing awareness of the content of Islamic doctrine and the differences between the mantras studied above in Chapter 9 and mosque-based prayer.

10.1 MUSLIM PRAYER IN SIXTEENTH CENTURY JAVA

When Islamic prayer entered Java, it was subject to Javanese influence. The Javanese are noted for the ease with which they adapt and incorporate foreign beliefs and practices from outside the archipelago. They provide a case study of adoption and adaptation. Syncretism is not the first word which comes to mind in describing Islam. Nonetheless Islamic prayer practice could not have taken root in Javanese soil without some "adaptations" undertaken by the Javanese, with repeated Islamic corrections of these adaptations over the centuries. There was a process of ebb and flow of what was still a marginal orthodoxy.

Examples from old texts are "thin" descriptions and cannot rival the "thickness" of contemporary socio-linguistic analyses. Nor do the citations from these literary witnesses make any pretence at balancing witnesses from all the currents in Javanese Islam, something which would require a full book in itself. We are not seeking to question the extent to which Java has become Muslim. That question should find answers from the mouths of the Javanese themselves, but in any case the massive impact of Islam on Javanese culture is everywhere present.

The acceptance by the Javanese of a new form of prayer, the five daily *salat* and the religious law (*sharī'ah*) that accompanies it, gained strength during the fifteenth century along the north coast (*pasisir*) of Java. It did not mean that older forms of prayer, with deep cultural roots in the countryside and in the aristocratic houses, were to disappear. The "conversion" process to a theistic monotheism, with links to India and the Middle East, can be seen as another religious landscape of an already diversified Indonesian religious geography. The stamping out of polytheism (*shirk*) or unbelief (*kupur*) was to the forefront of Muslim preoccupations, but nowhere totally successful.

In the sixteenth century one can distinguish three contiguous religious praxes in Java: the peasant ancestral traditions (*agama luri* or *agama jawi*), Javanese Siwaite yoga (*agama buda*), and Islam. Generally speaking, *agama luri* existed in the countryside and continued to flourish during and after the widespread acceptance of Islam. Indeed there are ample witnesses to its vitality today in rural regions of Java. The *agama buda*, practised in the princely urban centres, yielded ground more readily to Islamic influences except in one important sphere: the interface between court and traditional village praxis. It suffices to repeat what was shown in Chapter 4, that the Javanese kings held onto those traditional beliefs concerning cosmology which provided the shared structure on which the apanage and state organization was based (Strange 1992, pp. 537–39). Java's political and social morphology favoured the continuation of the village–urban/princely–religious links (*agama luri — agama budi*) which articulated the implicated kinship necessary for the tax-collecting mechanism. Apanage of tax-bearing lands was granted to members of the extended royal family. The accompanying rites for the protection of the realm and their corresponding rituals for the well-being of villages and individual households were intimately related, and remained largely outside the grasp of the Muslim framework.

AN EARLY JAVANESE CODE OF MUSLIM ETHICS

The point of view of the unnamed author of an Islamic ethical tract from the sixteenth century[1] reflects that of Muslims from the north coast of Java. It is clearly that of an apologist describing a newly introduced and still marginal belief system. Reminding us of the cosmopolitan commercial port cities in the Indian Ocean and elsewhere, he encourages the strict Muslim to remain inside his presumably coastal city (at home or in the mosque) and to avoid frequenting his slacker or pagan Javanese neighbours (Drewes 1978, vol. II, §1a, 2b, 9b). Muslims are confronted with a sceptical majority of indigenous Javanese population for whom the superiority of Islam was hardly a given. They are asking, "Which religion is better, Islam or the religion of the Javanese?" (Drewes 1978, pp. 36–37; §12a). The same text claims that *agama luri* still has its temples with their statues, offerings (*banten*), and its own law courts (*kerta*).

The document describes how the ancestral Javanese religion (*agama luri*) invokes the "foetus siblings" of Ego (cf. Chapter 1). Text II, cites one of these key social templates,

> …It is unbelief to say that among that which is born into the world together
> with you, namely, blood, "younger brother" (placenta) and amniotic fluid,
> it is the "younger brother" who torments you by trying to jump over
> (*lumumpat*) you without success. (Drewes 1978, pp. 38–39; §13b).

What the author meant by "jumping over" is not clear.

As we have seen, the Javanese "ancestral religion" associated the macrocosmic elements of fire, air, water, and earth with the four invisible birth kin of placenta, blood, amniotic fluid, and *vernix caseosa*. Many tables and charts from the fifteenth century onwards chart the traditional associations of these elements. Such primordial physiological and macrocosmic conceptions as the four macrocosmic (*pañcamahābhūta*) elements associated with the four foetus siblings of Ego (the fifth and central element) were not easily dislodged from their place in society, and is still found in Java today. Text I (Drewes 1978) showed the influence of these Javanese representations. It even correlated the moments of the *salat* (*ṣalāh*) with these primordial elements, attesting to the strength of the Javanese mentality. The "unbelief" associated with this traditional Javanese notion concerning the foetus siblings and denounced in verse 13b of Text II of *An Early Code of Javanese Ethics* is paradoxically reincorporated and adapted in another context. Here the four macrocosmic correspondents of the foetus' four sibling, fire, air, water, and earth (Arabic, *muthallathi*²) are matched with postures of prayer in the mosque:

> To stand is because of fire; to bow is because of air; to prostrate is because of water, to sit, because of earth. Fire represents Omnipotence; air his Majesty: water his Beauty; earth his Perfection. (Drewes 1978, pp. 50–51; §4a).

The polytheistic cults of *agama luri* began to die out with the complete abolition of royal rule (1949), the intense modernization of the Javanese countryside due to economic pressures, the advent of Muslim influence in the education system and the civil ethos of Pancasila government. As stated in Chapter 1, Islam was only one expression of the body social, and was treated with suspicion by the colonial authorities, both because of the great Java War (1825–30), which was led with an Islamic justification, and the Sarekat Islam which primed the nascent nationalist movement at the beginning of the twentieth century. Up to the 1980s, Islam's institutional hold on Javanese society was far from total. Its own institutions (*ulama* courts,³ *pesantrèn, mesjid, madrasah*) were important, but not pivots for the frames of social reproduction.⁴

Our witnesses to the earlier Javanese/Islamic systems of belief are old songs, poems, theological treatises, essays, etc. One of the most interesting continuing themes is the opposition between the Javanese preoccupation with cosmology and the Semitic, Greco-Muslim abiding concern with ontology, the exclusive claim of Allah to be the only Being. Prayer outside the mosque continued to follow its deep non-Muslim river beds, because that prayer often adequately expressed the relation between man and the cosmos (*jagad alit/gedhé*).

10.2 THE ASCETIC LANDSCAPE OF PRAYER IN THE SEVENTEENTH CENTURY

Just as myths are told against a mythological landscape (M. Leenhardt, *Do Kamo*, 1947), prayers are expected to mediate a given cosmological space within which one tries to involve the Deity as a interlocutor. To the Javanese this was a local cosmology. Leaving his village used to mean that a peasant was virtually unable to pray to the protecting spirit (*dhanyang dhusun*) once his hamlet was out of sight. The hierarchy of the pantheon compensated for this to some extent by including deities venerated in other places, but the only real exception was the high religion of Sivaism (*agama buda*) where one confronted the forces of chaos with offerings in the great temple complexes or by deliberately entering the jungle to meditate alone. It is in such a landscape of prayer that the earliest Muslim-Javanese poetry sets descriptions of canonical *salat*.

KIDUNG CANDHINI

For Behrend[5] this poem is fundamentally a story of unnatural separations and searches following the sacking of a palace of Sokaraja (unidentifiable toponym). Amongraga, the wandering son of the deposed ruler, is separated from his wife Tambangraras (Silabrangta) who goes off in search of him. Names are often allegorical. Thus the three royal siblings are called: Amongraga (seeker of body), Rasakapti (feeling desire), and Jayèngsastra (victorious in letters). Although the main topic is religion, Behrend is struck by the anti-textual nature of authority here. Normally Islam is expressed rationally by reference to canon law (*fikh*) and to the *sharī'ah*. Here, however, the main figure is a thaumaturge; the arguments used in theological discussion are not logical ones; and, unlike its literary descendant, the 1814 *Centhini*, which has long lists of Koranic references,[6] the *Kidung Candhini* has no citations of textual authorities. It is just this stress on asceticism (fasting, meditation in mountain caves) that appears in its description of *salat*.

In practice *salat* involves ten different postures of which six are repeated two times each. They are accompanied by the *sotto voce* repetition of short prayers in Arabic. The successive prayers and postures[7] used for each *salat* at the mosque employ a certain number of obligatory, optional, or supererogatory elements (*fard, sunan,* and *nafl*). Their presence or absence gives a distinctive shape to the prayer, inaccessible to anyone one who does not know the standard order by heart, just as in the monastic hours in the Benedictine monasteries. Each posture bears its own name. For example one begins with the determining of intention (*niat*), then the upright posture (*qiyam*), a bowing (*ruku'*), and a prostration (*sujud*). The whole sequence composes a *rak'ā*.[8] Below I have summarized a *salat* from the *Kidung Candhini* canto III:[9]

> Woken in the afternoon by a bird's call, Silabrangta (=Tambangraras) is reminded of her nostalgia for her Lord (*Tuhan*). Preceded by her servant, Silabrangta does her ritual ablutions (*asambyangan* or *wudu*). The Lord had already touched the veil placed in the place of prayer; they had already said the *kamat* (*iqāma* or call to prayer). Having concentrated her thoughts and her eyes toward the *kiblat*, her heart is filled by the return of the command

for the servant to worship by *sembah* [*wus rumangsa yen kinen amba amuji sembahira wangsula*]. With the words *Allahu Akbar* she weaves together tightly her intention and conviction and the law (*sharī'ah*). Her communion (*munajat*) veils all that is spoken, as her prayer is internalised. This is called *tungadil* (=?), i.e. *sembah* or worship wherein through God's love one disappears as the moon does at dawn when the sun rises.

Silabrangta next says the *Iftitah* and the *al Fatihah* and the names of the Generous and Loving one: Praise be to Allah who loves the world and the faithful therein. He is King at the day of Judgement to forgive men's sins. Follow the way of the Nabi and Wali. The "Praise be to ..." (*Alhamdu*) is said by Silabrangta according to adat, bowing her hands to her knees. Standing upright she says, "God, if possible, listen to the words of your servant." Like water descending from the mountains to the sea, all bow in the seven ways to the Lord. Sitting, Silabrangta magnifies the Lord, then prostrates twice as before and stands for the next unit of prayers (*rak'a*). After that she says the greeting (*tahyat sunnah*). The third and fourth *rak'a* conclude the third or late afternoon prayer (*asar salat*). Then is the initial greeting (*tahyat awal*). If one misses the three kinds of works of proper conduct (*sunnah af'āl*), they can be replaced by the "forgotten" (i.e. replacement or *sahwî sujud*). Silabrangta finishes the *salat* and begins to use her prayer rope, taking her heart beats for its rhythm. This is the highest worship (*sembah*). The apostle of God says that when we pray we should not shout, but murmur in the heart.

Candhini [the servant] for her part is always bothered by her five senses. She has to calm them again and again to obtain sincere faith (*usalli*). This clarifying her heart's intention coincides with the falling of a single *aksara* (letter). This is too fast and is classified as middling worship (*sembah*). Another kind of worship follows the voice and that without comprehending. Many people do this useless worship.

Silabrangta mortifies her self-will and along with Candhini enters the great forest, submitting herself to the Almighty. Having done her *puja* (adoration), she sees a deep ravine and a great stone barring the stream making the water foam up over it. The impatient flowers, ferns and black bamboo lie scattered around its banks. *Gesing* trees grow out into the stream. Pandanus flower petals fall on its rocks. In the shelter of the *praba* trees, tender young ferns sprout. *Sanggahasa* flowers blossom in brilliant colours. High above all this in the banyan trees the monkeys clamour while eating their fruit. They alert their companions at the approach of humans. Candhini smiled to herself seeing the animals watching them.

The two women rested in a cave. They neither slept nor ate, purifying their bodies and restraining their desires. Their bodies became like corpses.

As an ascension (*miraj*) or a sublime musing (*tapakur ing luhung*) she traverses the four worlds (*alam*). In the world of humanity (*nasut*), behaviour is called *sharī'a*. In the second world of angels (*malakūt*) the feeling of holding oneself in the presence of God is centred in the heart. In the third world of power (*jabarūt*), the high spirits adore unceasingly. The fourth world of divine essence (*lahut*) takes on this form only after death; the adoration of worship of the body and the soul are all perfectly destroyed. There is nothing left to be said. What can be seen is no longer twofold but exists in the past (*purba*). The body's passions are already exhausted and it resembles a corpse. Only the heart beat subsists.

Candhini weeps over the corporeal mortification of her mistress. Silabrangta, surprised by the weeping, gently tells Bibi Candhini not to cry for this was her intention since she left home. Candhini says, "I am like a person trying to salt the ocean as I ask for my mistress to return. My destiny is to meditate in the hustle of the world, to dissimulate myself in the world, but nonetheless to observe the taboos (*batal haram*). Fatimah is the model for women. It is their fate to be abandoned by men.

Nyi Silabrangta replies gently to Candhini telling her to return to Wanamarta and report her death to her family. Henceforth she is to be freed from her domestic service. Silabrangta asks Candhini's forgiveness and in turn forgives her any offence. Candhini's answer is mixed with sobs as she is unable to accept her dismissal. Candhini expresses in her own passionate, confusing way that she must remain faithful according to the teaching of a single letter (*aksara*). Thus Silabrangta, promising herself a short life, continues to practice severe corporeal mortification. While Silabrangta stays in the cave, Candhini enters the thick jungle, sitting alone. She wanders on miserably.

{Canto 4} Candhini next comes upon a newly-felled and well-planted clearing (*babadan*) with tobacco [imported cultigen] etc. Nearby is a well-kept *mesjid*. There Syeh Mangunarsa, his *santri* students and two servants are praying in their mosque. Once they have left, one of the *santri*, Montel, comes to greet Candhini in the field and a new episode starts.

This canto requires little comment. The fruits of canonical prayer are quickly transposed to a classical countryside familiar to Old Javanese pre-Islamic religious poetry (cf. Zoetmulder 1974, pp. 173–85). Here ascetic endeavour occurs in the isolation of a cave in the depths of the jungle. An encounter with Muslim *santri* in a clearing in the forest occurs at the end of the episode, the community established there being already provided with a mosque. Historically speaking, this is unlikely, as until the late twentieth century most mountain villages still had no *mesjid*. What it does reflect of course, is the desire of the poet that Islam should go and meet the lively tradition of *agama buda* ascetic endeavour on its own ground. Later texts are full of stories of Muslim friends of Allah (*wali*) converting "Buddhist" monks and ascetics.

The early sixteenth century ethical treatise discussed above was more "orthodox" in its prescriptions and advice, reflecting a newly arrived Islam. The *Kidung Candhini*, early forerunner of the major 1814 *Kadipatèn Centhini*, reflects an indigenous Javanese Islamic world. It is less sophisticated in its appreciation of the doctrine of the unicity (*tawhīd*) of the Godhead than its descendant, the nineteenth century *Centhini* (cf. §3.3). This supposedly seventeenth century *kidung* is directly interested in the fruits of *salat* prayer interpreted in terms of the union with the absolute. The merit of obeying a religious law pales by comparison with the rapture of intimacy with Allah. Such a Javanese notion of the different levels of worship (*sembah*) reappears continuously down to the nineteenth century *Wédhatama* poem studied below.

10.3 SITI JENAR AND THE HERITAGE OF RADICAL MONISM

The ever popular poem, *Serat Siti Jenar*, presents a council of nine *wali* discussing the unicity of the Godhead (*tawhid*) in the kingdom of Giri.[10] At this council, Siti Jenar conducted a flamboyant polemic against the notion of a personal God (Allah). He defended the existence of a universal soul where man was portrayed as the coarse envelope, a physical body which must be shed to become one with the Invisible (*Suksma*). This world is death and the hereafter is life. For having said "I (*ingsun*) am the supreme Reality", Siti Jenar was put to death, but his blood, spilt on the ground and, changing colour only to proclaim in *dhikr* style,[11] the exclusive godhead. The date of this text is too complex a problem to be dealt with here. Here is the scene described by the *Serat Siti Jenar*.

(Canto V, kinanthi meter[12]:)
5.7. Sire Siti Jenar, once / he was summoned to Giri, / having arrived there / followed by seven companions, / kept shaking his head persistently, / not changing (his attitude?), as in the past.
5.8. Sunan Kalijaga hurriedly / signalled to Sunan Giri / (who) quickly drew a sword. / At the same time saying sweetly / "E, Ki Sanak (relative) this way." / Sire Siti Jenar said,
5.9. It is called secret, / certainly it will be. / He departed (this life) by Allah's grace and mercy. / When he was struck dead, / he immediately went to heaven, / the conclusion was the "final" world.
5.10. The noise was loudly shouted out, / its joint is an authentic secret. / Now it will all at once / be perfectly pure, / known everywhere in the world / (as) the disguised destination.

5.11. The sword once made to drop / on Sire Siti Kuning, / once neck his neck was broken, / bled glittering blood / momentarily appearing red. / Sunan Kalijaga said, half smiling,

5.12. Oh, this is the colour / which forcefully speaks of death. / This is only normal. / His blood is not white. / His corpse keeps its original / form as can still be seen.

5.13. Then blood shortly / changed colour to white. / which the dying corpse soon / emitted a little at a time. / momentarily visible / (to) the All-Seeing Lord of the world who knows.

5.14. When the sword had been withdrawn, / there remained to be seen its glint, / four-coloured: / red, black, yellow, white.

5.15. Shortly after it let lose / a flash of five-coloured light. / At first a purple beam, / (then) secondly a blue beam, / thirdly a green beam, / (and) fourthly a light-red one.

5.16. The maroon five-fold light / shortly died again. / Thus the shining ray, / with its awesomeness brilliance, / like a kind of ivory, / shortly thereafter was hidden.

5.17. (Once) its existence was ended, / the white blood / at once appeared as letters. / They were read by the wali (= friends of Allah). / The letters said, / "*La illaha illullahi.*"

5.18. Once this blood/dispersed without a trace, / Ki Sunan Kalijaga / said fiercely, / "That was like the death of a devil, / (for) the corpse disappeared without a trace." (translation: S.C. Headley).

Siti has been called the Javanese al-Hallāj because he withdrew the veil (*miyak warana*) of the *sharī'ah*. It had protected the profoundest experiences of worship from being construed as pantheism. Zoetmulder (1994, pp. 297–300; 308) writes that Siti Jenar and al-Hallāj are not practising the same religion. The free thinker Siti Jenar is an unambiguous monist of the Indian tradition, while al-Hallāj was only accused of revealing the divine secrets (*ifsā al-asrār*) and is an orthodox Muslim, albeit a *sufi*.

So far we have loosely referred to pre-Muslim "Indian" or "Hindu" religious beliefs. But clearly there was no Hinduism in Java, only a Javanese religion that drew on Indian religious praxis and mixed it with local ones. What were the pre-Islamic, Javanese sources of our heretical figure? Siti Jenar did, in fact, remain faithful to the pre-Islamic notions expressed in the *Bhuwanakośa* (Harun Hadiwijono 1967, pp. 9, 45), but changed the terminology and used that of Islam. For pre-Islamic *agama buda* the reality of soul (*puruṣatattwa*) arises from the Absolute and is the Absolute itself. The *Bhuwanakośa* no longer refers to the yogic axis of six *cakras* and the network of veins (*nādi*) (Harun Hadiwijono 1967, pp. 48–49). A fuller description of that is found in an earlier Javanese text, the *Wṛhaspatitattwa*. There the seven worlds of the macrocosm are found in the body of man: the three lowest in the navel; the four upper worlds in the stomach, heart, chest and neck (Harun Hadiwijono 1967, p. 50). But in the *Bhuwanakośa* (Harun Hadiwijono 1967, p. 61) a single *dhyāna* (meditation) has replaced the *Wṛhaspatitattwa*'s more complete and traditional six-part (*saḍanga*) yoga. What is clearly absent in all these experiences of the yogi is the Islamic notion that the Creator's image is in any way reflected in an analogy of being with the humans he creates. This difference makes worship in yoga, that is to say the manifestation of the *suksma* (immateriality of the Universal Soul) in oneself, very different from prayer in Islam.

In the *Serat Cabolek* (Soebardi 1975, p. 104; §6.5), written two centuries later, one sees how much ground orthodox Islam has gained. This text speaks of Siti Jenar and then goes on to say that other and later councils of *ulama* in each subsequent kingdom have all known a "Siti Jenar" and how all have ended branded as heretics. This ostracism was not totally successful because Siti Jenar's magical powers surpassed those of a banal *ulama*. Despite the marginalization of heretics, these unorthodox Javanese figures retained fame and influence. In everyday life the Javanese continued to turn towards corporeal ascetical practices to control the physical world around them, both kings and peasants believing that the spirit world could be controlled by mortification and mantra. Adherence to Muslim beliefs has never meant automatic abandonment of this Javanese praxis.

10.4 THE ANALOGY OF BEING IN THE EIGHTEENTH CENTURY

By the eighteenth century, theological discussion is sufficiently evolved that one can speak of a veritable spectrum of doctrinal convictions. At opposite ends of this spectrum one finds Javanese *agama luri* with its "peasant" cosmic pantheism and radical monism of the Indian non-dualistic (*advaita*) sort. In between and closer to monism, one finds orthodox (not radical) monism which claims that there is an analogy of being linking the Creator to his creation, but in no way rendering him dependent on it. This was a commonplace notion in Hellenistic philosophy, and was borrowed by Muslim philosophers to express the relationship of Allah with man. The basic idea that the creator leaves an ontological relationship with himself in the humans he creates can be unpacked in many ways. In Java the understanding of this was given a different cultural spectrum.

Pantheism ◀━━━▶ Radical Monism		
Creator identifiable with energies found in Cosmos (*agama luri*) by tables of regular correspondence between the microcosm and the macrocosm.	Islam affirms a diminishing analogy of being as being emanates downward from Allah towards the created world.	The creation does not exist (*Sivaïte maya* or illusion); all being is in the Godhead.

In this overly simplified spectrum, it is apparent that the Sivaïte and Muslim visions of creation are closer to each other than they are to the Javanese peasant's cosmology. Of course such a simple presentation is not to be found in practice, but the different protagonists are beginning to understand each other's positions.

Zoetmulder has made a similar useful distinction between two Javanese literary genres, the *suluk* of the eighteenth century and the later nineteenth century *primbon*.[13] In normal Javanese speech these designate, respectively, mystical poetry and almanac-like compendia of wisdom of all sorts. Zoetmulder (1994, p. 144, note 21) characterizes them as follows:

> ...we mean by *primbon* those Modern Javanese writings in which the subject matter, especially religion, is systemised and assembled without a great understanding of its exact meaning, and by *suluk* a discussion of religion (mostly mystic and esoteric) doctrines in *tembang* form, showing a deeper understanding.

It is, then, to the eighteenth century *suluk* which we must turn to find an intellectual interface between earlier Javanese Sivaïte (*agama buda*) notions of worship and the Muslim vision involving man's return to his Creator. They are indeed very different visions, but they sometimes use the same terminology. For instance, there are different understandings of the worship of the "void". This term captures succinctly the differences between Javanese Sivaïte and Muslim worship. For both, it can designate the ineffable. Zoetmulder (1994, p. 273), however, separates the different Javanese visions of the "empty godhead" by analysing the mirror analogies found in Muslim (and ultimately Neo-Platonic) philosophy. For example, the sufi Ibn al-'Arabi contrasts an "image" of Allah found in created Being with the absolute Being itself. The two, man and his Creator, bear an analogy to each other. One Javanese *suluk* (Leiden Codex 1796) also provides a clear expression of this:[14]

> (19) His body is like a mirror. The true Immaterial, which governs all, sees His own (mirrored) image. That image (*wayang*) is an indication of relative

Being (*wujud ilapi*). In reality it is the attribute (*sipat/sifa*) of the Most High. Now that attribute is really the essence, not to be distinguished from the essence of God, and in truth they are one.

In the following section we will see that the monism of Islam, described by Ibn Arabi, situates the created attributes of Allah in Allah's essence. This is different from the Javanese who, while using the same Arabic terminology, are preoccupied with the identification of the microcosmic "I" with the macrocosmic "I" (*ingsun*), which is immaterial and whose eternity is often expressed by the terms "empty" or "void".

SEH BARI'S BASIC PRINCIPLES OF MYSTICISM: ON PRIMORDIAL VOID

How could such divergent views of worship be expressed in the same terminology? The well-known eighteenth century figure, *wali* Sunan Bonang, putative author of a text presenting the teaching of Seh Bari,[15] illustrates the Javanese capacity for accommodation. Seh Bari does not present a general doctrine of being, but uses the term "void" to describe the monodic existence of Allah before the creation of the Apostle. While seeking to present an orthodox doctrine, Seh Bari can claim in this sense Allah is a kind of void. Here is Seh Bari's treatment of the primordial void (*liwung sadya*):

> ...(§7) The Primordial Void is the *dhātu 'llāh*, the Essence of the Adored Lord, but this Divine Nothingness, this Divine Void is not empty, (...) but before the creation of Muhammad the Apostle, the only one in existence was the Lord and he alone without any servant ... This is the meaning of the Essence of Allah being the Void, the Nothingness as such ... i.e. There was no one to know His Self, no one to worship His Being; only his Attributes worshipped His Essence which mean that before (§8). He had created the Apostle of Allah there was no one beside Him, and He was comparable to Nothing. The Essence of Allah as the Void was like that.[16]

So, by the word "void", Seh Bari has expressed the total independence and isolation of the Being of Allah. However Seh Bari uses the term "non-being" or "void" in a second way. To become one with Allah is not only to participate in his attributes of love, but also to be "lost in the sea of [one's own] non-being (*ma'dūm*)". This second non-being is not to be confused with a third non-being, that of things before they come into existence, *'adam mumkin*. Thus by strict logic, if the essence of polytheism (*shirk*) is to ascribe partners to God, one should see in created being nothing but God.

Describing what happens in ecstasy when one is overwhelmed (*kandheh*) and replaced (*kagantèn*) by God, Seh Bari says that the soul in worship becomes utterly passive before God, like a walking corpse (*batang lumampah*).[17]

Seh Bari affirms emphatically that the divine names, Allah's attributes, are one with his essence. Here to participate in God, to commune with Allah in worship, is in no way analogous to the proportional aligning of macro- and microcosmic correspondences teased out by Javanese peasant rituals.

Seh Bari repeatedly states that it is God who sees and who is seen. So on the level of worship, during the five daily *salat*, it is said that God uses man's tongue to praise himself. Using the mystery (*sirr*) of man's soul, the act of worship remains totally Allah-centric. Allah does not "depend" on man for praise. This is close to the formulation, but not identical in content, with the union of self (*ingsun*) and *Suksma* (universal soul) of Siti Jenar. Obviously this can quickly be turned around, as the Javanese often did, to envisage creation pantheistically. Zoetmulder (1994, p. 85) aptly called this Javanese "deviation", cosmic monism.

KITAB PATUHULRAHMAN: TERMINOLOGY FOR AN ISLAMIC COSMOLOGY

During the eighteenth century, the debates over "heretical positions" contributed to the clarification of the expression of the unity of Allah (*tawhid*). The Javanese were colonized by their technique of self-defence. An example of this is the early eighteenth century *Kitab Patuhulrahman*.[18] According to Drewes (1978, pp. vii–viii) this treatise was written to counter the influence of the doctrine of the seven grades of being (*wujūdiyya*), the emanationist Islamic cosmology, introduced into the archipelago *circa* 1590 by Muhūmmad ibn Faḍlallāh al-Burhānipūrī's work the "Gift addressed to the Prophet" (*al-Tuhfa* ...; Johns 1965). The doctrine of the *Tuhfa* was already known in Sumatra by the 1610–20s. It was just this emanationist doctrine of creation which had proved so useful in introducing the categories of "being" and "attribute" used by all participants in the debates about the status of the monad, Allah.

What is striking in this eighteenth century Javanese poem, *Kitab Patuhulrahman*, is its author's use of truly Javanese metaphors rather than Arabic ones. At the same time the poet strives for an orthodox cosmology. He feels free to adopt truly local similes from Javanese culture, and uses indigenous images in his search for precise terminology to paraphrase Arabic Muslim theological vocabulary. He clearly expresses worship in terms of ontology. Creation is not to be divided into macrocosm and microcosm whose energies are retrievable by classificatory cosmology. Quotations from the third canto will demonstrate this:

> ...essence, attributes and works (*dat sipat apengalipun*) are comparable to a wayang play / they are not self-subsistent (*wujud tan adhéwéki*) [III.4]

...but are leaning on the Lord / Being of limited existence (*ananing wujud mukayad*) / is in conformity with Real Being...This is indeed the essential of real *tawhīd*. [III.5]

It is named 'permanent prayer' (*salat da'imat*) / permanent homage and praise... [III.6]

God said / When desirous / of meeting Me, / you intend to do that / this intention springs from Me. Do not fancy / that it is your own. This is what is meant by 'return homage' (*sembah wangsulan*). [III.8]

...the outward is the being of 'things' (creation; *asya*) / the inward are their intelligible forms (dalem ilmī). ...[III.13]

...All things / are in fact the Reality (jatining ehak)...These is no difference between the inward and the outward;... [III.14] (translation Drewes 1977: 53–57)

By assigning a pejorative status to creation, that of limited Being fading away from Allah, he places man in the position of a creature who only lives if he is turned towards Allah. Man's worship binds him to the undivisible monad, the unity of the Godhead (*tawhīd*). Javanese cosmological orientations are totally excluded here and worship, prayer, has become the axis of what the Javanese would call the reabsorption of the cosmos into the Godhead, only here it has become the annihilation of the self.

THE ISLAMIC ANALOGY OF BEING AND JAVANESE MONISM

The term "analogy of being" has been widely used in Aristotelian philosophy, Christianized Platonism, and later medieval Latin scholasticism. Its Christian variant derives ultimately from the first book of the Torah where it is said that man is created in the image and likeness of God (Genesis I: 26–27). It designates the fact that man is created by God and that his creatureliness reflects both the mark and the distance of his maker. Islam also stresses that this link is only an analogical one and that the ontological chasm which separates their two kinds of being is unbridgeable. At the end of eighteenth century in certain unorthodox cantos of the *Centhini*, the analogy of Being between Creator and created mankind are completely obliterated as the two are fused, for instance in Ragayuni's threefold teachings to the two brothers Jayèngresmi and Jayèngraga concerning true worship and prayer (*Centhini*, Canto 155, pp. 7–8; 12–15):

(7) To reach the true secret, one must know the true *shalāt*, the *shalāt* which consists in three parts, which are the exalted ways of worshipping God. It is like water which flows down from a mountain to the sea. (8) Many stand before the river mouth, but the true *shalāt* is located in the middle (of the

sea). There are only a few who penetrate so far. ...(12) And furthermore one must know the light and its transformation into darkness. Then it is sufficient. We who once had much which we feared, now become brave and unfrightened, defying all difficulties, for we know the truth of all uncertainties. We do not see our bodies as God. (13) nor the empty firmament (*tawang-tawung*), nor the written table, nor a sound or word, not Being or Non-Being. We do not see knowing as God, nor the multiplicity of separate things, nor the coarse or fine. (14) We do not have as Lord the Immaterial, nor prophets or *wali's*, nor teachers or kings, nor our fellow humans, nor our own selves, nor created things, nor bustle or solitude. (15) There is only the disappearance of (all, including) the depths of the heart, so that not the least trace remains... (translation Zoetmulder 1995, pp. 211–15)

Deep worship involves the disappearance of all conceptual content. In this radical monism, *Ingsun* (Allah-as-self) speculations, the perfect man becomes all that exists: God, heaven, and all that is on earth. Here the motif of the perfect man (*insan kamil*), the perfect realization of mankind on earth, is detached from the Muslim doctrine of the seven emanations of the cosmos, and also from any distinction of inner and outer relation such as is found in the Koran *surat* 28.88; for in a rapture of praise, Allah speaks with humanity's tongue by a transposition (*shath*) of roles. Examining Canto 155 of the *Centhini* where Ragayuni in the silence of the night communicates the third and last stage of such prayer, Zoetmulder (1995, p. 219) concludes that, "...there is little evident connection with Islam. A hint of Islam glimmered only in the division of essence, attributes, works and names and the Arabic terms for these." Note that the *Kitab Patuhulrahman's* orthodox Muslim expression of worship (*sembah*) in no way monopolized centre stage during the course of the eighteenth century. Late eighteenth-century recensions of the *Serat Centhini*, prolonged other pre-Islamic doctrinal positions just as Siti Jenar had some two centuries earlier. In its encyclopaedic character the compendia called *Serat Centhini* could embrace both orthodox Islamic discussions and many unorthodox ones. For the authors of the *Centhini*, Islam is in Java and Java is in Islam!

10.5 WORSHIP AND SELF IN THE NINETEENTH CENTURY: THE WÉDHATAMA

By the beginning of the nineteenth century the major *Kadipatèn Centhini* (1814)[19] refers to the merging (literally marriage; *dhaup*) of Islam and Javanism (*agama buda*).[20]

The *Wédhatama* (translation: the Highest Wisdom), which dates from the 1970s, is traditionally attributed to Mangkunagara IV of Surakarta although it was most likely written by a Javanese poet in his court. It is considered a classic *piwulang* or didactic essay in poetry, and provides us with a window on the progressive acculturation of Islam and the persistence of other kinds of invocations. It is widely used even today in Central Javanese high schools, and still often sung,[21] not read. The *Wédhatama* illustrates how typically Javanese notions of self, of personhood, have persisted in the practice of prayer.

When Javanese pray at the mosque, very little they do differs externally from what is done in mosques throughout the Middle East. The *Wédhatama* I.10[22] points out that prayer obeys rules, presumably the same rules as elsewhere in the Muslim world. The translation used here is by Robson (1990, pp. 39–47).

> …There are also the rules and principles of kingship / and all that pertains to worship / which are to be observed by day and night/…[23]

As a means for attaining union with the Absolute, the prolongation of the five daily *salat* in mantra-like *dhikr* is common to Muslim practices worldwide. But here when the author describes this prolongation, one begins to hear something distinctly Javanese. The author designates worship not as *salat*, but by the more general label of *sembah* (worship). Spiritual power derives from regular observance of prayer and that force that overpowers all other kinds of power (*wisésa*), as verse 14 of canto I claims:

> Truly such a man / Has been granted grace by God; / He has returned to the realm of the Void / …What had the quality of power has itself been overpowered…[24]

As we have seen repeatedly above, the notion of the void is an ancient one and the poet is expressing a very Javanese nostalgia for that more Javanese style of prayer and notion of self. The levels of interiority, going into oneself, are more explicitly described in canto (*pupuh*) IV. The poet speaks of the four kinds of worship (*sembah*): bodily, conceptual, soul and inner. These are levels of self, hierarchically arranged. The first and lowest kind of worship, the bodily one, designates the five daily prayers at the local prayer house (*langgar*) or mosque. Traditional Muslim wisdom does not classify prayer in this way.

This extract of the fourth canto of the *Wédhatama* mentions these rules in passing in verses two and six:

Wédhatama, canto IV (meter-*gambuh*)

(1) Now I shall teach / the four kinds of worship (*sembah*) so that you may acquire them: / firstly, that of the body (*raga*), then thought (*cipta*), the soul

(*jiwa*) and the essence (*rasa*), my boy; / The acquisition of these / is a sign of favour from the All-Seeing (*nugrahaning Manon*).

(2) Worship with the body / is the work of an apprentice; / Its ablution (*susuciné*) is made with water, / and the usual custom is five times; / this has the nature of an established rule.

(3) In former times secret teachings (*wulang*) / were not made public, / but now the punctilious make a show of their fabrications, / in order to let their cleverness be seen / their precepts are most strange.

(4) It is rather like the adherents of the Agama Dul (=? *kidul*), / as I recall, like the *santri birai* of the south, / Along the Pacitan coast. / There are thousands who believe them / whenever they start talking gibberish.

(5) They are in a hurry to see / the divine light (*cahya hyang*) that they imagine they know well; they look forward to its glow in order to throw themselves upon it;[25] They do not understand that such a life / has its brains in the wrong place............

(7) As for Islamic law (*syari'at* or *sharī'ah*), / it can be called a discipline: / firstly it calls for regularity, and in the second place for diligence. / Its use, my son, is to keep refreshing the body in order to improve it.

(8) For when the body is refreshed, / muscles, flesh, skin, bones, and marrow, this passes on into the blood, causing peace of mind. / The peace of mind becomes focused / and banishes inner confusion...

(11) Now the worship of the heart, / if it is sustained can also be a way of practising asceticism; / it is a grand way, such as befits a king. / It is precisely the certainty of knowledge / that leads us to acknowledge Providence...

(14) When the path has been embarked upon / the means is calmness in everything we do; / it is reached by inner stillness, clarity and mindfulness. / Feeling then dies away / and there we find the rightness (*adiling*) of the All-Seeing (*hyang Manon*)....

(16) What is taught now / is the third kind of worship, which verily is offered / to God; absorb yourself in it day by day, / take care to master it, / this worship of the soul (*jiwa*), my son! ...

(18) One prepares for it by aiming to bring together, / bind up and tightly tie the three worlds; being gathered up / the macrocosm (*jagad agung*) is mastered by the microcosm (*jagad alit*). / Believe with your whole heart, my boy, / that you will catch a glimpse of the world yonder.

(19) To sink in it, brings forgetfulness, / and barely conscious one is swept into the universe;...

(20) It is sought through a fading of the wakeful state: complete calm, and any means of inspiring rapture (*panganyut*).

(22) That is the heart opening, / the revelation of what contains and is contained. / Its whole content is contained within you, But you yourself too are contained / by what was compared to a glittering star.

(23) Now I shall teach you / in its turn the fourth kind of worship, / the worship of the essence (*rasa*), which is felt to be the core of creation (*wosing dumadi*). How it happens cannot be pointed out, / only that it is achieved by inner firmness. (Translation, Robson)

Reflections on the ever deepening levels of *salat* are, of course, found in many forms in Islam, but not employing such Javanese expressions. In canto IV.8 of the *Wédhatama*, the poet claims that worship by the body (*raga*), and the discipline of Islamic law (*saréngat* or *sharī'ah*) that regulates it, is refreshing. Peace of mind follows on the purification of interior confusions (*angruwat ruwéding batos*). That is exactly what the Javanese *dhalang* claims to do during ritual exorcism using the Javanese creation myth of the Birth of Kala (*Murwa Kala*)! Language here betrays other ways of thinking, not because there is any deliberate syncretism between Javanese peasant religion (*agama luri*) and Islam, but because the poet is using the same words to describe different processes. The verb purify (*ruwat*) means to render powerless an evil influence, here a distraction, a dispersal (*ruwed*) of concentration. Whereas in Islam this is accomplished by the physical act of worship five times a day of Allah, in a Javanese exorcism "dirt" (*reged*) is annihilated by the dhalang (the delegate of Siwa) when he 'writes' the letters of the formula (*rajah*) of the mantra on the body of Kala. This dirt is in fact the fallen seed of Siwa described in the creation myth as a shower of jewels which turns into the parasites of rice and illnesses that attack humanity, and which Kala epitomises. As a transition figure between the two, between the ritual of exorcistic purification and the ritual of purification in the mosque by five daily salat, we find the body praying (*mintaraga*) by ever interiorized *sembah*.[26]

Ritualised Cosmology	←――――→	Submission to the Monotheos, Allah, and his Prophet
The Birth of Kala: a physical body is described in myth as the victim of an attack by an ogre (Kala). The person and his body is freed from dirt and father's seed by writing the creation of the world on the victim's head.	In the *Wedhatama*: Sembah is described in terms of four levels of increasingly interior worship. Liberation is achieved by self "being swept into the universe" and enraptured (*panganyut*) by what is contained within one.	Orthodox Islam: The use of the body and words to publicly confess every day Allah and his prophet in the mosque both by postures and words.

RECENT DISCUSSION

The proof that this analysis of *salat* in the *Wédhatama* poses a problem is that two scholars in the contemporary Islamic Institutes (IAIN) felt they had to explain its unconventional approach. Without making rapprochements between non-Muslim and Muslim prayer styles, by presenting four progressive kinds of worship, the *Wédhatama* has opened the question of the value of different kinds of worship. A doctoral thesis by Mohammad Ardani in the Islamic university of Yogyakarta will serve to illustrate these questions.[27]

In his chapter (1988, pp. 66–163) on *Wédhatama's* teaching concerning worship (*sembah*), Ardani is at pains to distinguish between the gesture of *sembah* (i.e. the Indian *anjali*) and what he calls (1988, pp. 72, 79) *taharah* (*tahāra*, purity). This he situates in the perspective of healthcare legislated by the *sharī'ah*.[28] Ardani equates holiness and bodily freshness (*segaran jasmani*) which refers to desirable coolness obtained by traditional Javanese meditation techniques (*tapas semedhi*) and the undesirable heat associated with sickness and passions. Ardani associates purification in the *Wédhatama* (canto IV.8 "*angruwat ruweting batos*") with that of the *Surat al-Baqarah*, *ayat* 222 in the Koran: "Truly God loves those who repent, and He loves those who cleanse themselves."

The author is deliberately seeking to prove that *sembah* in the *Wédhatama* corresponds to what is to be found in certain sections of the Koran under the name of *taharah* and *ibadat* (prayer). The very fact that Ardani feels the need to reinterpret a great nineteenth-century poet in this way belies a malaise, whose origin is easily located. In canto II we read (Robson translation 1990, pp. 30–33):[29]

> (10) If you insist on imitating / The example of the Prophet / Oh my dear, you overreach yourself: / ...Seeing that you are Javanese / Just a little will be enough...
> (13) ...That as the son of an official, / If I should strive to be a *Kaum* [=strict Muslim] I would degrade myself-"

Why is the poet insisting that Javanese are so different? What could have been the literary poetic sources from which the author of the *Wédhatama* drew his understanding of this word for worship, *sembah*? Most probably his understanding came from what he had read or heard sung in late eighteenth-century and nineteenth-century *suluk* and selections of the *Centhini*. The royal manuscript library of the Mangkunagaran palace contained an abundant selection of these poems. These were collected and copied for the benefit of its residents. If the *suluks* are not always the product of orthodox Islam, any more than certain teachings found throughout the *Centhini* (Drewes 1992, pp. 22–30), nor are they blatantly sectarian. Two examples of the use of the word "worship" taken from Zoetmulder's study of *suluk* literature will illustrate a possible source of the vocabulary of the *Wédhatama*. Their religious universe has not necessarily been effaced as the following extract shows. This is not to say that we have here direct or faithful traces of *Saiva-siddhanta*.[30]

> 1. Know well: in death the true *sadat* (oneness of essence) is the same as in life. For one no longer has one's own doings, but acts according to the will of God.
> 2. The true *adat* is as much worship (*sembah*) as it is the (state of death). It is the disappearance of one's own doing. But they who wish to (see) that it is one, that which does (all) acts.[31]

As Zoetmulder says (1995, p. 174),

> ...we should see in *pati* (death) a description of Allah in His utterly undifferentiated stage. ...so also in contrast to the plurality of manifested Being (Rasul, Muhammad) stands the absolute oneness of God (Allah), only describable by saying what it is not (stanza 226), unknowable and yet encompassing all existence, of which it is the origin and simultaneously the final destination into which everything vanishes and finds perfection.

It is common in the *suluk* literature to find simplified versions of the Neo-Platonist emanation cosmology used to focus on the path of man's return and the identification with Allah. This process may be called *sadat*. This word combines the concept of the Muslim confession of faith (*shahāda*) with that of true *salat*, i.e. *sadat* one (*sa-*) in essence (*-dat*), thus the union of God and Man. This ancient Javanese religious theme is here readily expressed in Javanese by these authors whose mystical lexicon has become entirely Arabic in origin. Sanskrit, which represented fully 50 per cent of the Old Javanese vocabulary, has been left behind.

As for the superiority of certain kinds of worship over others described by the *Wédhatama*, such a hierarchy appears clearly in the following passage from an eighteenth-century *suluk* collection. Its choice of words and modes of thinking remind us of the passage from the nineteenth-century *Wédhatama* above.

> 15. He who praises (God) must not share with pleasure in (common) praise and tribute. To have true insight into life and death is the divine worship (*sembah*) of the superior one.
> 17. The divine worship (*sembah*) of such (a superior one) is perfect. To him who has true insight there remains no praise (*sembah*) of God, in his words he departs from the normal path.[32]

From the last verse one gathers that everyday worship, or *salat* is composed of words which seem incompatible with the state of "death", that "the disappearance of one's own doing" mentioned in verse two (p. 18). So the use of the word worship has several meanings in verses fifteen and seventeen (p. 19). Claiming that there is a higher (*utama*) worship that is no worship, the poet admits that this is a departure from the "normal" path.

JAVANIZED ISLAM: THE *WIRID HIDAYAT JATI* OF RANGGAWARSITA

A figure who died at the period when the *Wédhatama* was being composed, Ranggawarsita, provides us with an even older Javanese understanding of worship. If the *Wédhatama* gives four levels of increasingly interiorized worship, the *Wirid* of Ranggawarsita reverts to a cosmological format. He takes the emanation of the cosmos as it is described in Arabic Islamic terms and, by emphasising reabsorption over emanation, uses this borrowed terminology to express the return of the human soul to the Godhead at death. The result is highly idiosyncratic.

Ranggawarsita is also intriguing because, being the *pujangga* of the elder palace of the Susuhunan of Surakarta, and being widely known in the younger palace of the Mangkunagaran, today he is considered by Javanese like Simuh and Ardani as capable of reconciling Islam and Javanese religion. In 1983, at the same IAIN *Sunan Kalijaga*, in Yogyakarta where Ardani was later to present his thesis on the *Wédhatama*, Simuh defended a doctoral thesis on the "Islamic Javanism" and the mysticism of Ranggawarsita.[33] The basic position of his thesis was that the *Wirid Hidayat Jati*, although not directly consonant with the doctrines of the Koran, provided a useful introduction to Muslim ethics and teaching. He labelled Ranggawarsita's teaching a "literary revelation" (*wahyu kapujanggan*). If Arjani took a Muslim perspective on the *Wédhatama*, Simuh had already enlarged the perspective on the Javanese experience of Islam further by not judging the *Wirid Hidayat Jati* to be un-Islamic as had Harun Hadiwijono in 1967 (pp. 150–51).

How can we situate Ranggawarsita in the theological evolution we have been describing? Teachings concerning the seven grades of creation (*martabat*), are always delicate for an Islamic monistic doctrine of creation to handle. Pantheism is a very small step away from a doctrine of creation where the universe exists only to reflect the greatness of Allah. The ultimate protection against pantheism in Islam lies in the claim that Allah is so independent as not to be conscious of the existence of what he had created. It is man that turns towards Allah in worship and not the reverse. This should be the sole source for any and all worship, the only reason of man's existence. The

Javanese understood that the Islamic theory of emanation (the seven *martabat*) was not really a cosmogony in the mythological sense, but they also saw there the possibility of "perverting" its doctrine of the creation of man, defining new possible contents for human prayer. Let us see how.

For earlier seventeenth century Sumatran Muslim writers, the divine creative fiat (*kunfayakun*; cf. Ch. 9, translation of the mantra "Letters on the Chest") was manifested in the descent of the exterior, outgoing realities from the "spirit of relation" (*ruh idhāfī*).[34] The third stage shows a devolution into four successive worlds. The fact that the undifferentiated absolute Being of Allah descends, differentiates (*tanazzul*) or manifests its essence and then returns or ascends (*taraqqī*) conflates the dimensions of cosmology with man's return to Allah through worship. Harun Hadiwijono remarked that the Javanese presentation of these seventeenth century emanationist theories had been harmonized (?unconsciously) with a similar devolution in Javanese Sivaism. Set into tabular form the Javanese Sivaite tripartite division of the cosmos has been made to match the presentation in three phases of the seven stages of emanation in an Islamic cosmogony.

Javanese Sivaism

1. Niśkala (Indivisible)

2. Sakala—Niśkala (Divisible & indivisible)

3. Sakala (the three-faced godhead or Trimurti)

Sumatran Islam

1. La Ta'ayyun
(=Ahadiyya or first differentiation; the sea)

2. Wahda (also called: the Light or Reality of Mohammad and the stirring of the waves of the sea) & Wāhidiyya (also called *roh ilapi* / *rūh idhāfī*, or spirit of relation) [The Divine fiat: kun fa yakūnu = "Be and it is!" (i.e. Koran 23:82)]

3. A'yān Khārija (outgoing realities):
—'alam arwāh (world of souls)
—'alam mithāl (world of similitudes)
—'alam ajsām (corporeal world
—'alam insān (world of man)

Assent to Allah may begin even before death. Ranggawarsita, like the later Javanese almanac authors, will give a detailed description of the process of man's death.[35] In the sixth stage preceding death Ranggawarsita writes in his *Serat Wirid*:

> Sixthly, when one's own colour is visible, that is the sign that fifteen days remain, that is the time for worship (*pamuja*), for inquiring after the will of the Almighty, in this way, that every time he is going to sleep he has to say

the following: 'There is the one whom I worship, his Essence is also my Essence, his attributes are also my attributes, his name is my name, his works are also my works; I worship him in united meeting;…then one's thought should be concentrated to one object of worship, as for instance: the parents, the ancestors, the family, grandchildren and so on. What is concentrated in the thought is that they may be united (with him) in the hereafte.[36]

These prayers for extended family recall almost word for word those of the protective songs[37] also addressed to the four foetus siblings of Ego mentioned above. Ranggawarsita has simply introduced extracts into his *Wirid.* This can be seen when the liberation of the "ascending perfect man" cannot take place without the purification of the foetus sibling (amniotic fluid, placenta, blood, and *vernix caseosa*) found in the late sixteenth century text evoked at the beginning of this chapter.

Ranggawarsita's speculations here are in large part the reflection of a social reality of his time, although it has probably much disappeared today. Rituals relating the transient microcosmic self to their eternal macrocosmic constituent elements are attested elsewhere.[38] Certain verses Ranggawarsita uses for liberating the four foetus siblings (that came into the microcosm at the moment of one's birth) are again taken from a *kidung*, still used today, the *Jiwawedha*:[39]

> I release (*angruwat*) my 'four relations (with) five centres (*kadangingsun papat lima pancer*) which are my own body, i.e. elder brother (*amniotic fluid*), younger brother afterbirth, blood, navel, all my relations which come forth through motherly (*ina*) ways, and which do not come forth in dishonourable ways, and my relations which are born simultaneously with me, that they all are perfect, stainless, restored in the real existence, by my power. *Serat Wirid*[40]

Other correspondences between man and macrocosm of the kind contained in these four relations with five centres are less personal. The indwelling of the Absolute in man is referred to by Ranggawarsita describing the parts of Adam's body as pervaded by these five *mudah* (?essence of the servant) from the fontanelle down. Thus the tripartite division or the coming into existence of the prototype of man is as follows (Harun Hadiwijono 1967, pp. 133–34):

> —the house of liveliness (*bait al-ma'mur*) concerns the head, the brain, the pupil, the body, the inclination (*napsu*), the suksma and the rahsa.
> —the forbidden house (*bait al-muhāram*) concerns the chest, the liver, the heart, the mind, thought, suksma (soul) and rahsa or atma.

—the sacred house (*bait al-muqaddas*) concerns the scrotum, the testicles, the semen (*mani*), the essence of seed (or *madi*), the essence of *madi* (*wadi*), the essence of *wadi* (*manikem*) and *rahsa* or the essence of *atma*.

Several scholars[41] remark that this triadic division of the body has been made to parallel the triadic division of cosmology. They note that the Javanese consider their own bodies as a microcosm. Now for Muslims the sacred house (*bait al-muqaddas*) is literally the temple in Jerusalem, but an author like Ranggawarsita resituates it not in the heart of man as Islam had it, but in his scrotum. The influence of Sivaite *linga* worship and its use of the six *cakra* axis (scrotum to fontanelle) is at work here.

In fact Ranggawarsita is more interested in adapting the Islamic doctrine of the creation of man to Javanese notion of yoga. The meagre concepts he finds in Islamic cosmology hardly retain his attention. There are also occasional traits reminiscent of Javanese *Manikmaya* cosmology (cf. Ch. 11).[42] And as the *Wirid* (Harun Hadiwijono 1967, p. 124) proves, expressions of popular Islamic emanation (*martabat*) theory are presented only to be reused in an original manner.

Void

1. The lime tree on the boundary (*shajarat al-yaqīn*) manifests the undifferentiated world (*'alam ahadiyya*).
2. The Light (*Nur Muhammad*, like a peacock in a white jewel according to the *hadith*) radiated by the concealed point (nukat gaib), revealing the first differentiation, the *'alam wahda*.
3. The mirror of shame (*Mirat al-hayāi*, according to the *hadith*; it faces the Light of Muhammad above) revealing the second differentiation, the *'alam wāhidiyya*.

A'yān Khārija (outgoing realities)

The spirit of relation (*roh idāfi*) manifests:
4. the *'alam arwāh* (world of souls)
5. the lamp without fire (*qandīl*) "hanging without a hook"[42] *'alam mithāl* (world of similitudes)
6. *'alam ajsām* (corporeal world)
7. *'alam insān* (world of man)

The seventh and lowest reality, the world of man, is for the Muslims usually the furthermost point from the Essence (*dhat*) of the Absolute. Yet for Ranggawarsita, at the moment of death one identifies this level where one existed with the first and highest stage, that of *ahadiyya* or non-differentiation.

This void is where the "I" (*ingsun*) awakens to the revelation that "There is no Lord except Me" (Koran 20:14). Here is his description of death:

> The secret revelation of the existence of the Essence (*Dāt*): In reality nothing existed, because when there was void (*awang-uwung*), when nothing existed, the first that existed was *Ingsun* "I". There is no Lord except Me, the true most holy Essence, embracing my attributes, participating in my names, manifesting myself in my works.[43]

Ranggawarsita has managed to present Islamic worship in this treatise as if the manifestation of Allah was the manifestation of man. Loosely speaking, Siti Jenar's radical monism is hiding in Arabic religious terminology, or to use Harun Hadijono's (1967, p. 150) Javanese metaphor,

> It is, according to the Javanese expression, as a frog that is tucked in by its hole (*kodok kinemulan ing lengé*). God is in man because man is in reality God himself.

10.6 ISLAMIZATION TREATED AS HISTORY

The persistence of divergent concepts and visions of this mystical reality down to the end of the nineteenth century is well attested. If Ranggawarsita reintroduced the sexual centres of energy found in yoga into an unorthodox soteriology using much Islamic terminology, others have openly challenged the identities of the prophets. For instance, in the nineteenth-century *Serat Gatoloco*, after the final destruction of self with its sense perception, in short after a kind of death, the final destination of man is accomplished through oneness of the Godhead:

> One must prostrate oneself before Nabi Adam, but this is not the prophet Adam; rather "*adam*" signifies empty non-being (*suwung wungwang*) whose being is eternal.[44]

This recalls the primordial void of some two centuries earlier. Related to the same literary genre as the *Serat Gatoloco* is the *Derma Gandhul*. The opening of a new school for the sons of native chiefs in Panaraga (East Java) in 1878 was the occasion for an author to rework a local history, the *Babad Kedhiri*, into a brand new poem the *Derma Gandhul*. In it he prophesied that the foreign religion of Islam would eventually be replaced by indigenous Javanese ancestral belief, *agama luri*, and the cult of reason (*budi*; Drewes 1966, pp. 327–31).

Reflecting local traditions from Kedhiri (East Java) concerning the fall of Majapahit, he explains the confusion in the Javanese books on history and religion. These derived from the seventeenth-century Demak Muslims' burning of these older books after the sacking of the non-Muslim kingdom of Majapahit. When in later centuries the kings of Mataram tried to rewrite these books on the basis of those few copies that survived, mouldy with age, in the villages, their language was obscure and each of the king's scribes produced a different version:

> What was written by them was not the same / (since) every one of them / had found something different; / therefore, the Javanese history books / do not conform to one rule; / there are two or three versions. (Drewes 1966, p. 327)

The author apparently regrets the loss of a mono-vocal history, a loss which he attributes implicitly to the introduction of Islamic religion. In the beginning of canto IV (Drewes 1966, p. 337) Derma Gandhul asks why his ancestors abandoned their native religion to become Muslims. This is explained in terms of the consequences of the marriage of Brawijaya (the last king of Majapahit region in the beginning of the sixteenth century) with a Cham Muslim princess and the arrival of Islamic preachers who later followed her to Java's north coast.

In canto V describing the missionary campaigns of Sunan Bonang, a local titulary demon, Buta Locaya, exclaims,

> People should keep to this book (*Derma Gandhul*) instead of believing all kinds of stories about Arabia which escape their judgement...for I am well acquainted with the situation in Arabia. Its inhabitants are an uncleanly crowd; they hold their fellow-men as slaves and have sexual intercourse with their female slaves without marrying them; there is little water and almost no rain; the soil is stony, the vegetation scanty and the temperature exceedingly hot. In the opinion of sensible people it is an unlucky country, cursed by God. On the other hand, the Kedhiri region is a blessed country. (Drewes summary 1966, pp. 339–42)

After Raden Patah had overthrown his father, king of Majapahit, and himself become sultan of Demak, he repented of his harsh treatment of his father, Brawijaya. The poet tells us how the new king sends the Muslim missionary Sunan Kalijaga out to bring his father to Ngampel so that he can beg his forgiveness, and asks him to return to his throne. Drewes (1966, p. 352) summarizes the king's answer as follows:

> Taken aback Brawijaya first wants to reconsider the offer delivered by Sunan Kalijdaga. What he dreads most is that at his return to Majapahit he will be ill treated by Raden Patah, (his son) be castrated and vigorously scrubbed in a pond (circumcision and ritual ablution!), so that all the same he will be forced to embrace Islam.

Sunan Kalidjaga eases his mind by replying that in the Islamic religion the confession of faith is more important than the regular practising of ritual prayer. However intent a man may be upon performing his prayers, if he does not understand the meaning of the *shahāda* (Javanese *sahadat*) he will remain an infidel. Now the first phrase of the shadat means: "to acknowledge the Spirit and the Essence of God (as the active principles in creation; "*ngesahken roh lan dat ing Hyang*"). Man is instrumental in the operation of these principles by propagating the human race and, therefore, what the common confession of the faith (*sahadat sarengat*) really means is sexual union. The same with ritual prayer; the place to perform this *masjid al-haram* (forbidden mosque in Mecca) is woman.

Going on in the same strain Sunan Kalijdaga gives phallic interpretation of various Islamic and other terms, in such a way that sexual intercourse is the pivot on which everything turns.

Many more quotes of this Rabelais-like satirical history could be quoted, but the main point should already be clear. By the latter part of the nineteenth century, a well-read aristocrat from East Java could so totally distance himself from the ambient Islamization that he could write a satirical-prophetic poem about Muslim *dakwah* (proselytism). He could make use of Javanese yoga's sexual metaphors to recommend the five daily prayers in the mosque in terms of sexual postures. The *Derma Gandhul* remains popular today. The work relativises the centrality of *salat*, ridiculing it by word play, reducing Arabic formulae to Javanese terms for coitus and all that accompanies it. The author avoids Islam by localizing his society in history and returning with a vision every bit as cosmopolitan as that of the network of *ulama* that linked Java to Gujarat and the holy pilgrimage cities of the Arabian peninsula since the seventeenth century (Azra 1994). His literary flare is in the finest Javanese tradition, one which he knows well. When the servants of their now Muslim king, Brawijaya, are given names (Sabdapalon and Nayagenggong; Canto XIX; Drewes 1966, p. 359), these names' etymologies are slipped into the text (cf. italicized sections below) to give credence to their prophecies that the new Muslim faith will decline. Indeed, as in Javanese *wayang*, these servants are only disguises for the ancestral great gods of the land.

> Sabdapalon's *words are utterly reliable* and Nayagenggong is the eternal and *unchanging face of Java*....In reality he (Sabdapalon) is Manikmaya, otherwise called Semar, the elder brother of Sang Hyang Guru and the real builder on the hell on top of Mount Meru. He too equilibrated Java, which island in former times lay reeling in the ocean, by his mighty flatus which blew the tops off mountains and brought about the craters of the volcanoes so that the subterranean fire found vent and the motion ceased.

COSMOGONY VERSUS ONTOLOGY: ORIENTATIONS OF PRAYER

The very notion of prayer seems to be quasi-universal. This seems strange because the implied dialogical dimension of most prayers is thwarted by the status of their addressee (the divinities) who are bereft of any words humans could hear in reply. Let us give an example (Kittel, vol. III, 1965, pp. 67–73).

Just as in ancient Greece the word *théos* designated the cosmic righteousness, that regularity of being to whom prayer appeals, the word for cosmos meant "well-ordered world". *Théos* was the word later used in the New Testament to translate the Semitic Tetragammon (*Yahweh*). If the Greek pantheon of anthropomorphic *théoi*, with their eternal youth lacking moral seriousness, are just as much victims of *moīra* (fate) as we are, then they do not stand in relation to the created world as Creator to creature. They are at best the achievement of an order, an intrinsic meaning. The *théoi* permit man to objectify reality, but in no way to set up an immediate "I-Thou" relationship, which under the influence of Judeo-Christian tradition, has come to be associated with the monotheistic Muslim concept of a prayer. So if classical Greek religion could not have created "dialogic" revolution, what about Islam on its arrival in Java?

For a pseudo museum of certain earlier Javanese prayer practices, Bali may have preserved in modified form certain Javanese pre-Muslim Majapahit cultural heirlooms after this Javanese kingdom finally fell (1527 A.D.). At least this is true of Javanese literature, even if it is not really the case of Javanese invocations because Balinese society is so different structurally from Javanese. The kind of anthology of *stuti* and *stava* (praise and hymns) which Hooykaas and Goudrian published in 1971 on the basis of Balinese Bauddha, Saiva, and Vaisnava materials displays an inextricable mixture of worship (*puja*), i.e., offerings, hymns and praises of the divinities on the one hand and formulaic *bija* mantra syllables on the other. The use and possession of the latter must have been mostly restricted to the specific groups of Balinese priests.

It is in this sense that the advent of Islam would have revolutionized the oral rites to which the Javanese was accustomed. Henceforth, every Muslim had access to the same prayers, hence the "populist" quality of *salat* prayer. Certainly one of the reasons Muslim prayers have retained their vitality down to the present day is the availability the five daily mosque prayers. This was achieved in the very foreign tongue of Arabic. In the mouths of their new adepts, the words of prayer had to be kept pure of local traditions and their peasant connotations. Yet the earlier invocations, some of which were known to the population at large, as are simple village mantra in Java today, were just as formulaic as the Arabic Muslim prayers and sometimes just as obscure. But they were controlled by private needs and political integration of the landscape of Javanese kingdoms. Islamic prayer, rigidly imitative of the Prophet's own tongue and style, was everywhere just as it had been. One's personal religion was not the religion of one's king.

But it was not just a question of overthrowing peasant practices. The very Javanese notion of the domination of the world by asceticism and help from the spirit world was central to Javanese notions of kingship. In the *Wédhatama* II, pp. 3–5, we see rulership over the spirits exercised by Senapati, founder of the second Mataram in the early seventeenth century. Remember that this poem was written in the Mangkunagaran court after the Java War (1825–30), that is to say, once Dutch domination was complete. The nostalgia for an earlier grandeur was pervasive.

> ...And there on the shore of the ocean / In the midst of his austerities he was visited by an inward sign: He (Senapati) surveyed the circumference of the sea / Roundabout, and having swept it with his eye, / He entered it into his heart by magic, / Where he held it, no bigger than a fistful; So that he might take dominion over it, / And verily the Queen of the South Sea / arose soaring into the sky, / and came before him beseeching/her majesty as an inferior to the Great Man of Mataram. Earnestly she begged / to be allied to him as companion. / In the realms of the invisible / whenever he frequented lonely places, / she took upon herself to undertake / whatever he might determine as his wish. / Her intention was merely to beg / blessing from his austerities...

Here the ultimate titular deity, to take a Durkheimian perspective, was society, that of the kingdom itself, served by the king's dominion, both political and spiritual. In this sense the king's pretended dominion over the cults of protecting spirits paved the way for another and more universal religion, Islam. The king marginalized the more parochial village protective spirits by worshipping their "generals", Durga and the Queen of the southern seas. The Muslim prayers came with a new religious landscape, a mosque, oriented towards Mecca. In short, a more cosmopolitan landscape was created to show their larger community. A self-conscious uniformity was introduced. In Javanese traditions, diverse invocations existed for each locality, for instance, those to request the permission to cut down certain trees and to take them away out the forest. On the other hand, Islam sought to define who prays to whom. Village ancestral religion did not convey any such theo-linguistics. The written traditions dealing with the ascetic means for union with the Siwa lying in the heart of the yogi was attacked as pantheism.

What were the alternatives? One could pray at one's local village shrine following the cosmic cyclical calendar, or one could follow Islam which enlarged using new oral rites which made prayer possible anywhere and any time. The Javanese never forgot their nostalgia for a more intimate cosmos. The monotheistic ontology proved universal only by its philosophical rigour. But the equation the Javanese sought between being a Javanese person living on their ancestral lands and their collective experience of its reproduction in that limited space and time was frustrated. To them "here" was not one of many islands in the midst of the South China seas, but their whole world. Why abandon one's own self nestled in a protecting cosmology when one could try to better understand the new more individualistic religion, Islam, by analogies and metaphors taken from the old?

The twentieth century would complicate this simple picture considerably. Islam was instrumental in the nascent nationalist movements in the early decades. By the time independence was achieved, however, Islam was overwhelmed by its separatist puritan movements. They proved more sectarian than the archipelago's diverse ethnic groups and the new republic could tolerate. Their armed rebellions were temporarily contained. The final and complete fall of the old aristocratic system led to the spread of commoner lineages (*trah*) and reinforced Muslim ones. Traditional Javanism took refuge in new religions, *kabatinan* or "interiority" sects. Christianity spread, with its Western schools and hospitals. Only secular altruism failed to thrive. It was not till the 1970s that a non-political Islam would revive. The articulating axis of prayer remained as strong as ever, but the unanimity of Javanese tradition was lost forever.

World history had become a conscious category, relativizing commitments, obliging Muslims scholars to go abroad, not only to Mecca, but also to Europe to better know their own traditions and to learn from the sciences that would allow them to contextualize such religious diversity. A whole sociology of religious institutions had grown up and needed to be administered. The extent to which Pancasila's civil religion, as an official ideology, was not a secularized faith but a political use of religious diversity in the interest of stabilizing a complex polity lies beyond the scope of this book. Clearly a conflictual "sociology of theology" had existed for centuries in Java and little unanimity had been achieved around the orthodox norms of Islamic faith. Prayer, for the Javanese, has remained an intense personal concern.

10.7 *SALAT* AS A MIRROR OF ALLAH'S SOCIETY

In pious Muslim tradition, prayer in the mosque is said to cleanse the soul, as if it were a mirror (*mir'āh*), allowing it to reflect the light of the divinity of Allah. One could add from a sociological point of view that not only is his worshipping congregation (*jema'at*), but his whole *umat* or religious community, is configured in the accomplishment of this oral rite. But this sociology is also shaped by other factors. Even if *salat* has the upper hand amongst all other forms of congregational worship, side by side to the Muslim *umma'* other worship communities have persisted. Even in that most famous form of a society in which Islam is completely dominant, the caliphate, the *dhimmitude* (Ye'or 1996), the "tolerated" monotheistic minorities, were envisioned. Short of making Muslim norms the obligatory centre of attention by a *djihad* or a *dakwah* (*da'wā*) campaign (Peletz 1997), Islam everywhere reflects the differences of the Muslims who enter the mosque and those who do not. Recently ministries of religion, in Indonesia for instance, have "entered the mosque". They have devised strategies to make Islam a civil religion.[45] Meanwhile, alongside of all of this, individuals everywhere have continued their own discreet and private *bricolage* of oral rituals. Religious inventiveness has not been stamped out.

This heterogeneity has a potential for social and political disruption so great that controlling Islam's impact on the life of the polity has been at the centre of the pre-occupation of nation-states throughout the twentieth century. The double dimension of public and private implicated in worship is reproduced by the very nature of invocation. As a conversation with an invisible partner, a deity, prayer is a *prima facie* paradox. It does resemble everyday conversation. When one is praying, one usually tells a deity what He is presumed to know already. Invocation, like many conversations, is designed only to make or prolong contact and not to inform or direct (Tannen 1989; Jacques 1988). So prayers are said in order to manifest that one is present *before* the divinity who in turn is *in front of* the local community. Its psychological "salience" (Bouyer 1990) derives from the cont(r)act made between the first two parties before the third party, the community.

How do we know what people believe when they pray? Prayer, all by itself, is a *credo*, a gift of credit to the divinity as the etymology of the word creed (cred-do) suggests. The way men put into practice their faith in prayer is in conformity with the contents of their faith, otherwise faith would disappear. This is reflected in an adage of fourth century Mediterranean Christianity: *lex orandi, lex credendi.* This could be paraphrased: (tell me) how you pray (and I will tell you) what you believe. Muslims also often claim that one is only really a *Muslimin* when one is praying. So to turn your face in public to the invisible Other is a gesture of defining significance. It defines the person, *vis-à-vis* the *umma'*, the Muslim community.

Usually conversion takes place during a group movement towards recognition of a new divinity. Individual creation of a new religion is rare

(Macdonald 1981), even if individual conversions to mass religions is common. Naturally these collective credit networks, these religions (from *re-ligio*, to bind; Lewis and Short 1962, p. 1556), are of many kinds. Such networks of religious "credit", Pulleyn (1998, ch. 2) examined on the basis of classical Latin and Greek rhetorical models of reciprocity and favour (*xápis*).[46] He found that in classical Greece the relationship of a host to a guest, or that between friends characterized the link between the orant and his deity. By Chapter 9 of his study however, Pulleyn is brought to wonder why the Greek gods crave honour and recognition. In the case of Islam honour is clearly related to worship.

For Muslims, *salat* is technically speaking not prayer, which is called *du'ā'*. *Salat* is worship, a canonically ritualized invocation. The term *salat* is borrowed from the Aramaic. In its root form, it means to bend, i.e., to bow; *salat* as a verbal noun means "to bow in prayer". As A. J. Wensinck (1934, pp. 99–100) pointed out, the *salat* created by Mohammed resembles historically speaking the contemporary seventh-century models found in Jewish and Syrian Christian canonical prayer. Already in the Meccan period (*surat* 17.50 and 84.21) *salat* is linked to the recitation of phrases from the Koran, and the recitation of the Koran is linked to the prostrations. The word *koran* means recitation. In Muslim terminology bowing is called *rukū'* and prostrations, *sujūd*. The postures that accompany this memorized recitation are possibly its most personal feature. They are the corporeal signature of the orant that he is making the words of the *salat* his own.

Do the postures which are so basic to the execution of this canonical prayer help us to understand this apparent similarity of prayer with conversation? The fact that everyone performs the successive postures together and acknowledges each others' participation during its course, makes *salat* a congregational form of invocation. There exists here a form of *tour de parole*. The identity of the individual members of the community (*umat*), possibly jeopardized by segregating men from women, is reinforced on the socio-linguistic level, by the uniformity of body language employed. No one stands before Allah as a husband or a wife, let alone a family. Anthropologists concerned with the way that societies communicate with deities, don't usually investigate how individuals are taught to pray personally.[47] But, in *salat*, the implied reciprocity of invocations, their "credit structure", does underline the fact that the exchange is tripartite, between the community, the orant, and the deity. The overwhelmingly oral nature of the Muslim praxis of public prayer in the mosque encourages the use of conversational modelizations. As Paul Mus tried to show more than fifty years ago, the "adequation" that permits communication between partners in the same society passes through their common reference to the same sociological reality. There are few hermits and even fewer prophets who communicate with God entirely alone.

Canonical *salat* still uses today the model constructed in the seventh-century Meccan community, while the personal and private *du'ā* (Indonesian *doa*) participates in more contemporary social lingusitic repertories. *Du'ā* is, in this sense, an innovation (*bid'ah*) and potentially heretical. Heresy (*shirk*) was traditionally defined as placing a companion next to Allah, i.e., instituting polytheistic dialogue with idols reflecting the constitution of the created world. Since Islam claims that ultimately only Allah exists, *shirk* dissipates the being that is Allah's. Combatting heresy occupies a very different slot in the social horizon than we might imagine coming from Europe. Nihilism and other extreme forms of atheism are rare around the Indian Ocean. *Salat's* centrality to community worship presupposes, as a backdrop, an even more traditional polytheism. The sophisticated nihilism of contemporary European secularization jeopardizes the place of Friday noon prayer in European mosques in a very different way than polytheism does, say in India. This is clear if we examine the specific self-consciousness Western European Muslims have had to develop in order to accumulate an Islamic identity which these Western secularized societies withhold from them (Metcalf 1996).

The difference between *salat* and *doa* (Arabic *du'ā*) reflects their role in society. The supplications for a specific answer or aid in *du'ā* are of a more private and personal nature. As general prayers of praise and adoration of the deity of the society, *salat* refers to Allah as the all-Merciful creator and sustainer of the world. Which world, whose world? *Du'ā* deals with this issue. The world at large is not always *my* society, the one to which I belong, but only the one in which I try to behave. A second dimension arises everywhere. What is the definition of the social boundaries of the *umat*, the praying community. From the ethnic group, in the past from the kingdom, and now most clearly from the nation-state, competing demands on the definition of the *umat* are rampant (Hefner and Horvatich 1997). The recent pressure for the creation of Islamic states should not disguise the fact that the very definition of such a theocratic state has also be challenged as idolatrous just as recently by Muslims like the Indonesian Nurcholish Madjid (1987; cf. ch. 1).

PERMANENCE OF JAVANESE COSMOLOGY: OF A SPIRITUAL GEOGRAPHY — *SEMBAH* AND *SALAT*

The sociological form of the congregational prayer of the *umat* implies that Allah assists the regeneration of society, guaranteeing theodicy, the justice of the deity. Without opening the immense historical issues of the roles of the *imâms* and the caliphate (Levy 1957, ch. 7), it is certain, politically speaking, that oral rites create social solidarity. Attracted to this *sui-generis* nexus of power, a variety of parties, not all of them religious, but each possessing smaller or larger clienteles, covet the social forces tapped in oral rites of invocation. The more public the worship, the more the solidarity its generates and hence is coveted by self-proclaimed orthodoxies.

Given this competition, it is significant that adherence to the one God as a criterion for belonging to the *political* community (supposedly the case of Saudi Arabia) has *not* been imposed in large areas of the Indian Ocean's periphery (Metcalf 1997, pp. 309–19). In areas like Indonesia, negotiated pluralism has even been considered, by many, as the hallmark of Islam (Hefner 1996). In Pakistan, a nation created for Muslims, the ethnic differences between the various groups and regions have been identified by their political parties, *inter alia*, with otherwise minute differences in the way *salat* is executed.[48] These phenomena show that the identity of Islam is woven differently by the various component groups of a nation.

Why is prayer outside the mosque, which responds so well to the network of credit and debt that links members of a given society amongst each other and to local deities, the object of such suspicion on the part of those inside the mosque? Why not *salat* and *du'â*? In a word, why do those inside the mosque crave the honour rendered to spiritual forms outside the mosque? The usual reason given for monotheistic intolerance of what is otherwise such a clearly demonstrated social need, is that *du'â* eventually involves the honouring of the full variety of local spirit relations within the indigenous mythological geography. At the same time, if Islam claims to offer everyone access to the same prayers (Parkin 2000), Muslims are famously required to restrict the variety and modalities of prayer to those which partake of their monotheistic presuppositions. Dogmatically, this translates as: one should pray as Muhammad was taught to, full stop.

Salat defends more than the needs of the individual Muslim to be heard by Allah when he bows in monophonic praise of his merciful creator. The distinctions reciprocal / non-reciprocal / indirect and reflexive cited by Parkin (2000, pp. 5–8) help us to capture the social dimensions of prayer inside and outside the mosque. But they are only operative if one uses them in a comparative study of *all* the oral rites a given society employs, which is what this volume has been undertaking to do. The distinctions concerning the reciprocal dimensions of prayer are confirmed each time that *salat* is envisaged as a *fait social total*, implicating more than two parties (orant and deity), that is to say including the community. Variations on reciprocity allow us to account for the different social responses to this oral rite. For instance, Lambek describing Mayotte, claims that certain oral rites *outside* the mosque weave a social structure. In Mayotte during the *shijabo*, a collection of prayers (*du'ā*) is recited as a blessing, which as Lambek notes (2000, p. 71), is a praxis that cannot be completely distinguished from the "duties, constraints, and interests of kinship, friendship, and citizenship". Is this also true of *salat*?

If these localities with their own cultures refuse Allah his "exclusivity", a second cosmological map of a society's ritual relations comes into focus like a palimpsest revealing an earlier text underneath. To the sustaining forces of the cosmos, everywhere important for family health, abundance of crops, the harvest of the seas, and trading surpluses, sacrifices need to be made. The setting aside of such a polytheist cosmology in favour of Muslim ontology (cf. Chapter 11), does not automatically introduce these dimensions of gift and reciprocity which people were used to experiencing in their prayer to the ancestors, etc.? Why not maintain two kinds of benediction, Allah's and the ancestors, calling them both *berkah*?

Allah as "creator" possesses a monadic quality as the sustainer of entire yearly cycle in the high state-sponsored forms of religion. The pressure against divisions in divine functions, hence for the unity of divinity exists, for instance in the Balinese Hindu trinity (creator-sustainer and destroyer). The Balinese, who had refused Islam for centuries, were encouraged to devise creeds for their polytheism to bring it in line with the Indonesian governments insistence on "Pancasila" monotheism (Picard forthcoming; Howe 2001). At the folk level the well-known phenomena of prayers around mutually venerated Javanese and Muslim saints creates a harmonizing convergence at least before the appearance of post-Soeharto communalism (on India, cf. Assayag 1995, ch. 4). In Indonesia the state-induced monotheism everywhere jeopardized this pattern of co-existence irrespective of whether it was Islam or Christianity that was to "replace" the indigenous polytheism (for the case of the Salvation Army, cf. Aragon 2000).

In the pluralist societies of the Indian Ocean, participation in mosque-based prayer may not show to which "religion" one belongs. In Parkin's understanding of *salat* the praxis of canonical prayer is constitutive of the person's public persona. Clearly, just as the execution of *salat* can define the orant's relation to his Creator, it also can be the criterion for judging others' performance of invocations. What Parkin (2000, pp. 1–22) calls the templates of procedure invoked by daily prayer are strengthened, or weakened, by being a Muslim majority or minority in an overwhelmingly atheist, Hindu or Christian society (Metcalf 1996). The social spectrum is redefined in each cultural area (Europe, the Middle East, the Indian subcontinent, insular

Southeast Asia).[49] *Shari'a* can be more or less limited in its practical application to marriage and inheritance law, or at the other end of the social spectrum, the practice of Islam can be the *sine qua non* to make one a citizen of a nation-state. When Muslims' cultural and economic occupations bring them into contact with infidels on a daily basis, these are to be regulated or avoided on a predetermined basis. These segregating or integrating forces extend well beyond the mosque.

NOTES

1. This pair of texts written, on palm-leaf manuscripts, were edited and translated by G.W.J. Drewes (1978). Text II is a tract on ethics. Drewes estimates that this second and more important text "could well date back to a period still earlier than the end of the sixteenth century; though the MS. must be of more recent date (1978, p. 4)". M. Ricklefs in his review of Drewes' 1978 publication contests this dating and says the text could be as late as eighteenth century Blambangan (East Java). That is one way of saying that it is not only in sixteenth century that Islam and non-Islamic religions confronted each other.
2. In Muslim astrological tables these are made to correspond to their companions: Lord of the day, Lord of the night, signs of the Zodiac, etc.
3. Drs. Muhamad Hisyam is researching these courts. Cf. *INIS Newsletter*, vol. XIV (1997), pp. 9–12. Strange (1992, pp. 536–37) stresses the millenarian and magical strands of revolt in the twentieth century which resulted in the Darul Islam revolts in Java and elsewhere.
4. Cf. Robert Hefner's, *Civil Islam: Muslim Democrats and Sate Violence in Indonesia*, Chapters 1–5.
5. Behrend is the only one to have studied this *kidung*. According to Behrend (1997), this is the earliest version (recension A) of the *Serat Centhini*. Sudibyo says it was adapted (*tinedhak*) from an earlier version in 1616 A.D., but, as Behrend points out, that date (1538 A.D.) falls ten years before the introduction of the Muslim lunar calendar by Sultan Agung of Mataram so the question of its date is still awaiting confirmation. The manuscript used was a May 1832 copy of the original and even this is temporally lost. Composed entirely in *dandhanggula* meter, it is nonetheless divided into seventeen separate cantos whereas usually cantos serve to introduce new meters.
6. *Serat Centhini* (1991, vol. 12 canto 708ff). This lengthy encyclopaedic (12 vols.) text contains a multitude of theological perspectives.
7. Cf. for a detailed description, cf. Juynboll (1925, pp. 59–63); Wensinck (1934, pp. 99–109); the Javanese vocabulary of this is explained in such pamphlets as Hadiwiyata (1974); Dja'far Amir (Yogya, no date); S.C. Headley (1996, pp. 195–234) in "Trois styles de prière à Java: écriture sur le front; offrandes et purification du coeur" gives a description of the sequences of words and gestures in a given *rak'a*.

8. Or *raka'at* from the Arabic *rak'ā*.

9. 1983, Javanese text, pp. 178–89; Indonesian translation pp. 13–24.

10. In East Java, during sixteenth and much of the seventeenth century an important port city state, Cf. Pigeaud and de Graaf (1976, pp. 14–15); (1974, pp. 137–55).

11. On the general background to *dhikr*, cf. *Encyclopaedia of Islam* (1977, vol. II, pp. 230–33).

12. *Boekoe Siti Djenar ingkang toelèn*, fifth canto, pp. 25–26 (2nd ed., Tan Khoen Swie, Kediri, 1931).

13. Just how many of the *suluk* studied by Zoetmulder in nineteenth century manscript compendium are from the eighteenth century is not yet clear. Ricklefs (1998, pp. 241–42 and *sub voce* in index) has identified some eighteenth century *suluk*.

14. Translation Zoetmulder (1994, pp. 144–46); *"Sarirané anglir péndah carmin / Hyang Jati Suksma ingkang amurba/andulu wawayangané / wayangan puniku / upamané wujud ilapi / jatiné iku sipat / ing Hyang Mahaluhur / sipat iku yèstu edat/tan apisah saking ing dat ing Hyang Widi / jatiné iku tunggal."*

15. Drewes (1969, pp. 8–13) rejects the authorship of Sunan Bonang in favour of Seh Bari, but then has troubled identifying who Seh Bari was. A teacher from Karang or a legendary figure? In any case the ascription to Sunan Bonang is of early date.

16. Drewes (1969, pp. 42–45): *"...kang liwung sadya iku, iya iku dhātu 'llāh, sab(e)ner-b(e)nere Pangeran kang sinembah...tatapi ta nafining Allah, liwunging Allah iku nora yan suwunga...tatapi sadurunging andadeken nabi Muhammad...aning sira Pangeran kang ana dhewek tanpa rowang, norana kawula sawijia,...iya iku t(e)gesing liwung nafi dhātu 'llāh, nora ing dheweke,...norana i(ng)kang angawikana, ing dhewekira, norana (ingkang) amujia ing anane, (§8) anging sifate amuji ing dhate, iku sadurung(ing) andadeken ra/sulullah, norana sakutunira, nora kaya apa, kaya iku liwung nafi dhātu 'illāh."*

17. Cf. Zoetmulder (1994, pp. 83–86).

18. According to Drewes (1977, p. 3), "...at the latest in the early part of the eighteenth century, it was put into verse in Cerbon; or rather that a Javanese composed a poem claiming to be a poetical version of this commentary." The Javanese poet, author of the *Kitab Patuhulrahman*, himself belonged to the older school of spirituality represent by al-Junaid (died in 910). His knowledge of this master came to him via Zakariyyā' al-Ansārī's *Kitab Fath al-Rahmān*, itself a commentary on an earlier work by Walī Raslān al-Dimashqī (A.D. 1145–46) Cf. Ricklefs (1998, pp. 259–60).

19. Canto IX: 299 quoted in Zoetmulder (1995, p. 217), note 6: "...*dhaupé kadi punendi / lawan élmi sarak land agama Buda...*"

20. A proper anthropological study of conversion should have abundant comparative material. This is beginning to appear for Western Indonesia. For instance for the work of Bowen on the Gayo (Sumatra; 1991 and 1993) and the work of Pelras

on the Bugis (Sulawesi, 1984 and 1996*a*). Space will not allow us to give the Indonesian comparative backdrop of Javanese Islamization in this chapter.

21. For instance, the Semarang musician Ki Nartosabdho *"dipersembahkan"*, offered with veneration, the *Wédhatama* in a 1983 double cassette recording by his group Panguyuban Karawitan Jawi "Condong Raos" at Lokanata. The text of the poem was printed on the fold-out inside the jacket.

22. Available in a 1990 English translation with accompanying Javanese text and notes by Stuart Robson (KILTV Working Papers no. 4, KITLV Press, Leiden); cf. also for a selection of his other works, Karangan Pilihan KGPAA Mangkunagara IV (Yayasan Centhini, Yogyakarta, 1992) compiled by Kamajaya. Pigeaud's 1928 Java Institute edition in four volumes of Mangkunagara IV's complete works was reissued in 1953, again in Surakarta by the Mangkunagaran Palace.

23. Robson 1990: 24 "... / *Ana uga angger-ugering kaprabon / abon-aboning panembah / kang kambah ing siyang ratri/...*"

24. Robson (1990, p. 24) "*Sejatiné kang mangkana / Wus kakenan nugrahaning Hyang Widhi / Bali alaming asuwung / ...Ingkang sipat wisésa winisésa wus ...*"

25. This seems to recall the passage from the *Serat Centhini* (vol. 8, 1989, p. 119, canto 446) where they actually throw themselves into the fire.

26. Cf. Headley "Trois styles de prière à Java: écriture sur le front; offrandes et purification du coeur." (1996, pp. 195–234).

27. I have not been able to consult the published version of this thesis.

28. "*Suci dan bersih adalah dasar dan sendi segala peraturan agama Islam.*" Ardani cites as his authority for this the 1968 study of Dr. Med. Ahmad Ramali, *Peraturan-peraturan untuk Memelihara Kesehatan dalam Hukum Syar'Islam*, (third edition) Balai Pustaka, Jakarta.

29. "*(10)Lamun sira paksa nulad / Tuladaning Kangjeng Nabi / O nggèr kadohan panjankah... / Rèhné ta sira Jawi / Sathithik baé wis cukup...*

    (13) ...Rèhné ta suta priyayi / Yèn muriha dadi kaum temah nistha."

30. Which is not to say that we have here direct or faithful traces of *Saiva-siddhanta*; cf. Zoetmulder's comments (1994, p. 174) on the term death (*pati*) as a name of Siva.

31. Leiden Oriental Codex no. 1796, pp. 198–206; translation Zoetmulder / Ricklefs 1995, pp. 19 and 151):

    1) Kawruhana ing pati sadat sajati / tan béda ngegesang / pan ana polahnèki / polah saking karsaning Hyang.

    2) Sasat jati iya sembah iya pati / sirnané kang polah / anging kang sedya ngrawuhi / tunggal kang adarbé polah.

32. Leiden Oriental Codex 1795, pp. 164–65; translation Zoetmulder 1995, p. 185:

    15) Wong amuji sampun kesengsen ing puji / sembah sanalika / kang awas ing urip mati / sembahé ingkang utama.

    17) Kang mengkana sampurna ing sembahèki / ingkang sampun awas/ sembahé tan ana kari/sebdané amurang dalan.

33. *Mistik Islam Kejawen: Radèn Ngabèhi Ranggawarsita. Suatu studi terhadap Serat Wirid Hidayat Jati*, published in 1988 by the University of Indonesia Press.

34. Stage 2–3 in diagram below adapted from Harun Hadiwijono (1967, p. 101).

35. Harun Hadiwijono (1967, p. 140, note 4) remarks that Goris (1926, p. 124) has also found this in connection with a discussion of liberation (*kamoksan*) from duality (Rwa Bhinéda or the "two differentiated").

36. Simuh (1988, p. 190); Harun Hadiwijono (1967, p. 141): "*Ingkang kaping nem, jèn sampun katingal warninipun pijambak, tanḍa kirang setengah wulan. Ingriku panggénaning pamudja, aneges karsanipun Ingkang Kuwaos, patrapipun saben angangkat jèn badé saré, pamudjanipun kasebut ing ngandap punika. Ana pudjaningsun sawidji, daté ija datingsun, sipaté ija sipatingsun, asmané ija asmaningsun, pangalé uja pangalingsun, ingsun pudja ing patemon tunggal....ingriku tjiniptaa ingkang pinudja satunggal, kadosta: bapa-bijung, kaki-nini, garwa putra...*"

37. Cf. Wirid text transliterated by Simuh (1988, p. 191); for the "*kidungan rumeksa ing wengi*"; cf. Bernard Arps' extensive article in Headley (1996, pp. 47–113).

38. *Serat Memulé Sadherek Sakawan Wasiyat Saking Sultan Mangkubumi*, 102 Ra (SMP-KS 587) in the Sasana Pustaka (Surakarta Palace Library): 7 pp.

39. The darkened words show up in the third stanza of the "Song of Soul Knowledge" (Kidung Jiwawedha) in the *Kitab Primbon Atassadhur Adammakna* (1979, p. 106) translated in Headley (1987*a*, p. 145).

40. Harun's translation (1967, p. 144); Simuh's transcription (1988, p. 191): "*Ingsun angruwat kadangingsun papat lima pancer, dumunung ana in badaningsun dhéwé, kakang kawah adhi ari-ari, getih, puser, sakèhing kadangingsun kang metu ing marga ina, lan kang metu saka ing marga ina, sarta kadangingsun kang metu bareng sadina, kabèh padha sampurnaa, nirmala waluja ing kahanan jati kalawan kodratingsun*".

41. Kraemer (1921, p. 98); van Akkeren (1951, pp. 36–37) and Harun Hadiwijono (1967, p. 139).

42. "*gumantung tanpa canthélan*" commonly desribes the primeval bell found in the cosmologies of the Manikmaya texts.

43. Translation Harun (1967, p. 104); transliteration Simuh (1988, p. 174): "*Wisikan ananing dat. Sajatiné ora ana apa-apa, awit duk maksih awang — uwung durung ana sawiji-wiji, kang ana dhingin iku Ingsun. ora ana Pangéran amung Ingsun, sajantining dat kang amaha suci, anglimputi ing sipatingsun, anartani ing asmaningsun, amratanḍani ing apanglingsun.*"

44. Zoetmulder / Ricklefs' translation (1994, p. 175); "*kinèn sujed nabi Adam / iku dudu Adam nabi / adam iku suwung wungwang / ingkang langgeng kahanané.*" *Serat Gatoloco*, edition Tan Khoen Swie (Kediri 1913, p. 51).

45. David Szanton at the Social Science Research Council in New York initiated a whole series of studies on the relation of the sacred and the secular in Muslim societies in the late 1980s. Several of these volumes have already appeared edited by W.R. Rolff, G. Keppel and Y. Richard, B. D. Metcalf and J. Piscatori.

46. Cf. review by S.C. Headley of S. Pulleyn, *Prayer in Greek Religion*, Oxford

Classical Monographs (Oxford: Clarendon Press, 1998); in JASO (*Journal of the Anthropological Society of Oxford*) 28(1997): 2.

47. But cf. Adeline Masquelier, *Prayer has Spoiled Everything. Possession, Power and Identity in an Islamic Town of Niger.*

48. Personal communciation Dr. Muhammad Saleem, St. Antony's College Oxford.

49. By way of comparison, the appearance of *hindutva*, Hindu Indian identity, is more than a rage against Islam. The difficulties of ascribing and agreeing on the causes of communalsim in India are described in Ludden (1996, pp. 1–26).

11

JAVANESE COSMOGONIES AND MUSLIM COSMOGRAPHIES
An Encompassing Knowledge?

11.1 INTRODUCTION: EXPLORING THE
JAVANESE *MANIKMAYA*

Cosmography usually designates descriptive astronomy. Here the term is used to designate the Muslim notion of the progressive emanation of the universe from Allah's fiat described in Chapter 10 as opposed to Javanese conceptions of the genesis of the cosmos and the gods designated by the term cosmogony. Since at least the sixteenth century Javanese genesis narratives have been retold in mantras and in compilations of myths. Beginning in the middle of the eighteenth century numerous collections were entitled *Manikmaya* (Made of Jewels). These constitute a new mythological landscape resulting from the new spiritual geography of the island. What is meant by "jewels" may be Guru's fallen seed from which the world is constructed. In later versions, it was from this seed that appeared Guru's monstrous son Kala and the rice parasites.[1] The usual Javanese formula which introduces a cosmology is "when the void still existed and there was neither heaven or earth". This signals either portions of these Javanese creation myths or, from the eighteenth century onwards, emanations from Allah's divine fiat.[2]

These longer eighteenth century *Manikmaya* poems began to incorporate Muslim cosmographies by "weaving" them around the narrative of which the Birth of Kala ("fallen seed") myth was the coda. Episodes from these related

Javanese myths include: the fall of Guru's "jewel" (*manik*), the death of a Sri, a beautiful maiden who appears from a jewel box, and the creation of the first rice fields attacked by Kala's animal army led by Puthut Jantaka. In this chapter I will concentrate on the persistence of the Javanese cosmogonies, giving the relevant history of existing scholarship, description of recensions with quotes, and their analysis. These narratives combine several successive origin myths into one long tale. Under the influence of the Pasisir (Javanese north coast) Kandha, Book of Tales traditions,[3] these *Manikmaya* then go on to tell the "history" of the Javanese world down to Jaka Tingkir and the realm of Pengging (late fifteenth century). The fallen seed episode is the best remembered from these cosmogonies because of its purification/exorcism (*ruwatan*) rituals. These texts clarify the links which existed in the minds of the Javanese compilers of mythology between the myth of creation, the myth of the origin of rice and the myth of Kala hunting down humans with bad destinies (*sukerta*). The link between first and third myths is found in the motif of Guru's fallen seed which gives birth to Kala preying on humanity.[4]

Collation, in and of itself, may be used as a strategy of interpretation. Late eighteenth-century *Serat*[5] *Manikmaya* combine serially both Islamic creation myths and the just cited Javanese creation stories. The liberties taken with the cosmographic terminology borrowed from Arabic sometimes reflects a lack of interest of the compilers in the terminology of these Muslim cosmologies. These narrators are sometimes more interested in *their* place in the cosmos than theodicy.

In a way the nineteenth-century *Manikmaya* present an intimate juxtaposition and compilation between full-blown Javanese cosmogony and Islamic cosmography. In the twentieth century, most Javanese Muslims have avoided further writing in this literary genre encompassing diverse mythologies. These late eighteenth-century *Manikmaya* with Islamic cosmographies never completely replaced pre-Muslim myths. Indeed there exists a contemporary wayang *Manikmaya*, entitled "Unfolding of World", *Jagat Ginelar*, which preserves the framework of the earlier sixteenth/seventeenth-century cosmology unfamiliar with Allah's creative fiat.

An anthropological approach to the spread of Islam in Central Java, by studying these *Manikmaya* compilations can better understand the communities of the contemporary Javanese. In trying to understand the place that this myth has in their daily lives, I was drawn into the ethno-history of a literary genre. My approach is not that of a philologist or a literary critic, but that of someone who went back to the compilations of older myths in order to go forward and better understand the contemporary religious communities.

The word *manik-maya*, "made of jewels", is already a composite, a *nomen actionnis*, as mentioned above. And grammatically speaking it is not just the common noun. *Manikmaya* may also designate several personages, prayers or objects. This is attested to by contemporary *wayang* lore where *Manikmaya's* identity is defined in terms of separate and conflicting genealogies accounting for the different deities it designates. In the *Silsilah Wayang Purwa Mawa Carita* (1979, vol. 1, pp. 62–67), a contemporary compilation of genealogies (*silsilah*) of the gods and kings, S. Padmosoekotjo tries to locate the written sources of these lineages. In his own way he is making a new kind of compilation, genre which the *Manikmaya* epitomized in the nineteenth century. The titles of literary works are underlined below:

> The word "Manikmaya" according to the *Paramayoga*, the *Layang Sejarah Wayang Purwa* and *dhalang's* tales is the name of one god (*dewa*) who is also known as:
> Bathara Guru,
> Sang Hyang Trinetra (the Three-eyed one),
> Caturbuja (the four-armed one),
> Nilakantha (the blue-necked one),
> Jagadnatha (ruler of the world),
> Jagadpratingkah (Action of the world),
> Randhuwana (Kapok forest),
> Kalawisaya (dominion of Kala),
> Tuguwisesa (paramount pillar),
> Trilocana (three-eyed),
> Girinata (lord of the mountain),
> or Pramesthiguru (paramount master).
> But according to the *Manikmaya* and the *Arjunasasrabahu* (thousand-armed Arjuna) this is the name of two gods Bathara Manik (Bathara Guru) and Bathara Maya (Ismaya, Semar). While according to the *Kanda*, Manikmaya is the name of a devil (*iblis*, Arabic) who is also called Ijajil. (Arabic, *Azāzīl*).
> 'According to the *Paramayoga*, sang hyang Manikmaya or Bathara Guru held court in Triloka whose heaven is in the Arga Dumilah (jewelled mountain), his mount being the cow Andini.

By providing a framework of literary sources for *Manikmaya*, contemporary writers on wayang lore, such as Padmosoekotjo, accomplish a very different sort of compilation. What Padmosoekotjo's twentieth-century approach has added is the notion of the *separate but equal* legitimacy of divergent Javanese sources. On the other hand, the initial chapters of the *Manikmaya* in the eighteenth century, by overlaying and interweaving Muslim cosmographies on top of Javanese cosmogonies, created a synthetic, encyclopaedic perspective that would endure some one hundred and fifty years before the appearance in the twentieth century of a phylogenetic view point derived from academic perspectives. As Muslim cosmographies were woven into these texts, Javanese myth codes appeared to ensure their narrative integrity in these compendia. Mythological codes articulated eventual contradictions by juxtaposition of these oppositions between creation Javanese myths. During this earlier period no similar effort was made for Islamic creation legends and the resulting articulations between episodes is often ragged. In the course of the twentieth century it would be rejected by both Javanists and strict Muslims.

To understand the evolution from the earliest *Manikmaya* would involve a huge amount of codicological spadework. This chapter simply opens a window on the compilations of cosmologies with the hope that further research will be undertaken by proper philologists. As an anthropologist it is easier for me to address the issues posed by the evolution of the cosmogonies in mythological corpus than those of literary genre by which they are transmitted and developed. But the determination of genres through exhaustive codicological investigation is a methodological prerequisite, as Behrend has shown (1995, ch. 8).

11.2 SOURCES FOR AND RECENSIONS OF *MANIKMAYA*

The longer Javanese *Manikmaya* style, or cosmogonic compendium by another name, seem to present a double vision in their initial sections. Having given the recently arrived Muslim versions pride of (first) place, they next present the purely Javanese creation myths deriving from the fifteenth century in several variants and at such length that they create a bridge from a Muslim "universal" cosmography to local Javano-centric mythology. Other approaches were also tried, as the discussion below of the Amir Hamzah shows. There an historical figure, Amir Hamzah, his children, and servants, are the object of legends of Islamization which gained great popularity from Malaya all the way to Lombok from the seventeenth to the nineteenth centuries.

These *Manikmaya* myths would have been recited separately as sung poetry and performed in wayang; their narrative codes originally need not have been homogeneous. The series of these "secondary" Javanese myths concerning the origins of plants and social order are woven together according to a mythological code which suggests more than just compilation.[6] The elaboration of such codes for a collective articulation might well have taken several generations of story-telling, given the length of the myths. The purpose of this exploratory study is to find a way through the early cosmogonies at the beginning of the *Manikmaya* and then to sketch out their evolution in later recensions.[7]

SOURCES OF THE *MANIKMAYA* COSMOLOGY

The indigenous Javanese cosmogonies which were retained to go alongside the Muslim ones were not the pre-fifteenth century Sivaitic ones written in Old Javanese (*kawi*), as paraphrases of Sanskrit *śloka*'s treating the process of creation of man and the world (cf. Sudarshana Devi 1957, 1958, 1961). By the eighteenth century few could understand these religious texts (*tutur*). So we must look for more recent cosmogonies. Goris (1926, pp. 124–35) gives an example of such a myth, the *Dharma Wiśeṣa*. He calls it a cosmogony in the "younger style" (possibly post-fifteenth century). Although still presenting itself as an Old Javanese *tutur*, the language is "younger", more recent, and so is the cosmogony itself. At the very beginning of this genesis, a mysterious amorphous figure of Harttha-heto (Artha-hetu) appears,[8] followed shortly by "Manik Maya". It is noteworthy that in the *Dharma Wiśeṣa* Manik already designates several different figures. In Goris' Dutch résumé the beginning of the *Dharma Wiśeṣa* runs as follows:

> Opening "ornament verse": Thus the earth, thus the interior (? *dalem*), thus the *cam* (?) wind god, thus the sun, thus the moon, thus the *kaśi* (?), thus the eight-year cycle (*windu*), thus the decoration, thus the creation (*yoga*[9]), thus the undivided (*nishkalem* = ? *nishkala*); thus the prose story (*parwa*), thus the subtle body of the god.

After this list of topics, an explanation is given of the shapeless Hartha-heto (Artha-hetu) who gave his being to a body *nir-awayana* (without limbs[10]), and his descendants. This occurs by creation (yuga = yoga). Thus:

> "Without limbs" gives rise to Lohana (? *loha* = iron in Sanskrit) who gives rise to Grana Wiśeṣa, gives rise to Ananta Wiśeṣa by whom the creation (*yuga*) arose. From this spirit a seed of millet arose, a tree as "tall" as a millet seed, in full bloom with flowers white, shining, spotless. The spirit called it Manik-Anungku-Rat (Jewel, ruling the world), there after it moved and it was called Manik Meleng-meleng (Glittering Jewel).

Later in the *Dharma Wiśeṣa*, *sang hyang Manik* also designates a protective formula (cf folio b26–a27) in which are mentioned each of eight "teaching jewels" (*aguguron*).

> *Sang hyang manik* Amreta(ni); Angkayani; Suntagi Manik (= jewelled girdle); Antiwani (= waiting); Gandhapurwa wangi (also title of a text); Arcana-

Wiséṣa; Astaguna; Darma-Wiséṣa. [After this genealogy follows the story of how: *bhathari* Uma arose out of the rubbing of the ankles of *bhathara* Guru.[11] She arose from him such that she was "male not male, female not female". The shower of seed also led to various episodes corresponding to what is represented in the Birth of Kala *ruwatan*.]

Next is given the directions of the eight winds (*nawānga*), then the five demiurges called sages (*rṣi*) are listed and finally the older four guardians of the four quarters of the universe (*catur lokapāla*).

Despite the initial obscurity of its "ornament verse", the outline of the rest of this cosmogony will serve as a benchmark for the new genre of genesis. The concluding horizontal orientations, the mapping of the cosmos, are permanent feature of the pre-Muslim Javanese sense of space. A serious effort at dating would require a careful comparison with the compendium of traditions found in the *Tantu Panggelaran*,[12] which is pre-1635, so possibly late sixteenth century (Pigeaud 1924, p. 47) as well as several other of the younger cosmologies.

The question of the genre of such cosmogonies was already posed by H. Kern (1887, p. 576) in his study of the *Tantu Panggelaran*. In order to understand what genre of compilation this text presented, Kern examined its title. One translation of *Tantu Panggelaran* could be "(Javanese) world theatre". But for Kern the Javanese word *tantu* is better translated as the equivalent of the Sanskrit, *pratiṣṭa* (foundation). Zoetmulder also notes their semantic overlap (1982, pp. 1933–34): *tantu* may mean thread (as in Sanskrit: cause of continuity, thread of a story; establishment of world order[13]). And indeed in the *Tantu Panggelaran* 61.18 (parallel to 104.22), the two words (*pratiṣṭa* and *tantu*) are used as synonyms of one another.[14] The placing piecemeal of Mt Meru in Java, the main cosmogonic gesture of the beginning of the *Tantu Panggelaran* would seem to indicate that "founding of the world" is the proper translation. This particular myth of the "foundation" of Java is adapted here from the Javanese *Ādiparwa*, and ultimately from the Indian myth of the churning of the milk ocean (Poerbatjaraka and Tardjan 1952, p. 58). Yet this is far from being the only cosmogonic motif in Javanese creation myths.

The *Tantu Panggelaran* also gives snippets of other "purely Javanese" cosmogonies like the transformation of Siva into Kala-Rudra.[15] This metamorphosis is well illustrated in the east Javanese Tengger *Purvaka Bumi*[16] where the five sages (*rṣi*) initially refuse to create the world. They are made into monsters and exiled to the four cardinal points. After humanity has been created, it is attacked by Durga and Kala Rudra. The battle ends in a contract between the gods and man, enjoining prayer and respect for the ancestors. To make a first rough approximation for this preliminary exploration, it seems that, starting from an indigenous Javanese cosmology enriched by Indian Samkhya classifications, tables of correspondences initially found at the end of the younger cosmologies are put centre stage (cf. Figure 11.1). They will eventually be taken over in "Islamic" *primbon* in the form of numerological classifications of time and space.[17]

In resumé, "younger" cosmogonies like *Dharma Wiśéṣa* describe creation in terms of the division of body of a macro-anthropos and then its distribution of the cosmic co-ordinates. This is a typically western Indonesian feature. This cosmogony may be taken as the point of departure of the *Manikmaya* genre which will be investigated below.

RECENSIONS OF THE *MANIKMAYA* COSMOLOGY

Three manuscripts[18] were used for J. J. de Hollander's 1852 short verse *Manikmaya* edition.[19] Its purported *kawi* original was entitled not

FIGURE 11.1
Cosmological table (used in the contemporary Tedjokusuman school of kanuragan, Yogyakarta)

	Amniotic fluid (elder) *Legi* East White Smell Purity	
Umbilical cord *Wagé* North Black Taste Gluttony	Soul/subtle essence *Kliwon* Centre Multi-coloured Subtle sense (heart/liver) Compassion	Blood *Paing* South Red Hearing Anger
	Placenta (youngest) *Pon* West Yellow Sight Lust	

Note: In order of presentation 1–6: foetus sibling; market day of the five-day Javanese week; cardinal direction; colour; five senses; and character.
Source: Adapted from J.-M. de Grave (2001, ch. 3)

Manikmaya but *Jitapsara*.[20] The author of LUB/LOr. no. 1858 was supposedly a Sundanese, Karta Mosada, working in Kartasura (the capital from A.D. 1680 to 1745), who would have used the *Jitapsara* to write a modern Javanese *Manikmaya*. The common supposition found in the manuscript catalogues (cf LUB/LO 6414; Pigeaud 1968, vol. I:371) is that a *kawi Jitapsara* is a genealogy of the gods from Adam to Pramesthi Guru. The *Jitapsara*, which according to Brandes comes from *jitāksara*, meaning "learned", is not related to the old Javanese didactic *kakawin* poem *Dharmaśūnya* (Dharma Palguna 1999). The problem here is that this *Jitapsara* has not been found.[21] Yet, clearly, this prototype *kawi* text was not forgotten, for in the second half of the nineteenth century Ranggawarsita (or his entourage) did a pseudo Old Javanese version of the *Jitapsara* of which there are at least two ms. in Europe.[22]

To further complicate the question, it is not clear that there is any relation between the *Jitapsara* and the *Dharmaśūnya*. (Palguna 1999). Ricklefs mentions (1992, p. 673) that a *Dharmaśūnya Keling* was copied at the court of Kartasura in November 1716 and there are at least four representatives of the *Dharmaśūnya* poem in the Leiden collection alone. So we are as yet unsure how or even if, the Kartasura *Manikmaya* actually paraphrases any earlier *tutur* or its *kakawin*.[23]

According to C. F. Winter (1843, pp. 1–2), this work of Karta Mosada (or Mursadah?) is a modern Javanese *Manikmaya* written in Kartasura in 1725 just before the reign of Paku Buwana II (1726–49). Winter notes its close relationship with the Raffles *Manikmaya*. Winter, senior, worked from a manuscript copied by (the order of?) Pakubuwana VI while he was in exile in Ambon (in the 1830s?). J. J. de Hollander had three ms. to work from for his 1852 published edition. Yet, it is not simply a rice myth as claimed in Pigeaud's catalogue. There is, of course, a myth of the sprouting of the rice from Sri's/Tiksnawati's corpse following on her rape by Guru, but this is encoded into a larger mythic corpus. If the overall evolution of these tales both "upstream and downstream" in the later *Pustaka Raja Purwa* and *Pustaka Raja Madya* were researched, they might well illuminate something of the earlier evolution of the *Manikmaya*.

In the eighteenth century some of these modern poetic *Manikmaya* link cosmogony to the Birth of Kala story. This suggests that during the eighteenth century this Birth of Kala myth, as a follow up to a genesis myth, began to replace older exorcistic tales such as *Sri Tanjung, Calon Arang*, etc.[24] Perhaps the older indigenous cosmogonies were already forgotten at the time that the compilations of indigenous Javanese and imported Muslim cosmogonies were just beginning.

The PNRI/NBS codex 74 (dated 1794) is just such a version of these short, verse *Manikmaya*. Among the dozen found in the Perpustakaan Nasional, the PNRI/KBG 1074 supposedly dates from Kartasura, *circa* 1725, but the manuscript itself is a copy done when Paku Buwana VI was in exile in Ambon after 1830. Carey confirms (1992, p. 495, note 466) the interest in the eighteenth century *Manikmaya*, reporting that Pangéran Panular was copying this "popular" text in c. 1782 in Yogyakarta.

A *Manikmaya*,[25] dated 1780 (BL/IO Javanese no. 71), was translated by Vincent (BL/IO, MacKenzie Private collection no. 69). This is purportedly related to the short *Manikmaya*, which served Winter for his 1843 article on "Javaansche Mythologie".[26] Yet according to my own brief examination of this manuscript, it already shows a strong influence of the same kind of Javanese Islam one finds in the *Centhini*. This India Office *Manikmaya* begins with a description of a forty-day gestation period (*ghaib al-ghuyub*) of a concealed point (*nukat* (=? *nukta*) *ghaib*) followed by the appearance of fixed essences (*a'yān thābitah*) in the world of spirits (*alam arwāh*.) From the "spirit of relation" (*ruh idhāfī*) God formed Sri Wesi in the world of men.

Neither Winter's text nor the *Manikmaya* translated by Raffles contain such a Muslim pairing of the stages of the descent of the absolute and the terminology of the gestation of the human foetus. However, a passage in the *Centhini* (II: 399–401; translation, Harun Hadiwijono 1967, p. 136) contains just such a description. Here we see the interface of Javanese and Muslim cosmologies. What the Sumatran seventeenth-century poet Hamzah Fansuri (Drewes and Brakel 1986, p. 17) describes as creation, is an "ontological" (*wujūdiyyah*) descent. This was also received wisdom for some time in Malaysia and Sumatra (Al-Attas 1970). As shown in Chapter 10 above, in Java, however, certain authors stressed the second part of this cycle of manifestation and absorbtion, that is to say rather than focusing on the description of the creation as emanation (*fayḍ*), they highlighted the creation of *man as microcosm and his ascent* to Allah. The self-disclosure of the absolute involves a double movement. Says Ibn al-'Arabī (Chittick 1989, p. 324), "The ascent belongs to us, the descent belongs to Him".[27] This balance was later distorted in favour of the ascent by Ranggawarsita in his *Jitapsara* (LUB/LOr 6414) written in the 1850s.

The three Surakarta manuscript collections surveyed in the Cornell University Surakarta Manuscript project include some seven texts under the title of *Manikmaya*. However under other titles[28] similar contents are found, i.e. histories of archaic Java, developing the left and right genealogies with cosmogonic prefaces of varying length. Because of the heterogeneous character of what it has compiled, the limits of the *Manikmaya* genre remains vague.

A century after the shorter *Manikmaya* described above, we find a Kraton Surakarta *Manikmaya* (SMP/KS 14), commissioned by Paku Buwana VII (1830–58) in 1840 and written by R. Ng. Sindusastra. This recension ran to some 459 pages (Florida 1993, p. 66), and the three volumes of a Mangkunagaran *Manikmaya* (ms. B97a, B99, and B97b) ran to some eight hundred pages. It is clear that the *Manikmaya* cosmogony is lengthened in these large compendia to include not just the creation of Java but all of Javanese pre-modern history.

11.3 WAYANG COSMOGONIES

In the eighteenth and nineteenth centuries the *wayang kulit* or shadow puppet theatre *Manikmaya* (or *Jagat Ginelar*, Unfolding of the World) refer to these cosmogonies and origin myths. The translation of a late eighteenth-century *Manikmaya* in Raffles' *History of Java* (1817/1988) is based on just such a *wayang* version of this cosmogony. The twentieth century Probohardjono version below is surprisingly similar.

During the last two centuries, when it came to ritual performances, cosmogonies have often been used to purify: re-creation by retelling creation. The Birth of Kala exorcism gradually absorbed the earlier cosmogonies like those still used in East Javanese Tengger ancestor rites (*entas-entas*). These older cosmogonies survived encoded in the mantra (Ch. 9: *Sastra Pedhati, Mandala Giri, Kumbala Geni*) used in the Birth of Kala or the *Maésa Lawung* rituals.

Another genre, intermediate between the three volume "historical" *Manikmaya* and the short *wayang* plays is the *Serat Kandhaning Ringgit Purwa*[29] and the *Serat Pustaka Raja Purwa*.[30] Here the full narration of the "historical" *Manikmaya* genre is compartmentalized (*dipakemaké*) in the framework of an individual play (*lakon*) on the model of *wayang* résumé (*pakem*). This genre will only run its course after Ranggawarsita and his associates had drawn it out to uncopiable, but not unpublishable lengths in the *Pustaka Raja Purwa* and *Madya*. Because these belonged to the first generation of printed texts, they overcame this obstacle and became accessible to a wider public whose use of this literature has yet to be studied. The origins of this use of *pakem* as a model for résumés needs further research. Dutch influence existed, but may not have been determining.[31]

A LATE EIGHTEENTH-CENTURY *MANIKMAYA* COSMOGONY

Although the Javanese original for the *Manikmaya* translated in the appendix of Raffles' *History of Java* (1817) and p. 407 above is not yet identified with complete certainty,[32] there seems little reason to imagine that it was written for foreign consumption. It strongly ressembles a *wayang* résumé (*pakem*). The printed English translation Raffles gives a close resemblance to the contemporary Surakarta *Jagat Ginelar wayang* play. To complicate matters, the source for Probohardjono's modern version is also unknown, at least to this author. Curiously, its title seems to be a paraphrase of the *Tantu Panggeleran*, but its cosmology is not derived from the *Tantu*.

> *Résumé of the beginning of the Raffles Manikmaya:*
> Ch. I. There was the void (*awang-awang uwung-uwung*). Wiséṣa was! He wished, then followed desire, then a storm, then a ball or a bell[33] which separated into three parts: heaven and earth; sun and moon; and man, that is to say Manikmaya or Guru.
> Wiséṣa concedes the world to Guru and vanishes. An unstable universe ensues. The sun and moon are made to alternate.
> Guru, without wife, has nine sons and five daughters, who are disposed in the cardinal directions. Each brother takes one of the sisters for a consort. These directions are classified in terms of palace, metal, a sea of a certain milk, a bird of a certain colour, a group of five letters and a day of the five-day week.
> The four remaining figures: Pratancala/Kuwera/Mahayakti/Séwa, are placed in the intermediary directions (NE/NW/SW/SE). Guru is under the earth.

The Raffles' *Manikmaya*, if late eighteenth century, is similar to later *wayang* cosmogonies, but what kind of myths did it derive from? It certainly bears partial resemblance to the much earlier *Dharma Wiséṣa*. But it also shows similarities to:

1. the *Séwa Sāsana*,[34] a collection of laws and edicts containing a cosmogony. This text's date is unreliable. As in the *Tantu Panggelaran*, Kandhyawan is given as second in a list of ancient culture heroes or *rahyangta's*.
2. the *Medhang Alas*,[35] an old Javanese(-Balinese) cosmogony with some Sanskrit *sloka's*. It begins with Windu, the Creation of *manuh* (man), male and female; Brahma and Wisnu, further mentioning *rahyangta* Kandhyawan, King of Medhang; the *pancawara* (five day week); the seven *rṣi*, etc. It concludes with the end of the *kertayuga*.
3. the *Tatwa Sawang Suwung*,[36] an old Javanese prose cosmogony, beginning with creation by *sang hyang* Taya;[37] mentioning Brahma as patron of

blacksmiths and ending with a rice myth connected with Sukra and Sri. Here, Suwung (= *sunya*, empty), is a mythical "empty" mountain, residence of Siwa and Indra.

Further research on texts like these three is needed. The topic of these younger post-fifteenth century Javanese cosmogonies, the *jagat awang-uwung*, (the "void" world) became a popular theme in Arabic script manuscripts like LUB/LOr. 7724 from Surakarta. But how does popularity, frequency of treatment of a theme affect the genre of compilation?

ISLAMIC COSMOLOGY IN THE NINETEENTH-CENTURY *MANIKMAYA*

H. A. R. Gibb, in his Preface to the first edition (1964; 1993, pp. xv–xvi) of Seyyed Hossein Nasr's *Introduction to Islamic Cosmological Doctrines*, claims that behind the Ptolomaic concentric spheres, the Aristotelian elements of fire, water, earth, and air and the Plotinian emanations of pure intelligences in a world of similitude (*'ālam al-mithāl*), the ancient Middle Eastern notion of a unified controlled cosmos, a divine justice, underlies all the rest. This can be seen in the fact that real government is in the hands of the hidden saints or the Poles (*kutub*/*quṭb*) to whom this mystical cosmos has been revealed. For them religious experience lay in knowing their creator's words and not how Allah created the world.[38] They wanted to understand the descent of the Absolute and experience an ascent to it. This is what we have called cosmography. The Koran readily took over what Plato's *Timaeus* and Aristotle's *Metaphysics* had said about a single universe. In contrast earlier Greek philosophers and Hindu theology allowed for an endless number of worlds.

In the Javanese *Manikmaya*'s treatment of cosmogony, are the Muslim elements only nominally present? A familiarity with Islam (and ultimately Neo-Platonic emanationist terminology) is visible, but it seems to me that the basic oppositions and linkages that pervade the *Manikmaya* myths are largely Javanese.

Zoetmulder (1995, p. 115) has remarked that the relation between the world and Allah in eighteenth-century Javanese religious poetry (*suluk*) is generally treated through the prism of the relationship between an "I" and God. Perhaps "over-compilation" in nineteenth century *Manikmaya* banalized and secularized cosmography by detaching it from its textual origins. One author, H. M. Rasyidi (1977, pp. 32–33), admits that he is at a loss to explain the diversity of the nineteenth century conceptions of creation and its theories of the "light of Muhammad" (=second or *wahda* stage in the emanation of reality). It is tempting to see in this variety of cosmologies, the result of the nineteenth-century encyclopaedic compiling of mythology.[39] The compilers don't claim only one exclusive origin myth describing primordial phenomena. By the 1850s Ranggawarsita can even use the technical terminology of Islamic cosmology to present a profoundly Javanese path of union of "Ingsun" (self) and the Absolute. The diversity here reveals a disintegration of Muslim cosmologies in certain Javanese adaptations. The careful study of the *Serat Kanda* genre, roughly contemporary to the *Manikmaya*'s, made by Kuznetsova (section 11.4 below) fills out the picture given here. The *Serat Kanda* text is more cogent in its Islamic description of the descending manifestations of the primeval light.[40] On the other hand the codes of purely Javanese mythology continue to articulate their traditional origin myths to create larger ensembles.

The myths studied here do not "seriously" present creation in the perspective of Muslim theology, even if they display some familiarity with its terminology. The next-to-last emanation from Allah will illustrate their treatment using vague polysemic associations. The sixth emanation, world of bodies (*alam ajsam*), is both equated with a jewel [(*sosotya* (beam) or *durrah* (pearl essence)] and considered as a descent or lineage (*dharah*). This popularity in Java of the notion of jewel or *manik*[41] in the recyling of older Javanese notions of creation probably accounts for the widespread use of the indigenous metaphor of jewel for seed. This was reinforced by the Javanese-Arabic association of the Javanese word lineage or descent (*dharah*) with the Arabic word jewel (*durrah,* note also *dharra* = "atom"). To make this play on words all the more obvious, the descent, the fall of Guru's jewels (i.e., seed) was considered a cosmic procreation and therefore a sort of lineage in the sense of emanation (*fayd*)involving grades of being (*martabat*).

In Malay texts such as Nuruddin al-Ranīrī's *Bustan as-Salatin*, Book I, the notion of emanation of the world from the light of Muhammad has already been accepted as traditional. A *Hikayat Nur Muhammad* referred to in the *Bustan as-Salatin* was translated early into Malay and deals with this theme. G. F. Pijper's translation *Het Boek der Duizend Vragen* (Leiden 1925) presents another version of this vision of cosmology where the non-differentiation of the essence (*dhāt*) is immediately followed by several set stages of manifestation of being. However according to K. Steenbrink (personal communication), such a cosmological treatment of the light of Muhammad would not be found in any classical Arabic Muslim cosmologies, such as Tabari's *Tarikh* or al-Kisai's *Qisas al-Anbiya*. According to the Islamic traditions already well entrenched, the destiny of each creature is already inscribed in Allah's providence.

In his nineteenth century Javanese "classic", the *Serat Wirid Hidayat Jati* (Simuh 1988, p. 191), Ranggawarsita indigenizes this notion of emanation further by placing the focus on reabsorption: that the ascent to the absolute involves purifying (*angruwat*) one's four foetus siblings and five relations (*sadhulur papat lima pancer*). It was from these that ego was created out of the constituent elements of the cosmos. This last example allows us to envisage a spectrum of cosmologies stretching from orthodox Islamic cosmology to purely Javanese-Hindu esoteric teaching veiled in Islamic terminology.

Their popularity extends down to semi-illiterate professions like those of masseuse (Headley 1996*b*; 2000*a*). Contemporary kiosk literature of Java simplifies this theology radically. The creation of the world and man's forthcoming from the being of Allah by divine fiat are presented to the general public as due to Allah's fiat: "Be and it is!" (*kun faya kun*). This differentiation of creation from the essence (*dhāt*) of Allah explains how all being, including man, derives from God without any change in His being. From the Muslim point of view, this divine fiat is the first phenomenon and the last positively-intelligible description of Allah's being before reaching those negative apophatic names of God: unknowable, undividable, ineffable, etc. Nonetheless such popular treatises as Yoedi Parto Yoewono's the *Treatise of Guidance Explained* (*Serat Wedaran Wirid*, 1957, 1984, and 1991); *Science of Pure Reality and "Be and it is"* (*Ilmu Khak Sejati & Qun Fayakun*, (1979) and Soewarno's *The Teaching of Islam Javanised* (*Ajaran Islam di Jawakan*, 1984) are still read. These mix in elements from the pre-Muslim cosmogonies that we have examined above.

11.4 THE GENRE OF MYTHOLOGICAL COMPENDIA

To sum up, in the sixteenth century the use of "younger" Javanese creation myths to purify the evil destiny of an impure (*sukerta*) person eventually led to the narration of the Birth of Kala to free one from danger. A creation myth entitled *Manikmaya*, initially associated with the Birth of Kala became a separate *lakon*, the "Spreading out of the World". When during the following two centuries the Javanese cosmogony and the Muslim cosmography were juxtaposed, they were never completely fused. The nineteenth century *Manikmaya* preserved both of them side by side. The inclusion of Muslim creation myths and theological terminology in the mid-nineteenth century *Manikmaya* (1984: vol. I, cantos I–VIII) gave pride of place to Muslim cosmography before continuing on to the Javanese *Manikmaya*/spilt-seed creation myths.

In an important article on the *Manikmaya* and *Babad Kandḥa*'s Javanese conception of the world, Seda Kuznetsova wrote (1992, p. 79):

> Various things or properties — elements, or classifiers, of each series — are considered to be not only the "synonyms" and "antonyms", but also the members of a specific family who "come from" a common "ancestor" represented by the centre and who again "return to" and "re-unite in" it. In the two/three fold classification, the elements of the right and left series are the junior and senior brothers begotten by the Creator (Sang Hyang Wenang). In the five-fold classification they are grandfathers, fathers, sons, and grandchildren descending from the demiurge Bathara Guru. This explains why the reverse side of the classification-integration principle is constituted by the concept of genealogical order of the cosmos which plays such an important role in both the Javanese "picture of the world" and those of other peoples in Indonesia ...

Although a synchronic comparison of the *Manikmaya* and the *Babad Kandḥa* does provide a clear formal contrast, the inclusion of the vagaries of the appearances of younger old Javanese cosmologies, their gradual transformation and juxtaposition with the Muslim imported cosmologies provides a more complex tissue of diachronic developments.

Vladimir Braginsky (personal communication, June 1999) has suggested that there are Malay parallels to the *Manikamaya* description of Bathara Guru's creation of a celestial abode (Indralaya), with the difference that the Malay celestial cities claim to rival Allah's paradise. These Malay versions derive ultimately from the Koranic (*sura* 89:7) legend of a city with many pillars, Iram Dhat al-Imad, built by Shaddād, king of the 'Ad, to whom the Nabi Hud prophesied that any earthly city imitating paradise would be destroyed along with the king who built it (*Shorter Encyclopedia of Islam* 1961, pp. 171–72; and 13; 140). Just as the incorporation of the "pseudo"-Koranic Adam and Sis legends and the Neo-Plantonic Sufi "light (*nur*) of Muhammad material into the *Manikmaya*, this material about the country of Zamin Ambar in the Malay *Amir Hamzah*, provided the narrative intervals allowing expansions. The seven-storied city built by Syamsul Alam, complete with angels and a bridge, is conquered by Amir Hamzah's servant Umar Maya.[42] Thus incorporating secondary cosmographic legends into the earlier *Manikmaya* and *Kandḥa* texts, had more or less contemporaneous precedents in Malay cosmographies, if that is what they are. These episodes are certainly not cosmogonies and are not juxtaposed to the mythological material dealt with above.

At the very end of the Amir Hamzah epic,[43] one finds a seven-tiered heavenly city being finished on earth where kings becomes angels. In the

Javanese Yasadipura Ménak of 1832 A.D.,[44] the *Ménak Jamintoran* and *Ménak Jaminambar* (vols. 21 and 22), contain lengthy descriptions of this exploit, where admiration vies with condemnation. Marrison (1999, pp. 26–50), the most recent writer to have studied the corpus of Ménak tales from Java (and Lombok), makes several valuable observations. First of all he identifies Jamintoran (Zamin Turan) with Transoxania, and Jaminambar with the Persian Zamin Ambar, a locality in Khurasan. He then goes on (1999, p. 38) to suggest that the self-apotheosis (Malay, *didéwakan*) of these kings may reflect the strength of Buddhism in this area.

This "heretical" material seems to me as drifting further and further away from the opposition of cosmogony and cosmography enunciated in the introduction to this chapter. It presents only the sinful dimension of presumption such as found in the tower of Babel (Genesis 11:19), minus the confusion of languages. In *Ménak Jamintoran*, canto 14:14 states that three kings had deified themselves (Javanese, *binathara*). Marrison suggests (1999, p. 50) that when Malay prose translation appeared in Javanese seventeenth century poetic versions and travelled along the Pasisir or North coast of Java, "an important aspect of such texts is the implied continuity of the sacred history of Islam as included in the Qur'an and the traditions with that of the conversion of Indonesian countries to the religion of the prophets." Now if the point of certain of the Ménak romances were to present an increasingly clear delineation of *kafir* practices from Islamic ones, this incident suffices and at the same time makes good listening. What it doesn't present is a contemporaneous "kafir" cosmography juxtaposed to a Javanese cosmogony juxtaposed to a Muslim one, such as we found in the *Manikmaya*.

11.5 CONCLUSIONS

An oral corpus of Javanese mythology couldn't have been compiled indiscriminately when committed to writing. The first twenty cantos of *Manikmaya* contained mythological codes whose narrative articulations commanded respect from its performers, because they were myths not romances. But for composers/compilers adding Muslim elements to the *Manikmaya*, the way to jump over the structure of the Javanese mythological codes was reiteration, treating the same topic, i.e., creation, in successive myths. The seven successive emanations (*fayḍ*) or *martabat* of Muslim cosmography seems to have favoured this reiterative approach. The mythological codes inside a given myth did not permit it to be strung together without a corresponding surface-level narrative structure. Such compilations of myths had their limits. They could not be as encyclopaedic as in the *Serat Centhini* which treated knowledge of blatantly diverse kinds. Another approach deriving from these tales use in wayang was "*pakemization*"; telling tales in *lakon* or scenario format remained strong down to the twentieth century.

The *wayang Manikmaya* escaped Islamic influence as did other *lakon* like the *Buda Respati* dealing with the chronological divisions related to the planets. This is not to say that *dhalangs* did not read the Koran assiduously. The claim here is that certain juxtapositions persisted, for instance, left and right-hand genealogies. These permitted the two main strands, Javanese and Muslim, of this island's culture to continue side by side. Javanese cosmogonies were usually not in conflict to Islamic ones over the last three centuries, just as the annual *wuku*-dated festivals for the local protecting deities (*dhayang dhusun*) were part of a larger annual calendar including Muslim religious feasts. The *Manikmaya* in its different avatars, both written and theatrical, is an important source for understanding these "encompassings". It permits us to study this mentality as it brought forward two radically different visions of genesis side by side (*wayang* and Koran). Ultimately the introduction of individualism into Javanese sociology in the twentieth century benefited from the restrictions that Muslim cosmography gradually exerted on Javanese cosmogony. Episodic even constructed history of mentalities could now be constructed based on individual destinies. The price to be paid for such new histories henceforth was to be the impossibility of finding a frame for total history since society was no longer presented as a whole.

The passage from mythology to historical narrative was such a watershed in the sixth and fifth century B.C. Greek culture,[45] that we have trouble realizing that the Javanese by delaying this passage to the nineteenth and twentieth have maintained a closeness to their mythological origins that the West has often lost. This is what Walter Ong called sound-sight split of chirographic culture (1967, pp. 76–79). Having brought forward into Modern Javanese during the eighteenth century parts of Old Javanese literature, old Javanese died. No "dead" language like Latin or Sanskrit existed only in writing to preserve the past.

Still the past had not yet been devocalized (Ong 1967, p. 72); it lived on as an oral performance in *wayang*. "Ancient" history became a play. As nineteenth-century literary genre, the *Manikmaya* became one cultural mode for encompassing knowledge. Since the *macapat* groups that recite *Manikmaya* are now on the point of extinction, the longer *Manikmaya*, so much a product of the nineteenth century, will finally probably die out before the post-fifteenth century mythology concerning cosmogony falls out of the *wayang* repertory.

Did the nineteenth-century *Manikmaya* fail to "tie up the past into a discourse", *angiket purwanipun* (1981, canto I.1)? Was the source of these compilations really shadow puppet theatre? The popular oral *wayang* repertory continued to function as kind of shared knowledge drawing on many sources of oral tradition. Myths reappeared in all-night *wayang* performances long after they seemed to have disappeared from the peasants' oral repertory. They are so much a part of Javanese history that their own evolution becomes a kind of history.

NOTES

1. In contemporary *wayang* lore, Javanese myths recounting the creation of the world are part of the Birth of Kala (*Murwa Kala*) play which is used as an exorcism. At the end of this play one or more creation myths have been fragmented into a series of obscure mantras. The fragmentation of the cosmogonic material in the Birth of Kala mantra is such that no one mantra is a complete myth. Conversely, strands from several different myths could be at the origin of a single mantra. Such treatment is not a new phenomenon in the evolution of Javanese ritualized myths.

2. The two versions of the *Usulbiya* (Book about the Origins of the Prophets: the first written in 1729–30 A. D.; canto 23:31 and the second written in 1743 A. D. canto 27:7) studied by Ricklefs (1998, pp. 83, 297 and 358–59) both have a "before the earth and the heavens" cosmogonic formula followed by a statement concerning cosmographic activity of the word (*sabda*) or fiat (*kun*) of Allah.

3. Cf. Day (1978) and Ras (1986).

4. The Javanese attitude towards Muslim daily prayer (*salat*) followed a different evolution. Cf. Headley 1996*a*.

5. It is a well-known fact that Javanese titles may indicate the literary genre of the text (*layang, serat, babad, kandha,* or *suluk*), but not its subject. A topic indicator like *Manikmaya*, suggests a given content, but similar Javanese works are known to hide behind the most diverse titles.

6. The influence of the codes of two different Austronesian corpus of myths on the figure of Sri and Kala is discussed in Headley (2004, forthcoming) "Les moitiés d'homme à Java:…"

7. As yet we have no study of the complex relations of the recensions of the *Manikmaya* corpus like those constructed by Behrend for the *Serat Jatiswara* (1995) and the *Centhini* (1997) corpuses. The text of the *Manikmaya* was published by the Departemen Pendidikan dan Kebudayaan in three volumes from a nineteenth century Mangkunagaran Palace library Reksapustaka manuscript [B97 (211 pp.); B99 (339 pp.); B100 (254 pp.)]. In her catalogue of the Mangkunagaran Reksapustaka collection, Nancy Florida (2000, pp. 110–11) has noted that the third volume was probably composed by Mas Ngabèhi

Rongga Panambangan II who served as *patih* under Mangkunagara I (r. 1757–96) and Mangkunagara II (r. 1796–1835). The first volume, including up to canto 38 of P dan K volume two, p. 266, was also published in Semarang in 1984 by the Departmen Pendidikan dan Kebudayaan, Proyek Pengembangan Perpustakaan, Jawa Tengah). These two printed texts show a few discrepancies despite having been made from the same ms. (Reksapustaka B 97a, 97b & B99). Although published, neither versions were ever for sale publicly.

8. As he does in the nineteenth century Surakarta Palace mantra *Tata Winanci*. I have attempted a translation of a genesis involving Artha-hetu in Headley (2000*a*: ch. 5). The persistence of much earlier mythological motifs in the eighteenth and nineteenth century amalgam of lore is a witness to these mythological figures' resilience.

9. *yogamaya*, meaning, as in the Old Javanese (Zoetmulder 1982, p. 2364), a deity's power to create the world.

10. The limbs of the deity are both the source of certain cosmogonic powers. So the rubbing of the ankles of Siwa produces the goddess Uma in the Tengger Purwa Bumi myth and the creation of the world out of the movements of a macrocosmic giant in one of the *Maésa Lawung* mantra (cf. Headley 1979*b*, pp. 54–55).

11. This episode is present in the modern Balinese and East Javanese (Tengger) "Beginning of the World (*Purvaka bumi*)" myths.

12. Pigeaud (1924, p. 2327), after Kern (1887), treats the question of the names of divinities in the *Tantu Panggelaran* by identifying them with early indigenous Javanese deities. Thus, Wisnu designates Kandyawan, Guru is a volcanic mountain god, etc. What preoccupied both authors were the discrepancies with the borrowed Indian nomenclature. Pigeaud tends to see the *Tantu Panggelaran* as the watershed for modern Javanese compendia. Thus (1924, p. 52), "Although there is not a little difference to distinguish them, a comparison of the *Tantu Panggelaran* with a text like the *Manikmaya* seems to be not without importance. It is not to be excluded that some of the stories in the *serat Kaṇḍa* or older *lakon* (*wayang* plays) display common origins with certain stories treated here, in the same way that generally the representation of *bhathāra* Guru and his court in the new literature is quite close to that of the *Tantu*." Zurbuchen on the other hand (1979), seems to consider the *Tantu Panggelaran* as showing the Indian origins of much of Javanese mythology.

13. I.e. Javanese *tata* as in the *Tata Winanci* cosmogony; cf. R.M.T. Bratadinigrat et al., *Kuwajiban Abdi-dalem Juru Suranata, Maésa Lawung, Donga-donga, Nglabuh, Pados Sekar Jayakusuma, Saha Mriksa Kasegedan Juru Suranata*. SMP/ KS 189.1. Transcription by Nancy Florida (1985). Related to *Bundel Slamentan dan labuhan serta Kebo Maésa Lawung*. Mangkunagaran Reksopustaka ms. above. Cf. also note 1 in Kern (1887, p. 576) for Malayo-Polynesian parallels centred on the semantic field for "stable".

14. "…*kahucapa ta srī bhatāra Mahākārana magawé tantu pratista ri Yawadipa, tuminggalekna tantu hyang, ya a gumlar ing anda bhuwana, kemendeng tan pegat rumeka tan lbur.*" Same double in 81.20; 90.4; and 99.22.

TP 57.4: "...*kacaritanikā nusha Jawa ring asitkala. Iki manusha tanana; nguniweh sang hyang Mahāmeru tan hana ring nusha Jawa; kunang kahananira sang hyang Mandalagiri, sira ta gunung magông aluhur pinakalinggāning bhuwana.*" In the nineteenth century Murwa Kala *mandalagiri* becomes the name of a mantra.

15. Cf. Pigeaud text (1924, p. 102); translation (1924, p. 169).

16. Nancy Smith-Hefner (1996, 295–300). For the Balinese version, cf. Hooykaas (1974, pp. 11–51, especially pp. 13 & 33). In the Balinese cosmogony there is a god of the Void (*sang hyang* Sunya).

17. Library manuscript abbreviations are found at the beginning of the Bibliography at the end of this volume. Cf. In the mid-nineteenth century *Manikmaya* canto 10 (1981) where such a system of oriented correspondences are presented in table form. In the early *Manikmaya* these represent the finished form of the cosmos and in later *primbon* literature they are exploited to identify favourable and unlucky days, directions, dates, etc. The influence of Amir Hamzah tales would later be so great that one of the standard contemporary Javanese almanacs containing these tables of divination is called after the father of Amir Hamzah's servant (Umar Maya), Bétal Jamur.

18. The LUB/LOr 1858 (1), as well as LUB/LOr 2034, and LUB/LOr 2101 dated 1794 A.D. are short manuscript (56, 62, 27 pp.). Cf. Vreede (1892, pp. 13–15).

19. Cf. *Verhandelingen Bataviaash Genootschap*, vol. 24; A. C. Vreede (1892 p. 13) and Pigeaud (vol. II, 1968, p. 44).

20. What is the relation of the late nineteenth/early twentieth century *Serat Jitapsara, Jitsara, Sastraharjèndra* (SMP/KS 574.6 in Florida 1993, p. 313) to the *kawi* text mentioned as existing in the beginning of the eighteenth century? If one were to find that the calendric/cardinal direction classification system was all the lore of *Jitaspara* retained by later centuries, that would mean that it was similar in content to some of the seventeenth century Merapi *lontar* in Gunung or Buda script. Clearly cosmographic co-ordinates were given in many kinds of old Javanese texts (*Panca Mahābhūtā, Bhuwana Kośa, Tiga Jñāna, Kamoksan* etc.) and not only those bearing the title *Jitāpsara*.

    The evolution of these texts will certainly turn out to be complex. For instance *Sri Tanjung*'s later exorcistic mantra seemed to have been just such classificatory tables. In the *Sri Tanjung* (edition Prijono 1938), Durga re-animates and exorcises Sri. The text interpolates seventeenth-century East Javanese invocations for this occasion, but itself is written in "younger" middle Javanese (Poerbatjaraka and Hadidjaja 1952, p. 95). Nothing more specific can be said of the date, although the text may belong to the sixteenth century.

21. Poerbatjaraka and Tardjan Hadidjaja (1952, pp. 135–40) repeat Winter's assertion that the *Manikmaya* originated in the Kartasura court, but admit not knowing if there was ever an *sekar-ageng* Old Javanese version. Ricklefs (1978, p. 152) suggests that Kartasura was the cradle of several Modern Javanese adaptations of Old Javanese works like the *Dharmaśūnya* I. Kuntara Wiryamartana (1990, p. 462) says that the Merbabu-Merapi monastic scriptoria were in contact with the valley palace milieu. Unfortunately no mention is found of the *Jitāpsara* or

the *Manikmaya* in Ricklefs (1988) very thorough study of Pakubuwana II's reign (1726–49) at Kartasura where one might have suspected to find it. *Cabolek* (canto 2:13; Soebardi 1975, p. 73) shows that so-called Buda traditions were still alive in a period which Ricklefs (1988, ch. 4) argues corresponds to Pakubuwana II reign in Kartasura (1726–49).

22. LUB/LO 6414 and Berlin's Staatsbibliothek Preussischer Kulturbesitz (no. 157 in Pigeaud 1975, p. 187).

23. The 1999 doctoral thesis on the *Darmaśūnya* text by Dharma Palguna at Leiden University did not bring to light any relation of the *Darmaśūnya* recensions with the later *Dharma Wisésa* genre. On the *Darmaśūnya* classical poem Palguna's M.A. thesis (*Kakawin Darmaśūnya*, 1993) and 1999 Leiden University doctoral dissertation.

24. Cf. Headley (1991, pp. 77–89).

25. Cf. Ricklefs and Voorhoeve (1977, p. 69) and C.O. Blagden (1916, pp. 206–207).

26. Cf. *Tijdschrift voor Nederlands Indië* (1843), 5è jaargang, 1è deel, pp. 1–88.

27. Cf. also Chittick (1989, pp. 15–16) and Braginsky (1993).

28. *Serat Kandha, Serat Sajarah awit Kangjeng Nabi Adam lan Babu Kawa tumurun dhateng ngarcapada, dumugi Prabu Makukuhan ing nagari Medangkamulan, Serat Pustaka Raja Purwa, Serat Sri Mahapunggung*, etc. In the Perpustakaan Nasional in Jakarta ones finds juxtapositions (or simply odd bindings together?) of *Manikmaya saha Serat Baron Sakender* (KBG 133) and *Amibya Manikmaya* (NB8).

29. Leiden Oriental Codex 6379. Djambatan & KITLV, Jakarta 1985.

30. *sampun kadhapuk balungan lakon*. Private edition, Solo 1983.

31. cf. Kenji Tsuchiya (1991, *passim*).

32. A candidate might be RAS Raffles Java 10 or 17, but cf BL/IOL Javanese 71 dated 1780 A.D., translated in BL/IOL Mackenzie collection no. 69 (cf. Blagden 1916, pp. 206–208).

33. This bell is often presented as suspended "without a hook" (*gumantung tanpa cantélan*) as in Probohardjono's *wayang* cosmogony presented below. Even in a mid-nineteenth century text replete with Arabic terminology like Ranggawarsita's *Serat Wirid Hidayat Jati* (Simuh 1988, p. 182), there is a lamp without fire, and a jewel suspended just like the bell "without a hook".

34. Cf. Pigeaud (1968, vol. 2, p. 557); LOr. 9379.

35. Cf. Pigeaud (1968, vol. 2, p. 595); LOr. 9748 = Kirtya 1361.

36. Cf. Pigeaud (1968, vol. II, p. 163); LOr 3931 (3).

37. Cf. Zoetmulder (1982, p. 1968) *taya* = there is not. This may be the same sort of expression as *tanana* (= "there is not anyone" or "there is no one" (woman the equal of…) which is used as an epithet of Durga.

38. Cf the articles *khalk* (creation, in vol. VI) and *fayḍ* (emanation/effusion of being, in vol. IV) of the *Encyclopaedia of Islam*.

39. Four seventeenth-century authors active in Sumatra (Hamzah Fansuri, Shamsu'l-

Din both accused of pantheism) and Al-Raniri and 'Abdu'l-Ra'uf, (considered orthodox), set the stage for the later and less rigorous nineteenth-century debates in Java on the emanation of the created world from Allah. A Javanese translation and adaptation of the text *Tuhfa* (Johns 1965) was written in Tegal on the north coast of Java before 1690. It is probably the earliest treatment, in a Sufi perspective, of the being of God. The seven stages of emanation *(martabat)* ordered by Allah, the unique being, create the world, provoking no change in the godhead. (Johns 1965, pp. 5–12).

In the nineteenth century, Ranggawarsita popularized the notion of sevenfold emanation. Simuh (1988, p. 234) presents a useful comparative table of the correspondences of the emanations. Ranggawarsita in his *Wirid Hidayat Jati.* summarizes them thus:

"...I first created *hayyu* (existence), named it *sjaratul yakin*, (the true tree) that grew up in the eternally old world of *adam-makdum* (= *ma'dūm*, non-being). Then I created the light and named it Nur Muhammad (light of M.). Then the mirror and called it *mir'atul haya'i* (mirror of shame). Then the soul and named it *ruh idlafi* (spirit of relation). Then the lamp and called it *kandil* ("flameless" lamp). Then the jewel and named it *dharrah* (beam). Then the wall before the majesty and called it *hijab* (veil) of divine glory. Those were the ends of Myself." (Ranggawarsita, *Wirid Hidayat Jati.* II:26 in Simuh, 1988, p. 182).

40. Cf. descent of the absolute in the form of light *(nur)*, in Poerbatjaraka and T. Hadidjaja (1952, pp. 142–51); H. Hadiwijono (1967, pp. 71–78).

41. From the Sanskrit *mani* = jewel, cf. Zoetmulder (1982, pp. 1102–103); and *Serat Wirid* in H. Hadiwidjono (1967, pp. 108–109), where *mani* is the seed and *manikem* is the essence of *mani*. There exist more standard Muslim description of Adam's fall.

42. For the construction of the seven-storied city by Syamsul Alam, cf. *Hikayat Amir Hamzah* (1987, pp. 608–609) and for the destruction of the same city by Amir Hamzah, cf. pp. 668–69.

43. Hamzah ibn Abu Muttalib, a companion or *sahabat* of the Prophet was killed in the battle of Uhud in 625 A.D.

44. In the *Proyek Penerbitan Buku Sastra Indonesia dan Daerah* edition of 1982 cf. *Ménak Jamintoran*, vol. 2, canto 24 down to the end of following volume, *Ménak Jaminambar*, where the heretical king Rabius Samawati (= Malay, Syamsul Alam) is subject to Amir Hamzah. For a resumé of this episode in the 1715 A.D. Kartasura *Ménak* cf. Vol. IX (Vreede resume (1982, pp. 59–60). Poerbatjaraka (1940, pp. 9–33) gives another resumé of all nine volumes of the 1715 A.D. manuscript. The even earlier Pasisir Ménak greatly influenced the *wayang léndong* or *wayang* Sasak in Lombok (Marrison 1999, p. 27).

45. Cf Marcel Detienne (1981; 1994). Cf. also Paul Ottino (1986, pp. 523–80) on the encounter of Malagachy and Indo-Muslim culture.

PART IV

COSMOLOGY, CONVERSION, AND COMMUNITY IN CENTRAL JAVANESE ISLAM TODAY

12

JIHAD IN JAVA
An Islamic Appropriation of Individualism

If the coherence of a representation resides in bringing together its elements in the order of their meaning, *jihad* in contemporary Java can be analysed as three successive processes. *Jihad* enables Javanese Muslims to: (1) reinvent Islam in Indonesia as the *umat* writ large;[1] (2) face down the secularizing state; and (3) confront the growth of individualism promoted by state-centred nationalism. Nevertheless, these *jihad* campaigns fail to convince many Javanese Muslims that they fully represent Islam. For the unconvinced, Islam is already that whole which allows Indonesians to think through all of Javanese society, and so by definition Islam peacefully cohabits with all that is "other" in Java.

Here is an example of the difficulties of thinking of Java as a whole.[2] The major conservative Javanese Muslim party, the Nahdlatul Ulama (NU) in its July 2002 congress in Jakarta (25–28 July 2002), defended suicide bombing as a legitimate weapon to defend Islam. But at the same time it moderated that stance, insisting that it was necessary to prepare students to face relativism in ways other than monolithic rejection of alien opinions: the study of the Koran and *hadith*, the study of Islamic jurisprudence (*fikh*). These two positions were not irreconcilable. Calls for *jihad* are barometers of storms concerning alterity in a socially disintegrating Java. To combat this disintegration, many Javanese Muslims perceive an advantage in coexisting with contemporary non-believers (*kafir*). The opposite strategy for dealing with this social fragmentation is *jihad*, which imagines Java as a seamless

Islamic whole and attempts to represent, to render present (*prae esse*), Islam as an exclusive totality, thus condemning the non-Islamic margins of Java.

What is the value of tolerance? In this less combative perspective, it appreciates the value of difference (*ikhtilāf*), used by some Muslims trying to create inclusive visions of their relation with other Javanese. Difference is thought of as an inherent dimension of society, consolidating their own community or *umat*. There is more to the Islamization of Javanese society than a militant communalism treating other religions as foreign to Javanese society. An Islamic current is trying to "civil"-ize the multi-confessional Javanese society through a religious encompassing. This is possible to the extent that all confess Allah, the standard word all Javanese use for God. Behind this tolerant approach, just as behind the concept of *jihad*, there lie two related questions: how is Javanese society composed; where can we gain a vision of the whole of Javanese society?

Any conception of totality in Java will have a decisive effect on the shape of the Muslim community. The stakes are high. Theologically speaking, it is the very existence of Allah that is the *sine qua non* of a conception of totality. Only the "perfect unity of Allah" permits one to conceive of an "all". Society is not a whole; the word "society" is itself a neologism. In Central Java the Muslims represent more than half the population, and in East and West Java even more, yet to be "the whole" is a morphological not a demographic reality. A small community can possess a holistic hierarchy of values, while a much larger one may lack it. Java presents three competing sociological visions of itself: (1) a holistic village-based society; (2) Islamic *umat*-based community of believers; and (3) a nation-state. Beatty has shown (2002) that a certain relativism permits the ambient hierarchy of values to validate the claims of these three visions to be "true", almost simultaneously.

1. The village communities traditionally were based on local residence in the same bounded space, and cults of local village spirits. In the past this vision ranked values and people internally and allotted social space to outsiders moving into the village. In a word the village territory was the landscape of belief. By the beginning of the twenty-first century often only 10 per cent of the villagers owned any agricultural land. The post-1997 economic crisis has thrown the great percentage of these villages into subsistence labour in the informal sector, while the opportunities for migration out of the village to find temporary employment elsewhere have dried up.

2. In the Muslim community, the limits of the *umat* are not territorial. Neither the social space of the local mosques, nor that of the rural

Koranic schools (*pesantrèn*), are territorially bound. The *pesantrèn* recruit from many regions, near and far, and thus present a horizon of universality based on a common faith.[3] The social styles of the mosques and these *pesantrèn* are very well integrated into Javanese life, in contrast to the more "modern" Catholic parishes (*kapastoran*) that physically resemble those in Holland. They are centred on the authority of the priest and occupy large well-equipped parish compounds.

3. The nation-state claims the "imagined community" of the entire archipelago as its territory.[4] In this sense it is a universal community just like the traditional village. The current move to include the word "Islam" in Article 29 of the 1945 Constitution was recently opposed by the July 2002 Nahdlatul Ulama Congress who protest that it is sufficient to say that the state is based on one God in order to apply Islamic teachings in a "secular" state. Nominally this clause defends freedom of religion in Indonesia, but ideologically the universal monotheism, creates a vision of society as a whole, for the monadic alterity of Allah is its own hierarchy, relegating the multiplicity of the created world is a lower level. The real problems lie elsewhere. As Munir (head of the Advisory Board Commission for Missing Persons and Victims of Violence, or KONTRAS) wrote recently,[5] the real challenge posed by integration into the unitary state of the Republic (of Indonesia) is that, "… there is no space for the issue of human security. For the sake of national unity, humans are not important; absolute power and control is more acceptable."

In this chapter and again in Chapter 14, we will try to see how the contemporary resistance to communalistic violence and the promotion of tolerance has taken the Javanese vision of society as a whole for its starting point. These moral combats reveal significant sociological resources, which thirty years of the Soeharto dictatorship (1966–98) had forced the Javanese to ignore.

12.1 THE FRAGMENTATION OF THE JAVANESE MUSLIM COMMUNITY

One cannot describe a society[6] such as Java in terms of "modernity"; the use of binary categories, like nature and culture, private and public, facts and values, is not appropriate. These categories fit western European societies with developed individualistic ideology. Even if Java has been described in post-modernist terms (Pemberton 1994), it is more a post-traditional society whose traditions refuse to disappear. In Javanese society the ways persons relate form patterns of sense, institutions of meaning, that are inherited from generation to generation and reproduced in quasi-institutional norms. The insular *society* of the Javanese is not only a matter of geography. Their shared social space partially structured by a common hierarchy of traditional values, contains systemic regional variations. In Central Java this "whole" embraces a higher order than the separate norms that go to make it up. These norms are not evaluated by Javanese individually in a quest for authenticity; they are accepted implicitly; one grows up with them. There is still an unspoken but strong sense of custom (*adat*). Javanese are simply not asocial enough to justify discarding the notion of social fabric as Pemberton has suggested; they are more tribe than crowd. To describe a Javanese outside of his social milieu is to forsake any description of his context and level of insertion in a totality which gives meaning to it. To simply add up the imagined communities which go to make up Javanese "society"[7] is to try to look at Java through a shattered mirror. Certainly individual Javanese have their own strategies for constructing a life for themselves; but when these fail or are postponed, they are still very much part of a network that gives a sense to their lives.

There is a non-Javanese Java. Millions of Madurese or Sundanese, who do not speak Javanese as their mother tongue, live on this small island. Inter-ethnic relations between them and the Javanese are an ever present dimension, in both urban and to some extent rural milieus. Madurese and Sundanese tend to be Muslim, but are separated from one another by Central Java. Divisions due to religious pluralism do appear among reforming Muslims of the various Neo-Wahabi persuasions when they are confronted with subaltern varieties of Islam, but never to the extent "provoked" by Chinese or Javanese Christians, who are a unique case. Like Muslim monotheists, Christians refer to a universe created by a *monothéos*, but when they refuse the status of prophet to Muhammad, to which cosmos do they refer? To break the line of prophets in Islam is equivalent to breaking apostolic succession in the Catholic Church. The ontological leap from creatures to their creator (Allah) without any intermediaries as is proposed by Islam suspends any accommodation of the stranger, the non-Muslim, on the immediate personal recognition of the Almighty's *rahmat* (mercy).

Currently (1996–2002), political manipulations have produced conflict between these two communities of monotheists. Christian-Muslim dialogue (LiKIS, and DIAN/Interfidei in Yogyakarta; Forum Suara Hati Kebersamaan Bangsa, or FSHKB, in Surakarta, etc.) attempts to limit the damage and propose another approach to this pluralistic society. To control instances of Muslim violence against Christians (church burning and bombings during services), these forums emphasize the common ground of adherence to the norms of mutual respect and tolerance that these monotheisms require. This is more than common sense moralization. There is a real effort to recapture the Javanese sense of society and its cosmic wholeness. Urban *kampungs* are territorially based communities; there one finds Muslims and Christians sharing the same yards. The status and morphology of these communities' insertion into the larger Javanese society is, however, the subject of much tension. Are non-Muslims heathens to be excluded in such an individualistic vision of Javanese society? Contemporary *jihad* against Christians inverts the earlier (eighteenth to twentieth century) social encompassment of Muslims and non-Muslims. The fact that most Javanese Muslims do not agree with such *jihad* gives us a unique opportunity to observe their understanding of their society its morphology.

In a traditional society, inhabitants subscribe to norms which direct the flow of their collective lives.[8] Custom is less an institution than a way of making social (not private) sense out of relationships and articulating them. Such is the case in Java where one finds attempts to incorporate the unusual, the foreign and the unknown,[9] making them ordinary, usual and common (*biyasa, lumrah, umum*) which has very positive connotations. Thus society can be described holistically since the norm, the *adat* (custom) in Indonesian, is recognized by all and adhered to by many. The non-normative feels very uncomfortable in Javanese society. Adopting the stranger means evaluating real life situations in terms of the value of the harmonious whole and hence articulating it within a hierarchy which functions by inclusion. It is this very Javanese vision of "society" that is sometimes attacked by Muslims. From an Islamic point of view, traditional Javanese custom offers no salvation, but for the moderate Muslim Javanese it permits society to be in harmony with the cosmos and its constituent members. It functions as a social net of very broad spectrum. It is no small achievement to permit Javanese to live together in mutual respect and tolerance. Are these goals possible in an increasingly individualistic Javanese society based on contract, lacking a cultural determinism like *adat* (custom)? What is the value of still being able to envisage the nature of the society as a socio-cosmological whole? In other words, if Islam is becoming individualistic, can its community (*umat*) really create the social harmony (*rukun*) its pretends to?

There is more to Javanese society than just Islam, and this "more" despite being old is resilient. Since the Javanese conception of society at large is not identical with the Muslim community or *umat*, the place of the Muslim community (*umat*) in Javanese society needs to be defined before any attempt at its description can be undertaken. To have a common horizon of transcendence is implicitly to share a common cosmology. Do Javanese

Muslims still describe themselves as being a community or *umat* when sharing social space with non-Muslims? If so, where is the totality?

If, on the other hand the Javanese *umat* is not a community, is it then a "transposable landscape of belief", i.e., no community at all, since many different ethnic groups in Indonesia are Muslims and have accommodated Islam to their customs (*adat*) and vice versa? One of the main ideological tasks of the nascent Indonesian anti-colonial movements was to project a vision through the motto of an imagined independent Indonesia as a society where all ethnic groups were "different (yet) one; separate (yet) united" (*bhinneka tunggal ika*).

Since the main task of the twentieth century was nation-building, it is not surprising that Javanese society is no longer a well-integrated, holistic one, but it is certainly not yet one that is animated only by the values of individualism.[10] The open holism that Marcel Mauss envisaged can be employed here. I suggest four levels and contexts which need to be distinguished to describe the morphology of the Javanese Muslim community:

- the Southeast Asian context of Javanese Islam;
- the incorporation of Islam into a pre-existing Javanese cosmology;
- the role of an emerging Javanese individualism in the anti-colonial, nationalism movements' treatment of inter-island ethnicity as different yet equal; and
- the changing morphology of the Javanese Muslim community or *umat* under the influence of political parties.

Javanese sociology starts from the village (*dhusun*), and from its indigenous Austronesian notion of inhabited space (*wanua*). Despite the increasing deterritorialization of Javanese villages — where very few villagers actually own any arable land — they are still the benchmark of any other form of society. In the village sociology, a territory that is not animated by kinship, by ancestral graves and local offering grounds (*pepundhèn*) for local deities, no matter how lossely, is either neutral (*tawar*) or empty (*suwung*). In villages one finds the locus of the traditional generalized normative structure (*adat*), incarnate in this its lowest common sociological denominator: networks of families interacting in a village. Even in communities as marginalized as those of landless squatters occupying strips of land on the edge of urban roads (cf. Ch. 14), these notions of custom (*adat*) survive and animate their struggle to justify their right to land.[11]

The relations between neighbours (*tatangga*), with diverse religious affiliations and economic statuses, have always and are everywhere taken as the unit of commensality in which ritualized harmony needs to be created.

Cosmic social embeddedness is expressed in sharing ritual food, and harmony is woven from diverse formal institutional religious adherences. Thus the Muslim *umat* is only one kind of community in the larger society. Not surprisingly then, the mosque of the Muslim community is rarely the social centre of this inhabited space in Java. Despite increasingly serious consciousness in the prayer life of the *umat*, the worshipping community is only one among others village ritual and commensality centres.

History tells us the *umat* has been refounded on several occasions.[12] The most serious challenge to date has come from the nation-state (post-1949). The Pancasila state ideology reduced Islam to one of the five expressions of "monotheism". Each foundational crisis in the last fifty years of Indonesian political life has had to do with the place of Islam, i.e., its inability to represent the whole of society and its discomforture at being reduced to the status of just one among several communities, despite its obvious numerical superiority. Below, Javanese material from the months following the al-Qaeda attack on the World Trade Centre in New York City shows how communalism was treated by Muslims who stood for social wholeness and tolerance. The

FIGURE 12.1
Director of El Mukmin (Ngruki) Foundation praying (fourth from left)
at an inter-religious forum (RUU Kerukunan Umat Beragama) at the
Pondok Pesantren Al-Muayyad Windan, Surakarta, on 9 September 2003.
Kyai Haji Dian Nafi is behind the microphone.

stranger, the non-Muslim, in these visions is to be displaced. The experience of others leaves a trace in the image projected of Java that does not accord with that of *jihad*. We will try to relate these two different approaches to the notion of community (*umat*).

12.2 A MUSLIM COMMUNITY'S STRUGGLE (*JIHAD*) WITH DIFFERENCE (*IKHTILAF*)

What is *jihad*? The initial and most important meaning of *jihad* is to be found in the Meccan chapters (*sura'*) of the Koran. There it means an effort to contain one's passions (i.e. directed towards oneself), the so-called *jihad 'ala nafs*. The word appears twenty-five times in the Koran but not always with the same connotations so that over time its meaning has been understood differently according to context. For example, in the branch of Islam represented by Sūfism, the meaning of ascetical struggle with oneself has remained primordial. Perfection is a struggle (*mujāhada*), an interior combat (the "great *jihad*") to be conducted under the guidance of a *shayykh* or spiritual director (*murshid*). By exercises of contemplation (*fikr*), prayer, *dhikir* (repetitive invocations), and examination of conscience,[13] this struggle was conducted against one's evil tendencies. And in chapter 29 of the Koran, the Ant (*al-Ankabut,* 29:6), "Whoever struggles, struggles only to his own gain; surely God is All-sufficient nor needs any being." This is a solitary struggle, unlikely to be attractive to the power hungry.

If the great struggle (*al-jihad al-akbar*) is against one's own defects, it is waged most especially during the month of Ramadan. Altogether different is the aggression towards non-believers (*kafir*) and eventually their forced conversion in a combat called *al-jihad al-asghar*. For instance in a later *sura'*, *Repentance*, from Medina, where the word appears nine times (more than any other *sura'* in the Koran), *jihad* is identified with a holy war. There one reads (9:36) "That is the right religion .... And fight the unbelievers totally, even as they fight you totally; and know that God is with the God-fearing." In the twenty-fifth sura' entitled Salvation (*al-Furqan*), one reads (verse 50[14]): "… so obey not unbelievers, but struggle with them thereby mightily." After the *hédjra* (flight in the year O (CE 622) of Muhammad to Médina) the importance of war against polytheism and its supporters (the tribes in Mecca and elsewhere) gained ground. Such fighters for Allah (*moujahidin*) may become martyrs (*chahid*; plural *chouhada*). These martyrs are described in the Koran (9:111 and 113) as follows:

> God has bought from the believers their selves
> And their possessions against the gift of Paradise

They fight in the way of God; they kill and are
killed; that is a promise binding upon God
in the Torah, and the Gospel, and the Koran;
and who fulfils his covenant truer than God?
It is not for the Prophet and the believers
To ask for pardon for the idolaters, after that it
Has become clear to them that they will be the inhabitants
of Hell.

These two associations of the word for effort (*jihad*),[15] the ascetical one and the combative one, are articulated by the notion of two abodes or lands. Inside the territory of Islam (*dar al-Islam* or *dar as-soulh*) is a territory of peace. The atheist, the polytheist, or the evil doer should be chased away, but no violence against a Muslim is tolerated. After Muhammad's death, the territory of war (*dar al-harb*) coincides with the frontiers, with the borders for Muslim society's potential expansion, making the "struggle" a divine institution (*al-qayrawani*). This leads el-Bokhari (an early collector of the *hadīths*) to say, "Paradise lies in the shadow of the sword." The key to the problem is the nature of authority: who can lead these movements. The *shari'a* legislates answers which are blatantly ignored by any well-financed militia. Let us return now to a historical and sociological perspective, since no presentation of jihad and the incorporation of strangers into an Muslim society can be complete without a discussion of secularization.

Has the modernist democratic promise proved to be a mirage for the majority of the world's population? Instead of seeing the WTC collapse in this light, the media reports on terrorism that have circulated since 11 September 2001 have massively propounded the secular creed that only private expressions of religion can create the conditions of tolerance. Religion when it enters the public, and above all the political, sphere is said to create social tensions and violence. But so does an independent secular ethos, as one sees with the contemporary "liberalism" allowing the free capital ebb and flow throughout the globe.

Certain Westerners reading the history of Islamic and Christian relations come to the conclusion that Islam is a social and political organization with a religious cover (Bat Yé'or 1996). While it is true that Islamist political parties sometimes seek to enflame the intolerance latent in these religious cleavages, the irony of the increased *Western* intolerance of religion expressed in the public sphere is that "we" fail to see that Western individualism is of such ambiguous ethical stuff that it no longer produces any public ethos, religious, or otherwise. It is heresy in Europe to suggest that perhaps countries with a strong public ethos, be it religious or ethnic, are in a better position than those of the West. Many countries in Europe have had to strengthen their "civics" courses in high schools because the students were learning little at home that would enable them to participate in, let alone work to build up, a civil society. The individualistic ideological foundations of Hobbes' philosophy of civil society (Milbank 1990) are not explored as the outcome of a social evolution comprising an ever-increasing indifference to communitarian bonds. The religious response to this is to say that only the person, not the individual, could really respond to a relational crisis. But the Christian vision and experience of personhood brought onto the social stage during the Middle Ages, has faded away in Europe (M. Gauchet 1985). Muslim intellectuals around the world have remarked on this disenchantment.

This is not the place to attempt to prove these claims historically, but Muslim intellectuals generally and non-Arab Indonesian *ulama* in particular, schematize Western history using the standard (i.e. Troeltsch's) secularization theory. A stenographic version runs something like this. Secularization originated when political economy and hence philosophy, first of all in Western Europe, and then elsewhere, found it expedient to marginalize the creator of society, God, who until then in fact had been indispensable to conceiving a total social order inside of which the occurrence of alterity could be accommodated. Once the state has taken God's place and conceptualizes the nation-state as a pseudo-whole, the hierarchy of values previously drawn from the Christian ethos fades, and this *anomie* favours the growth of an ideology of individual evaluation indifferent to *any* hierarchy of values. The only clear values that remain are economic ones. Once the Western papo-caesarist church was neutralized and communitarian parish links were weakened, the state could further pursue in its own interests through taxation authorized by representative government.

The creation of the Indonesian nation-state took place in a very different post-colonial context. Sukarno's vision of the place of the nationalist ideology of *pancasila* in the formulation of the Indonesian state,[16] gave the unity of men and place priority over any *désir d'être ensemble* (E. Renan). For Soekarno speaking on 1 June 1945, the nation was to be dominated by mutual co-operation (*gotong-royong*), a very idealized reciprocity that guaranteed freedom of religion through representative government. The fact that Soekarno had been able to speak the language of the people while using such basically imported foreign concepts shows that the medium was the message and that these five principles (*pancasila*) would be applied in a Javanese social morality. This morality continues to be propounded in many Christian, Muslim, and purely Javanese forms.[17]

Scott Thomas wrote in the *Tablet* (6 October 2001):

Taking religion and culture seriously means recognising that the cosmopolitan values of Western liberalism, rooted in the European Enlightenment, may no longer provide an adequate basis for what is becoming a genuinely multicultural international society for the first time in history. Can the West and Islam live together, and if so, how? This will not be possible if the West expects Muslims to exchange the beliefs, practices, and traditions which are constitutive of Islamic communities for those of Western liberalism, which appears to be what many people in the West expect.[18]

In that non-Arabic periphery where the majority of the world's Muslims are found, the political calls for *jihad* against the worldwide economic empire led by American interests, reproduce a variant of an individualizing, social evolution idealizing reinvented communities that Europe experienced under the guidance of the ideology of state governance over the last three centuries.[19] This seems to be something that Islam is allowing to happen to itself.

There is resistance, however. An example is the well-known Javanese Muslim, A. Mustofa Bisri, the director of the Raudlatut Thalibin Islamic boarding school in Rembang (Central Java). In an opinion column of the Jakarta weekly magazine *Tempo* (6–12 November 2001) he presented an article entitled "America, Terrorism and Islam". The first page of his argument is devoted to his understanding of the anti-imperialist cause. But Mustofa Bisri goes on to say that the attack on the WTC and the attack on Afghanistan are equally cruel and equally unjust. Why implicate religion in issues of one's own making, he asks? Both protagonists, Al-Qaeda and the United States, are defending their own political interest and not any religious cause. Islam, he claims, is exceedingly clear: it totally renounces injustice and ruthlessness in the act of upholding justice and truth. This means that one should help the unjust and the cruel to cease to be so. Their destiny is in God's hands, not ours. Do Mustofa Bisri's references to Allah's benevolence suffice to give the Muslim community a vision of society at large?

12.3 "*JIHAD* IS THE SOLUTION"[20]

In the third week of October in front of the great mosque of Al-Azhar in Cairo, demonstrators trooped by with banners proclaiming "Jihad is the Solution!". This is Islam as a language of dissent, commented the *New York Times* (Douglas Jehl, 20 October 2001). It is also the language of the tens of millions of Muslims bitterly disillusioned by the promises of "modernity". To economic rationalists, the social engineers of development, the word "solution" sounds like rhetorical overkill given the complexity and intractability of the social problems involved. There certainly is a thick layer of semiotics in this apparently simple affirmation. The exaggeration derives from the desire to avoid taking into consideration other issues. There is also the implication that in a perfect world, fully Muslim, this would be true. Verisimilitude is sacrificed to a categorical assertion of a transformation. Why is it all that simple? Why are the demonstrators "moving the goal posts on modernity"?

Rather, we should ask, why can we not see where their frustrations lie? What has generally been the experience of being a Muslim in the modern world? One important frustration derives from the fact that in a tolerant milieu, the community of believers is hard to mobilize.[21] The renaissance (*al-Nahda*) of the *umma* has been a long time coming. To oversimplify, the history of these last two hundred years of Islam is one of spiritual renewal directed at this passive centre and militant action directed at the borders. The capacity of the centrifugal actions to galvanize the centre is best illustrated by the Wahabite nineteenth century consolidation of Saudi Arabia.[22]

In Java there are submerged, constructive voices, appealing to the vision of a complete society which have been ignored by the commercial media. Violence sells, as long as you don't have to live in its aftermath.[23] In the aftermath of 11 September 2001 in the Indonesian archipelago, the young Muslims of the Bureau for the Study of Islam and Society in Central Java (LKiS) distributed their broadsheet *al-Ikhtilaf*, The Difference, in mosques serving some twenty million Muslims in Central Java every Friday morning. Three days after the terrorist attacks, the edition of 14 September was entitled "From individual piety toward social devotion", that of 19 October "*Shalat*[24] an effort to restrain oneself from the desire to go on the rampage", and the edition of 26 October, "The feeling of humanity, torn apart". Behind the choice of topics and headlines, one can feel the frustration mounting. Each issue expresses need for peace and tolerance based on a vision of the whole of Javanese society. Their work was not reported by the media, local or international.

Sometimes small anecdotes of daily life form a pretext to re-evaluate the Javanese mentality. In the issue of *al-Ikhtilaf*, of 15 September 2001 — a year before Al-Qaeda attacks — an article was entitled "To expose the prejudices between communities of believers". Wening Tandas Ati recalled a middle-aged woman who said to him, after a Javanese forgiveness (*silaturrahmi*) meeting[25] in the town of Parakan:

> "Sir, you're a Muslim aren't you? How is it that you have such a feeling of love. What moved you to become like this?" I was stunned by this question. What I understood was that a Muslim cannot possess a feeling of love. If I speak about attention to, receiving and respecting difference (*al-ikhtilaf*)

this lady finds it strange that the person speaking in this way is a Muslim. As a Muslim who has inherited the *hadīth* (saying of the Prophet reported only by oral tradition) stating that it is not enough to believe, if one doesn't not love one's brother as oneself, I was quite wounded by her question. But seeing the woman's innocence, I began to reflect. This mother had probably had an ugly experience of living with Muslims. As a follower of the Catholic religion, she may often have been marginalized and ostracized by her neighbours. Most likely she was mocked and condemned for practising (her) religious practices that fulfil a call from God. And the Muslims who acted arbitrarily towards her would not have felt that there was anything wrong in what they did.

This is where the real drama of Islam's treatment of "alterity" (i.e., non-Muslims) is being played out. Does the model of the Muslim believer whose sense of *umat* leads him to assign a status to the non-believer lead to a greater unity of Javanese society or not? The international press is speaking at a level of indifference towards that religion where their own agnosticism is never put into question by any local Muslim hierarchy of human values. Or as Bernard Lewis[26] wrote almost twenty years ago, for the "developed" West, to categorize oneself by one's religion adherence is already a reflection of one's backwardness. Thus Salman Rushdie in a recent op-ed (*New York Times*, 2 November 2001) discussing the hijacking of Islam by obscurantists, emphasizes that Muslims themselves are calling for a reformation of Islam. He interprets this as reflecting the need for an evolution towards private personal expression of their faith. By personal he means de-politicized, which can *only* (*sicut* Rushdie) be accomplished by adopting the secularist-humanist foundations of modernity. Since Muslims have suffered most from this kind of violence, many recognize that Islam has become its own enemy and that terrorism is a disease within it. But it is not common amongst Muslims to find someone who wants to abandon the public sphere to secular humanism. On the contrary Islamic reform movements in Indonesia want to take the public sphere out of the hands of the oligarchic political parties whose greed and ambitions have created such an uncivil society. Reduced to its basic concepts, religion deals with the status of "alterity" in a divinely organized society that is the *topos* of all relations. Therefore religion is public or else it ceases to exist as anything other than a private fantasy.[27]

12.4 WHAT IS A MUSLIM COMMUNITY (*UMAT*[28])?

L. Gardet says (1954, p. 194) that in Islam, *everything is given as a whole*. But then one must ask "Whose whole?". What does it mean to speak of "a whole", especially in terms of a *jihad*, for to speak of a *jihad* is a metaphorical procedure designed to reinforce or persuade all to follow this horizon of transcendence. One is not yet at war; it is as though one was at war. This register of metaphor belongs as well to verification as to falsification. *Jihad* is encouraging to Muslims who, as Gunawan Muhammad said recently (A.A.S. Roundtable; Washington, D.C., 15 April 2002), suffer from the "anxiety of decentering". It cannot rhetorically guarantee the unicity of the praxis of only one religion, but it does mean that all of human society may be viewed as becoming Islamic. The coherence of the faithful is a given, a function of its sobriety in the five daily prayers (*salat*). This seemingly simple observation is pertinent, for by its very nature Islam is both a religion and a community which *qua* grouping fixes the conditions and rules of daily life. The solidarity of the community realizes its vocation of being a whole, in the image of Allah's oneness. There is little place for gradual, progressive realization of God's law on earth. If on the one hand this guarantees the integrity of the praxis of the religion, analysed as dogma, the simplicity of Muslim monotheism is such that it lends itself to be taken for granted intellectually and, where it lacks a real ascetical depth, is quickly converted into an ideological package.[29]

Ideally Islam tends towards a cosmos-free theocracy, completely Allah-centric, without any ecclesiastical organization, where no member has any spiritual power over another. Loosely structured leadership implies a strong notion of authority often located in charismatic individuals. This being so, its pure Islamic traditions and customs are also consolidated in the community by their bond of unity which is an uncreated and eternal one, namely the word of Allah, in the Koran. It is in this context and by such a yardstick, that one should try to evaluate the calls for a *jihad* which the extremist groups have been brandying about in the streets of Java's main cities since mid-September 2001. The question that we will try to answer here is the following: in Java why and when does the solidarity of the community of the faithful translate into a *jihad* against the *kafir* or infidel?

Here is a typical discussion of the danger of Islam's place in the Indonesian political arena. In a dialogue with the journalist A. Thonthowi Djauhari that appear in *Tekad*,[30] the well-known historian of Indonesian Islam, Azyumardi Azra (dean, IAIN Syarif Hidayatullah, Jakarta) expressed his fear that the multiplication of Indonesian political parties (currently some ten besides the two main Islamic movements, Nahdlatul Ulama and Muhammadiyah), will make of the community of believers nothing more than the foam on the waves of the ocean of these political manoeuvres. Azyumardi Azra stresses (2000, p. 61) that, if the objective of political parties is only the acquiring of power, then it can only harm the solidarity and authority of the community, the *umat* of the faithful.[31] The élite politicians' horse trading mentality[32] destroys the capacity of the *umat* to represent the wholeness of the community of Islam. Even at the highest level of governance, the president of the republic is hamstrung by this political bargaining. The downfall of Abdurrahman Wahid, who was sincerely committed to the promotion of a civil society, *inter alia*, illustrates this. Political manoeuvring wastes the authority of the *umat*. What is more, the instability created by these Muslim political parties renews the question of whether the *umat* should be politically represented at all.[33] Since the Darul Islam revolt of the 1950s,[34] this has been the Indonesian military's point of view and the pretext for their eventual intervention into civilian life. The solidarity of the *umat* has already been weakened by such fighting for "power" in the name of their political parties who, using strategies for accumulating identity by claiming to be Islamic, are really destroying the Muslim faithful's community fabric. In brief, Islam is being marginalized. This debate first emerged in Indonesia in 1970–71 when Nurcholish Madjid[35] condemned the ideal of a Muslim state as idolatry. One must "secularize" the political in order to preserve the *tauhid* (unity of Allah) in which the *umat* finds its coherence; otherwise social solidarity (*ukhuwwah Islāmiyyah*) is weakened by the manoeuvres of parasitical politicians. What solidarity is can be answered once we know where the totality is situated.

In order to grasp what kind of group Muslims constitute, one has to separate out the behaviour, the sociology of this group (if it is a group), from the ideas of those who claim to be able to describe it in the name of Islam. A Java-based militia, the Laskar Jihad[36] (the soldiers of the Struggle), has recently cowed many provincial governments in Indonesia.[37] This well-funded militia of fanatic Muslims was founded by Ja'far Umar Thalib, after his return from Afghanistan in 1999. Their website <Laskar.Jihad.or.id> reflects a preoccupation with propaganda and publicity. But they are also capable of operations of massive provocation resulting in thousands of deaths, for instance in Ambon. As others in Bosnia and Kosovo have done, their strategy is to create Christian–Muslim hatred. One instance was the anti-Christian riots organized by outsiders (i.e. non-Sasak) that broke out in 1999 in the capital of the island of Lombok, Mataram. The results were not only the destruction of Christian Churches, but the devastation of the tourist industry for a full year. The economic consequences were of course borne by the local population. In late September of that year, when Ja'far Umar Thalib returned to Mataram (Lombok) to organize anti-American protests, he was met in his hotel rooms by Hadi Faishal (director of the local development organization and son of a Muslim *adat* leader[38]). Together with some friends, they explained to him that violence was not going to be tolerated a second time round. They then escorted the Laskar Jihad leader back to the port and sent him away. To make sure that he would not return on 15 October 2001, they organized some five hundred Muslims leaders in a conference with the theme "Non-violence and religious tolerance". The tourism industry and Muslim non-violence founded an unusual alliance here. What is the structure of the Muslim community that permits it to resist violence in certain instances and participate in it in others?

It is not enough to say that Islam is an egalitarian theocracy; one needs to specify the nature of the communitarian religious bond in Islam, how it excludes and how it includes non-believers. Gardet (1981, p. 195) claims that their common good and the bond of unity is the Koran, described as a miracle in itself, because Mohammed recited it word by word under the dictation of the archangel Gabriel. The great hope of the Puritan reformers of Islam has always been the unification of Islam around the Koran and its commentary. The "people of the *qibla* (direction for praying)" from the very beginning of Islam formed a worshipping community (*jamā'a*). Personal error is effaced by a common accord (*ijmā'*); in this sense the community or *umma* is a state of law or *hukm*. Muslims have great confidence this divinely inspired society of law. It gives them what Gardet calls a dignity and calm pride. This may well be so but the focus seems to be on those who confess the faith to the exclusion not only of those who do not or who do not yet. In the *umat* one needs to include those (ancestors) who already confessed the faith and to exclude those who never did. Territorially-based communities like the Javanese village seem resistant to such separation on the basis of the confession of a given faith and prefer the homogenization of all its members to a single status, more ancestors (*leluhur*) than souls (*arwah*).

To put it another way, the immediate jump from creatures to their creator without any intermediaries is such an accommodation of the stranger that it is impossible on any other basis than an immediate personal recognition of the Almighty's *rahmat* (mercy). All men belong to this Muslim community thanks to a pre-eternal covenant (*mīthāq*). While the pillars of Islam are personal and individual (the creed (*shahāda*), prayer, alms, fasting and pilgrimage), there is one *collective* duty, the "effort (*jihad*) to spread the right[39] (*huqūq*)" of Allah to the ends of the earth. Such a conception of the unity of the community does not permit secession. An apostate is to be put to death. The severity of the traditional conception of this *umma* is not fanaticism, says Gardet (1981, p. 202), but simply the spiritual and temporal expression of its cohesion. Originally for Islam the world was divided only into the house of Islam (*dār al-Islām*) and the world of war (*dār al-harb*). The approach of the former to the latter is that of the *jihad* which in periods of religious reform usually takes on a missionary character.

What is the place of the individual in this community? His dignity derives from the fact that Allah placed him there. By belonging to the *umma* he acquires a very existential dignity, expressed by a living sense of fraternity. This is a community (*umat*), not a communion. While Islam requires outward conformity to its law, it does not judge inward adherence (Gardet 1981, p. 205). It recognizes that the believer must have correct intentions (*niyya*). So if man exists only through his community (*umat*) he nonetheless presents himself alone before his Maker. Intercession or mediation on another's behalf, as it is stressed by the Sufis, cannot replace individual private action. While the *umat* is man's sole spiritual community, as a society the *umat* remains outside of man. This is not to say that Islam shares the German distinction between society and community. Nowadays Islam is confronted with two other conceptions of man's social settings: modern individualism for which the absence of any distinction between person and individual leads towards democratic ideologies; and a materialist individualism where the earthly city is the only possible objective of all social communities. Because Islam does not distinguish between the temporal and the spiritual (Gardet 1981, pp. 297–98), these distinctions are irrelevant. Muslim individuals feed off the community, irrespective of its concept of alterity (believer/non-believer). The *umat* does not transcend earthly cities, but unifies them. Historically, unification in the Middle East has involved a lower public status for Jews, Armenians, and Orthodox Christians. The fact that armed *jihad* led to an ascribed status of servitude for other monotheists in conquered lands makes the religious, commercial, and political protection provided for the subject populations pale in comparison to the combination of oppression and gratitude they were forced to accept.[40]

The Muslim community thus presents itself as a universalism: believers are brothers. The coat of arms of Islam is the social character of religious duties, although unlike the Jewish law of Leviticus and Deuteronomy, larger sectors of life go unqualified. As Gardet says (1981, p. 232) underneath the rigidity of the forms there is a whole world of suppleness and imprecision. Mutual help, interdependence, and solidarity are important dimensions of daily life and a Muslim "is encouraged to identify his personal drama with the primordial care and defence of the interests of the community". This is not the practice of fraternal love in the Christian sense, but rather "mutual understanding and faithfulness guaranteed by the promises of God" (Gardet 1981, p. 239). While the predominance of social relations and a collective mentality over the individual is real, individualism is expressed as a certain scepticism and suspicion of one another. This value of individualism however is subverted when confronted by a foreigner; one closes ranks for the offensive moments of *jihad* and *da'wa* (missionary endeavour). The desire to live independent of foreign influence is very deep even where the adoption to modern technology is accepted. It is obvious that after the First World War with the collapse of the Ottoman Empire a painful awakening occurred which neither the sombre Puritanism sponsored by Saudi Arabia nor the orthodox reformers like the Muslim Brotherhood were able to assuage in the course of the twentieth century. Muslims are still looking for a vision to organize their common life. The shared values which construct this common lifestyle are their most natural defence against individualism, ethnic nationalism and the sense of belonging to a given social class. While a country like Turkey may have progressively become more and more laicized, the latent values of the *umma* resemble so many norms that determine the real daily behaviour of people (Gardet 1981, p. 266). But in Java...?

12.5 THE *UMAT* BEHIND THE *JIHADS* IN JAVA

To ask how Javanese Islam incorporates "strangers", notably non-Muslims, requires discussing not only its appropriation of modern pluralism in a given cultural setting, but also the multi-culturalism of insular differences, that which characterizes the Islam of the archipelago. Between Javanese Islam and that Islam practised by the other ethnic-linguistic groups on Java and the other islands of this archipelago, there are indeed differences, but not of the kind that today would fragment the Muslim community along ethno-linguistic lines. Islam in Indonesia has already responded to subaltern varieties of Muslim practice since the first coastal sultanate appeared in Sumatra (Samudra Pasai) in the late thirteenth century. The conditions of its own traditional sense of community regularly had to be renegotiated. That adoption and the adaptation of Muslim notion of identity, has already been achieved in Java; that the Javanese identified themselves as Muslims before they identified themselves as Javanese, sometime around the end of the eighteenth century (Ricklefs, forthcoming).

Orthodox Islam in Java for centuries has presented a certain kind of individual praxis (but not individualism), complementary to communitarian worship. The Persian Shiite, Sohravardi (eleventh century), said: "Read the Koran as if it was revealed only for you!". The Islam first encountered in Indonesia was aware of these currents favouring personal revelations. Many recent studies of the poetry of eighteenth and nineteenth century Javanese literature stress the ways in which these works restructure older Javanese culture in terms of a Muslim hierarchy of values: knowledge of Allah (*ma'rifa*), repentance (*tawba*), and abandonment to Allah (*tawakkul*); love of Allah (*mahabba*) and meeting with Allah (*wajd*).[41] The Islamization of the 1970s–1990s has, on the other hand, created a contrast between traditional rural conservatives and urban fundamentalists.

The undeniable renaissance of orthodox Islam in Java over the last quarter of a century is also partially a response to the challenges of Javanism. The decline of the Sufi brotherhoods, despite of a spate of popular books on this branch of Islam, has continued. The modernists, i.e., the Muhammadiyah movement, do not consider their fundamentalism to be Islamization, but the indigenization of a pure Islam (*pribumisasi Islam murni*).[42] The demographic reality of an Islamic "majority", poses major problems to religious pluralism. For instance, in the second half of the twentieth century, the issue of the prohibition by the Department of Religion of mixed marriages between Muslims and non-Muslims refuses to go away.[43] However traditional the "mix" of Islamic values and traditional Javanese culture, and the ethnic heterogeneity of the population in major cities on the island of Java, none of that changes the fact the Javanese Muslims have a bipolar adherence to Javanese society and a Muslim community. Visually the strongest image of this is the immense crowds that fill the squares in Javanese cities as the Ramadhan fast is broken early in the morning of *Lebaran* (*Idulfitri*). Indubitably this is the feast of feasts and the holy day of holy days for the immense variety of Javanese. This being so: (1) how is the hierarchy of values proper to the Muslim community mediated in such a society; (2) how does that society integrate communities of belief systems in a higher whole? The answers to these two questions elucidate the different kinds of calls for *jihad*.

Such a mediation does not take place in the streets, on the media stage with video cameras and satellite phones relaying the news of the latest demonstration where everyone, not only the news media, is paid to create an event. This is *jihad* as political manipulation by the political élite. These politicized media theatrics alienate the members of the *umma* from local communities who consider them menaces to daily living. Political scientists tell us that the "weak legitimacy of local regimes leaves the most essential themes of the social and political destiny hanging, creating a vacuum to be filled by populist politicians and extremist groups, by wars and civil wars".[44]

Is this true? Do weak regimes really make citizens more malleable in this sense? On the contrary, in the recent outbreaks of violence in Java (1997–2001) the typical reaction was one of downscaling to better protect inter-community tolerance (cf. Ch. 14). By this we understand that when local Javanese communities are threatened by insecurity they pull inwards their parameters of defence, creating communities on a smaller scale where the hierarchy of values remains the same, but endowed with greater control. The street demonstrations, these so-called appeals, often have little to do with piety or human rights; they are the effort on the part of politicians with a dwindling clientele to get attention in tomorrow's papers.

In Indonesia at least two phenomena are taking placing simultaneously, which explains why they are often confused. While in the last twenty years of Soeharto's regime (1980–98) a wave of re-Islamization, spearheaded by an outreach in preaching (*dakwah*; Arabic, *da'wah*), gathered steam, at the same time the *premanisme*[45] (gangsterism) that was used during elections by Soeharto, became under Habibie, Abdurrahman Wahid, and Megawati, a permanent feature of political life. What were initially very different movements stemming from the Middle East and the Egyptian Muslim Brotherhood inspired by Sayyid Qotb, the Pakistani Mawdoudi's Society for the Propagation of the Faith (Tablighi Jama'at) to the more ephemeral recent ones like the Hisbollah Front, the Laskar Jihad, the Front Pembela Islam, and all the militias of the Islamic political parties,[46] are not likely to affect the mentality of average Javanese Muslims who are busy scaling down the frontiers of their residential community to a size which they can reasonably expect to defend. This is only to say that it is in the village hamlets and the inner city *kampung* (villages), and not in the capital Jakarta, that the real evolutions we want to observe are taking place.

Generalizations about the *umat* are only possible when they correspond to a consensus stepping off from shared Muslim religious belief. In many Central Javanese towns the efforts of Nahdlatul Ulama leaders have aimed at creating a consensus among Muslims that tolerance towards Christians best reflects the meaning of Javanese society. In a country like Indonesia many of the best sociological observations of the country are to be found in weeklies, and the daily newspapers, before they are published as collections of short essays on society. In an article entitled the "Spirit of *Jihad* for Peace-making" (*Semangant Jihad untuk Perdamaian*),[47] Azyumardi Azra (2000, pp. 96–101) discusses the "universal values" of *jihad* which he translates as "exerting oneself". As seen above, this indeed is the basic meaning of the word. For Azyumardi, a Minangkabau from Sumatra teaching in Jakarta, the community of mankind (*umat manusia*) in all its pluralism can benefit from the mercy and divine grace that flows from Allah through Islam to all mankind. To practise *jihad* as war against non-aggressive Christians as in Ambon, for instance, is totally forbidden. It would only be permitted if the Muslims were attacked by the Christians and their government was unable to defend them. To Azyumardi's knowledge Christians have not perpetrated any such crusade, so the only Muslim *jihad* in Indonesia can be one for peace. While security is the province of the government and the military, social peace is everyone's responsibility. It first of all involves learning how to control one's own appetites, passions, and that for the benefit of mankind. In this article, Azyumardi having expressed his fear that the *umat* will become like the foam of the waves on the ocean, says that the unity of the *umat* can only be preserved by ascetic *jihad*. Then the *ulama* and *kyai* (Muslim leaders) will, as was in the case in Mataram (Lombok), come to the defence of social peace by chasing out the extremists. In a country as out of control as Indonesia this is not a vain hope; it is the only hope. This is the reason we need to take seriously what the grassroots Muslims in their mosques and *madrasah* think and say.

In the Malay world the charisma of governance[48] used to be *daulat*. This is a blessing the ruler receives from Allah that allows him to be "God's shadow on earth". Clearly this divine gift cannot be bestowed on the president of a secular government like that of the Republic of Indonesia. It can only be realized in the context of a society articulated by the ethos of the *umat*. This is what certain Muslim teachers in Indonesia have been striving for over the last century. But the fruits of decades of *dakwah* can be destroyed by the violence of the *jihad* militias. In Java an anti-terrorist, non-violent reform movement can only come from local *kampung*-centred Islam. The Indonesian Government has not, does not, and will not control its extremist groups for reasons of short-term political expediency.[49] Every one has the "right" to raise its own private militia. With the police as well as the judiciary in total disrepute, standard methods of control by governance have had to take a back seat to modes of consensus findings (*mujarrawah*). Yet the prospects of a civil society are not as bleak as one might suspect. Many Muslims comparing the experiences of Islamic regimes elsewhere realize that this utopia has been exhausted by the test of time and the negative records of these regimes (the bankruptcy of Sudan, the mollaharchy of Iran, and the fanaticism of Afghanistan, and abuse of human rights everywhere, etc.). The Southeast Asian cult of "Asiatic" values and the primacy of the community over the individual, propagated in Malaysia, has turned out to be a smokescreen for Mahathir's repressive regime. And despite all these reasons for discouragement, not many Islamic political thinkers look for the way forward through dissolving the Islamist ideology in favour of that of pure economic liberalism.

Following the failure of nationalism and economic development to fulfil their promises (1950–60) and after thirty years (1960–90) of "Islamism", the most sophisticated Muslim analysts[50] extrapolate from their disillusionment with the violence of *jihad* and the poor quality of governance of the regimes that have sponsored it, questions about the post-fundamentalist (salafist;[51] jihadist) future. The failure of the Islamist regimes produced lessons that were not lost on their populations. As Gilles Keppel (2000, p. 545) notes, the concrete modes of political socialization these regimes engendered have rendered useless the ideological precepts that they stood for.

The head of the Nahdlatul Ulama's research department, Ulil Abshar-Abdalla, who works for inter-faith dialogue and promotes pluralism, stated to the FEER (22 November 2001) that, "After the tragedy (of September 11), radical Islam is beginning to dominate public opinion." The élite may be uneasy, but closer to the grassroots; note that the jargon of the Muslim militias is often incomprehensible to the man in the street.[52] For example: the militias periodically request that foreigners in hotels in Yogyakarta or Surakarta leave these cities. There is no reason why the word for this "sweeping" (i.e., jargon for "emptying" foreigners from hotels), would mean anything in Indonesian (*menyapu*). This is the militia's newspaper "talk". When confronted *in situ* by a demonstration, what the man in the street does sometimes say is: "You don't represent me or Islam."[53] We need to understand what it means to such man to belong to a community. Unlike the militia's theatrics, such a person clearly has a hierarchy of values he is ready to defend, at least verbally. Paradoxically this is not the case with the militants. Their abusive calls for *jihad* reflect their marginal status, their "democratic deficit". On Friday, 16 November 2001, the day before Ramadan in the main streets of Surakarta (*Suara Merdéka*, 15 November 2001) there was another demonstration on motorcycles to demand the shutdown of all dens of sins (*kemaksiatan*) during Ramadan. The pleasure of getting together and riding around town with Muslim flags on the back of one's scooter is undeniable, even in the driving rain. The Front Pemuda Islam Surakarta provides an outlet for frustrations as the fasting period approaches. They go on to say that not only is America the source of pornography, gambling, and hard liquor, but it is also responsible for a plot to ruin Indonesia's economy. If the hotels are empty, one person added, this is due to the Americans' war (literally *gara-gara*) and not to the Laskar Jihad. Fixing blame is part of the motorcycle parade.

Abdel Wahab El-Affendi, in a recent essay "The 'Democratic Deficit' in the Muslim World"[54] has shown that despite massive research on the question, neither those identifying the deficit with unchanging cultural norms (i.e., E. Gellner 1995), nor those trying to identify resources in Islamic tradition that would support authoritarianism, can identify the reasons for the general democratic deficit in Muslim countries. It is important to remember here that it is a debate internal to Islam. As Abdurrahman Wahid has asked (Feillard 1995, p. 313), what Islam do the Javanese want? Normative content of the values is always problematic in cross-cultural contexts. But what in Java is the value of "civility" (*madani* from the word *medan* or public square). What is its analytical worth in a society where there is both more and less pluralism than, for instance, in Great Britain. The debate launched in the 1980s by Nurcholish Madjid and Abdurrahman Wahid about what it might means to create a Muslim version of a civil society is still very much alive, in spite of the corruption of much of the political élite and the severe depression of the economy.[55] There is growing awareness that there can be a Muslim civil society and that, if the terminology is new, the concept is an ancient one (cf. R. Hefner 2001, *passim*).

Of course, it poses the contrast between the urban and rural components of Javanese Islam, where the latter are usually viewed by the Muhammadiyah as practising an impure Islam influenced by the traditional socio-cosmological fit. The post-Soeharto decompression (and perhaps abolition) of the Ministry of Religion's component of Islamization by presidential decree, allows everyone to think more clearly. But the bureaucratization of Islam, where the cadres are just petty bureaucrats teaching Islam for a living, will not go away so soon, nor will the Indonesian military's suspicion and brutal exploitation of religious cleavage be removed for another generation. And if there is to be an *umat*, a younger generation inevitably will not copy the New Order model, but will learn from the current disintegration and the violence that it has accompanied. The foundation of their evaluation of Java will be Javanese Islam taken as a whole, for that is the horizon of harmony. After all it was in large part the renaissance of Islam that brought down Soeharto in 1998. The next *jihad* may not be so naïve about where the real solutions lie.

More questions have been asked than answered by our approach, but we have seen how issues of tolerance and resistance to violence, alive and well in this part of the Muslim world, are obliged to engage the traditional notion that the Javanese held of their society as a totality. Integration of believers and *kafirs* (non-Muslims) in the past had been possible thanks to an encompassing cosmogony. In Java today the integration of the stranger or non-believer (*kafir*) is being currently addressed using several social models. Many Javanese advance that local intra Muslim–Christian religious tolerance is "more" Javanese. If some of the positions of these tolerant Indonesian Muslims quoted in this article sound banal or trite to our ears, it is important to remember that the two major Indonesian political parties and Muslim movements, the Nahdlatul Ulama and the Muhammadiyah,[56] represent some seventy million Muslims. What they lack in incisive rhetoric, they make up in their ability to influence grassroots behaviour. When they do mobilize their members, their *encadrement* is impressive, for it is not a demonstration where the hired crowd gets a free lunch and some cash, but thousands of young people who participate in mosque and *madrasah*-based study groups on a weekly basis and who are learning to think about what it means to integrate difference as a reappropriation of Javanese society and not of some illusory modernity.

At recent seminars on the effect of the attacks on the World Trade Centre, Indonesia Javanese Muslims recognized that they have let the fringe groups (the motorcycle, turban, and sabre crowd) seemingly become the spokespersons for Indonesian Islam. These two parties are currently seeking ways to counter the militant groups which indeed have a head start in elementary strategies of public relations. Mainstream Muslims are realistic about how the society they are living in works, and have a positive vision of the role that the common values of Javanese can play in peace-making. In a post-traditional society where the two major "universal" monotheisms are struggling to share in Allah's *rahmat* or mercy, denying the revelation of the other is a less effective way forward towards social harmony than insisting on stricter adherence to the values of their own traditions that tend to forge a unified society. This may be only a reinvented expression of the totality, but it demonstrates cohesiveness. In a word, Allah's sovereignty depends on the *umat* (community) uniting in his *rahmat* (mercy).

NOTES

1. Our understanding of the invention of tradition differs from that of the book of the same name which made this terminology popular. We are more interested in why societies try to reinvent their tradition than by the artificiality of these recently invented customs. Cf. Eric Hobsbawm and Terence Ranger, *The Invention of Tradition* (1983).

2. The Middle Eastern Islamic groups that operate out of Indonesia are not representative of any Nusantarian society and are not taken into account here. For instance the Jordanian Hizbut Tahrir (Party of Liberation); cf. Chris McCall's article in the *South China Post*, 8 August 2002.

3. Zamakhsyari Dhofier, *The Pesantrèn Tradition. The role of the Kyai in the Maintainence of Traditional Islam in Java* (1982 Indonesian edition; 1999); Pradjarta Dirdjosanjoto, *Memilihara Umat. Kiai Pesantrèn — Kiai Langgar di Jawa* [Caring for the *Umat*. Koranic school *kiai* and prayer house *kiai* in Jawa] (1999).

4. Cf. several articles in *Jakarta Post* on 16 August 2002, the eve of Indonesia's Independence day. In the article by Fitri Wulandri on nationalism among the Indonesian youth, he found that many young people felt that geography alone

defined nationhood and that the reform movement had failed to forge large-scale social solidarity.

5. *Jakarta Post*, 22 July 2002; article "The Year of Living Pragmatically without Humanity".

6. Here we juxtapose society to community, and not the state, the individual, or culture. Nonetheless society in this sense can still be taken in two different meanings: a human group's population, institutions, and relations, or its cultural ideology. Tönnies used the notion of association to describe complex, contract-based rational and individualistic societies. In post-traditional societies, these bonds of association are often seen as the links between family and the society (*polis* in Aristotle's terms), and as a means to revive dimensions of status-bound traditional communities. Cf. E. Vivieros de Castro, "Society", in *Encyclopedia of Social and Cultural Anthropology*, A. Barnard and J. Spencer (1996), pp. 514–22. Cf. Stéphan Vibert's paper, "The Ideal of Community as a Paradoxical Apropriation of Modernity", shows how by becoming aware of society as culture (i.e., an identity), one can reinvent a tradition under the cover of continuity.

7. Political and economic social boundaries in the case of insular Southeast Asia are quite recent and sociologically not always relevant to the discussion of Java.

8. Cf. Vincent Descombes, *Les Institutions du Sens* (1996, p. 257).

9. In Javanese these three terms: *anèh; manca; séjé / sanes* do not correspond exactly. "Unknown" is not precisely "different" (*séjé*), "foreign" (*manca*) can also be expressed by "overseas" (*sabrang*); and "strange" (*anèh*) is more "odd", than "not yet familiar".

10. Cf. Peter van der Veer, *Religious Nationalism: Hindus and Muslims in India* (1996, p. 18). In Jakaratan political circles in 2001, there was a debate whether Article 33 of the Indonesian Constitution on the founding principle of collectivism (*asas kekeluargaan*) should be replaced by individualism supposedly more suited to the market economy (*Jakarta Post*, 15 June 2001 article by Ari A. Perdana). Our use of the term *individualism* here is not meant to convey the full panoply of the values contained individualistic ideology found in modern Europe. In Java a "moral" person alienated by the Javanese holistic hierarchy of values tries to evolve in a pseudo-holistic ideology created by the Indonesian state. To do so he "ceases" to be Javanese and adopts and Indonesian persona thereby escaping from the constraints of Javanese social life.

11. Maria Rawiastuti, "Menuju Pluralisme Hukum Agraria" (2000, pp. 77–104).

12. Cf. in the Introduction our periodization of the adoption of Islam in Java into four stages: (1) its appearance in the north coast ports among foreigner traders (pre-1500); (2) a raja-centric period among the Javanese sultanates (1650–1750); (3) its implantation in rural Koranic schools after its withdrawal from the courts as they came under VOC (160?–1799) and the colonial state influence (1799–1949); (4) its effort to adjust itself to the nascent nationalist movement and its refounding as an urban political force after independence (1900–2000).

13. G. C. Anawati and Louis Gardet, *Mystique Musulmane. Aspects et tendances, expériences et Techniques* (1986, p. 42).

14. All translations from the Koran used here are taken from: A. J. Arberry, *The Koran Interpreted* (1955).

15. To describe in any detail the chain of exegesis on this theme of *jihad* over the centuries would take many pages and is not necessary here where our interest is in the reaction of the community of believers to periodic calls for a holy war.

16. Cf. G. McT. Kahin, *Nationalism and Revolution in Indonesia* (1952, pp. 122–26).

17. For a few titles in Javanese or Indonesian: Damarjati Supadjar (a professor of philosophy), *Kridha Graita*. (Yogyakarta: Kridha Martana, 1994); Yudi Partojuwono, *Serta Wedharan Wirid*, 3 vols. (Surabaya: Djojobojo, 1991+); Tanpoaran (anonymous), *Sangkan Paraning Dumadi* (Surabaya: Djojo Bojo (1988); Y. B. Mangunwijaya (a well-known Jesuit author), *Ragawidya. Religiositas Hal-hal Sehari-hari* (Yogyakarta: Yayasan Kanisius, 1975); Marbangun Hardjowirogo, *Manusia Jawa* (Jakarta: Idayu, 1983); *Sasangka Jati*, 10th ed. (Jakarta: Pangestu, 1975). The latter text is the basic text of the interiority sect Pangestu dating from the 1930s.

18. This is the point of view, for instance, of Myriam Revault d'Allones in her article, "Faut-il avoir peur de l'universel", *Le Monde*, 24 November 2001, p. 15.

19. Cf. B. Anderson, *Imagined Communities* (1991); and E. Hobsbawm and Ranger (1983).

20. I have reproduced the word *jihad* in the title of this chapter for its irony. During the demonstration in Cairo (October 2001) in front of the al-Azhar Islamic University: "*Jihad* is the solution" implicitly accredits policies which, consciously or unconsciously, will ultimately marginalize the public expression of Islam by destroying the Muslim community's (*umma*) social fabric (cf. for the Palestinian case, Gilles Keppel, *Jihad. Expansion et déclin de l'islamise* (2001, pp. 327–48; 478–91). Gilles Keppel argues that these one-off calls for *jihad* disillusion individual Muslims, who, according to him, are less and less susceptible to "Islamist" manipulation of religion for potential political gains.

21. Robert Caspar, *Traité de Theologie Musulmane*, tome I (1987, pp. 259–446).

22. *Sub voce* Wahhābīya in *Encyclopedia of Islam* (1953, pp. 618–21).

23. Apart from the commercial benefits of reporting on violence, its ritualization in Indonesia is examined in the context of the local apocalyptic narratives (Muslim and Christian) by Nils Brabandt, "Malukan Apocalypse, Themes in the dynamics of violence in Eastern Indonesia" (2001).

24. The five daily Muslim prayers.

25. These take place during the month following the end of Ramadan (ninth month of the Muslim lunar year) and consolidate social solidarity at all levels of society: factories, political parties, hamlets, etc.

26. "Islamic Revolution", *New York Review of Books*, 30 June 1983.

27. The distance that separates the mentality of Europeans from the average Muslim

is sometimes immense. In the 3–4 November 2001 edition of the Parisian newspaper *Libération* (p. 9), a reader (Jean-Luc Delacroix, Dieppe) wrote quite simply that Islam had to respect *laïcité*, a totally French social value.

28. As our references indicate, most of the ideas for this section are taken from the classic exposé of Louis Gardet, *La Cité Musulmane. Vie sociale et politique* (1981).

29. One Christian parallel here would be William of Occam (Franciscan, 1285–1347) who while trying to justify the riches of the Franciscan orders with their vows of poverty, invented legal nominalism to get around the contradictions posed by this wealth.

30. Reproduced pp. 60–62 in *Islam Substantif. Agar Umat Tidak Jadi Buih* (2000).

31. In a two-part article in the *Jakarta Post* (21–22 November 2001) Azyumardi Azra quotes Robert Hefner's (2000) view that part of the confusion of the *umat* is due to nation-building and market globalization which have increased pluralism and confrontation generally in the Muslim world. Azyumardi remarks that although generally accepted the secular nation-state, by failing to perform according to its promises, has generated considerable scepticism. The marginal Muslims groups call for a "universal caliphate" where a single caliph could unite and strengthen the Muslim *umat*. But as Azyumardi points out the "rightly guided caliph" (*al-kulafā' al-rashidun*) was quickly replaced by the despotic caliph of Umayyads, Abbasids and the Ottomans.

32. In Indonesian, water buffalo market (*pasar kerbau*).

33. In 1984 the Nahdlatul Ulama by a step or decision (*khittah*; Arabic, *khathwa*) withdrew from the unique Muslim party (PPP) altogether and more basically decided not to participate in practical politics. For the debate on this decision, cf. Robert Hefner, *Civil Islam: Muslims and Democratisation in Indonesia* (2000).

34. Cf. K. van Dijk, *Rebellion under the Banner of Islam. The Darul Islam in Indonesia*.

35. Cf. N. Madjid *Islam, Kemodernan, dan KeIndonesiaan* (1987).

36. Cf. Michael Davis, "Laskar Jihad and the political position of conservative Islam in Indonesia" (2002); Kees van Dijk (2001, p. 482) provides a photo of the Lakar in their theatrical dress.

37. Cf. Dan Murphy, *Christian Science Monitor*, 5 November 2001. I haven't been able to trace this report on the Indonesian language online newpapers (cf. <Jendela.Indonesia.com>. This discrepancy between the provincial and the international press is sometimes a question of self-censorship, an effort to avoid counter-attacks, and in other cases one is left to wonder whether the event ever happened. As Kees van Dijk says repeatedly in *A Country in Despair: Indonesia between 1997 and 2000* (2001, p. 483), when several press reports are contradictory, it is near impossible to really know what happened.

38. Cf. on Sasak (i.e., Lombok) Islam, cf. Erni Budiwanti, *Islam Sasak; wetu telu versus waktu lima* (2000).

39. As in French and English, *huqūq* in Arabic means the rights (*droits*); presumably the rights of Allah that are to be defended here are to prescribe good and to

outlaw evil. Ethically speaking this makes no sense in modern Europe, where individuals, not gods, have rights.

40. Cf. Bat Ye'or, *The Decline of Christianity under Islam: From Jihad to Dhimmitude* (1996).

41. Cf. for instance. Zainuddin Fananie, *Restrukturisasi Budaya Jawa. Perspektif KGPAA Mangkunagara I* (2000). The opposite trend, the Javanization of Islam has often been developed, for instance Simuh, *Sufisme Jawa. Transformasi Tasawuf Islam ke Mistik Jawa* (1999) discussed in ch. 11.

42. Cf. Abdul Munir Mulkhan, *Islam Murni dalam Masyarakat Petani* (2000).

43. Cf. *Laksmana Net*, 7 November 2001, "Marriage Bill: Against the Current".

44. Hazem Saghiey, *Time*, 15 October 2001.

45. Cf. Institut Studi Arus Informasi, *Prémanisme Politik* (2000); James Siegal (1998).

46. For an overall survey, cf. Gilles Kepel (2000).

47. This originally appeared in the Muslim journal *Panji Masyarakat*.

48. Cf. Jajat Burhanudin, "The Making of Islamic Political Tradition in the Malay World" (2001).

49. Cf. U.S. Dept. of State, International Religious Freedom Report 2001. For instance the Crisis Centre Diocese of Amboina report 210 (dated 16 November 2001) reported that Laskar Jiahd leader Jaffar Umar Thalib after staying one week in Ambon had left for Sorong, Papua while he was supposed to be under house arrest in Jakarta.

50. Cf. for "Londonstan" <http://www.islam2.net> and the newspaper *Al-Qods al-Arribia*.

51. On Rashīd Ridā (1865–1935), and on the Salafiyya, cf. Robert Caspar (1987, pp. 287–95).

52. Cf. article on "Elite Jargon" in the *Jakarta Post*, 30 October 2001, and "Hundreds of applicant for the GPI brigade don't know what the jihad stands for", *Washington Times*, 12 October 2001.

53. Cf. Dini Djalal and John Mcbeth, "All talk, no action", *Far Eastern Economic Review*, 25 October 2001.

54. <http://www.islam 21.net/pages/key issues/key3-7.htm>.

55. Cf. *Membongkar Mitos Masyarakat Madani* (2000) and Ahmad Baso, *Civil Society versus Masyarakat Madani. Arkeologi Pemikiran "Civil Society" dalam Islam Indonesia* (1999).

56. Cf. *Jakarta Post*, 9 November 2001 article by Muhammad Nafik.

13

OF SACRED WELLS AND SHOPPING MALLS
Glimpses of the Reconstruction of Social Confidence in Solo after Soeharto

13.1 INTRODUCTION

It was not immediately after the turmoil of May 1998 that calls for *jihad* appeared. The initial efforts to deal with the fractured Javanese society came from a healthy reform movment that wanted to promote social solidarity. Élite competition for the spoils of the defunct dictatorship came later. It could be many years before historians, economists, and other social scientists have a clear perspective on the changes wrought in Indonesia by the fall of General Soeharto's regime in 1998. In this chapter and the following one we will move our focus away from the rural area north of Surakarta and study the rituals and social healing practised in the city of Solo following these traumatic events. The urban scene south of the district of Kaliasa is chosen because of the apocalyptic disturbances that led to the sacking of the city of Surakarta. Theatre appears crucial for representing to the victims the trauma of these events.

Javanese *wayang*, a highly "traditional" art form, might be expected to evolve more slowly than other social indicators, artistic or otherwise, in reaction to such political upheaval. However, the very nature of *wayang* theatre, and the nature of any living "tradition," is indeed to evolve within its own structures. For once "tradition" becomes a completely static and immovable entity it is in textbooks and museums but not in the streets in tense times of rapid social change. Within *wayang*, the purification, or *ruwatan* genre, occupies a receptive place for change. For how can one claim to purify unless one heals today's ills? The agency of *wayang* during exorcisms addresses the current needs of the local populace. But how does it do so? More specifically, how can it address such all-encompassing social crises as the fall of the New Order regime?

The fall of General Soeharto created many new social currents in the later half of 1998 and during 1999. The social reconstruction of confidence, required for society to continue, took many forms. The economy had been going through a total crisis (1997+). Local neighbourhood committees in the town of Surakarta (Solo), as in many other places, were mobilized to protect the neighbourhoods (*kampung*) at night and help the poorest to get by through aid in kind and money.[1] The major Muslim movements increased their stress on religious tolerance and could be called upon to protect churches threatened with being burned down.[2] After the fall of Soeharto in May 1998, the status of the state was in question due to the daily lack of order and confidence. For instance, no one in Solo believed that the police were really police, just cowards and profiteers. The police, knowing they had lost their authority, kept a low profile. During the course of thirty lengthy interviews with Solonese of all walks of life in January and February 1999, I listened to descriptions of various types of efforts for the social reconstruction of confidence that had occurred after May 1998: new labour unions, aid associations (*panguyuban*), NGO legal aid networks, and pedlars' co-operatives.

Eldar Braten has asked what relationship exists in Java between contemporary experience and cultural representation.[3] Against the backdrop of rapid social change, we are asking: how did *wayang* react? More precisely, one month or six months after the events of May 1998, did cultural representations in Solo reflect public experience? Many things changed in the Javanese way of being in the world in 1998–99. Obviously, that had to be true on a personal level, but what were the changes on the social plane?

Collective experience had always been reflected in ritual and theatrical discourse. In the purification rites I studied between 1983 and1993,[4] the *dhalang* always included in his monologues and dialogues references to the persons purified and their place of habitation, family background, and so on. The 1996 ecologically oriented earth purifications (*ruwatan bumi*) as well as the farcical imitations by live actors of political figures resonated with the concerns surrounding current events. Commenting on the recent debacle of Soeharto, Ward Keeler (2002) stressed that not only the Javanese *dhalang* but also his sponsors and fans would be likely to take *wayang* in new directions in the coming years. In a recent article, Jan Mrazek (2002) showed how the *dhalang* Enthus Susmono married Islam in a commercially oriented *wayang* borrowing techniques from television. Yet during the second half of 1998 theatre often illustrated a tendency that Barbara Hatley describes: "If performances of traditional theatre genre ... celebrate the world as it is, modern theatre typically interrogates and problematises from a distance."[5] Indeed, contesting the Soeharto regime had been a major feature not only of traditional Javanese theatre, but also of other more innovative theatrical genres. But, once the regime fell, *wayang*, with its epic metaphors and tropes, set to work on the new situation, that is to say, post-Soeharto Indonesia.

What it meant to be Solonese was being reviewed in the wake of the "war", as the inhabitants often called the chaos that had devastated their town. The issue of who organized the May 1998 riots has never really been clarified, but it was clear that the impoverished population had not been hard to provoke and that outside criminal elements had been employed to destroy the city by those in the army "loyal" to Soeharto. This pattern was avoided *in extremis* in Yogyakarta in the same period by means of a remarkable alliance of the court, the population, and the universities.

During the night of 6 February 1999, I attended a purification (*ruwatan*) of a Solonese shopping plaza followed by the performance of the *wayang pandhawa timbul* (The Pandhawa Appear) by *ki dhalang* Mantep Sudarsono. That evening ritual is compared here to the offering of another *wayang* play, *Wahyu Kamulyan*, by the *ki dhalang* Warseno Slenk at another purification ritual, this time at the well of Mbah Meyek in the nearby neighbourhood of Bibis Kulon.[6] The latter took place on 11 June 1998, after having been delayed for a month by the May riots in Solo and the collapse of the Soeharto regime.

During a shadow puppet performance, the dialogue between a wizened old mother (Cangik) and her plump and slow daughter (Limbuk) deals with many topical issues. The final chapter of Jan Mrázek's dissertation[7] has demonstrated the importance of these Limbukan exchanges for understanding the place of *wayang* theatre in the social debates of the late 1990s. Tony Day's discussion of the treatment of hybrid identities in East Javanese *wayang* (2002) also encouraged me to scrutinize the ritual accompanying the play and the dialogues of Limbuk and Cangik in these two Solonese *wayang* performances for glimpses of the social reconstruction of confidence in Central Java.

Both theatrical events described below contained a distinct ritual dimension. They also both provided ample opportunity for the *dhalang* to comment on events. The village well purification was an annual event that never before had occurred in such an atmosphere, coloured as it was by the recent riots. When the village well purification was celebrated, the city was still a series of burned-out ruins. The purification of the burned-out shopping mall took place eight months later, and occurred next to the cleaned up but not rebuilt commercial centre. The Beteng Plaza purification was a direct reaction to the rioting that took place in Solo seven days before Soeharto's fall. The parallel dimensions in the two performances, one in an urban village and another in a shopping mall just northeast of the main Solo palace, across the street from the eighteenth-century Dutch fort, suggested that a comparison should include at least two levels, the ritual and the dialogic. The long-necked, scrawny peasant Cangik and her plump, indecisive daughter Limbuk could not ignore the recent events, which had encroached massively on every aspect of Solonese life. I present the earlier village purification after the later shopping mall purification. The village *ruwatan* presented neighbourhood bonds and social linkage with home that the non-lieu of a shopping mall cannot claim to possess. On the other hand, the shopping mall ritual united the Beteng Plaza merchants with mutual economic interests far greater than those of the villagers of Bibis Kulon. How purification (*ruwatan*), the communal ritual meal (*slametan*), and *wayang* theatre relate aspects of social morphology and facilitate the exchange of values will be taken up in the conclusion (Ch. 15).

13.2 PURIFICATION RITUAL AT BETENG PLAZA

At the beginning of the evening of the purification ritual, after the committee of sponsors had presented the evening's schedule and one of its members, Bapak Suhardi, had prayed, the sponsors handed over the puppets of Bathara Kala and Bathara Wisnu to their respective *dhalangs* (*ki* Suloto Guno Sukasno and *ki* Mantep Sudarsono). This brief purification play began with a request:

> SPONSOR: Please Sir, I request your assistance that you stop at the Beteng Plaza here. I request that younger brother *dhalang* be willing to do a Birth of Kala purification of the Beteng market plaza here in order that our families [literally, "siblings"] who are merchants in whatever, might [do business] smoothly and that later on no impediments whatsoever may appear.

> DHALANG KANDHA BUWANA:[8] Yes, I have already received your request. I, an ordinary mortal and subject to the authority of the Almighty Lord, my action will initiate the purification of the Beteng Plaza here and so expedite prosperity without any obstacles. After I hold the exorcism ritual, every trader (*bakul*) here will be prosperous. Later no obstacles will

FIGURE 13.1
The burning of Beteng Plaza on 14 May 1998

Source: Reproduced from *Rekaman Lensa: Peristiwa Mei 1998 di Solo* (p. 49) (Solo: Aksara Solopos, 1998), with permission of the publisher.

be encountered. Those I have "cooled" will be healthy, selling quickly, whoever has suffered also. They will be able to carry things out according to [their] plans. Let's start holding this purification, for the authority of Hyang Widi can make one impervious to any obstacles.

After the second mantra, the second sequence showed how Kala came to identify the *dhalang* Kandha Buwana with the person of *ki dhalang* Suloto Guno Sukasno, who was representing the "family" of the shopping mall merchants. This recognition and the fact of his descendance in six generations from Bango Thonthong qualifies the young *dhalang* to open the purification mantra book and purify "the household earth" (*banjar bumi*) of the mall. Afterward, anyone using common sense (*ngupaya duga*) in trading will experience fluency (*lancar*). The *dhalang* claimed that he knew every one of Kala's desires. Then Kala asked if the *dhalang* could read the distinguishing marks (*cap*) on the nape of his neck. The *dhalang* replied that the "letters of clarity" or "clear letters" (*sastra cetha*)[9] were at the top of Kala's forehead, and he recited the third mantra. After this "reading," which was done reciting from the *dhalang's* heirloom mantra book, Kala described what has come over him:

> KALA: Oh, oh, oh, Dhalang, you've made my heart feel so relieved. That is the good feeling of the "light letters". Mankind should worship each according to his own beliefs. Since this is the way it is, sire Dhalang, never again will I create obstacles [or] riots in the Beteng Plaza here. May those who are engaging in commerce, operate with ease. Let there be no obstacles whatsoever. I will return to the Southern Ocean.

This extremely short version of the play ended with the *dhalang* asking the "Broom of the World" to cleanse the plaza of any remaining members of Kala's army. Sapu Jagat accepted the task of sweeping this filth back to the Southern Ocean. Once he declared that all this *rereged* had been dumped into the ocean, the *dhalang* implored that the shopping mall remain clear and transparent (*padhang trawangan*) and free of any further dirt or obstacles. The *dhalang* then evoked, in a *suluk*, the unsettled, agitated earth and the quaking sky, which looked as if it has been distanced (*katon lir cuncanging*). The pronouncing of the syllable "Om" ended this episode.

In the final exchange between the *dhalang* and the sponsor, the *dhalang* implored the Lord to fulfil the aspirations (*gegayuhanipun*) of all the families installed in the Beteng Plaza, and asked Allah to grant their hopes, which were expressed in these prayers (*ngijbahi*). The sponsor replied, saying that he acknowledged that he was ready to receive these prayers/offerings for the well-being (*puji hastuti*) of the *dhalang*.

Day (2002) describes a *ruwatan* that lasted only twenty-five minutes, beginning at 4 a.m. Until ten years ago, purification plays had to take place in the morning and lasted roughly four hours. For the older generation of Javanese, this performance at the Beteng Plaza represented a change in scheduling and a radical shortening of the performance. The purification play has become an increasingly familiar ritual to many Solonese during the last two decades due to grouped exorcisms of several families; in the last five or so years, its half-hour version has also become common. Therefore a very short purification play after an all-night performance of a first play or before, as is here the case, does not present insurmountable obstacles to situating the concise selection in the remembered context of the full-length play. Little about the contents, except the brevity, innovates if one is aware of what a full telling of the myth entails. It is almost as if the perceived formulaic quality of the purification mantra allows the play itself to be performed in a *pars pro toto* manner.

Although the upper and more luxurious floors of the mall were still burned out and remained unrepaired, the basement section of the Beteng

Plaza had been reoccupied by dozens of modest cloth merchants, representing a cross section of social and religious categories similar to the nearby but much larger Pasar Klewer batik and cloth market. The diversity of ethnic and religious commitments represented that evening by the Beteng traders' association required the tolerance of all concerned. The *dhalang* was also discrete, as was seen above, when he said: "Mankind should worship each according to his own beliefs." At the beginning of the play, the *dhalang* modestly claimed to be only a mortal man at the same time that he used the traditional name of Kandha Buwana, indicating that he was an incarnation of Wisnu. Allah is prominently mentioned at the end as the one who will grant the fulfilment of prayers. The story is told without the habitual spilled seed motif, which explains the presence of Kala and his ogre army on earth, where they destroy human destinies by eating these prey (Headley 2000). If one wanted to find a way to slip a purification play into an evening's entertainment without running any risks of offending Muslim conservatives, this certainly was a successful arrangement. But this is, in itself, a surprising strategy because, although the Javanese are not given to "in your face statements", the purification ritual is what is supposed to eliminate the risks, not present any.

The *Solo Pos* newspaper discussed matter-of-factly that it had been eight months since the plaza had been ravaged and that only 20 per cent of it had been refurbished. In its editions on 5 and 6 February, it gave front page coverage to the *ruwatan* event, with a discussion on the second day of the appropriateness of the choice of the day in terms of its character (*watak*) as judged by Javanese divination. The eve of that Sunday's character was "windblown" (*lebu katiyup angin*), a negative prognostic. The *Solo Pos* report said that a "mass" (*massal*) *ruwatan* was deemed to be more flexible in its calendrical dating because of its intentions (*tergantung pada tujuannya*). What seemed to characterize the post-Soeharto social crisis in Solo was both a new openness in expression and concern that it not further jeopardize social harmony. This was to be done by expressing concern for the "intentions" of others. Steering clear of what might be perceived as doctrinaire points of view, the reconstruction of social confidence is favoured by the classic Solonese commercial sphere of cloth and garment sellers who had been hard hit by the economic deflation that began in 1997.

THE PANDHAWA BROTHERS STAND OUT: SCENARIO OF THE *WAYANG* PLAY

At around 10.30 p.m., we quickly moved on from the ritual play dealing with Kala to an epic narrative that lasted seven hours. This second performance described the emergence of the Pandhawa brothers after their exile from their kingdom of Astina, which had been lost at the gambling table. The recovery of freedom, the need for reconciliation, and the risks of subversion are the main themes that structure this play. During the twelve years, the Padhawa had wandered in exile in their forest kingdom and spent a thirteenth year, after their return, incognito. The play begins with the sage Bima, one of the Pandhawa brothers, counselling Duryadana, the king of the Kurawa, to reconcile with his exiled cousins. The sage describes the virtues that each one of these five brothers has imparted to a given site. The vizier, Sengkuni, plots deception so that the Pandhawas can be exiled for another thirteen years. Then King Sukrasuno arrives, seeking Duryadana's help to attack the weaker kingdom of Wirata. The sages Bisma and Dorna violently upbraid Sukrasuno for proposing this unethical and ill-considered war, concluding that, although Wirata is weak, it has many allies.

At this juncture, a conversation ensues between two peasants, Cangik and her daughter, Limbuk. Their dialogues are called Limbukan, after the unresponsive daughter. One isn't far enough into the Pandhawa Timbul story to be able to predict how it is going to be interpreted, so the dialogue is doubly detached from all that precedes it in the play. Surprisingly, the *wayang* by this famous *dhalang, ki* Mantep Sudarsono, was poorly attended. Perhaps one should ascribe this to the light rain that night or to fears of insecurity in the centre of town in the early hours of the morning. Anyway, the small audience relaxed for what was expected to be a lively interlude drawn from the Pandhawa Timbul epic narrative.

THE CANGIK–LIMBUK DIALOGUE

Cangik starts out by saying that although nepotism (*wong sak omah maju breng ki*) is understandable, it is better that artists don't take part in government. Artists only get pensioned off at death. "What heavy work — sitting here cross-legged till four in the morning. The *dhalang* gets so tired … [first song]."

Cangik suggests that she and her daughter will pray for the large family of Beteng Plaza traders (*tanggi brayat ageng pedagang Beteng Plaza Solo*). Cangik goes on to give an extended commentary on the *ruwatan*. In order that the damage of the rioting (*ontran-ontran*) in the recent past be repaired and that it not be repeated, the Solonese must return to an inner serenity (*rasa katentreman*). Social solidarity is linked to group aspirations:

> Let us pray together! Besides tonight performing the *ruwatan*, let us never cease in our devotions. To perform devotions is to follow religious belief

with conviction. Pray to God so that the present situation may soon become calm. May we have peace and calm again, like the puppeteers who return to the rules of performance.

Limbuk asks for an example of these groups' aspirations. Cangik says that this must have practical, concrete repercussions, for instance, by the government promulgating new regulations inspired by *reformasi* movement and promoted by the students. This way, the name Indonesia won't connote "wild forest". True justice must be created by standing before Allah and seeking the will of God. This way, religion, entrusted to mankind, brings order on earth. Otherwise, all this commotion (*ramé-ramé*) exhausts our strength. The students' struggle was a just one. Let us not retreat from it to further our private ends. Let no one jump on the bandwagon (*mboncengi*). Let the provocateurs stop. "Don't ransack [the town], don't create disturbances. Have mercy on the little people!" (*Aja nggawé rusak, do nggawé kisruh. Mesaké rakyat cilik!*).

Cangik goes on to explain that if the price of hot peppers has risen so astronomically, it is because of dishonest (*culika*) people. Anyway, by June everything will be better, once the elections have taken place. Limbuk is not so sure. But Cangik remembers that as a child there were lots of political parties presenting candidates (with images of Gareng, flat irons, and hoes). Now that we are free, not like the ducks (in a row) we used to be, regimented all day long. The election spirit means to stand firm: "In a time like this it is difficult to think" (*Jamané kaya ngéné mikir abot-abot*).

The dialogue returns to the relatives of the large family of Beteng Plaza. The spirit of mutual love that should characterize nationalism is defined as the sensation of love towards the light of life (*Rasa kebangsan kuwi rasa tresna marang papadhanging urip*). Three explicit examples of mutual aid are given to illustrate this: a person who falls down, a person who is in a bus accident, and a person who asks for help. Now, if others have different opinions, says Cangik, let's hear about it!

The exchange now moves on to the calculation of the right day according to Pancasuda Paarasan (i.e., *pawukon* horoscopes), almanac calculations for ritual events like this *ruwatan*. Here the *dhalang* repeats the caveat about proper intentions, for if the intention is pure then God blesses [whatever date is chosen] (*nèk niaté ki resik mesti Gusti ki ngeparengaké*). The six female singers are then introduced, each singing a popular (*ngetrend, baru ngetop*) song chosen from written requests by fans. Finally, Cangik says that even if a *dhalang* doesn't have the proper *ruwatan* genealogy this doesn't matter, for it all depends on one's inner intention.

What are we to make of this departure from tradition in order to validate an authentic inner self? Are we spectators to the re-emergence in the shambles of post-Soeharto Central Java of the secularization of this archaic ritual? It doesn't feel like it. The ritual's very marginality seems to equip it for new tasks. In 1996–97, Cangik puppets across Java were mouthing GOLKAR party slogans during these dialogues and only occasionally making critical political remarks.[10] However, after the fall of Soeharto, Cangik is represented as believing that the social reconstruction of mutual confidence is more than simply getting back to regular business and commercial exchange. Cangik believes in *reformasi*, in mobilizing goodwill. To this extent, Cangik really reflects popular aspirations. She is a "healthy" conformist to her audience's aspirations. That is another way of saying that *dhalangs* are, like any good public speaker, well aware of what their audience needs to hear.

13.3 CLEANSING OF THE WELL OF *MBAH* MEYEK IN BIBIS KULON

Bibis Kulon is situated in the urban village (*kelurahan*) of Gilingan on the outskirts of Solo. Every year, during the month of Sura on Kliwon Friday, Bibis Kulon proceeds with a ritual purification of its territory. Local community leaders organize the event. In the government officials' clichéd explanations, they claim that this event celebrates Java's traditional culture. Such descriptions are often called secularized ones (literally, "culturated" *dikabudayaké*) as opposed to the more traditional "religious" ones. In fact, the village prayers and offerings are made to the local spirits (*roh leluhur*) and personifications of sacred pools, trees, and so on, capable of protecting the village. About 30 per cent of the population of this *kelurahan* is registered as non-Muslim. Despite the proximity of markets, Legi, Ngeplak, and Mojosongo, the majority of its population is, or was, employed as construction or industrial workers. Apparently, differences in religion present few impediments to respecting the custom, or *adat*, considered to be an inheritance from one's ancestors. To accomplish the purification of Bibis Kulon, there are six complementary events:

1. The co-operative labour of cleaning the sites.
2. The offerings and *slametan* at the sacred place (*pundhèn*).
3. The procession of the puppets (*kirap wayang*), involving worship at each offering site (*sungkeman pundhèn*).
4. The village communal meal (*slametan dhusun*).
5. The night-long *wayang*.
6. The following morning's *wayang*.

The final two elements, the *wayang* performances, are the only ones openly treated as entertainment, whereas in fact they all involve both worship and communal eating. There are four *pundhèns*:

1. The pool (*sendhang*) of *mbah* [Grandparent] Meyek.[11]
2. The well or Sumur Bandung.
3. The tamarind tree of *mbah* Asem Ageng.
4. The tamarind tree of *mbah* Asem Kandhang.

According to a villager, Prawirowidjojo, the choice of the Javanese calendrical date goes back to 1937. A well-known village official (*bayan*) named Tirtawidjaja, who was in office between the wars, dreamed that a girl with Chinese features wearing a *kain kebaya* was walking along "belaboredly". Her *pundhèn* has been called *mbah* Meyek ever since.

During the Japanese Occupation, these village purification ceremonies were outlawed until an outbreak of illness in 1944, when *bayan* Tirtawidjaja and the *demang* Pantjanarmada asked the Mangkunagaran palace for permission to reinstate the ritual. Ever since that date, lest further outbreaks of illness occur due to the curse of the local "protecting" deity or *dhanyang*, who when unpropitiated become angry, these annual ceremonies have been carried out. There is a collective village memory of the *dhalang* chosen to perform the all-night play as well as the play selected to be presented. In 1991, *ki* Mantep Sudarsono put on the play Anoman Obong (Hanoman Burns); thirty-five days later, the Bibis Kulon furniture factory went up in flames. This was considered to be the consequence of the poor choice of play. In 1998, the choice for the *dhalang* fell on a young and popular *dhalang*, *ki* Warseno Slenk.[12]

The organization of these annual rites involves large numbers of villagers organized into nineteen separate sections, each with its own tasks. The Kamis Wage and Jum'at Kliwon of 1998 fell on 14–15 May. On the morning of the fourteenth the "spontaneous" work teams for weeding and cleaning the four *pundhèns* began. Cleaning (*nguras*) the well involves draining it and descending into the shaft, out of which a tree is growing.

By eleven o'clock the Islamic prayer leader, or *modin*, Achmad Charun, began the offerings (*sajèn*) at two *pundhèns*, those of *mbah* Meyek and *mbah* Sumur Bandhung. Sarwanto commendably reproduces the entire invocation or *ujub* used by the religious leader.[13] It proves to be a *mélange* of explicit Islam (the closing third is in Arabic) and an affirmation that the connections between the offerings and the cardinal directions will guarantee the same distancing of the hindrances we heard about during the Birth of Kala play at the Beteng Plaza. The attendees were young and mostly male; seated *slametan strictu sensu* are of course exclusively male.

At three in the afternoon, representatives of the village population dressed in formal Javanese clothing carried the five Pandhawas (Puntadewa, Bima/Werkudara, Janaka, Nangkula, and Sadewa), Kresna, Bathara Guru, Bathara Narada, and the panakawans (Semar, Gareng, Petruk, and Bagong) as well as a sign (reading "Bersih Desa Bibis Kulon"), the national and the village flags, and a hoe laden with in-between harvest crops (*palawija*) and rice. This procession was followed by the Panji lion-headed trance dances (*reyog Singa Manggala*) and proceeded clockwise (*pradaksina*), symbolizing, so we are told, the process from birth to death. The route taken is shown in Figure 13.2; the village is not at the centre but on the periphery of the procession. At each *pundhèn*, the men stand around the tree or well carrying the *wayang* puppets upright and a prayer is said. At this moment, the *wayang* figures are made to bow to the female spirits associated with the tree or well, thus paying their respects. This is followed by the communal meal (*slametan kampung*) to the west of the shrine of *mbah* Meyek. The individual families do not each bring the rice accompanied by vegetables (*sekul ambengan*), as is customary in village harvest festivals, although they will later eat these offerings together. The offerings are prepared by the appropriate section of the organizing committee, which has already solicited contributions to this effect.

FIGURE 13.2
Order of the procession in the Bibis Kulon Purification

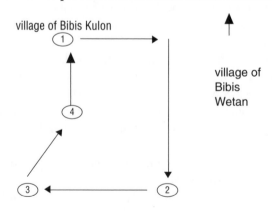

1) pundhèn of Mbah Meyek
2) pundhèn of Mbah Kandhang
3) pundhèn of Mbah Asem (or Mbah Kaji)
4) pundhèn of Mbah Sumur Bandung

In general, offerings are classified by the number nine, symbolizing the nine *wali* of Javanese Islam, the nine directions of the compass, and the nine elements (water, fire, wind, earth, star, moon, sun, mountain, and fire). In the Javanese system of correspondences, this act of synthetic classification is in and of itself a request for cosmological blessings from these three sets of nine. This refers to the belief that a man who is able to shut the nine openings/appetites of his body (*nutupi babahan hawa sanga*) may obtain these blessings. In addition, the nine complete sets of offerings correspond to the nine gods (Wisnu, Sambu, Iswara, Mahaswara, Brahma, Rudra, Mahadewa, Sangkara, and Siwa). The Muslim prayer pronounced here, explicitly prayed against looting (*mangké ora kena rayahan inggih*), is kept well away from any reference to the cosmological destination of the food offerings,[14] stressing the mutual reciprocity or *guyuban* resulting from village togetherness, free from accidents (*sambékala*).

REVELATION RESTORED: SCENARIO OF THE *WAYANG* PLAY

The play performed to invoke the multiple divinities and ancestral spirits (*hyang*) and the village protecting spirit, or *dhanyang*, ensured that the obstacles presented by evil spirits were removed and that blessings (*restu, pangestu*) would reward the villagers' good intentions and ritual endeavours. Sarwanto's informant, Pak Prawirowidjojo, insisted on the fact that the good spirits became the bad spirits if not propitiated and that therefore the choice of the shadow puppet play was critical. Other offerings left for the spirits during the *wayang* performance are not there to be shared by the participants like those made during the earlier village *slametan*. The *dhalang* may give them away after the performance. The *dhalang* is there not only to give the village a spectacle but also to provide a role model by praying. It is the village that sponsors the performance, just as it makes the offerings, but the *dhalang*'s role is to execute the ritual duties.

The first spectacle, the all-night *wayang* performance, had been scheduled to take place beginning at nine o'clock in the evening after the afternoon village communal meal or *slametan*. In the meantime, rioting and looting had engulfed the entire city in connection with the imminent fall of thirty years of military dictatorship. Some of the youths had gone out to participate in the looting and/or observe the excitement. Most were hiding in village alleyways, hoping to be spared any violence. Some were ready to defend their neighbourhood. The committee quickly postponed both *wayang* performances from Wage Thursday (i.e., the eve of Jum'at Kliwon, 14 May). Later they were rescheduled for Pahing Thursday (the eve of Jum'at Pon, 11 June). *Ki*

Warseno Slenk from Makam Haji (Sukoharjo) was the *dhalang* chosen. It was thus to him that the puppet Puntadewa was to be presented before the performance. He was considered ideal, for he was popular with the youth for his trendy Limbukan dialogues as well as his action-packed war and turbulence scenes (*gara-gara*). The bicycle and motorcycle parking attendants and the food hawkers also liked him because of the crowds he brought, an important financial consideration after the recent riots. Nonetheless, the *camat* (subprefect) of Banjarsai, Iman Sutop, was consulted before the final choice of *dhalang*. The late morning *wayang* play The Marriage of Wisnu (*Wisnu Krama*) of Jum'at Pon, 12 June, was performed by the elder cousin of *ki* Warseno Slenk, the *dhalang ki* Wijiyanto from Juwiring, Klathen.

The choice of which all-night main *wayang* play to present is important. This is not only an aesthetic consideration, but it must fit the needs of the sponsoring community. For a rural village purification (*bersih dhusun*) ceremony a play about planting rice, Sri Mulih, or in urban "villages" a "construction" theme is often used. A revelation (*wahyu*) play is considered to have a good effect. The dedication (*diujubaké*) of these good effects of the play is usually to be found in the mouth of Semar at the end when a leather puppet, representing a cosmic tree or *kayon*, is being planted.

Sarwanto provides a scenario sketch of the first play, *Wahyu Kamulyan*, which he claims is an original composition of the *dhalang*.[15] The background to this drama begins when Prabu Baladewa arrives in the court of Dwarawati to ask Prabu Kresna, in the presence of Samba and Setyaki, why Prabu Puntadewa of Amarta has left without informing his siblings. Before they have had the time to finish this conversation, Begawan Sidik Wacana arrives, delegated by the court at Astina to borrow the Kembang Wijaya Mulya (the flower of august victory). Kresna refuses him this request. On the square in front of the court of Dwarawati, Begawan Sidik Wacana then tries to take it by force and is defeated in combat by Prabu Baladewa. The rest of the drama revolves around another amulet or *aji*, the Wahyu Kamulyan, which Puntadewa receives during the act Kahyangan Alang-Alang Kumitir. Two masks or disguises permit members of the two families to deceive one another as to their identity. In the final scene in Amarta, Sanghyang Wenang disguises himself as a crow before Puntadewa until this king, Prabu Puntadewa, proves his total inner serenity by preparing to sacrifice himself for the life of a sparrow (*Passer montanus malaccensis*), which the crow is pursuing. The final act ends with Puntadewa facing Prabu Kresna, Baladewa, Seno, and Semar. Puntadewa giving thanks for having received the revelation, Wahyu Kamulyan, which has brought back peace and happiness to the entire kingdom of Amarta.

THE CANGIK–LIMBUK DIALOGUE

This lengthy exchange[16] seems a likely place to find reflections on the reconstruction of social confidence in Surakarta. Their conversation starts out with an affirmation. The mother and daughter are in fact divinities incarnate as peasant women intending to make their annual visit to *mbah* Meyek. The opening dialogue between the mother, Cangik, and her "most lovely daughter", the Crisis Goddess (Dewi Krisis), now incarnate as Limbuk, presents a vision of their function in the play. Afterward most of the Limbukan is devoted to thanking the sponsors, introducing the singers (*pesindhèn*), satisfying song requests, improvising in Sundanese with a singer from Bandung (West Java), and presenting brief instrumental selections of the drum and separate instruments of the gamelan. Their opening exchange is translated below:

LIMBUK: What did you say mother?

CANGIK: You and I see in true perspective the incomparable revelation that we have received from the Lord. We accept that immeasurable honour.

LIMBUK: Why is that?

CANGIK: Ever since I became Cangik and you become Limbuk, thirty-three years of age, during the village purification, we pay a visit to Mbah Meyek, who lives in Mbibis.

LIMBUK: Yes.

CANGIK: Because you and I have a fortunate destiny, namely, that of benefiting humans so that they not become jealous, right?

LIMBUK: Yes.

CANGIK: What is more, my child, mankind can receive that good fate by following the sayings of the elders and the wise that must be based on [the following]: One must fast (from sleep and food) a great deal and pray (*prihatiné*); second, one must be diligent and careful as well as honest in every aspect of what one is working on.

LIMBUK: Like that.

CANGIK: Be unremittingly responsible in furthering mankind's existence.

LIMBUK: Yes, like that.

How does this compare to other general statements about the relation of the play to the collective consciousness of the villagers? During the *dhalang*'s first introductory words (the *janturan jejer*, Sarwanto's transcription 1999, p. 210), one hears the following pronouncement:

Dhalang is going to pray for the existence of life.[17] Under the sign of the Bhinneka Tunggal Eka (unity in diversity), becoming the inner strength of cultured life, as a tool for fivefold guidance, that is to say worship of the

Almighty (*panembah mring hyang Kuwasa*), love for one's equals (*tresna asih mring sesama*), ethnic brotherhood (*kedadang sami bangsa*), consultation as a path to wisdom (*sarasihan sarana wicaksana*), working for the ideal of a just and good [society] (*kinarya anggayuh adil lan para marta*). This cultural fragrance reaches even abroad; shadow puppet theatre flourishes in Java, providing a model, a means of teaching the highest wisdom, conveyed by the nine holy Muslim *wali* [saints]. Thus, wayang kulit contains teachings concerning the refined and the coarse [*alus agal*, i.e., the spiritual and the physical] for the people now gathered together here, so there is nothing strange in the fact that the essence of these teachings accords with the purpose of reinforcing harmony and unity while not diminishing the sentiment of submission (*tawakal*). Evil traits of character (*watak*) must be thrown away, the sentiment of jealousy and envy destroyed and cut off, for good deeds will dispose (of them) by the magnitude of the blessing.

The *dhalang's* capacity to perform a *wayang* that cleanses evil destinies depends on his genealogy and his capacity to intercede. The modelisation of the Solo city crisis is never explicit, it is indeed scrupulously avoided, but the claim to be able to annihilate evil traits implicitly reflects the need for restructuring society by social groups rather than individually. The Mangkunagaran palace of Surakarta held such a rite to calm the unrest in Solo in 1949, and many other precedents exist for using *ruwatan* to combat pests, epidemics, and so on.[18] The *dhalang*, as the priest of a ritual, addresses present needs. This is reflected in Semar's assessment of the accomplishments of the performance just before the end of the play (*tancep kayon*; Sarwanto's transcription, pp. 310–11). These are the final words of the *dhalang* said by Semar, the paramount ancestor:

> Thus is the supplication, now complete. Let us put out of our minds [all that, now that] well-being, peace, and prosperity have been given. Let us give thanks for Almighty God, who so wills. May He always give [us] victory from above (*jaya2 wijananti*), interior and exterior serenity, serenity for the people and the village, interior and exterior purity, far from any troubles and chaos (*retu*), that the village might be increasingly cleansed from feelings of greed, anger, and meanness and thus secure, secure and giving thanks unto the Lord.

Without any of the *ruwatan's* mythic structure (a cosmogony retold to re-form the present destinies of the sponsors), the Bibis Kulon village purification by moralistic exhortation performatively accomplishes a cleansing of the village from hindrances and moral obstacles. In 1997 the words "chaos" (*retu*) and "rioting" (*rebut*) would not yet have appeared; the need for the conventional purification of the village was certainly felt more pressingly in 1998 than in other years.

13.4 CONCLUSIONS

It remains to be seen how a theatrical production like a *wayang* materializes a perceived ritual and moral need. Both the Beteng Plaza traders and the villagers in Bibis Kulon had suffered direct material loss as a result of the riots and looting in Solo in late May 1998. The people felt strongly about their need to restore a vanished equilibrium, but their requests appear to have been contained in a few nearly incomprehensible mantras recited during the Birth of Kala or in the prayers in front of the village shrines and offerings displayed at the well of *mbah* Meyek. The two plays, however, incorporate these desires in a different and lengthier discourse, articulating and embedding in a less explicit manner all the aspirations placed in the plaza and village rituals of purification. These entertaining spectacles bring together and hold the attention of the local social agents by providing theatrical relief and occasional invocations. The *dhalang* didn't moralize about private personal serenity (*iklas*), patience (*sabar*), and acceptance (*trima*). He articulated a social aspiration, speaking directly of its realization: a healthy, tolerant community.

The crowd present at a popular *dhalang*'s performance is already a sign that things are getting better, even if the village provided a clearer focus for these rituals than did the commercial plaza. The Limbukan dialogues and *gara-gara* turmoil are the most prominent scenes (*adegan*) to crystallize this popular confidence by focusing on the personal taste in music and humour of a *dhalang* and that of his spectators. Through the interplay of the identities of the actors, masked in the leather puppets, the puppeteer and spectators attain mutual attunement, providing one kind of the inner satisfaction (*kapuasan bathin*) that contributes to the inner clarification (*pernyataan jati diri*) needed after such a trauma as the sacking of Solo city. The endless verbiage of Panca Sila moralism may have been vacuous, but moral exhortation has certainly always occupied a large place in Javanese discourse. It is only in indiviudualistic societies that such encouragement seems vacuous.

F. Tonnies, writing in 1887, observed that communities based on kinship, neighbourhoods, and friendships differed from those where the typically social acts of exchange brought together perfect strangers in contractual relationships. Even if this broad distinction has limited use in Java, such a social construction of confidence is still the main issue.[19] Both of these performances stress socially constructed confidence as an essential factor for social cohesion, providing a passage from suspicion and defiance to confidence. It was not a culture of law that was invoked but a culture of trust in mutual dependence.

Certain social attitudes are crucial. Confidence institutes society by maintaining and guaranteeing alterity, otherness. Confidence is initially a sign of alienation. As Levinas has written, "The future is another person." The violent attacks on private property, the abuse, rapes, beatings, and killings that occurred in May 1998, convinced the Javanese of Solo that their social fabric was unravelling; "society" was coming to an end. The two performances presented above in the media of invocation and spectacle provide an alternative vision of Solo, a virtual return to the desired normality of social harmony. It was a very long time coming. As far back as April 1982, Goenawan Mohammad was writing in his weekly column in *Tempo* that when a state ceased to be a state serving the nation it is normal that it no longer exist as a focus of loyalty and service. What seems to have reappeared gradually over the last twenty-five years is an understanding of society composed of organic social bonds at many different levels, each demanding mutual confidence one from another. The role of NGOs was primordial here.[20] The communality of the *wayang* that arises while these issues are being discussed provides the perspective that mutual confidence, the topic of many of the dialogues, can be achieved. Therein lies a catharsis to the burning of Solo.

How do purification (*ruwatan*), the communal meal (*slametan*), and *wayang* theatre facilitate the circulation of values inside the Javanese social morphology? What does the exchange of values mean when we are talking about the end of the New Order regime? In Chapter 3 (cf. Figure 3.5), we saw that the difference in scale between palace and village mutually reinforced this exchange of values sought in the cult of the Javanese goddesses, as long as the villages were not in revolt. In the classical Javanese kingdom, it is clear that the circulation of values redistributed from the centre, and by apical demotion through high social status, was completed by intervillage networks of exchange between households. Royal kinship granted the privilege to raise taxes through the apanage system; taxes allowed one to raise armies, and armies guaranteed rights of succession, which in turn permitted the royal kinship to reproduce itself, at least in times of stability. The hypertrophy of universality in the the territorial pretentions of the nation-state had under the Soeharto's regime proved untenable. One knew the regime would fall once the people lost their fear of its capacity to be a dictatorship, to be a pseudo whole. That moment was distinguished by the people's mocking of the corrupt government cadre, police, judges, etc.

In all events described — these two Surakarta rituals, purification rituals, the communal meal, and *wayang* theatre — there was a coming together on the basis of a communal intention (*niat*) and a spoken common declaration (*ujub*) over the offerings. In Indonesia, during Gayo (Sumatra),[21] Tengger Hindu (Java),[22] or Banyuwangi Osing (East Java)[23] *slametans*, the unsaid and underinterpreted (Gayo), the hiding of communal rites from public exegesis (Tengger), or, on the contrary, the systematic integration of disparate ideas (Osing Javanese) all display a variation of the same value seen in the two events in Solo, namely, a refusal to contest common social qualities on the basis of doctrinal disagreements. So how are the Solonese, celebrating their social body in the ruins of their city, demonstrating their harmonious belonging to a community? What do these groups imagine to be their permanence? What founds and charters their social bonds?

The expression of their shared values is manifest in the food offerings. There the four foetus siblings,[24] of which Ego is the fifth and central partner, are materialized out of the cosmos. There one finds the correspondences with that cosmos, which is, as Pigeaud puts it, one's community.[25] The micro–macrocosm (*jagad alit / jagad gedhé*) linkage becomes accessible through these protective four-five sets on which Ego as a member of the community is centred. The Javanese over the centuries have developed their interpretations of food offerings with great subtlety. Although orthodox Muslims may treat this Javanese lore as custom, *adat* in its present form is in fact the fruit of earlier generations of Javanese reflections on Islam, especially Muslim cosmography. As Beatty has shown in his analysis of the Banyuwangi rituals, the formal properties of this conceptualization of the whole as centre are of two kinds:

1. The centre encompassing the four outer components.
2. The centre presenting their combination.[26]

Now if the Solonese purification ceremonies (*ruwatan*) explicitly sweep away to the Southern Ocean the parasitic Kala and re-create the constellation of four-five harmony, the *wayang* plays used in village purification ceremonies contain prayers and declarations of intention for much the same thing but in a more muted and discreet way. Islam is embedded here and there in a single age cosmogony, but it is not the same cosmogony that Islam first encountered in the sixteenth century on the north coast of Java, for that one did not yet reserve a place for Allah in its pantheon. At the beginning of the twenty-first century in Solo however, Islam is fully identified with the well-being of Javanese society, indeed it is its principle guarantee as we will see in Chapter

14. One can no longer separate out Islam from Java; one can even allow oneself to minimalize the Muslim dimension of belief knowing that it will return centre stage in other circumstances.

In both cases studied above, the community sponsoring the two events is busy cleansing its body social of obstacles and dirt. So much is said about obstacles and dirt being expelled that one forgets to ask what is actually being cleansed? Clearly, here a real sociological community senses that its welfare is linked to a healthy connection to its cosmic matrix. But what is this Javanese community as family's relation with the macrocosm (*jagad gedhé*) about which it expresses so much concern? Startlingly to our "modern" mind, these "individuals" conceive of themselves, of their community, as grounded in an other, greater, outer world.[27] Their sociological vision focuses on this macrocosm. Whereas "we" situate all humanistic values, and indeed all human beings who lie outside ourselves, in this world, the Javanese, despite all the acculturation and economic remodelling of 350 years of Dutch presence, at the end of the twentieth century still aspires to be a holistic society. Their supreme value lies in society as a whole, identified with the macrocosm (*jagad gedhé*) and not in the individual. Such a category of person as community is well expressed in these two recent events centred on a shopping mall and a sacred well as the Solonese try to re-centre their society on the patterns of the cosmos. We may want to consider central Java a pseudo-whole but the hierarchy of values is still very far from individualism.

NOTES

1. I was able to consult a very complete general survey of the prefecture of Surakarta that was prepared by the Lembaga Pengembangan Teknologi Pedasaan. A preliminary version was finished in March 1999 by this non-governmental organization (NGO) based in Solo. When this was published in late 1999, it gave a very full description of the sociological background of ethnic relations in Solo, its tradition of social radicalism, a chronology of events, and an analysis of the alienation of the population at the end of Soeharto's rule.

2. Interview with *kyai haji* Dian Nafi' of the Solo branch of the Nadhlatul Ulama (2 February 1999). Few foreign observers, reading about the provoked and unprovoked outbreak of inter-ethnic and religious violence in Indonesia in 1998–99, have been able to integrate into their vision, an Indonesia seeking better relations between Christians and Muslims. Robert Hefner's study, *Civil Islam* (2000), is an important exception to this failure.

3. Eldar Braten, "Recapturing 'Java': A Call for a Javanese Anthropology", manuscript, 4, 9–10.

4. Cf. S. C. Headley (2000*a*).

5. Barbara Hatley, "Cultural Expression and Social Transformation in Indonesia" (1999).

6. My understanding of the event in the village of Bibis Kulon is based entirely on Sarwanto's thesis (1999), "Wayang Kulit Purwa Dalam Upacara Bersih Desa di Bibis Kulon, Surakarta", Gadjah Mada University, 1999. This study included a transcription of the play and the invocations.

7. Jan Mrázek, "Phenomenology of a Puppet Theatre: Contemplations on the Performance Technique of Contemporary Javanese Wayang Kulit" (Ph.D. dissertation, Cornell University, 1998), chap. 8. A revised version of the chapter was published in *Indonesia* no. 68–69.

8. Literally, "Telling the World", that is, *ki dhalang* Suloto Guno Sukasno.

9. Cf. Soewito Santoso, "Sastra Harjendra Yuningrat in the Wayang" (1991).

10. This point was called to my attention by Jan Mrázek.

11. The greatest of the four is the *putat* tree (Planchonia Valida BL.) and tamarind (*asem*) of *mbah* Kaji are called the *pundhèns* of *mbah* Asem Ageng.

12. Slenk is an acronym for "I prefer watching you" (*Saya lebih enak nonton kamu*).

13. Sarwanto, "Wayang Kulit Purwa", pp. 54–55.

14. Such *takhayul*, or superstitions, are formally not approved of by reform or Muhammadiyah Islam.

15. Sarwanto, "Wayang Kulit Purwa", pp. 115–20.

16. Ibid., pp. 227–49.

17. This is Sarwanto's free adaptation of the opening formula: *Swuh rep data pitana*.

18. At the time of writing (summer 2000) this chapter, the most recent notable example of a national *ruwatan* took place on 18 August 2000 in Yogyakarta for the president of the Indonesian Republic, Abdurrahman Wahid. Cf. Headley (2000*a*, p. 24).

19. Cf. Philippe Bernoux and J.-M. Servet, eds., *La Construction Sociale de la Confiance* (1997).

20. Cf. Muhammad A.S. Hakim, "Non-governmental Organisations and the Empowerment of Civil Society" (1999).

21. Chapter 10 of John Bowen, *Muslims through Discourse: Religion and Ritual in Gayo Society* (1993).

22. Chapter 1 of Robert Hefner's *Hindu Javanese: Tengger Tradition in Islam* (1985).

23. Chapter 1 of Andrew Beatty, *Varieties of Javanese Religion: An Anthropological Account* (1999).

24. Cf. Stephen C. Headley, "The Body as a House in Javanese Society" (1987*a*).

25. Th. G. Th. Pigeaud, "Javanese Divination and Classification," in *Structural Anthropology of the Netherlands* (1928/1983).

26. Beatty (1999, p. 41).

27. To use Louis Dumont's terminology. Cf. Chapter 1 of his *Essais sur l'individualisme: Une perspective anthropologique sur l'idéologie moderne* (1983).

14

THE SOCIAL RECONSTRUCTION OF CONFIDENCE
Community and Islam in Surakarta Today

14.1 THE *UMAT'S* APPROPRIATION OF MODERNITY

In the introduction to this volume, we justified the need for an anthropological study of the nineteenth century Central Javanese *umat* by invoking the historical contrast opposing enveloping cosmologies to elective citizenship.[1] We claimed that any effort to understand the appropriation of modernity by the *umat* of Javanese Muslims would need to take that route. Their community's morphology could only be grasped through a study of its changing forms. More fundamentally, one could only decide what kind of community the *umat* is by investigating to what extent it is encompassed. Our starting point was the attempt to show how the Javanese Islam had become the higher value by representing that society towards the exterior world, while *vis-à-vis* the older insular orientation of this island, the values of "Javanism" have remained primordial to this day. In this chapter their interface will be explored; the processes that led to this inversion of their value helps explain the emergence of communalism in the period after the fall of the Soeharto dictatorship (May 1998). Using contemporary data, it is no longer possible to confine ourselves to material from the village of Krendawahana and the area of Kaliasa, for the village has become "sub-urban", or as its villagers say *wis kota*, and at the sociological level, the village has in some respects been assimilated to that of the urban neighbourhood (*kampung*). The village that used to lie on the northern frontier of the Mangkunagaran kingdom, now lies at the northern limit of the industrial influence of the city of Surakarta with its population of more than half a million people. Taking the framework of the greater (*raya*) Surakarta into which Kaliasa now belongs has the advantage of giving greater scope to the conclusions of our earlier chapters. As the revival of Islam in the 1980s moved from the city to the countryside using techniques of popular preaching (*dakwah*) it was no longer a question of the Islamization (*Islamisasi*) of the countryside but of the indigenization of a pure Islam (*pribumisasi Islam murni*), where "pure" was defined by urban Muslim values.[2] And it was in this same urban milieu that after the fall of Soeharto in May of 1998, that a power vacuum was created into which the new reformers of the Javanese village communities rushed. It is to these that we now turn.

Nasr Abou Zeid (1999, p. 132) claims there are three sources of authority in contemporary Islamic discourse: anathema (*takfir*), sovereignty (*hākimiyya*), and textuality (*nass*). The use by the Indonesian Muslim community of the term, *jihad* (struggle), as we saw in Chapter 12, touches on the semantic fields of the three preceding terms. The *jihad* is often qualified as "the solution" in the slogans of demonstrators. It is tempting to claim that such a solution implies a "*fuite en avant*". Claiming to speak in the name of the praying community (*jemaah*), the armed militias also claim that in view of some perfect world to come, *jihad* is the solution. Verisimilitude is sacrificed to a categorical assertion of a transformation, which I call "*jihad* in front of the mosque". The most evident contradiction to their claims comes from the fact that the community (*umat*) inside the mosque is being represented politically by a vocal minority.[3] The primary identifying referent of the universal *umma* is the Koran, which surpasses all more limited ethno-cultural references. The silent majority who remain in the mosque are trying to remain a community, true to the broader ascetic meaning of the word *jihad*: involving knowledge of Allah (*ma'rifa*), repentance (*tawba*), and abandonment to Allah (*tawakkul*); love of Allah (*mahabba*) and meeting with Allah (*wajd*).

To almost all Indonesian Muslims a more peaceful notion of "alterity" (relations with non-Muslims) propagated by the fervour of ascetic *jihad* does not mean assassination of the unbelievers (*kafir*), but reconciliation with difference through mastery of one's own passions. The broadsheet *al-Ikhtilaf* (The Difference; cf. ch. 12), distributed in mosques throughout Central Java every Friday morning, illustrates the dimensions of this struggle through concrete incidents in Javanese daily life and their corresponding foundation in Koranic texts. Sovereignty is Allah's; the idolization of the Islamic state is treated as unbelief. What in Java is called the "secularization" of Islam derives from a movement to take Islam out of the political arena, initiated by Nurcholish Madjid in the 1970s. Otherwise, the community (*umat*) risks becoming "foam on the waves" of political competition through the financing of so-called *jihad* militias (*laskar*); there will then be no more *umat*.

What is at risk here? First of all, a blurring of the distinction between revealed texts and human thought, the textuality (*nass*) of the revelation of the Koran referred to above. Secondly the distinction between lay ('*ilmānī*) or terrestrial (*dunyawiyya*) and the world of Allah will no longer be possible because the human thought will have taken Allah for an object. When private political motives move people to speak of Islam in the absolute, the distinction between text and a Muslim's understanding of the sacred word is lost. Anathema then plays a primordial role, and the difference between the moderate and extremist versions of Islam is reduced almost to nothing, for each side claims to have a direct hold on Allah's *wahyu* (revelation). Views on Javanese society seen from inside the mosque as opposed to outside the mosque differ:[4] moderates insist that social reproduction includes everyone, Muslims and non-Muslims alike.

14.2 A JIHAD FOR INTEGRATING OTHERS INTO JAVANESE SOCIAL MORPHOLOGY AFTER 1998

Key social values require successive evaluations. For instance, J. Fox (1971) has claimed that centralized kingdoms have more history than societies lacking a strong hierarchy while M. Bloch (1977) asserted that domination and inequality were able to create a past in the present. On the contrary, J. Hoskins (1993, p. xiii) proposed that historical traditions in the broadest sense of the word provide as many opportunities for innovation as for the reproduction of their earlier forms. Despite the decentralizing impact of the introduction of Islam and the successive V.O.C. onslaughts, on the social plane in Java a similar hierarchy linked heaven and earth in the eighteenth century. During the twentieth century, public violence destroyed much of what remained of these commonly held values. Late colonialism, nascent nationalism, the Japanese Occupation, and finally the Soeharto military dictatorship disabused them concerning the strength of their sacred canopy, and reordering the world of a Javanese in days of uncertainty was a difficult task.

When the modern state is dysfunctional, formerly traditional societies often recall an earlier social morphology, in contemporary garb, and older forms of evaluation return even if the cosmic vault has faded. The need to manage the diverse religious and ethnic rifts which have arisen in the meanwhile, subjects ethnic kinship practices to new constraints, gradually introducing the phenomenon of "dissociated" identities. For Kipp, studying the Batak (1996), adherence to ritual is not identical with belonging to the local society. These in turn eventually generate secularized identities created in part by the impact of religious pluralism. Roughly speaking, this was the situation in the urban areas of Java at the end of the twentieth century in which we will plunge *in medias res*.

In Chapter 10 we skteched out the sociological parameters of the Muslim *umat*. Prayer with one's Muslim brothers in the mosque serves to clear to the mirror of the soul so that it will clearly reflect the divinity of Allah. At the same time the mosque space is a sociological stage where these rites are accomplished by the local *umat*. All *salat* (the five daily canonical prayers) have this double dimension. One of the supposed demands of Muslim monotheism put forth in the ethos of the *sharī'ah* is the construction of a Muslim polity. However the Javanese experience of the Darul Islam and PRRI revolts in the 1950s led the Indonesian army to distrust their state-building endeavours, and led to the marginalizing of Muslim political ambitions (Hefner 2000, ch. 3). The longevity of Soeharto's military dictatorship (1966–98) created a pseudo metamorphosis in Javanese society.

Contemporary religious and kinship praxis bring with them a present memory of older socio-cosmic ritual bonds. Adherence to these practices is often only "individually" achieved, even if they claim to be a total sociology. What has happened? With the advent of the New Order Pancasila ideology in Indonesia (1966+), monotheistic faiths bureaucratically endowed with a monopoly on the label *agama* (religion)[5] by the state Ministry of Religion. This created a crisis that made that past more visible in the present. One of the characteristics of ideological control in the second half of the twentieth century in Indonesia was the appearance of an "evaluative indifference" often propagated by such totalitarian regimes (Sers 2001, ch. 2). The Pancasila ideology tried to avoid experience of its own ideological impotency by refusing the population the right to choose and practise polytheisms. Since all "religions" were put in the same category (monotheisms) by the government, all religions could be placed under the same umbrella of Pancasila orthodoxy. Through the false appearance of a popular consensus, religion is made to seem well defended by the obligatory adherence to a monotheistic religion, that recorded on each citizen's personal identity card. Of course all these religions were not that monotheistic, and, as Umar Dani once said,[6] all this civil religion did was to encourage atheism. This also left the Muslim citizens, in many cases initially nominal Muslims, as *individuals* belonging to an *umat*, but an *umat* which could no longer claim exclusivity to a socio-cosmic and monotheistic harmony which was pre-empted by a basically secular, state-controlled Ministry of Religion.

Outside the mosque throughout Java, a diverse theo-linguistics reflected a diversity of local spirit cults encrusted in the local mythological landscape (Headley 1996*a*). These diverse religious landscapes "presented" these divinities to the local community. A gift of credit ("cred-o") to the divinity that tied up (*re-ligio*) a network of relations within the whole community was implied.

The characteristic of the five daily *salat* in the mosque was that immediately one stood before Allah as an unranked individual. An equivalency was thus obtained between partners in prayer through their communicative common reference to Allah. Often both Muslim prayer in the mosque was practised, as well as *donga* (*du'a*) to local spirits outside the mosque (Parkin and Headley 2000). Once reified, this ambivalence led to competing demands among the participants. Allah was a creator, regenerating society by theodicy and therefore all honour should be returned to him. Another contradiction was that since all collective oral rites create some sort of solidarity, Muslim orthodoxy coveted control over this sort of social capital.

It is easier to understand now what kind of religious orthodoxy the New Order of General Soeharto wanted to guarantee. Clearly it was not a Muslim-centred Indonesia, in which the military government would find their own position marginalized from the centre.[7] As the Karo Batak example has shown (Kipp 1996, ch. 12; Vignato 2000), in *some* of the smaller ethnic groups religious pluralism led to a transformation of the role of kinship networks. For the Karo Batak, it is hard not to see that the separation of religion from community today does consolidate the basis of community (Kipp 1993, ch. 12). Indeed where these networks contributed to religious tolerance, the kinship aspect of *adat* became more influential than its religious dimension.

The problem posed by inter-faith marriages is less that of protecting the purity of one's faith than with how to protect kinship ties from dispersal. The trade-off is clear. If one joins a "universal" religion like Christianity or Islam, then one can secularize kinship and culture on which the links between the social and the cosmic formerly rested. Those entering the middle class were the most likely to accept this, while those faithful to the older *adat*-based religion are the least likely. The kin ties also protect the emerging class distinctions between a given wife-taker or wife-giving group from becoming too prominent. Thus in northern Sumatra which entered the colonial "state" three centuries after Java, ethnic identity was reinforced *vis-à-vis* the Malay and Dutch only fifty years before their religious identity was redefined by massive conversions to Christianity. The result, as Kipp says, is that religion was shunted off into the private sphere, where it gained in importance as a consciously held individual value, while kinship became more important socially, but in the form of disenchanted custom, no longer important in circulating values. It is this odd pairing that she calls a secularized identity. General Soeharto cynically used the values shared by many Indonesians concerning the collectivity to hide the fact that enforced monotheism was in fact leading to the transformation of "total life values …(into) part time norms" (Luckman 1967, p. 39, cited by Kipp). Here secularization favours the compartmentalization, the emerging heterogeneity, and the fragmentation which allows the centre to assume control. Kipp stressed that by pretending to purify religion (*agama*) of superstition (local beliefs), the government could reinforce secularized local culture which was good for tourism at the same time as favouring the emergence of religious pluralism among ethnic groups. Henceforth ethnic diversity would come to mean cultural diversity, and the umbrella ideology of Pancasila would override class-based or religiously-based divisions in the name of a peaceful collectivity.

14.3 HIERARCHIES OF VALUES IN CENTRAL JAVA TODAY

In the nineteenth century Javanese and Muslim value systems were rarely juxtaposed. In the imagery of every opening scene of the shadow puppet theatre (*wayang*), if the cosmic tree (*kayon*) or mountain (*gunungan*) showed instability, twirling out of kilter, the holistic nature of society returned in a matter of hours as the references evoked in the myths reinstalled it in a horizon of transcendence. While this *wayang* theatre recognized the existence of frequent upheavals, it did not create a "new order" as did the Soeharto regime (1966–98). This dictatorship tried to play the role of an ideological cosmic tree *(gunungan* or *kayon)*, using the Pancasila ideology to stabilize society, but its purposes were cynical and its means violent. When the New Order lost its brutally enforced control, when its violence no longer intimidated a large enough portion of its population, and society started to shed its habits of submission in order to be rid of Soeharto, while rogue elements from the old regime helped to destabilize the President, free speech and information technology (mobile phones, e-mail, and websites) enabled the Javanese to react in many instances collectively and not just individualistically. Instinctively they sought to restore a traditional form of social confidence that was holistic in the sense used above, "housing" society in a larger hierarchical relationship with the cosmos. This process quickly fell apart in the capital, and several regions (Moluccas, South Kalimantan, and Aceh) were torn apart by communal violence. It was often local mechanism (peace pacts, etc.) that alone proved capable of restoring order in these areas. Throughout Java, more discreetly, social tensions remained very high.

Social frustrations at the end of the New Order (ORBA) military rule of Indonesia (1990–98) ran very high. Citizens had become desperate and, as the economic situation worsened, people lost their fear of the "authorities". When a prospect of toppling the regime appeared, the wave crested. In a final effort to stall the "reformation" movement, on 14–15 May 1998 the city of Surakarta or Solo[8] in Central Java was burnt and sacked by mobs led into action by New Order intelligence officers. Although the population eventually participated in the looting, it did not initiate it. What the riots were intended to provoke were potentially violent expressions of sectarian regroupings (anti-Chinese, anti-Christian). These, in turn, stimulated counter efforts to rebuild social confidence which will be described here. Notwithstanding this initial provocation and many others elsewhere in Java, five days later Soeharto was forced to resign in Jakarta. The population had no trust in the police or the army and, what is more, they were no longer afraid of them. The army and the police stayed well away from many urban areas, knowing they would be threatened there. Indeed there was little authority left, and the imminent anarchy made everyone afraid that Solo would again become a war zone. Communalism, called "primordialism" in Indonesia, had made its entry here, shrinking social horizons. By communalism we understand that when a culture begins to be used as a repertoire for identifying difference, the cosmologies that in the past had accommodated both Javanism and Islam, are no longer any kind of sacred canopy but a secularized one. As Arjun Appadurai said (1996, p. 13), "culture is a pervasive dimension of human discourse that exploits difference to generate diverse conceptions of group identity".

With the fall of the dictatorship in May 1998, more than thirty years of ideological control came to an end. Not only could their lessons on *Pancasila* ideology[9] be unlearned, but many new norms of behaviour needed to be integrated into the public sphere of civility. Indeed there was an urgent need to reflect sociologically on what was happening. A deluge of new papers, weeklies, and new books appeared. By the spring of 2001 retrograde groups would begin to make "anti-communist sweepings" against bookstores as they began to realize the importance of the freedom of expression in changing perceptions of reality. Despite the first euphoria of *reformasi* during 1998–99, it soon became apparent that this reformation of society was going to take time.[10] Neither the creation of a consensus about what social values were lacking nor the installation of new forms of evaluation required to conceive of the new society to be built, was a priority of those who rushed in to the power vacuum. In the meanwhile "tolerance", "civility", and "pluralism" quickly became overused words with little precise content. The jargon of New Order ideology was replaced by the jargon of the reformation movement with an increasingly discouraged (*putus asa*) constituency. After the relatively clean and fair election of May 1999, the rhetoric of a deep social change seemed too weak to deal with so much élite-sponsored public violence. Many positive aspirations faded into the uncertain future. On the local level nonetheless changes were taking place and it is to these that we must turn to find evidence of the process of rebuilding of social confidence.

As claimed above, in times of such radical loss of social confidence, one gets glimpses of the articulation of social morphology which in more normal periods are hidden away behind a wall of so-called "self evident" assumptions and goals. When these "obvious" assumptions fall apart, the social bonds are consciously re-thought, often with perspicacity. Observing these public thought processes prompted our own reflections on the evolution of the city Surakarta given below.[11]

Below is a brief summary of several hundred pages of transcribed interviews and documents, concentrating on three major themes:

1. Even though regionalization is creating opportunities for new fiefdoms, local authorities in villages and urban villages (*kampung*) are no longer invariably co-opted by centralized state institutions. Regional (provincial) autonomy, if it is accomplished, will have to make certain aspects of sub-prefectural and prefectural (*kecamatan* and *kebupaten*) more responsive to local territorialized solidarity, instead of the reverse.
2. Horizontal and vertical solidarity's being realigned on the basis of new possibilities of self-defence by the population, both urban and rural.
3. The invigorating effect of free speech on inter-religious, legal and cultural networks.

The importance of current speech styles as indicators of new ways of thinking is emphasized throughout our evocation of the three themes above. The examples used are taken from four distinct fields of social interaction:

1. Two legal aid NGOs: the Foundation of the Upholding of Indonesian Law or YAPHI and the consortium for Agrarian Reform.
2. Two Muslim groups working for religious tolerance: the Pondok Pesantren Al-Muayyad (Windan branch) in Kartasura, a "suburb" of Solo; and the Yogyakarta-based LKiS or Institute for Islamic and Social Studies.
3. A full day (27 January 2001) "ritual" (*upacara*) for social peace organized in Surakarta by the Panitia Nasional Doa Sedekah Bumi or the National Committee for a Prayer Offering to the Earth, comprising a morning

speech at the Surakarta palace by a Javanese philosopher, Damarjati; an evening procession by delegates of all the provinces of Indonesia, ending with six prayers by different religious groups, and an all-night shadow puppet theatre. The *dhalang* was *ki dhalang* Mantep and the play, a variant of the Sajèn Raja Suyo (the offering of the Suyo king), the "In-gathering of the Pandhawa".

4. A seven-part presentation of music, dance, and theatre by the STSI or Surakarta Graduate School of the Arts on 7 February 2001.

The first two of these are quite self-conscious efforts on the part of the Javanese to be empirical, that is to say to describe and formulate social realities they wish to influence. The other two describe and briefly analyse ritual activities. Here there exists a whole set of assumptions that by definition precludes self-conscious reflection about what is going to happen. Rituals proceed through performatively efficacious speech and gestures. The performers here have introduced a self-reflective dimension through the traditional satire and irony with which these art forms are treated. In conclusion, I will briefly contrast the efforts to reconstruct social confidence in Solo with those in the city of Medan in the province of Northern Sumatra. These comparisons give the urban particularities of Surakarta a sociological backdrop that permits us to situate them in the general Indonesian context.

14.4 LAW, TERRITORY, AND AUTONOMY

The beginning of the end of the co-opting of local communities' authority by centralized state institutions can be seen in many ways. Historically speaking, it began with the taxation of village lands via the apanage system under the Eastern, and later Central, Javanese kingdoms in the seventeenth and eighteenth centuries, yet their notion of eminent domain targeted people not land; the nineteenth century colonial state after the revolt of the Java War (1825–30) targeted both (cf. Ch. 4).[12] A recent study of the nineteenth century apanage system[13] and the Javanese rentiers or tax farmers, widely read by the Javanese, has popularized a vision of nineteenth century aristocrats as social parasites that lived off the apanage land tenure system. The elements of such an analysis were already identified by the Dutch historians Rouffaer (1905). Now one hears in the mouths of NGO activists[14] such expressions as the "rentier mentality" inherited from the nineteenth century. The issue of just access to land for the landless farmer has never been more acute than at the beginning of the twenty-first century. Since the fall of the Soeharto regime it has been raised constantly.

The contemporary sociological perspective of young lawyers working in legal aid NGOs has opened up a broader understanding of the New Order regime (1966–1991) using anthropological and historical perspectives. Before May 1998, one heard much discussion of the New Order's lack of respect for law, but now one hears more about the general Javanese lack of *culture* of law. Yet knowledge of how to use the law to defend oneself is not sufficient. First of all, equality before the law is not conceivable in Java. After thirty years of illegal governance under Soeharto, legal actions to redress injustices have to be based on a renewed vision of social bonds. Fortunately, if a culture of law is lacking, an understanding of the culture of sociality, of social networks, is to be found in abundance. Holism may have been fractured but it lies in wait as a value ready to be represented. So after more than thirty years of near total lawlessness, many legal aid foundations have chosen, as will be shown below, to educate the peasants or urban proletariat in techniques for acquiring a sense of their *collective* rights,[15] as well as in how to use the law as a means of personal defence.

NGOs, hard put to appeal to any popular confidence in the corrupt legal system, encourage their lawyers offering to defend their clients without charge. Although the existence of legal aid centres (LBH) in Jakarta dates from 1982, when Adnan Buyung Nasution opened a bureau there, free (*Pro Déo*) consultation with lawyers in Solo is a more recent phenomenon. The two NGOs described here are YAPHI or the Foundation for the Upholding of Indonesian Law and the KPA or Consortium for Agrarian Reform. The first is a legal aid NGO, founded in Solo in 1992. It is an outgrowth of the LBKS (Yayasan Bimbingan Kesejahteraan Masyarakat, a Protestant NGO) and the YISR (Yayasan Ignatius Slamet Riyadi, a Catholic NGO). It has branches in Kebumen and Kudus. They both share the critique that NGOs should not just be middlemen siphoning off overseas sponsors' funds for nominal projects. As Maria Ruwiastuti (interview Solo, 29 February 2001) said, it is strange that some NGOs in Solo sometimes ask their clients to pay for their services, for, if their clients cannot pay, then how are they being "aided"?

Whether dealing with labour or land disputes, both organizations stress that truth their clients are trying to bring to light must be based on hard facts. YAPHI handles a large number of cases each year.[16] This is all the more impressive as they are trying to "transform" their clients, to teach them to learn not only how to end the injustices to which they are subjected by resorting to legal aid, but also how to become independent of the legal aid facility in order to be able to deal with these conflicts themselves. Individual clients come to the Solo YAPHI office, but if a whole village or a whole factory work-force is involved, then YAPHI goes to where they live or work. After 1998 free speech and free access to information began to be introduced to the villages or to the factories. One cannot exaggerate how great a change this is after more than a generation of enforced silence under the New Order. The mass is no longer floating: it is finding its feet.

What are the problems encountered? YAPHI finds that to prevent people from using the law for their own private ends, it is necessary to insist on the cohesiveness (*kerekatan*) among the villagers or factory workers, especially in Central Javanese factories where the tactic of buying off a fraction of the workers in labour dispute or the peasants in a land dispute is a common tool to oppose labour from organizing. In a conversation (22 January 2001), Haryati Panca Putri, the director of the Solo YAPHI, described the need to increase awareness among the poor of their common destiny (*senasib*) since the Solo riots of May 1998. Those who share a common destiny can constitute a community.[17] Exploration of the shared dimensions of the problem they are facing, being cornered (*disudutkan*), is such a common and painful experience to the Javanese that the realization of a common destiny, or *senasib*, is an important event. The reality of being unjustly handled (*diperlakukan*) by a landlord or factory owner, or of being arbitrarily oppressed by the government, requires factual description that only becomes *imaginable*, and thus useable for self-defence, when one is aware that the law could be on one's side. The value attributed to workers and peasants by factory owners and real estate investors is so low that the initial difficulty is to convince those to whom injustices are done that they can best evaluate their situation by considering first of all that they are worthy of some respect. And this begins, says Haryati Panca Putra, by gathering together as "friends". The adhesiveness (*kerekatan*) that characterizes farmers will be different than that which characterizes factory workers who are not all from the same hamlet, but, in both instances, what is advocated by the YAPHI is cross-political party, trans-religious solidarity. Refusing to support the actions of labour unions in other factories is treated as an expression of individualism. Even if it is intuitively contra-factual, the law is presented as being potentially the same for everyone.

The negative corollary of this is that the individualism, expressed in sectarian groupings, is clearly a danger, as will be explained in Section 14.7. By increasing their awareness of the dangers of individualism, YAPHI tries to increase solidarity between the members of these factions or *kelompok*. Ganging up (*dikeroyok*) on those who do not share one's factions views, says Haryati Panca Putra, should be branded as an individualistic awareness using religious, political or regional ideology in ways that lead often to rioting and other forms of violence. She adds that regional autonomy will certainly aggravate these conflicts because each region will have to provide for its own local needs on the basis of limited local resources.

To further this end the Catholic YAPHI works with Muslim legal aid foundations in such a way that no NGO can ever be accused of defending a case on the grounds of religious sectarianism. Haryati Panca Putra[18] stated that this was very carefully done by the five Legal Aid foundations during the recent trial of Ahmad Welson, sentenced to five years in prison for having claimed on a Solo radio station that Mohammed had initially been a Christian. As a pagan (*kafir*) to be combated, Welson excited street actions around the Solo court house that made its sessions very dangerous. On another occasion, YAPHI was accused of Christianization, as in Kebumen where certain Muslims took a vow not to be defended by Christians. In such a situation religious soldiarity was evaluated negatively.

The Javanese pesasants began to lose control of their land in the 1830s when the Dutch started taking it over for plantation economy. Prior to that, although the traditional system was collapsing and many *priyayi* (aristocrats) sub-rented their apanage to the Dutch, Chinese, and Javanese, basically the peasants were kept on the land because they were required as farmers. After the introduction of the *cultuurstelsel,* and down to the present time, this bond between the tillers of the land and different usufruct rights to it, have been jeopardized. As claimed in Chapter 4, the question of the feudal inheritance of the two former principalities of Central Java, Yogyakarta and Surakarta, is crucial. In the urban area of the special district of Yogyakarta, more homogeneous than that of Surakarta with its numerous and juxtaposed social groupings, the last two sultans of Yogyakarta[19] have created a climate of political development that advanced well beyond feudalism at the same time as reinforcing the prestige of the sultan. In Surakarta on the other hand, the political passivity of the disenfranchised Susuhunan and the Mangkunagaran houses left the city in 1998 with no respected leader with any experience in a construction of social confidence in the face of the numerous political and economic challenges faced by Solo since independence in 1949. This discredit of the local government in Surakarta is also found at the level of the provincial government. The rentier mentality led prefectural and provincial level officials to steal land from the villages and towns and resell it to the industrialists or private individuals. Many of these injustices occur when converting one kind of ownership (*andarbeni, duwé désa, pesini, milik yasan, agrairisch eingendom,* etc.[20]) into another (cf. Ruwiastuti 2001, pp. 89–91). The legitimacy of *local socially recognized ownership* at the village level began to be marginalized in the nineteenth century by land grants by the Kasusunan of Surakarta (*Wenang Nganggo Run-Tumurun*). The danger of complete marginalization, says

Ruwiastuti (2001, p. 97) is that, "for a people as religious but also as naïf as the Indonesian populus, law is still believed to be sacred and a prolongation of the decisions of God, since they themselves are called just and good." The lack of credibility of the government and the reputed arbitrariness of its use of the legal system is difficult of redress.[21] A truly landless peasantry quickly turns to banditry, as the recent (1997–2001) pillaging of the Central Javanese teak forests has shown.

In the second half of the twentieth century, demographic pressure and poverty have created a large class of defenceless and landless peasantry, often more than 75 per cent of a given village. During the thirty odd years of the New Order regime, in the greater Solo area, land-grabbing by the military, by the bureaucrats, and by the wealthy became more blatant with each passing year. The peasants and urban poor knew that they had no way of defending their action, from being forced off their land. Recently, when land has been unilaterally reoccupied by displaced peasants, one of the advantages of defending their takeovers legally, as opposed to "taking the law into one's own hands" (*main hakim sendiri; aksi sepikah*), is that it brings out this hierarchy of social values. Treating people as persons (Javanese, *diuwongaké*), coming close to them, enables them to believe in the themselves. These legal aid actions are finally not based on any existing culture of law, but on the fact that even the most mistreated Javanese is still sensitive to such an appeal: *Manggo sesarengan*, "Let's do it together".[22] This belief in the power of a collectivity to bind together as an englobing, higher level social unit is often called a *paguyuban* (mutual aid society). Without this belief in a communal dimension that encompasses and englobes the individual, no recourse to undo injustices would be viable. We will call this hierarchy of values social confidence.

The Consortium for Agrarian Reform (KPA) founded in 1994 with the support of sixty-five NGOs, benefits from its national linkages and wide regional experience. It is specifically dedicated to the land issues. The co-ordinator of its expert council, Maria Ruwiastuti, with whom I talked, is based in Solo. Taking stock of the consequences of more than three decades of violations of that most elementary right, the occupation of the land that serves to house or feed one's family, she and her colleagues refused to be scared off, after an interval of nearly forty years, by the danger of reformulating the question of land reform. In the villages of Central Java in 1965–66, it was the aftermath of the efforts towards land reform in the early sixties that served as the pretext for much of the violence that led to the death of tens of thousands of so-called communists.[23] One of the reasons for the numerous thefts of land at the village level under the New Order regime was the interdiction and hence disappearance of political activity below the prefectural level, the so-called "floating mass" policy. The purpose of this depolitization and security approach to the village life was that it deprived the peasants of the local space necessary to articulate their interests and rights. Political development in this situation could only be that of the nation-state institutions with their downward reach towards the local context. The alarming increase of conflicts over land indicates that the village notions of ownership, so-called *adat* or customary law, are alive, even if they are ignored, and demand to be recognized.[24] As a recently published book shows, regional autonomy will only be viable if some dimension of social justice is introduced into the conflicts over landownership, those acquired by clearing the land (*hak ulayah*), by occupation, as opposed to the simple possession of a certificate of ownership recognized by the government. If the sociological weight of that piece of paper is greater than that of the livelihood of a whole group of villages, the results will resemble the area of Kedungombo,[25] said Ruwiastuti. This huge irrigation project showed up the government's incapacity to make an elementary social analysis of the area of this artificial lake. The result was a twenty-five-year long battle on the part of its inhabitants to remain near their villages and the graves of their ancestors. Such can be the effects of uprooting a Javanese village.

14.5 MUSLIMS' RELIGIOUS TOLERANCE

A discussion (3 March 2001) in Yogyakarta (Gambiran) office of the Lembaga Kajian Islam dan Sosial (LKiS, Institute for Islamic and Social Studies) treated the reports of three team surveys in the Central Javanese cities of Yogyakarta, Solo, and Salatiga. Their theme was the way these populations experienced relations between individuals or groups of different religious affiliations. These young researchers[26] expressed their surprise to find that each town displayed major sociological differences.

The first report concerned Solo. The Javanese interviewed there never felt that differences of *religious* belief were an obstacle to contacts with people of different religions. This goes against the commonly accepted opinion that Muslims keep their distance from non-believers (*kafir*), avoiding marriage with them, etc. The same was true for certain neighbourhoods in the urban context in Yogya (i.e., Sorowajan) where many families displayed mixed Muslim, Christian, and Hindu religious affiliations. That having been said, the great anti-Communist massacres that followed 30 September 1965, religion as opposed to Communist "unbelief" gained an institutional importance. Once the New Order government made it obligatory for everyone to have a religious affiliation and have that written on their identity card, for many people their adherence to Islam, the majority faith, was purely a formal one. By its interference in the domain of religious belief, the government made religion a category of civil behaviour, and people felt freer than before to change that adherence for another one, since the government only asked them to belong to a faith. On the other hand, because they were dealing with the government (i.e., in the Ministry of Religion), the different faiths were in part conditioned by the decrees and rules of the province in which they operated. The most obvious example of this was the Muslim marriage law. As one person said, religion became a part of the nation-state and thereby part of an institution that controlled people's lives. Another person claimed that by the 1980s building a mosque became a political gesture as much as a religious one. That created the conditions for SARA,[27] intolerance of ethnic origin, religion, and race and denied the 1945 Constitution (UUD 45) which guaranteed their freedom of expression. Furthermore, as the effects of the 1997 economic crisis deepened, religious antagonism became the *national* expression for a despair that was manipulate by the moneyed political interests in Jakarta.

Once religion entered the political arena the conditions were set for it to become a factor of separation between regions on an ethnic basis; local culture became a distinguishing factor. In Medan, where the dominant ethnic group are the immigrant Batak Protestants, despite the older Malay Muslim presence, racial heterogeneity is such a daily fact of life that one cannot isolate Christians as readily as in Central Java. Gradually each person grew accustomed to finding his ethics from his own religion's authoritative texts and no longer from the ties that bound them together where they lived. Religious practices began to undermine traditional cultural values and made people forget their earlier common identity, in favour of reinvented religious "traditions". For the first time one read criticisms, not only of the government-sponsored violence, but also of the way in which religions are part of the mode of operation of state terror.

The LkiS survey teams' discussion then turned to the town of Salatiga which its inhabitants characterized by four specific traits: education as a goal in the life for the youth (a prestigious university is situated there); the population's closeness with the military personnel residing there; the influence of the retirement community on the urban life; and finally the strength of religious life, manifested in the religious communities' independence from the provincial government's effort to control them, and so the lessening the influence of the Ministry of Religion. The strength of traditional religion (*agama leluhur*) made it hard for the Islamic reform movement (Muhammadiyah) to make progress in Salatiga, while the Nahdlatul Ulama and the Greja Kristen Jawa's accommodative stance *vis-à-vis* customary religious practice gave them a hearing with the Salatiga's residents. Here, already in the 1980s, inter-religious dialogue arose directly between Islam and Christianity, partially due to their independence from the local Ministry of Religion.

In Yogyakarta where Christian religious adherence is also strong, there were few inter-religious conflicts until the late 1990s; the ethic of neighbourliness is not empty words. On the other hand, there has recently appeared serious friction between currents representing the militias of political parties and these that have led to violence. For these young researchers of LKiS the diversity of Central Javanese sociology was seen as motivating the local use of sociological inquiry.

Outside Java, LKiS is most widely known for its publications (some one hundred titles currently) which concern mainly the interface of Islam and social sciences in Indonesia. They represent a high level of social science research. On a much more popular local level, its notoriety stems from its weekly (Friday) bulletin, *al-Ikhthilaf* (the Difference) mentioned in Chapter 12. Its subtitle explains its purpose: "to deal with difference (is to) fill the national with mercy". This single sheet (four-page) bulletin is distributed freely in mosques throughout Java, before the Friday noon *salat* service. Its message is not well received everywhere and in some mosques, self-designated conservative Muslims promptly put it out of sight so that the faithful will not have the chance to take one. So at the bottom of the first page there is a suggestion: "It is hoped that this will not be read during the *khotib's* sermon."

As mentioned in Chapter 12, all issues of this bulletin are concerned with the social difference, hence its title *al-Ikhtilaf.* Their main question turns on how should the *umat* Islam react to religious alterity? The titles of a few random issues already give the flavour of this modest, but pertinent publication: *The Pillar of Justice* (2 February 2000); *Jihad is not the same thing as War* (April 2000); *Combating Harshness passing as Religion* (26 January 2001); *Building Humanitarian Tolerance* (12 January 2001); *Zakat (Alms) for the People* (15 December 2000); *Fasting for Reconciliation* (1 January 2000); *The Simplicity of the Muslim Community (Umat)* (23 November 2000); *Coincidence in Difference* (17 November 2000); *Justice in Difference* (13 October 2000); *Dakwah (Mission) in the Composition of Religion* (6 October 2000). More simply stated, their theme is often: how do we deal with non-Muslims? The answer to this question is less an issue of what to do, than of how to think about them. It is surprising that some of these bulletins use the rhetorical style of social sciences to define the basic ethical issues they are propounding. Illustrating the congruence of their stance are verses (*ayat*) quoted from the Koran, even if the authors admit that other interpretations are possible.[28] Often the authors are alumni of the IAIN (National Institutes of Islamic

Religion). Their use of these proof text from the Koran clearly favours the depth and purity of intention on the part of the believer, above and beyond the simple fact of public adherence to the faith of the Prophet. One could interpret this a promoting deeper individual conviction, but it might just as well be seen as the *umat* guaranteeing the authenticity of its members. Thus in the bulletin entitled *Education which Values Complexity* (20 October 2000), Saud el Hujaj cites the chapter of the Koran entitled *Al-Baqarah* (*ayat* 62; Arberry 1955, p. 36), where Allah affirms that non-Muslims who believe and pray sincerely will indeed receive their wage from their Lord. The author is at pains to show that to respect someone who does not share our Muslim belief does mean that our faith is shallow, for faith is judged by its quality and the social works that accompany it. Saud el Hujaj claims, that the real danger comes from politicians making political use of religious symbols. He goes on to say that since every religion has its own *kiblat*, Muslims can deepen their faith through the experience of dialogue, for this openness will give us the experience of a justice and love of our fellow man. This experience of *tafahum* (mutual understanding) will build up in us an ethnic concerning similitude and differentiation enabling us to judge other people not by their religion or ethnic origin, but by the quality of their actions.

Throughout these short texts (some nine hundred words), the issues of religious pluralism and tolerance are dealt with by trying to teach Muslims how to evaluate the situation in which they live in Java today. This evaluation requires a conscious understanding of the values vehiculed by Islam. Their inclusiveness is sorely put to the test, not only by the direct political party manipulations of the *umat*, but more deeply by the demands made on the Javanese body social to divide itself on ethnic or religious lines in order to be able to express greater internal solidarity in these lesser social units. In the introduction to this chapter, we called this phenomenon the challenge of evaluative indifference. Here manipulated horizontal and vertical social solidarities risk destroying the holistic reference of society (*masyarakat*) who, for Muslims, *as a whole* have the responsibility of replying to the call to mercy from Allah. The *ayat* quoted here deals with the role of the prophets in fulfilling the *eschaton* by announcing the oneness of Allah throughout the ages and is from *Al-Anbiya* (107): "We have not sent thee, save as mercy unto all beings."(Arberry 1955, vol. II, p. 26) For the LKiS, providing the people with new ways of thinking about the dangers of particularistic, individualistic endeavour, means giving them new ways of discerning what are the deeper social links between believers created by Allah's all-encompassing compassion, irrespective of religious beliefs. This necessitates becoming conscious of how the negative solidarities, which Islam is being prompted to provide politicians, can operate in Java today. The hierarchy bonds of the socio-cosmic links that once characterized the eighteenth century synthesis between Javanism and Islam are no longer functioning, and religious pluralism risks denying basic human rights to those who do not share "our" way of living Islam.

A very different approach is taken in the relations between Muslims and Christians by the director of the pondok pesantren Al-Muayad. Its director Haji M. Dian Nafi' in a position paper delivered on 6 November 2000 at the Koranic school Ar-Risalah in Ponorogo in front of an audience of fundamentalist Muslims, tried to escape dogmatic confrontation between Muslims and Christians by addressing their social, as opposed to their confessional reality. In so doing he raises a number of issues that are important to bring into focus at this point in our discussion. Discussing the social capital of the Muslim *kaum* or *umat* in his conclusion (2000, p. 11), he contrasts their manner of belonging to Islam with that what he calls the membership (*warganya*) of the Christian churches where membership in a parish is relatively fixed. Muslims on the other hand have no such hindrances to their social mobility, nor any system of church administration resembling the Catholic hierarchy. Coming as this does after his discussion of the separating out of state and religion through secularization (2000, p. 8), Dian Nafi' clearly interprets the abandonment of religious confrontation based on *extra ecclesia nulla salus* on the part of the Catholic Church in Indonesia, as part of a minority denomination's strategy to create condition of peaceful coexistence in a majority Islamic country.

Although his citations of the Koran (*al-Baqarah* 256; *al-An'an* 108; *al-Maidah* 48) are aimed at showing how Allah deliberately created a religiously diversified humanity, this hardly seems like the universal value (*syumul*) that he claims it is when one reads these three Koranic passages in context. By universal, however, Dian Nafi' means eternal (*kakal*). There one finds a ambivalent ethos which both respects *and* challenges Jews and Christians to progress to a fuller revelation by leaving their holy books behind them. By addressing the reality (*kenyataan*) of the Indonesian nation sociologically, Dian Nafi' hopes to encourage the local Muslim *umat* to deal with the effective presence of Christians in their midst, rather than dreaming of an ideal Muslim community that lives harmoniously under the *sharī'ah*. For this Solonese Nahdlatul Ulama leader, son and grandson of *pesantrèn kyai* and himself director of a progressive *pesantrèn*, the task of nation-building can only be accomplished by an empirical approach, which in Indonesia means admitting that only in a few areas is Islam the dominant form of religious expression. Here he cited the regions of Aceh, Minangkabau, Riau, Banten, Madura, Banjar, Melayu, Makassar, Bugis, Buton, Sasak, and Halmahera.

Dian Nafi's presentation of the diversity of the Muslim *umat* in Indoensia poses a problem. The triangulation of ethnicity, religious adherence, and kinship must be read sociologically before it is read regionally or ethnically. The issue that Dian Nafi' is trying to come to grips with concerns the nature of relations between divergents faiths shared by members of the same ethno-linguistic group, the Javanese, as discussed generally at the beginning of this chapter. To promote tolerance, Dian Nafi' has created a forum for inter-faith dialogue[29] and gives lectures to conservative Muslim groups like the one we have just presented. The issue he poses is clear. Can the Javanese rebuild their social confidence and strengthen their shared identity when they do not share the same religious faith? One can have recourse at one or the other end of the spectrum: either secular individualism, ignoring religious affiliations; or sectarianism ("primordialism" in Indonesian), which only admits one religion and so tolerates those of their own faith. The second recourse has intuitive appeal in the face of the current wave of secularism.

Take the example of Medan, the large capital of the province of northern Sumatra. The effect of individualism on the behaviour of religious groups has recently been posed by Silvia Vignato in her book, *Au Nom de l'Hindouisme* (2000) which treats this province of north Sumatra. It describes the reconfiguration of the Tamil and Karo Batak communities in and to the west of Medan (Sumatra) through their respective adherence to Hinduism.[30] She brings into focus the requirements of monotheism forced upon these two ethnic groups by the Indonesian state's Ministry of Religion during the New Order period (1966–98). Her conclusion is that for the Karo, their ancestral religion had bound them together as the Karo became secularized in the process of disguising itself as Hinduism. This was a successful mutation in the sense that it did consolidate Karo, ethnic identity, but at the price of eliminating its cosmic reference, any non-Christian horizon of transcendence. Vignato (2000, ch. 13) finds this *natural* in the sense that for her a modern pluri-ethnic society cannot admit a given ethnic group as the centre of any religious universe. However her use of Louis Dumont's analysis of the Indian caste system to explain how the Tamil minority of Medan, together with the Karo Batak (albeit for different reasons), enter the officially tolerated Indonesian version of "Hinduism", throws some doubt on her analysis.

In India the major evolution of the caste system, analysed by Dumont and others, is summarized by the word *substantiation*. For Dumont the traditional nineteenth century network of relations between sub-castes (*gotra*) was interactive and relational. Their *dharma* was to maintain personal and collective *purity* brought in and defined by these interactions between high and low castes. As Susan Bayly says, they were bound together in an asymmetrical symbiosis (1999, p. 309). Thus far there is nothing qualitatively different from the Karo experience in the multi-ethnic social tissue of the city Medan. But in the mid-twentieth century India, there appeared the notion of an inviolable caste substance which was indifferent to the personal and collective endeavours practised by what Bayly (1999, pp. 310–11) calls the "open-ended array of divergent sub-caste units …. what members of particular kin groups … might do or fail to do towards the preservation of personal or collective purity". Surprisingly enough this evolution was the outcome of the early caste uplift movements and the post-independence anti "casteist" campaigns of politicians. Caste came to be treated as an imagined community with an idealized allegiance just when the modern nation India was making supra-local claims on the identity of the sub-caste members.

How Indian pride in caste becomes an expression of selfless virtue especially among the urban middle classes, where it was least expected, can be explained by the solicitations from the supra-local sphere. What had occurred in the pre-modern "states" in India had been something very different. Historically the origins of caste society conflated the sub-caste or *gotra* and royalty. "With this flow of assets and retainerships went the provision of 'caste' identities to the king's subjects….The forms of caste which were thus embraced identified such people as a part of a 'community' in their lord's image, or in the image of his affiliates and retainers." (Bayly 1999, pp. 43 and 61). The competing claims and allegiances to rival local lordships enhanced the possibility of successful royal houses to claim bloodlines to royal house.

Did something similar occur in Javanese polities? In Sumatra and the north coast of Java in the coastal trading sultanates, there was more ethnic diversity and hence ethnicity was more of a factor. And of course were Indian and Indonesian experiences of kingship comparable. In the Sumatran coastal sultanates, competition among royal retainers of course existed behind the codes of Javanese royal kinship, real and fictive. Even if in Java recruitment for the royal houses was often a very bloody affair, nonetheless in the central part of the island where the Javanese kingdoms have been located since the seventeenth century, the major social segmentation officially admitted was kin-based. It was that bond which related the apanage holders to the king's royal house through the networks that entitled them to become royal rent farmers. Kinship was simulated in the royal houses, making of it the main social recognized social bond for governance; as Kumar has shown (1997, pp. 399–405) the ideal for the Muslim Javanese aristocrat was service imbued with filial devotion.

My point here is that what happened in Java to the Muslim *umat* is simply another version of what occurred in the Sumatra Batak *warga*. In Java today group membership (*warga*), especially family membership, negotiates between the *adat* kinship obligations and of religion. Exclusive individualism is never a practical option. When Dian Nafi' writes that *warga masyarakat* (groups of the people) have to struggle together, i.e. no one their own, for reconciliation and social peace, he is both expressing his confidence that this is possible (and indeed it is on the local level), and also admitting that the society (*masyarakat*) can be divided up into groups, i.e. *warga* in this new sense. The damage of state violence under Soeharto and the programmed destabilization of the Reformation period (1998–present) appealed to secularized polities for lack of any other social capital. There is a generalized lack of credibility. Dian Nafi' implies only that *warga* can overcome the conflicts introduced from somewhere "outside". By a higher "inner" loyalty, that of belonging to each other on the local level, *warga* become harmonious. He does this by appealing to the universal values of religion (*nilai-nilai agama universal*). So when a local Nahdlatul Ulama leader like Dian Nafi' appeals in his Friday *Solo Pos* columns to the spirit of forgiveness (*Solo Pos*, 24 December 2000) and the need for volunteers (*rélawan*; *Solo Pos*, 19 January 2001) to calm social tensions, he is describing a group (*warga*) that is no longer a group and needs refounding. To base *warga* membership exclusively on kinship in Central Java is no longer credible since the social and economic mobility of these Javanese families stretch these bonds beyond their territorially viable limits. To base the *warga* on religion is no longer possible because of the large number of Christians and members of traditional Javanese religious sects. The *warga* now needs to have a local territorial base smaller than the former kingdoms and at least as large as a hamlet (*dhusun*). Historically speaking the Javanese are still waiting for a replacement of the old apanage system's link between the peasant and his land, hence the importance of the different kinds of rights over land discussed above. They have been in flux for almost a hundred years now and need to be stabilized legitimately. In the next section we will see what multi-confessional and yet territorially based rituals have appeared in Solo since the fall of the Soeharto regime. There are broader and larger than rituals described in Chapter 13 and provide an image of community within an urban network.

14.6 RICE CONES FOR PEACE AND OFFERINGS TO THE EARTH

Our example of urban networking between local communities in Solo began with a so-called Long March for Peace on 27 August 2000, including a procession of torches, a *reyog* dance troop and speeches. As the end of the year

2000 came to an end, this was followed by preparations for the Feast of the Rice Cones for Peace (*pahargyan tumpengan perdamaian*). This culminated on Sunday, 14 January 2001 with a procession of rice cones to the great pavilion (*pagelaran*) of the Solo palace. Organized by the Forum for the Heartfelt Cry for the Togetherness of the Nation (Suara Hati Kebersamaan Bangsa[31]), it coincided with four religious feasts: the Muslim Idul Fitri, the Christian Christmas, the Balinese Galungan[32] and the Chinese New Year (Imlek). The theme of the coming together of a hundred different communities, each with their own rice cone for a communal meal, was seen as a lesson that peace is not a gift from Allah, but something to search and struggle for. It was not clear until the morning of the feast how many communities would actually send delegations to participate; this was supposed to be a spontaneous effort on their part. Finally five hundred community representatives showed up each having paid for their rituals offerings (*sajèn*) themselves. Politically motivated sponsorship had been avoided. During a speech at this meeting, Haji Dian Nafi' presented the distortion of information as one of the principal dangers to be combated, if social peace is to be preserved. Social conflicts will break out, he insisted, if all religious, cultural and political relationships are not improved. An appeal for unity of society (*masyarakat*) was made by the Solo king Paku Buwana XII before he cut the main rice cone into portions before the some five thousand people. In attendance at the festival were

FIGURE 14.1
Long March for Peace, 2000

FIGURE 14.2
Palace officials (*abdi dalem kraton*) praying at the gathering of Rice Cone for Peace Meeting at the Pagelaran (Mangkunagaran Palace, Solo) in 2001

FIGURE 14.3
Paku Buwana XII cutting the rice cone for peace at the Pagelaran (Mangkunagaran Palace, Solo) in 2001

FIGURE 14.4
Poster for peace at Surakarta during the Iraq War, 2003

Christian and Muslim children who later collaborated in a music and dance programme. The impoverished day labourers from Kléwer wholesale batik market across the street also participated enthusiastically, knowing that the offerings would be given as food to all those in attendance.

At the other end of the spectrum from such spontaneity, two weeks after the event just mentioned one finds the National Human Rights Committee's (KomNasHam) sponsoring a twenty-four-hour "ritual" for peace. This is a GOLKAR (Soeharto's) party controlled organization. Protected by more than a thousand police and private militia, this top-heavy event received well-placed local press coverage, treating everything from the Javanese mystical relationship with their earth to the supposed expected presence of the President and the Vice-President of the Indonesia, Gus Dur (Abdurrahman Wahid) and Megawati. Neither showed up.

The "earth" prayer for the "peace of the land, the unity and unification of the Indonesian nation" began at the same Solo palace pavilion (*pagelaran*) just mentioned, on Saturday morning at 10 a.m., with a *gambyongan*[33] dance; then prayers from the Koran were read, followed a brief report of the president of the preparation committee Slamet Suryanto from the Solo town hall and a wide-ranging speech by a Yogyakarta Gadjah Mada professor of philosophy, Damarjati Supajar (cf. analysis below). Greetings from the Sri Susuhunan, Paku Buwana XII and Akbar Tanjung (president of the DPR and the GOLKAR party), present in the front of the hall, concluded the morning segment of the "rite".

At eight o'clock on Saturday evening, around the Pillar of National Awakening (the "candle pillar"),[34] a procession was launched from the palace by the crown prince, Haryo Gusti Dipakusuma and led by the palace guards followed by scouts, six religious delegations (Hindu, Buddhist, Catholic, Christian, Islamic, and Confucian) and members of all the twenty-six provinces of Indonesia (plus East Timor) in local costumes. It crossed Solo on foot, carrying torches, to arrive at the candle pillar. The six religious groups then performed their respective prayers for peace until ten o'clock. That evening Akbar Tanjung had apparently found better things to do, so after brief allocutions by the regional head of the regional branch of this committee, a stand-in for the mayor of Solo, Slamet Suryanto, and the Solo delegate (Ing. Sujadi) of the govenor of Central Java Mardyanto, the president of the National Committee Drs. Bambang W. Suharto gave his speech. After these pro forma interventions, Drs. Suharto gave the puppet of Puntadewa (the elder Pandawa brothers in the Mahabharata mythic cycle) to B. Radèn Ayu Brotodiningrat who in turn gave it ceremoniously to *ki* Mantep, the *dhalang* (puppeteer) of that evening's all-night performance of the shadow puppet play. At this point the town's bourgeois for the most part went home, and the local poor flooded in around the stage where the orchestra and the *dhalang* prepared to begin the performance of the "Offerings for the Royal Consecration", here called the "In-gathering of the Pandhawa". This play lasted till dawn.

We will discuss in some detail Damarjati's speech, the prayers said around the candle pillar and the wayang play. The organizers of this day can hardly be called free of political interests, but the event is nonetheless interesting on the socio-linguistic level, which they could hardly pretend to totally control or manipulate.

Damarjati, who gave the long morning speech at the royal reception hall (*pagelaran*) of the Solo palace, is a professor of Javanese philosophy[35] in Yogyakarta. He began by explaining that he did not need a written text any more than would have the President of the Republic (Abdurrahman Wahid) due to his handicapped external vision, which Damarjati hoped was not doubled by inward blindness as well. In greeting the distinguished guests, Damarjati moved from Indonesian to Arabic to Javanese, and back to Indonesian, saying that to greet these guests was an inner movement of a well-concentrated heart, a prayer which was like a four-edged arrow released from a bow with the blessing of Sultan Agung. Such a sacred heirloom should reach their minds. He interjected here what a pity it was that certain sons of Adam made bombs to terrorize their fellow man rather than realizing that we are all servants of the Lord (*abdining pangeran*). This Javanese greeting was then reiterated in Arabic: *Assalamualaikum warrahmatulahiwabarotaku.*

He went on to say, using *jarwa dhosok* (the modern Javanese equivalents of an Old Javanese sayings), that real feudal (*ning/rat*) philosophy was not feudalistic, i.e. disintegrative while grasping (*rebut*) at power as today we see occurring, in the country's capital Jakarta, but serene (*ning* = *hening*) in its outward-looking dimension and releasing an indescribable power (*rat* = *serat*). His talk was to explain how this occurs.

The nature of the Javanese word play, *plèsètan*, obliges the speaker to precede by zigzags. After the first of many excursions, here into obligatory and voluntary fasting during the current month of Syawal (tenth Muslim month), which follows the fasting month of Ramadan, Damarjati started to explain Gus Dur's reliance on Megawati (his Vice-President and rival who at that time often read speeches for him). The speaker then claimed that the period they were living through could be called a "Durga" time because when the goddess Uma (Megawati) does not follow Gus *Dur*'s orders, she becomes the demon named *Dur*ga.

This relatively meaningless word play served as a transition back to the theme of the insane period (*zaman edan*) they were living through due to the many acts of terrorism. What is the purpose of having an *ulama* for president if he can't read the signs of the times? We now need horizontal reconciliation (*silaturahmi*). Returning to the Muslim religious calendar, Damarjati said that we are living in a period of "ripped mats" (*klasa bedhah*). Here he weaved into his remarks on the cycle of the five (Subuh, Lohor, Asar, Maghrib, Isya) daily canonical prayer, the ten verses of an ironic ditty which goes as follows:

> The guests arrive; the mat is unrolled; it has rips in it; fill them with sticky rice; the glutinous rice is rotten; give it to the dog; the dog dies; throw it in the river; the river overflows; the shore is flooded.[36]

The point is that, as in the song, when the guests arrive one finishes dealing with a dead dog on the banks of a flooded river, so in our times (after the fall of Soeharto) there are too many aborted reconciliations. A third dimension to this word play is brought in when the speaker changes the last syllable of the word for reconciliation in Arabic *silaturahmi* to *silatu-rahim* (womb) and begins a series of parallels concerning the chosen sperm's (*winih pinilih*) trip to the mother's womb, which ends with his concluding that modern technology's aims are unclear. Just as in the song where one fills holes in the welcome map with rotten rice, so today reconciliation is not consistent, and one's efforts to welcome one's guest are deflected into dead dogs or irrelevant concerns, as in the recent controversy over the supposed non-*halal* ingredients in Ajinomoto. Introducing a *pantun* (Malay word for a quatrain of two couplets[37]), Damarjati reiterates its last line ("walk with mincing little steps") to describe how those who follow after Gus Dur have to walk, for the President refuses to walk backwards (i.e., resign, *mundur*) if only because advancing slowly is already difficult for him. At this point Damarjati returns to his enumeration of the kinds of fasting and how they give us serenity when confronted with the distressing events we are living though. The fast of David (Daud) should have calmed the head of the MPR, Amien Rais', ambitions. There follows a comparison between the six-pointed star of David, the Hexagon, and the five-pointed form of the Pentagon which it dominates by its spiritual superiority.

The interweaving of so many literary genres and languages, and the retrieval of so many incompletely developed topics coupled with lightly provocative remarks about major political figures and diverse sexual innuendo, typifies the kind of refined persuasion that the 1990s revived with the coming of greater freedom of speech. The Javanese are charmed by the virtuosity and appreciate the soft indoctrination the speaker develops. Where Europeans would be looking for a logical construction to further the argumentation, the nature of the event in the Solo palace pavilion calls for an appeal to commonly held references and a shared culture. The dominance of Arabic and Muslim theological motifs does not disguise the extremely Javanese treatment they are given.

The relation between reconciliation, i.e., *halal-bihalal* or *silaturahmi* gatherings taking place nightly during the month of Syawal, and the recent provocation of the Laskar Jihad in the Solo region, was on everyone's minds. About two-thirds of the way through his speech, Damarjati is prepared to make his second point.

> If there are any members of the Laskar Jihad here, I must let you know that the great struggle (*jihad akbar*) does not consist in drawing a sword to threaten someone, the great struggle is to change awareness of fire (*nar*) into an awareness of light (*nur*). Without sincere religious practice it is "impossible" (in English) for us to enter into the ocean of the light from light. To do so the required condition is to pass through the gateway of

lohburu rohim (?). For in the Koran there are no requests for forgiveness that do not (imply) forgiving.

In the last third of his speech Damarjati is anxious to call into question the political and financial turpitudes of the Jakarta élite. He introduces this by saying how disappointed he was after the 1 August 2000 meeting in Yogyakarta (Damarjati lives in the northern suburbs of this nearby university city). Hamengku Buwana X, Akbar Tanjung, Amien Rais, Megawati, and Abdurrahman Wahid met there nominally to reconcile their differences. The result was that their relationship worsened! Had they forgotten how many demons (*buta*) were then abroad: Eggplant (*terong*) demons in the National Assembly doing nothing except taking money; Flaming Hair demons setting forest fires everywhere; Gaping Ravine demons and above all Cakil demons with their undershot jaws who are penniless (*sepeser*), like Soeharto, because their billions are in foreign banks.

There follows a presentation of the Javanese, Arabic, and Chinese alphabets (i.e., writing systems) which serve to introduce successive themes. The Javanese alphabet and its local genius is the occasion for mentioning the need for a genuine regional autonomy, and the futility of culturally illegitimate children, those endless demonstrations which show they are products of social body that has lost its cultural soul. The Arabic writing system is compared to the body language of the five daily prayers (*salat*) which should not be performed as does General Soeharto, or the cadets of the National Military Academy who are rolling stones, and do not truly submit by such bowing before Allah. The sixty-year old speaker then prostrated himself and continued into a somersault. Just as in the sacred dance of the *bedhaya ketawang* with its nine virgin dancers whose movements caused an invisible tenth one to appear who will become the consort of the king, so during the body language of the *salat*, it is forbidden to stand upright and place limitations on Allah.

Damarjati then turned to address the Solo king (*susuhunan*) seated to his right, Paku Buwana XII, saying that the image of the *calif* (*kalifatulah*) of his predecessors was noble (*linuhung*) because, passing though the gateway of forgiveness they created an ethnos of co-operation. Twelve centuries of Indian acculturation, three centuries of Islamic wisdom, three and a half centuries of Dutch colonialism, three and a half years of Japanese fascism, and now fifty year of independence have left the Indonesian Republic like an only child in the grips of the man-eating demon Kala. Allah must exorcise (*ruwat*) this nation completely and quickly. The blessing of social justice for all is needed; new disinterested leaders should arise. Money may be in the hands of bankers, but blessing is in the hands of Allah alone.

After the entertaining knot work of Damarjati's morning speech, the evening prayers at the Candle Pillar were more pious, and, in spite of the fair-like surroundings, remained prayers, even if their messages were so similar that they are difficult to compare. The juxtaposition of six religions each with their own languages for invocation (Sanskrit, Arabic, etc.) and hymnographic culture in front of an audience who had come to listen to what was "happening" deprived the event of the organic, natural quality that characterizes Javanese prayer (Headley 1996a). And it is true that one can only be a spectator confronted with another person's faith, even if each short service had a second part in Indonesian, comprehensible to all. Everyone said approximately the following: "From Sabang to Merauke ... for the blessing of well being on our nation, 'Diverse yet One', ... in this multi-dimensional crisis ... we turn to you all Merciful One ... to grant us harmony, brotherhood and peace, etc., etc." This is far from the kind of traditional ritual speech one finds in Eastern Indonesia where authority is created by the performance because of the sociological capacities of the communities who performed it (cf. on the Weyewa, Kuipers 1990; 1998). Here the confrontation of different invocational styles seemed to dissipate their potency, although the organizers seemed unaware of this. The final cutting of the rice cone before the beginning of the *wayang* theatre was anti-climatic compared to the event organized two weeks before where five hundred communities had made and brought their own rice cones to the pavilion.

The most interesting reflections on this part of the all-day ritual were found in newpaper reports. The *Solo Pos* Saturday morning edition (27 January 2001, i.e. before the event took place) presented an editorial describing the hollowness of the notion of *sedekah bumi* unless it was "actualized". The editorialist claimed prayers to the earth were an out-of-date traditional cultural expression. What is important is to slip the reins of such mythological thinking about mother earth (*ibu pertiwi*), to restore moral values through the rational transformation that will allow individuals to adopt morally consistent behaviour. Indeed "mother earth" should not be the object of the communal meal (*sedakah*), but the object of the prayers and should be understood to be the Indonesian nation rent by conflicts between religious communities. This editorialist certainly sounds as though he was from Muhamadiayah or the Javanese Dutch Reformed Church.

From the opposite end of a spectrum of commentaries, just the day before, the same newspaper ran three feature articles on the great "(ritual) work" (*gawé*) that the city of Solo was going to undertake Saturday. The main article, entitled *Sedakah Bumi*, by Riyanta, was based on an interview with Supariadi, a lecturer in history at Universitas Nasional Surakarta. He described the bond that linked Javanese farmers with the land and leads them to honouring it with offerings and invocations. This takes many forms: the Tengger (East Javanese) *kasada* harvest ritual, the *unda-unda* plowing rituals in Mojowarno (Jompang), the Ponorogo *jawab goda rencana*, and the Ngawi *bukak bumi*, etc. The reactualization of the farmers' respect for "their" land traditionally followed natural disasters such as landslides, floods, and volcanic eruptions. Returning to the earth to re-establish the harmony of their relationship, the correspondence of the microcosm (man) with his environment (the macrocosm or natural world) was imbued with of respect and concord (*rukun*). Supariadi defines respects as follows: "Respect means that values must coincide with social status." In the *hierarchy* of Javanese society, asking mutual forgiveness within the group (*warga*) becomes essential, but, adds the lecturer, in the national context of this ritual should also be given a legal framework. The well-known Javanese adage quoted in Chapter 7, used to describe the sacred forests, is next quoted to illustrate the dangers of not respecting the natural world: "the large sacred forest, a human who enters it, is a person who dies".[38] Javanese beliefs are said to protect man and the natural world in which he lives, crediting indigenous lore with an understanding of how to protect social harmony. In fact society and nature are not be opposed but are part of a higher whole.

The journalist does not deal with the relationship between these principles and the recent ecological disasters in Java or caused by Javanese transmigrants elsewhere in Indonesia (cf. Whitten et al., 1996, ch. 2). Perhaps like the farmers inhabiting the high slopes of the volcano Merapi to the west of Solo, he feels that despite the daily eruptions of lava (*lahar*), there is nowhere else to go, so they just keep on farming while the "wooly sheep" (clouds of carbon monoxide, hydrogen sulphide and/or sulphur dioxide) roll down the slopes unexpectedly. Claims like that of this *Solo Pos* correspondent, Riyanta, that the continuing eruption of Merapi is the marriage of the World Broom (*kyai Sapujagat*) and the Queen of the Southern Seas (Ratu Kidul) show that there is a contradiction between these two ways of speaking about volcanic eruptions.

14.7 GOOD AND BAD MAHARAJA: COLLABORATING IN A CORONATION

Of course there are more than two ways for speaking about the same reality. Javanese rarely use the Western term "myth" to describe a genre of tale or a level of discourse. The mythological intrigue recounted in that evening's *wayang* play, describes social realities not described in ordinary parlance. The evening *wayang* theatre was the one spontaneously attended event of the whole day. Well attended by the local populace who poured in as the middle class left following the handing over of the puppet of Puntadewa (the elder of the five Pandwa brothers) to the well-known *dhalang, ki* Mantep from Karangpadan(?), the choice of the play was made to fit with the theme of the day, reconciliation, and for that reason the play's title, normally *Sesaji Raja Suyo* (the Offerings for the royal Consecration) had been paraphrased as the "Gathering together of the Pandawa brothers".[39] Here is the outline of the plot:

Act I: In the semi-historical (fifth century B.C.) kingdom of Magadha, on the Gangetic plane of northern India, King Jarasanda (or Jalasandha) is telling three vassal kings that he wants to perform a Lodra[40] offering since he is a king who worships *bethara* Kala. The pre-eminent ingredient for this offerings is a human sacrifice (*mbekakak*)[41] of one hundred kings to roast (for a meal) for Kala. So far Jarasanda has imprisoned ninety-seven kings, so there are still three missing. Jarasanda wants to capture Puntadewa (the king of Amarta), Kresna (the king of Dwarawati) and Baladewa (the king of Mandura), and gives instructs to the kings under his sway to find a way to emprison these three kings before sacrificing them.

Act II: A parallel discussion, but with very different conclusions, is taking place in the kingdom of Amarta where king Puntadewa (i.e. Yudhistira, the eldest of the five Pandawa brothers, (cf. V. Mani 1975, pp. 226–31) is asking for Kresna's advice concerning his long-planned celebration of his own royal consecration and the offerings required. Kresna insisted that for the consecration to be valid (*sah*) one hundred knights (*ksatriya*) from one hundred different countries must attend of their own free will and witness the event. As to the offerings (*syarat*) one must have the standard *ubo rampé* (rice; barley; underground, spreading and hanging roots; and vegetables). These express the Pandhava's thanks to the mother earth (Ibu Pratiwi) for nourishing them and all mankind who live off her abundant goodness and who will later be buried and reunited to this earth. Furthermore Kresna adds that the *dharma* also requires a sacrifice. This implies a knight who is willing, without counting on any reward, to accomplish a just duty, to eradicate a ruthless enemy. Puntadewa feels this will be possible once the visit of the seven Brahman has taken place, but he would cancel any consecration involving a human sacrifice. Baladewa says that Puntadewa should not rush to cancel the consecration and should let the other brothers deal with the issue of human sacrifice. Werkudara then tells Kresna that each of the five brothers has different capacities. He then lists their dispositions (*watak*), starting from those of eldest brother. He states that Werkudara (Bima) is physically gifted for war and ready to capture the dangerous enemy that is to be sacrificed. Kresna agrees on the condition that Werkudara ask his elder brother Puntadewa for permission (*palilah*) first. All aflame, Werkudara says he set off anyhow. Baladewa reminds him that if Puntadewa is both his brother but also his king. Puntadewa differs to Kresna saying that it is his decision, and Kresna confirms that Werkudara is entrusted with obtaining this sacrificial victim, but asks whom he should attack?

At this point king Hamsa appears at the court of Amarta as a delegate from Magada and, on identifying Puntadewa, laughs unseemingly. Kresna suggests tolerance, saying that customs may be different in different cultures. Hamsa then requests the Amarta kingdom's heirloom Kalimasada (etymologically from the *kalimat sahadat* or "Islamic profession of faith") for the relief of the kingdom of Magada's suffering. Werkudara replies ironically that everyday he has been trying to sell off this heirloom. Hamsa doesn't get the sarcasm of the remark[42] and Werkudara says they will settle this on the *alun-alun*. Kresna tells Werkudara that Hamsa is not the victim, but that the victim will be the king Magada, Jarasanda, who with avarice and his cruelty promotes sacrificial worship of *betara* Kala which causes suffering. Werkudara's killing one evil king to save ninety-seven good ones will not be a sin, says Kresna. Puntadewa tells Werkudara to accomplish his duty without animosity. Baladewa continues to moralize on the themes of humility and honesty and then insists that he accompany Werkudara.

In the following scene Cangik and Limbuk are discussing what it means to hold a *sedakah bumi*. Cangik tells her daughter that it is already over, but that she wants to understand the idea behind it. She feels it is explained in Ranggawarsita's writing found in the palace manuscript written in *aksara* (Javanese script).[43] It is implied that the time of Allah's retribution (*kala bendhu*) is discussed there. In any case, with a transcription into Latin letters Cangik has been able to understand some of it, in which she sees a connection with this evening's *wayang*, which as she notes, is not just entertainment (*cengegesan*) but ritual. Cangik says her task tonight is to express the opinion of the little people of Solo. She is not there to teach, but to suggest. If you don't agree with her, just forget it. The first point Cangik learned from reading Ranggawarsita is that our nation is being tested by the Lord and Creator. By dint of farming the land indiscriminately, for instance, forcing the harvests to up to eight times a year, instead of giving thanks to the earth for her fruits, the land no longer gives crops for it is ruined. The second point Cangik has extracted from Ranggawarsita is that the rapacious political élite has "fenced in the plants" through their political corruption and greed. Their actions harm the nation rather than help it. Even religion is turned into a point of dispute and instead of being the torch that guides our steps has lost itself in the trivia (*rèmèh*) of what is *halal* and what is *haram*. What is important? The fact that all the religions gathered tonight to pray together, that is important. There are no bad religions, only bad persons.

In Solo the *dhalang* continues, "we are sick of all the screaming and disputes. These only produce scavenging beggars. It is so hard to get food and find work that we even sleep badly. All this is because of the bomb threats, placing grenades in the trains … what is a nation coming to? Let's pray together, rather than blaming each other. Let's build together, and not criticize each other. Let's use our own ethics and not American ethics. You see, my child (Limbuk), I only took, as my compass, two from the eleven verses in *gambuh* meter. Indonesian culture fits here and American democracy is not like Indonesian democracy. It's not feudal to respect people and for the younger generation to be polite to the older generation." (Here they play the Reformasi melody.)

I believe that the conversation between Cangik and Limbuk may be taken at face value. Just as in this *wayang* play there are two kinds of royal consecrations, the one requiring whole-hearted co-operation and the other the putting to death of a hundred kings, so there is a local Javanese ethos of collectivity that even the market women of the likes of Cangik understand and which mobilizes the goodwill of their peers.

14.8 MOCKERY AND SOCIAL RECONSTRUCTION

A seven-part presentation of music, dance and theatre by students of the Solo and Yogya conservatories was organized at the beginning of February in conjunction with a seminar on tourism held in a conservatory's *pendapa* in the eastern suburbs of Surakarta. These performances which took place at the Surakarta Graduate School of the Arts (STSI) on 7 February 2001, are typical of the vitality of Central Javanese art forms, classical and contemporary. As the "student" performers' own programme description shows, its interest was more than entertainment; these spectacles were to elevate the vision of the participants in the seminar. The cultural vitality Central Java has experienced since the 1990s, is displayed in their increased honesty and outspokeness since the fall of Soeharto. The three parts of the programme translated below, are in fact interpretations by the performers of the significance of their artistic creations. The didactic cohabits with the artistic in the first resurgence of hope during the early "reformasi" period; two years later (2002) one would have felt much more anger and despair.

The Candra Kirana Bedhaya[44] dance
Human problems often arise at the moment when mankind is attacked by feeling of envy in his heart, revenge wrapped up in hate. The above feelings

can drag men down to behave criminally both violently or with subtlety. Nonetheless this criminality or brutality can be tamed using gentleness, humility and personal human dignity.

The above idea (here) becomes the rungs of a ladder arranged to focus on the figure of Candra Kirana (Moon Beam), object of the jealousy of her younger sister and her mother in law, who treats her meanly and calumnies her. But all these attacks are repulsed by her gentleness, generosity, her nobility of heart and largesse of spirit.

This dance is performed by nine young female dancers who hope that it will incarnate symbolically Dewi Sekar Taji or Galuh Candra Kirana confronted with the problems of life. The choreographer was Nora Kustantina Dewi, S. Kar., M. Hum.

This dance, in the words of one of the Surakarta palace dancers, is a paradigm of "pure task" (*tugas suci*; Brakel 1992, "Concluding Remarks") since it provides a "model for social activities". As original (*asli*) and complete (*wutuh*) the *bedhaya* possesses full ritual function. The *bedhaya* Semang, for instance, recounts choreographically the meeting of the queen of the southern ocean and Sultan Agung (cf. Ch. 3). Other twentieth century *bedhaya* depicting Panji tales are animated by two principles: *bathara* Kala's frustrating the male hero Panji's attempts to recover his wife Candra Kirana (Moon Beam) (cf. *Sang Nasib*, Braginsky 1998, pp. 109–25); and the theme of male infatuation (*cinta birahi*) as a passion that needs to be exorcized. Part and parcel of the exorcizing are parodies and comic scenes animated by the grotesque followers (*punakawan*) of the heroes which regularly interrupt the narration of the two main themes. As we will see here, the relation between purification tales and grotesque comedy is very close. The reference to the current social and political situation need not be made explicit for the audience to benefit from the spectacle of the victory of the refined heroine Candra Kirana over her coarse kinfolk. At the end of this evening's programme there was an inverted, farcical performance of this first *bedhaya* dance. Here is the explanation which introduced this final satirical dance. The authors have taken the precaution of expressing their respect of these court traditions before turning them on their head:

The Bedhaya Mocked (Préeg)
Bedhaya is a work of choreography that has been highly esteemed ever since the kingdom of Mataram [c. 1584–1755, Treaty of Giyanti]. From historical data it is claimed that the *bedhaya* dance was originally conceived of by Sultan Agung Anyakrakusuma. Sultan Agung received inspiration from a spiritual event that occured in the kingdom of the Southern Ocean ruled by the Queen of the South (Ratu Kidul). His meeting with the ruler of the

southern seas inspired him to make a holy dance to which he gave the name *Bedhaya Semang*. Each king who reigned over the palace at Yogyakarta seized the opportunity to create a *bedhaya* dance that legitimized them as the king of Jawa. *Bedhayas* are presented in the most respected place in the palace surroundings, that is to say the Golden Room (*Bangsal Kencana*). In former times all the *bedhaya* dancers formed a corps which was highly respected by the king and society. In conclusion the *bedhaya* dance is a sacred dance that is venerated by the palace milieu.

Préeg (mockery) is an instance of exchange which takes the form of a verbal reproach/curse (*umpat*) on the part of a person who is dissatisfied. Originally *préeg* was only used by certain people who were considered vulgar. For aristocrats or officials what was strictly forbidden was called designated *préeg*. However with the subsequent developments, *préeg* became a temporary form of discourse for all layers of society. *Préeg* has found a place among the elite. *Préeg* has already been hurled by President Abdurrahman Wahid in the hall of the Popular Assembly (MPR). This means that that *préeg* has already changed from a marginal speech form to a form used by the political elite, or to use a parallel from past times, *préeg* has already penetrated the ruling elite. *Préeg* has thus already been diffused becoming a discourse for all social groups. In fact *bedhaya* has also already become the property of the people because it is often employed in diverse events, whether the occasion be entertainment or marriages or the ceremonies of various social groups.

A formal apology was made by the choreographer, Kristadi, after this performance. He expressed his regret for any offence and reassured the audience that these transvestite male dancers were just making a joke and not deriding the sacred character of *bedhaya*. There is nothing unusual about the use of the grotesque in modern Javanese and Malay literature. Satire and blasphemy in the Panji tales is already traditionally handled during the comic interludes (Poerbatjaraka 1940/68). The ugliness of the clowns conceals their divinity (Wieringa 2000, p. 251). This is especially clear with Semar, the father of the clown servants.

How can one speak of the mediating roles of these tricksters during these dance performances, which are direct travesties of *bedhaya* with no change of characters? The programme explains that during the current social crisis, mockery (*préeg*) has now spread to all levels of society. The difference between mockery and defamation (*fitnah*) lies in the fact that while calumny attacks a person's reputation, mockery allows one to attain a certain social distance from the institution ridiculed. Bakhtin has shown how in medieval Europe the grotesque aspects of carnival culture consolidated social breaches by renewing social reflexes. Just as Bakhtin used his reflections on Rabelais to overturn the seriousness of Soviet social realism in the 1930s, so Kristiadi here is renewing with the wild (*gelak*) or Tantric side of the holiness of these *bedhaya* dances through vulgarity, the momentary suspension of taboos. The commentary on another of the STSI performances that night indeed suggests that this was the case. Here is the introduction to the satirical musical composition by Surono entitled "Joke" (*Glenyengan*).

> *Glenyengan (Joke)*
> This idiom (joking) always touches (our) mentality and is everywhere present in Javanese culture. It is a way to transfer, council, propose and tease by light insinuation with a joke that is not stubborn and often involves no follow up.
>
> To apologize to the teased person is an exploration in porcelain *gendèr* and the person given peaceful advice has two basic characteristics with different touches: to ask forgiveness of the person who is contested employs a strange sound with short vibrations. We certainly must develop joking in order to confront confrontation without conflict. Yes this paradoxical firmness needs (first of all) to be undertsood by ourselves. Composer Surono.

What is constructed by in these grotesque travesties where male impersonators of virgin women dancers flash their bare behinds at the audience? Are they simply prostituting the *bedhaya*? In fact these shocking tricks value the source of the dance, that is to say the social protection that comes from the original ritual. They indeed believe that social protection comes from the original form of the ritualized dance, but that this morality or custom is not obliged to be integrated into a deadly seriousness that would cut it off from willingness to play (*lila*).[45] Ultimately this *lila* is a willingness to be social, to be civil, and allows the artistic tradition to be preserved through innovations. When social bonds are tired, they need a good thrashing which is both comic and refreshing. In conclusion Chapter 15 will place in historical the difficulties of recreating social confidence generally and the role of a Muslim vision of the society and their place in this regeneration.

NOTES

1. Mitsuo Nakamura (1977, p. 8) has described the sociologicy of a breakaway (*firaq*) *umat* in Kotagedé, but here we are using the term *umat* or Muslim community in its most inclusive sense, the whole of the Muslims who feel part of the faithful whose native language is Javanese.
2. Cf. Abdul Munir Mulkhan's (2000) study of East Java.
3. The sociological value of the juxtaopposition between the prayers made inside and outside the mosque in a given local lies in the fact that entire society is not represented by either perspective taken separately.

4. Cf. *Islamic Prayer across the Indian Ocean. Inside and Outside the Mosque*, edited by David Parkin and Stephen Headley, ch. 9 (2000).
5. Cf. Benedict R. O'G Anderson, Mitsuo Nakakmura, and Mohammad Slamet, *Religion and Social Ethos in Indonesia* (1977).
6. The first director of the Akademi Seni Karawitan Indonesia (now, Sekolah Tinggi Seni Indonesia); personal communication in 1983.
7. The New Order government's ministries of religion and of education were so successful in co-opting the centre that they provoked the exit from the political scene of the major Muslim party, the Nahdlatul Ulama, in 1984. [Through his well-known appeal, Nurcholish Madjid for a secularization of Islam, he hoped to obtain a freedom from control the Pancasila military state.]
8. The best study of the radicalization of the Solonese prior to the great 1998 riots is Hari Mulyadi and Soedarmono's *Runtuhnya Kekuasaan "Kraton Alit". Studi Radikalisasi Sosial "Wong Solo" dan Kerusuhan Mei 1998 di Surakarta* (1999). A photographic essay in the Rekaman Lensa series entitled *Peristiwa Mei 1998 di Solo* was published in 1998 (72 pp.).
9. Cf. Marcel Bonneff, et al. *Pantjasila, trente ans de débats politiques en Indonésie* (1980).
10. Cf. the chronology provided by Kees van Dijk in *A Country in Despair: Indonesia between 1997 and 2000* (2001).
11. The research was undertaken in three stages:
    • Fieldwork in 1993 in the town of Solo focused on the population's ambient dissatisfaction (in Javanese, *kurang marem*). By collecting some thirty biographical accounts of religious conversion, efforts to achieve greater serenity via religious praxis were described. These interviews took place before any hope of genuine political reformation became widespread.
    • In 1999 the impact of the burning of Solo was studied through thirty biographical narratives relating personal experiences of the collapse of General Soeharto's regime. Some of these people had been interviewed in 1993, while others were drawn from people I had come to know over the preceding two decades of work in Central Java.
    • Then in the beginning of 2001, some of the same persons were recontacted. A provisional assessment of the first two and a half years of the *Reformasi* period in the town of Surakarta was attempted, including interviews with students, artists, and selected NGOs and Muslim leaders. In this last phase I deliberately focused on the positive side; expressions of discouragement are widely reproduced in all sorts of printed forms, hence well documented. If good news doesn't sell newspapers, it is, on the other hand, interesting sociologically. To work out well, these social movements knew they had to be grounded in reality, to concentrate on the refounding of social bonds as manifest in concrete projects that inspired mutual respect is instructive. What visions of their social bonds were inspiring Solonese in their attempts to reconstruct public confidence? The answers to this question reflect very local

urban realities, but, as elsewhere, people only have a clear vision of where they live and work.

- In September–October 2003 I re-examined the trends discussed in this chapter to see if they were confirming what I had written.

12. Cf. B. O. J. Schrieke, "Uit de gecheidenis van het adatgrondenrecht: De theorie van het zoogenaamde 'vorstelijk eigendomsrecht' " in *Tijschrift van het Bataviaasche Genootschap van Kunsten en Wetenschappen* (1919–21).

13. Suhartono, *Apange dan Bekel: Perubahan Sosial di Pedesan Surakarta 1830–1920* (1991). For the basic study of the evolution of Javanese law on land tenure: Soepripto, R. *Ontwikelingsgang der Vonstenlandsche Wetboeken* (1929). Many recent (post-Soeharto) studies of land tenure problems have appeared from a historical or sociological point of view: Fadjar Pradikto, *Gerakan Rakyat Kelaparan: Gagalnya Politik Radikalisasi Petani* (2000). Gunawan Wiradi, *Reform Agraria. Perjalanan yang belum Berakhir* (2000). Soegijanto Padmo, *Landreform dan Gerakan Protes Petani Klaten 1959–1965* (2000).

14. The first legal aid NGO (Lembaga Bantuan Hukum) was established in Jakarta by Buyung Nasution in the 1971. Cf. Philip J. Eldrige, *Non-Government Organizations and Democratic Participation in Indonesia* (1995, ch. 6).

15. Cf. Maria Ruwiastuti, "Menuju Pluralisme Hukum Agaria", in *Otonomi Daerah dan Sengketa Tanah. Pergeseran Politik di Bawah Problem Agraria*, edited by Noer Fauzi (2000, pp. 77–104).

16. Cf. *Laporan Proyek. Periode July 1999 s/d Juni 2000*, pp. 10–30. The cases concern dismissal without severance pay (*pesangon*); impediments to the construction of "free" labour unions; all kinds of illegal land dealings, illegal allocation of state-supplied rice and infrastructural materials, etc.

17. Even local government now encourages this, cf. Damar Harsanto, "People urged to enhance neighborhood security", *The Jakarta Post*, 2 September 2002.

18. YAPHI and ATMA are Protestant; Nurani, Catholic; and LBH Universitas Sebalas Maret and Jakalata have a Muslim colouring. Cf. Articles in the *Solo Pos*, 25 May 2000 and *Bernas*, 26 May 2000.

19. Cf. on Hamengku Buwana IX, the magazine *Tempo*, *Sri Sultan Hari-hari Hamengku Buwono IX* (Grafitipers, 1998).

20. For the definition of these terms, cf. D. van Hinloopen Labberton, *Dictionnaire de Termes de Droit coutumier Indonésien* (1934).

21. Cf. Donna Woodward, "Rule of Law or Tyranny of law?", *Jakarta Post*, 8 March 2001.

22. *Reroyikan*, or *kroyok*, meaning to work or fight as a group, can have connotations of violence or ganging up on that are absent from the term *sesarengan*.

23. For Java, cf. Robert Cribb, ed., *The Indonesian Killings, 1965–66: Studies from Java and Bali* (1990). For Bali, cf. Geoffrey Robinson, *The Dark Side of Paradise: Political Violence in Bali* (1995, chs. 10–11).

24. In a book edited by Noer Fauzi, *Otonomi Daerah dan Sengketa Tanah. Pergeseran Politk di Bawah Problem Agaria* [Regional Autonomy and Land Lawsuits. Political

Frictions behind the Agrarian Problems] (2001), Maria Ruwiastuti in Chapter 3 entitled "Towards an Agrarian Legal Pluralism" (pp. 77–104), describes the marginalization of law in general and in particular *adat* law as incorporated in the UUPA (Decrees of Agrarian Law of 1960).

25. Area north of Solo where the inhabitants were brutally forced off an immense area of land to make way for a large artificial lake and which opened, now for more than twenty-five years, a social battle that is not yet over.

26. In the resumé below I have not distinguished their opinions by name.

27. Prejudice on the basis of ethnic, religious, racial, and orientation identity (*suku, agama, ras, dan aliran*).

28. The textuality of the Koran is a much-discussed question in Indonesian Muslim exegesis, for instance, cf. Nasr Hamid Abu Zaid, *Teksutalitas Al-Quran: Kritik terhadap Ulumul Qur'an* (2001).

29. In a *Jakarta Post* article dated 29 May 2001, Hery Haryanto Azumi points out that in the euphoria of the last three years of "reformation" the two major Islamic groups have abandoned their social roles for political ones. Using their religious legitimacy to justify their political partys' interests has been a disaster for what he calls cultural discourse.

30. Of course a certain objectification of *adat* took place already in the beginning of the twentieth century. Cf. R. S. and R. D. Kipp, eds., *Beyond Samosir* (1983, *passim*).

31. *Bangsa* originally meant nobility, and later came to mean ethnic group, nation, and race.

32. Day of the descent of the souls of the dead to earth, cf. Kersten (1984, p. 262).

33. A non-court dance usually performed by a single female dancer, hence also a performer of this dance.

34. This had been constructed to commemorate the twenty-fifth anniversary of the founding of the Budi Utomo in 1933.

35. Cf. his *Kridha Graita* (Yogyakarta: Kridha Martana, 1994).

36. *E dhayohé teka; é gelarna klasa; é klasané bedhah; é tambalen jadah; jadahé mambu; é papakna asu; asuné mati; buangen kali; kaliné banjir; cemplungno pinggir.*

37. In Javanese: *Dondong opo salak ; duku cilik-cilik/ gendong opo mundak ; mlaku thimik-thimik.* Meaning "(Please choose) between a *dondong* fruit or a small *duku* fruit/ (chose between) being carried on a person's back or shoulders, (then) walk in mincing little steps."

38. *"Alas gung liwang-liwung ; jalma mara, jalma mati."*

39. The source of this play is the Mahabharata, cf. G. Dumézil, *Mythe et Epopée II. Types Epiques Indon-Européens: un héros, un sorcier, un roi* (1995). Cf. ch. IV, on Jarāsandha, pp. 96–108. Elsewhere (Headley 2003) I have analysed the Javanese treatment of Jarasandha as a half-man myth.

40. Lodra is neither Javanese nor Sanskrit according to my dictionaries.

41. These were also encountered in the offerings to Durga described in Chapter 8.

42. The witness that Werkudara requires of Hamsa on the *alun-alun*, the five hundred well-armed soldiers, is later explained to Hamsa by Togo who says that Werkudara was challenging him to battle. Hamsa says he didn't feel challenged, but Tagog explains that the Pandhawa are polite, and that it was nonetheless a challenge. Bilung says it is not too late to find a bus and they should all go home because no one wants to fight Werkudara. Furthermore his children will be there with him. In Solo they are Anatarejo and Gatutkoco; in Yogyakarta, the preceding two and Antasena; while in Banjumas, Srenggini is counted as the fourth.

43. It is not clear on the tape what text is referred to, although the meter, *gambuh*, is noted. It sounds like the *Serat Jaka Lodhang* (the carefree young man; edition Kamamjaya 1985, pp. 80–88), but the *dhalang* Mantep may be referring to a prophecy (*jangka*). Jangka and Jaka are easily confused in the midst of the noise of the performance.

44. The *bedhaya* is the most famous and most hieratic of the classical court dances in Central Java. It used only to be celebrated in front of the king in his palace. The standard work on these dances is C. Brakel, *The Bedhaya Court Dances of Central Java* (1992).

45. During the evening programme the composer Guntur Sulistiyono *lila* (willingness; play) to "sincerity" defined as follows:

    "That willingness (*lila*) to be sincere (*iklas*), that cursed sincerity, that abused sincerity; any whole-heartedness (*iklas*) is based on pure-heartedness. Of course to attempt to be sincere is hard, but decency adheres to sincerity as the path that leads to blessedness/happiness. That blessedness will appear where ever piety (*rasa salèh*) becomes dominant."

15

ENCLOSING COSMOLOGIES
AND ELECTIVE CITIZENSHIP

In this conclusion, I would like to lift this documentary monographic contribution on the introduction of Islam to Central Java to the level of a theoretical one. Throughout the preceding chapters our perspective on Java has frequently been contrasted to those of Andrew Beatty and John Pemberton. But our unnamed opponent has been Emile Durkheim and an untenable opposition of individual and society (Ingold 1996, pp. 57–98). If in the *Elementary Forms of Religious Life* (1912) the society is present in the individual, his search for a positive definition of religion, discourages Durkheim from starting from God/Allah as totality and pushes him in the direction of a distinction between the sacred and the profane. Our disagreement with this dichotomy is that our description of Java has made it clear that a Javanese may not perceive division between the sacred and the profane, since the social space created by his relations with others projects him immediately as part of a whole. It is less a question of collective representation of types of ideas which individuals accept, than individual(istic) participation in a common cosmology. A person with no relation of any kind would have no existence in society. It is in this sense of society that brings a man to life. As often as possible we have described how Javanese persona are formed by these relationships into which they enter.

In former times there was no precise word for this formative matrix. The word in Javanese now used is *masyarakat* which originally meant group or association before being used to translate the imprecise concept of society.

514

Now during the 1980s Javanese themselves say, for instance, of the *dakwah* ("propagating" the faith) campaigns, that Javanese society (*masyarakat*) was still being Islamized. It was not Western social sciences that brought about the possibility of distancing oneself from the object of observation (society) to better understand it. As Jonathan Spencer has pointed out "this distinction lay at the very heart of colonial practice ... orderly government without active reform of local society" (in Ingold 1996, p. 79). Already Boeke in his 1930 inaugural address in Leyden University had described Java as a dual (native and colonial) society. Needless to say, the Javanese had realized that long before. Hence the appearance in twentieth century Javanese of the word society (*masyarakat*) is not only of ethnographic interest,[1] but also of theoretical consequence. It shows that a consciousness of colonial exploitation has been politicized in nationalist circles and is used to characterize Java as a whole. This whole is henceforth named society, but it is not unique since other "societies" on other islands were treated the same way by the Dutch. This new self-consciousness carries with it both an older individuation (inter-island trade was pluri-millenial), but also a new vision of a possible unity on the level of the Dutch East Indies themselves. They could become a nation, an imagined community of individuals for whom there was no question of using Javanese as the lingua franca.

The ambiguity we have focused on concerned the Muslim community's mode of appropriating this modernity. How across the newly-defined Javanese "culture", "society" and nationalist political "parties" would the *umat* be articulated? How long would it take it to find its place in this fast-moving process of historical redress, we call independence movements? Perforce at this specific moment in twentieth century Javanese history, competition arises for who can claim to describe Java. This is Pemberton's overarching paradigm. Java has become a subject of debate, but who is entitled to describe it and with which agendas is disputed. To counter Durkheim, to take description beyond the invested political interests in controlling the representation of Java, I have persistently proposed that human relationships are not extrinsic to the persons who create society, but that personal experience of "others" constitutes society. Society is not beyond but inside the persons animating it. The whole point of entitling this volume *Durga's Mosque* was to scrap the neat distinction between Javanese paganism and Islam. Religions outlast the conversions of those who cease to practise it because coeval with the history of the people who continue to live in Java in the new Islamic codes of experience. Dichotomies do not explain conversion, as the observed socialization of the Javanese presented above testified. Not all Islam was politicized. As Hefner (1990, p. 220) has shown for the Tengger highlands of East Java, although the Soeharto government denied Islam a major role in national politics until the late 1980s, popular religious NGOs were active in these remote regions and, as taste for urban life styles increased, the authority of village religious traditions declined.

A social order cannot be conjured up out of individual representations of it, but out of those institutions of meaning that are society's social creations. There are hierarchies of values, even relativistic ones. As Beatty has shown (2002), an institution like the *slametan* (communal meal), both fragment and articulate the collectively sponsored events. Grid and group are strictly dependent on one another. Islam is said to aspire to be society, to incarnate its values. Unfortunately Islam excites the covetousness of politicians who objectivize, reify and finally distort it in order to be able to manipulate its electoral constituencies. These short-term strategies have still not undermined the long-term goals of the two mainstream political parties, the Muhammadiyah and the Nahdlatul Ulama. This later movement continues to represent a tolerant synthesis with the older Javanese values that we have seen above as early as the seventeenth century. The Nahdlatul Ulama is trying to recycle an open holism found in the Javanese countryside at the end of the nineteenth century. It has been worthwhile focusing on the lifestyles of these Javanese Muslims in and around Krendawahana. They have shown how the input of recent historical events (the 1825–30 Java War, etc.) as well as the rural landscapes of belief were integrated in their earlier hierarchy of values. In Java ideological imagination changes slowly and reforms social morphology without necessarily adopting any orthodoxy.

Admitedly the writing up of fieldwork is perilous recomposition of description. A foreigner describing Java is drawn towards an arbitrary order, that of his discovery of "the facts", or a rationale of them which he or she can perceive. One pretends to be able to represent that other order, social structure, or the "history" behind a culture, in any case another supposedly coherent perspective. The subject of this study was the introduction of individualism into the morphology of Javanese society as seen through the prism of the changes in the religious landscape after the appearance of Islam. It presents a coherence that lies beyond the scattered facts that have come down to us. For me the context of their mutual intelligibility appears when three "orders" are triangulated making a single field of oppositions: village communities, the Muslim community (*umat*), and the construction of the nation state, the Republic of Indonesia.

Even if all the religious history of Java in the nineteenth century were available, there would still be enormous problems of interpretation. India, for which the data on Islamization is much more complete, shows that scarcity of data is not the only problem (Wink 1990, 1997; Vaudeville 1996, ch. 1). Furthermore religious adherence among Javanese is an ongoing experience mixing personal conviction and a much sought after integration into a social hierarchy. The Javanese over the centuries have rarely completely lost anything from their past religious praxis. Usually avoiding obvious syncretism, they have continued to add new dimensions to their religious repertory. Finally our history of past forms of worship should never be allowed to overshadow the ongoing popularity of worship itself.

What does the appearance of a deterritorialized religious community imply for the earlier territorially, village-based Javanese ancestral religion? The freedom to flee the web of rural kinship and neighbourhood networks of hereditary custom (*adat*) for the "freedom" and individualism of urban life above all reflects the devaluation of these earlier Javanese public norms. Their unity had been put into question. In our opening chapter we argued that to study the appearance of individualism in Java, a view of the whole of Javanese society is a prerequisite for the study of its component parts. To this end our study of Central Javanese Islam has tried to keep in focus four distinct sociological processes resulting in recognizable forms. Each of these social "orders" has its own time frame so below we describe them from the most ancient and tenacious towards the most recent, and more rapidly evolving:

1. Before the appearance of an "authentic" *umat*, fully Javanese and fully Muslim, Islam and the ancestral religion cohabited under the same tradition-bound Javanese cosmic canopy. The forest of Krendawahana is taken as a sign for this cohabitation and has given this volume its title, *Durga's Mosque*. These earlier village societies and their cults articulated the whole on the level of the village.
2. The formation of a separate deterritorialized Javanese Islamic community around mosques that were not neighbourhood-based. It was from their pan-Indonesian network of Koranic schools (*madrasah*, *pesantrèn*) that the Muslim reform movements in a colonial and later nationalistic social space developed.
3. During the course of the twentieth century, the differences in these Muslim reform movements, each having created their own political parties, were exacerbated by the consolidation of individualism deriving from the secular political ideologies of nation-state.
4. In the aftermath of the collapse of state terror in 1998, the vacuum left behind permitted efforts for the reconstruction of social confidence to emerge using mechanisms of social cohesiveness that many imagined had

definitively vanished. For the first time individualism as an ideology was challenged, however tentatively.

These four social orders are related by their reactions one to another. They are discussed separately due their distinct even overlapping chronological frameworks. These four social orders behave like a quadruple helix, four coils with a common axis developing a complex surface of social history. The four processes constantly associated and dissociated themselves as they evolved, as they "turn" together temporally. Even if social reality itself is more subtle, the complexity of these relationships requires us to use heuristic models (holism: individualism) to bring them into focus. For instance, when the appearance during the age of commerce (1400–1600) of a specific Muslim variety of individualism, (number three above) was initially introduced by Islam and when roughly speaking it replaced cosmology with soteriology is hard to decide. It depends entirely on where we are talking about. Likewise the local mosque community (*jemaah*) is a much smaller unit than the *umat* which in principle is transnational. In a certain sense one could identify this transnational *umat* with a pseudo-holism in the sense that belonging to it does not change much of one's place in Javanese society whereas being part of a village shapes one's entire view of society.[2] Does this mean that individualism became tangible only with the creation of an Indonesian state? During the colonial period it certainly characterized the behaviour of the Javanese aristocrats subservient colonial administration of Java? The post-Soeharto period of Indonesian history (1998+), which is just beginning, suggests that Javanese are downscaling the size of the communities they feel capable of working in and that in a climate of rampant political sectarianism.

Separation of social space rather than sharing spaces can occur in any society at any time. The question one needs ask is where the lines of demarcation fall. The second of the four processes cited at the beginning of this chapter concerns the divisions in the Javanese Islamic community nominally brought about by the neo-Wahabi reform movements in the late colonial and early nationalistic period. In fact it began much earlier. Among the factors which have favoured these divisions, Boland (1982, pp. 205–11) suggested that the increasing importance of Javanese Muslims over non-Javanese among the leaders of Indonesian Islam during the first half of the twentieth century might have diminished religious tolerance towards non-Muslims. Since he has written this, non-Indonesian influences in Indonesian Islam have further decreased tolerance. But what we are analysing in this volume is the shape of society in Central Java and not currents of contemporary thought of Indonesian Islam.

If the Koran teaches how to organize social life, in Java since the nineteenth century all the institutions of meaning[3] that society throws up include Islam as an important instance of articulation and mediation. One can divide these institutions up, triangulating three kinds of social space: village social space; that dispersed, chequered space of the Muslim mosque-based communities (*umat*); that supposed homogeneous space of the Indonesian nation-state (*negara*). The first and the third share a similar sense of scale in that they pretend or have in the past pretended to represent a whole. Because it is not territorially based, the *umat* can only appeal to monotheistic and transnational coherence of belief. We are now in a position to understand how this threefold juxtaposition came about historically. As is diagrammed in Figure 15.1, Javanese custom (*adat*) was shattered by the accumulated impact of a universal religion, Islam, and the implantation of a racial colonialism. Afterwards all that was left of custom (*adat*) was the extended family, often spread over separate non-contiguous villages.

The fissures in Javanese communities caused by these competing reform movements were exacerbated by the appearance of a more standard variety of individualism brought in with the secular ideologies of nation-state during the course of the twentieth century. The secular by definition is this worldly, preoccupied by the ever-pressing present. The nation-state in this archipelago

FIGURE 15.1
Triangulation and fractioning of Javanese custom

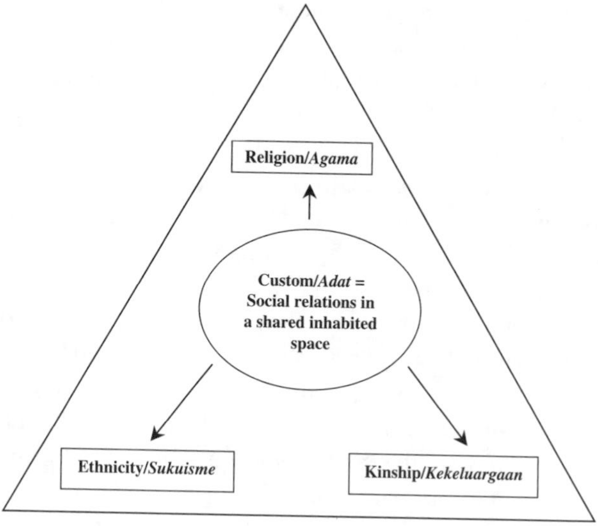

could have hardly acted otherwise; nothing guaranteed its permanance. By stipulating that in principle all its ethnic components are different yet equal, they created a national pseudo-whole in this pluri-cultural maritime zone. Its founders tried to rivet it to a single foundation through the invented ideology of the Pancasila. The higher divinity of the nation was an umbrella over the gods of Islam, Catholicism, Protestantism, and Hindu-Buddhism. The only way to reconcile such an ideology with local socio-religious practices was through a massive input of individualism. This left the state as the only institution capable of making sense of the whole of society. It led its citizens into an epistemological cul de sac.

The fall of the Soeharto dictatorship should not lead us to practise only a history of facts and events but also one of coherence and the ongoing structure of Javanese history. The post-1998 vacuum, which regenerated institutions of meaning that many imagined definitively marginalized, was studied in several cultural discourses in Chapter 12 to 14. Here Javanese Islam struggles to maintain its footing. The meta-Javanese discourse of Damarjati's speech (Chapter 14) interweaves Islam with other layers of meaning dominated by the value of security, peace and social solidairty. By his virtuosity in juxtaposing Muslim, Hindu-Buddhist and traditional Javanese semantic fields, Damarjati made his case for a social tolerance of difference. Yet there are more responses to the violence of 1998 than pious public rituals and clever speeches. What is constructed in the grotesque travesties of *bedhaya* dances (Ch. 14) where male impersonators of virgin women dancers flash their bare bottoms at the audience? Are they simply prostituting the classic palace dance of the *bedhaya*? In fact these shock tricks also value the source of the dance, that is to say the social protection that comes from the original ritual. They indeed believe that social protection comes from an original form of the ritualized dance, but that this morality or custom is not obliged to be integrated into a deadly seriousnessness of Pancasila which would cut it off from willingness to play (*lila*). Ultimately this *lila* is a willingness to be sincere, to be civil. "Play" allows artistic tradition to be preserved through innovations. When social bonds are tired, they need a good thrashing which is both comic and refreshing.

The four parts of our study concerned successively: the general anthropology of Central Javanese rural society; a reconstruction of the religious history of Kaliasa by local lineages; the structures of this landscape as seen through the rituals and prayers pre-Muslim and Islamic used at Durga's tertre in Krendawahana and in the Kaliasa mosques; and finally in the fourth section an assessment of the place of individualism in post-Soeharto Surakarta as reflected in the effort at the reconstruction of social confidence.

Historically, these four social orders were brought into focus by data describing the facets of the introduction of Islam into the area of Kaliasa. For the modern period (Part IV), Krendawahana was viewed as a village in the suburban orbit of the nearby urban centre of Surakarta with its half a million inhabitants. These lines of argumentation of all the chapters can now be brought together here to present a more concise assessment of the adaptation of the earlier religious landscape to the Muslim one.

Paradoxically in Indonesia the less the "house" is founded on kin-based social organization of an objective sort, the greater its capacity for inclusion (Ch. 1). The extension of the idiom of siblingship to encompass the Javanese peasants' real or foetus siblings was hierarchized by socially prominent families who dominated village life. The idiom of siblingship, as a vehicle for an axiomatic "house", appeals to a principle, yet their kin-based "house" took into account the biographical vicissitudes of real life. This lies in an imagined community where siblingship conveys the bonds of a family "house"; since siblings relate to one another laterally, eventually forming a locally recognized order. Even if the idiom of siblingship could create conditions of alienation propitious to the introduction of an urban derived individualistic evaluation of that household hierarchy of values, individualism per se could not begin to describe the bonds forged by such a "house".

Thus in the first chapter we foregrounded two features of Javanese social morphology, lineages and the foetus siblings. Both play an important role in the creation of worship communities as well as the articulation of the Javanese society within the cosmos. Despite the strength of the Asiatic commercial networks and a certain cosmopolitan cachet at this Javanese "crossroads", the particularity of these cognatic features endured in Javanese social organization sandwiched between India and China. The social inheritance of the concentric medieval kingdoms, and the divine right rice agriculture with its strict royal hierarchy economically founded on an apanage system, were harmonized as a well-articulated whole, so that cohesion and equlilibrium were constant preoccupations (Lombard 1990).

Next we saw how during the life of a person myth and ritual wove him/her into a web of correspondences together with his/her foetus siblings' macrocosmic (*jagad agung*) dimensions. The conclusion of this chapter concerned the semantics of Ego's generation in comparison with other Austronesian kinship classifications. If elder sister–younger brother marriage appeared in Javanese myths, in every day Javanese life spouses are classified by a distinctive use of elder/younger. They are assimilated to the category of near cross-siblings. The inversion of this opposition permits the articulation of two orders: temporality (elder and younger) and gender (male and female).

At the beginning of the twenty-first century, Sri (Chapter 3), the ultimate elder sister, can be described the last "goddess", that is to say value, left over from the second Mataram dynasty (1613–1755) with a full sweep of clients and hence a nearly total social network (Ch. 3). She has left the palaces and now stays on in the "primordial" Javanese village, Medhang Kamulan, where she first appeared, associated with the origin (*kamulan*) of the rice shaft (*medhang*). As long as her myths and the dangers she protects against are spoken of, it seems unlikely that her place in the Javanese hierarchy of spirits will disappear. Indeed the Javanese have been caring (*ngopèni*) for Sri's invisible body for so long that to speak of her disappearance is in fact to miss what the myth has always been about. She "disappeared" into the rice granary with the beginning of society. The same cannot be said for the cult of Durga and Lara Kidul, whose political role as protectors of the king have eroded, while that of Islam's hierarchy of social values has been strengthened throughout the last century, eventually moving towards modern forms of leverage in the young nation-state.

In Chapter 3, it was claimed that the profoundly village-centred *topos* of well-being was homologous to a larger matrix, the whole society. Their difference lay in the scale of the circuit through which similar values are passed. In the countryside, a blessing is invoked for that particular place, whereas in the palace invocations the ruler, his body, and his palace incarnate the whole. Since the village perspective is so strongly rooted in an inhabited space, it proved important to understand how the evolution of the princely polities effected the village communities in terms of their land tenure and taxation procedures. Without this outside influence alienating peasants through indirect land tenure and exploitive *faire valoir*, it is difficult to understand the transformation from membership in a village to a non-territorial community like the Javanese Muslim *umat*. Did Islam offer a dignity valued by certain landless peasants who were no longer full-fledged village members? Often the élite were allied with the most pious (*salèh*). Membership in the village involved many alliances and as many constraints. One could not leave the village and settle in another one since all able-bodied family heads and farmers, called *cacah*, were bound by economic indebtedness to the ruler. The relationship of servant to master (*kawula-gusti*) was first and foremost economic. The king measured his resources in terms of numbers of *cacah*. On the other hand, the destiny of the village was perceived in large part as a communal one; local spirits protected the frontiers of that particular space and the residents who honoured its deities (*dhanyang*) at offering sites, sacred trees and wells, etc. The local ritual calendar involved the annual farming cycle as it related to these local deities. Communal meals were held, and communal labour was necessary for rebuilding houses and restoring bridges and wells. The king held no royal eminent domain (*vorstelijk eigendomsrecht*[4]) over the village land; the local Javanese princes did not even measure these lands. What they did count was the number of farming families on them. They were preoccupied by sociology, not by territory measured in square metres of rice fields. Gradually during the course of the eighteenth and nineteenth centuries precedence for membership in the village began to be based on outside economic and political networks unrelated to principalities.

Lea Jellinek wrote of Jakarta slum dwellers (1991, p. 51), "As in most societies, crisis brought out a sense of unity among the kampung dwellers." However the memory of strict village reciprocity may take a perverse turn, and pretensions of solidarity may be shown to be hollow. The recent crisis in Javanese villages has created mistrust of the poor on the part of the village élite, who on occasion have refused to allow exceptional distributions of inexpensive rice set aside by the government's social safety net programme during "Special Market Operations". Certain shop-owners stopped selling rice altogether so as not to have to extend credit to buy it. As Breman and Wiradi conclude (2002, p. 308): "The crisis in Indonesia has stopped being a purely monetary-economic recession and has escalated into a far-reaching disruption of society as a whole." It is this whole, society at large and the place of a Javanese within it, that is being shown to be untenable if individualism is allowed free rein. Where no value is attributed to redistribution, then the exclusive circulation of monetary value proves an obstacle to protection of social cohesiveness.

In Chapter 4 the agent of the deterritorialization of the Javanese village communities was shown to be the Javanese rural *bekel*, the tax farmer. This role of the *bekel* and his followers were often in blatant contradiction to the territorial integrity of the village (Elson 1997, pp. 28–30). To begin with the function of tax-farmer was usually bought, often by an outsider. Where there existed a certain distance from the kingdom, the village settlement could develop their common interests in the margin of the stratified centralization of the divine right rice agriculture administered by the kingdom. Between the village cults and the royal cults there existed a massive gap that was sometimes furnished by regional cults, albeit not too pretentiously for fear of royal suppression.

As shown in Chapter 4, the erosion of the economic foundation of the royal apanage system prepared the restructuring of the religious landscape of Krendawahana-Kaliasa by Islamic and aristocratic lineages presented (Part II, Chs. 5–6). The basis of these local narratives were often other meetings, for instance that of Durga with Natakusuma. It was more in the tradition for Javanese to vanish as did Natakusuma, than to be captured and exiled by the Dutch as was Paku Buwana VI. When Paku Buwana VI did leave his palace, to go to Mancingan to consult his deity (*déwa*) and to seek the Queen of the Southern Seas, he met instead the resident of Yogyakarta. Arrested, he was taken to Semarang to be exiled to Ambon where he wrote his *Babad Bangun Tapa* (Wieringa 1994). An Ambonese prison was not part of the mythological landscape of the Javanese. What the 1979 recyling of the *Maésa Lawung* ritual unsuccessfully tried to refurbish was the tarnished reputation of Paku Buwana VI's lineage. Surprisingly the dusting off of an important and ancient ritual showed it to be no worse for having been in storage. Durga was certainly still present in Krendawahana, and now the princely cult would be encouraged by the various people who came there to venerate her.

The exclusivity of royal lineages had been brutally challenged by placing the Javanese king in an Ambonese jail. The power to appoint tax farmers in the royal apanage system was definitively put into question and commercial renting of royal tax lands began to take over. Once this apanage system had been abolished, their mode of calculating proximity to a ruling or former king interested only themselves. The Muslim lineages, on the other hand, responsible for the worship communities linked to the cemeteries in the Kaliasa-Krendawahana area, permitted contacts stetching out from the graves there; over time they were able to draw together increasingly large numbers of people living throughout the island. These worship communities constructed a number of mosques, and recently a minaret at the Koranic school which constituted a means of uniting religious endeavour via a large network of common ancestors. Clearly the prestige that came from descending from such a lineage had become as valuable, if not more so, than calculating one descent from Paku Buwana VI. Descent was no longer a royal privilege.

Nonetheless the reactivation of the cult of Durga in Krendawahana in 1979,[5] did nothing to raise the prestige of the palace aristocrats among the Muslims of the nearby villages and probably little to raise their own status as the palace no longer ruled the kingdom (Ch. 6). In Kaliasa the lineage (*trah*) now has deep regional roots; it represents more than four thousand people, both present locally and linked to Kaliasa from afar. The lineages (*trah*) are in an intermediary position between the village and the *umat*. On the one hand they are deterritorialized like the *umat* and on the other hand they are kin-based like the villages. Clearly the pretensions of a Javanese lineages are only valuable as long as one remains on the island of Java. Although some middle-class Javanese are willing to participate in the Surakarta palaces' efforts to propagate neo-feudalism on the basis of an ancient cult to Durga, they could also opt for these Muslim networks. To say that the sociology of Islam has escaped the *priyayi* aristocrats' vision of social hierarchy, is really to say that there is no longer a global hierarchy recognized by all Javanese. Now there are several kinds of lineages in Java. Other genealogies have been written in the landscape of the area's graves and mosques, and over Durga's tertre. Despite the continuing annual pilgrimages from the palace on the occasion of the buffalo sacrifice (*maésa lawung*) commemorating the anniversary of the king's coronation, the invisible kingdom of Durga meant less to the local inhabitants than the assembling of the bones of their ancestors buried there. On the other hand the sociological "work" of Muslim burial rites, as well as the renewal preaching (*dakwah*) of the Muslims during the 1980s, insured that social memory was increasingly an Islamic one.

To understand better this transition from Javanese raja-centric and ancestral traditions to Islam Durga as the slayer of the demon buffalo, Mahishāsuramardanī, was studied. This victory is assimilated with the repulsing of the demons armies that would destroy the world order, finally making a demonic (*asura*; *daitya*) into divine dharma. Paradoxically in East Java, Durga's son Kala is assimilated to Kalāgni, the destructive fire. How this assimilation took place in detail still escapes us, but in the course of Chapter 7 we saw the elements that produced the assimilation: the iconographic canon of the Durgā's victory over the buffalo, royal cults at temples, but also at obscure forest shrines like Krendawhana. Outside the Javanese palaces, after the fifteenth-century indigenized "Hindu" rituals were destined to gradually disappear for want of royal support, while the Muslim *umat* in the course of the nineteenth century chose to distance itself from the royal centres and to resist colonization with ever greater support among the exploited peasantry. Not all resistance to the Dutch was Islamic, but after the Javanese *jihad* (1825–30) against the colonial government the die was cast, Islam was indelibly Javanese.

The grafting of the myth from the first book of the Mahābhārata, the *Ādiparva*, onto an Indian iconography of Durga's victory over the titan buffalo was overtaken in the popular mentality by Kala, Durga's son, becoming the subject of individual exorcism rites (Ch. 8). For if Durga's cult was always in sacred forests (Krendawahana, Gandamayit), cemeteries and the like, Kala attacked anywhere in Java. Rather than the king sending buffalo blood or his clothes to Durga's forest, in the case of the Birth of Kala exorcisms, the exorcists *dhalang* goes to the house of the afflicted to perform the myth of Kala's birth in shadow puppet theatre. Their house became the temple of his ritual. Although group exorcisms exist, this is essentially a rite for an individual. Recently a whole family or group of families have joined together to be prayed over in group exorcism (*ruwatan masal*). The ritual boundary scales seem very different from mosque-centred prayer. This seeming contrast is lessened once we examined the actual corpus of invocations used in the royal rituals and in the personal family-based exorcisms. In fact the mantra for the royal offering of buffalo meat to Durga are nearly the same as those said of Kala who "devours" the destinies of Javanese peasants (Ch. 9). Both include Arabic formulae.

The corpus of prayers used in a given Javanese offering ground (*pundhèn*) provides the outside observer with some important indications of the evolution of the scales of these religious landscapes. If one compares the corpus used with that of other cults, the invocations of the local protective deities are usually not generic, i.e. found elsewhere in Java.[6] These local prayers are often related to the founders' intentions and as such distinguished between that cultic figure's jurisdiction (*wilayah*) and the sphere of influence of the deities worshipped in the palace or at other royal shrines arranged around the kingdom. The exceptions to this are the standard Arabic invocations which impregnate most rural cults. These are generic in the sense that they are used as such in many different settings throughout the Malayo-Indonesian world. Here, however, universal blends into individualistic through their monotone fit throughout this area. In not being context sensitive, they are a vehicle of individualism, detaching the peasant from his personal set of bonds to the present community and its local protective spirits.

The "redeeming" quality of offerings requires a sacrifice on the part of the intercessor. In prayer one has to give up, abandon, and dedicate (*labuh*) an offering, along with offering one's attention, while awaiting the response of the deity addressed. This is guided by a socially-instituted precedent, a convention that if one implicates oneself this way, one can redeem and prevent the evil obstacles from arising. If the dialogic aspect of invocation, so important in Muslim prayer, is formally absent in the Krendawahana *Maésa Lawung* ritual, one can describe its prayers pragmatically. The presence of the chorus chanting "well-being" at the foot of Durga's tree after every verse of the *Sastra Pedhati* mantra at the buffalo spearing ritual insures a dialogic ambience for the royal delegates to the ritual. One is witnessing the transformation of the debris of cosmogony narratives (the sources of the mantra used here) into a protective purifying invocations (Headley 2000*a*).

Public Muslim prayer in Java reflects society in three very different ways. *Salat* is potentially a mirror distinguishing itself from the non-Muslim (*kafir*) society outside the mosque (Ch. 10). This varies from mosque to mosque and region to region Secondly, in pious Muslim tradition, prayer in the mosque cleans the soul, compared with a mirror (*mir'āh*), allowing it to reflect the divinity of Allah. Finally the coherence of the religious community (*umat*) is also reflected in their collective accomplishment of this oral rite. Muslim monotheism creates an ethos proposing that Muslim society at large follow its *sharī'ah*[7] leading towards a polity structured by the Muslim *fikh*. None of the societies around the Indian Ocean have yet reached the situation found in parts of the Arabian peninsula where national frontiers are ideologically covered and bounded as if by the roof of one great mosque. Everywhere else, even if *salat* is paramount among all other forms of congregational worship, different worship communities persist. Even in that most famous form of a society in which Islam is completely dominant, the caliphate, the dhimmitude (Bat Ye'or 1996), the "tolerated" monotheistic minorities, were envisioned.

The greatest difficulty when describing the development of Muslim prayer in Java comes, not from its admixture to ancestral Javanese rites, but from our own inexperience in listening to Muslim prayers in the same polyphonic, plurivocal ways they are heard by the Javanese themselves. Beatty (1999) has shown that these Arabic formulae can be understood in many different senses. The social production of prayer in Java is partially a function of this inclusion of heterodox in its recitation. Mosque prayer (*salat*) thus contains at least two elements of social reproduction: its pretension to represent Allah's command of the world and its ability to be the prayer of all Javanese.

Societies, "modernized" by the forces of the nation-state, although lacking strong atheistic currents, have often seen Islam temporarily marginalized away from the centres of power in their capitals (Feillard 1995, Ch. 9), not prepared to share in the mastery of society. Nonetheless we find here an instance where Muslim rituals contribute to the reproduction of the society at large through an inclusive monotheism. The simple fact is that societies deploy oral rites, be they monotheist or polytheist. These are best understood as a result of the religion's unique ability to relate to society as a divine whole. Of course the nascent Indonesian state needed that capacity of encompassment to bind together the diversity of the archipelago and therefore Soekarno "included" monotheism in the Pancasila ideology. But as Milbank writes:

> Sociology fails to encompass religion in space as the whole, the outside, or the transitional. It also fails to encompass religion in open time as the growth of knowledge, or a necessary transitional phase. Its [sociology's] third device is to encompass religion as the concealed temporal process of social self occlusion, or as ideology (1990, p. 133).

What Milbank says of sociology can be applied *mutatis mutandis* to modern secular thinking about religion which is hard put to accept the demands of fundamentalists striving for greater public expression of what the state had hoped would become an increasingly private faith whose doors onto the street would be "closed" by tolerance. This is to misunderstand the capacity of public prayer to represent society before the divine. During conventionalized canonical prayer (*salat*), the praying community (*jemaah*) pretends to be at one through the use of identical prayers with the whole Muslim world) and yet sociologically still typify the whole of Java not even excluding the heterodox who use certain Muslim formulas as every day greetings.

Chapter 11 addressed the issue of how the Javanese past remained vocalized (Ong 1967, p. 72); how it lived on as an oral performance in different genres of plays. "Ancient" history finally became a play. As nineteenth-century literary genre, the long poem *Manikmaya* (Ch. 11) became one cultural mode for encompassing knowledge. Since the *macapat* (a genre of sung poetry) groups that recite *Manikmaya* are now on the point of extinction, the cosmogony at the beginning of *Manikmaya*, so much a product of the eighteenth century, will finally probably die out before the post-fifteenth century mythology that composed this cosmogony falls out of the *wayang* shadow puppet repertory.

The nineteenth century compilation of Javanese mythologies, the *Manikmaya*, did in a sense fail to "tie up the past" into a discourse (*angiket purwanipun*; 1981: canto I.1). But in the course of the nineteenth century this particular genre of "history" was to begin to die out while the source for these compilations reappear in the popular oral *wayang* repertory where they continued to function as kind of shared knowledge drawing on many sources of oral tradition. Myths (like *Sesaji Raja Suyo* in Chapter 14) reappear in all-night *wayang* performances long after they seemed to have disappeared from the peasant's oral repertory. While their written poetic source lay unconsulted in palace scriptoria, they are so much a part of Javanese history that their own evolution becomes a kind of history. As mentioned above, this is the case of the rice goddess Sri.

In the introduction to this volume, we justified the need for an anthropological study of the nineteenth-century Central Javanese *umat* by invoking the historical contrast opposing nineteenth-century enveloping cosmologies to twentieth-century elective citizenship in the new Indonesian republic.[8] We claimed that any effort to understand the Javanese Muslims appropriation of modernity would need to account for this transition. The *umat's* morphology could only be grasped through a study of its changing recursive efforts to encompass Java. More basically one could only decide what kind of community the *umat* was/is by investigating its ability to "encompass" Java as a whole. Our stepping off point was the ambition to show how Islam for the Javanese had become the higher value by representing all of that society towards the exterior world, while *vis-à-vis* the older insular orientation on this island, the values of "Javanism" to this day have remained important. We claimed that the study of the processes that led to this inversion of their hierarchy of values would go a long way to explain the emergence of communalism in the period after the fall of the Soeharto dictatorship (May 1998). Using contemporary data from the village of Krendawahana and the area of Kaliasa, for the village is already "sub-urban", as its villagers say "*wis kutha*", drew us towards the nearby city of Surakarta. The sociological level of the village has in some respects been assimilated to that of the urban neighbourhood (*kampung*). The village that used to lie on the northern frontier of the Mangkunagaran kingdom, now lies at the northern limit of the industrial sphere of greater (*raya*) Surakarta with its population of more than half a million people. Taking the framework of the greater Surakarta into which Kaliasa now belongs has the advantage of giving greater scope to the conclusions of our earlier chapters. As the revival of Islam in the 1980s using techniques of popular preaching (*dakwah*) moved from the city to the countryside, it was no longer a question of the Islamization (*Islamisasi*) of the countryside, but of the indigenization of a pure Islam (*pribumisasi Islam murni*), where pure was defined by urban Muslim values.[9] And it was in this same urban milieu that after the fall of Soeharto in May 1998, that a power vacuum was created into which rushed the new reformers of the Javanese village communities.

In the fourth part of this study the place of individualism was examined in the post-Soeharto Javanese Islam. Beginning in Chapter 12, it was shown that *jihad* enables Javanese Muslims to reinvent Islam in Java as society writ large,[10] but that *jihad* campaigns in Java, once hijacked by militant agendas, fail to convince many Javanese Muslims that these radical movements fully represent Islam. This conscious downscaling of the local *umat* on the part of the militants of partisan Islam usually appeals to the outrage at injustices perpetrated against other *umat* in a "universal" brotherhood of all. *Jihad* also has been brandished to face down the secularizing state to be a greater whole than Islam and to confront the growth of individualism promoted by this nationalism for whom individualism is a comforting social feature. But one could claim that individualism is also inherent to Islam which claims a universal but equal status for all believers. Islamic theology refutes this accusation by saying, "each believer must feel at home in himself and travel throughout this territory in the shadow of his faith" (Boubakeur 1985, p. 50).

For the majority of Javanese, Allah remains a whole which allows Indonesians to think through all of Javanese society, and so by definition Islam peacefully cohabits with all that is "other" in Java.

At recent seminars on the Al-Qaeda attacks in New York City, Javanese Muslims recognized that they have let the fringe groups (the motorcycle, turban and sabre crowd are for hire) become the spokespersons for Indonesian Islam, in the international media as well as locally. The two major associations, Muhammadiyah and Nahdlatul Ulama, are currently seeking ways to counter the militant groups' head start in strategies of media relations. In a post-traditional society like Java, Islam's credibility rests on its capacity to represent the social totality of this island world "ruled by Allah's mercy". Insisting that the revelation of the "other" is an effective way forward towards social solidarity they propose a stricter adherence to those values of their own traditions that tend to forge a unified society. This may be only a reinvented expression of the totality, but it demonstrates an authentic cohesiveness. In a word, Allah's sovereignty depends on the *umat* (community) uniting in his *rahmat* (mercy) in a the recognition of social difference (*ikhtilaf*). The importance of the outside world seeing the *umat* as just (*adil*; Koran 2:143) here comes to the fore. The Friday morning weekly of the same name published by LKiS in Yogyakarta illustrates this approach forcefully.

It was not immediately after the turmoil of May 1998 that calls for *jihad* appeared. The initial efforts to deal with the fractured Javanese societies came from a healthy reform movement (*reformasi*) promoting social solidarity. Élite competition for the spoils of the defunct dictatorship came later. It will take many years before historians, economists, and other social scientists have a clear perspective on the changes wrought in Indonesia by the fall of General Soeharto's regime in 1998. In Chapters 13 and 14, we moved our focus away from the rural area north of Surakarta and studied the social healing rituals practised in the city of Solo following these traumatic events. The urban scene south of the district of Kaliasa is chosen because of the apocalyptic disturbances accompanying the sacking of the city of Surakarta.

Theatre (Ch. 13) often appeared at the centre of efforts to represent the trauma of the victims of these events. If the Solonese purification ceremonies (*ruwatan*) after the fall of Soeharto explicitly sweep away to the southern ocean the parasitic Kala and re-create the constellation of four-five harmony, the *wayang* plays used in village purification ceremonies contained prayers and declarations of intention for much the same thing. Muslim ritual is more devotional and discreet. Here and there Islam is still embedded in older Javanese cosmogony, but it is not the same cosmogony that Islam first encountered in the sixteenth century on the north coast of Java. That one did not yet reserve a place for Allah in its pantheon and, in this sense, was less compromising. So at the beginning of the twenty-first century in Solo, Islam is not identified with this older cosmic canopy. Its large networks of social activists (Muhammadiyah and Nahdlatul Ulama) struggle to consolidate the fault lines of social violence in order to consolidate the well-being of Javanese society. They are its principle guarantee, even if some Pentecostal Christians would say they were its main danger. Chapter 14 showed that one can no longer separate out Islam from the rest of Java even in times of crises. One can even minimize the Muslim dimension of belief knowing that it will shortly return centre stage in other circumstances.

In both "non-Muslim" rituals held in Surakarta (Ch. 13), the community sponsoring the two events was busy (*ramé*), cleansing its body social of generic obstacles and dirt. So much is said about the obstacles and dirt being expelled that one might miss the discreet references to what is actually being cleansed, social violence and state terror. Here an empirical community senses that its welfare is linked to a healthy connection to its cosmic matrix using a complementary dynamics.

- The centre encompassing the four outer components;
- The centre presenting their combination.[11]

Such a strong sense of embeddedness of the microcosm (local Javanese society), here a shopping plaza and a village well, implies a territory that is community centred. It also implies a centripity that is inside (*dalem*) society, not outside it (*lahir*). This explains that its centre "encompasses" and recomposes society more that it surrounds it. What is this Javanese community or family's relation with the macrocosm (*jagad gedhé*) about which it expresses so much concern? Startlingly to our "modern" mind, these "individuals" conceive of themselves, of their community, as grounded in another, greater, higher world.[12] Their sociological vision focuses on the benefits from co-ordinating corresponsability with this macrocosm. Whereas "we" situate all humanistic values, and indeed all human beings who lie outside ourselves, in this world, the Javanese, despite all the acculturation and economic remodelling of three hundred and fifty years of Dutch presence, at the end of the twentieth century often aspire to such a holistic society. Value lies above all in society as a whole, identified with the macrocosm (*jagad gedhé*) and not in the individual's private choices or personal preferences which lack any scope. These fail to place the person in community as is well expressed in these two recent events centred on a shopping mall and a sacred well where the Solonese try to recentre their society on the patterns of their ancestral cosmos. We may want to consider Central Java a pseudo-whole, but the hierarchy of values is still very far from individualism.

So our most general claim is that beliefs, religious adherence, change more quickly than the values ensconced in the morphology of society. This desynchronization is well captured by the relation of Durga's mosque to Islam. This is an important example of the seventeenth and eighteenth-century cohabitation of Islam and the royal religion which by the end of the nineteenth century will be called into question by Islamic reform. By then the principalities were "hollow crowns". As Henk Schulte-Nordholt (1996, p. 335) remarked about the effect of Dutch colonialism on traditional Balinese customs, "ritual care of the crucial style of life no longer rested with the royal centre, and was not looked after by the colonial state either". But Bali is and has remained massively Hindu-Buddhist. In Java the demise of Durga's cult at Krendawhana was paradoxically slowed down through the implantation of local Islam in the area of Kaliasa. Durga's tertre at Krendawahana, *inter alia*, serves locally as a historical monument to the recent Islamization, somewhat in the manner of the Kurawa who highlight their righteous cousins in the Pandava in the *wayang* theatre. After the Treaty of Giyanti in 1755, and with the full dominance of the V.O.C. (Dutch East India Company) in Central Java, one would have expected that the cult of Durga would have gradually disintegrated, once its royal sponsors lost the remaining vestiges of their pretense to power. In fact it also proved useful for the princes to continue their ritual activity as if they were still fully empowered. Juxtaposition with Allah consolidated Durga's domain in the same sense that the royal mosques were located to the northwest of the palace or that the the Muslim pioneers, *kyai*, now buried on either side of the Cemara River in Kaliasa initially penetrated into the twin sacred forests there to challenge the demonic powers with a greater truth. This was not a once and for all confrontation. We saw in Chapter 1 how Nalakirdha at the end of the eighteenth or beginning of the nineteenth century sought the meaning of Allah's name and found it finally from the mouth of a "Muslim" Durga.

In what sense can we compare the characteristics and the qualities of the cult of Durga in the "forest" of Krendawahana with that of the two early mosques that built in Sambirejo and the "forest" of Jaga Patèn? If we abstract the details of the décor and its theology, we are left with Javanese sitting facing in a given *direction*, awaiting an ineffable *meeting* to *protect* them. If these first three characteristics provide similarities, the traits four to seven display dissimilarities, as sketched out.

TABLE 15.1
An Islamic morphology of Durga's mosque

1. *Orientation*: On the steps up to Durga's tertre are "doors" to her invisible kingdom (*karaton* and *kobongan*).	The mosques' *kiblat* (niche) points towards an invisible but geographical mosque in Mecca.
2. *Meeting*: Encounters with Durga are dangerous, even fatal.	One cannot meet with Allah, only submit to him and thus receive blessing (*berkah*) and mercy (*rahmat*).
3. *Protection*: Durga possesses a demon army which serves the Javanese king.	Allah's prophet Mohammed established the institution of *jihad* to protect the Islamic polity.
4. *Creation*: Durga is associated with the consequences of creation more than as a creator: mankind makes offerings to divinities in exchange for protection.	Creation by Allah *ex nihilo* has its direct corollary, complete self-extinction or *fanā'* of those who in ecstasy approach Allah.
5. *Location*: Durga's cult is outside the village, on the borders of society, in a "forest".	Even the mosques founded for rural Koranic schools (*pesantrèn*) clearly belong to the inhabited social space of villages.
6. *Coupling*: Formerly the spouse of Guru (Siwa's), Durga is a cursed goddess with ambivalent magic powers (*sakti*).	Allah is a monad and beyond gender. This is neither the Indian radical (*advaita*) monism nor the Javanese 'Saiva-siddhānta which envisaged the unity of man in God.
7. *Invocation*: Durga is approached with buffalo meat recalling her victory over the demon general Mahisha.	The five canonical prayers (*salat*) are verbal invocations where the only sacrificial elements are marked corporeal postures and gestures.

Behind this comparison lies the obvious fact that even when one changes gods, the morphology of early cults shapes the succeeding ones for several centuries. This volume, however, has attracted our attention to a deeper level of the sociology of these rituals. At the foot of Durga's tertre for the annual *maésa lawung* ritual came the aristocratic delegates from the king on the anniversary of his coronation. Everyone's behaviour, including that of the king was determined by who they were in a hierarchical social framework. When a person entered the mosques in Kaliasa, they were viewed (even when they did not so view themselves) as on an equal footing one to another before Allah. In the secular world outside the mosque they might be rich, esteemed members of the local Muslim society, but this could not be ascertained from their place in the mosque. The case studied here followed how the Javanese cosmos was conceived and portrayed when invoking Durga, and later how it accommodated Allah to the eventual exclusion of Durga altogether. This definitive "conversion" was to a monotheistic individualism; it was incapable of perpetuating the earlier social webbing. Here the permanence of a religious geography or landscape meets its limits. Could individualism take over a society? Dumont (1983, p. 22; translation S.C. Headley) thought that, "individualism ... was never able to function without holism contributing to its life in an unremarked and in some ways clandestine manner". He continues (1991, pp. 29–30; translation S.C. Headley):

> When under the impact of modern civilization, a given culture adapts to what is for her modernity, she constructs representations which justify herself in her own eyes *vis-à-vis* the dominating culture. Thus it was with Germany, Russia and India [just discussed]. The representations are a sort of syntheses, which can be more or less radical: something like an alloy of two kinds of ideas and values, on the one hand being indigenous of holistic inspiration and on the other borrowed from the predominant individualist configuration. These new representation have two faces, one face turned inwards, particularistic and self-justifying, the other turned outwards towards the dominant universal culture ... thanks to their universal face these products of acculturation of a given culture can enter into the dominant culture, the world culture of that period ... the dominant (culture) borrows from the dominated ... Not only do individualistic representations not dissolve or become insipid during the combination into which they enter, but quite to the contrary their draw from these associations with their opposites, on the one hand a superior adaptability, and on the other, increased strength.

What Dumont (1983, p. 29) said about Russia, I believe pertains to the Javanese when they combine a limited (interior) affirmation of their own culture with that of the dominant individualist universalism, which the nation-state proclaims for the entire cultural area of the Indonesian archipelago are equal. Dumont (1983, pp. 31–31) claims that individualism is a powerful ferment of transformation putting in place a blind mixture of opposing values instead of a clear hierarchy. This ideology is capable of being vehiculed by the most contrary assemblage of concepts, values, and institutions.

Is the history of Islam that of its expansion, of Islamization? If the same question were asked of Muslims in Western Europe, they would probably reply that its history is not that of its expansion, but of its "*approfondissement*", of its maturation. So the pertinence of such a question about religious history is determined by one's experience of it: on the one hand as praxis, on the other hand as an outside observer. The later is the perspective of expansion. We have tried to describe the Islamization of Java from the point of view of what one experiences if one lives there. My argument has been that local sociology changes much more slowly than individual religious adherence. Islam had to adapt to the earlier landscape of ascribed status in a closed society. When at the beginnning of the twenty-first century, Dian Nafi' appealed in his weekly Friday columns (Ch. 14) to the spirit of forgiveness (*Solo Pos*, 24 December 2000) and the need for volunteers (*rélawan, Solo Pos*, 19 January 2001) to calm social tensions in Surakarta, he is describing a group (*warga*) that is supra-village, supra-ethnic, surpa-kin, and supra-religious. This "*umat*" of pure unadulterated humanity, free of constraining hierachies, has to be freed of all those very values which when Islam first appeared on the island had enabled Javanese society to be fully social.

NOTES

1. As late as W. J. S. Poerwardarminta's Javanese-Javanese dictionary of 1939 (completed in the late 1920s), the *Baoesastra Djawa* (p. 297) under the spelling *masarakat* gives the definition: "*pasrawoengan lan bebrajaning ngaoerip*" (association and harmony of the living). The word is absent from Janz's 1877 dictionary as well of course from the Winter and Ranggawarsita dictionary begun in 1844 and finally published in 1980.

2. V. Descombes (1996, p. 121) gives a similar definition of pseudo-holism, "... collectivism is basically a pseudo-holism, for it does without any analysis of the relations of the parts of the whole." (translation S.C. Headley)

3. Manners of doing and thinking of which the individuals are not the authors according to Mauss; Descombes (1996, section 20.4).

4. On the Dutch misunderstandings on this question, cf. critique of P. Roo de la Faille, *Over het Grandenrecht onder Javaansch Vortsenbestuur* by B. Schrieke in *Tijdschrift voor Indische Taal-, Land- en Volkenkunde* 59 (1919–20): 122–90.

5. Cf. Headley (1979*b* and 1980*b*).

6. For a general presentation of the "overlap" in Javanese invocations, cf. Headley, "Trois styles de prières à Java: écriture sur le front; offrandes et purification du cœur" (1994).

7. Literally the path that leads to the water trough, hence the clear path for the faithful to follow, the canon of Allah's commandments (in the singular, a *hukum*). For a comparison of the impetus to world empire between Christianity and Islam, cf. G. Fowden, *Empire to Commonwealth, consequences of montheism in late antiquity* (1993).

8. Mitsuo Nakamura (1977, p. 8) has described the sociology of a breakaway community of worshippers (*firaq jemaah*) in Kotagedé. Here we are using the

term Muslim community in an inclusive, even if national sense, the whole of the Muslims *umat* who feel part of the faithful whose native language is Javanese.

9. Cf. Abdul Munir Mulkhan's (2000) study of East Java.

10. Our understanding of the invention of tradition differs from that of the book of the same name which made this terminology popular. We are more interested in why societies try to reinvent their tradition than by the artificiality of these recently invented customs. Cf. Eric Hobsbawm and Terence Ranger (1983).

11. Andrew Beatty (1999).

12. To use Louis Dumont's terminology. Cf. chapter 1 of his *Essais sur l'individualisme: Une perspective anthropologique sur l'idéologie moderne* (1983).

BIBLIOGRAPHY

ABBREVIATIONS USED IN THIS BIBLIOGRAPHY

LUB, MS Lor.	Leiden Universiteit Bibliothek, Leiden Oriental MS
BL/IO	British Library/India Office library
LUB/LOr	Leiden Universiteit Bibliothek: Leiden Oriental manuscript
KITLV	Koninklijk Instituut voor Taal-, Land- en Volkenkunde
PNRI: KBG	Perpustakaan Nasional Republik Indonesia (Indonesian National Library): Koninklijk Bataviaasch Genootschap
NBS	Netherlands Bible Society, loan collection, Leiden
RAS	Royal Asiatic Society (London)
SMP/KS	Surakarta MS Project: Karaton Surakarta
SMP/MN	Surakarta MS Project: Mangkunagaran (Palace library)
SMP/RPM	Surakarta MS Project: Radyapustaka Museum, Surakarta

MANUSCRIPTS

Babad Mangkunagaran, LUB, MS LOr. 6781.

"Bundel Slametan dan Labuhan serta Kebo Maésa Lawung", Mangkunagaran Palace Archives. Ms. 102 Ra.

Fatwa-fatwané para Pinituwa ("Councils to the Elders"). Radèn Tanoyo. 1971.

Gambar2 kanthi keterangan plabuhan dalem dhumateng redi2 saha dhateng seganten kidul nuju tingalan dalem jumengan mawi 11 lembar (verjaardag van troonsbestigang) from Ir. Moens Platen Album, no. 9 Museum Pusat, Yogyakarta, ms. 934 Dj.

Kraemer, H. Autograph note on prayers (*donga*) important *slametan* and the Maésa Lawung with *donga*'s (LUB, MS LOr. 10.846 §4).

Mangkunagaran Archives M.N.VI: (box 31) In 1915 the population of Krendawahana: 127 *bau* of cultivated fields and only 26 *bau* of rice fields.

Mangkunagaran Archives: (box 5.256) As a sort of *terminas ad quem* for deforestation by 1947 the village of Krendawahana had 139 ha. under cultivation (all classes combined) and was paying an annual tax to the Mangkunagaran of 300 guilders.

Pangruwatan. Leiden Oriental Ms. 6525 (1).

Pradata (*Ngabèhi Arya*), Klathèn 1890. Information on 67 *palabuhan* offerings, with Dutch notes by Rouffaer. KITLV Or. 240.1 (22 pp.).

Pranatan ing bab laku-lakuné amajegaké bumi désa, of 1837. Leiden Univ. Bibl. Cod. Or. 10,735 (12 pp.).

Rinkes collection LUB, MS LOr 8652j, no. 15: Penyayang ("Amateur", a pseudonym). "Dibinasakan". *Djawi Hisworo* 15 March 1915 (X.29) from LUB, MS LOr 8652 F: D. Rinkes, "Notes".

Rouffaer, G. P. Dutch translation made in 1889–90 by (1860–1928) figures in KITLV (Leiden) under H699 (*cf.* H. J. de Graaf, *Catalogue van de Westerse Hansdschirften*, p. 23. The Hague, 1963.)

Sejarah Negari Dalem Surakarta. Surakarta: Museum Radya Pustaka no. 341.

Serat Memulé Sadhèrèk Sakawan Wasiyat Saking Sultan Mangkubumi, SMP/KS Ms. 587, 7pp. [there exists a transcription by Miftah Alim Harphanta, 1985].

Soekro Djagosakaro. "Kisah ringkas perjuangan R.A. Sumirah, R.A. Khadiyah, R.A. Marwiyah and Kyai Suhodo Som membantu Pengeran Diponegoro perang melawan penjajahan Belanda (1825–1830)". Mimeographed, Karanganyar, 23 July 1976.

Suluk Nalakirdha, LUB, MS LOr. 6385.

Tanaya, Radèn. *Serat Raja Weddha*. Mimeographed, 14 pp., Solo, 1937.

———. *Karahardjaning Braja Desa*. Typescript 72 pages. Surakarta, 1971.

Yasadipuro, Riyo. "Sejarah Dalem Sampeyandalem Ingkang Sinuhun Kangjeng Susuhunan Palubuwono VI, Pahlawan Kemerdekaan Nasional Republik Indonesia". Mimeographed, 1980.

DOCUMENTARY FILMS AND RECORDINGS

Headley, Stephen C. *Le Buffle et la Reine: Quatre Rituels à Java Central*. Fifty minute High Eight film, (NTSC). Paris: CNRS Audio-Visuel, 1984.

Headley, Stephen C. *La Prière à Java, trois styles sur le corps, avec des offrandes et dans la mosquée*. Documentary film 50 minutes. Paris: Co-production CNRS/ORSTOM, 1989.

Wignyasarana, *Murwa Kala*, at the Mangkunagaran Palace, Surakarta. Recording by K.R.M.T.H. Sanyoto Sutopo Kusumohatlodjo. March 1983.

BOOKS, ARTICLES, ETC.

Abdullah, Taufik. "Pahlawan dalam Perspektif Sejarah". English translation in *Prisma, Indonesian Journal of Social and Economic Affairs* 4 (1976): 27–32.

Adam, L. "Het Vorstelijke offer aan den Lawoe". *Djawa* 20 (1940): 107–18.

Adiwidjaja, P. A. "Kalioso-Krendawahana". *Pustaka Jawi*, no. 6 (1927): 55.

Agrawala, P. K. *Goddesses in Ancient India*. New Dellhi: Abhinav, 1984.

Agrawala, Vasudeva S. *The Glorification of the Great Goddess*. Varanasi: Ramnagar, 1963.

Ahmad, A. Samad, ed. *Hikayat Amir Hamzah*. Kuala Lumpur: Dewan Bahasa dan Pustaka, Kementerian Pelajaran Malaysia, 1987.

Aichele. "Lor-Kidul". *Bijdragen tot de Taal-, Land- en Volkenkunde* 115, no. 4 (1959): 328–35.

Alatas, Syed Husein. *The Myth of the Lazy Native*. London: Frank Cass, 1977.

Al-Attas, S. M. N. *The Mysticism of Hamzah Fansuri.* Kuala Lumpur: University of Malaya Press, 1970.

Allen, N. J. "The Hero's Five Relationships: A Proto-Indo-European Story". In *Myth and Mythmaking. Continuous Evolution in Indian Tradition,* edited by Julia Leslie, pp. 1–20. Richmond, Surrey: Curzon Press, 1996.

Anawati, G. C. and Louis Gardet. *Mystique Musulmane: Aspects et tendances, expériences et Techniques.* Paris: Vrin, 1986.

Anderson, Benedict R. O'G. "The Idea of Power in Javanese Culture". In *Culture and Politics in Indonesia,* edited by Claire Holt, pp. 1–10. Ithaca and London: Cornell Univesity Press, 1972.

———. "Notes on Contemporary Indonesian Political Communication". *Indonesia* 16 (1973): 39–80.

———. *Imagined Communities: Reflections on the Origin and the Spread of Nationalism.* New York: Verso, 1991.

———, ed. *Violence and the State in Suharto's Indonesia.* Ithaca: SEAP, Cornell University, 2001.

———, Mitsuo Nakakmura, and Mohammad Slamet. *Religion and Social Ethos in Indonesia.* Clayton, Victoria: Monash University, 1977.

Andy A. Mangkunagaran. *Apa yang Terjadi?* Solo, 1994.

Anonymous. "Alas Krendawahana". *Tjundaka,* no. 3 (1972): 38–49.

Anonymous. "'Caos Dahar' di Patilasan Krendowahono dari Kraton Surakarta". *Buana Minggu,* 13 March 1983, pp. 4 and 10.

Anonymous. "Sesaji 'Mahesa Lawung' untuk Memperingati Kembalinya P. Sambernyawa". *Suara Merdéka,* 31 March 1982, pp. 12 and 20.

Appadurai, Arjun. *Worship and Conflict under Colonial Rule.* New York: Cambridge University Press, 1981.

———. *Modernity at Large: Cultural Dimensions of Globalization.* Public Worlds, vol. 1. Minneapolis: University of Minnesota Press, 1996.

Aragon, Lorraine. *Fields of the Lord: Animism, Christian Minorities and State Development in Indonesia.* Honolulu: University of Hawai'i Press, 2000.

Arberry, A. J. *The Koran Interpreted.* New York: Macmillan, 1955.

Ardani, Muhammad. "Konsep Sembah dan Budiluhur dalam Pemikiran Mangkunagara IV Surakarta ditinjau dari Pandangan Islam: Suatu Studi mengenai Serat-Serat Piwulang". Dissertation, IAIN Syarif Hadayatullah, Jakarta, 1988.

Arps, Bernard. *Tembang in Two Traditions: Performance and Interpretation of Javanese Literature.* London: School of Oriental and African Studies, 1992.

———. "The Song Guarding at Night: Grounds for Cogency in a Javanese Invocation." In *Vers une anthropologie de la prière: études ethnolinguistiques javanaises,* edited by Stephen C. Headley, pp. 47–113. Aix-en-Provence: Publications Universitaires de Provence, 1996.

Asad, Talal. *Genealogies of Religion: Discipline and Reasons of Power in Christianity and Islam.* Baltimore: Johns Hopkins University Press, 1993.

———. *Formations of the Secular: Christianity, Islam, Modernity.* Stanford: Stanford University Press, 2003.

Ash-Shiddieqy, T. M. H. *Pedoman Shalat.* 12th ed. Jakarta: Bulan Bintang, 1983.

Asmussen, V. A. "Asking for Blessings, Warding off Misfortune: The Poetics and Politics of Rituals in a Muslim Community in Central Java". Ph.D. dissertation, Aarhus University, Denmark, 1999.

Aspinall, E., H. Feith, and G. van. Klinken. *The Last Days of President Soeharto.* Clayton, Australia: Monash Asia Institute, 1999.

Assayag, Jackie. *Au Confluent de Deux Rivières. Musulmans et Hindous dans le Sud de l'Inde.* Monographies EFEO no. 181. Paris: Ecole Française de l'Extrême-Orient, 1995.

Auerbach, E. *Mimesis: The Representation of Reality in Western Literature.* Princeton: Princeton University Press, 1953.

Augé, Marc. *Génie du Paganisme.* Paris: NRF, Gallimard, 1982.

Azra, Azyumardi. *Jaringan Ulama: Timur Tengah dan Kepulauan Nusantara Abad XVII dan XVIII.* Bandung: Mizan, 1994.

———. *Islam Substantif: Agar Umat Tidak Jadi Buih.* Jakarta: Mizan, 2000.

Babad Tanah Djawi in proza Javaansche Geschiedenis, translated by W. L. Olthof. 2 vols. The Hague: M. Nijhoff, 1941.

Babcock, Tim G. *Kampung Jawa Tondano.* Yogyakarta: Gadjah Mada University Press, 1988.

Baker, J. W. M. (Rachmat Subagya). *Agama Asli Indonesia.* 3rd ed. Seri Pustaka, no. 95. Yogyakarta: Sekolah Teologi Katolik Pradnyawidya; and Jakarta: Sinar Harapan, 1981.

Baker, R. W. et al. *Indonesia: The Challenge of Change.* The Netherlands and Singapore: KITLV and Institute of Southeast Asian Studies, 1999.

Barton, Greg. "Neo-Modernism: A Vital Synthesis of Traditonalist and Modernist Islamic Thought in Indonesia". *Studia Islamika* 2, no. 3 (1995): 1–75.

———. "*Indonesia's Nurcholish Madjid and Abdurrahman Wahid as Intellectual Ulama: The Meeting of Islamic Traditionalism and Modernism in Neo-Modernist Thought*". Paper presented in a panel on Southeast Asia in the AFEMAM and EURAMES conference, Aix-en-Provence, 6 July 1996.

Baso, Ahmad. *Civil Society versus Masyarakat Madani: Arkeologi Pemikiran "Civil Society" dalam Islam Indonesia.* Bandung: Pustaka Hidayah, 1999.

Bayly, Susan. *Caste, Society and Politics in India: From the Eighteenth Century to the Modern Age.* The New Cambridge of India vol. IV.3. Cambridge: Cambridge University Press, 1999.

Beane, W. C. *Myth, Cult and Symbols in Sakta Hinduism.* Leiden: E. J. Brill, 1977.

Beatty, Andrew. *Varieties of Javanese Religion; An Anthropological Account.* Cambridge Studiers in Social and Cultural Anthropology, no. 111. Cambridge: Cambridge University Press, 1999.

———. "Changing Places: Relatives and Relativism in Java". *Journal of the Royal Anthropological Institute* 8, no. 3 (September 2002): 469–91.

Behrend, T. E. "Kraton and Cosmos in Traditional Java". M. A. dissertation, University of Wisconsin, 1983.

————. *Katalog Induk Naskah-Naskah Nusantara, jilid 1, Museum Sonobudaya, Yogyakarta.* Jakarta: Djambatan, 1990.

————. *Serat Jatiswara: Struktur dan Perubahan di Dalem Puisi Jawa 1600–1930.* Seri INIS XXIII. Jakarta: INIS, 1995.

Behrend, Tim. "Technical Prolegomena to any Further Centhini-Critique. Manuscript Survey of the Textual Corpus and Outline of Recensions". Draft paper ESF Workshop on "Encompassing Knowledge: Indigenous Encyclopaedias in Indonesia in the 17th and 20th Centuries", 1997.

Benda, Harry J. and Lance Castles. "The Samin Movement". *Bijdragen tot de Taal-, Land- en Volkenkunde* 125 (1969): 207–40.

Benjamin, G. *Semang, Senoi, Malay: Culture, History, Kinship and Consciousness in the Malay Peninsula.* Canberra: Dept. of Prehistory and Anthropology, ANU, 1980.

Berg, C. C. *Herkomst, Vorm en Functie der Middel-Javaanse Rijksdeelingtheorie.* Verhandelingen Koninklijk Nederlandse Akademie van Wetenschappen Afd. Letterkunde, Nieuwe Reeks, vol. LIX, no. 1 (1953).

————. "The Javanese Picture of the Past". In *An Introduction to Indonesian Historiography*, edited by Soedjatmoko et al. Ithaca: Cornell University Press, 1965.

Bergsma, W. B. *Eindrésumé. Onderzoek naar de Rechten van den Inlander op den Grond op Java en Madoera.* 3 vols. Batavia: Landsdrukkerij, 1876–1896.

Berkson, Carmel. *The Divine and Demonic: Mahisa's Heroic Struggle with Durga.* Delhi: Oxford University Press, 1994.

Bernoux, Philippe and J.-M. Servet, eds. *La Construction Sociale de la Confiance.* Paris: Association d'Economie Financière et Montchrestien, 1997.

Berthe, Louis. "Aînés et Cadets. L'Alliance et la Hiérarchie chez les Baduj (Java occidental)". *L'Homme* V (1965): 189–223.

————. "Parenté, Pouvoir et Mode de Production agricoles de l'Indonésie". In *Echanges et Communications*, vol. II, edited by P. Maranda and J. Pouillon, pp. 707–38. Paris: Mouton, 1970.

Bertling, C. T. "Huwverbod op grond van verwantschaps posities in Middel-Jawa". *Indisch Tijschrift van het Recht* 2 (1936): 119–34.

Bhatt, P. Gururaja. *Studies in Tuluva History and Culture.* Manipal, 1975.

Bhattacaryya, N. N. *Indian Mother Goddess.* Calcutta: R. D. Press, 1971.

Biardeau, Madelaine. *Théorie de la Connaissance et Philosophie de la Parole dans le brahmanissme classique.* Paris/Lattaye: Mouton, 1964.

————. Etudes de Mythologie Hindous". 3rd part. *Bulletin de l'Ecole Française de l'Extrême Orient* 58 (1971): 17–90.

————. "Etudes de Mythologie Hindous". 3rd part. *Bulletin de l'Ecole Française de l'Extrême Orient* 63 (1976): 111–263.

————. *Histoires de Poteaux: Variations védiques autour de la Déesse hindoue.* Publications de EFEO 154. Paris: EFEO, 1989.

Blagden, C. O. *Catalogue of Manuscripts in European Languages belonging to the Library of the India Office. Vol. I: The Mackenzie Collection.* London: Oxford University Press, 1916.

Bloch, Maurice. "The Past and the Present in the Present". *Man,* new series 12 (1997): 278–302.

Blust, Robert. "Linguistic Evidence for some early Austronesian Taboos". *American Anthropologist* 82 (1981): 285–319.

———. "Austronesian Sibling terms and Culture History". *Bijdragen tot de Taal-, Land- en Volkenkunde* 149 (1993): 22–76.

Boeke, J. H. *The Structure of the Netherlands Indian Economy.* New York: Institute of Pacific Relations, 1942.

———. *Economics and Economic Policies of Dual Societies, as Exemplified by Indonesia.* New York: Institute of Pacific Relations, 1953.

Boeles, J. J. "Het Groote durga Beeld te Lieden". *Cultureel Indie* 4 (1942): 37–50.

Boland, B. J. *The Struggle of Islam in Modern Indonesia.* Verhandelingen KITLV 59. The Hague: Martinus Nijhoff, 1971/1982.

Bonneff, Marcel. "Le Renouveau d'un Rituel Royal: les garebeg à Yogyakarta". *Archipel* 8 (1974): 119–46.

——— et al. *Pantjasila, trente ans de débats politiques en Indonésie.* Paris; Editions de la Maison des Sciences de l'Homme, 1980.

Boomgaard, Peter. "A Bird's-Eye View of Economic and Social Development in the District of Comal, 1740–1940". In *Beneath the Smoke of the Sugar-Mill. Javanese Coastal Communities during the Twentieth Century,* edited by H. Kano, F. Huskens, and D. Suryo, pp. 9–37. Yogyakarta: AKATIGA and Gadjah Mada University Press, 2001.

Boubakeur, Cheikh Si Hamza. *Traité Moderne de théologie Islamique.* Paris: Maisonneuve et Larose, 1985.

Bouyer, P. *Tradition as Truth and Communication: A Cognitive Description of Traditional Discourse.* Cambridge: Cambridge University Press, 1990.

Bowen, John. *Sumatran Politics and Poetics. Gayo History, 1900–1989.* New Haven: Yale University Press, 1991.

———. *Muslims through Discourse: Religion and Ritual in Gayo Society.* Princeton: Princeton University Press, 1993.

Brabandt, Nils. "Malukan Apocalypse: Themes in the Dynamics of Violence in Eastern Indonesia". In *Violence in Indonesia,* edited by Ingrid Wessel and Georgia Wimhöfer, pp. 228–53. Hamburg: Abera, 2001.

Braginsky, Vladimir. *Tasawuf dan Sastra Melayu: Kajian dan Teks-Teks.* Jakarta: RUL, 1993.

———. *Yang Indah Berfaedah dan Kamal: Sejarah Sastra Melayu dalam Abad 7–19.* Seri Inis 34. Jakarta: INIS, 1998.

Brakel, Clara. *The Bedhaya Dances of Central Java.* Leiden: E. J. Brill, 1992.

———. "Sandhang-pangan for the Goddess: Offerings to Sang Hyang Bathari Durga and Nyai Lara Kidul". *Asian Folklore Studies* LVI-20 (1997): 253–84.

Brakel, L. F. and G. W. J. Drewes. *The Poems of Hamzah Fansuri.* Dordrecht: Foris, 1986.

Brakel-Papenhuyzen, Clara (with S. Ngaliman). *Seni Tari Jawa: Tradisi Surakarta dan Peristilahannya.* Jakarta: ILDEP-RUL, 1991.

Brandes, D. J. "Pararaton (Ken Arok) of het Boek der Koningen van Tamapël en van Majapahit". *Verhandelingen Bataviaasch Genootschap*, vol. 49, 1897.

Brataisiswara, Harmanto. *Ensiklopedi Adat Tatacara Jawa*, vol. I. Surakarta: Reksapustaka, Istana Mangkunagaran, 1994.

Braten, Eldar. "Recapturing 'Java': A Call for a Javanese Anthropology". Manuscript, pp. 4, 9–10.

Breman, Jan. *Control of Land and Labour in Colonial Java: A Case Study of Agrarian Crisis and Reform in the Region of Cirebon During the First Decades of the 20th Century.* KITLV, Verhandelingen 101. Dordrecht: Foris, 1983.

——— and Gunawan Wiradi. *Goods Times and Bad Times in Rural Java.* KITLV, Verhandelingen 195. Leiden: KITLV Press, 2002.

Bringa, Tone. *Being Muslim the Bosnian Way: Identity and Community in a Central Bosnian Village.* Princeton: Princeton University Press, 1995.

Brinkgrave, Francine. "Offerings to Durga and Pretiwi in Bali. *Asian Folklore Studies* 56 (1997): 227–51.

Brontodiningrat. *The Royal Palace (Kraton) of Yogyakarta, Its Architecture and Its Meaning.* Yogyakarta: Kraton Museum, 1975.

Budiman, Arief, B. Hatley, and D. Kingsbury. *Reformasi, Crisis and Change in Indonesia.* Clayton, Australia: Monash Asia Institute, 1999.

Budiwanti, Erni. *Islam Sasak. Wetu telu versus waktu lima.* Yogyakarta: LkiS, 2000.

Burger, Peter. *The Sacred Canopy: Elements of a Sociological Theory of Religion.* Garden City, New York: Anchor Books (Doubleday), 1967.

Burhanudin, Jajat. "The Making of Islamic Political Tradition in the Malay World". *Studia Islamika* 8, no. 2 (2001): 1–54.

Carey, Peter B. R. *The Cultural Ecology of Early Nineteenth Century Java.* Occasional Papers no. 24, Singapore: Institute of Southeast Asian Studies, 1974.

———. "Pangéran Dipanagara and the Making of the Java War: Yogyakarta History 1785–1825". Pts. I and II, Ph.D. thesis, Oxford University, 1975.

———. "The Residency Archive of Yogyakarta". *Indonesia*, no. 25 (April 1978): 115–50.

———. "Aspects of Javanese History in the Nineteenth Century". In *The Development of Indonesia*, edited by Harry Aveling, pp. 45–105. St. Lucia: University of Queensland, 1979.

———. *Babad Dipanagara: An Account of the Outbreak of the Java War (1825–30).* The Malaysian Branch of the Royal Asiatic Society Monograph no. 9. Kuala Lumpur: M.B.R.S., 1981.

———. *The British in Java; A Javanese Account. A Text Edition, English Synopsis and Commentary on British Library Additional Manuscript 12330 (Babad Bedah ing Ngyayogyakarta).* Oriental Documents X. British Academy. Oxford: Oxford University Press, 1992.

Carsten, Janet. "Analogues or Opposites: Household and Community in Pulau Langkawi". In *De la Hutte au palais: sociétés "à maisons" en Asie du Sud-Est insulaire*, edited by Charles Macdonald. Paris: Editions du CNRS, 1987.

Carsten, Janet. "Houses in Langkawi: Stable Structures or Mobile Homes?". In *About the House. Lévi-Strauss and Beyond*, edited by Janet Carsten and Stephen Hugh-Jones, pp. 105–28. Cambridge: Cambridge University Press, 1995.

Caspar, Robert. *Traité de Theologie Musulmane*, vol. I. Rome: PISAI, 1987.

Chabot, H. Th. *Verwantschap, Stand en Sexe in Zuid-Celebes*. Groningen and Jakarta: J. B. Wolters, 1950.

———. *Kinship, Status and Gender in South Celebes*. KITLV, translation series 25. Leiden: KITLV Press, 1996.

Chambert-Loir, H. and C. Guillot. "Indonésie-La tombe de Sunan Gunung Jati". In *Le culte des saints dans le monde musulman*, pp. 235–59. Etudes Thématiques no. 4. Paris: Ecole Française de l'Extrême-Orient, 1995.

Chittick, William C. *The Sufi Path of Knowledge: Ibn al-'Arabī's Metaphysics of Imagination*. Albany: State University of New York Press, 1989.

Chronos [pseud.]. "Asal moela aksoednja Sekatèn. Sekatèn tahoen Dhal". In *Suluh Sekaten*, pp. 3–14. Solo: B.T. Tjoe, 1940.

Coedes, Georges. *Les Etats Hindouisés d'Indochine et d'Indonésie*. (1st ed. 1949). 3rd ed. Paris: E. de Boccard, 1964.

Cribb, Robert, ed. *The Indonesian Killings, 1965–66: Studies from Java and Bali*. Clayton, Victoria: Monash Papers on Southeast Asia, no. 11, 1990.

Damais, Louis-Charles. "Etudes Javanaises I: Les Tombes musulmanes dates de Tralaya". *Bulletin de l'EFEO*, no. 48 (1957): 353–415.

———. "Etudes Javanaises III: A propos des couleurs symboliques des points cardinaux". *Bulletin de l'EFEO*, no. 56 (1969): 75–118.

———. *Etudes d'Epigraphie Indonésienne*. Paris: Ecole Française d'Extrême Orient, 1990.

Damardjati, Supadjar. *Kridha Graita in Rèh Silayu*. Yogyakarta: Kridha Martana, 1994.

Danandjaja, James. *An Annotated Bibliography of Javanese Folklore*. Occasional Paper no. 2. Berkeley: Center for South and Southeast Asian Studies, University of California, 1972.

———. *Kebudayaan Petani Desa Trunyan di Bali*. Jakarta: Pustaka Jaya, 1980.

Darrow, William R. "Ummah". In *Encyclopedia of Religion*, vol. 15, pp. 123–25. New York, 1987.

Daud, Alfani. *Islam dan Masyarakat Banjar*. Jakarta: RajaGrafindo Persada, 1997.

Davis, Michael. "Laskar Jihad and the Political Position of Conservtive Islam in Indonesia". *Contemporary Southeast Asia* 24, no. 1 (2002): 12–32.

Day, J. Anthony. "Babad Kraton, Babad Kandha, and Modern Javanese Literature". *Bijdragen tot de Taal-, Land- en Volkenkunde* 134, no. 4 (1978): 433–50.

Day, Tony. "Wayang Kulit and 'Internal Otherness' in East Java". *Puppet Theatre in Contemporary Indonesia: New Approaches to Performance Events*, edited by Jan Mrázek, pp. 189–98. Ann Arbor: University of Michigan Press, 2002.

de Hollander, J. J. *Manik Maja. Een Javaansch gedicht (tembang)*. Verhandelingen Bataviaash Genootschap 24. Batavia, 1852.

Descombes, Vincent. *Les Institutions du Sens*. Paris: Editions du Minuit, 1996.

Detienne, Marcel. *L'Invention de la Mythologie*. Paris: NRF Gallimard, 1981

————, ed. *Transcrire les Mythologies*. Paris: Albin Michel, 1994.

Devereux, Georges. *Ethnopsychoanalyse complémentariste*. 2nd ed. (Original edition 1943). Paris: Flamarion, 1975.

Dewi Sri: Ceritera Rakyat dari Daerah Surakarta, Jawa Tengah. Collected and translated by Jumeiri Siti Ramadjah. Tim Penyusun Naskah Cerita Rakyat Daerah Jawa Tengah. Proyek Pengembangan Media Kebudayaan. Jakarta: Departemen Pendidikan dan Kebudayaan, n.d.

Dharma Palguna. *Dharma Sunya. Memuji dan Meneliti Siwa*. Denpasar: Yayasan Dharma Sastra, 1999.

Dhofier, Zamakhsyari. "Kinship and Marriage among the Javanese Kyai". *Indonesia*, no. 29 (1980): 47–58.

————. *Tradisi Pesantrèn: Studi Tentang Kepandangan Hidup Kyai*. Jakarta: LP3ES, 1982.

————. *The Pesantren Tradition: The Role of the Kyai in the Maintenance of Traditional Islam in Java*. (Indonesian original ed. 1982). Program for Southeast Asian Studies Monograph Series. Tempe, Arizona: Arizona State University, 1999.

Dirks, Nicholas. *The Hollow Crown: Ethnohistory of an Indian Kingdom*. Cambridge: Cambridge University Press, 1987.

Divakaran, Odile. "Durgā the Great Goddess: Meanings and Forms in the Early Period". In *Discourses on Siva*, edited by Michael W. Meister. Philadelphia: University of Pennsylvania, 1985.

Djatikusumo. "Sejarah Politik: Hingkang Sinuhun Kandjeng Susuhunan Paku Buwana VI". Mimeographed, 20 pages, 1971.

Djogosarkoro. *Sukro Serba-serbi di Gunung Lawu*. Karanganyar, 1973.

Dobbin, Christine. *Kebangkitan Islam dalam Ekonomi Petani yang Sedang Berubah, Sumatra Tengah 1784–1847*. Indonesian-Netherlands Co-operation in Islamic Studies 12. Jakarta: INIS, 1992.

Drewes, G. W. J. "The Struggle between Javanism and Islam as Illustrated by the Serat Dermagandhul". *Bijdragen tot de Taal-, Land- en Volkenkunde* 122, no. 3 (1966): 309–65.

————. *The Admonitions of Seh Bari*. Bibliotheca Indonesica no. 4, KITLV. The Hague: Martinus Nijhoff, 1969.

————, ed. and translator. *An Early Javanese Code of Muslim Ethics*. Bibliotheca Indonesica no. 18, KITLV. The Hague: Martinus Nijhoff, 1978.

————. "Wat valt er te verstaan onder het Javaanse woord Suluk?". *Bijdragen tot de Taal-, Land-, en Volkenkunde* 148, no. 1 (1992): 22–30.

Du Bois, J. W. "Meaning Without Intention: Lessons from Divination". *IPrA Papers in Pragmatics* I (1987): 80–122.

Ducrot, Oswald and Tzvetan Todorov. *Dictionnaire encyclopédique des sciences du langage*. Paris: Editions du Seul, 1972.

Dumézil, Georges. *Mythe et Epopée II. Types Epiques Indon-Européens: un héros, un sorcier, un roi*. Edition Quarto. (Original edition 1971). Paris: Gallimard, 1995.

Dumont, Louis. *Homo Hiérarclucus Le Système des Castes et ses implication.* 2nd ed. (original edition 1966). Paris: Gallimard, 1979.

————. *Essais sur l'individualisme. Une perspective anthropologique sur l'idéologie moderne.* Paris: Edition du Seuil, 1983.

Duranti, A. "Language in Context and Language as Context: The Samoan Respect Vocabulary". In *Rethinking Context. Language as an Interactive Phenomenon,* edited by Lessandro Duranti and Charles Goodwin, pp. 77–100. Cambridge: Cambridge University Press, 1992.

Dwitjjo Sukando. *Tantrik Mataram.* 1966.

Eaton, Richard M. *The Rise of Islam and the Bengal Frontier, 1204–1760.* Berkeley: University of California Press, 1993.

Eggan, Fred. "The Sagada Igorots of Northern Luzon". In *The Social Sturcture of Southeast Asia,* edited by George Peter Murdock, pp. 24–50. Viking Fund Publications in Anthropology, no. 29. Chicago: Quadrangle Books, 1960.

Eickelman, D. F. "National Identity and Religious Discourse in Contemporary Oman". *International Journal of Islamic and Arabic Studies,* no. 6 (1989): 1–20.

Eldrige, Philip J. *Non-Government Organizations and Democratic Participation in Indonesia.* Oxford: Oxford University Press, 1995.

Elson, R. E. *The End of Peasantry in Southeast Asia. A Social and Economic History of Peasant Livelihood, 1800–1990s.* Basingstoke, Hampshire: Macmillan, 1997.

Errington, Joseph. *Language and Social Change in Java: Linguistic Reflexes of Modernisation in a Traditional Royal Polity.* Monographs in International Studies Southeast Asia Series, no. 65. Athens, Ohio: Ohio University Center for International Studies, 1985.

————. *Shifting Languages. Interaction and Identity in Javanese Indonesia.* Studies in the Social and Cultural Foundations of Lanauge, no. 19. Cambridge: Cambridge University Press, 1998.

Errington, Shelley. "Incestuous Twins and the House Societies of Insular Southeast Asia". *Cultural Anthropology* 2, no. 4 (1987): 403–44.

————. *Meaning and Power in a Southeast Asian Realm.* Princeton: Princeton University Press, 1989.

Fananie, Zainuddin. *Restrukturisasi Budaya Jawa. Perspektif KGPAA Mangkunagara I.* Surakarta: Muhammadiyah University Press, 2000.

Feillard, Andrée. *Islam et Armée dans l'Indonésie Contemporaine. Les pionniers de la tradition.* Cahiers d'Archipel 28. Paris: L'Harmattan and Archipel, 1995.

————. "Traditionalist Islam and the State in Indonesia: The Road to Legitimacy and Renewal". In *Islam in an Era of Nation States. Politics and Religious Renewal in Muslim Southeast Asia,* edited by Robert Hefner and Patricia Horvatich, pp. 129–56. Honolulu: University of Hawai'i Press, 1997.

Florida, Nancy K. *Javanese Literature in Surakarta Manuscripts,* vol. I. Ithaca: SEAP Cornell University, 1993.

————. *Writing the Past, Inscribing the Future: History as Prophecy in Colonial Java.* Durham and London: Duke University Press, 1995.

Fokkens, F. "Vrije desa's op Java en Madoera". In *Tijdschrift van de Bataviaasch Genootschap* (T.B.G.) XXXI (1886): 477–517 .

Forrester, G. and R. J. May. *The Fall of Soeharto*. Singapore: Select Books, 1999.

Fowden, Garth. *Empire to Commonwealth: Consequences of Monotheism in Late Antiquity*. Princeton: Princeton University Press, 1993.

Fox, James J. "A Rotinese Dynastic Genealogy: Structure and Event". *The Translation of Culture*, edited by T. O. Beidelman. London: Tavistock, 1971.

———. "The Ordering of Generations: Change and Continuity in Old Javanese Kinship". In *Southeast Asia in the 9th to the 14th Centuries*, edited by D. F. Marr and A. C. Milner, pp. 315–26. Singapore: Institute of Southeast Asian Studies and the Research School of Pacific Studies, 1986.

———. "Ziarah. Visits to the Tombs of the Wali, the Founders of Islam on Java". In *Islam in the Indonesian Social Context*, edited by M. C. Ricklefs, pp. 19–38. Clayton: Monash University, 1991.

———. "Who's Who in Ego's Generation: A Consideration of Malayo-Polynesian Same Generation Kinship Terms". In *Austronesian Terminologies: Continuity and Change*, edited by A. Pawley and M. Ross, pp. 127–39. Canberra: Pacific Lingualies, 1994.

———. "Austronesian Societies and their Transformations". In *The Austronesians. Historical and Comparative Perspectives*, edited by Peter Bellwood, James J. Fox, and Darrell Tryon, pp. 214–28. Canberra: Comparative Austronesian Project ANU, 1995.

———, ed. *The Flow of Life: Essays on Eastern Indonesia*. Cambridge: Harvard University Press, 1980.

Fox, James J. and Clifford Sather, eds. *Origin, Ancestry and Alliance. Explorations in Austronesian Ethnography*. Canberra: Comparative Austronesian Project, Australian National University, 1996.

Fox, Robin. *Kinship and Marriage: An Anthropological Perspective*. Cambridge: Cambridge University Press, 1967.

Franke, R. W. "Limited Good and Cargo Cult in Indonesian Economic Development". *Journal of Contemporary Asia* (1972): 366–81.

Frick, H. "Principles of Ritual Purity in Traditional Spatial Concepts and House Structures in Central Java". Paper for Seminar on Cultural Constructions of Architecture and Space in Indonesia and Africa, Leiden, 29 October 1991.

———. "Rite de Passage of house and man in Central Java". Paper for the Seventh Annual Workshop on "Social Change and Social Movements" of the European Social Science Java Network, London, 21–22 April 1994.

Gaboriau, Marc. "Islamisation de l'Inde et de l'Asie orientale". In *Etats, sociétés et cultures du Monde Musulmanes Médiéval, Xè-XVè siècles*, edited by Jean-Claude Garcin et al., pp. 431–59. Paris: P.U.F., 1995.

Gadjahnata, K. H. O. and Sri-Edi Swasono. *Masuk dan Berkembangnya Islam di Sumatera Selatan*. Jakarta: Penerbit Universitas Indonesia, 1986.

Gardet, Louis. *La Cité Musulmane. Vie Sociale et Politique*. Etudes Musulmanes I. (1st ed. 1954). Paris: J. Vrin, 1981.

Gauchet, Marcel. *Le desenchantement du Monde*. Paris: NRF Gallimard, 1985.

Geertz, Clifford. *The Religion of Java*. New York: Free Press of Glencoe, 1960.

——. *Kinship in Bali*. Chicago: University of Chicago Press, 1975.

Geertz, Hildred. *The Javanese Family: A Study of Kinship and Socialization*. New York: Free Press, 1961.

Gellner, Ernest. *Muslim Society*. Cambridge: Cambridge University Press, 1981.

Gericke, J. F. C. and T. Roorda. *Javaansch-Nederlandsch Handwoordenboek*. Leiden: Brill, 1901.

Gibert, P. *Bible, Myths et Récits de Commencement*. Paris: Seuil, 1986.

Gibson, Thomas. "Having Your House and Eating It: Houses and Siblings in Ara, South Sulawesi". In *About the House: Lévi-Strauss and Beyond*, edited by Janet Carsten and Stephen Hugh-Jones, pp. 129–48. Cambridge: Cambridge University Press, 1995.

Giddens, Anthony. *The Transformation of Intimacy. Sexuality, Love and Eroticism in Modern Societies*. Oxford: Blackwells, 1992.

Godelier, Maurice. *L'énigme du don*. Paris: Fayard, 1996.

Gonda, Jan. *Het Oud-Javaansche Brahmānda-Purāna. Prozatekst en kakawin*. Bibliotheca Javanica 5. Bandung, 1932.

——. *Sanskrit in Indonesia*. Nagpur: International Academy of Indian Culture, 1952.

——. *L'Hindouisme Récent*, vol. II. Les Religions de l'Inde. Paris: Payot, 1965.

Goodwin, C. and A. Duranti. "Rethinking Context: An Introduction". In *Rethinking Context: Language as an Interactive Phenomenon*, edited by Charles Godwin and Alessandro Duranti, pp. 1–42. Cambridge: Cambridge University Press, 1992.

Goody, Jack. *Death, Property and Ancestors*. Stanford: Stanford University Press, 1962.

Goris, Roelof. *Bijdrage tot de Kennis der Oud-Javaansche en Balineesche Theologie*. Leiden: Vros, 1926.

Goudriaan, T. and C. Hooykaas. *Stuti and Stava (Bauddha, Saiva and Vaisnava) of the Balinese Brahman priests*. Verhandelingen der Koninklijke Nederlandse Akademie van Wetenschappen, afdeeling Letterkunde, nieuwe reeks, no. 76, 1971.

Graaf, H. J. and Th. G. Th. Pigeaud. *De Eerste Moslimse Voerstendommen op Java. Studien over de Staatkundige Geschiedenis van de 15de en 16de Eeuw*. KITLV, Verhandelingen 69. 's-Gravenhage: Martinus Nijhoff, 1974.

Graaf, H. J. de. *Catalogue van de Westerse Handschriften*, p. 23. The Hague, 1963.

Grave, Jean-More de. *Initiation, Rituelle et Arts Martiaux. Trois écoles de Kanuragan javanais*. Paris: Harmattan/Archipel, 2001.

Guillot, C. "Le rôle historique des *perdikan* ou 'villages francs': le cas de Tegalsari". *Archipel*, no. 30 (1985): 137–62.

Hadiwidjojo. "Wiludjengan Mengeti Pamindahipun Lajondalem I. S. Banguntopo Dawung Tengah no. 10, wismaipun R. M. Soebardjo". Pamphlet commemorating the transfer of Paku Buwana VI from Batugajah in Ambon to the royal cemetery in Imogiri. Privately published, 1966.

————. "Danse Sacréé à Surakarta: la singnification de Bedhojo Ketawang...". *Archipel*, no. 3 (1972): 117–30.

Hadiwijono, Harun. "Man in the Present Javanese Mysticism". Ph.D. dissertation, Vrije Universiteit te Amsterdam. Baarn: Bosch & Keuning, 1967.

Hadiwiyata, S. *Pasalatan Jawa*. 10th ed. Sala: Ab. Sitti Syamsiyah, 1974.

Hagestijn, R. *Circles of Kings. Political Dynamics in Early Continental Southeast Asia.* KITLV, Verhandelingen 138. Dordrecht-Providence: Foris Publications, 1989.

Hakim, Muhammad A. S. "Non-governmental Organisations and the Empowerment of Civil Society". In *Indonesia: The Challenge of Change*, edited by Richard Baker et al., pp. 217–32. Leiden and Singapore: KITLV Press and the Institute of Southeast Asian Studies, 1999.

Hall, D. G. E. *A History of South-East Asia* (1st ed. 1955). London/Singapore: Macmillan, 1985.

Hall, Kenneth R. "Ritual Networks and Royal Power in Majapahit Java". *Archipel*, no. 52 (1996): 96–118.

Hamonic, Gilbert. "Pour une étude comparée des cosmogonies de Célébes-Sud. A propos d'un manuscrit inédit sur l'origine des dieux bugis". *Archipel*, no. 25 (1983): 35–62.

————. "L'histoire, comme éclatée... Deux ordres du passé en pays bugis-makassar". In *Transcrire les mythologies*, edited by Marcel Detienne, pp. 114–30. Paris: Albin Michael, 1994.

Hardjadisastra, M. and M. Jasasoeparta. *Tjarijos Redi Lawoe*. Batavia: Balé-Poestaka, 1936.

Hardjopandojo, Ng. "Sanggaran Krendawahana". *Djawa* 21, no. 2 (1941): 109–10.

Hassan, A. *Pengajaran Shalat*. Bandung, Diponegoro, 1930 (23rd ed. 1987).

Hatley, Barbara. "Cultural Expression and Social Transformation in Indonesia". In *Reformasi: Crisis and Change in Indonesia*, edited by Arief Budiman, Barbara Hatley, and Damien Kingsbury, pp. 267–86. Clayton, Australia: Monash Asia Institute, 1999.

Headley, Stephen C. "Il n'y a plus de Cendres: description et historie du finage d'un hameau javanais". Ph.D. dissertation, Univ. Paris V et EHESS, 1979*a*.

————. "The Ritual Lancing of Durga's Buffalo in Surakarta and the Offering in the Krendowahono Forest of Its Blood". In *Between People and Statistics. Essays on Modern Indonesian History presented to P. Creutzberg*, edited by Francien van Anrooij et al., pp. 49–58. The Hague: Martinus Nijhoff, 1979*b*.

————. "De l'Apanage au Métayage, l'exemple de Java central". In *Sociétés Paysannes du Tiers-Monde*, edited by Catherine Coquery-Vidrovitch, pp. 111–24. Lille: Presses Univ. de Lille, 1980*a*.

————. "Recyclage Rituel au Centre de Java: Le 're-lancement' du Buffle de Durga". *Cheminements, écrits offerts à Georges Condominas. Asie du Sud-Est et Monde Insulindien*, vol. XI, no. 1–4 (1980*b*): 401–13.

————. "Le Lit Grenier et la déesse de la fécondité à Java: rites nuptiaux?". *Dialogue 'Le Lit'* no. 82 (4è trimestre 1983): 133–52.

Headley, Stephen C. "The Body as a House in Javanese Society". In *De la Hutte au Palais. Sociétes "à maison" en Asie du sud-est insulaire*, edited by Charles Macdonald, pp. 133–52. Paris: Editions du CNRS, 1987*a*.

———. "The Idiom of Siblingship". In *De la Hutte au Palais Sociétés "à maison" en Asie du sud-est insulaire*, edited by Charles Macdonald, pp. 209–18. Paris: Editions du CNRS, 1987*b*.

———. "The Javanese Exorcisms of Evil: Betwixt India and Java". In *The Art and Culture of South-East Asia*, edited by Lokesh Chandra, pp. 73–110. Delhi: Aditya Prakashan, 1991.

———. "Biographical Approaches to Conversion in Contemporary Java: Javanese from Solo". Paper presented at the EUROSEAS conference on "Religious Revival in Southeast Asia", Leiden, Netherlands, 29 June–1 July 1995. (35 pp.)

———. "Trois styles de prière à Java: écriture sur le front; offrandes et purification du coeur". In *Vers une anthropologie de la prière: études ethnolinguistiques javanaises*, edited by Stephen C. Headley, pp. 195–234. Publications de l'Université de Provence, Aix-en-Provence, 1996*a*.

———. "Notes sur les types de soignants à Java". In *Soigner au pluriel; Essais sur le pluralisme médical*, edited by Jean Benoit, pp. 225–50. Paris: Karthala, 1996*b*.

———, ed. *Vers une anthropologie de la prière: études ethnolinguistiques javanaises*. Aix-en-Provence: Publications Universitaires de Provence, 1996*c*.

———. "The Islamisation of Central Java: The Role of Muslim Lineages in Kalioso". *Studia Islamika* 4, no. 2 (1997): 52–82.

———. *From Cosmogony to Exorcism in a Javanese Genesis: The Spilt Seed.* Oxford Studies in Social and Cultural Anthropology. Oxford: Oxford University Press, 2000*a*.

———. "Sembah/Salat: The Javanisation of Islamic Prayer; the Islamisation of Javanese Prayer". In *Inside and Outside the Mosque: Islamic Prayer across the Indian Ocean*, edited by David Parkin and Stephen C. Headley, pp. 169–212. Richmond, Surrey: Curzon, 2000*b*.

———. "Combining Javanese Cosmogonies and Muslim Cosmographies in the Manikmaya". *Indonesia and the Malay World* 28, no. 82 (2000*c*): 280–300.

———. "Afterword: The Mirror in the Mosque". In *Inside and Outside the Mosque: Islamic Prayer across the Indian Ocean*, edited by David Parkin and Stephen C. Headley, pp. 213–39. Richmond, Surrey: Curzon, 2000*d*.

———. "Nier allah? Réflexions javanaises sur la conversion à l'islam". In *Nier les Dieux. Nier Dieu*, edited by Gilles Dorival and Didier Pralon, pp. 393–404. Aix-en–Provence: Publications de l'Université de Provence, 2002.

———. "Of Sacred Wells and Shopping Malls: Glimpses of the Reconstruction of Social Confidence in Solo after Soeharto". In *Puppet Theater in Contemporary Indonesia: New Approaches to Performance-Events*, edited by Jan Mrazek, pp. 220–34. Ann Arbor: University of Michigan Press, 2003.

———. "The Purification of Rice Fields in Java". In *The Art of Rice*, edited by Roy Hamilton, pp. 101–18. Los Angeles: Fowler Museum UCLA, 2003.

————. "Les moitiés d'homme à Java: Leur engendrement, nourritures et assemblages". In *L'Homme, Revue françaosie d'anthropologie*. numéro spécial, *Les Moitiés d'Hommes*, textes réunis par Stephen C. Headley, no. 174 (forthcoming).

Hedman, Eva-Lotta E. "Contesting Sate and Civil Society: Southeast Asian Trajectories". *Modern Asian Studies* 35, no. 4 (2001): 921–51.

Hefner, Robert. *Hindu Javanese. Tengger Tradition and Islam*. Princeton, Princeton University Press, 1985.

————. *The Political Economy of Highland Java: An Interpretive History*. Berkeley: University of California Press, 1990.

————, ed. *Conversion to Christianity: Historical and Anthropoloigcal Perespectives on a Great Transformation*. Berkeley: University of California Press, 1993.

————. "Secularisation and Citizenship in Muslim Indonesia". Paper presented in a panel on Southeast Asia in the AFEMAM and EURAMES conference, Aix-en-Provence, 6 July 1996.

————. *Civil Islam. Muslims and Democratisation in Indonesia*. Princeton: Princeton University Press, 2000.

————, ed. *The Politics of Multiculturalism. Pluralism and Citizenship in Malaysia, Singapore and Indonesia*. Honolulu: University of Hawai'i Press, 2001.

———— and Patricia Horvatich, eds. *Islam in an Era of Nation States. Politics and Religious Renewal in Muslim Southeast Asia*. Honolulu: University of Hawai'i Press, 1997.

Heringa, R. "Dewi Sri in Village Garb: Fertility, Myth and Ritual in Northeast Java". *Asian Folklore Studies* 56, no. 2 (1997): 355–78.

————. "Mbok Sri Dethromed: Changing Rice Rituals in Rural East Java". In *The Art Rice Spirit and Sustence in Asia*, edited by Roy W. Hamilton, pp. 469–88. Los Angeles: UCLA Fowler Museum, 2003.

Héritier, Françoise. "Symbolique de l'inceste et de sa prohibition". In *La Fonction Symbolique. Essais d'anthropologie,* edited by Michel Izard et Pierre Smith, pp. 209–43. Paris: Gallimard, 1979.

————. *L'Exercise de la Parenté*. Paris: Le Seuil-Gallimard, 1981.

————. *Les Deux Soeurs et leur Mère*. Paris: Odile Jacob, 1994.

Hidding, K., ed. *Nji Pohatji Sangjiang Sri*. Leiden: M. Dubbeldeman, 1929.

Hinloopen Labberton, D. van. *Dictionnaire de Termes de Droit coutumier Indonésien*. The Hague: M. Nijhoff, 1934.

Hoadley, Mason C. *Towards a Feudal Mode of Production. West Java, 1680–1800*. Singapore: Institute of Southeast Asian Studies, 1994.

————. "The Archive of Yogyakarta and Javanese Administrative History". In Appendix I of *The Archive of Yogyakarta. Documents Relating to Economic and Agrarian Affairs* 2 (2000): 438–39.

Hobsbawn, Eric and Terence Ranger. *The Invention of Tradition*. Cambridge: Cambridge University Press, 1983.

Hooykaas, C. *Tantri Kāmandka. Een Oud Javaansche Pañtjatantra Bewerking in tekst en vertaling*. Bibliotheca Javanica 2, 1931.

Hooykaas, C. "Het Verhaal van den Halve op Java, Bali en Lombok". *Mededeelingen van de Kirtya Liefrinck van der Tuuk,* aflevering 13 (1941): 1–15.

———. *Balische verhalen van den Halve.* The Hague: van Hoeve, 1948.

———. *Cosmogony and Creation in Balinese Tradition.* KITLV, Bibliotheca Indonesica, 9. The Hague: M. Nijhoff, 1974.

———. *Drawings of Balinese Sorcery.* Leiden: E. J. Brill, 1980.

Hooykaas, Jocoba. "De godsienstige ondergrond van het praemuslimse huwelijk op Java en Bali". *Indonésië* 10 (1957): 109–36.

———. "The Myth of the Young Cowherd and thee Little Girl". *Bijdragen tot de Taal-, Land- en Volkenkunde* 117 (1961): 267–78.

Hoskins, Janet. *The Play of Time. Kodi Perspectives on Calendars, History and Exchange.* Berkeley: University of California Press, 1993

Hossein, Sayyed. *An Introduction to Islamic Cosmological Doctrines.* Rev. ed. (Original ed. 1964.) Albany: State University of New York Press, 1993.

Hostetler, Jan. "Bedhaya Semang: The Sacred Dance of Yogyakarta". *Archipel,* no. 24 (1982): 127–42.

Houben, J. H. *Kraton and Kumpeni. Surakarta and Yogyakarta, 1830–1870.* KITLV, Verhandelingen 164. Leiden: KITLV Press, 1994.

Howe, Leo. *Hindu and Hierarchy in Bali.* Oxford: Hames Curry; and Santa Fee: School of American Research in Bali, 2001.

Hunger, J. D. *Javaansche Wetten,* 3 vols. Djogjakarta: H. Buning; and Semarang: G. C. T. van Dorp, 1910–11.

Hüsken, Frans. "Een drop op Java; Sociale differentiatie in een boeren gemeenschap, 1850–1980". Ph.D. dissertation, Universiteit van Amsterdam, 1988.

———. "Cycles of Commercialization and Accumulation in a Central Javanese Village". In *Agrarian Transformation. Local Processes and the State in Southeast Asia,* edited by G. Hart, A. Thurton, and B. White, pp. 303–31. Berkeley: University of California Press, 1989.

———. "Declining Welfare in Java: Government and Private Inquiries 1903–14". In *The Late Colonial State in Indonesia: Politics and Economic Foundations of the Netherlands Indies 1880–1942,* edited by Robert Cribb, pp. 213–28. KITLV, Verhandelingen 163. Leiden: KITLV Press, 1994.

———. "Living by the Sugar Mill: The People of Comal in the Early Twentieth Century". In *Beneath the Smoke of the Sugar-Mill: Javanese Coastal Communities during the Twentieth Century,* edited by H. Kano, F. Huskens, and D. Suryo, pp. 73–110. Yogyakarta: AKATIGA and Gadjah Mada University Press, 2001*a.*

———. "Continuity and Change in Local Politics: The Village Administration and Control of Land and Labour". In *Beneath the Smoke of the Sugar-Mill: Javanese Coastal Communities during the Twentieth Century,* edited by H. Kano, F. Huskens, and D. Suryo, pp. 231–63. Yogyakarta: AKATIGA and Gadjah Mada University Press, 2001*b.*

Hyung-Jun Kim. "Reformist Muslims in a Yogyakarta Village. The Islamic Transformation of Contemporary Socio-Religious Life". Ph.D. dissertation, Department of Anthropology, Australian National University, Canberra, 1996.

Ingold, Tim, ed. *Key Debates in Anthropology.* London: Routledge, 1996.

Ikhtilaf, Bulletin Juma'at Al-. LKiS, Yogyakarta.

Institut Studi Arus Informasi. *Prémanisme Politik.* Jakarta: 2000.

Izikowitz, Karl and P. Sorensen, eds. *The House in East and Southeast Asia. Anthropological and Architectural Aspects.* London: Curzon, 1982

Jacques, Francis. "Trois Stratégies interactionnelles: conversation, négociation, dialogue". In *Echanges sur la Conversation,* edited by J. Cosnier, N. Gelas, and Kerbrat-Orecchioni, pp. 45–68. Paris: CNRS, 1988.

Janz, P. *Practisch Javaansch-Nederlandsch Wordenboek.* (6th edition) Semarang: G. C. T. van Doys, 1918.

Jay, R. R. *Javanese Villagers. Social Relations in Rural Modjokuto.* Cambridge and London: MIT Press, 1969.

Jellinek, Lea. *The Wheel of Fortune. The Listing of a Poor Community in Jakarta.* Asian Studies Association of Australia. Southeast Asia Publications Series No. 18. London: Allen and Unwin, 1991.

Johns, A. *The Gift Addressed to the Spirit of the Prophet.* Canberra: Australian National University, 1965.

Jonge, de J. K. J. *De Opkomst van het Nederlandsch gezag in Oost-Indie,* edited by M. L. Deventer, vol. XII. 's-Gravenahage: Martinus Nijhoff, 1862–1909.

Jordaan, Roy. "Test, Temple and Tirtha". In *The Art and Culture of South-east Asia,* edited by Lokesh Chandra, pp. 165–81. Delhi: Adity Prakashan, 1991.

———. *In Praise of Prambanan.* KITLV Translation Series 26. Leiden: KITLV Press, 1996.

———. "Tārā and Nyai Lara Kidul: Images of the Divine Feminine in Java". *Asian Folklore Studies* LVI, no. 2 (1997): 285–312.

——— and P. B. Josselin de Jong. "Sickness as a Metaphor in Indonesian Political Myths". *Bijdragen tot de Taal-, Land- en Volkenkunde* 141 (1980): 253–74.

——— and Robert Wessing. "Human Sacrifice at Prambanan". *Bijdragen tot de Taal-, Land- en Volkenkunde* 152, no. 1 (1996): 45–73.

Jurumantani, K. R. T. *Tuwuhan Manten ing Pura Pakualaman.* Yogyakarta: Gadjah Mada University Press, 1980.

Juynböll, H. H. *Katalog des Ethnographischen Reichmuseums: Band V, Javanische Altertümer.* Leiden: E. J. Brill, 1909.

Juynboll, Th. W. *Handleiding tot de kennis van de Mohammedaansche Wet.* Leiden: E. J. Brill, 1925.

Kahin, George McTurnan. *Nationalism and Revolution in Indonesia.* (Original ed. 1952). Ithaca: Cornell University Press, 1970.

Kamajaya, ed. *Pilihan Karangan KGPAA Mangkunagara IV.* Yayasan Centhini: Yogyakarta, 1992.

Kanō, Hiroyoshi. *Land Tenure System and the Desa Community in Nineteenth-century Java.* Institute of Developing Economies Special Paper no. 5, 40 pp. Tokyo, 1977.

———. "The Economic History of Javanese Rural Society: A Reinterpretation". In *The Developing Economies* 17, no. 4 (December 1979): 4–21.

Kartika Setyawati, I. Kuntara Wiryamartana and Willem van der Moten. *Katalog Naskah Merapi-Merbabu Perpustakaan Nasional Republik Indonesia.* Semaian 23. Leiden/Yogyakarta: Sanata Dharma and Univ. Leiden, 2002.

Kartodirjo, Sartono. *The Peasants' Revolt in Banten 1888. Its Conditions, Course and Sequel. A Case Study of Social Movements in Indonesia.* Verhandelingen KITLV no. 50 's-Gravenhage: M. Nijhoff, 1966.

———. "Agrarian Radicalism in Java: Its Setting and Development". In *Culture and Politics in Indonesia,* edited by Claire Holt, pp. 71–125. Ithaca and London: Cornell University Press, 1972.

———. *Protest Movements in Rural Java.* Singapore: Oxford University Press, 1973.

Kats, J. "Dewi Crī". *Tijdschrift voor Indische Taal-, Land- en Volkenkunde* 57 (1916): 177–99.

Keeler, Ward. *Symbolic Dimensions of the Javanese House.* Working Paper 29, Centre for Southeast Asian Studies, Monash University, 1983.

———. "Wayang Kulit in the Political Margin". *Puppet Theatre in Contemporary Indonesia. New Approaches to Performance Events,* edited by Jan Mrázek, pp. 92–108. Ann Arbor: University of Michigan, 2002.

Kenji Tsuchiya. "Javanology and the Age of Ranggawarsita: An Introduction to Nineteenth Century Javanese Culture". In Translation Series. Translation of Contemporary Japanese Scholarship on Southeast Asia vol. 1; *Reading Southeast Asia,* pp. 75–108. Ithaca: Southeast Asia Program Cornell University, 1990.

Keppel, Gilles. "Jihad". *Expansion et déclin de l'islamise.* Paris: Gallimard, 2000.

Kern, H. "Eene Oudjavaansche Cosmogonie". *Bijdragen KITLV,* deel 36, no. 4 (1887): 573–85.

Kern R. A. *I La Galigo, Cerita Bugis Kuno.* Yogyakarta: Gadjah Mada University Press, 1989.

Kersten, J. *Bahasa Bali.* Ende, Flores: Nusa Indah, 1984.

Kinsley, David. *Hindu Goddesses. Visions of the Divine Feminine in the Hindu Religious Tradition.* Berkeley: University of California Press, 1987.

Kipp, Rita Smith. *Dissociated Identities. Ethnicity, Religion and Class in an Indonesian Scoiety.* Ann Arbor: University of Michigan Press, 1996.

Kipp, R. S. and R. D. Kipp, eds. *Beyond Samosir.* Athens: Ohio University Southeast Asia Program, 1983.

Klokke, Marijke J. "On the Orientation of Ancient Javanese Temples: The Example of Candi Surowono". In *International Institute for Asian Studies Yearbook 1994,* edited by Paul van der Velde, pp. 73–85. Leiden: International Institute for Asian Studies, 1994.

Kodiron. *Pedhalangan Jangkep: Lampahan Sambadra Larung.* Surakarta, 1962.

———. *Sembadra Larung.* Surakarta, 1968.

Koentjariningrat, R. M. *A Preliminary Description of the Javanese Kinship System.* Yale University Southeast Asian Studies Cultural Report Series. New Haven: Yale University, 1957.

———. "The Javanese of South Central Java". In *Social Structure in South-east Asia,* edited by G. P. Murdock. Chicago: Quadrangle Books, 1960.

————. "Javanese Data on the Unresolved Problems of the Kindred". *Ethnology* VII (1968): 53–58.

————. *Anthropology in Indonesia: A Bibliographical Review.* KITLV, Bibliographical Series 8. 's-Gravenhage: Martinus Nijhoff, 1975.

————. "Javanese Terms for God and Supernatural Beings and the Idea of Power". In *Readings on Islam in Southeast Asia,* edited by Ahmad Ibrahim et al., pp. 286–92. Singapore: Institute of Southeast Asian Studies, 1985*a*.

————. *Javanese Culture.* Singapore: Oxford University Press, 1985*b*.

Kooij, K. R. van. *Worship of the Goddess According to the Kalikāpurāna.* Leiden: E. J. Brill, 1972.

Kosambi, Damodar D. *Culture et Civilisation de l'Inde Ancienne.* Paris: François Maspero, 1970.

Kraemer, H. *Een Javaansche Primbon uit Zestiende eeuw.* Leiden, 1921.

Krauskopff, Gisèle. *Maîtres et Possédés: Les Rites et l'ordre social chez les Tharu.* Paris: Editions CNRS, 1989.

Kreemer, J. *De Kaerabouw, zijn beteknis voor de voken van Indonesiche Archipel.* s'-Gravenhage/Bandung: W. van Hoeve, 1956.

Kruijt A. C. "Gebruiken bij den Rijstoogst in enneiger streken op Ooost-Java". *Mededelingen van wege het Nederlasch Zending Genootschap* 47 (1903): 125–39.

Kumar, Ann. "The 'Suryengalangan Affair' of 1883 and its Successors: Born Leaders in Changed Times". *Bijdragen* no. 138 (2–3), 1982.

————. *Java and Modern Europe: Ambiguous Encounters.* Richmond, Surrey: Curzon, 1997.

Kuipers, Joel C. *Power The Creation of Textual Authority in Weyewa Ritual Speech.* Philadelphia: University of Pennsylvania Press, 1990.

————. *Language, Identity and Marginality in Indonesia. The Changing Nature of Ritual Speech on the Island of Sumba.* Cambridge: Cambridge University Press, 1998.

Kuntara Wiryamartana. "The Scriptoria in the Merbabu-Merapi Area". In *Bijdragen tot de Taal-, Land- en Volkenkunde* no. 149-III (1993): 503–10.

Kuntowijoyo. "Serat Cabolek dan Mitos Pembangkangan Islam: Melacak Asal-Usul Ketegangan Antara Islam dan Birokrasi". In *Paradigma Islam: Interpretasi untuk Aksi,* edited by A. E. Priyono, pp. 123–37. Bandung: Mizan, 1991.

Kuznetsova, S. S. "Some Remarks on the Traditional Javanese Conception of the Historical Process (with special reference to the *Babad Tanah Jawi*)". In *Looking in Odd Mirrors: The Java Sea.* Semaian 5, edited by V. J. H. Houben et al., pp. 76–96. Leiden: Vakgroup Talen en Culturen van Zuidoost-Azië en Oceanië. Rijksuniversiteit te Leiden, 1992.

Laksono, P.M. *Tradition in Javanese Social Structure, Kingdom and Countryside.* Yogyakarta: Gadjah Madah Univ. Press, 1986.

Lambek, Michael. "Localising Islamic Performances in Mayotte". In *Islamic Prayer across the Indian Ocean. Inside and Outside the Mosque,* edited by David Parkin and Stephen C. Headley, pp. 63–98. Richmond, Surrey: Curzon, 2000.

Larson, George D. *Prelude to Revolution. Palace and Politics in Surakarta, 1912–1942.* KITLV, Verhandelingen 124. Dordrecht, Providence: Foris Publications, 1987.

Lebar, Frank M., ed. *Ethnic Groups of Insular Southeast Asia,* vol. I. New Haven: Human Relations Area Files Press, 1972.

Leclerc, Jacques. "Vocabulaire social et répréssion politique: un exemple indonésien". *Annales* (March–April 1973): 407–28.

Leenhardt, Maurice. *Do Kamo: Personne et le mythe dans le monde. Mélanésien.* Paris: Gallimard, 1947.

Leur, J. C. van. *Indonesian Trade and Society, Essays in Asian Social and Economic History.* The Hague and Bandung: van Hoeve, 1955.

Lévi-Strauss, Claude. "Anthropologie Sociale". *Annuaire du College de France* (1977–78): 493–99.

———. *La Voie des Masques.* Paris: Plon, 1979.

———. *Histoire de Lynx.* Paris: Plon, 1991.

Levinson, Stephen C. *Pragmatics.* Cambridge: Cambridge University Press, 1983.

Levy, R. *The Social Structure of Islam.* Cambridge: Cambridge University Press, 1957.

Lewis, C. T. and C. Short. *A Latin Dictionary.* Oxford: Clarendon Press, 1962.

Lind, Elisabeth. *The Ideal Equilibrium.* Mimeographed. University of Stockholm, 1975.

Lombard, Denys. "La vision de la forêt à Java", *Etudes Rurales* no. 53–56 (1974): 474–85.

———. *Le Carrefour Javanais: Essais d'hsitorie globale.* 3 vols. Paris: Edition de l'Ecole des Hautes Etudes en Sciences Scoiales, 1990.

Lombard, D. and J. Aubin, eds. *Marchands et Hommes d'Affairs Asiatiques dans l'Océan Indien et la Mer de Chine, 13e–20e siècles.* Paris: Edition de l'Ecole des Hautes Etudes en Sciences Sociales, 1988.

Louwerier, D. "Bijgeloovige gebruiken, die door de Javanen worder in act genomen bij de verzoring en opvoedig hunner kinderen". In *Mededeelingen van wage het Nederlandsche Zendelinggenootschap* IL (1905): 252–57.

Loyré, Ghislaine. *A la Recherche de l'Islam philippin. La Communauté Marono* Paris. L'Harmattan, 1989.

Luckman, Thomas. *The Invisible Religion: The Problem of Religion in the Modern World.* New York: Macmillan, 1967.

Ludden, David, ed. *Making India Hindu. Religion, Community and the Politics of Democracy in India.* Delhi: Oxford University Press, 1996.

Mabuchi, T. "Tales Concerning the Origin of Grains in the Insular Area of Eastern and Southeastern Asia". *Asian Folklore Studies* 23 (n.d.): 1–91.

Macdonald, Charles. "Exstase et Esthétique, réflexions sur des formes rituelles à Palawan". In *Orients pour Georges Condominas,* pp. 85–98. Paris: Sudestasie/Privat, 1981.

Maclaine Pont, H. "Javaansche Architectuur". *Djawa* 111, no. 2 and 4 (1923): 79–89; 159–171; *Djawa* IV, no. 1 (1924): 44–73.

Madjid, Nucholish. *Islam Kemodernan dan Keindonesiaan.* Bandung: Mizan, 1987.

Mahābhārata, edited and translated by J. A. B. van Buitenen. Chicago: University of Chicago Press, n.d.

Mahābhārata, vol I. Critical edition of Vishnu S. Sukthankar. Poona: Bhandarkar Oriental Research Institute, 1933.

Maijer, L. Th. *De Javaan, als mensch en als lid van het Javaansche Huisgezin.* Batavia-Solo: Albrecht & Rusche, 1894.

Malamoud, Charles. "Cuire le Monde". *Purusārtha* I (1975): 91–135.

Mangunwijaya, Y. B. *Ragawidya: Religiositas Hal-hal Sehari-hari.* (1st ed. 1975). Yogyakarta: Yayasan Kanisius, 1987.

Mangunwiryatmo. *Kawruh Bubak Kawah — Langkahan Tingkeban.* Surakarta: Cendrawasih, 1990.

Mani, Vettam. *Purānic Encyclopedia.* Delhi: Motilal Banarsidas, 1975.

Manikmaya, 3 vols. Proyek Penerbitan Buku Sastra Indonesia dan Daerah. Jakarta: Departemen Pendidikan dan Kebudayaan, Balai Pustaka, 1981.

Manikmaya. Proyek Pengembangan Perpustakaan, Jawa Tengah. Semarang: Departemen Pendidikan dan Kebudayaan 1984.

Manning, C. and P. van. Dierman. *Indonesia di Tengah Transisi. Aspek-aspek Social Reformasi dan Krisis:* Yoyakarta: LKiS, 2001.

Marbangun Hardjowirogo. *Manusia Jawa.* Jakarta: Idayu, 1983.

Marrison, G. E. *Sasak and Javanese Literature of Lombok.* KITLV Working Papers 14. Leiden: KITLV Press, 1999.

Masquelier, Adeline. *Prayer has Spoiled Everything: Possession, Power, and Identity in an Islamic Town of Niger.* Durham: Duke University Press, 2001.

Masselman, George. *The Cradle of Colonialism.* New Haven and London: Yale University Press, 1963.

Mayer, L. Th. *Een Blik in het Javaansche Volksleven,* 2 vols. Leiden: E. J. Brill, 1897.

McKinley, R. "Cain and Abel on the Malay Peninsula". In *Siblingship in Oceania: Studies in the Meaning of Kin Relations,* edited by MacMarshall, pp. 335–87. Ann Arbor: University of Michigan Press, 1975.

McKinnon, Susan. "Hierarchy Alliance and Exchange in the Tanimbar Islands". Ph.D. dissertation, University of Chicago, 1983.

———. "Houses and Hierarchy: The View from a South Moluccan Society". In *About the House. Lévi-Strauss and Beyond,* edited by Janet Carsten and Stephen Hugh-Jones, pp. 170–88. Cambridge: Cambridge University Press, 1995.

McLaughlin, S. "The Book of Aji Saka: A Literary Analysis". B.A. Honours thesis, University of Sydney, 1975.

Membongkar Mitos Masyarakat Madani. Yogyakarta: Pustaka Pelajar, 2000.

Mershon, Katharane. *Seven plus Seven: Mysterious life-rituals in Bali.* New York: Vantage Press, 1971.

Metcalf, Barbara D. "Islam in Contemporary Southeast Asia: History, Community, Morality". In *Islam in an Era of Nation States. Politics and Religious Renewal in Muslim Southeast Asia,* edited by R. Hefner and P. Horvatich, pp. 309–20. Honolulu: University of Hawai'i Press, 1997.

Metcalf, Barbara D., ed. *Making Muslim Space in North America and Europe.* Berkeley: University of California Press, 1996.

Metcalf, Peter. *A Borneo Journey into Death: Berawan Eschatology from its Rituals.* Philadelphia: University of Pennsylvania Press, 1982.

Milbank, John. *Theology and Social Theory. Beyond Secular Reason.* Oxford: Blackwells, 1990.

Miyazaki, Koji. *Javanese Classification Systems: The Problem of Maximal Correspondence.* Institute of Cultural Anthropology Publications no. 35. Leiden: Institute of Cultural Anthropology, Leiden University, 1979.

Moll, J. F. A. C. and H. 's. Jacob. *De Desa-Volkshuishouding in Cijfers.* Amsterdam: Algemeen Syndicaat van Suikerfabrikanten in Nederlandsch-Indïe, 1913.

Mrázek, Jan. "Phenomenology of a Puppet Theatre: Contemplations on the Performance Technique of Contemporary Javanese Wayang Kulit". Ph.D. dissertation, Cornell University, 1998.

———. "Javanese Wayang Kulit in the Times of Comedy". *Indonesia* 68–69, pts. 1 and 2 (October 1999 and April 2000): 38–128, 107–172.

———, ed. *Puppet Theatre in Contemporary Indonesia: New Approaches to Performance-Events.* Ann Arbor: University of Michigan Press, 2002.

Mukhan, Abdul Munir. *Islam Murni dalam Masyarakat Petani.* Yogyakarta: Bentang, 2000.

Mukherjee, B. N. *Nana on Lion, a study in Kushāna numismatic art.* Calcutta: Asiatic Society, n.d.

Mulyadi, Hari and Soedarmono. *Runtuhnya Kekuasaan "Kraton Alit": Studi Radikalisasi Sosial "Wong Solo" dan Kerusuhan Mei 1998 di Surakarta.* Solo: Lembaga Pengembangan Teknologi Pedesaan, 1999.

Murdock, George Peter, ed. "Cognatic Forms of Social Organization". In *Social Structure in Southeast Asia,* pp. 1–14. Viking Fund Publications in Anthropology, no. 29. Chicago: Quadrangle Books, 1960.

Murhono Hs. "Sunan Paku Buwono VI Berperan Dalam Perang Diponegoro". *Sinar Harapan,* 14 January 1983.

Mus, Paul. *Borobudur, esquisse d'une histoie du bouddhisme fondée sur la critique archéologique des textes.* 2 vols. Hanoi: Ecole Française de l'Extrēme Orient, 1935.

———. *Barabudur, Sketch of a History of Buddhism.* Translated by A. W. Macdonald. New Delhi: Sterling Publishers, 1998.

Nafi', Dian. "Memahami Agama Kristen sebagai Realitas Sosial". Pondok Pesantrèn Ar-Risalah, Ponorogo, 6 November 2000, 13 pages.

Nagaswamy, R. *Tantric Cult of South India.* Delhi: Agam Kala Prakshan, n.d.

Nahuys van Burgst, H. G. *Herinneringen uit het openbare en bijzondere leven (1799–1849).* Utrecht: van de Weijer, 1852.

Naipaul, V. S. *Beyond Belief: Islamic Excursions among Converted Peoples.* New York: Random House, 1998.

Nakamura, Mitsuo. *The Crescent Arises over the Banyan Tree: A Study of the*

Muhammadiyah Movement in a Central Javanese Town. Yogyakarta: Gadjah Mada Press, 1983.

Nama dan Alamat Pondhok Pesantrèn Indonesia. Proyek Pembinaan dan Bantuan Kepada Pondhok Pesantrèn. Direktorat Jendral Pembinaan Kelembagaan Agama Islam; Departemen Agama R.I., 1982–83.

Nasr Abou Zeid. *Critique du discours religieux.* Arles: Sindbad, Actes Sud, 1999.

Nasr Hamid Abu Zaid. *Teksutalitas Al-Quran: Kritik Terhadap Ulumul Qur'an.* Yogyakarta: LKiS, 2001.

Nasr, Seyyed Hossein. *An Introduction to Islamic Cosmological Doctrines.* Albany: State University of New York Press, 1993 (1st edition 1964).

Natawidjaja. "Krendawahana-Kaliasa". *Pustaka Jawi,* no. 6 (1927): 21–25.

Needham, Rodney. "Remarks on the Analysis of Kinship and Marriage". In *Rethinking Kinship and Marriage,* edited by Rodney Needham, pp. 1–34. London: Tavistock, 1971.

Noer Fauzi. *Otonomi Daerah dan Sengketa Tanah. Pergeseran Politk di Bawah Problem Agaria.* Yogyakarta: Lapera, 2001.

Norse, Jennifer W. *Conceiving Spirits: Birth Rituals and Contested Identities among the Lauje of Indonesia.* Washington and London: Smithsonian Institution Press, 1999.

Nugraha, Iskandar P. *Menikas Batas Timur dan Barat: Gerakan Theosofi dan Nasionalisme Indonesia.* Jakarta: Komunitas Bamboo, 2001.

Nwiya, P. *Exégèse cranique et langage mystique. Nouvel essai sur le lexique technique des mystiques musulmans.* Beyrouth: Dar-al-Machreq, 1970.

Ong, W. J. *The Presence of the Word: Some Prologomena for Cultural and Religious History.* Minneapolis: University of Minnesota Press, 1967.

Ottino, Arlette. "Origin Myths, Hierarchical Order, and the Negotiation of Status in the Balinese Village of Trunyan". *Bijdragen tot de Taal-, Land- en Volkenkunde* 150 (1994): 481–517.

Ottino, Paul. *L'Etrangère Intime. Essai d'anthropologie de la Civilisation de l'ancien Madagascar.* 2 vols. Montreux: Editions des Archives Contemporaines, 1986.

Oudheidkundig Verslag 1917. Oudheidkundige Dienst in Nerderlansche-Indië. [Notes on the site of Nusukan] (1917): 3–5, 74.

Padmasoesastra. *Serat Tatatjara ngadat sarta kalakoewanipun titijang Djawi, ingkang taksih loemèngkèt dhateng goegontoehon.* (Original ed. Batawi, 1907). Reprint. Semarang: Balai Pustaka 2, 1911.

Padmosoekotjo, S. *Silsilah Wayang Purwa Mawa Carita,* vol. I. Surabaya: Citra Jaya, 1979.

Padoux, André. *L'Energie de la Parole. Cosmogonie de la Parole Tantrique.* Paris: Le Soleil Noir, 1980.

Pagnol, Marcel. *César.* Paris: Presses Pocket, 1976.

Pak, Ok-Kyung. "Royauté et parenté chez les Minangkabau de Sumatra". *L'Homme,* no. 124 (1993): 89–113.

Palmier, L. H. *Social Status and Power in Java.* London Schoool of Economics Mongraphs on Social Anthropology, no. 20. London: Athone Press, 1960.

Pargiter, F. Eden. *Markandeya Purāna*. Calcutta: Bibliotheca Indica, 1904.

Parkin, David. "Invocation: Salaa, Dua, Sadaka and the Question of Self-Determination". In *Islamic Prayer across the Indian Ocean. Inside and Outside the Mosque*, edited by David Parkin and Stephen C. Headley, pp. 137–69. Richmond, Surrey: Curzon Press, 2000.

———— and Stephen C. Headley, eds. *Islamic Prayer across the Indian Ocean. Inside and Outside the Mosque*. Richmond, Surrey: Curzon Press, 2000.

Peacock, James L. *Muslims Puritans. Reformist Psychology in Southeast Asian Islam*. Berkeley: University of California Press, 1978.

Peeters, Jeroen. *Kaum Tuo — Kaum Mudo: Perubahan Religious di Palembang 1821–1943*. Indonesian-Netherlands Cooperation in Islamic Studies 31. Jakarta: INIS, 1997 (Dutch language dissertation, Leiden 1994).

Peletz, M. G. " 'Ordinary Muslims' and Muslim Resurgents in Contemporary Malaysia: Notes on an Ambivalent Relationship". In *Islam in an Era of Nation-States: Politics and Religious Renewal in Muslim Southeast Asia,* edited by R. Hefner and P. Horvatich, pp. 231–75. Honolulu: University of Hawai'i Press, 1997.

Pelras, Christian. "Religion, Tradition, and the Dynamics of Islamisation in South Sulawesi". *Indonesia*, no. 57 (1984): 133–54.

————. *The Bugis (Peoples of South-East Asia and the Pacific)*. Oxford: Blackwells, 1996*a*.

————."Islam and Pre-Islamic Traditions among the Bugis of Sulawesi (Indonesia)", Xè Réunion de l'AFEMAM, "Les Chantiers Européens de la Recherche", Aix-en-Provence, 7 juillet 1996*b*. (7 pp.)

Pemberton, John. *On the Subject of "Java"*. Ithaca and London: Cornell University Press, 1994.

Picard, M. "What's in a Name? *Agama Hindu Bali* in the Making". In *Religion and the Nation State: Hinduism in Modern Indonesia*, edited by M. Ramstedt. Richmond: Curzon, forthcoming.

Pigeaud, Theodore. G. Th. *De Tantu Panggelaran. Een Oud-Javaansch Prozageschrift, uitgegeven, vertaald en toegelicht*. 's-Gravenhage: Nederl. Boek en Steendrukkerij voorheen H. L. Smits, 1924.

————, ed. *Serat-Serat Anggitanipun K.G.P.A.A. Mangkunegara IX*. 4 vols. Surakarta: Java Institut, 1928/1953.

————. *Java in the 14th Century: A Study in Cultural History. The Nāgara-kertāgama by Rakawi Prapañca of Majapahit, 1365 A.D.* KITLV Transation Series 4, in 5 vols. The Hague: M. Nijhoff, 1960–1963.

————. *Litterature of Java*, 3 vols. The Hague: Martinus Nijhoff, 1967.

————. *Javanese and Balinese Manuscripts and some Codices written in Idioms spoken in Java and Bali. Descriptive Catalogue. Verzeichnis der Orientalischen Handscriften in Deutschland*, band 31. Weisbaden: F. Steiner, 1975.

————. *Literature of Java vol. IV Supplement*. Leiden: Leiden University Press, 1980.

————. "Javanese Divination and Classification". In *Structural Anthropology of the Netherlands*, edited by P. E. de Josselin de Jong, pp. 61–82. KITLV Translation Series, no. 17. Dordrecht: Foris, 1983.

————. *Javaans-Nederlands Woordenboek*, 5th ed. Leiden: KITLV, 1994.

Pigeaud, T. and H. J. de Graaf. *Islamic States in Java 1500–1700*. KITLV, Verhandelingen no. 70. The Hague: M. Nijhoff, 1976 .

Pijper, G. *Het Boek der Duizend Vragen*. Leiden, 1925.

Pijper, G. F. *Studi tentang Islam Indonesia 1900–1950*. Jakarta: University of Indonesia, 1985.

Pink, Peter. "Ya maraja or Yamaraja: Notes on a Javanese Verse". In *Vers une anthropologie de la prière: études ethnolinguistiques javanaises*, edited by Stephen C. Headley, pp. 235–58. Aix-en-Provence: Publications Universitaires de Provence, 1996.

Poensen, C. "Iets over Javaansche Naamgeving en Eigennamen". *Mededeelingen van wage het Nederlandsche Zendelinggenootschap* XIX (1870): 304–21.

————. "Javaansche Woningen en Erven". *Mededeelingen van wage het Nederlandsche Zendelinggenootschap* XIV (1875): 101–46.

Poerbatjaraka, R. M. Ng. "Mengeling". *Tijdschrift van Nederlands Indie* (1940*a*): 291–93.

————. *Beschriving der Handschriften: Menak*. Bandung: Nix, 1940*b*.

———— and Tardjan Hadidjaja. *Kepustakaan Djawa*. Djakarta/Amsterdam: Djambatan, 1952.

————, P. Voorhoeve, and C. Hooykaas. *Indonesische Handschriften*. Bandung: A.C. Nix, 1950.

Poeroebaya, B. P. H. "Rondom de huwelijken in de Kraton te Jogyakarta". *Djawa* 6 (1939): 295–329.

Poerwadarminta, W. J. S. *Baoe Sastra Djawa*, vol. I. Ngajaogja: Triwikrāma, 1939.

Pott, P. H. *Yoga and Yantri*. KITLV Translation Series 8. The Hague: M. Nijhoff, 1966.

Pradikto, Fadjar. *Gerakan Rakyat Kelaparan. Gagalnya Politik Radikalisasi Petani*. Yogykarta: Media Pressindo, 2000.

Pradjarta Dirdjosanjoto. *Memilihara Umat. Kiai Pesantrèn — Kiai Langgar di Jawa*. Yogyakarta: LKiS, 1999.

Prapañca, Mpu. *Deśawarṇana (Nāgarakṛtāgama)*. Translated by Stuart Robson. KITLV, Verhandelingen no. 169. Leiden: KITLV Press, 1995.

Pratelan Para Dalem Soewargi Kangdjeng Goeti Pangeran Adipati Arja Mangoennagara I hing Soerakarta Hadiningrat. Surakarta: Privately published, 1973.

Prawiroatmodjo, S. *Bausastra Jawa-Indonesia*, 2 vols. Jakarta: Gunung Agung, 1981.

Prémanisme Politik (Institut Studi Arus Informasi). Yogyakarta: LKiS, 2000.

Price, P. G. *Kingship and Political Practice in Colonial India*. University of Cambridge Oriental Publications 51. Cambridge: Cambridge University Press, 1996.

Prihohoetomo, M. *Nawaruci. Inleiding, Middel-Javaansch prozatekst, vertaling*. Groningen, 1934.

Prijono. "Sri Tanjung, een oud Javaansch verhaal". Ph.D. dissertation, Leiden University, 1938.

Pringgodigdo. *Geschiedenis der Ondernemingen van het Mangkoenagorosche Rijk*. 's-Gravenhage: Martinus Nijhoff, 1950.

Probohardjono, R. Ng. *Serat Kidungan. Babon asli saking Karaton Surakarta. Sakawit saking pituwahipun Kangdjeng Susuhunan in Kalidjaga Waliullah ing Nusa Djawi.* 2nd ed. Solo: Ratna, n.d.

Probohardjono. *Pakem Wajang Purwa.* 3rd ed. Lawijan, Solo: Ratna, 1961.

Pulleyn, S. *Prayer in Greek Religion.* Oxford: Clarendon Press, 1998.

Purwosugiyanto, ed. *Panguyuban Trah R. Tumenggung Secodiningrat Yogyakarta, Buku Riwayat dan Silsilah.* 41 pp. 2nd ed. 1985.

Quinn, George. *The Novel in Javanese.* KITLV, Verhandelingen 148. Leiden: KITLV Press, 1992.

Radcliffe-Brown, A. R. *Structure and Function in Primitive Society.* London: Oxford University Press, 1952.

Raffles, T. S. *The History of Java.* London: Cox and Baylis (republished by Oxford University Press), 1817 (1988).

Rajeshwari, D. R. *Sakti Iconography.* Delhi: Intellectual Publishing House, n.d.

Ranggawarsita, R. Ng. *Serat Pustakaraja Purwa,* vol. 3. Surakarta: Yayasan Mangadeg; and Yogyakarta: Yayasan Cethini, 1994.

Rao, *Mārkandeya-Purāna,* 1914.

Rapoport, A. ed. *House Form and Culture.* Englewoods Cliffs, New Jersey: Prentice Hall, 1996.

Ras, J. J. "The Panji Romance and W. H. Rasser's Analysis of its Theme". *Bijdragen tot de Taal-, Land- en Volkenkunde* 129 (1973): 411–56.

———. "The Babad Tanah Jawi and its Reliability: Questions of Content, Structure and Function". In *Cultural Contact and Textual Interpretation,* edited by C. D. Grijns and S. O. Robson. Dordrecht: Foris Publications, 1986.

Rasyidi, H. M. *Documents pour servir à l'histoire de l'islam à Java.* Publications de l'Ecole Française de l'Extrême Orient, 112. Paris: Maissonneuve, 1977.

Ratnaesih Maulana. "Durgāmahisāsuramardini". B.A thesis, Fakultas Sastra no. 2376, University of Indonesia, n.d.

———. "Variasi Ciri-ciri Arca Durgā Mahīsāsuramardani". *Majalah Arkeologi* II, no. 4 (1979): 3–19.

Rawiastuti, Maria, "Menuju Pluralisme Hukum Agraria". In *Otonomi Daerah dan Sengketa Tanah,* edited by Noer Fauzi. Yogyakarta: Lapera, 2000.

Reid, A. J. S. "The Origins of Poverty Indonesia". In *Indonesia: Dualism, Growth and Poverty,* edited by R. G. Garnaut and P. T. McCawley, pp. 441–54. Canberra: Research School of Pacific Studies, Australian National University, 1980.

Reid, Anthony. *The Lands below the Winds.* Southeast Asia in the Age of Commerce 1450–1650, vol. 1. New Haven and London: Yale University Press, 1988.

———. *Expansion and Crisis.* Southeast Asia in the Age of Commerce 1450–1650, vol. 2. New Haven and London: Yale University Press, 1993.

Rekaman Lensa Peristiwa Mei 1998 di Solo. Solo: Aksara Solopos, 1998.

Renou, Louis and Jean Filliozat. *L'Inde Classique. Manuel des Etudes Indiennes.* 2 vols. Paris: Payot, 1947.

Reuter, Thomas. "Precedence in Sumatra: An Analysis of the Construction of Status in Affinal Relations and Origin Groups". *Bijdragen*, 148, no. 3–4 (1992): 489–520.

Ricklefs, Merle C. "Dipanagara's Early Inspirtional Experience". *Bijdragen* 130 (1974): 227–58.

———. *Modern Javanese Historical Tradition: A Study of an Original Kartasura Chronicle and Related Materials*. London: School of Oriental and African Studies, University of London, 1978.

———. *A History of Modern Indonesia*. London: Macmillan, 1981.

———. "Unity and Disunity in Javanese Political and Religious Thought of the Eighteenth Century". *Modern Asian Studies* 26, no. 4 (1992): 663–78.

———. *War, Culture and Economy in Java, 1677–1726: Asian and European Imperialism in the Early Kartasura Period*. Asian Studies Association of Australia, no. 24. Sydney: Allen and Unwin, 1993.

———. *The Seen and the Unseen Worlds in Java, 1726–1749: History, Literature and Islam in the Court of Pakubuwana II*. Asian Studies Association of Australia. St. Leonards, NSW and Honolulu: Allen and Unwin and University of Hawai'i Press, 1998.

———. "Mystic Synthesis in Java: A History of Islamisation from the Fourteenth to the Early Nineteenth Centuries". Manuscript.

——— and P. Voorhoeve. *Indonesian Manuscripts in Great Britain*. Oxford: Oxford University Press, 1977.

Ricoeur, Paul. "Nommer Dieu". In *Theolinguistics,* edited by J. P. van Nappen Studiereeks Tijdscrifts, new series, 8 (1981): 342–67.

Robinson, Geoffrey. *The Dark Side of Paradise: Political Violence in Bali*. Ithaca: Cornell University Press, 1995.

Robson, Stuart. "Java at the Crossroads". In *Bijdragen tot de Taal-, Land-, en Volkenkunde* 137, nos. 2 and 3 (1981): 259–92.

———. "The Terminology of Javanese Kinship". *Bijdragen tot de Taal-, Land- en Volkenkunde* 143, no. 4 (1987): 507–18.

———, ed. *The Wédhatama, An English Translation*. KITLV Working Papers no. 4. Leiden: KITLV Press, 1990.

Ronggowarsita, K. *Wirid Hidajat Djati*, edited by R. Tanojo. Surabaya: Trimurti, 1966.

Roo de la Faille, P. de. "Over het Grondenrecht onder Javaansch Vortsenbestuur". In *Tijdschrift van de Bataviaasch Genootschap* (T.B.G.) 59 (1919–20): 21–84, 84–121.

Rosaldo, Michelle. *Knowledge and Passion. Ilongot Notions of Self and Social Life*. Cambridge: Cambridge University Press, 1980.

Rouffaer, G. P. "Vorstenlanden". *Adatrechtbundels* 34 (1931; original 1905): 233–378.

Saeed, Abdullah. "Approaches to *Itjihad* and Neo-Modernist Islam in Indonesia". Paper presented in a panel on Southeast Asia in the AFEMAM and EURAMES conference, Aix-en-Provence, 6 July 1996.

Sagimun. *Kyai Maja*. Jakarta: Dept. Pendidikan dan Kebudayaan, 1981.

Sairin, Sjafri. *Javanese Trah. Kin-Based Social Organisation*. Yogyakarta: UGM Press, 1982.

Salhins, M. *Islands of History*. Chicago: University of Chicago Press, 1985.

Santoso, Soewito. *Sutosoma*. Satapitaka Series 213. Delhi: International Academy of Indian Culture, 1975.

————. "Sastra Harjendra Yuningrat in the Wayang". In *The Art and Culture of South-East Asia,* edited by Lokesh Chandra, pp. 337–54. New Delhi: International Academy of Indian Culture and Aditya Prakashan, 1991.

Saraswati, Bandana. "Amba-Nana-Durgā". *Journal of the Asiatic Society*, VII (1965): 95–102.

Sarwanto, Ki. *Sesaji Raja Suyo*. Surakarta: Cendrawasih, 1991.

Sarwanto. "Wayang Kulit Purwa Dalam Upacara Bersih Desa di Bibis Kulon, Surakarta". Thesis, Gadjah Mada University, Yogyakarta, 1999.

Sasangka Jati. 10th ed. Jakarta: Pangestu, 1975.

Sastra Amidjaja. "Het Bouwen van het Javaansche Huizen". *Djawa* 4, no. 2 (1924): 105–18.

Schrieke, B. J. O. "Iets over het Perdikan-instituut". *Tijdschrift voor de Indische T.-, L.- en Volkenkunde*, no. 58 (1919): 391–423.

————. "Uit de gecheidenis van het adatgrondenrecht: De theorie van het zoogenaamde 'vorstelijk eigendomsrecht' ". *Tijschrift van het Bataviaasche Genootschap* (T.B.G.) (1919–21): 122–90.

————. "Naschrift" Bosch, F. D. K. "Het Lingga-Heiligdom von Dinaja". *Tijdschrift Bataviaasch Genootschap* vol 64 (1924): 286–91.

————. *Ruler and Realm in Early Java*. Indonesian Sociological Studies, 2 vols. The Hague/Bandung: W. vn Hoeve, 1957.

Schulte-Nordholt, Henk. *The Spell of Power: A History of Balinese Politics*. KITLV, Verhandelingen 170. Leiden: KITLV Press, 1996.

Sear, Laura J. *Shadows of Empire. Colonial Discourse and Javanese Tales*. Durham and London: Duke University Press, 1996.

Serat Centhini Latin. Vol. I. Yogyakarta: Yayasan Centhini, 1985

Serat Centhini. Vol. II. Transcribed by Kamajaya. Yogyakarta: Yayasan Centhini, 1986.

Serat Centhini. Transcribed by Kamajaya. Yogyakarta: Yayasan Cethini, 1991.

Serat Centhini (Suluk Tambangraras). Transliteration by Kamajaya. Yogyakarta: Yayasan Centhini, 1998.

Serat Jaka Lodhang. Yogyakarta: Kamajaya, 1985.

Serat Pustaka Raja Purwa. 11 vols. Surakarta: Privately published by Tristuti Rachmadi, 1983.

Serat Pustakaraja Purwa. R. Ng Ranggawarsita. Vol. 3. Surakarta: Yayasan Mangadeg; and Yogyakarta: Yayasan Cethini, 1994.

Sers, Philippe. *Totalitarisme et Avant-Gardes*. Paris: Les Belles Lettres, 2001.

Setten van der Meer, N. C. *Sawah Cultivation in Ancient Java: Aspects of Development during the Indo-Javanese Period 5th to 15th Century.* Oriental Monograph Series no. 22. Canberra: Australian National University, 1979.

Shamsul, A. B. "Inventing Certainties: The *Dakwah* Persona in Malaysia". In *The Pursuit of Certainty. Religious and Cultural Formulations,* edited by Wendy James, pp. 112–33. London: Routledge, 1995.

Sidamukti R. S. S. *Peringatan 40th.-5 Windu, Sri Paduka K. G. P. A. A. Mangkunagoro, Ke VI.* Surakarta, 1928.

Sidel, John. "Riots, Church Bombings and Conspiracies: The Moral Economy of the Indonesian Crowd in the Late Twentieth Century". In *Violence in Indonesia,* edited by Ingrid Wessel and Georgia Wimhöfer, pp. 47–63. Hamber: Abera-Verl, 2001.

Siegal, James. *A New Criminal Type in Jakarta. Counter-Revolution Today.* Durham: Duke University Press, 1998.

Silsilah Leluhur Kaliasa, 408 pp. Published privately, *circa* 1976.

Simuh. *Mistik Islam Kejawèn. Raden Ngabehi Ranggawarsita. Satu Studi terhadap Serat Wirid Hidayat Jati.* Jakarta: Penerbit Universitas Indonesia, 1988.

———. *Sufisme Jawa. Transformasi Tasawuf Islam ke Mistik Jawa.* 4th ed. Bentang: Yogyakarta, 1999.

Sircar, D. et al. *The Sakti Cult and Tara.* Calcutta: Calcutta University Press, 1967.

Slusser, M. S. *Nepal Mandala. A Cultural Study of the Kathmandu Valley,* 2 vols. Princeton: Princeton University Press, 1982.

Smith-Hefner, Nancy. "Language and Social Identity. Speaking Javanese in Tengger". Ph.D. dissertation, Department of Linguistics, University of Michigan, 1983.

———. "Pembaron: An East Javanese Rite of Priestly Rebirth". *Journal of Southeast Asian Studies* 23, no. 2 (1992): 237–75.

———. "The Litany of the 'World's Beginning': A Hindu Javanese Purification Text". In *Vers une Anthropologie de la Prière: etudes ethnolinguistiques javanaises,* edited by Stephen C. Headley, pp. 259–306. Aix-en-Provence: Publications de l'Univertsité de Provence, 1996.

Snouck Hurgronje, C. "Desa Perdikan", chapter IX, pp. 771–80, advisiezen dated 7 March 1895. In *Nasihat-nasihat C. Snouck Hurgronje semasa kepegawaiannya kepada Pemerintah Hindia Belanda, 1889–1936,* Seri Khusus INIS, jilid V, Jakarta, 1991.

———. *Aceh, Rakyat dan Adat Istiadatnya.* (1st Dutch ed., 1893). Indonesian-Netherlands Co-operation in Islamic Studies 28, vols. I and II. Jakarta: INIS, 1996.

Soebadio, Haryati. *Jñanasiddhānta.* KITLV Translation Series, no. 7. The Hague: Martinus Nijhoff, 1971.

Soebardi, S. *The Book of Cabolek.* KITLV, Bibliotheca Indonesica 10. The Hague: M. Nijhoff, 1975.

Soedjijono et al. *Struktur dan Isi Mantra Bahasa Jawa di Jawa Timur.* Jakarta: Departemen Pendidikan dan Kebudayaan, 1987.

Soedjono Tirtokoesoemo. *De Garebeg in het Sultanaat Jogjakarta.* Jogjakarta: H. Buning, 1931.

Soegijanto Padmo. *Landreform dan Gerakan Protes Petani Klaten 1959–1965.* Yogykarta: Media Pressindo, 2000.

Soejatno. "Revolution and Social Tensions in Surakarta, 1945–50". *Indonesia* 17 (1974): 99–111.

Soekomo. "Candi: Fungsi dan Pengertiannya". Positions de these presenté par W. Arifin. *Bulletin de l'EFEO* 62 (1975): 441–46.

Soepomo. *De Reorganisatie van het Agrarische Stelsel in het gewest Soerakarta.* 's-Gravenahge: Gerretsen, 1927.

Soepomo, Poedjosoedarmo, and M. C. Ricklefs. "The Establishment of Surakarta. A Translation from the Babad Giyanti". *Indonesia* 4 (1967): 88–108.

Soepripto, R. *Ontwikelingsgang der Vonstenlandsche Wetboeken.* Leiden: Eduard Idjo, 1929.

Soeratman, Darsiti. *Kehidupan Dunia Keraton. Surakarta 1830–1939.* Seri Pustaka Keraton Nusantara 4. Yogyakarta: Yayasan untuk Indonesia, 2000.

Soeratno, Siti Chamamah. *Hikayat Iskandar Zulkarnain,* 2 vols. Jakarta: Balai Pustaka, 1991–92.

Soeryohoedoyo, Soetardi. *Pepali Ki Ageng Solo.* Surabaya: Citra Jaya, 1980.

Soewarno, Muhammad Hari. *Ajaran Islam di Jawakan.* Jakarta: Damar Wulan, 1984.

Sollewijn Gelpke, T. H. F. "De Rijstkultur op Java". *Bijdragen Koninklijk Instituut voor Taal-, Land- en Volkenkunde* 21 (1874): 109–96.

Sri Sultan Hari-hari Hamengku Buwono IX, Jakarta: TEMPO, Grafitipers, 1998.

Srinivasan, K. N. *Cave-Temples of the Pallavas.* 1964.

Steenbrink, Karel A. *Beberapa Aspek tentang Islam di Indonesia Abad ke-19.* Jakarta: Bulan Bintang, 1984.

Stein Callenfels, P. van. "De Sudamala in de Hindu-Javaansche kunst". *Verhandelingen van het Bataviaasch Genootschap van Kunsten en Wetenschappen* 66: 1–181.

Stein, Burton. "Mahanavami: Medieval and Modern Kingly Ritual in South India". In *All the King's Men: Papers on Medieval South Indian History,* edited by B. Smith Madras, pp. 67–90. Delhi: New Era Publications, 1984.

Steurs, F. V. A. de *Mémoires sur la guerre del'île de Java de 1825 à 1830.* Leiden, 1833.

Stuart-Fox, David J. "Pura Besakih: Temple State Relations from Precolonial to Modern Times". In *State and Society in Bali: Historical, Textual and Anthropological Approaches,* edited by H. Geertz, pp. 11–42. Leiden: KITLV Press, 1981.

———. *Pura Besakih: A Study of Balinese Religion in Bali.* KITLV Verhandelingen no. 193. Leiden: KITLV Press, 2002.

Stutterheim, W. F. "De Oudheden Collectie van Z. H. Mangkoe nagoro VII te Soerakarta". *Djawa* (1937): 72–79.

———. *Studies in Indian Archeology.* The Hague: Martinus Nijhoff, 1956.

Sudarshana, Dewi. *Ganapati-tattwa.* Satapitaka Series no. 4. New Delhi: International Academy of Indian Culture, 1957.

———. *Wṛhaspati-Tattwa, an old Javanese Philosophical text, critically edited and annotated.* New Delhi: International Academy of Indian Culture, 1958.

———. *Tattvajñāna and Mahajñāna.* Satapitaka Series no. 23. New Delhi: International Academy of Indian Culture, 1962.

Sudibjo, ed. *Kidung Candhini*. Jakarta: Proyek Penerbitan Buku Sastra Indonesia dan Daerah, Departemen Pendidikan dan Kebudayaan, 1983.

Suhartono. *Apanage dan Bekel: Perubahan Social di Pedesaan Surakarta, 1830–1920*. Yogyakarta: Tiara Wacana, 1991.

Suleiman, Satyawati. "Durgāmahisāsuramardanī". In *Monuments of Ancient Indonesia*. Proyek Pelita Pembinaan Kepurbakalaan dan Peninggalan Nasional, Jakarta, n.d.

Sunar Tri Suyanto. *Pahlawan Kemerdekaan Nasional RI Sinuhun Banguntapa*. Solo: Tiga Serangkai, 1984.

Sunarto, M. *Sasangka Jati*. 10th ed. Solo: Pangestu, 1978.

Sutherland, Heather. "The Priyayi". *Indonesia* 18 (1975): 99–111.

Suwandi, Rahardjo. *A Quest for Justice. The Millenary Aspiration of a Contemporary Javanese Wali*. KITLV, Verhandelingen 182. Leiden: KITLV Press, 2000.

Swellengrebel, J. L. *Korawasrama*. Santpoort, 1936.

Tanakun, Mpu. *Siwatātrikalpa*, edited by A. Teeuw, Th. P. Gaestin, S. O. Robson, P. J. Worsely and P. J. Zoetmulder. Bibliotheca Indonesica 3. The Hague: M. Nijhoff, 1969.

Tanaya. *Bima Suci*. Jakarta: Balai Pustaka, 1979.

Tannen, Deborah. *Talking Voices: Repetition, Dialogue and Imagery in Conversational Discourse*. Cambridge: Cambridge University Press, 1989.

Tanpoaran (anon.). *Sangkan Paraning Dumadi*. Surabaya: Djojo Bojo, 1988.

Tatacara Upacara Mantu. Surakarta: Reksapustaka, Mangkunagaran Palace, n.d.

Teeuw, A. *Hariwangsa*. KILTV, Verhandelingen 1 and 2. 1950.

——— and Stuart O. Robson, eds and translators. *Kuñjarakarna Dharmakanthana. Liberation through the Law of the Buddha. An Old Javanese by Mpu Dhusun Poem*. Bibliotheca Indonesica 21. The Hague: M. Nijhoff, 1981.

Tiknoparnoto. *Buku Pengetan bab Pamiwahaning Agesang*. Solo: Pelajar, 1962.

Tinopranoto, R. M. N. *Primbon Pamiwahaning Ngegesang: Metu, Manten, Mati*. Solo: Pelajar, 1962.

Tjariosipoen Benawi Sala. Volklectuur no. 645. 14 pp. Batavia: Balé-Poestaka, 1924.

Tjerita Rakyat. Vol. I. Djakarta: Balai Pustaka, 1963.

Ton (Pak) "Sesaji Wiludjengan Nagari Mahesa Lawung". *Jayabaya* (December 1990): 8 and *Jayabaya* (December 1993): 40 and 51.

Traube, E. G. "Incest and Mythology". *Berkshire Review* 14 (1979): 37–53.

Tuuk, H. N. van der. *Kawi — Balineesch — Nederlandsch Woorderboek*. 4 vols. Batavia, n.d.

Van Akkeren, Ph. *Een Gedrocht en toch de Volmaakte Mens*. 's-Gravenhage, 1951.

van Bruinessen, Martin. *Tarekat Naqsybandiyah di Indonesia*. Bandung: Mizan, 1992.

———. *Kitab Kuning. Pesantren dan Tarekat*. Bandung: Mizan, 1995.

van der Veer, Peter. *Religious Nationalism. Hindus and Muslims in India*. Berkeley, Los Angeles and London: University of California Press, 1996.

van Dijk, Kees. *Rebellion under the Banner of Islam: The Darul Islam in Indonesia*. KITLV, Verhandelingen 94. The Hague: M. Nijhoff, 1981.

van Dijk, Kees. *A Country in Despair: Indonesia between 1997 and 2000.* KITLV, Verhandelingen 186. Leiden: KITLV, 2001.

van Groenendael, C. M. C. *The Dhalang behind the Wayang.* KITLV, Verhandelingen 114. Dordrecht: Foris 1985.

van Mook, H. W. "Koeta Gede". *Koloniaal Tijdschrift,* no. 15 (1926): 353–400.

van Neil, Robert. "The Effect of Export Cultivations in nineteenth-century Java". *Modern Asian Studies* 15, no. 1 (1981): 25–58.

van Ossenbruggen, F. D. E. "Java's *monca-pat*: Origins of a Primitive Classification System". In *Structural Anthropology in the Netherlands,* edited by P. E. Josselin de Jong, pp. 61–82. KITLV Translation Series 17 (Dutch original 1916). Holland/U.S.A.: Foris Publications, 1983.

Varenne, Paul, translator. *Célébration de la grande Déesse (Devī-Māhātmya).* Paris: Les Belles Lettres, 1975.

Vaudeville, Charlotte. *Myths, Saints and Legends in Medieval India.* Delhi: Oxford University Press, 1966.

Viaro, A. *Urbanisme et Architecture traditionnels du Sud de l'Ile de Nias.* Paris: UNESCO, 1980.

Vibert, Stéphane. "La quête russe de l'Universel. Mouvement slavophile et hiérarchie de valeurs socio-communautaire (1825–1855)". Ph.D. dissertation, Ecole des Hautes Etudes en Sciences Sociales, Paris, 1999.

————. "The Ideal of Community as a Paradoxical Appropriation of Modernity". In the Symposium "Integrating Others and the Appropriation of Modernity", University of Munster, Germany, *Sonderforschungbereich* du Wesfälische Wilhelms Université de Munster; programme on "State and Society in Southeast Asia: Continuity, Discontinuity, Transformation", November 2001.

Vignato, Silvia. *Au Nom de l'Hindouisme. Reconfigurations ethniques chez les Tamouls et les Karo en Indonésie.* Cahiers de l'Archipel 32. Paris: L'Harmattan, 2000.

Vincent, Jeanne-françoise, Daniel Dory, and Raymond Verdeir. *La Construction Religieuse du Territoire.* Paris: L'Harmattan, 1995.

Vivieros de Castro, E. "Society". In *Encyclopedia of Social and Cultural Anthropology,* edited by A. Barnard and J. Spencer, pp. 514–22. London and New York: Routledge, 1996.

Vreede, A. C. *Catalogus van de Javaansche en Madoereesche Handschriften der Leidsche Universiteits-Bibliotheek.* Leiden, 1892.

Wahhābīya. In *Shorter Encyclopedia of Islam,* pp. 618–21. London: Luzac, 1953.

Watson, C. W. *Of Self and Nation: Autobiography and the Representation of Modern Indonesia.* Honolulu: University of Hawai'i Press, 2000.

Weber, Max. *The Protestant Ethic and the Spirit of Capitalism.* Translation by Talcott Parsons. New York: Scribner's, 1958.

Weck, Wolfgang. *Heilkunde und Volkssturm auf Bali.* Stuttgart: Enke, 1937.

Wedyamanta, Siman, ed. *Adiparva.* 2 vols. Jogyakarta, 1958.

Weiss, Jerome. "Folk Psychology of the Javanese of Ponorogo". Ph.D. dissertation, Department of Anthropology, Yale University, 1977.

Wensinck, A. J. "Salat". *Encyclopédie de l'Islam*. Leyde, vol. IV (1st ed.) (1934): 99–109.

Wertheim, W. F. *Indonésië, van Vorstenrijk tot Neo-kolonie*. Amsterdam: Boom Mappel, 1978.

Wessing, R. "Nyai Roro Kidul in Puger: Local Applications of a Myth". *Archipel* 53 (1997*a*): 97–120.

———, guest ed. *The Devine Female in Indonesia: Asian Folklore Studies*, vol. 56, no. 2 (1997*b*).

White, B. and G. Wiradi. "Agrarian and Nonagrarian Bases for Equality in Nine Javanese Villages". In *Agrarian Transformations: Local Processes and the State in Southeast Asia*, edited by A. Thurton and B. White, pp. 266–302. Berkeley: University of California Press, 1989.

Whitten, Tony, R. E. Soeriaatmaja, and Suraya A. Ariff. *The Ecology of Java and Bali*. Hong Kong: Periplus Editions, 1996.

Wibisono, Singgih. *Kirap Pusaka*. Surakarta: Radya Pustaka Museum, 1972.

Wieringa, Erwin. "Babad Bangun Tapa. De Ballingschap van Pakubuwana VI op Ambon 1830–1849", 2 vols. Ph.D. dissertation, University of Leiden, 1994.

———. "Taming a Text: The Incorporation of the Shi'itic Hero Muhammad Hanafiyyah in a Sundanese Version of the Prophetic Tales". *Society and Culture of Southeast Asia: Continuities and Changes*, edited by Lokesh Chandra, pp. 355–64. New Delhi: International Academy of Indian Culture and Aditya Prakashan, 2000.

Wierner, M. J. *Visible and Invisible Realms. Power. Magic, and colonial conquest in Bali*. Chicago and London: University of Chicago Press, 1995.

Wilkinson, R. J. *A Malay–English Dictionary*, 2 vols. London: Macmillan, 1959.

Williams, Michael Charles. *Communism, Religion and Revolt in Banten*. Ohio University Monographs in International Studies. Southeast Asia Series, no. 86. Athens, Ohio: Ohio University, 1990.

Wink, André. Al-Hind. *Early Medieval India and the Expansion of Islam 7th–11th Centuries*. The Making of the Indo-Islamic World, vol. I. Delhi: Oxford University Press, 1990.

———. *The Slave Kings and the Islamic Conquest of the 11th–13th Centuries*. The Making of the Indo-Islamic World, vol. II. Delhi: Oxford University Press, 1997.

Winter, C. F. "Javaansche Mythologie". *Tijdscrift voor Nederlands-Indies* 5, no. 1 (1843): 1–88.

———. *Javaasche Zamenspraken*, 2 vols. Vol. 1, edited by T. Roorda. Amsterdam: Johannes Müller, 1848.

———. *Javaasche Zamenspraken*, 2 vols. Vol. 2, edited by S. Keyzer. Amsterdam: Johannes Müller, 1858.

———. *Kamus Kawi-Jawi*. Yogyakarta: Proyek Javanologi, 1983.

Wiradi, Gunawan. *Reform Agraria. Perjalanan yang Belum Berakhir*. Yogyakarta: Insist Press, 2000.

Wiryapanitra. *Serat Kidungan Kawedhar*. Translated by T. W. K. Hadisoeprata. Alih aksara: Siswoyo. Jakarta: Proyek Penerbitan buku Sastra Indonesia dan Daerah, DepDikBud, 1979.

Wiryosuparto, Sutjipto. "Ghatotkacāsraya Kakawin". Ph.D. dissertation, University of Indonesia, 1960.

Wolters, Willem. "From Corvée to Contract Labour: Institutional Innovation in Central Javanese Village Around the Turn of the Century". In *The Late Colonial State in Indonesia: Politics and Economic Foundations of the Netherlands Indies 1880–1942*, edited by Robert Cribb, pp. 173–90. KITLV, Verhandelingen 163. Leiden: KITLV Press, 1994.

Ye'or, Bat. *The Decline of Christianity under Islam: From Jihad to Dhimmitude*. Madison, Teaneck: Fairleigh Dickinson University Press, 1996.

Yokochi, Yuko. "The Warrior Goddess in the Devīmāhātmya". In *Living with Sakti: Gender, Sexuality and Religion in South Asia*, pp. 71–113. Senri Ethnological Studies 50. Osaka: National Museum of Ethnology, 1999.

Yosodipuro the elder. *Babad Giyanti*. 21 vols. Batavia: Balai Pustaka, 1937–39.

Yudi Partojuwono. *Serat Wedharan Wirid*. 3 vols. Surabaya: Djojobojo, 1991.

Zoetmulder, P. J. *Kalangwan, A Survey of Old Javanese Literature*. KITLV, Translation Series 14. The Hague: M. Nijhoff, 1974.

————. *Pantheism and Monism in Javanese Suluk Literature: Islamic and Indian Mysticism in an Indonesian Setting*, edited and translated by M. C. Ricklefs. KITLV Translation Series 24. Leiden: KITLV Press, 1995.

———— and S. O. Robson. *Old Javanese–English Dictionary*. 's-Gravenhage: M. Nijhoff, 1982.

Zurbuchen, M. " 'Weaving the Text' in Old Javanese". In *Papers from the Second Eastern Conference on Austronesian Languages*, edited by P. B. Naylor. *Austronesian Studies. Michigan Papers on South and Southeast Asia* 15 (1976): 285–99.

Zurbuchen, Mary. "Weaving the Text in Old Javanese". In *Austronesian Studies*, edited by F. B. Naylor, pp. 285–300. Papers on South and Southeast Asia, no. 15. Michigan: Michigan Center for South and Southeast Asian Studies, 1979.

INDEX

ABOUT THE AUTHOR

Stephen C. Headley (1943) has held a post at the National Centre for Scientific Research (CNRS) in Paris since 1981, where he works on the social anthropology of the Javanese. For several years he was associated with a research centre founded by Louis Dumont (+1998) and continued by Daniel de Coppet (+2002). This centre had a special interest in those hybrid societies that were recently animated by traditional social cosmology, and which are not yet thoroughly individualistic, and thus presented unique possiblities for exploring questions about these three kinds of social morphology. Over the last ten years, he has published five volumes on mythology, Islam, and the anthropology of prayer in Indonesia:

Forthcoming: *Ebauche d'hommes et corps et sociétés inachevés*, numéro spécial de la revue *l'Homme*, no. 174, textes réunis par Stephen C. Headley.

2000: *From Cosmogony to Exorcism in a Javanese Genesis: The Spilt Seed.* Oxford University Press, Oxford.

2000: *Islamic Prayer across the Indian Ocean: Inside and Outside the Mosque,* edited by Stephen C. Headley and David Parkin. Curzon Press, U.K.

1996: *Vers une anthropologie de la prière: études ethnolinguistiques javanaises,* textes réunis par Stephen C. Headley. Publications Universitaires de Provence, Aix-en-Provence.

1994: *Anthropologie de la prière: rites oraux en Asie du Sud-Est.* numéro spécial de la revue *L'Homme*, no. 132, vol. XXIV.4 (oct–déc 1994), textes réunis par Stephen C.Headley.

The common theme of these studies had been the hierarchy of Javanese values. Despite the introduction of individualism along with evaluative indifference during the twentieh century, Javanese values have not entirely disintegrated. The successive political crises in Indonesia in the second half of the twentieth century have in certain sense underlined the necessity for preserving these values which the promise of democracy at the beginning of that century seem to require abolishing.